9 ✓
14 ✓
15
10
11

UNDERSTANDING ORGANIZATIONAL BEHAVIOR

A MANAGERIAL VIEWPOINT

UNDERSTANDING ORGANIZATIONAL BEHAVIOR
A MANAGERIAL VIEWPOINT

ROBERT E. CALLAHAN
Seattle University

C. PATRICK FLEENOR
Seattle University

HARRY R. KNUDSON
University of Washington

Charles E. Merrill Publishing Company
A Bell & Howell Company
Columbus   Toronto   London   Sydney

Published by Charles E. Merrill Publishing Co.
A Bell & Howell Company
Columbus, Ohio 43216

This book was set in Novarese and Univers
Cover Designer: Cathy Watterson
Text Designer: Cynthia Brunk
Production Coordination: Mary Harlan

Photo credits: Part One photo by Tom Brunk; Part Two photo courtesy of Bell &
Howell; Part Three photo by Freda Leinwand; Part Four photo courtesy of Hewlett-
Packard Company.

Library of Congress Catalog Card Number: 85-61494
International Standard Book Number: 0-675-20198-5
Printed in the United States of America
  2 3 4 5 6 7 8 9—91 90 89 88 87 86

To Shirley for the freedom and support
To Kim and Kevin for allowing me to work weekends
To Robert and Kathleen for just being my parents

To Margaret and the Heuriger of Vienna

To Sallye and Sara and Eric

PREFACE

Our original conception of this book grew from our personal views that other textbooks in the area of organizational behavior did not do what we wanted them to. As we used these books in our teaching we found that they did not—for a variety of reasons—provide the kinds of material that resulted in the level of analytical behavior and practical understanding that we desired in our students.

Consequently, we decided to develop a book that would help a student acquire the knowledge and skills that we thought were important for a student of organizational behavior to have. Specifically, we wanted this book to provide information about fundamental concepts of organizational behavior in a clear and understandable fashion, without the jargon that is prevalent in the field. Further, we wanted this material to have a strong managerial emphasis, based on the assumption that many, if not most, of our readers would be interested in understanding this material from a manager's point of view and with an appreciation of how the theoretical constructs could assist a manager in making decisions. Finally, we wanted the book to have a strong emphasis on application of the concepts in organizational settings to prevent the sterility that, in our judgment, seems to be present in many of the books currently available. Thus, we have devoted a significant part of each chapter to application of the concepts covered, drawing from a variety of sources, including many not usually found in textbooks.

In short, we have tried to provide some important information about organizational behavior in an understandable, concise fashion, emphasizing a managerial approach and demonstrating how this information comes into play in the dynamics of the organization.

This orientation comes from our considerable experience in teaching organizational behavior and our belief that an effective experience for the student should go beyond a superficial understanding of theoretical concepts. Too often, that understanding lives only until the next examination! Our objectives for a course in organizational behavior are as follows:

- To provide the student with valid information about currently accepted theories of organizational behavior.
- To instill the realization that there are many different ways to approach a situation, and alternative ways of handling a particular situation should be developed and considered.
- To increase the ability to *predict* what will

happen in organizations so that a manager can move from a reactive to a proactive approach, anticipating organizational problems and opportunities before they occur.

- To provide the opportunity for each student to critically analyze the assumptions that he or she has about people and how they behave in organizations, and to evaluate the effectiveness of these assumptions, upon which managerial behavior is based. Note that we do not have a particular set of assumptions that we advocate—assumptions that are "better" than others. Our intent is to have our students—whether they be undergraduates or managers—understand the assumptions they now have and the impacts those assumptions are having in their organizational lives.
- To provide some managerial tools and approaches that have proven useful and that can be applied to a situation without great increases in resources, more skillful subordinates, a new boss, or any of the many other factors sometimes used as excuses for inaction.
- To have the concept of *tradeoff* become an integral part of the student thought process. We are continually amazed at the number of experienced managers who spend time looking for perfect solutions to the problems facing them, solutions with no negative outcomes. Any outcome has both positive and negative implications, and a manager should constantly assess the benefits of a proposed action against the costs of that action. We want our students to understand this and to develop skill in framing the tradeoffs involved in any situation rather than to waste physical, emotional, and intellectual energy searching for the perfect solution.

Although many of our students may not intend to become managers, the kind of approach to organizational behavior we advocate is favorably received because it allows an individual to become a more effective *member* of an organization, whether or not that person is a manager.

In addition to our strong emphasis on a managerial approach and the application of the theoretical concepts, we have included several topics not found in the typical text on organizational behavior. Nevertheless, these topics are important now and will gain more importance in the future. It is in the areas of computer technology, productivity, and international aspects of organizational behavior that the challenges of the future will come—perhaps more rapidly than we would wish. To ignore these areas of importance would detract from our ability to help students and managers prepare themselves for effective behavior in the organizations of today and tomorrow. Few texts deal well with either the nontraditional organizations of the present or the organizations of the immediate future, to say nothing of organizations that will exist ten or fifteen years from now. This new material is exciting and provides a different perspective from which to consider and evaluate the traditional material on organizational behavior.

We designed the book to be used by a broad range of readers, recognizing that what a reader takes away from the book will, to some extent, be determined by what the reader brings to the experience. Thus, a younger college or community college student will probably find much of the material new and will find the first challenge to be understanding the theoretical framework. An experienced manager, on the other hand, will probably be familiar, at least in an intuitive sense, with many of the concepts explored and may find the opportunity to analyze the concepts within the framework of his or her experience to be of greatest benefit. The graduate student may be more intrigued with some of the newer material and the references to certain research activities. Having used the materials with all three categories of potential readers, we are confident that they generate interest, enthusiasm, and understanding.

The materials have been extensively tested in learning situations of all kinds, undergraduate and graduate classes composed primarily of business students and classes at both levels composed of students from other disciplines—engineering, health sciences, architecture, law, education, nursing, and others. Similarly, the materials have been used in a large number of executive and management seminars in the United States and abroad.

Understanding Organizational Behavior is supplemented by an instructor's manual containing additional information, outlines, suggestions for lectures and discussions, class assignments, answers to text questions, and a set of transparency masters. A test bank is available in print form and on diskette for the IBM and Apple personal computers. A separate publication, *Understanding Organizational Behavior: A Casebook*, may be used in conjunction with this text or in other courses by instructors desiring greater emphasis on the case method.

Early drafts of this book were used as texts in undergraduate and graduate classes in the Albers School of Business, Seattle University, and at the Richland Center for Graduate Studies, a center for graduate study cosponsored by the University of Washington and Washington State University. We appreciate the efforts of the students in these classes and thank them for the many useful comments and ideas they provided. Most of their comments and suggestions were incorporated into the final version of the book.

We also wish to express our sincere appreciation to several people who were most helpful to our efforts. Many individuals permitted us to use materials that they had developed, and we thank them. They are acknowledged individually at the appropriate places in the book. Three people deserve special mention for their creative efforts and contributions to this book: Professor Diane Lockwood, Seattle University (chapter 16, Future Directions for People in Organizations); Dr. Gary Robinson, Boeing Marine Systems (chapter 15, International Aspects of Organizational Behavior); and Dr. Peter Scontrino, in private practice (chapter 10, Organizational Rewards and Performance Appraisal).

Many professional journals and newspapers permitted us to reprint materials that originally appeared in their publications. Much of this material is found in the "Applications" sections of the book, and provides invaluable information and perspectives.

Several colleagues provided very useful insights and suggestions after reviewing early drafts of the book. Among them are Professors Robert T. Woodworth, Dale A. Henning, and Fremont E. Kast, the Graduate School of Business, University of Washington; Professor Karl Wieck, University of Texas at Austin; Professor Jeffrey Ford, Ohio State University; Professor Mary Ann Von Glinow, University of Southern California, Los Angeles; Dr. Eric C. van Merkensteijn, The Wharton School of the University of Pennsylvania; Professor Thomas W. Dougherty, University of Missouri–Columbia; Professor James L. Nimnicht, Eastern Washington University; Professor H. Kirk Downey, Texas Christian University; Professor Anthony T. Cobb, Virginia Polytechnic Institute and State University; Professor Elmore R. Alexander III, Director, The Executive Training Center, Memphis State University; Professor Alan E. Omens, San Diego State University;

Professor Arthur La Capria, Jr., El Paso Community College; Professor Herbert G. Heneman III, University of Wisconsin–Madison; Professor Bronston T. Mayes, University of Nebraska-Lincoln; Professor Robert J. Ash, Santa Ana College; Professor M. Susan Taylor, University of Maryland; Professor Denise M. Rousseau, J. L. Kellogg School of Management, Northwestern University; Professor James R. Meindle, State University of New York at Buffalo; Professor Jack L. Mendleson, Arizona State University; and Professor Karen Paul, Rochester Institute of Technology.

Other colleagues were most helpful in using early versions of the book in their classes and providing useful reactions from the kind of reader toward whom this book is directed. Among these colleagues are Professors Sharon James and David McKee of Seattle University.

Both The Albers School of Business, Seattle University, and the Graduate School of Business, University of Washington, provided resources of various kinds, including relief from normal teaching duties, that were instrumental in the timely completion of the book. Professor John Eshelman, Dean of The Albers School of Business, Seattle University, and Professor Karl Vesper, Chairman of the Department of Management and Organization, University of Washington, deserve our special appreciation in this regard.

Our editors at Charles E. Merrill Publishing Company, Marilyn Freedman, John Nee, and Mary Harlan, deserve our special thanks. In addition to providing emotional support, encouragement, and friendly criticism, each at the appropriate time, they also provided a great deal of logistic support.

Two people who played major roles in the necessary research for the book and in the process of preparing the book for publication deserve special mention, Barb Tenny and Brenda Andrews.

Finally, each of us wants to thank, however inadequately, our families for the many contributions they have made to this project. Without their help in many tangible and intangible ways, we would not have been able to successfully complete our efforts. We appreciate very much what they have done, and trust that the lavish gifts we have settled upon them recently will deter them from proceeding with the oft-threatened legal actions that would so significantly affect our respective marital situations.

CONTENTS

PART ONE
Introduction

CHAPTER ONE
Work and Organizational Behavior

OUTLINE

OBJECTIVES

- Define the term "Organizational Behavior," and explain how three major fields contribute to our understanding of this field

- Describe the relationship between theory, research, and applications

- Describe the history of work from the time of the ancient Egyptians to the present

- Understand the major differences between Japanese and American management styles

- Discuss how the computer is beginning to affect individuals in organizations

- Define some of the changes in work-force values and the effects on the organization

- Identify and discuss the major managerial applications of this chapter

Ben Reed

Shortly after Ben Reed, twenty-seven, graduated from school with a degree in psychology, he took a job with the Acme Medical Association, a group health insurance organization. As assistant office manager, he was responsible for supervising approximately forty office employees who performed sorting, totaling, and recording operations concerning medical claims charged against Acme.

The workers, including Ben, were situated in a large room. His boss, Charles Grayson, had been with Acme for twenty years and was rather proud of his progress from clerical position to office manager and the increase in staff numbers over the years.

Ben Reed did not find his work especially challenging. His main duties were to check the time cards of the office workers each morning, to make sure that "everything was in order," and to answer questions concerning claims that might be brought to him. In addition, he did special statistical studies at the request of the controller's office or his boss. This additional work was very infrequent. His own estimate of time actually "worked" was no more than one or two hours a day.

Because of some courses he had taken at the university, Ben Reed had some strong convictions concerning the supervision of the office employees. He was concerned about the situation at Acme for two reasons: the high turnover of office employees—which averaged about 48 percent per year—and the apathy of many of the employees toward their work. He realized that he was new in the organization but nevertheless felt obligated to make some suggestions for improvement. Grayson, his boss, often did not agree with these suggestions.

For instance, Ben suggested developing some basic physiology courses to instruct the office staff, thereby helping them to process claims faster and more accurately. However, Grayson did not feel the same way and the classes were not developed. A second area of disagreement focused on the handling of D. Martin, a clerk-typist. Martin had approached Ben one day when Grayson was out of the office, to report feeling sick. Ben made the necessary arrangements for Martin to have the rest of the day off. When Grayson found out about the incident, he was very upset and told Ben that he did not have the authority to make those kinds of decisions. Although Ben felt that he had handled the Martin situation properly since no one else was present, he let the matter drop.

On December 10, Robert Colvin, controller for the firm, called Ben into his office to discuss plans for a new computerized claims processing department to replace the way claims were now being handled. Colvin spent two and a half hours with Ben explaining the proposed system and concluded the interview by stating that he felt that, as new people often had good ideas for improvement, he would welcome any thoughts that Ben might have.

Ben was enthusiastic about Colvin's approaching him, and spent several hours that night at home working out a plan that would permit the new process to be installed in his area with a minimum of difficulty. He submitted his ideas to Colvin the next morning. Colvin was very impressed with Ben's ideas and immediately called a meeting of several of the officials of the firm, including Grayson, to review the plan. This meeting was held during the early afternoon of December 11. About three o'clock that afternoon Grayson entered the area in which the office workers' and Ben's desks were located, approached Ben's desk, and slammed down the folder containing Ben's plans, exclaiming, "What in the hell is this?" Before Ben could reply, Grayson began in a loud voice to lecture on the necessity of going through channels when submitting reports, ideas, and suggestions. His remarks attracted the attention of the office workers, most of whom stopped work to watch the disturbance. Ben interrupted Grayson to suggest that they might continue the discussion in Grayson's office. Grayson snatched the folder from Ben's desk and stalked into his office, where he continued his tirade. After Grayson had concluded, Ben stated that he had not been satisfied with his relationship with the firm and felt that maybe he should resign. He then left the office.

The next day, Grayson asked Ben to step into his office, where he apologized to Ben for the previous day, remarking that he had had several things on his mind that had upset him and that he certainly had full confidence in Ben's abilities. Ben accepted his apology, remarking that he might have flown off the handle a little bit himself. The meeting ended on a cordial note.

On the following day, December 13, Ben Reed submitted his resignation and left the Acme Company on December 24. Ben did not have another job at the time of his departure.[1]

INTRODUCTION

What Is Organizational Behavior?

While the story of Ben Reed ends on a negative note, it clearly shows the complexities of human behavior in an organization. It raises some interesting questions that managers need to appreciate and begin to answer:

- Why is there turnover and apathy among the office workers?
- Why was Ben's suggestion for conducting classes rejected?
- Did Ben handle the "sick worker" incorrectly? What would you have done?
- How would you describe the leadership style of Grayson? Reed?
- What suggestions would you make to Mr. Colvin about introducing computers to the work force?
- Why did Grayson react the way he did to Ben's report?
- Why did Grayson apologize the next day?
- Why did Ben leave?

This situation is rich in various aspects of why and how people behave in organizations. How many answers can you develop that you feel are an accurate portrayal of the dynamics of the situation? And how comfortable are you that you can now give some recommendations that will solve the problems in this firm?

In order to study Organizational Behavior, we need to define what is meant by the term. "Organizational Behavior" is a subset of management activities concerned with understanding, predicting, and influencing individual behavior in organizational settings.

This definition may still have you wondering: What is meant by a "subset"? What is an "organization"? Do organizations actually behave? Isn't this just another name for psychology? Or sociology? Most importantly, how is this going to help me on the job?

Answering these questions, as well as the many others that we and you will raise throughout the book, will be a process of exploring the dimensions and dynamics of human behavior. By actively studying organizational behavior, we can understand how human behavior can be effective and satisfying for both the employee and the manager.

As you progress through this book, we will present a number of theories that will help you understand and explain human behavior. We will also present some cases and situations to test these theories, and we will relate how managers and organizations view these particular explanations of behavior and present some of their unique prescriptions for handling the situation.

What is the purpose of this approach? You should come to understand some of the important advances in the behavioral sciences. But our underlying objective is that you develop your own theory of organizational behavior, one that will allow you to be more productive in dealing with others in organizations.

Why Study Organizational Behavior?

We live in a society built around organizations. How many organizations are you a part of today: Family? Church? Sports team? School? A student club? A job? It's almost impossible to avoid being a member of some kind of organization.

Why do we become part of an organization? Or why do we leave an organization like Ben did? We usually join an organization to satisfy our individual needs, whether they be social, emotional, physical, or monetary. We depend heavily on organizations to fulfill our own as well as their purposes. We can surmise that Ben felt some of his needs were not being met. But which needs?

Consider that we will probably work for forty or more years in one or various organizations. Since we spend so much of our lives within organizations, it seems reasonable that learning as much as we can about how they operate might help us be more effective within those settings. Maybe we can reduce some of the frustrations that Ben felt as we learn how to cope. Maybe we can prevent some of the problems which Mr. Colvin faced as he introduced new technology.

Working in organizations means having to work for other people, work with other people, or supervise other people. Thus we need to understand why other people behave the way they do (as well as understand why we do what we do). You may believe that it's just common sense to treat people the way you want to be treated. If this is true, why do organizations have so many "people" problems? Why is there so much dissatisfaction among certain work groups? Why is there such controversy about declining employee productivity and about how to correct it? Obviously, these types of questions will not be answered through just "common sense."

Theory and Research as a Framework for Application

Behavioral science does not operate according to formal and precise rules, as do the physical sciences. It does not have exact formulas for human behavior. But behavioral scientists can, and do, describe human behavior quite well. As a result managers will try to alter their own and others' behavior to become more effective. This process of theory and application is shown in Figure 1–1. While the model of relationship between theory and application has no actual starting and ending point, we will begin with theory development and research.

We utilize theory and research to develop an explanation for what we see. A theory is a model for relating certain variables in a systematic manner. For example, a manager may want to understand why Ben left Acme Medical Associates. The manager feels that Mr. Grayson's manner of handling employees (leadership style) is the reason why Ben left (dissatisfaction with the job). A possible theory might state: An autocratic style of leadership will lead to employees being dissatisfied with their jobs. Since we are interested in the leadership style as a predictor of subordinate satisfaction, the leadership variable is termed *independent*. Job satisfaction becomes the *dependent* variable. We then need to design research to measure both the independent and dependent variables. The leadership style could be measured by some previously identified behavioral characteristics (eg., number of one-way communications from superiors to subordinates) that the researcher observes in the organization. The job satisfaction of employees could be measured by a questionnaire focusing on individuals' attitudes.

Having collected data from the observations of a number of managers in this organization and an employee survey of their subordinates, we then would

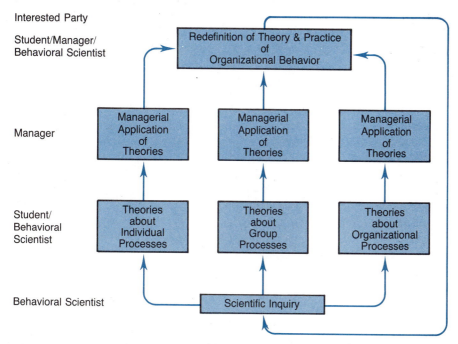

FIGURE 1–1
Model of relationship between theory and application

compare the results statistically to see if the resulting relationship between the leadership style and job satisfaction was significant from a numerical standpoint. If so, we and the concerned manager would have a possible explanation for the high turnover rate at Acme.

Based on this research and the resulting theoretical understanding, Mr. Colvin may wish to apply the findings. He may send Mr. Grayson to some training course to learn how to be less autocratic in his approach to employees. This is the application of theory and research.

However, there might also be other explanations for Ben's leaving the organization and the high turnover. The reasons for each might be completely different. Ben might want to go back to school for more education. The employees might only be bored with their jobs and are finding better positions elsewhere. Needless to say, we must be careful when trying to explain human behavior in organizations. If we feel that our theory needs refinement then, according to the model, we would redefine our theory and practice and suggest new research to develop more accurate theories of behavior at the individual, group, or organizational level.

What can the student and the manager learn from these theories about organizational behavior? In reality, few organizations or managers perform these theoretic steps of research and application. Yet some systematic study or planning must accompany each suggested solution if it is to increase our knowledge of human behavior and our success in treating people humanly and effectively. Being more questioning in our approach to human behavior may lead to an appreciation of the complexity involved. This appreciation may then create a desire to learn more about ourselves and to be more systematic and effective in solving organizational and individual problems.

Contributing Disciplines

The field of organizational behavior is heavily influenced by several other behavioral sciences and social sciences. In a manner of speaking, these other disciplines are the underpinnings for organizational behavior. Each contribute to our knowledge about humans in organizations.

The main disciplines are psychology, sociology, and anthropology. Although each is concerned with behavior, there are few commonly accepted theories among them. In addition, there are methodological controversies. Nevertheless, there is a common ideal to be systematic in approaching the study of behavior. A simplified view of this type of inquiry is: theory → research → application → new theory → research, etc. This is very similar to the model in Figure 1–1. While each discipline may be imperfect in being able to always predict and control behavior, it is the *attempt* that should interest us.

Psychology   This discipline has had the most influence on the field of organizational behavior. The reason is the focus of psychology—what determines the behavior of individuals? The attempt to answer this question in different settings has engendered a multitude of subdisciplines—industrial psychology, clinical psychology, and experimental psychology. The major areas researched to understand the determinants of behavior are individual motivation and learning.

Motivation refers to the mental and emotional processes that precede actual behavior under consideration. Learning is concerned with the changes and adaptations of behavior that occur over time. Obviously, understanding either motivation or learning would help clarify the individual behaviors in the Ben Reed situation.

Sociology   Sociology, while not as prominent as psychology, is nevertheless the basis for trying to understand social behavior. By social behavior we mean the dynamics of two or more individuals interacting. Therefore, sociology focuses attention on groups, organizations, and societies rather than individuals. Areas of concern to a sociologist might include the actual pattern of interaction (who talks to whom for how long), the effects of different social status on the interaction, and the effects of different roles on interaction.

This knowledge can help us understand the interactions between Ben and Mr. Grayson, Ben and Mr. Colvin, Ben and the workers, and Mr. Grayson and the workers.

Anthropology   Anthropology is a broad discipline that studies the origins and development of human cultures, how those cultures have functioned in the past, and how they continue to function in the present. While the study of culture may seem to be a very indirect approach for today's manager, this is rapidly changing as we deal more directly with other nations who do not share our values and standards of behavior. These differences will be highlighted in chapter 15. In addition, cultural anthropologists have made it obvious that what was believed to be an inborn instinct to compete is really a learned, culture-specific behavior. In other cultures this competitive behavior may be moderated by other culture-specific behaviors that explain the complexity and reality of "foreign" approaches to business. A popular example is the drive to adapt the Japanese style of management to American businesses and the resulting frustrations.

Furthermore, much has been written about corporate culture—a general consensus of beliefs, mores, customs, value systems, behavioral norms, and ways of doing business that are unique to each organization—as a method of understanding how the organization is consistent in the areas we will be studying in this text. For example, one researcher trying to understand the individuals in a functional subunit of a high-tech firm found that there may be multiple cultures within an organization.[2] These multiple cultures might be represented by sales, manufacturing, and administration, each having its own values, goals, and beliefs. The researcher suggests that management may have to understand the subunit's culture as well as the overall corporate culture when trying to redirect this unit.

We can see from this brief discussion of the contributing disciplines that organizational behavior draws from a rich array of research. What makes it a field in its own right is the attempt to integrate various aspects and levels of behavior.

Organizational behavior focuses on the individual, the group, and the organization separately and also on their interactional relationships. For example, an organization in a rapidly changing environment should have a corporate culture (new ideas are encouraged and valued) and structure (small work groups are formed around specific problems or suggestions for new products or services) that allow it to respond quickly to perceived new demands. At the group level, we need to examine how groups are formed and disbanded as new directions are explored and incorporated into daily activities. At the individual level, we need to see what motivational theories will explain how the individual worker responds to rapidly changing task demands and even security needs as work appears and disappears. We can see how important it is to bridge the gaps between these levels of study and try to integrate them for a more realistic understanding of behavior in organizations.

Plan of the Text

Our text is based on the premise that the study of organizational behavior is very useful to the student and the manager as they deal with others in organizations. Figure 1–1 provides a framework for this premise and a rationale for the two major sections—theory and applications—found in most chapters. The chapters are designed to describe the theoretical and applied elements needed to understand, appreciate, and predict human behavior in organizational settings. The emphasis is on the development of an effective working knowledge of organizational behavior.

With this as a model, the general plan of this text includes several elements: beginning story, concepts, applications, exercises, cases, boxed features, and questions. Most chapters start with a brief story or situation that illustrates the theory being presented. This story raises certain questions which the chapter helps us explore and answer. The conceptual section presents some of the most relevant research around a particular topic. You will note that there isn't always agreement about an issue, as in chapter 5, on leadership. Some researchers feel that one should change the job to match the leader, while others feel that a leader's behavior should be the focus of change efforts. We present both theories to give a balanced perspective. The major issues and points in the conceptual section are reviewed in the "Summary of Key Concepts" as a transition from theory to applications.

The applications section shows how the theory is applied in the "real" world, including what specific individuals or organizations are doing in that particular area. In certain chapters we have provided the negative (what not to do) as well as the positive perspective. The applications illustrate not every concept but some of the most influential.

An exercise and a case are then presented to highlight certain issues raised in the conceptual section. This allows you to apply your ideas to these situations and begin the process of integrating your learnings.

Finally, select boxed features illustrate the concepts and issues raised.

These stories usually cover many more ideas and complexities than the chapter does but, as a result, the boxed features provide a more realistic notion of how the theory is to be applied and understood and how situational considerations might affect the outcome.

The book is organized into four parts.

Part One: Introduction presents an overview of organizational behavior, the history and meaning of work, and current trends affecting this field.

Part Two: Basic Concepts examines several topics that are considered to be the foundations of organizational behavior: attitudes and values, perceptual processes, motivation, communication, leadership and power, group dynamics, and decision making.

Part Three: Organizational Aspects reviews some of the applications to organizational problems and issues: conflict resolution, organizational and job design, organizational rewards and performance evaluation, and management of change.

Part Four: Issues in Organizational Behavior highlights special areas that are beginning to get more attention in organizations: stress, implications of computer technology, productivity, international aspects, and future directions.

WORK AND ORGANIZATIONAL BEHAVIOR

Examples of Work and Behavior

To truly appreciate and understand organizational behavior, we must view behavior in its context, an organization. We must look and, if possible, experience the context as do the individuals who occupy it. As we explore the various concepts relating to organizational behavior throughout the book, we need constantly to remind ourselves that the study of organizational behavior includes the study of ourselves as we work.

The following short stories[3] are intended to help us focus attention both on the context of work and on the rich experience of working. As you read the incidents, try to answer some of the following questions:

- What is it like to work at this job for eight hours a day, five days a week, fifty-two weeks a year?
- What are the job's strong points? Its weak points?
- How would I like to have this job?
- How would I improve it?

Steelworker "I'm a dying breed. A laborer. Strictly muscle work . . . pick it up, put it down, pick it up, put it down. . . . You can't take pride any more. You remember when a guy could point to a house he built, how many logs he stacked. He built it and he was proud of it. . . . It's hard to take pride in a bridge you're never gonna cross, in a door you're never gonna open. You're mass-producing things and you never see the end result of it. . . . I got chewed out by my foreman once. He said, 'Mike, you're a good worker but you have a bad attitude.' My attitude is that I don't get excited about my job. I do my work but I don't say whoopee-doo. The day I get excited about my job is the day I go to a head shrinker. How are you gonna get excited about pullin' steel? How are you gonna get excited when you're tired and want to sit down. . . . It's not just the work. . . . It's the nonrecognition by other people. . . . Yes. I want my signature on 'em, too. Sometimes, out of pure meanness, when I make something, I put a little dent in it. I like to do something to make it really unique. Hit it with a hammer. I deliberately —— it up to see if it'll get by, just so I can say I did it. It could be anything."

Box Boy at Supermarket   "You have to be terribly subservient to people: 'Ma'am, can I take your bag?' 'Can I do this?' It was at a time when the grape strikers were passing out leaflets. They were very respectful. People'd come into the check stand, they'd say, 'I just bought grapes for the first time because of those idiots outside.' I had to put their grapes in the bag and thank them for coming and take them outside to the car. Being subservient made me very resentful. It's one of a chain of supermarkets . . . with music over those loud-speakers—Muzak. So people would relax while they shopped. . . . Everything looks fresh and nice. You're not aware that in the back room it stinks and there's crates all over the place and the walls are messed up. There's graffiti and people are swearing and yelling at each other. You walk through the door, the music starts playing, and everything is pretty. You talk in hushed tones and are very respectful. . . . When I first started there, the manager said, 'Cut your hair. Come in a white shirt, black shoes, a tie. Be here on time.' You get there, but he isn't there. I just didn't know what to do. The checker turns around and says, 'You new? What's your name?' 'Brett.' 'I'm Peggy.' And that's all they say and they keep throwing this down to you. They'll say, 'Don't put it in that, put it in there.' But they wouldn't help you. . . . Jim's the boss. A fish-type handshake. He was balding and in his forties. . . . Jim would say things like 'groovy.' You were supposed to get a ten-minute break every two hours. I lived for that break. You'd go outside, take your shoes off, and be human again. You had to request it. And when you took it they'd make you feel guilty. You'd go up and say, 'Jim, can I have a break?' He'd say, 'A break? You want a break? Make it a quick one, nine and a half minutes.' Ha, ha, ha. One time I asked the assistant manager, Henry. 'Do you think I can have a break?' He'd say, 'You got a break when you were hired.' Ha, ha, ha. Even when they joked it was a put-down."

Factory Owner   "I manufacture coin machine and vending machine parts— components. We also make units for amusement devices. . . . I have about two hundred employees. I never counted. They're people. We have tool and die makers, mold makers, screw machine. . . . You name it, we got it. I just stay in the background. Myself, I like making things. I make the machinery here. I'm not an engineer, but I have an idea and I kind of develop things and—they *work*. All night long I think about this place. I love my work. It isn't the money. It's just a way of expressing my feeling. . . . When I talk to people about plastic I take the position

I'*m* the plastic and how would I travel through the machine and what would I see. Maybe I'm goofy. . . . I'm here at six in the morning. Five-thirty I'll leave. Sometimes I'll come here on Sunday when everybody's gone and I'll putter around with the equipment. There isn't a machine in this place I can't run. . . . They tell me it don't look nice for the workers for me to work on the machine. I couldn't care less if I swept the floors, which I do. Yesterday some napkins fell on the floor from the napkin feeding machine. I said to the welder, 'Pick up the napkins.' He says, 'No, you pick it up.' I said, 'If you're tired, I'll pick it up.' So I'm pickin 'em up. . . . The workers say: 'You're the boss, you shouldn't do this. It's not nice. You're supposed to tell us what to do, but not to do it yourself.' I tell 'em I love it. They want me more or less in the office. . . . I'm making a machine now. I do hope to have it ready in the next couple months. The machine has nothing to do with helping humanity in any size, shape, or form. It's a personal satisfaction for me to see this piece of iron doing some work. It's like a robot working. This is the reward itself for me, nothing else. My ego, that's it. . . . Something last night was buggin' me. I took a sleeping pill to get it out of my mind. I was up half the night just bugging and bugging and bugging. I was down here about six o'clock this morning. I said, 'Stop everything. We're making a mistake.' I pointed out where the mistake was and they said, 'Holy —— we never thought of that. Today we're rebuilding the whole thing. This kind of stuff gets me. Not only what was wrong, but how the devil do you fix it? I felt better."

Director of Bakery Cooperative   "I'm the director. It has no owner. Originally I owned it. We're a nonprofit corporation 'cause we give our leftover bread away, give it to anyone who would be hungry. Poor people buy, too, 'cause we accept food stamps. We never turn anybody away. . . . We give bread lessons and talks. Sometimes school children come in here. We show 'em around and explain what we're doing. . . . Everything we do is completely open. We do the baking right out here. People in the neighborhood, waiting for the bus in the morning, come in and watch us make bread. We don't like to waste anything. That's real important. We use such good ingredients, we hate to see it go into a garbage can. . . . We have men and women, we all do the same kind of work. Everyone does everything. It's not as chaotic as it sounds. Right now there's eight of us. Different people take responsibility for different jobs. We just started dealing tea last week. Tom's interested in herbs. He bought the tea. . . . We start about five-thirty in the morning and close about seven at night. We're open six days a week. Sundays we sell what's left over from Saturday and give bread lessons. We charge a dollar a lesson to anyone who wants to come. It about covers the cost of the ingredients. Each person makes three loaves of bread. We tell why this shop uses certain ingredients and not others. . . . We try people out. We take them as a substitute first. You can't tell by words how someone's gonna do. We ask people to come as a sub when someone is absent. Out of those we choose who we'll take. We watch 'em real close. We teach 'em: 'This is the way your hands should move.' 'This is how you tell when your bread's done, if it feels this way.' . . . We try to discourage people from the start, 'cause it's hard having high turnover. . . . Some of them think it's something new or groovy. I let 'em know quickly it's not that way at all. It's *work*. Each person's here for a different reason. Tom's interested in ecological things, Jo enjoys being here and she likes working a half-day. . . . I get here at six-thirty. I stand at the table and make bread. I'll do that for maybe two hours. There might be a new person and I'll show him. . . . At eight-thirty or so I'll make breakfast and read the paper for half an hour. Maybe take a few phone calls. Then go back and weigh out loaves and shape 'em. . . . In the beginning our turnover was huge. It's slowing down now. I noticed as I was doing this tax thing at the end of the year, we've had only eleven people here the last three months, which is beautiful. That means only three people have left. In our first three months we had eighteen people. The work was unbearably hard at the beginning. As we've learned more, our work has gotten easier. So there's a big feeling of accomplishment. I get the same money as the others. I don't think that's the important issue. The decisions have been mainly mine, but this is getting to be less and less. Originally all the ideas were mine. But I'd taken them from other people. Now we have meetings, whenever anyone thinks we need one. Several times people have disagreed with me, and we did it the way the majority felt. . . . I believe people will survive if we depend on ourselves and each other. If we're working with our hands instead of with machines, we're dealing with concrete things, personal, rather than abstract things, impersonal. Unless we do something like this, I don't see this world lasting. . . . I am doing exactly what I want to do. Work is an essential part of being alive. Your work is your identity. It tells you who you are. It's gotten so abstract. People don't work for the sake of working. They're working for a car, a new house, or a vacation. It's not the work itself that's important to them. There's such a joy in doing work well."

From these brief stories we can begin to see work from the individual's perspective. We can feel some of the frustrations of trying to do one's job without the support of others. We can sense the pride workers can feel as they accomplish things they thought impossible. We can imagine the boredom of doing the same thing minute by minute, day by day, year by year. But to grasp the full meaning of this experience of work, we need to try and understand it historically.

History of Work

One of the most prevalent realities of human existence in the industrialized world is one's work experience in organizations. Most of us spend over fifty percent of our waking life engaged in some form of work. And like other human activities essential to our very existence, such as eating, sleeping, and socializing, work is well known experientially. If you asked some of the individuals from our short stories "What is work?" you would undoubtedly receive a variety of responses:

- It's a way to earn a living.
- I make my livelihood from work.
- It's what I do at WORK, INC.
- It's a boring waste of time.
- It's a real joy for me.

Yet if we ask for a definition of work we are likely to hear that work is something one does in an organization for money. While this basic conceptualization is true for most of us, it seems pretty bare in contrast to the richness of experience people can so easily relate about their work. In other words, people's conception of work provides few concrete, generally accepted clues as to why we experience work as we do. Why does the box boy feel so bored whereas the factory owner can actually see some value in sweeping a floor? How can a steel worker feel nothing exciting about his job and the bakery director enjoy making bread?

In addition, the very experience of work has changed from earliest times to the present. Prior to the Industrial Revolution work was extremely physical. With the advent of other sources of energy, work became mechanized and standardized. Now, if we believe the current literature, we are entering a new period—the post–Industrial Revolution—which can be called "the information society."[4] The result is a complexity that makes the study of work difficult to understand, much less predict and ultimately control.

Yet to understand and appreciate human behavior we must take a historical perspective to comprehend its richness and inherent dilemmas. Let us first look at one of the very earliest forms of work and organization. The ancient Egyptians were masters at organizing people for accomplishing tasks (the pyramids) that we today find extraordinary to duplicate (witness the difficulty of completing the nuclear power plants in various parts of the country). Next we look at how the craft-oriented work of the Middle Ages was accomplished on a very different level of human experience. We then compare how the Industrial Revolution transformed the concept of work and organization with which most of us are familiar today. And, finally, we see how the beginning of the information and technology revolution is redefining our present concept of work.

Ancient Egyptians   Some of the earliest written records currently available show human awareness of the importance of organization of work. The organizing problems faced by the early Egyptians are very apparent if one considers the construction of the great pyramids. One pyramid, for example, required 100,000 men working 20 years to complete. The pyramid covered 13 acres and measured 481 feet in height. It was constructed of approximately 2,300,000 stone blocks, each weighing an average of two and a half tons.[5] Just planning for and organizing the feeding and housing of 100,000 men over a 20-year period are monumental efforts in themselves, regardless of the complex end product.

The written records maintained by the Egyptians indicate that their concepts of organization had reached a high level. Indeed, it is quite reasonable to assume that without strong organizational abilities and understandings, the pyramids could not have been completed. Detailed written instructions were given to viziers (equivalent to today's manager) that defined their responsibilities. The following translation of parts of these instructions illustrate organizational problems and how they were dealt with.

Responsibility.   The overseers of hundreds and the overseers of (word not translated) shall report to Him their affairs. ("Him" refers to the top manager.)

Reports.   Furthermore, He shall go in to take council on the affairs of the kind and there shall be reporting to him in the affairs of the Two Lands in his house everyday. (Daily reporting)

Impartiality.   It is an abomination of the God to show partiality. This is the teaching: Thou shalt do the like, shalt regard him who is known to thee like him who is unknown to thee, and him who is near to thee . . . like him who is far. . . . An official who does this then shall be flourished greatly in the place. (Don't show favoritism.)

Staff advice.   Let every office, from first to last, proceed in the hall of the Vizier to take council with Him.

Authority.   It is He who appoints the overseers of the hundreds, in the hall of the king's house.[6]

While the records do not contain the feelings, reactions, or the attitudes of any of the 100,000 workers, it is probably safe to assume that the working conditions weren't as comfortable or safe as they are today. In addition, the vizier did not have to be as concerned about worker motivation since most of the labor was conscripted for the duration of the project.

A listing of the managerial problems, concepts, and attempted solutions to them over time could be greatly extended. Needless to say, we have faced problems of organizing work since the beginning of time. The distillation of human experiences (good and bad) with differing organizational arrangements, policies, methods of operation, and ways of managing work and workers over time is, to a great extent, reflected in modern organizational behavior theory. This certainly does not argue that organizations as we view them today represent the last step in their evolution.[7] Rather, this evolution has proceeded towards increasing levels of sophistication and ingenuity; it was not until the twentieth century that work and behavior became a topic of serious study. The advent of the Industrial Revolution was a major turning point in the study and design of work. Starting with the invention of the steam engine in the latter part of the eighteenth century and continuing into the twentieth century with the discovery that work and behavior could be scientifically analyzed and structured in a more efficient manner, the organization of work and behavior underwent a number of significant changes. Examining how these changes influenced the design of work provides a clearer understanding and appreciation of how people have come to manage work and behavior.

Craft-oriented Work   Widespread during the Middle Ages, the guild or craft was organized according to specific skill categories. Examples of the types of crafts include the cobbler guild, the furniture guild, the clothing guild, and the blacksmith guild. Each craft was concerned with control over learning and utilization of particular skills within a tightly defined membership. Those who aspired to membership were required to serve lengthy apprenticeships in which the art of the craft was learned from a master who was both teacher and arbitrator of craft skills. Craft knowledge and subsequent work were limited to guild members, who carried out their work with a good deal of freedom and involvement once they reached the master level.

Once an apprentice mastered the skills of the craft, that individual was able to exert considerable control—deciding upon the type and quality of goods and services to produce; choosing raw materials, tools, and methods of production; marketing the goods; and often developing new products and techniques of production. The performance of these activities allowed the involvement of total self, mentally and physically, in the craft. When certain sights, sounds, smells, feels, and even tastes were combined with know-how, intuition, and a highly trained neuro-muscular system, the artisan was able to manipulate a few simple tools and utensils to turn raw materials into useful and often artistic products. The co-op bakery is an example of this type of work experience. The new workers were instructed in the subtlety of kneading bread—how it feels and looks.

One only need to observe a modern-day artisan to appreciate the intricate balance and integration that exists among the different parts of the body. Each movement of arms, hands, and fingers is coordinated to produce a purposeful change in the product; the gestures are smooth and rhythmic, yet complex and intricate in ways that are difficult to discern. The muscles that control the movement of eyes contract and expand in ways that enable the artisan to pick up inconspicuous visual clues; the fingers are sensitive to slight changes in pressure, heat, and texture, while ears, nose, and tongue are keyed to sounds, smells, and tastes that are integral to the quality of the work. Facial expressions, breathing, and physical presence reveal a level of concentration and involvement that demands the full utilization of the whole being to produce a finished product.

In many ways, the results of craft-oriented work may be attributed to the ways in which it was "organically designed." That is, through the skillful use of the whole self, one was able to create a work structure both adaptive to environmental demands and responsive to one's own needs. The basis of this type of work design was the ability to regulate behavior in the face of change. By actively relating all facets of the self to the environment, the artisan was able to modify behavior or goals as well as influence the environment in a direction favorable to the individual.

INDUSTRIAL REVOLUTION

Mechanized Work   Watt's invention of the steam engine in 1782 revolutionized and displaced craft-oriented work. Once it became possible to replace man and beast as primary sources of physical work, people sought ways to mechanize their production processes.

In 1911, Frederick Taylor's scientific approach to analyzing and structuring tasks became the standard for designing work. The scientific approach involved analyzing tasks and combining them into the most efficient method for production. This approach, basically, involved decomposing work into its simplest elementary components, specifying in detail the tasks of each component, and recombining the components into a specific efficient sequence commonly referred to as a "production line." Using this method, it was possible to turn production tasks into "predictable determinate mechanisms which could be performed by machines or human beings behaving like machines."[8] Given the superiority of mechanical power over muscle power, production processes were converted gradually into long sequences of energy-driven machines, each performing repetitive tasks at a constant speed. The individual's role became one of assistant to the machine, performing those aspects which machines couldn't. The rationale was: "Man was simply an extension of the machine, and obviously, the more you simplified the machine (whether its living part or its nonliving part), the more you lowered costs."[9]

In contrast to the artisan, the production-line worker was constrained severely. Instead of having relative control over work life, the worker was now relegated to a limited set of highly specified quasi-mechanical operations. Decisions concerning the type, quality, and amount of goods to produce, the methods of production, the acquisition of raw materials, and the distribution of products were no longer made by production workers, but by other specialized units (such as sales, purchasing, and engineering). Since machines transformed raw materials into finished products, the individual's direct contact with the product was mediated through technological and mechanical components. This narrowed the variety of possible adaptive responses by restricting a worker's behavior to a few simple machine adjustments. Thus, the degree of self-regulation possible was confined to a narrow range. Since discretionary tasks were limited, the production-line worker did not have the opportunity to utilize fully the sense organs, brain, or the rest of the body. The steel worker provides an example when he relates how his movements are so regulated by the tasks that he can not sit down and rest because of the need to keep operations flowing.

One need only observe a modern day production-line worker to realize the extent to which the individual is not involved fully in work. The movement of the body is smooth and rhythmic, yet limited to a few simple operations that are repeated in a relatively fixed time cycle. The muscles flex and contract in ways that minimize wasted effort while establishing a uniform and continuous pattern. Raw materials and finished products are brought to and from the work area, thereby enabling the worker to continue the work cycle without interruptions. Social contact is limited to immediate work neighbors or to periodic visits from a superior who dispenses rewards and punishments. Facial expressions, gestures, and posture appear mesmerized by the repetitiveness of a work cycle that engages the physical self while neglecting emotional and cognitive sides.

If we use the criterion of economic efficiency, production-line work was extremely successful. The rate of produced goods was far superior to that of the craft method. This allowed various social and economic groups to obtain a higher standard of living while relieving them of much of the drudgery of physical labor. However, workers were relegated to a limited part of the production process. As a result, identification with a product or service was no longer a viable means of attaining social significance and community recognition. Because of the lack of challenge and self-control in production-line tasks, workers were left with little to which they could meaningfully relate or derive self-respect. Motivation to perform became dependent on extrinsic rewards as coercion was used to elicit relevant task behavior. Failure to operate according to specification resulted in reprimands from supervisors who controlled worker's behavior and coordinated the separate parts of the production process. Thus, the workplace gradually evolved into a social hierarchy. At the bottom of this pyramid stood the worker, reduced to performing a task that was no longer under the individual's control or that utilized full self-involvement.[10]

Computerized Work   We are again in the process of redefining work through the information revolution sparked by computer technology. While this subject is explored more fully in chapter 13, certain concepts and trends need to be examined at this time to fully understand the changes in our concept of work.

The potential of microprocessors as well as mainframes is awesome when we look at their usage in organizations. Certain mechanized work is being performed at computer terminals and by robots on the production line. The automation of factories and offices, once a pipe dream, is becoming a reality. Computer technology is to the information age what mechanization was to the Industrial Revolution: It is a threat because it incorporates functions previously performed by workers. How has this affected the experience of work?

There are some similarities between mechanized work and computerized work. First, both types of work have control over the worker in terms of the tasks having to be completed in a certain way to maintain quality. The information requested by the logic of a program needs to be addressed precisely or the work is rejected by the system. Second, the task characteristics are narrow in both computerized and mechanistic work. The jobs, especially in the clerical areas, still entail a limited variety of tasks because most of the paperwork processing was merely computerized without adding many additional responsibilities. Finally, the source of motivation is similar. Computerized work is no more intrinsically rewarding than mechanized work. Both provide the worker with feedback that is external to the work being performed. A printout of errors or time spent on various activities, while inherently faster than mechanized feedback, is still separated from the actual performance of the work.

One difference between mechanized work and computerized work is the physical involvement. Instead of using limited physical parts of the self, computerized work requires a great deal of mental attention to details. This has been one cause of increased complaints of stress reported by some researchers.[11] In addition, the close attention to the computer constricts the amount and timing of social contact between workers.

Table 1–1 shows the results of both the Industrial Revolution and the "information revolution" on the nature and design of work. As we can see from the table, mechanical power replaced wind, water, and animals as the primary source of energy. The development of a predictable supply of power provided the impetus for the mechanization of the workplace. Mechanized tools and complex

TABLE 1-1

Craft, mechanized, and computerized work: A comparison

	Craft Age	Industrial Revolution	Information Revolution
Prime Examples	Various guilds	Production lines	Computer terminals
Sources of Energy	Nonmechanical power (wind, water, animals, human beings)	Mechanical power	Electrical power
Types of Technology	Utensils, simple tools and machines	Mechanized tools and complex machines	Management information systems, computer programming, and electronics
Task Characteristics	Variety, challenge, autonomy, direct feedback and human contribution	Narrow, quasi-mechanical, indirect feedback and human contribution	Narrow, quasi-electronic, indirect feedback and human contribution
Human Requirements	Social, cognitive, and physical parts of self	Physical parts of self	Mental concentration
Source of Control	Self-regulation by worker	External regulation by superior or machine	External regulation by system and supervisor
Source of Motivation	Intrinsic rewards	Extrinsic rewards	Extrinsic rewards
Results	Economic livelihood, socially and psychologically rewarding	Economic efficiency, mass production, socially and psychologically inhibiting	Economic efficiency, rapid information processing, socially and psychologically inhibiting

Source: Adapted from Thomas G. Cummings and Suresh Sirvastva, *Management of Work: A Socio-Technical System Approach*, San Diego, CA: University Associates. Copyright 1977. Used with permission.

machines gradually replaced utensils and tools as methods of production. Through the scientific method the production process was reduced to its simplest components and the work became standardized. These scientifically designed jobs, mediated by machines, provided indirect feedback while limiting the direct contribution of the worker. Instead of fully engaging the social and mental parts of the worker as in the craft age, the new work required only the physical contribution.

Since the tasks allowed for little variety, challenge, autonomy, direct feedback, and individual involvement, sources of control shifted from self-regulation by workers to external regulation by supervisors. As a result, motivation to perform changed from intrinsic rewards derived from meaningful work to extrinsic rewards of money and praise.

With the advent of computers, even certain mechanized work was reduced to simpler functions controlled by information systems. The work now demands close mental concentration and can cause stress. Computer technology can also interfere with social interaction between coworkers. The source of control now resides in the information system and its demands for data. The result of this new work revolution is increased speed and accuracy of information processing and greater worker productivity.

Current Trends Affecting Organizational Behavior

In today's complex and changing state, an organization is affected by many variables both from within and from outside the organization's boundaries. Some of these variables make managing more difficult while others, if used properly, can provide solutions to management's current problems. This section, while not all inclusive, should prove beneficial to management as they strive to understand and apply the consequences of these trends.

Japanese Management Style   There has been widespread publicity about the economic and social miracle of Japan. Recently Japan has outperformed other countries in most of the sophisticated technological areas, excelling in electronics, ship building, and production of cameras, watches, video recorders, and the like. Japan has achieved these miracles while importing many critical raw materials from abroad. In many sectors of industry, Japanese wages have surpassed those of Britain and are approaching wage levels in the United States and West Germany. Behind the economic and social miracle of Japan, there are newly developed management philosophies, operating systems, and diligent workers. Japanese management systems have turned around many failing business organizations located in the United States.

While there are many reasons for their success, including governmental political support, homogeneous ethnic population, and a group-oriented culture, some credit must be given to the management style of the Japanese organizations. Japanese management style has been called Theory Z,[12] in contrast to Theory X or Y; "organic type" of management, in contrast to the American "system type" of management; and the art of Japanese management.[13] The cofounder of the Honda Motor Company once remarked that American and Japanese management are 95 percent alike, yet differ in all important respects.[14]

Japanese management can be characterized by three basic principles. These are (1) an emphasis on the group rather than the individual; (2) an emphasis on human rather than functional relationships; and (3) a view of top management as generalists and facilitators rather than as decision makers.

BOX 1–1

Nissan Utopia: Can It Work?

Smyrna, Tenn.—Marvin Runyon sat in his blue-collar uniform with his first name embroidered over the pocket and spoke recently of the team spirit and open communication between workers and managers under the 69-acre roof of the new Nissan truck plant here.

Contrary to appearances, he was not one of the production-line workers, known here as "technicians." Once an admittedly autocratic Ford Motor Co. executive in coat and tie, Runyon, 58, has become down-home, consensus-building "Marvin" now that he is president of Nissan's U.S. operations and in charge of this futuristic factory rising out of the cow pastures 18 miles southeast of Nashville. At $660 million, it is the largest investment in the United States by any Japanese company.

It boasts 220 robots to work beside 2,000 Tennessee humans whose selection from among 120,000 applicants was based in part on ability to be "team players." It has laser-controlled paint guns, streamlined die-changing, common cafeterias and uniforms for workers and bosses, Ping-Pong and picnics, wages competitive with industry averages, workers trained in many skills instead of just one, only half as many management levels as Detroit automakers and, in contrast to old-style tough Detroit straw bosses, supervisors who are required always to "enhance or protect the workers' self-esteem."

In short, it is an expensive selection of what Runyon and his staff deemed the best of both American and Japanese technology and philosophy, assembled from the ground up. "A once-in-a-lifetime chance," Runyon said.

In an industry where union organizers once fought club-wielding management goons for workers' basic rights, such an enlightened approach might have been hailed as industrial nirvana. Instead, it is a beam in the eye of the United Auto Workers Union.

As Runyon drove the first Nissan pickup off the production line here June 16, UAW President Owen Bieber issued a statement reiterating the belief of union officials that organizing the plant is a must, lest their negotiating powers be undermined in the industry.

The workers "have been led to believe they are the beneficiaries of a Japanese-style experiment in cooperative management which makes a union unnecessary," he said. "We respectfully remind Mr. Runyon that Henry Ford, the founder of his former employer, likewise believed a union could not improve the condition of Ford workers."

However, Nissan workers such as Frank Johnson, 29, present the union with a difficult task. He grew up in a farm family of 14 and previously belonged to the machinists' union while working

Source: Kathy Sawyer, *The Herald,* Everett, WA (26 June 1983): 3D. © The Daily Herald Co. Used by permission.

Instead of the rugged individualism so idealized in the United States, Japanese relish life in groups. The president of Nippon Steel, describing the difference between American and Japanese management, said that while a U.S. corporation is regarded as a cold, impersonal economic unit, the Japanese unit is regarded as a community with a common destiny.[15] By focusing on the group instead of the individual, Japanese corporations are able to unleash considerable

at a Tennessee air-conditioner assembly plant. "I believe unions have outgrown the intentions of what they were organized for," he said. "If you're going to do your job, and the company is going to recognize that things are changing and treat you fairly, you don't need a third party talking for you."

Johnson, who works in the paint booth touching up places missed by machines, was one of 383 employees, including 128 production-line workers, taken to Japan by Nissan to study Japanese teamwork and other techniques. . . .

The state also contributed $7 million to Nissan's unusually extensive $63 million screening and training program for employees. Nissan, in turn, agreed to hire Tennesseans instead of bringing experienced, unemployed auto workers from out of state. Only two vice presidents here are Japanese to aid in the start-up, and some 10 employee families are Japanese. . . .

Beverly Myers, 27, and her husband, Bruce, both work for Nissan. She puts on brake tubes, air conditioning, rear carpets, door locks, and does other jobs the robots can't do. A former factory worker, she applied two years ago and says she had to go through a test, three interviews, six weeks in the company's unpaid training program nights and weekends, and another interview.

At the union plant she worked in before, she said, "If somebody picked up something they weren't supposed to, somebody would file a grievance. It was too picky for me." At Nissan, she said, "I've learned every job in my zone—19 different jobs."

She and other workers meet every morning with their supervisors and talk about everything from softball to problems on the line. "They want you to come to them if something's wrong. . . . They want you to be happy and not dread coming every day. That way, absenteeism stays down and quality stays up and they'll make more money in the long run."

While the workers, new to the auto industry, have not yet developed "bad habits," officials said, the managers are another story. Many of them came from Ford or other American auto companies and they speak of the old traditions like smokers trying to quit.

"When you're in an autocratic environment, you tend to respond in an autocratic way," said Runyon. In changing styles, "We have to fight the old tendencies. It's tough when you know what you want to do but you are reaching a consensus decision. It takes longer."

Questions

1. List the trends affecting Nissan and what specific programs are being used to address them.
2. What work values does Nissan assume in setting up the Tennessee plant? How do you respond to Mr. Bieber's statement about the union being the only way to improve the condition of the workers?
3. What aspects of Japanese management are present in this story? Why do they seem to work? Under what conditions could this be applied elsewhere?

energy of the type usually reserved for college athletics, nationalism, or religion. Japanese companies seem to be able to elicit worker attitudes similar to school spirit, patriotism, and religious fervor.

Japanese management reinforce the group consciousness through a variety of methods. The first is to emphasize the permanence of the group. Those who are recruited into the core group of an enterprise enter with the understanding that they are joining for life. Pay and incentives for workers, which account for nearly a third of yearly salary, depend partly on company profits or on the financial health of the group. Group cohesiveness is supported by morning calisthenics, company songs, recitations of the company creed, and other activities. The ''us against them'' mentality in a Japanese company is likely to refer to the company against its competitors—not the workers against management.

The second major Japanese management principle is the emphasis on human rather than functional relationships. American organizations tend to view people as tools to fill slots that have specific job descriptions. In Japan, however, the permanence of the group forces managers to place more emphasis on people than on the system. This emphasis on human relation can be seen in careful recruitment practices, a concern for the whole employee, harmonious resolution of conflicts, and ambiguity in expressing differences, which minimizes hurt feelings and allows for saving face.

First, recruitment in Japan tends to be centralized, with the president of the company often personally interviewing the candidates to be hired. Virtually all new recruits in Japan are hired directly after graduation from schools and universities. Japanese rely heavily on schools to select the students with the best minds, who will then be offered the best jobs in government or business. Japanese paternalism and focus on social as well as economic relationships stem partly from Japan's early industrial period. During this period firms had to provide housing and healthy diets, and provide for the moral, intellectual, and physical well-being of their employees before their families would allow them to leave the farms to work in the city.

Finally, the Japanese feel that there should be harmony within and competition without. People resent being humiliated, publicly scolded, or fired. They will go to great lengths to defend themselves against any such action and will in the process dissipate considerable energy that could better be directed toward external competition. Japanese companies attempt to minimize the internal conflict by emphasizing harmony.[16] But maintaining harmony requires having a multitude of ways of saying no. Japanese use ambiguity and indirection instead of outright refusal. As a result, differences tend to be worked out through long discussions and an attempt to understand the viewpoint of others.

Japanese management tend to be generalists and facilitators much like elders in a tribe. Problems are usually solved by groups from middle management after consultation with superiors and then circulated for final approval. The decision-making process tends to be slow, but the implementation is faster with the full commitment of those in the organization. Having individuals trained from a generalist's perspective allows responsibility to be widely dispersed and the system to be highly flexible. Another aspect of this generalist orientation is the practice of consensus or participative decision making. The vehicle for formalizing the decision is the *ringisho*, a document outlining the decision, which circulates among various groups for their approval. Each affixes its seal after the group makes suggestions for improvement. This form of decision-making requires centralization and considerable face-to-face contact among managers. As a result the actual responsibility for the decision is also widespread among the employees of the firm.[17]

A summary of the differences between Japanese and American management practices is illustrated in Table 1–2. The overriding characteristic of Japanese management appears to be its emphasis on the organization as a community whose members share a permanent bond and fate.

Information Technology   In 1982 about one million computers or data terminals were added to the four million already in use in firms in the United States. It is expected that this number will increase by 25 percent each year for the next ten years.

TABLE 1–2
Characteristics of Japanese and American management styles

Japanese	American
1. Emphasis on group	1. Emphasis on the individual
Permanence of group	Transitory nature of group
Same fate shared by all employees	Own fate determined by each employee
Group incentives	Individual incentives
Group against outsiders	Individual against others
2. Emphasis on human relationships	2. Emphasis on functional relationships
"Lifetime" employment and recruitment	Short-term employment and recruitment
Harmonious resolution of conflicts	Adversarial resolution of conflicts
Holistic concern for employees	Segmented concern for employees
Desire for indirection, ambiguity	Desire for clarity, brute integrity
No formal distinctions between managers and workers	Frequently sharp distinctions between managers and workers
3. Managers as generalists	3. Managers as specialists
Manager as social and symbolic leader	Manager as professional
Manager as facilitator	Manager as decision maker
Management by consensus	Management by objectives
Decisions that come from middle up	Decisions that come from top down
Centralization	Decentralization
Wide dispersion of responsibility	Narrow assignment of responsibility
Nonspecialized career paths	Specialized career paths

Source: Adapted from Dick Kazuyuki Nanto, "Management, Japanese Style," in S. M. Lee and G. Schwendiman, eds., *Management by Japanese Systems,* p. 21. Copyright © 1982 Praeger Publishers. Reprinted and adapted by permission of Praeger Publishers.

No one doubts that the use of computers will not only increase but that almost every job will be affected by computers either directly or indirectly. Yet what will the impact be on the behavior of individuals within organizations as they adapt to this new technology? What will this change mean for the management of employees? How will individuals respond to management's pressure to learn how to use computers? Will this technology affect relationships between individuals on the job? These questions are only the beginning of concern felt by workers and management alike. While the answers are only in their infancy, some effects have been noted as firms begin to introduce computers into employees' jobs.

One of the first reactions employees have when notified that their job is about to be computerized is "OH, NO!" Computers mean change and change means that "I will have to do something different." But this reaction is typical of any change an individual faces and not necessarily just that of computer technology. More is said about the change process in chapter 11.

Nevertheless, there does seem to exist a form of reaction termed "computerphobia" or "cyberphobia," meaning fear, distrust, or hatred of computers.[18] One researcher interviewed several hundred managers and college students who used computers, and tested them by wiring them to a galvanic-skin-response measuring device while they worked at their terminals. He found that nearly one-third of these people were cyberphobic. About 5 percent of the participants actually showed the physical symptoms of classic phobia: nausea, dizziness, cold sweat, and high blood pressure. One frustrated worker actually dumped coffee and cigarette ashes into a computer console.[19]

Another organizational group often cited as fearful of the introduction of computers is the ranks of middle management.[20] One factor that contributes to cyberphobia seems to be middle management's fear that they don't actually manage anything—that in fact they are not really decision makers, but merely "information conduits," who could easily be replaced by the very computers that they are learning to use. This notion has also led to predictions of organizational structures becoming flatter over time as middle management is eliminated.

What can be done to overcome some of this fear? One suggestion is to gradually expose people to the computer. Attach the introduction to what most people have experienced before, such as calculations and games. One firm has bought "Pac-Man" and has the employee merely play the game.[21] Boston's First National Bank has set up a walk-in computer center where managers can get private instruction. John Martin, a vice president, says, "We have found that if they can go and practice someplace private, a little knowledge and interest will conquer their fears."[22]

Work Force Value Changes   Another trend having importance for the manager and the organization is the effects of the changing values and attitudes of today's workers. Much of the literature examines the value changes that result from the workers' search for meaningful, self-fulfilling work. Workers are seen as becoming more inner-directed and now seek and expect, among other things, autonomy in their work, respect for their superiors, open channels of communication, and the opportunity to participate in decision making.[23]

What are some of the factors which have brought about these value changes? Suggested factors include higher levels of education, more leisure time, greater affluence, the effects of today's "instant" culture, and growth of the media. Most authors agree, however, that the changes are rooted in the social upheaval of the sixties. The sixties were characterized by search for self-fulfillment, self-expression, and personal growth and a rejection of such traditional values as materialism and respect for authority. Two authors suggest that this clash between the Protestant work ethic of the older generation and the hippie counterculture produced a generation uncertain in its view of itself and its goals. Left with no clear role models, this generation was forced to look inside itself for direction and emerged the "Me Generation" of the seventies.[24]

Another author views workers today as seeing themselves as "total systems." She reports that American workers have "taken to heart the expanded personal freedom that accompanied the social upheaval" and now are focusing on self-fulfillment and personal happiness as ultimate life goals. She further suggests that "organizations may find employees harder to manage, but they will also find them highly motivated and committed to tasks they value."[25] A related view of the evolution of today's values revolves around Maslow's hierarchy of needs. This study reports that employees today perceive their basic needs for pay and good working conditions to be satisfied to the extent that they are now motivated to satisfy a higher level of need. The authors suggest that "when . . . employees perceive that their basic needs for adequate pay and job security are being fulfilled . . . esteem-related factors . . . become more salient. Employees' attitudes toward (these) factors . . . will probably continue to deteriorate unless concerted short-term efforts are made to correct (them)."[26]

The end result is that a large group of sixties baby boomers has arrived on the corporate scene with a new set of values and beliefs about what life should be. Whether you agree that the narcissistic culture of the "Me Generation" has brought about an intrinsic decline in the work ethic, or that organizations' lack of response to the natural evolution of workers' needs has caused a drop in morale, the fact remains that the issue is here to stay. "The value changes will be the *realities* that companies must face in the 1980s."[27]

Before the business world can attempt to deal with the changing demands of its workers, it must clarify exactly what today's employees are looking for. Studies agree that first and foremost is the workers' desire to find meaning and self-fulfillment in their work. Work is no longer seen as merely a means of supporting oneself, but a major factor in one's life. As employees have become more concerned with the quality of life in general, they also become concerned with the quality of life at the workplace. One researcher comments, "Humans today want more than to survive; they want to flourish. They want . . . their work places to be responsive to this need, to assist them in flourishing, to assist them in becoming whole."[28]

BOX 1–2

Mayor Keeps Date with Workers

The Edmonds Civic Center all but closed down from 1 to 2 P.M. Friday. Meanwhile, the parking lot at Wade James Theater held two fire engines, an aid car, police cars, half a dozen public-works trucks and assorted other city vehicles.

There was no fire at the theater, and city employees weren't attending a matinee. It was Edmond's first all-city staff meeting, a chance for new Mayor Larry Naughten to meet the 165 people who work for him.

He told employees he wanted to "get the whole city under one roof to tell you my plans . . . and to quiet some fears that some of you may have."

Naughten took the major's office away from 16-year incumbent Harve Harrison in November's election. He became the city's first full-time mayor on January 1.

The new mayor gave a 20-minute pep talk Friday, promising improved working conditions and stressing the importance of serving the public. Then he fielded questions for another 20 minutes before sending everyone back to work.

Employees had lots of questions, ranging from Naughten's plans to reorganize city departments to his feelings about annexation and shared services.

"I'm opposed to a lot of layers of management between myself and the employees," Naughten said, confirming that he and the Edmonds City Council plan to reshape departments. The subject will be discussed at a February 25 workshop, he said. . . .

A firefighter asked why the 1984 budget doesn't include money for three new firefighters, as Fire Chief Jack Weinz had requested. Naughten said the council set aside only $100,000 for new employees. One new firefighter probably will be hired, but the rest of the money may be needed for other workers, he said.

Naughten asked employees to help him improve the city's efficiency and working conditions. February paychecks will include a confidential survey, he said. He said he also plans to establish an employee suggestion program and revive a long-defunct employee newsletter.

Several city workers said later they appreciated the chance to meet with the mayor. "It shows there's interest in how we feel," said Robert Bentler, a 14-month employee of the water-sewer division. "It was time for a change."

"Morale was kind of low," agreed Marty Burns, who has worked for the water-sewer division for three years. "A lot of times there was a lack of communication. This kind of thing is going to help."

"I think he's taking all the right steps," said Deputy City Clerk Jackie Parrett.

Questions

1. Do you think what Mr. Naughten did was necessary? Why?
2. What values do you suppose Mr. Naughten has about his job? How does he view his employees' values?
3. If you were Mr. Naughten, what would you do during your tenure as mayor?

Source: Kathy Samels, *The Herald*, Everett, WA (Saturday, 21 January 1984): 3A. © The Daily Herald Co. Used by permission.

To achieve their goal of meaningful and fulfilling work, employees have come to expect and demand changes in organizational structure, management behavior, and the design and scope of their own jobs. Of primary importance are autonomy in one's job, respect from superiors, open channels of communication, and participation in the decision-making process. In addition, workers expect fair and equal treatment, opportunities for advancement, and employer concern for the employee's personal situation or problems.

Studies show, however, that employee expectations are not being met. And because these expectations are the motivating factors employees require to perform well, morale and performance levels have tended to drop. One study shows that while workers rate traditional motivators such as pay and job security favorably, overall job satisfaction is on the decline. The study shows dissatisfaction with perceived respect from management, opportunities for upward communication, and expectation of advancement. The study concludes

> Thus, the esteem-related items seem to account for the recent downturn in overall job satisfaction, while extrinsic items, such as satisfaction with pay, do not. These attitudes suggest that there are strong disincentives to perform well on a job, since some of the major rewards for good performance are missing.[29]

Another study makes a similar point and contends that the work ethic is thriving, while work behavior is faltering.[30] The researcher feels that American workers' self-esteem requires them to work harder and produce high-quality products. The fact that they are not doing so, he says, is related to flaws in the reward system; there is "growing doubt that hard work will bring the rewards people have come to cherish."[31]

What impact does this have for the study of organizational behavior? It is clear that organizations must undergo some major changes to cope with the demands of changing worker values. This is the result of the hypothesis that the supposed decline of the work ethic is merely a failure on the part of organizations to respond to the motivating needs of today's employees.

In the first place, it is apparent that the traditional hierarchical management structure is no longer effective. Workers are looking for upward communication and participation in decision making at all levels. In addition, workers want meaningful rather than tedious job tasks. They want to feel that they are contributing to the success of the organization and that they will be rewarded for their efforts through recognition and advancement. More than one researcher advocates more participatory management styles "where management recognizes that imagination and initiative cannot be legislated from the top down, but must rise spontaneously from every level and area of operation."[32] Concepts such as quality circles and suggestion systems, and frequent attitude surveys followed by tangible attempts at improving identified problems, are possible areas where organizations might start.

Summary of Key Concepts

1. Organizational behavior helps us answer questions concerning understanding, predicting, and influencing individual behavior in organizational settings.

2. Studying organizational behavior helps us cope with organizational life and develop insights beyond "common sense."

3. A theoretical model allows us to view the relationship between dependent and independent variables, such as leadership style and employee satisfaction. However, we must be careful to understand that individual behavior may have multiple causes.

4. Organizational behavior has a rich foundation in other disciplines, such as psychology, sociology, and anthropology. Each gives us insight into the various aspects of organizational life—individual, group, and organizational levels. Organizational behavior attempts to integrate this knowledge into a systematic study of behavior in organizations.

5. Whether one's job is at the bottom of the organizational hierarchy or at the top, we all experience frustrations, joys, problems, and opportunities that form the basis of our experience of work.

6. The history of work spans three periods—craft-oriented work, mechanized work, and computerized work. Each period has its uniqueness in terms of how it affected the individual worker.

7. It is our contention that several trends, such as Japanese management style, information technology, and work force value changes, will provide some challenge to today's management that can be beneficial in the long run as we cope with their demands.

Key Terms

Computerized work	Mechanized work
Craft-oriented work	Organizational behavior
Dependent variable	Participative management
Independent variable	Theory

ORGANIZATIONAL BEHAVIOR IN PERSPECTIVE—APPLICATIONS

As already noted, most of the chapters in this book consist of two parts—one part describing and explaining the pertinent, widely accepted theory in an area of specific interest in the field of organizational behavior, and the other part relating how some of these theories are applied by organizations and managers. As this is the first of the application sections, it might be useful to discuss some of the characteristics of these sections so that you can determine how they will be most useful to you.

Purpose of Application Section

In these application sections we describe some situations in which application of the theories has been highly successful and others in which application of the theories has met with failure. We look at the behaviors of managers who support the theory and at the behaviors of managers who oppose the theory—yet get impressive results. In short, we try to get you to look at the theory from the perspective of an action-oriented manager who is responsible for achieving some specific organizational goals. Much of what we see in textbooks today describes what ought to happen and how the theory ought to work in the real world of organizations. We first describe the pertinent theory, then relate a series of applications of that theory so that you can make your own judgements about its effectiveness and its usefulness to a manager.

Several different kinds of materials are included in these sections, from a variety of sources. There are descriptions of situations in which particular organizations have attempted to apply some of the theory. We look at a variety of instances from various kinds of organizations. There are also comments from managers about their experiences in using some of the theories. We'll find that some managers had very positive experiences while others were very disappointed in their attempts to apply what the theorists say ought to work.

Our materials come from a variety of sources:

- *Professional literature* in the field—materials intended primarily for researchers and academics studying organizational behavior. Often this literature is very technical and obtuse.
- *Popular literature* in the field—materials intended primarily for practicing managers and those interested in organizations from a very pragmatic viewpoint.
- *General literature*—materials related to organizational behavior and management published in the general press and intended for widespread consumption.
- *Management experience*—information drawn from the experience of managers in organizations—managers talking about their actual experiences.
- *Consultant experience*—information based on the experience of consultants to organizations. We draw on both our own consulting practices and the experiences of other consultants.

Each point covered in the theory part of the chapter could not be covered in the applications section, in the interest of space. One criterion for inclusion was that the material be interesting and that it have a managerial emphasis. We were not concerned, for example, that each theoretical point have a corresponding application, or that each point be supported by both a description of an organizational practice and a comment from a practicing manager. We weren't concerned that each of the previously noted sources be represented in each of the applications sections. We didn't look for items that would either support or oppose our prejudices as they relate to organizations and how they function. Because the overall purpose of the applications section is to give you some useful insights into how organizations and managers really function, we tried to keep this focus in selecting materials to be included.

We do not intend for the material presented to be prescriptive about how organizations and managers should behave. Even in those instances in which the results of a particular practice seem to be highly successful, we don't offer that practice as a recommendation for action. We always ask you to look at the trade-offs in following a particular course of action and to make the decision of whether or not it would be useful based on your analysis of the situation, not ours. The history of organizational behavior research indicates a strong attempt to discover some universal theories that could—and should—be applied in any situation. More recent efforts strongly indicate that the application of theory is highly situational, and must be appropriate for a particular situation. One of the major responsibilities of a manager is to determine if a particular theory is appropriate for a specific situation. The applications sections of the book should help you to develop the capacity to make those kinds of decisions.

Participative Management

One issue that comes through very strongly in the first part of this chapter is the tendency toward increased participation by workers in the decision making process in organizations. This was highlighted in the section "Work Force Value Changes." Today's worker is looking for a more meaningful relationship to the work being performed. In fact, participation has taken on many of the characteristics of a cult in some management circles. There have been some interesting studies done recently about the nature of participation and its effectiveness.

Rosabeth Moss Kanter indicates some of the dilemmas of managing participation.[33] Citing that many experiences in using participative management seem to be unsatisfactory, she notes that managers are often unrealistic about what can happen as a result of encouraging participation by workers in decision making. Managers simply expect too much. She also notes that in many situations managers fail to manage the participative process effectively.

Participation is often not the most effective process to use in an organization, and there are many circumstances in which authoritative, unilateral decisions or delegation to a single individual makes more sense. Participation seems to apply for the following kinds of purposes:

- To gain new sources of expertise and experience
- To get collaboration that results in synergism
- To allow those who feel they know something about a topic to get involved
- To build consenses on a controversial issue
- To balance or confront conflicting interests
- To address conflicting approaches or views
- To develop and educate people through their participation

But there are clearly times when participation is not appropriate:

- When one person clearly knows more than others
- When those to be affected by the decision accept the knowledge and expertise of that person
- When the "correct" answer is already known
- When there is no time for discussion
- When no one really cares all that much about the issue
- When people work more productively and effectively alone

Thus, the decision to have participation or not is not automatic, regardless of what much of the popular literature might say. There are conditions under which it is likely to be much more effective, and a manager must assess for the current situation whether or not those conditions are present.

An excellent example for understanding these sorts of guidelines for participation or nonparticipation can be seen by looking at the Ben Reed story in the beginning of the chapter. What criteria did Mr. Grayson use to decide about Ben's physiology courses? What was Ben's view of using participation with the office workers?

Another consideration we have not mentioned concerns the manager's style and comfort with the process of participation. We know many very effective managers whose style is such that participation is not a useful activity for them. When forced to engage in participative processes, they seem to lose a great deal of their effectiveness. We'll talk more about this element of managerial style in chapter 5; but you should recognize that managerial style has a lot to do with how any particular manager will evaluate the trade-offs in following any particular decision-making process.

In looking more closely at the participation process, Dr. Kanter notes that there are several kinds of dilemmas that arise. Some are concentrated around beginning the process of participation. Can participation be effective if an *order* to participate comes from the top of the organization? What if the people who are asked to participate feel that the request is just a form of paternalism? Should participation be limited to volunteers, or should participation be mandatory? These questions illustrate some of the problems that arise in starting a process of participation in an organization. In light of this dilemma, what advice would you give Mr. Grayson if he wanted to allow his employees more say in their jobs?

Another kind of dilemma concerns the structuring of the participative process. Supposedly simple questions regarding the amount of time devoted to participation become important at this stage of the process. How do you resolve the questions concerning decision making by a number of people when the area under discussion might be the responsibility of a single person? What happens when people want to be involved in decisions in which they should not be—because they don't have adequate information or a broad enough perspective?

Who decides whether or not they have adequate information or a broad enough perspective? These kinds of questions are not easy to answer.

There are dilemmas revolving around the dynamics of teamwork. Bringing people together to participate in decision making doesn't mean that all will flow smoothly or, even if it does, that an effective decision will be reached. Who is responsible for establishing the ground rules under which the participation will be enacted? Who, if anyone, monitors the process to assure that more powerful people are kept under control? What happens when a team becomes bogged down and makes no progress? Although such issues significantly affect a team's ability to perform, in much of the literature concerning participation, they are often not even considered.

Finally, problems can arise regarding the evaluation of the output of a team or other participative group. What if the solution is technically inappropriate? The group likes it, but it just won't work. What if the solution is not economically feasible? Or the manager doesn't like the solution because it is counter to the manager's values? Again, these kinds of issues often don't seem to have been taken into account in determining whether to use the participation.

It is these very questions regarding participation that speak to the criticisms of applying Japanese style of management. In America, individual orientation is more predominant than group orientation. The Japanese, therefore, have an advantage; they are able to use participation more effectively by applying some consistent rules of behavior to individuals in a group setting.

As we can see, participation may not be as simple as it seems. Although there is no question that we will see more of it, managers who understand some of the potential problems will be much more likely to use participation successfully than those who take the popular literature at face value.

Management in the Late 1980s and 1990s

In the conceptual section we noted that the experience of work changed with the Industrial Revolution and is changing as the effects of the information revolution are felt by more segments of our economy. We also noted some of the trends that will affect management and organizations in the future. A recent article in the Wall Street Journal [34] stresses that one of the most prevalent trends of the future is that managing will be tougher.

The period of sluggish economic growth forecast for the 1980s and 1990s will make management's job more difficult. According to Edward Jefferson, chairman of the duPont Company, "Everything is easier when the economy is bubbling along because growth can help to mask your mistakes. Slower growth is less forgiving because you simply have got to focus on the basics, such as competitive cost position. . . . And in a period of low growth, you have to redouble your emphasis on quality and service."[35]

Such comments are not peculiar to profit-making organizations. In a recent informal survey of Chief Executive Officers (CEOs) of all kinds of organizations, the authors found that one of the top concerns of these executives was the impact that reduced growth and decline in activity would have on their ability to manage their organization successfully.[36]

In the period immediately ahead, organizations must be especially alert to their own strengths, build upon them, and make growth happen—for them. There can be great variations in the fortunes of individual organizations in difficult times, and the successful organizations seem to be those that can "make something happen" rather than simply react to things that do happen. Some of the managers in those successful organizations seem to do things counter to "traditional" management theory.

One top executive states that the difficult times of the 1980s and 1990s will require a tough analytical discipline that will enable an organization to build on its strengths and eliminate its weaknesses. He states that more attention must be paid to operations and that increased managerial attention must be given to stressing an organization's "cultural values" in a way that instills employee loyalty and shared goals. In addition, a greater need for managerial vision is apparent.[37]

Obviously, this last comment about "cultural values" reflects the reality that the work force's values are changing and management can not assume that employee loyalty will result from just a paternalistic attitude and benefits on the part of management. Instead managers need to instill loyalty through more shared destiny—as the individual succeeds, so will the organization succeed. Can management connect the values of self-fulfillment and self-direction with the organization's need for a common vision and purpose?

Top Management and Computers

One of the major trends noted earlier in this chapter was the increasing impact of computers on how organizations are managed. Much of the information that supports this trend deals with managers at a middle level in organizations—managers who routinely use computers as an integral part of their activities. But what about top level managers? Do they use computers themselves—or is it just their staffs and subordinate managers? An article from the *Harvard Business Review* is revealing.

In the article "The CEO Goes on Line,"[38] the authors indicate that very top level managers are personally using computers at a rapidly increasing rate and are, in fact, changing the nature of some of the traditional communications patterns found in organizations. (We'll talk more about this in chapter 4.) More and more CEOs are depending less on their staffs for analysis and evaluation of operational data. They are personally doing more of this kind of activity—using computers.

While a great many top level managers still depend upon their staffs to provide both manual and computer-generated analysis, more and more top managers are moving away from this pattern—for a variety of reasons. Many top managers are analytically oriented. Computer technology can help them to gain a greater understanding of their organization and how it operates. Further, the technology has progressed to the point where it can be tailored to the needs of the individual top manager relatively easily, at least as compared with the possibilities of doing so just a few years ago. Finally, top managers can have a system developed for their personal use at a relatively low cost. For these reasons, we would expect the numbers of top managers using computers to continue to increase very rapidly, and at some point, not too far distant, would expect literally all top managers to have the capability to use computers and would expect most to actually do so.

Here are some comments from CEOs now using computers:[39]

- "Your staff can't really help you think. The problem with giving a question to your staff is that they provide you with an answer. You learn the value of the real question you should have asked when you muck around in the data."
- "It saves a great deal of time in communicating with functional staff personnel. Today, for an increasing number of problems, I can locate the data I want, and can develop it in the form I want faster than I could describe my needs to the appropriate staffer."
- "Some of my best ideas come to me at times between five in the evening and seven the next morning. Access to the relevant data to check something out right then is very important. My home terminal lets me perform the analysis while it's at the forefront of my mind."
- "The computer system provides me with a somewhat independent source for checking on the analysis and opinions presented to me by my line subordinates and my functional staffs. There is a great deal of comfort in being relatively independent of the analysis done by others."
- "A very real use of the system is the signal it gives to the rest of the company that I desire more quantitatively oriented management of the organization. I want my subordinates to think more analytically, and they are. I feel we're on the way to becoming a significantly better managed company."

Judging from the previous comments, CEOs find the computer to be an increasingly valuable managerial tool. As more and more people who will become CEOs receive education in computers early in their schooling, more and more executives will be very comfortable using computers when they reach the highest levels of management.

Other "application" sections aren't exactly like this one, but now you have an idea of the sorts of things that are included. We're very concerned that the theoretical part of the field of organizational behavior be presented in a meaningful context, and these application sections are one of the ways that we attempt to do so. We hope they help you to develop meaningful insights into the ways that organizations really function.

DISCUSSION QUESTIONS

1. Are today's jobs becoming more mechanized or more craft oriented? How do you view the introduction of computer technology in these terms?

2. What characteristics of Japanese management style can we use in the Western world? Which characteristics can't we use? Why?

3. How might you redesign your role as a student in this course using the changes occuring in work values? What obstacles may prevent you from implementing those changes?

4. If a manager or a family member asked you why you are studying a course about organizational behavior, what would you say?

5. Suppose your instructor said, "Today you may participate in deciding how to run this course. Tell me where we should start." What would your response be?

EXERCISE: VALUES

From reading this chapter, you are aware that human behavior in organizations has evolved over time from craft orientation to more specific task orientation. This means that on the whole jobs have less individual discretion attached to them, yet a current trend is a change in the workers' values from security to self-actualization. This contrasting picture could present some conflict between organizational needs and individual needs. This exercise allows you to collect some data from individuals in organizations to see how they view this situation.

Organize yourselves into small groups of three or four members and identify six individuals in various organizations to interview. Try to choose workers and managers from different levels and from union and nonunion firms. Using the following questions as a guide, construct your own questionnaire. After you collect the data, present your findings in light of what the chapter stated.

Questions

1. Tell me about your job responsibilities. What is a typical day like?

2. What are the positive aspects of your job? What excites you about doing your job?

3. What are the negative aspects of your job? What things would you like to change? Who could you tell about those changes? Would they listen and respond? Can you give an example?

4. What are the reasons you work? Can you give some examples?

5. Is this your first job? If you've had others, how does this job compare to the others? Better? Worse? Why? Examples?

6. Do you see any differences between the younger and older workers concerning why they work? What motivates them to work?

7. Is the organization changing over time? How? Can you give some examples? Do you see this as positive? Negative? Why?

8. What advice would you give someone like myself, who was considering work here in this firm?

NOTES

1. Copyright © 1976 by H. R. Knudson, Graduate School of Business, University of Washington. Reprinted with permission from Harry R. Knudson and C. Patrick Fleenor, *Organizational Behavior: A Management Approach* (Winthrop Publishing, 1978): 148–150.

2. Kathleen L. Gregory, "Native-View Paradigms: Multiple Cultures and Culture Conflicts in Organizations," *Administrative Science Quarterly*, vol. 28, no. 3 (September 1983): 359–76.

3. Adapted from Studs Terkel, *Working* (New York: Avon Books, 1974). Used by permission of author.

4. John Naisbitt, *Megatrends* (New York: Warner Books, 1982).

5. William L. Westerman, *The Story of the Ancient Nations* (New York: D. Appleton, 1912): 18–19.

6. James Henry Breasted, *Ancient Records of Egypt, Vol 11* (Chicago: The University of Chicago Press, 1906): 269–279.

7. John H. Jackson and Cyril P. Morgan, *Organization Theory: A Macro Perspective for Management* (Englewood Cliffs, NJ: Prentice-Hall, 1978): 13–14.

8. P. G. Herbst, "Socio-Technical Unit Design," Tavistock Institute of Human Relations, Doc. No. T.899 (1966): 1.

9. Louise E. Davis, "The Coming Crisis for Production Management: Technology and Organization," *International Journal of Production Research*, vol. 9, no. 1 (1971): 70.

10. Adapted from Thomas G. Cummings and Suresh Srivastva, *Management of Work: A Socio-Technical Systems Approach* (San Diego: University Associates, 1977): 5–10.

11. Craig Brod, *Technostress: The Human Cost of the Computer Revolution* (Reading, MA: Addison-Wesley, 1984).

12. William Ouchi, *Theory Z* (Reading, MA: Addison-Wesley, 1981).

13. R. T. Pascale and A. G. Athos, *The Art of Japanese Management* (New York: Simon & Schuster, 1981).

14. Ibid.

15. "Japanese Managers Tell How Their System Works," *Fortune* (November 1977): 126–138.

16. Pascale, *Art of Japanese Management*, p. 101.

17. M. Y. Yoshino, *Japan's Management System* (Cambridge, MA: The MIT Press, 1968).

18. Berkley Rice, "Curing Cyberphobia," *Psychology Today* (August 1983): 79.

19. Sanford B. Weinberg, John T. English, and Carla J. Mond, "A Strategem for Reduction of Cyberphobia," presented to the American Association for the Advancement of Science, Toronto, Canada, 1981.

20. *Business Week* (25 April 1983).

21. Personal interview, January 1984.

22. Rice, "Curing Cyberphobia."

23. Daniel Yankelovitch, "The Work Ethic Is Underemployed," *Psychology Today* (May 1982): 5–8; and Phillip Grant, "Why Employee Motivation Has Declined in America," *Personnel Journal* (December 1982): 905–909.

24. Ann Howard and James A. Wilson, "Leadership in a Declining Work Ethic," *California Management Review* (Summer 1982): 42.

25. Johanna S. Hunsaker, "Work and Family Life Must Be Integrated," *Personnel Administrator* (April 1983): 89.

26. M. R. Cooper, B. S. Morgan, P. M. Foley, and L. B. Kaplan, "Changing Employee Values: Deepening Discontent?" *Harvard Business Review*, vol. 57, no. 1 (January–February 1979): 123.

27. Rosemary J. Erickson, "The Changing Workplace and Workforce," *Training and Development Journal* (January 1980): 84.

28. Marsha Sinetar, "Management in the New Age: An Exploration of Changing Work Values," *Personnel Journal* (September 1980): 751.

29. Cooper et al., "Changing Employee Values," p. 124.

30. Yankelovitch, "Work Ethic Is Underemployed."

31. Ibid., p. 8.

32. Mary Cunningham, "Planning for Humanism," *Journal of Strategy* (Spring 1983): 83.

33. Rosabeth Moss Kanter, "Dilemmas of Managing Participation," in *The Changemasters: Innovation for Productivity in the American Corporation* (New York: Simon & Schuster, 1983): 5–27.

34. "The Outlook: Managing in the 1980s Won't Be an Easy Task," *The Wall Street Journal* (20 September 1982): 1.

35. Ibid.

36. Survey conducted by Professor H. R. Knudson, 1983. Presented as a paper to the Western Academy of Management, December 1982.

37. Ibid.

38. John F. Rockhart and Michael E. Treacy, "The CEO Goes On-Line," *Harvard Business Review* (January–February 1982): 82–88.

39. Ibid.

RECOMMENDED READINGS

M. R. Cooper, B. S. Morgan, P. M. Foley, and L. B. Kaplan, "Changing Employee Values: Deepening Discontent?" *Harvard Business Review* (January–February 1979): 117–125.

In this article, the authors present trends in employees' attitudes toward pay, supervision, and equitable treatment as well as more global attitudes toward the company and the job over a twenty-five-year period. What is most troublesome about their conclusions is the fact that their trends indicate a growing gap in satisfaction between managers and the hourly employees.

Marsha Sinetar, "Management in the New Age: An Exploration of Changing Work Values," *Personnel Journal* (September 1980): 749–755.

This article presents an argument that the '80s will bring an increased demand for worker self-actualization to which management will have to respond. The author contrasts the traditional work values of security, control, status, and power with the new age work values of self-esteem, relatedness to others, self-definition, self-actualization, and personal power.

Lester Manufacturing Company

One February morning, George Healey, personnel director of the Lester Manufacturing Company, received a document entitled "The Trouble with Lester" from Mike Bossart, one of his assistants. It had been given to Bossart by Frank Baxter during the customary exit interview which had followed Baxter's voluntary resignation the day before. The document read as follows:

THE TROUBLE WITH LESTER

DEDICATED TO THE FRUSTRATED SOULS WHO SPEND THEIR WORKING HOURS IN THE SUFFOCATING JUNGLE OF THE ACCOUNTING DEPARTMENT

Without the Lester Company the economy of our city and the state would collapse. This statement, constantly reiterated, is undoubtedly true. But even with Lester, unemployment in the state has reached one of the highest figures in the nation.

It follows that with the current changing product emphasis, Lester, like others in the field, will, in the future, be operating with less manpower. Thus, inevitable cutbacks and mounting unemployment will follow.

Lester could care less. They have their defense contracts. The Lester products, both military and commercial, are universally respected. The company will still reap financial profit.

But what will become of the state, and the people who live here? They have suffered, and are doomed to suffer more, from the weaknesses of an overbalanced economy. Nearsighted leadership and moss-backed legislation have made it difficult to attract new industry. In contrast to other states which promote new industries with lease-free land, our state offers prohibitive taxes.

Source: Reprinted with permission from Harry R. Knudson and C. Patrick Fleenor, *Organizational Behavior: A Management Approach* (Winthrop Publishing Co., 1978): 110–114. Copyright 1976 by Professor Harry R. Knudson, Graduate School of Business, University of Washington.

A remedy must be found. In the meantime, Lester, without competition, floats like a fat shark in a pool of shellfish, taking all, giving nothing, and spitting out the bones.

No, the picture isn't that morbid. Actually, Lester is benevolent. They provide a huge payroll. They have a rewarding Suggestion System, which benefits the ingenious employee (as well as the company). Cash awards are made on everything from designing a labor-and-expense-saving casting to suggesting that Maintenance install bigger signs over the restrooms for nearsighted personnel. Suggestions concerning the value of specific employees, or where they should go, are not accepted.

Lester supports the Community Chest, and they have a personal Blood Bank. They also have a Credit Union, where an employee can obtain a loan at a reasonable interest rate. Payments are deducted from the second paycheck of every month. It is not advisable to borrow too much, however. It is difficult to take a $500 loan payment out of a $175 termination check and end up with any money.

The company protects its employees with insurance. The rumor that they were forced into it by the federal government is false.

The company has a pension (?) plan. However, unless you work for Lester for 120 years, don't expect to retire to the Bahamas on the money they give you. Better line yourself up with a part-time job as a Western Union boy.

Lester provides schools where the employee can better himself. The courses are related to the company and its business. Supervision urges that employees take advantage of this built-in education system, and attend as many classes as possible. The fact that you have taken some classes goes in your personnel folder, and will help you advance. I know a fellow who has been with the company six years and has taken twenty-four classes. (That's an average of four a year). He's an expediter—at the next to bottom grade.

The company stimulates leisure activities. It has hobby clubs and athletics.

In addition, different departments (for example, the Accounting Department) sponsor social functions for their employees. This promotes a feeling of "togetherness" in the section. There are dances, picnics, mixed overnight camping trips, and assorted orgies.

For the employee working in Accounting, the Accounting Dance is a social must. This gives the peon a chance to cultivate his supervisor. An interchange of dances is a good approach. What do you care if his wife is a foot taller than you and has halitosis? So she wants to lead? When dancing, try to Charleston in front of the Chief's table. In this way you may be able to strike up an acquaintance with him. This is especially true if you kick him in the mouth.

Bowling is the best of departmental athletics. The whole gang is down at the alley. You can joke, and kid, and drink beer with your supervisors. It's a hell of a lot of fun. But don't try to win, or you'll be permanent second shift. (This is comparable to being permanent K.P., or permanent latrine.) And for God's sake don't laugh if some superior falls down delivering the ball or gets a split.

Lester provides for sick leave. But if you work in Accounting, don't take it unless you have polio. If you break an arm, put it in a splint and come to work. If you have malaria so bad your clothes are soaked through, put on another change and come to work. Supervision stresses attendance, and if they don't like the color of your ties, a bad attendance record (missing over two days a year) is a ready-made excuse for stopping your progress.

What happens to the employee working in the Accounting Department at Lester?

Foremost, his individualism is crushed. The bigness of the company, and its socialistic structure make him small. It's no wonder that he loses incentive.

He must conform. The proper dress is a white shirt and tie (conservative), and preferably a business suit. To get ahead, you should keep your suit coat on, even though it may be a rather sticky 95° , and four stenos have fainted.

Be intense. Furrowing the brow, and scowling, indicates that you have a business-like attitude, and are serious about your job, and not that you have a bad case of hemorrhoids. And for gosh sakes don't laugh during working hours. Laughing conveys frivolity, and may give some superiors the idea that you don't give a damn about your job. (A small chuckle is permitted at lunchtime.) Don't grin, and smile only at superiors.

When traveling to another area, walk briskly. Don't loiter. An efficiency expert may be watching. Carry a piece of paper. A paper gives the carrier an air of importance.

Being on good terms with your supervisor is essential at Lester. Cultivate him. Asking him questions about the job is one method. Chances are he won't know the answer, but he can direct you to some experienced employee who will. Asking questions shows that you're enthusiastic. That's the image you must create.

Discover your supervisor's interests. If he cuts out paper dolls, buy a pair of scissors.

Be cautious in talking with your supervisor, or, for that matter, any supervisor. The relationship is a delicate one. Never disagree, even though you know he's dead wrong, and a jerk besides. Contradicting the supervisor means that you are out of line, have a bad attitude, and are not pulling with the team.

Your supervisor can make or break you, depending on his whims, and whether or not he's had his coffee. Despite all the "hogwash" about a "scientific" personnel evaluation system, all individual progress at Lester is based on the personal relationship of the supervisor with those under him. The man who thinks he can succeed through merit alone is living in an "ivory tower."

If the supervisor likes you, and considers you "sharp" it's one step into the "Up" elevator. If he doesn't think you "fit in," or aren't aggressive, it's the basement.

Stock cover-up phrases are used by supervisors in the "P.E." interview to conceal personal feelings. Such mouthings as "You don't communicate well," "You don't write an effective memo," or "You don't show enough initiative" are typical.

Movement is vital in the Accounting Department. Many a good man has stayed at the same desk month after month, watching new hires pass him by, because a supervisor has taken a dislike to him. This man may be a good, conscientious employee, well qualified for a better job, but he won't get it. Eventually this man must go out the door. He isn't moving.

Once you are stopped, start reading the want-ads.

Security is a hollow word at Lester. Nobody uses it, unless they're talking of the market. Anybody who thinks he has it here should be advised to see a psychiatrist. When the cutbacks come, they can strike anywhere, both bottom and top. They will get worse.

After reading the document with a great deal of interest, Healey reviewed the personnel record of Frank Baxter. This record is reproduced in part in Figure A.

A few days after he had received the document Healey made the following comments concerning Frank Baxter. "I've really never talked with him, so these are just observations that I have. I became acquainted with him, originally, or rather I noticed him originally, because of his sloppy dress. He has a real talent for looking sloppy if you know what I mean. You know, the kind of guy who makes even the best clothes look unkempt. I really don't think he would comb his hair if he were paid for it. He's balding, about thirty-six or thirty-seven years old, single, and, rather suprisingly, a university graduate.

Work History		Position	Salary
Hired in	3/16/63		
Transferred to Accounting	5/25/64	Clerk C	$169.60/week
Reclassification	4/22/65	Accountant C	176.60
Merit raise	4/6/66		180.40
Reclassification	7/13/66	Accountant B	194.60
Merit raise	1/25/67		197.60
Merit raise	8/23/67		204.40
Reclassification	9/19/68	Controller B	210.60
Resigned	2/2/71		217.80

Evaluations (from Personnal Evaluation reports)

W. Bostrom	4/15/63 to 2/15/64—Group 4 to Group 3. Good steady worker. Improve accuracy factor.
R. Kast	7/20/64 to 7/18/68—Rating 60 to 72. Hard worker, good job knowledge. Needs to attain self-confidence and aggressiveness.
B. A. Lootkens	2/69 to 9/69—Comments same as above.
V. R. Cone	11/69—Reliable and cooperative. Needs initiative.
J. R. Lockover	6/70—Improve initiative, productivity, judgment. Shown some improvement over last P.E.

Merits (from Merit Increase Evaluation form)

M. R. Ballert	1/67 to 8/67—Good improvement, "Above average."
H. A. Berg	12/68—"Average."
B. A. Lootkens	3/69—Show more initiative & drive. "Above Average."
	9/69—"Below Average"—not concentrating.
J. R. Lockover	3/70—Room for considerable improvement in job performance. "Below Average."
H. E. Martin	9/70—Improved over past 6 months. "Average."

Memo dated 3/2/70: J. R. Lockover, regarding job performance. Placed on 30-day probation. Remarks: Needs to improve—initiative, reliability, response to Company needs, productivity, and judgment. Has capability to do good work, but needs to apply himself and show interest.

FIGURE A
Personnel record of Frank Baxter

"He is very interested in sports—really an authority on them. He's the kind of guy, for example, who can quote batting averages for years back, knows who is playing whom three years from now, and how many night games the Yankees played in 1958. He is also a participant in sports to some degree, and I've heard that he's been active in some of the company's recreational programs.

"He is a man who has frequently been suggested to me as someone who might fill vacancies of higher positions in the accounting department. But just as frequently I've said 'Not interested.'

"He's obviously quite well liked by his fellow employees. I've received many indications through the grapevine that they have been asking if something can't be done to get him moved up the ladder or some way worked out that he could progress faster than he had been. There is no indication at all that he had any difficulty in getting along with his people. Indeed, quite the opposite. It is strange, though, in noting the comments on his personnel evaluation reports and merit evaluation forms, that this matter of sloppy appearance never came up. Yet this was what first attracted my attention to him.

"I've done nothing about the document. The guy has some good points in there. There's a real message, I think. For example, his comments about 'conformity' may be quite pertinent. Some of the people I've talked with about the document have suggested that we get it reproduced and distribute it to all our supervisors. I'm not sure this is the right approach, though. I think we should try and gain what good we can from this incident, and I'm not sure that circulating it with wide distribution will let us realize any of the benefits that are here. You can get good ideas from this or anything like this, but I'm afraid that if we circulate the document those supervisors who weren't involved might treat it facetiously and tend to ride their fellow supervisors who had had contacts with Baxter. Maybe a better approach would be discuss it with the chief supervisors who were involved and see if there is, in fact, any good that we can get out of the situation. I'm really not sure what I should do. There's probably some element of 'sour grapes' involved in this but, on the other hand, Baxter does make some good points."

Questions

1. Using the letter from Mr. Baxter, what work values are present in Lester Manufacturing Company?
2. How do you evaluate the method used by Mr. Baxter to communicate his concerns? What alternatives would you suggest?
3. What does the personnel record tell you about Mr. Baxter? If you were his boss how would you handle him?

PART TWO
Basic Concepts in Organizational Behavior

CHAPTER TWO
Individual Behavior

OUTLINE

FRAMEWORK FOR INDIVIDUAL BEHAVIOR

Introduction
Values
Attitudes
Perceptual Process
Summary of Key Concepts

MANAGERIAL APPLICATIONS

Introduction
Effects of Attitude and Attitude Surveys
Influence of Values

OBJECTIVES

- Describe a value system and the various types of values

- Define the relationship between attitudes and behavior

- Describe the role consistency plays in attitude change

- Discuss the basic elements in the perceptual process and understand the factors that influence these elements

- Identify the major managerial applications of this chapter

A Measure of Individual Success?

Bob Lyons was a very successful manager in a large company. His superiors saw him as aggressive, with a talent for being able to get things done through others. During his ten years with the organization his hard work and vigorous pace led to several positions of increasing responsibility.

Lyons' athletic skills included swimming, hunting, golf, and tennis. During weekends one could find him in various rebuilding and repairing projects around the house, or engaged in some form of sports. He was also very active in his church and in the Boy Scouts. He and his wife enjoyed entertaining others in parties and social activities. Both shared much of themselves with their three children.

During the spring of his ninth year with the company, Bob Lyons spoke with the vice president to whom he reported. "Things are a little quiet around here," he said. "Most of the big projects are over. The building is now finished, and we have a lot of things on the ball that four years ago were all fouled up. I don't like this idea of just riding a desk and looking out the window. I like action."

About a month later, Lyons was assigned additional responsibilities. He rushed into them with his usual vigor. Once again he seemed buoyant and cheerful. After six months on the assignment, Lyons had the project rolling smoothly. Again he spoke to his vice president, reporting that he was out of projects. The vice president, pleased with Lyons' performance, told him that he had earned the right to do a little dreaming and planning; furthermore, dreaming and planning were a necessary part of the position he now held, toward which he had aspired for so long. Bob Lyons listened as his boss spoke. But it was plain to the vice president that the answer did not satisfy him.

Several months after their meeting, the vice president noticed that the replies to his memos and inquiries were not coming back from Lyons with their usual rapidity. In addition, he noticed that Lyons was beginning to put things off, which was extremely unusual behavior for him. He observed that Lyons became easily angered and disturbed over minor difficulties, which previously had not irritated him at all.

Bob Lyons then became involved in a conflict with two other executives over a policy issue. This was not unusual in this organization since there were varying points of view on many issues. The conflict was not personal, but it did require the intervention of upper level management before a solution could be reached.

A few weeks after this conflict had been resolved, Lyons went to the vice president's office. He wanted to have a long private talk, he said. His first words were "I'm losing my grip. The old steam is gone. I've had diarrhea for four weeks and several times in the past three weeks I've lost my breakfast. I'm worried and yet I don't know what about. I feel that some people have lost confidence in me."

They talked for an hour and a half. The vice president recounted his achievements in the firm to reassure him. He then asked if Lyons thought he should see a doctor. Lyons agreed that he should and, in the presence of the vice president, called his family doctor for an appointment. By this time the vice president was very concerned. He called Mrs. Lyons and arranged to meet her for lunch the next day. She reported that, in addition to his other symptoms, her husband had difficulty sleeping. Both were now alarmed. They decided that they should get Lyons into a hospital rather than wait for the doctor's appointment that was still a week off.

The next day Lyons went to the hospital. Meanwhile, with Mrs. Lyons' permission, the vice president reported to the family doctor Lyons' behavior and their conversations. When the vice president concluded, the doctor said, "All he needs is a good rest. We don't want to tell him that it may be mental or nervous." The vice president replied that he didn't know what the cause was, but he knew Bob Lyons needed help.

During the five days in the hospital, Lyons received extensive laboratory tests. The vice president visited him daily. He seemed to welcome the rest and the sedation at night. He said he was eating and sleeping much better. He talked about company problems, though he did not speak spontaneously without encouragement. While Lyons was out of the room, another executive who shared his hospital room confided to the vice president that he was worried about Lyons. "He seems so morose and depressed that I'm afraid he's losing his mind," the executive said.

By this time the president of the company, who had been kept informed, was also concerned. He had talked to a psychiatrist and planned to talk to Lyons about psychiatric treatment if his doctor did not suggest it. Meanwhile, Lyons was discharged from the hospital as being without physical illness, and his doctor recommended a vacation. Lyons remained at home for several days where he was again visited by the vice president. He and his wife took a trip to visit some friends. He was ready to come back to work, but the president suggested that he take another week off.[1]

FRAMEWORK FOR INDIVIDUAL BEHAVIOR

Introduction

The story of Bob Lyons is not unusual. Different people faced with the same situation, do *not* necessarily behave the same way. A real difficulty in studying organizational behavior is assuming that others would react to a situation the same way we would. In one sense, Bob Lyons has been extremely successful; consider the additional responsibilities he has been assigned, the interest that the vice president has shown for Bob's progress, the feelings of concern for Bob's health, and the reassurance that the vice president offered to Bob about his achievements in the firm. If you were Bob's boss, would you understand his reactions, his ill health, his lack of motivation, his conflict with the other executives, and his dissatisfaction with the idea of dreaming and planning that the new job required?

Yet, these individual differences illustrated in the opening story are extremely important for the manager and the student of organizational behavior to understand. The behavior of an employee is always a complex interaction of the person and the situation. For instance, people are influenced by others in the situation, the situation itself, and their own values and attitudes. What impact on Bob Lyons did his job have? His family? His boss? His background? His attitudes? His values?

Chapter 1 related how individuals may view the rich experience of their work. Some were very positive—the factory owner and the director of the bakery cooperative—while others were basically negative—the steelworker and the box boy. From those examples, we can simplistically conclude that management positions are more exciting than worker positions. But how do we explain Bob Lyons' reactions?

It becomes obvious that simple conclusions and quick observations will not help us fully understand why individuals behave the way they do. To understand and appreciate behavior in the context of an organization, we must delve deeper into the individual. To make the best use of other theories, such as motivation, communication, leadership, decision making, and stress, presented later in this book, we must develop a basic understanding of some of the internal or hidden workings of the individual.

To better understand the behavior of any particular individual, we need to know many things about that person—past experiences, values, attitudes, and how they view their surroundings—as well as a great deal about the situation or context the individual is in. This chapter focuses on the individual to develop a base for understanding behavior in organizations.

Values

Is offering a bribe to an official in another country where it is standard practice right or wrong? Is shutting down a polluting chemical plant in a small town that depends on the firm's taxes and payroll to survive right or wrong? The answers to these questions are value laden. Some might argue, for example, that other countries are offering bribes and getting the business we might lose if we don't follow the local customs. Others may argue, however, that our society and business practice find such a custom unethical.

The strong opinions voiced on both sides of just such questions are a sign of our values. Values represent basic convictions that "a specific mode of conduct or end-state of existence is personally or socially preferable to an opposite or converse mode of conduct or end-state of existence."[2] Values contain a moral premise; they are an individual's ideas as to what is right, good, or desirable.

But how do we know what values are or how many values there are? One researcher[3] has classified eighteen "end" values and eighteen "means" values, listed in Table 2-1.

"End" values are goals for which an individual may be striving. "Means" include the actual method the individual finds appropriate to reach the goal. For example, a person may want self-respect as the goal and feel that behaving independently and relying on one's self rather than others is a method of attaining self-respect. Reviewing the Bob Lyons story, we can safely say that he was striving for achievement as a goal and that he saw ambition and hard work as the appropriate means for reaching his goal. But what other goals or end values was Lyons pursuing and what "means" values did he apply? Could there have been some conflicting goals or means of which Bob was unconscious?

Value Systems   Table 2-1 suggests the multitude of values by which an individual behaves; yet the very number questions whether there exists some ordering of these values. In fact, each individual must order these values according to

TABLE 2-1
Types of personal values

End (Goal) Values	Means (Behavior) Values
Prosperity	Ambition and hard work
Stimulating, active life	Open-mindedness
Achievement	Competence
World peace	Cheerfulness
Harmony in nature and art	Cleanliness
Equality	Courage
Personal and family security	Forgiving nature
Freedom	Helpfulness
Happiness	Honesty
Inner peace	Imagination
Mature love	Independence and self-reliance
National security	Intelligence
Pleasure and enjoyment	Rationality
Religion and salvation	Affection and love
Self-respect	Obedience and respect
Friendship	Courtesy
Wisdom	Responsibility
Social respect	Self-discipline

Source: Adapted from Milton Rokeach, *The Nature of Human Values*. Copyright ©1973 by The Free Press, a division of Macmillan Publishing Company. Used with permission.

their relative importance in a given situation. In other words, we each have a set of values that forms a value system. Individuals differ widely in the degree to which they have these values and the actual priority a value has in an individual's value system. For example, a higher paying job with more responsibility is offered to an individual. In trying to make a decision the individual considers: "I will get more pay and responsibility"; "I will advance in my career"; "my spouse will have to give up his/her job and career position"; "we will have to leave our family and friends"; and "I like this area with its cultural and recreational opportunities." How an individual sorts these statements out and arrives at a decision gives us a hint of that person's value system.

Values are important to the study of organizational behavior because they lay the foundation for understanding attitudes, perceptions, and motivations. Values generally influence behavior. Suppose you enter an organization with the view that allocating pay on the basis of performance is right, while allocating pay on the basis of seniority is wrong or inferior. How are you going to react should you find that the organization you have joined rewards seniority and not performance? Would your behavior be different if your values aligned with the organization's pay policies?

Types of Values   Researchers have used various schemes to identify and categorize values. One researcher suggested that there is a hierarchy of levels that are descriptive of personal values and life-styles.[4] The seven levels are

BOX 2-1

Bluford Seen as Milestone, Role Model

During the middle of the night, the first black American astronaut traveled into space and reluctant heroism. He was Guion Bluford, 40, a scientist and Vietnam veteran who flew 144 combat missions and won 10 Air Force medals.

"A milestone? Yes," says Lt. Gen. Benjamin O. Davis, the first black Air Force general, who commanded the nation's first black airborne fighter squadron 40 years ago. "On the flying business, there is no question that we have come a long way—from a zero start."

Bluford is an achiever in a family of achievers. His father was a mechanical engineer, his mother, a teacher. An aunt, Carol Brice Carey, is a nationally known contralto. The family includes a pianist, a prep school founder, a college president, a newspaper editor.

Brother Kenneth, 33, says, "You had some kind of obligation to use your talents." Guy Bluford is not an atypical member of the black middle class "which has never had any real visibility in the media." In their family not achieving "was like having a garden, and letting it turn to straw."

Bluford's parents were Republicans. There was no liquor in the house, not much entertaining. Guy, whom Kenneth Bluford still calls by the nickname "Bunny," was "an advertisement for the Protestant work ethic." At Overbrook High,

Guy Bluford was captain of the chess team. He wanted to become an aeronautical engineer. Teacher Fred Hofkin recalls he sought challenge—"ignoring easy questions, raising his hand for hard ones."

Bluford took military correspondence courses while working on his Ph.D. At Wright Patterson Air Force Base, he was put in charge of 40 engineers before he finished his degree. He spent late nights at a laboratory computer calculating the air flow of a Delta wing—a first.

Bluford doesn't talk of heroes. Of his role, he says, "I recognize it from a historical perspective." He doesn't want to be larger than life. "My kids look upon me as 'Dad'. I consider myself carrying on a (family) tradition by carrying on a profession. I think the quiet professional way is more indicative of my own style."

When all that remains of the flight are news clippings, Bluford "would like people to think of the flight as a very successful flight—by a very professional crew."

Questions

1. What impact does Bluford's family and early childhood have on his values and their development?
2. What perceptual factors are likely to influence how Bluford sees the world and his job?
3. If Bluford is typical of astronauts, what values and attitudes does this group have? Do these match the job they have? Explain.

Source: *U.S.A. Today* (Monday, 29 August 1983).

Reactive (Level 1). Reactive individuals are unaware of themselves or others as human beings and react to basic physiological needs. Such individuals are rarely found in organizations.

Tribalistic (Level 2). These individuals are characterized by high dependence. They are strongly influenced by tradition and the power exerted by authority figures.

Egocentric (Level 3). These persons believe in rugged individualism. They are aggressive and selfish. They respond primarily to power.

Conforming (Level 4). Conforming individuals have a low tolerance for ambiguity, have difficulty in accepting people whose values differ from their own, and desire that others accept their values.

Manipulative (Level 5). Manipulative persons strive to achieve their goals by manipulating things and people. They are materialistic and actively seek higher status and recognition.

Sociocentric (Level 6). These individuals consider it more important to be liked and to get along with others than to get ahead. They are repulsed by materialism, manipulation, and conformity.

Existential (Level 7). Existential individuals have a high tolerance for ambiguity and people with differing values. They are outspoken on inflexible systems, restrictive policies, status symbols, and arbitrary use of authority.

This hierarchy has been used to analyze disparate values in organizations. Most people in today's organizations operate on levels 2 through 7. While historically organizations were run by level 4 and 5 managers, there is currently a rapid movement of level 6 and 7 types of managers into influential positions in organizations. The number of individuals holding existential and sociocentric values is increasing while probably still representing a minority. Most of us know of someone who has refused a promotion that required a move to another community and in doing so seems to exist above level 5.[5]

At what level would you place Bob Lyons? His boss? The organization? If Bob is operating on the lower levels and the organization is operating on a higher level, would this partially explain the ineffectiveness of merely trying to reassure Bob about his past performance? Would operating on the same level assure organizational and individual effectiveness?

The knowledge that people have different types of values has led a few of the more progressively managed organizations to initiate efforts to improve the values-job fit to enhance employee performance and satisfaction. For instance, Texas Instruments has developed a program to diagnose different values types and to match properly these types with appropriate work situations within their company.

Some individuals, for example, are classified as "tribalistic" people who want strong, directive leadership from their boss; some are "egocentric," desiring individual responsibilities and wanting to work as loners in an entrepreneurial style; some are "sociocentric," seeking primarily the social relationships that a job provided; and some are "existential," seeking full expression of growth and self-fulfillment needs through their work, much as an artist does. Charles Hughes, director of personnel and organization development at Texas Instruments, believes that the variety of work that needs to be done in his organization is great enough to accommodate these different types of work personalities in such a manner that individual and organizational goals are fused.[6]

Another set of research for measuring values that has been used with business managers is England's Personal Values Questionnaire (PVQ).[7] The PVQ, designed specifically for business managers, has been completed by thousands of managers from several countries. It provides a measure of a manager's personal values system, defined as "a relatively permanent perceptual framework which shapes and influences the general nature of an individual's behavior."[8] England found three primary value orientations, which refer to the orientation most descriptive of the respondent's most important values. If a respondent's primary orientation is moral or having a "right manner of acting," he or she would be termed a moralist. If a respondent's most important values are rated as successful and "dealing with only facts or reality," the primary orientation is pragmatic. If the pleasant or "achieving a state of pleasure" category is rated most frequently, the respondent is labeled an aesthetic.

Figure 2–1 shows the values of managers from five countries. As the figure indicates, pragmatism and moralism are the major value orientations that have been observed among managers.[9]

England suggests a theoretical framework for how these values can influence behavior through two processes: behavior channeling and perceptual screening. Behavior channeling is individuals entering or leaving situations based upon their understanding that the situation either matches or does not match their values. For example, an individual who has honesty as a value, when placed in a situation involving dishonesty, would be channeled away from the situation. In behavior channeling, values directly affect problem solving by providing a standard for generating and testing alternatives and for making decisions. Perceptual screening is the influence our values have on both what we select to see and hear and how we interpret what we see and hear. This process of perceiving is presented more thoroughly later in the chapter. Through perceptual screening, values can influence how managers perceive individuals and groups, what organizational events and processes get their attention, how they respond to those events and processes, and how they interpret their own and their organization's success or failure.

A few studies using this conceptual framework have found some interesting results. One study compared the values of college students and managers. It reported some similarities and differences and also found that students inaccurately attributed many values to managers.[10] Another study found that the value systems of business managers were more pragmatic than those of union leaders, who were found to be more moralistic.[11] Further, value systems have been shown to be related to managerial career success:

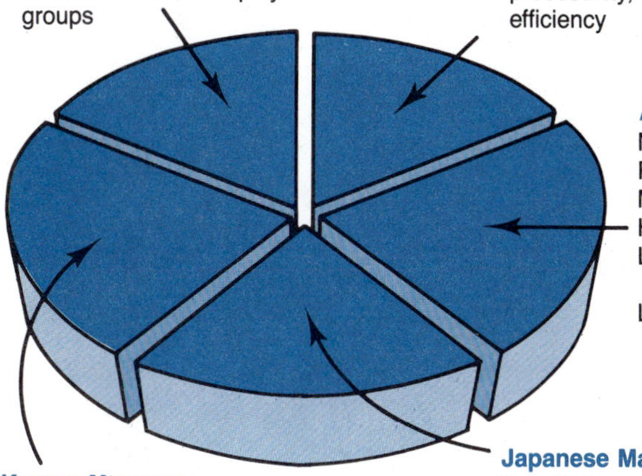

Indian Managers
N = 623
Pragmatists 34%
Moralists 44%
High value on stable organizations
    with minimal or steady change
High value on personal goals and
    status orientation
Low value on most employee
    groups

U. S. Managers
N = 997
Pragmatists 57%
Moralists 30%
High achievement and competence
    orientation
Emphasis on profit maximization, high
    productivity, and organizational
    efficiency

Australian Managers
N = 351
Pragmatists 40%
Moralists 40%
High level of humanistic orientation
Low value on organizational growth
    and profit maximization
Low value on achievement, success,
    competition, and risk

Japanese Managers
N = 374
Pragmatists 67%
Moralists 10%
High achievement and competence
    orientation
Most homogeneous managerial
    value system of the five
    countries studied

Korean Managers
N = 211
Pragmatists 53%
Moralists 9%
Low value on most employee groups
    as significant reference groups
Self-oriented achievement and
    competence orientation

FIGURE 2-1
Values of managers from five countries. (Source: G. W. England, "Managers and Their Value Systems: A Five-Country Comparative Study," *Columbia Journal of World Business* (Summer 1978): 35–44. Reprinted with permission.)

Viewing the value-success relationships of American managers provides the following picture. Successful managers favor pragmatic, dynamic, achievement-oriented values while less successful managers prefer more static and passive values, the latter forming a framework descriptive of organizational stasis rather than organizational and environmental flux. More successful managers favor an achievement orientation and prefer an active role in interaction with other individuals useful in achieving the managers' organizational goals. They value a dynamic environment and are willing to take risks to achieve organizationally valued goals. Relatively less successful managers have values associated with a static, protected environment in which they take relatively passive roles and often enjoy entended seniority in their organizational positions.[12]

Much has been written about the changing nature of the work force's values. We looked at some of those changes in terms of a shift from more traditional values of authority to self-fulfillment in chapter 1. If such shifts are occurring, how will they affect management practices in the future? What motivation theories will prove more useful to a student of organizational behavior?

As students and members of organizations, we must continually question what we believe. Is it the same as what others believe? Can we put ourselves in the place of others to better understand their reactions to us and their surroundings? Could we now place ourselves in the position of Bob Lyons and give his boss some advice to help Bob and the organization become more effective? If your answer is not yes, then maybe we need to proceed to the next level of individual behavior—attitudes—and see the relationship between values and attitudes.

Attitudes

Attitudes are evaluative statements concerning objects, people, or events. They reflect how one feels about something. When I say "I like my work," I am expressing my attitude about work. Attitudes are not the same as values. Values are the broader and more encompassing concept. Attitudes are more specific than values. "Discrimination is bad" is a value statement. "I support implementing a career path program to develop and train women for managerial positions in this organization" reflects an attitude.

An attitude is an evaluative reaction that has three components: emotional, cognitive, and behavioral. The emotional component refers to the feelings associated with an object, person, or event, whether good or bad, pleasing or displeasing, favorable or unfavorable.

The cognitive or belief component includes the information, beliefs, and ideas that a person has about something. For instance, you may believe that managers are intelligent or stupid, ethical or unethical, and good or bad. These beliefs may be true, or they may be false.

The behavioral component of attitudes contains our overt reactions to the object. That is, attitudes presumably represent a predisposition to behave in a certain way. For example, if you have negative feelings or beliefs toward an object, you will probably, given the choice, behave negatively toward that object. Behavioral reactions to the job may include the negative responses of complaints, grievances, absences, tardiness, and turnover or the positive responses of praise, consistent attendance, punctuality, and long tenure.

Attitudes and Change   In many everyday situations we as individuals and we as managers try to change other people's attitudes. By presenting ourselves in a favorable light (putting our best foot forward) we attempt to get others to develop favorable attitudes toward us. Organizationally, managers try to get employees to hold positive attitudes toward work standards, safety practices, fair day's work for fair day's pay, and changes in work procedures. But how can attitudes be changed? What techniques are most successful in altering individuals' feelings, beliefs, and behaviors? While research has given much attention to these questions, two approaches appear to be most useful.

A *persuasive communication.* While the concept of communication is developed in fuller detail later, it is possible to make some brief connection between attitudes and communications at this point. Perhaps the most common technique for inducing attitude change involves the use of persuasive communications. These consist of written, spoken, filmed, or televised messages. Many factors can influence the success of persuasive attempts to alter attitudes. The most important involve certain characteristics of the communicator (the person trying to persuade), the communication itself (the persuasive message), and the recipients (those to be influenced by the message).

The most crucial of the communicator's characteristics appears to be credibility. The more trustworthy or believable the communicator is in the eyes of the recipients the more likely that the message will change their attitudes. Our impressions of a communicator's credibility, in turn, depend largely on the person's apparent expertise and the motives that seem to lie behind the individual's behavior. Communicators who appear to be experts in the field they are talking about are generally perceived as being more credible, and so are more successful in changing attitudes, than those who are perceived as being less expert. Communicators who seem to have little or nothing to gain from altering our views are often perceived as more credible than those who have much to gain from inducing such changes.[13] For example, a safety program initiated by a union officer would likely be more convincing than one initiated by the company's accident insurance carriers. The latter would probably be seen as attempting to reduce claims costs. Similarly, union support for a shortened work week would probably induce more favorable attitudes than exhortations from the company president, who might be perceived as having increased productivity as the main goal of the change.

The content of a persuasive message is also important in altering attitudes. Obviously, the more cogent and forceful the message, the more likely it is to induce attitude change. Research indicates that one specific way for a message to produce changes in attitudes is to induce fear or anxiety among the recipients. Such fear-inducing messages are most successful in altering attitudes when (1) they generate moderate levels of emotional arousal (if too weak, the messages have no impact; if too strong, they are often rejected); (2) the persons who receive them believe that the dangers cited are real; and (3) these persons also believe that the recommendations for avoiding these dangers will be effective.[14] An example of fear appeal in the recent economic recession might involve a manager exhorting workers to work harder, lest the company go broke and they find themselves out of a job.

Finally, the effectiveness of persuasive messages also depends on the characteristics of the recipients. Persons with high self-esteem are more likely to feel that their attitudes are correct and are less likely to change them. Attitudes that are more central to a person are less likely to change. Highly intelligent persons are less affected by such communications than those of lower intelligence.[15] But it is difficult to predict precisely how different people will respond, even to the same persuasive communication.

Cognitive consistency.   Attitudes tend to remain stable when emotions, cognitions, and behaviors associated with something are consistent. For example, if you feel that your supervisor is fair, kind, and considerate and you like him or her and act respectful, your attitude will probably remain stable. In contrast, if you believe that your supervisor is fair, kind, and considerate, but you have negative feelings and avoid him or her, your attitude is in an unstable state. When two components in a person's attitude framework are inconsistent or opposite, they are said to be *dissonant.*

The most influential research of cognitive consistency is the Cognitive Dissonance Theory by Leon Festinger.[16] This theory argues that people dislike inconsistency. The inconsistency in our attitudes or between our attitudes and our behavior gives rise to a disturbing state of dissonance that people try to lessen or avoid. For instance, if a person who strongly advocates not smoking in public places because of the harmful effects on health buys a restaurant that has patrons who find smoking a pleasant compliment to their meal, the result is a situation of dissonance for the individual. The attitude toward harmful smoking and the attitude toward making a living by allowing the loyal and paying patrons to continue to smoke are causing internal conflict and dissonance for the restaurant owner.

The theory states that dissonance can be reduced in one of two ways: (1) change the attitudes, or (2) justify the behavior as not being truly inconsistent with the attitude. People may justify their behavior by either believing that the behavior was forced upon them, or believing that they were "bought off" by being rewarded excessively to behave as they did. Research has shown that attitude change is greater when the behavior was based on free choice and the amount of incentive offered for the behavior was small rather than large.[17]

What can we say about the Bob Lyons story and attitudes? Can we infer what Bob's attitudes are from the behavior that the storyteller relates? One comment during Bob's discussion with the vice president shows that Bob has an emotional and cognitive component—"I'm losing my grip. . . . some people have lost confidence in me." In addition, Bob describes the behavioral component—"I've lost my breakfast." In contrast, the vice president tries to persuade Bob to look at "his achievements." Was the vice president persuasive? No! Why? Was it the boss's lack of credibility? Or was Bob's attitude too central to his beliefs and values to be changed?

Can cognitive dissonance give us some clue of the internal conflict Lyons was experiencing? Consider his values and attitude of being a very hard worker both at home and in his organization. His boss wants to reward his hard work by allowing Bob to relax now that he has earned it and asks him to do some creative thinking and planning. Could this seem inconsistent to Lyons? At the end of the story, Lyons was ready to come back to work, but the president suggested that he take some more time off. How would Lyons react to this suggestion? Is it in Lyons' best interest to not return to work?

Job Satisfaction: An Important Attitude?   While we are talking about attitudes, we must mention job satisfaction. Job satisfaction is defined as the degree of positive feeling one has about one's work situation.[18] Obviously, one can have degrees of dissatisfaction with the job situation as well.

The issue of job satisfaction becomes very complex when we try to link this attitude with worker behavior or performance. Intuitively, we might feel that a satisfied worker is a productive worker. Some researchers have tried to develop this conceptually—job satisfaction causes good performance.[19] Another possible view is that performance and its related rewards cause job satisfaction.

Reviews of studies that tried to settle this linkage question failed to support either that performance leads to job satisfaction or that job satisfaction leads to performance.[20] Instead, there is some indication that some third (or more) variable(s) are important—perhaps leader behavior, work group, self-esteem, job values, or ability.[21]

Returning to Bob Lyons' story, which causal linkage would you use to describe Bob's performance? How do you explain the high performance as seen by his boss, yet Bob's seemingly high job dissatisfaction? Perhaps Bob defines his performance differently. Maybe Bob's view of his intrinsic rewards—"I'm not performing a useful job by just planning"—is very different from the extrinsic rewards—high pay and promotion—that he has received. Maybe Bob's self-esteem is the key third variable linking his job dissatisfaction and his high performance.

Since the linkages are still being researched and defined, we must take a holistic view of the individual and try to integrate more of what we find out about human behavior. Therefore, until we cover some other topics such as leadership, group dynamics, and job design, the topic of job satisfaction remains incomplete.

Perceptual Process

What is perception? Perception involves the process by which individuals select, organize, and interpret sensory stimuli, such as from seeing, hearing, and touching, into meaningful information about their surroundings. The perceptual process in a simplified form is illustrated in Figure 2–2.

Perception influences our behavior through our ideas and attitudes. The influence that our perceptions have on our relationships with other people is especially important to understand. Errors in our ability to sense accurate information, to select appropriate data, and to correctly organize the information may lead to misperceptions about people. These misperceptions can cause conflicts and tensions between individuals, units, or departments, and affect an organization's performance.

| How We Sense Our Environment | Functions of the Perceptual Process | Results of the Perceptual Process |

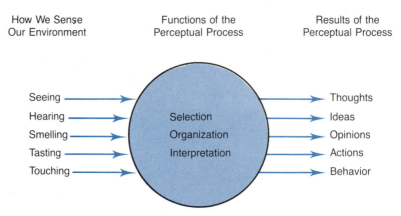

FIGURE 2–2
The perceptual process

Perceptual Selection   Much of the information in one's surroundings is not perceived. Perceptual selection is the process by which individuals decide to pay attention to some things and to ignore or avoid others. An employee who decides to listen to the shop steward about a potential grievance on the job and to avoid the supervisor until the grievance is filed is involved in the selective process. Part

FIGURE 2–3
Young woman or old woman? If you see an attractive, elegantly dressed young woman, your perception agrees with a majority of first-time viewers. Did you see an ugly and poor old woman? Your perception is closer to the minority of first-time viewers.

 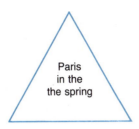

FIGURE 2-4
Perceptual selection: When you read the phrases printed in the triangles, did
you see what was really there? Or did you see what you expected to see? Most
people see "bird in the hand" and omit the extra "the" in the triangle.

of this selection involves filtering out information that an individual does not
want to be consciously aware of. Employees are able to tune out the constant
noise of machinery on the production line. Students are able to ignore noise
made by others in a class when they are listening to a lecture. Perceptual
selection is affected by an individual's needs, expectations, attitudes, values, and
personality. Figures 2–3 and 2–4 illustrate examples of perceptual selection.

Perceptual Organization   Each individual has to try to organize a sensible and
coherent world out of surroundings that may not make sense. This tendency is
referred to as perceptual organization. This is a process by which individuals
group the surounding stimuli into recognizable patterns. One basic organizing
principle is the concept of figure-ground. Figure-ground is our tendency to perceive any scene as consisting of objects (figure) and the space between them as
background (ground). For instance, as you read this page, you do not perceive a
random set of black marks and white space. Rather, you see letters or words
standing out from a white background. Illustrations of our tendency to divide our
surroundings into figure and ground are provided by the ambiguous figures in
Figure 2–5, in which figure and ground can be readily interchanged.

Another method of organizing our perceptions is called perceptual grouping. We tend to group isolated stimuli together on the basis of proximity,
similarity, closure, and continuity. In other words, we tend to perceive separate
stimuli as clustering together when they are next to one another, when they are
similar in some manner, and when organizing them in this fashion allows us to
complete some relatively simple pattern.

The concept of proximity means that a group of objects may be perceived as
related because of their nearness to each other. When individuals work together
in a department they may be perceived as very similar by others outside the unit.
Accountants in a department may be viewed as having similar personalities and
values.

Similarity means that the more alike objects are the greater is the tendency
to perceive them as a common group. Work groups may use this concept to
distinguish themselves by wearing similar clothes, such as team jackets or hats. A

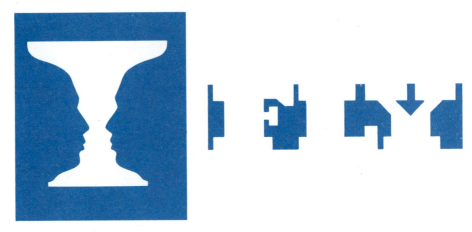

FIGURE 2–5
Figure-ground illustrations: Concentrate on the colored shapes. Do they form any recognizable pattern? Now try to concentrate on the white space between the colored shapes. This shifting is an illustration of our tendency to organize the world into figure and ground.

company might require workers to wear different colored badges to differentiate various security clearances.

Closure refers to the tendency to complete an object so it is perceived as a constant, overall form. It is the ability to perceive a whole object even though only part of the object is evident (see Figure 2–6). This can happen when we know how to finish a sentence a friend started but didn't complete.

The concept of continuity means perceiving objects as continuous patterns. Individuals who are inflexible or unbending may require not only themselves but others to follow certain continuous patterns. Inflexible managers may insist that employees follow set, step-by-step procedures. They may not tolerate individual self-direction since it upsets their unbending need for continuity.

Perceptual Interpretation   The way anything is interpreted depends on its surrounding, or the context in which it appears. The context in which information appears affects what you think you see or hear. Suppose the same message is

FIGURE 2–6
Closure: Despite the fact that the lines are broken, we tend to see the figures as a triangle and a circle because of our tendency to fill in the missing parts.

given to employees by the company president and by the union president. Ask the employees to interpret it and you will get two different interpretations. In addition, the interpretation is heavily influenced by personal characteristics of the individual. Have you ever bought a new car and suddenly notice a large number of cars like yours on the road? It's unlikely that the number of such cars suddenly increased. Rather, your own purchase has influenced your perception so that you are now more likely to notice them. Among the more relevant personal characteristics affecting our interpretation are values, attitudes, motives, past experience, expectations, and personality.

Factors Influencing Perceptions   How can we explain the fact that individuals may look at the same thing, yet perceive it so differently? A number of factors shape and sometimes distort our perceptions. In other words, we perceive reality through various colored "sun glasses." And like sun glasses, sometimes they help by reducing glare; and sometimes they may hinder our vision, as night approaches or in the shade. Influencing factors include stereotyping, selective perception, halo effect, set expectations, emotional state, and projection.

Stereotyping.   Stereotyping is a means of forming an impression of someone by using a list of characteristics assumed to be held by the group of which the person is a member. Various categories exist upon which a stereotype might be based, including race, age, sex, ethnic background, social class, occupation, and so on. People select characteristics to identify groups of people and attribute those characteristics to each person in the group. For example, accountants are often stereotyped as compulsive, precise, and one-dimensional; while engineers may be perceived as cold and calculating. Labor and management often hold stereotypic views of each other. Stereotyping limits our ability to perceive other people accurately and can prevent us from finding out how a person is unique and different from a group.

Selective perception.   Another factor that can lead to inaccurate perceptions is called selective perception. We have already mentioned the fact that our current needs and past experiences partly determine what we attend to and what we perceive. It is also true that the more ambiguous the situation, the more we rely on our internal cues.

A classic study by Dearborn and Simon[22] shows how vested interests can significantly influence what problems we see. Twenty-three business executives read a comprehensive case describing the organization and activities of a steel company. Six of the executives were in the sales function, five in production, four in accounting, and eight in miscellaneous functions. Each of these executives was asked to list what he or she thought was the major problem that a new president of the steel company should deal with first. The data from the study is presented in Table 2–2. It is clear from this data that managers tend to see problems in those areas of major interest to themselves. Accountants and sales executives were

BOX 2–2

The Successful Entrepreneur:
A Personality Profile

What makes an entrepreneurial winner? Someone with intellectual creativity, boundless energy, vision, and a patience quota of zero.

Those were the conclusions drawn by McKinsey & Co. after a study of midsized, high-growth companies that have more than doubled in size over a five-year period. The companies studied achieved annual sales growth of 21% and annual income growth of 27%. Most are run by their founders.

Bill McGrowan, the founder and chief executive officer of the telecommunications company MCI, is typical of this group who can't put up with corporate bureaucracy. McGrowan brings his newly hired managers together for an orientation session in which he tells them "I know that some of you, with your business-school backgrounds, are out there already beginning to draw organization charts and to write manuals for operating procedures. As soon as I find out who you are, I'm going to fire every last one of you."

These same CEOs are almost inevitably consummate salesmen who radiate enormous, contagious self-confidence that often translates into respect and esteem from their employees. They take pains to communicate their strong sense of mission to all. For example, Albert Snider of Bourns Inc., an electronics manufacturer in Riverside, California, visits with every one of his 7,000 employees at least twice a year.

A predominant trait of the successful entrepreneur is perseverance to the point of obsession. They routinely work seven days a week. In addition, the elite of America's entrepreneurial talent is composed of self-made people, often from lower-middle-class backgrounds, who demonstrate extraordinary motivation, tenacity, and will to succeed. Contrary to the popular perception, entrepreneurs are not reckless gamblers, but they don't hesitate to take substantial risks and will even "bet the company" in their efforts to remain competitive or protect a lead in technology.

Perhaps the most significant difference between the successful entrepreneur and the corporate executive who has worked his way up is that the entrepreneur/CEO is likely to be the founder of the company and the architect of its success. He knows all the details of the business and is a hands-on operator. He stresses informality rather than a highly structured environment. Unlike his traditional counterpart whose next promotion or pension is often keyed to short-term results, the entrepreneur can invest heavily in the future and is freer to focus on the long-term outlook.

Questions

1. Using the quote from McGrowan about organization charts, what kind of people does this organization hire?
2. What are the major perceptual processes that might be used to describe successful entrepreneurs? Could other employees be trained to adopt these same characteristics?

Source: Arthur Levitt and Jack Albertine, *The Wall Street Journal,* (Monday, 29 August 1983): 10. Reprinted by permission of *The Wall Street Journal,* © Dow Jones & Company, Inc. 1983. All rights reserved.

TABLE 2-2
Selective perception among managers

Department	Total Number of Executives	Number Who Mentioned		
		Sales	Clarify Organization	Human Relations
Sales	6	5	1	0
Production	5	1	4	0
Accounting	4	3	0	1
Miscellaneous	8	1	3	4
Totals	23	10	8	5

Source: DeWitt C. Dearborn and Herbert A. Simon, "Selective Perception: A Note on the Departmental Identification of Executives," *Sociometry*, 21 (1958): 143.

concerned with financial sales problems. Production people were anxious about
clarifying various production issues. Two executives in public relations and industrial relations saw human relations as the biggest problem. The participants
perceived aspects in the situation that related specifically to the activities and
goals of the unit to which they were attached.

On a somewhat broader level, selective perception has a major impact on
the communication and decision processes. We hear what we want to hear and
screen out other information. We overestimate the importance of past trends. We
simplify complex situations to fit an already determined pattern.

Halo effect. Another bias in our perceptual process is the halo effect. This refers to
the process whereby one's impression (either favorable or unfavorable) of a
person in one area tends to influence judgement about that person in other areas.
Frequently this phenomenon occurs when students appraise their instructor. For
example, Nisbett and Wilson had subjects observe a videotape of a college
instructor.[23] On one tape, he acted in a warm and friendly manner. On another, he
behaved in an aloof and arrogant fashion. After watching one of these tapes,
subjects rated the instructor's overall likability as well as several specific traits:
his physical appearance and mannerisms. As predicted, those who had seen the
instructor behave in a warm and friendly manner reported liking him much more
than those who had seen him act in a cold and arrogant fashion. Further, there
was a large spill-over from these global impressions to ratings of the instructor's
specific traits. Subjects who had seen the "warm" instructor rated his appearance
and mannerisms much more favorably than those who had viewed the "cold"
instructor.

In organizations, halo effects may have serious impact on performance
ratings. In most cases a supervisor only observes a small sample of an employee's
actual behavior. If, for some reason, the supervisor samples an area where the
employee does well, the supervisor may judge the individual's performance to be

excellent in other areas about which he or she has little information. The reverse can also happen. As a result, the employee may be more concerned with not making a noticeable mistake than with excellent performance.

Set expectations.   Another tendency to bias perceptions can result from our expectations about a person or situation. These expectations are derived from our experience and therefore each individual's set expectations about a situation or a person may be different. These perceptions are not universally held, as is the case with stereotyping. Expectations can distort our perceptions in that we see what we expect to see. If we expect old people to be forgetful, young people to be unambitious, or top executives to be ruthless, we may perceive them this way regardless of their actual traits or behavior.

The impact of set expectations was found in a study that manipulated the degree of supervision given to subordinates.[24] The supervisor was required to ensure that the performance of two subordinates was maintained at an acceptable level. In the first round, the supervisor was given almost constant surveillance reports on the performance output of one employee, but only periodic reports on the other. Because of the experimental conditions, the supervisor had to have greater trust in the loosely supervised employee. After the first round, the supervisor received identical output reports for both employees. In the second round of the experiment, the supervisor was free to monitor either or both of the employees whenever he wanted. The behavior of the supervisor in the second round demonstrated that, in spite of the equal performance records in the first round, the supervisor did not trust the two subordinates equally. Instead, he monitored more the subordinate who had been placed under high surveillance during the first round. Thus prior set expectations, based on various trust levels, resulted in different degrees of surveillance even though there was no difference in productivity to justify the different degrees of supervision.

Emotional state.   Most of us have at one time or another said, "Don't approach the boss yet, he's in a bad mood today." Our emotional state, whether positive or negative, can impact our view of what is happening around us. Research has shown that the perceiver's emotional state to some extent influences perceptions. For instance, one study asked several women to judge photographs of faces after they had played a frightening game called "murder." The women perceived the faces as more menacing than did women who had not played the game.[25] In another study, the participants were frightened because they were told that they were going to experience an electric shock. They were then asked to make judgements about some other individuals, whom they perceived as also being fearful.[26]

From these studies we see that our emotional state causes us to sense, select, and organize information in a manner consistent with that state. On days when we are happy and excited, we may perceive others as exuberant and cheerful. When we are sad and depressed, we may see others more negatively and suspiciously.

Projection.   The tendency to attribute one's own characteristics and feelings to others is called projection. In some cases, projection is an efficient and sensible practice. After all, people with similar backgrounds and interests often do think and feel similarly. A familiarity among people can result in effective communications around those specific subjects.

In other situations, however, these misperceptions may cause problems. We may make inferences about the causes of people's behavior based on what we would do in similar circumstances. If we want a raise, we may be suspicious of the motives of subordinates. In many instances our judgements are incorrect. Perhaps the subordinate wants the raise because of the status attached to getting more money. Or perhaps the subordinate butters up the boss because he or she actually likes the boss.

Consider again Bob Lyons' story. Can the perceptual process help explain some of Bob's reactions? If we review Bob's initial successes and increased responsibilities, we can understand how Bob expects to succeed and to deal with problems—"Most of the big projects are over. . . . we have a lot of things on the ball that . . . were all fouled up." Having expressed his concern about the lack "of action," he was assigned additional responsibilities and was happy again. Might not selective perception be hindering Bob from viewing his new job in terms of challenge? How does Bob view dreaming and planning? Once Bob reached a state of emotional unrest and depression, how did he view more time off? Did he see it as concern and faith that he only needed some rest?

This brief discussion allows us to appreciate that organizational behavior must begin at the individual level before we undertake the subjects of motivation, communication, decision making, or organizational design or look at the impact of computer technology and productivity. As managers, we must continually place ourselves in the position of the people we supervise.

Summary of Key Concepts

1. To understand individuals we must go beyond simple observations and explore how past experiences, values, attitudes, and perceptions influence their reactions to various situations. We must use their perspective to understand, and not ours.

2. Values can be viewed as both the goal towards which an individual is striving and as a basis for the behavior that helps the individual reach that goal.

3. Values can be a source of one's lifestyle, which will influence the interaction between the organization and the individual as the demands of the organization either match or don't match the individual's lifestyle.

4. Both behavioral channeling and perceptual screening can influence how an individual behaves in certain situations.

5. Attitudes are more specific than values and have three components: emotional, cognitive, and behavioral.

6. Two methods for changing attitudes are persuasive communication and cognitive consistency.

7. The perceptual process describes how individuals make sense out of their surroundings. While certain aspects of this process are essential to effective interaction between individuals in their environment, certain perceptions are distorted and as such can lead to miscommunication and conflict between individuals.

8. The perceptual process is based on past experiences, values, and attitudes of individuals.

9. Job satisfaction is a complex attitude that cannot be simply linked to individual performance but, rather, seems to be related to performance through a third variable, such as leader behavior, work group, ability, self-esteem, or job values.

Key Terms

Attitudes	Perceptual screening
Behavioral channeling	Projection
Cognitive consistency	Selective perception
Halo effect	Set expectations
Job satisfaction	Stereotyping
Perceptual process	Values

MANAGERIAL APPLICATIONS

Introduction

The preceding section leaves no doubt that our perceptions and attitudes are not always shared by others, but the implications of those differences are worth exploring. Let's put our perceptions and attitudes to a test.

In terms of quality of life among the world's countries, where would you rank the United States? If you are a U.S. citizen, the chances are that you will immediately rate the U.S. as first, or perhaps second. In a survey of quality of life in 107 countries, the U.S. came in not first, not second, but forty-second![27]

The study addressed forty-four factors, including such things as literacy and education, health and welfare provisions for citizens, political participation, women's rights, weather, economic growth, inflation, infant mortality, influence of the military, and per-capita income. The top five countries in the survey were Denmark, Norway, Austria, the Netherlands, and Sweden. The bottom five were Ethiopia (worst), Chad, Uganda, Burundi, and Mauritania. How did the Soviet Union rate? Forty-third—just behind the United States.

What was your reaction when you read the preceding paragraph—disbelief? Perhaps a little anger? When we receive information discrepant to strongly held attitudes, such reaction is common.

What we must clearly understand as managers, or indeed as citizens, is that our own attitudes, perceptions, and beliefs are not universally shared in the world, in an organization, or even in the classroom. Once we have accepted that notion, we can then use what we know about those phenomena to become more effective managers and citizens.

Some of the behavioral and cognitive elements covered earlier in this chapter have proven more useful than others in the practice of management. Let's look at a few uses and abuses of the concepts in organizations.

Effects of Attitudes and Attitude Surveys

We infer people's attitudes from their behavior. For example, if a student yawns, stares out the window, and frequently checks the time during a lecture, the lecturer is likely to infer that the student is bored and uninterested (has a "bad" attitude). The student who maintains eye contact, laughs in the right places, and takes copious notes is inferred to be interested, perceptive, and probably a superior student (has a "good attitude").

There is always some chance that our inference about another person's attitude will be wrong, but we act upon our own attitude about what we see.

For example, Weis and Fleenor found that managers as a group feel that employees who smoke are less productive than those who don't.[28] The implication? More than 53 percent of the 223 managers surveyed indicated that they choose nonsmokers over smokers when faced with a choice between otherwise equally qualified applicants. The other respondents saw the choice as a toss-up. None chose a smoker over a nonsmoker. For top executives, the result was even more dramatic: 70 percent reported that they would hire a nonsmoker over a smoker if other attributes were substantially the same. An increasing number of firms are refusing to hire smokers at all (it is not illegal). Though there is no evidence that smokers are in fact less productive than nonsmokers, if managers believe it to be true, they will act as if it is true.

Cox found some interesting attitudes toward evaluation and promotion of female executives.[29] Over 34 percent of the executives surveyed felt that women executives need greater sponsorship (than men) for promotion. Over 33 percent believe women have a lower risk of being fired, and 19.6 percent felt the woman executive is at a disadvantage if she has children. There is a mixture of positive and negative implications for the aspiring woman executive if these attitudes are strongly held by the more numerous male executives.

Attitude surveys are frequently used by organizations in making decisions. Surveys are ubiquitous during election years, and the popular press displays the results frequently. But most of the surveys are commissioned by the political parties, and the results are used in strategy development as well as the marketing and "packaging" of the candidate.

Hampton and Fleenor examined the attitudes that Americans have toward foreign investment in the United States.[30] They hypothesized that significant differences existed in the evaluation of foreign investments by Americans on the basis of the national origin of the investment. Countries investigated were Canada, United Kingdom, Japan, Mexico, Brazil, Taiwan, South Korea, the Philippines, Greece, Iran (before the hostage episode), Saudi Arabia, West Germany, and the United States. The favorability of investment by country is shown in Table 2–3.

The differences in favorability were all statistically significant except for the differences between the U.S., Canada, and West Germany. Therefore, these data would be useful to banks and investment groups in developing both investment and public relations strategies. While this is not a direct application of organizational behavior theory to managing an organization, the important point is that attitudes can be measured, and used in decision making.

A more direct application for organizations is the attitude survey. Many organizations use attitude surveys to gather opinions from employees or other groups about some aspect of the organization or its operations. The data may then be used in making decisions about operations or personnel matters. The organization may choose to develop its own questionnaire, usually with the help of a consultant, or may use any of literally hundreds of questionnaires already available. Numerous questionnaires are available to measure attitudes toward work, supervision, pay, intergroup relations, communications, career development, training, or even reaction to the survey itself. A brief example from a lengthy attitude survey is shown in Figure 2–7.

Some major businesses survey employees on a regular basis. Xerox corporation has designated a "Delta Branch." This is not a physical Xerox branch, but a cross-section of employees selected nationally for periodic data gathering. Whenever there is a specific area of interest, questionnaires are mailed to the Delta Branch employees. Their responses are evaluated and used as one element in decision making.

Xerox has sophisticated staff support, including people with training in survey techniques and questionnaire design. Development of a good survey

TABLE 2–3

Favorability ranking of investing nations

Favorability Rank	Country
1	U.S.A.
2	Canada
3	West Germany
4	Japan
5	Philippines
6	Mexico
7	United Kingdom
8	Taiwan
9	Iran
10	Greece
11	Brazil
12	South Korea
13	Saudi Arabia

SECTION V: SUPERVISOR-SUBORDINATE RELATIONS

On the following eleven scales describe the nature of the relationship that exists between you and your supervisor. Indicate your responses by placing an "X" in the appropriate space in each scale.

Pleasant	:__:__:__:__:__:__:__	Unpleasant
	1 2 3 4 5 6 7 8	
Friendly	:__:__:__:__:__:__:__	Unfriendly
	1 2 3 4 5 6 7 8	
Bad	:__:__:__:__:__:__:__	Good
	1 2 3 4 5 6 7 8	
Worthless	:__:__:__:__:__:__:__	Valuable
	1 2 3 4 5 6 7 8	
Distant	:__:__:__:__:__:__:__	Close
	1 2 3 4 5 6 7 8	
Cold	:__:__:__:__:__:__:__	Warm
	1 2 3 4 5 6 7 8	
Quarrelsome	:__:__:__:__:__:__:__	Harmonious
	1 2 3 4 5 6 7 8	
Self-Assured	:__:__:__:__:__:__:__	Hesitant
	1 2 3 4 5 6 7 8	
Efficient	:__:__:__:__:__:__:__	Inefficient
	1 2 3 4 5 6 7 8	
Gloomy	:__:__:__:__:__:__:__	Cheerful
	1 2 3 4 5 6 7 8	
Stressful	:__:__:__:__:__:__:__	Unstressful
	1 2 3 4 5 6 7 8	

FIGURE 2–7
Example from an attitude survey

instrument is no job for amateurs. One manager in a small company wanted information about work load in the plant, so he included the following question and scale:

The work load in my section is

____Very good ____Good ____Fair ____Poor ____Very poor

The average score was between poor and very poor. Unfortunately, the scaling does not allow interpretation. Does "poor" mean too heavy—or too light? Does it mean it is poorly planned? The manager also neglected to code the question-naires by department, so he had no way of identifying unit scores. The manager did want to know if the work load was too heavy. A simple change of the scale and coding by section would have retrieved the answer:

The work load in my section is

          ____Much too high ____Somewhat too high ____About right
          ____Somewhat too low ____Much too low

In this case, the manager spent a good deal of his time and a lot of employee time (filling out the questionnaire) to achieve no results.

All too often surveys are done simply to "find out what people think." Employees are generally pleased to be asked to participate, but in return they usually expect some reaction from management. Too frequently, neither the results of the survey nor the management reactions are communicated to the employees.

For management, an inflexible rule should be: "If you don't really want the answer, or if you will not act on the answer, *don't ask the question!*"

Influence of Values

As mentioned previously, another important aspect of an individual's reactions to others is based on values and value systems. While most organizations do not directly address or survey this issue, some work has been done to try and to understand the implications for managing organizations in various countries.

G. W. England's study, covered earlier in this chapter, compared the values of American managers with the values of managers from a number of different countries. He found the outstanding value characteristics of American managers to include

1. a large element of pragmatism
2. a high achievement and competence orientation
3. emphasis on traditional organizational goals such as profit maximization
4. organizational efficiency and high productivity
5. high value placed upon most employee groups as significant reference groups[31]

The value pattern of American managers was most similar to that of Australian managers and least similar to that of Korean managers. More is said about comparative values in chapter 15, but consider briefly the interesting problems inherent in communicating or negotiating with managers holding different values from your own.

On a smaller scale, values of a corporate founder can permeate an organiza-tion, attracting like-minded people. While Edwin Land was still with Polaroid

Corporation, brilliant scientists and skilled marketers vied for jobs at the company. The high-risk, rapid-growth atmosphere attracted people who valued challenge and innovation. Exotic new consumer products were produced regularly, including some with phenomenal sales potential.[32]

After Mr. Land's departure from the company, the new CEO began moving the firm away from its almost exclusive emphasis on consumer products, and reduced the portion of research and development funds used for new technology. Despite the fact that some industry analysts believe the company is better managed today, many key people have left. One Polaroid employee summed up the change: "Polaroid used to be *the* company. Now it's just *a* company."[33]

DISCUSSION QUESTIONS

1. Values have been described as the foundation of individual behavior. On what basis do you think such a statement was made?
2. How might a manager influence the attitudes of employees?
3. "Job candidates for a sales position are more likely to be successful if they hold egocentric values." Discuss.
4. "Young people today just don't have the same values of hard work and company loyalty that my generation has." Do you agree or disagree with this middle-aged individual's statement? Support your position.
5. Discuss the importance of attitudes to managing a work group.
6. Give examples of how people might perceive the same situation differently. Explain why.
7. When evaluating a subordinate's job performance, what perceptual tendencies might cause the manager problems? How might these tendencies be reduced?

EXERCISE: PERCEPTIONS AND VALUES

The following exercise has several goals: (1) to let individuals identify to what degree certain characteristics are seen as similar or dissimilar to what they possess and (2) to help individuals define the dimensions of human similarity and dissimilarity they believe are important in terms of values.

Each participant uses the Peer Perceptions Ranking Form. Each person identifies ten persons with whom they are familiar. These can include friends, family members, work associates and supervisors, and others. The participant then ranks all ten people, from the person he or she considers *most* similar to himself or herself to the person he or she considers *least* similar. Beside each name, the participant lists the characteristics he or she had in mind.

After completing this form, answer the questions following it.

PEER PERCEPTIONS RANKING FORM

	Your Ranking of Other Individuals	Characteristics You Considered
Most Similar to You	1._____	_____
	2._____	_____
	3._____	_____
	4._____	_____
	5._____	_____
	6._____	_____
	7._____	_____
	8._____	_____
	9._____	_____
Least Similar to You	10._____	_____

Questions

1. What perceptual processes may have contributed to your views of others?
2. What values are underlying your choosing certain people as most like you? Why did you classify certain people as least like you? What does that say about your value system?
3. How would you describe the way values helped or hindered you in looking at the other people?

NOTES

1. Reprinted by permission of the *Harvard Business Review*. Excerpt from "What Killed Bob Lyons?" by Harry Levinson (March–April 1981). Copyright ©1981 by the President and Fellows of Harvard College; all rights reserved.
2. Milton Rokeach, *The Nature of Human Values* (New York: Free Press, 1973): 5.
3. Ibid.
4. Clare W. Graves, "Levels of Existence: An Open System Theory of Values," *Journal of Humanistic Psychology* (Fall 1970): 131–155. Copyright © 1970 by *Journal of Humanistic Psychology*. Reprinted by permission of Sage Publications Inc.
5. Stephen P. Robbins, *Organizational Behavior: Concepts and Controversies and Application*, 2nd ed. (Englewood Cliffs, NJ: Prentice-Hall, 1983): 53–54.
6. W. Clay Hammer and Dennis W. Organ, *Organizational Behavior: An Applied Psychological Approach* (Dallas: Business Publications, 1978): 187.

7. G. W. England, *The Manager and His Values: An International Perspective from the United States, Japan, Korea, India, and Australia* (Cambridge, MA: Ballinger, 1975).

8. England, ibid., p.1.

9. W. Whitely and G. W. England, "Variability in Common Dimensions of Managerial Values Due to Value Orientation and Country Difference," *Personnel Psychology*, 33 (1980): 78.

10. D. N. DeSalvia and G. R. Gemmill, "An Exploratory Study of the Personal Value Systems of College Student and Manager," *Academy of Management Journal*, no. 14 (1971): 227–238.

11. G. W. England, N. C. Agarval, and R. E. Trerise, "Union Leaders and Managers: A Comparison of Value Systems," *Industrial Relations*, no. 10 (1971): 210.

12. G. W. England, "Personal Values of Manager—So What?" *Personnel Administrator*, no. 20 (April 1975): 20–22.

13. W. Wood and A. N. Eagly, "Stages in the Analysis of Persuasive Messages: The Role of Causal Attributions and Message Comprehension," *Journal of Personality and Social Psychology*, no. 40 (1981): 246–259.

14. C. R. Mewborn and R. W. Rogers, "Effects of Threatening and Reassuring Components of Fear Appeals on Psychological and Verbal Measures of Emotion and Attitudes," *Journal of Experimental Social Psychology*, no. 15 (1979): 242–253.

15. M. Zellner, "Self-esteem, Reception, and Influenceability," *Journal of Personality and Social Psychology*, no. 15 (1970): 87–93.

16. L. Festinger, *A Theory of Cognitive Dissonance* (Stanford, CA: Stanford University Press, 1957).

17. B. R. Schlenker and R. W. Miller, "A Self-presentational Analysis of the Effects of Incentive and Attitude Change Following Counter Attitudinal Behavior," *Journal of Personality and Social Psychology*, no. 39 (1980): 553–577.

18. E. A. Locke, "What is Job Satisfaction?" *Organizational Behavior and Human Performance*, vol. 4 (1969): 316.

19. V. H. Vroom, *Work and Motivation* (New York: Wiley, 1964); and D. W. Organ, "A Reappraisal and Reinterpretation of the Satisfaction-Causes-Performance Hypothesis," *Academy of Management Review*, vol. 2 (1977): 46–55.

20. A. H. Bradfield and W. H. Crockett, "Employee Attitude and Employee Performance," *Psychological Bulletin*, vol. 52 (1955): 396–424; and F. Herzberg, B. Mansner, R. Peterson, and D. Capwell, *Job Attitudes: Review of Research and Opinion* (Pittsburgh: Psychological Services of Pittsburgh, 1957).

21. C. N. Greene and R. E. Craft, Jr., "The Satisfaction-Performance Controversy Revisited," in H. K. Downey, D. Hellriegel, and J. W. Slocum, Jr., eds., *Organizational Behavior: A Reader* (St. Paul, MN: West Publishing, 1977): 189.

22. DeWitt C. Dearborn and Herbert A. Simon, "Selective Perception: A Note on the Departmental Identification of Executives," *Sociometry* (June 1958): 140–144.

23. R. E. Nisbett and T. D. Wilson, "The Halo Effect: Evidence for the Unconscious Alteration of Judgements," *Journal of Personality and Social Psychology*, no. 35 (1977): 450–456.

24. Lloyd H. Strickland, "Surveillance and Trust," *Journal of Personality*, vol. 26 (1958): 200–215.

25. N. A. Murray, "The Effect of Fear Upon Estimates of the Maliciousness of other Personalities," *Journal of Social Psychology*, no. 4 (1933): 310–329.

26. S. Feshback and R. P. Singer, "The Effects of Fear Arousal and Suppression of Fear Upon Social Perception," *Journal of Abnormal and Social Psychology*, no. 55 (1957): 283–289.

27. "Measuring the Quality of Life," *International Herald Tribune*, (26 November 1982): 7W.

28. W. L. Weis and C. P. Fleenor, "Cold-Shouldering the Smoker," *Supervisory Management* (September 1981): 31–35.

29. A. Cox, *The Cox Report on the American Corporation* (New York: Delacorte Press, 1982).

30. G. M. Hampton and C. P. Fleenor, "Attitudes Towards Foreign Investment in the United States." Research Paper, 1980, Albers School of Business, Seattle University, Seattle, WA.

31. G. W. England, *The Manager and His Values*, p. 10.

32. "Losing Its Flash," *The Wall Street Journal* (10 May 1983): 1.

33. Ibid., p. 20.

RECOMMENDED READINGS

M. R. Cooper, B. S. Morgan, P. M. Foley, and L. B. Kaplan, "Changing Employee Values: Deepening Discontent?" *Harvard Business Review* (January–February 1979): 117–25.

This article, which analyses survey data over twenty-five years, indicates that there has been a major shift in the attitudes and values in the work force.

T. T. Ivy, V. S. Hill, and R. E. Stevens, "Dissonance Theory: A Managerial Perspective," *Business and Society* (February 1978): 17–25.

Dissonance theory is shown to be especially relevant in predicting consequences of decision situations and suggesting methods by which undesirable consequences can be avoided.

B. Z. Posner, and J. M. Munson, "The Importance of Values in Organizational Behavior," *Human Resource Management* (Fall 1979): 9–14.

This article describes values and how they are measured, and argues that values are important to study and important for managers to know about.

Space Utilization

Sherman Adder, assistant plant manager for Frame Manufacturing Company, was chairman of the ad hoc committee for space utilization. The committee was made up of the various department heads in the company. The plant manager of Frame had given Sherman the charge to see if the various office, operations, and warehouse facilities of the company were being optimally utilized. The company was beset by rising costs and the need for more space. However, before okaying an expensive addition to the plant, the plant manager wanted to be sure that the currently available space was being properly utilized.

Sherman opened up the first committee meeting by reiterating the charge of the committee. Then Sherman asked the members if they had any initial observations to make. The first to speak was the office manager. He stated, "Well, I know we are using every possible inch of room that we have available to us. But when I walk out into the plant, I see a lot of open spaces. We have people piled on top of one another, but out in the plant there seems to be plenty of room." The production manager quickly replied, "We do not have a lot of space. You office people have the luxury facilities. My supervisors don't even have room for a desk and a file cabinet. I have repeatedly told the plant manager we need more space. After all, our operation determines whether this plant succeeds or fails, not you people in the front office pushing paper around." Sherman interrupted at this point to say, "Obviously we have different interpretations of the space utilization around here. Before further discussion I think it would be best if we have some objective facts to work with. I am going to ask the industrial engineer to provide us with some statistics on plant and office layout before our next meeting. Today's meeting is adjourned."

Questions

1. What perceptual principles are evident in this case?
2. What concept was brought out when the production manager labeled the office personnel a bunch of "paper pushers"? Can you give other organizational examples of this concept?
3. Do you think that Sherman's approach to getting "objective facts" from statistics on plant and office layout will affect the perceptions of the office and production managers? How does such information affect perceptions in general?
4. What would you suggest Sherman should do instead (that is, if you don't agree with his approach to gather facts)?

CHAPTER THREE
Motivation

OUTLINE

MOTIVATIONAL CONCEPTS

Introduction
Types of Motivation Theories
Content Theories
Process Theories
Reinforcement Theory
Summary of Key Concepts

MANAGERIAL APPLICATIONS

A Case of Success
A Case of Failure?
Money as a Motivator
Do Worker-Owners Perform Better?
What About Reinforcement Theory?
What Does the Future Hold?

OBJECTIVES

- Define motivation and the three main approaches to the study of motivation as well as the differences between them

- Describe the following theories of motivation: need hierarchy, two-factor, ERG, achievement, equity, expectancy, goal setting, and reinforcement

- Identify and discuss the major managerial applications of motivational theory

MOTIVATION – THE PROCESS WHICH CAUSES BEHAVIOR TO BE ENERGIZED, DIRECTED, AND SUSTAINED.

Million Dollar Motivation Plan

During the late 1970s and early 1980s, the employees at Diamond International faced an uncertain future. The company's main product is paper egg cartons.

The uncertain future resulted from not only stiff competition among styrofoam egg carton manufacturers but the deep economic recession with its high interest rates and high unemployment. This meant that profits were reduced to less than the minimum expected by the parent company. The director of personnel, Daniel Boyle, stated, "Relations between labor and management were strained at best."

Out of the desperate situation, Boyle designed and introduced a productivity and motivation system called "100 Club." The actual mechanics of the program are simple in nature. Above-average performance for an employee results in the allocation of points. A few possible schemes include 20 points for no job accident for one year and 25 points for 100 percent attendance. On the program's anniversary date, points are totaled and a letter sent to the employee. Once an employee reaches 100 points, he or she receives a light blue jacket with the company logo and a patch identifying the wearer as a member of the "100 Club." Additional gifts can be gained for points over 100.

How is it working? Well, all 325 employees have a jacket. Productivity is up 16.5 percent; quality related errors are down 40 percent; grievances have decreased 72 percent; and lost time from job-related accidents has dropped 43.7 percent. The result of these changes has meant a financial return of $1 million dollars to the parent company.

In summarizing what's happened, Boyle says, "For too long, the people who have got the majority of attention have been those who cause problems. The program's primary focus is the recognition of good employees."[1]

MOTIVATIONAL CONCEPTS

Introduction

As in this brief story, managerial concern for motivation usually stems from a firm's lack of financial success. However, once management has made a commitment to deal with some of the conditions of worker motivation there seems to be some indication that the situation can be changed for both the worker and the organization.

This story also raises some interesting questions. Is it that simple to motivate employees? Do they just want some recognition? Can't we just say "You did a good job" and not give prizes away? Does this mean people are motivated by some form of money? If one firm can get such great results, why aren't others doing this?

Managerial concern about the subject of motivation has become an issue of great importance and study. Much of the concern centers around improving productivity. Granted, many approaches feature large technological improvements; nevertheless, many of the programs aim at involving the worker or manager more directly to improve their performance. We look more carefully at some of these programs in chapter 14. But to appreciate and evaluate their possible success we need to look more closely at the theories of motivation on which most are either explicitly or implicitly based.

Factors other than insufficient productivity have made managers aware that motivating employees is part of their job. These include the recognition that employees want more from their job than just economic rewards, that the work force is more educated and sophisticated, that external control and authority are not as effective as in the past, and that employees are becoming more militant in making demands to have more of their needs satisfied in the workplace.

Types of Motivation Theories

People differ not only in their ability to work—that is, their skills and talents—but also in their "will to work," or motivation. Motivation is hard to define, much less understand. The literal meaning is from the Latin word "movere," to move. Yet in most cases a manager is really concerned about worker performance. Therefore, a basic definition that allows us to begin looking at various theories of motivation might be "the process that causes behavior to be energized, directed, and sustained."[2]

The introductory story shows clearly that the workers were energized to improve productivity. We can imagine that they must have received some direction, because errors were reduced and accidents were down. We can also surmise that the program was sustained to allow the workers to accumulate enough points to get jackets and gifts and the firm to earn a million dollars. But we are still left with the same questions raised earlier.

To explain motivation, we are basically trying to understand the "whys" of behavior. Why does an individual choose to act one way rather than another? Why does the individual stop doing something that needs to be done?

In attempts to understand the "whys" of individual behavior, three major categories of motivation theories have been developed—content, process, and reinforcement. These are summarized in Table 3–1.

Content Theories   Content theories of motivation focus on what arouses individuals' behavior—that is, what specific things motivate people. Various theorists have provided insight by discussing the needs, drives, and incentives that cause people to behave in a certain manner. For example, good working conditions, friendly supervisors and co-workers, fringe benefits, and adequate wages are rated in various studies.[3]

Content theories provide managers with an understanding of the particular work-related factors that arouse employees to behave certain ways. These theories provide little understanding, however, of *why* an individual chooses a particular behavioral pattern to accomplish work goals.

TABLE 3-1
Types of motivational theories

Type	Characteristics	Theories	Managerial Examples
Content	Concerned with factors that arouse, start, or initiate motivated behavior	1. Need hierarchy theory 2. Two-factor theory 3. ERG theory	Motivation by satisfying individual needs for money, status, and achievement
Process	Concerned not only with factors that arouse behavior, but also the process, direction, or choice of behavioral patterns	1. Expectancy theory 2. Equity theory	Motivation through clarifying the individual's perception of work inputs, performance requirements, and rewards
Reinforcement	Concerned with the factors that will increase the likelihood that desired behavior will be repeated	1. Reinforcement theory (operant conditioning)	Motivation by rewarding desired behavior

Source: From *Organizational Behavior and Performance*, 3rd ed., p. 85, by Andrew D. Szilagyi, Jr., and Marc J. Wallace, Jr. Copyright © 1983, 1980, 1977 by Scott, Foresman and Company. Reprinted by permission.

Process Theories   In contrast, process theories attempt to explain as well as describe how people start, direct, sustain, and stop particular behavior. While content theories talk about different needs that motivate a person, process theories discuss how these needs interact and influence one another to produce certain kinds of behavior.

Three well-known process theories developed to explain, predict, and influence behavior are the equity theory, the expectancy theory, and goal setting.

Both content and process theories deal with the individual's internal workings of motivation. As a result, it can be difficult to specify and develop programs to meet these internal dimensions.

Reinforcement Theory   This theory of motivation is primarily a behavioral approach. It does not concern itself with the internal conditions of employee motivation. If the manager wants a certain behavior that would be effective for the organization, then the manager schedules a definitive program of external reinforcements to create that desired behavior. These reinforcements—for instance, a salary increase—are in the employee's environment, unlike needs that are internal. Yet, from the managerial perspective, motivating employees by reinforcement still necessitates energizing, directing, and sustaining behavior and, therefore, can be considered a theory of motivation, a la pragmatic. The manager's job of motivation centers around maintaining and/or changing environmental conditions.

Content Theories

The most popular content theories of motivation are Maslow's need hierarchy, McClelland's achievement motivation, Herzberg's two-factor theory, and Alderfer's ERG theory.

Maslow's Need Hierarchy Theory   The most widely recognized need classification scheme was proposed by Abraham Maslow over a quarter of a century ago.[4] His list of needs is conveniently short, yet covers most of the dimensions that psychologists have found to be important.

There are three basic premises of Maslow's need hierarchy theory. First, a satisfied need does not motivate. When a need is satisfied, another need emerges to take its place, so people are always striving to satisfy some need. Second, various needs are arranged in hierarchy such that individuals attempt to satisfy some needs before moving on to others. Third, there are more ways to satisfy higher-level needs than lower-level needs.

Maslow suggests that human needs can be arranged into five levels (see Figure 3–1). He places the physiological needs first because they tend to have the greatest strength until they are somewhat satisfied. These are the basic human needs to sustain life itself—food, clothing, and shelter. Until these basic needs are met to the degree needed for sufficient operation of the body, the majority of activity will probably be at this level. When the physiological needs have been sufficiently satisfied, other levels of needs become important and provide motivation for the individual's behavior.

The next level of needs—safety or security—essentially includes the needs to be free of the fear of physical danger and deprivation of the basic physiological needs. In other words, these needs involve self-preservation. There is concern for the future as well as for the present. Will individuals be able to maintain their property and/or jobs so that they can provide food and shelter for themselves and their families? This could have been part of the motivation of the Diamond employees as they saw profits decline to the point where the parent company might sell or liquidate the plant.

After physiological and safety needs are fairly well satisfied, Maslow's theory suggests that social or affiliation needs become dominant. Because people are social beings, they have a need to belong and to be accepted by various groups. When social needs become dominant, a person will strive for meaningful relations with others. As the "100 Club" became a reality, with certain employees wearing a blue jacket, we can speculate that others may have begun to see this group as desirable.

After individuals begin to satisfy their need to belong, they generally want to be more than just a member of their group. They feel the need for esteem—both self-esteem and recognition and respect from others. Satisfaction of these esteem needs produces feelings of self-confidence, prestige, power, and control.

Once esteem needs begin to be adequately satisfied, the final level—self-actualization needs—becomes more important. Self-actualization is the need to

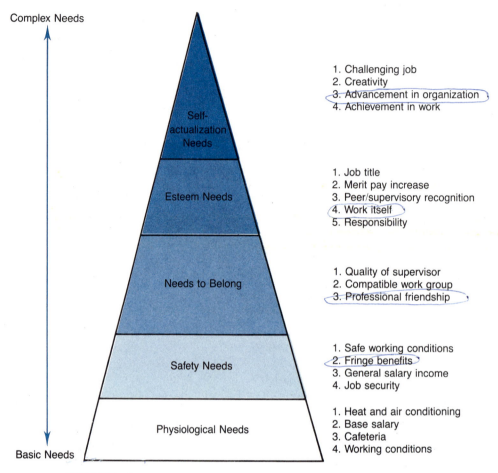

Complex Needs

1. Challenging job
2. Creativity
3. Advancement in organization
4. Achievement in work

Self-actualization Needs

1. Job title
2. Merit pay increase
3. Peer/supervisory recognition
4. Work itself
5. Responsibility

Esteem Needs

1. Quality of supervisor
2. Compatible work group
3. Professional friendship

Needs to Belong

1. Safe working conditions
2. Fringe benefits
3. General salary income
4. Job security

Safety Needs

1. Heat and air conditioning
2. Base salary
3. Cafeteria
4. Working conditions

Physiological Needs

Basic Needs

FIGURE 3-1

Maslow's need hierarchy and examples of each level in an organization (Source: Data (for diagram) on Hierarchy of Needs in ''A Theory of Human Motivation'' in *Motivation and Personality,* 2nd ed., by Abraham H. Maslow. Copyright © 1970 by Abraham H. Maslow. Reprinted by permission of Harper & Row, Publishers, Inc.)

maximize one's potential, whatever it may be. A welder must weld metal, a professor must teach students, a manager must manage people, an engineer must design technology and products, and a student must learn as much about a subject as possible. Thus, self-actualization is the desire to become all that one is capable of becoming at that point in time.

Maslow's categories of need have a common sense appeal that has ensured them wide discussion and application. Yet, for such a widely accepted view of need structure, Maslow's theory has received little research support. One study of managers in two different companies shows not a hierarchy of five needs but only two levels of needs—a biological level, and a global level covering the higher level needs.[5] Other research has shown differences in need levels between managers in smaller and larger firms and between American managers working abroad and foreign managers.[6] For instance, managers in larger firms placed less emphasis on safety and security needs and more importance on higher level needs than did managers in smaller firms. This may be partially explained by the fact that there is more security in a large organization than a smaller, but still not totally established, firm. Yet managers find this conceptualization of individual needs a convenient way to appreciate some of human complexity and diversity.

Herzberg's Two-Factor Theory   Another view of human needs that has been a major influence on managerial practice and education is the "two-factor" or "two-need" theory suggested by Frederick Herzberg.[7] The theory was originally derived by analyzing critical incidents written by 200 engineers and accountants. These incidents were supposed to describe times when the engineers and accountants felt particularly happy and particularly unhappy at work. This same approach has often been repeated with a variety of other jobholders. The data from analyzing such incidents were interpreted by Herzberg to reveal that there are two types of needs in the work environment—"hygiene" or "dissatisfiers" and "motivators" or "satisfiers." The specific job factors that influenced individual attitudes are illustrated in Figure 3–2.

Hygiene factors can be viewed as the need to avoid pain in the workplace. The need is met by factors such as the type of supervisor, fringe benefits, company policies, salary, and working conditions. In general, hygiene factors prevent employees from being dissatisfied or unhappy in their jobs.

Motivation factors meet the need for employees to use their talents and to grow. These factors include recognition, responsibility, advancement, personal growth, and the nature of the job itself. Herzberg considers achievement to be the most important motivator. Motivators make people satisfied with their jobs, and may thus improve their job performance.

How are these two sets of factors, hygiene and motivators, related? According to Herzberg, the factors leading to job satisfaction are separate and distinct from those that lead to job dissatisfaction (see Figure 3–3). Therefore, managers who seek to eliminate job dissatisfaction can bring about an equilibrium but not necessarily motivate individuals to use their full potential. They are placating their work force, not motivating them. When hygiene factors are sufficiently fulfilled, people will not be dissatisfied; however, neither will they be satisfied. Herzberg suggests emphasizing achievement, recognition, the work itself, and growth. People find these factors intrinsically rewarding and, therefore, will be motivated to use their full range of skills and talents to improve their job performance.

Which set of factors does the Diamond "100 Club" represent? Is the gift a fringe benefit or compensation? How do you explain Boyle's comment about the

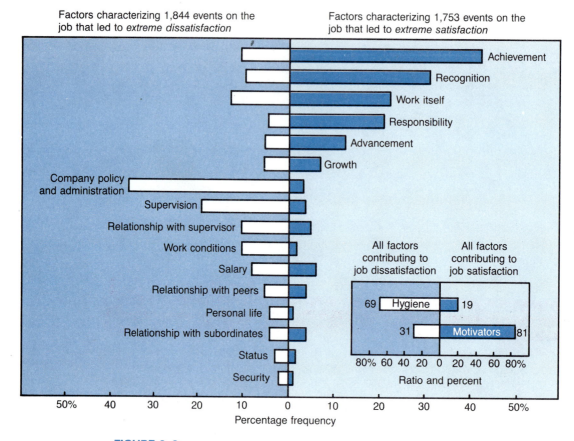

FIGURE 3–2

Comparison of satisfiers and dissatisfiers and their effects on job attitudes
(Source: Reprinted by permission of the Harvard Business Review. "One More Time: How Do You Motivate Employees?" by Frederick Herzberg (January–February 1967): 57. Copyright © 1957 by the President and Fellows of Harvard College; all rights reserved.)

"bad" employees (those who caused problems) getting recognition and not being motivated? These types of questions have raised criticisms of Herzberg's theory as an explanation of individual motivation.

One criticism centers around research showing that a given factor, such as pay, may cause satisfaction in one situation and dissatisfaction in another.[8] Other criticism concerns the lack of testing the motivation and performance implications and relationship.[9] This merely suggests that the focus of Herzberg's work is employee satisfaction, not actual motivation and performance. Motivation is associated with some behavior that the manager wants accomplished, while satisfaction is an attitude that results from behavior whether managerially directed or not.

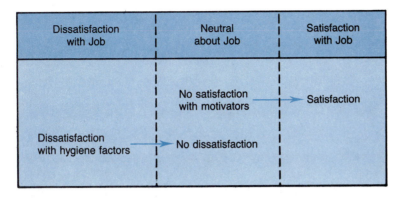

FIGURE 3-3
Satisfaction-dissatisfaction relationship

While criticism of Herzberg's two-factor theory continues to be developed and debated, the theory is widely known by managers. Many business organizations have used the theory as a basis for job redesign (covered in chaper 9) and for personnel training and development. Herzberg should be credited with having made an important contribution to management understanding and practice.

Clayton P. Alderfer's ERG Theory ERG theory, while somewhat related to Maslow's theory of needs, has gained its own popularity as an area of study. Alderfer suggests three broad categories of needs: existence, relatedness, and growth.[10]

Existence needs are constantly and pervasively important in the work setting. Specific examples are needs for some degree of job security, suitable working conditions, reasonable working hours, and adequate pay and fringe benefits. According to ERG theory, a person's existence needs must be relatively satisfied before the individual can concentrate on satisfying relatedness needs.

Relatedness needs involve relationships with significant others—family, supervisors, coworkers, subordinates, friends, and so on. Significant others can be groups of individuals as well as specific people. A basic characteristic of relatedness needs is that, unlike existence needs, their satisfaction depends essentially on the process of sharing with others. Furthermore, satisfaction of relatedness needs can be met by expressing anger and hostility as well as by developing close, warm relationships with others.

Growth needs are those that compel a person to make creative or productive efforts for himself or herself. The satisfaction of growth is what a person needs to experience in a sense of completeness as a human being. Satisfying growth needs results from fully utilizing and perhaps extending one's capacities and talents further than was thought possible.

ERG theory holds that the less existence needs are satisfied, the more they will be desired; but the more existence needs are satisfied, the more relatedness

BOX 3-1

How to Earn "Well Pay"

The woman in blue jeans and a logger's shirt looks up from the production line and says grimly: "I can't miss work today. It's almost the end of the month, and I'm going to earn that 'well pay' if it kills me."

At Parsons Pine Products Inc. in Ashland, Ore., "well pay" is the opposite of sick pay. It is an extra eight hours' wages that the company gives workers who are neither absent nor late for a full month. It is also one of four incentives that owner James W. Parsons has built into a "positive reinforcement plan" for workers: well pay, retro pay, safety pay, and profit-sharing pay.

Beating the Tax Man   The formula, Parsons says, enables him and his wife to beat the combination of federal and state income taxes that leaves them only 14% of any increase in earnings; it allows them to pass along much of the potential tax money to the workers. Under the Parsons system, an employee earning $10,000 a year can add as much as $3,500 to his income by helping the plant operate economically.

Parsons Pine employs some 100 workers to cut lumber into specialty items—primarily louver slats for shutters, bifold doors, and blinds, and wooden bases for rat traps. It is reportedly the U.S.'s biggest producer of these items, with sales last year of $2.5 million.

The company began handing out "well pay" in January, 1977. "We had a problem with lateness," Parsons explains. "Just before the 7 A.M. starting time, the foreman in a department would take a head count and assign three people to this machine and six over there. Then a few minutes later someone else comes in and he has to recalculate and reshuffle. Or he may be so short as to leave a machine idle."

"Well pay" brought lateness down to almost zero and cut absenteeism more than Parsons wanted it reduced, because some workers came to work even when they were sick. He dealt with this awkwardness by reminding them of "retro pay." Says Parsons: "I'd say, 'By being here while not feeling well, you may have a costly accident, and that will not only cause you pain and suffering, but it will also affect the retro plan, which could cost you a lot more than one day's well pay.'"

Reducing Accidents   The retro plan offers a bonus based on any reductions in premiums received from the state's industrial accident insurance fund. Before the retro plan went into effect in 1976, Parsons Pine had a high accident rate, 86% above the statewide base, and paid the fund accordingly. Parsons told his workers that if the plant cut its accident rate, the retroactive refund would be distributed to them. The upshot was a 1977 accident bill of $2,500 compared to a 1976 bill of $28,500. After deducting administrative expenses, the state will return $89,000 of a $100,000 premium, some $900 per employee.

Source: Reprinted from the 12 June 1978 issue of *Business Week* by special permission, ©1978 by McGraw-Hill, Inc.

needs will be desired. The less relatedness needs are satisfied, the more both existence and relatedness needs will be desired; but the more relatedness needs are satisfied, the more growth needs are desired; and so on.

The retro plan did not improve the accident rate unaided, Parsons concedes. "We showed films and introduced every safety program the state has," he says. "But no matter what you do, it doesn't really make a dent until the people themselves see that they are going to lose a dollar by not being safe. When management puts on the pressure, they say, 'He's just trying to make a buck for himself,' but when fellow workers say, 'Let's work safe,' that means a lot."

The 'Little Hurts' Employees can also earn safety pay—two hours' wages—by remaining accident-free for a month. "Six hours a quarter isn't such a great incentive," says Parsons, "but it helps. When it didn't cost them anything, workers would go to the doctor for every little thing. Now they take care of the little hurts themselves."

As its most substantial incentive, the company offers a profit-sharing bonus—everything the business earns over 4% after taxes, which is Parsons' idea of a fair profit. Each supervisor rates his employees in four categories of excellence, with a worker's bonus figured as a percentage of his wages multiplied by his category. Top-ranked employees generally receive bonuses of 8% to 10%. One year they got 16½%. Two-thirds of the bonus is paid in cash and the rest goes into the retirement fund.

To illustrate how workers can contribute to profits, and profit-sharing bonuses, Parsons presents a dramatic display that has a modest fame in Ashland. Inviting the work force to lunch, he sets up a pyramid of 250 rat trap bases, each representing $10,000 in sales. Then he knocks 100 onto the floor, saying: "That's for raw materials. See why it is important not to waste?" Then he pushes over 100 more, adding: "That's for wages." And pointing to the 50 left, he says: "Out of this little pile we have to do all the other things—maintenance, repairs, supplies, taxes. With so many blocks gone, that doesn't leave much for either you or me."

A Vote for Work The lunch guests apparently find the display persuasive. Says one nine-year veteran: "We get the most we can out of every piece of wood after seeing that. When new employees come, we work with them to cut down waste."

The message also lingered at the last Christmas luncheon, when, after distribution of checks, someone said: "Hey, how about the afternoon off?" Parsons replied: "O.K., our production is on schedule and the customers won't be hurt. But you know where the cost comes from." Parsons recalls that someone asked him, "How much?" and he replied that the loss would be about $3,000.

"There was a bit of chatter and we took a vote," he says. "Only two hands were raised for the afternoon off. That was because they knew it was not just my money. It was their money, too."

Questions

1. What aspects of Parsons' benefits can be described using Herzberg's theory? Maslow's theory? Alderfer's theory? Now use the reinforcement theory of motivation (p. 99) to compare with your previous answer.
2. Do you foresee any potential problems with Parsons' motivation plan? How will workers be treated who continually want to go against what the group wants?

As yet, there has not been much research on ERG theory; however, many behavioral scientists tend to view it as the most current, valid, and researchable theory based on the need concept.[11]

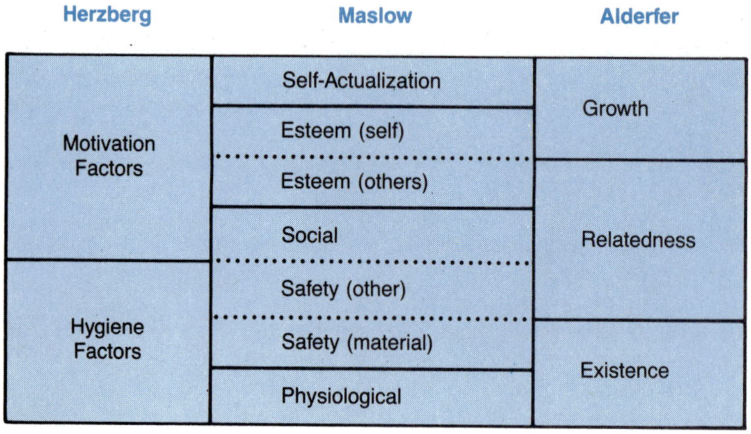

Herzberg	Maslow	Alderfer
Motivation Factors	Self-Actualization	Growth
	Esteem (self)	
	Esteem (others)	Relatedness
	Social	
Hygiene Factors	Safety (other)	
	Safety (material)	Existence
	Physiological	

FIGURE 3–4

Need classifications compared across three content theories

Figure 3–4 compares the levels of needs in the three content theories. Remember, however, that there are differences between the theories when needs are either satisfied or frustrated.

McClelland's Motivation Theory Another theory, advanced by David Mc-Clelland, began with the use of Thematic Apperception Test (TAT) to measure human needs. The TAT asks people to view pictures and write stories about what they see.

In one situation McClelland tested three executives using an identical photograph. One wrote of an engineer who was daydreaming about a family outing. Another described a designer who had picked up an idea for a new gadget from remarks made by others. The third saw an engineer who was intently working on a bridge-stress problem that he seemed sure to solve because of his confident look.[12] McClelland scored the stories given by the executives according to the amount of achievement thinking present or absent on each story, as follows:

Person dreaming about family outing   Achievement need = +1
Person pondering new idea for gadget   Achievement need = +2
Person working on bridge problem   Achievement need = +4

McClelland's theory applies projection. Individuals faced with an ambiguous situation will project their own feelings and motives on the situation to explain it. The written stories explaining the situation are self-reports of what motivates each writer.

McClelland, using the TAT stories, distinguishes three themes. Each theme corresponds to an underlying need that he feels is important for understanding individual behavior.

Achievement. The achievement need (n = Ach) requires a relatively stable disposition or potential behavioral tendency to strive for achievement of success.[13] It is a desire to do something better or more efficiently than it has been done before. A sign of strong achievement motive is the tendency of a person, who is not being required to think about anything in particular, to think about ways to accomplish something difficult and significant. Remember the executive who saw the engineer working on a bridge-stress problem and solving it.

There are three major characteristics of self-motivated achievers. First, they like to set their own goals. They do not want to drift aimlessly and they want to have a high degree of control over goal achievement. Second, self-motivated achievers set goals that are neither too easy nor too difficult to achieve. High achievers tend to set realistic goals, since they want to win. Third, those high in n = Ach like frequent and concrete feedback about their performance. High achievers like to know how well they are doing.

Affiliation. The need for affiliation (n = Aff) is the desire to be with other people regardless of whether anything else is gained thereby. Positive feelings toward social relationships and being concerned about the happiness of others is associated with n = Aff. It has been suggested that the number of groups to which an individual belongs can be taken as a measure of n = Aff.

In one study of forty-nine line managers it was found that managers who were high in n = Aff generally were less effective than managers who were high in the need for power (n = Pow).[14] One possible explanation for this finding is that high n = Aff managers, with their strong desire to be liked by their subordinates and others, make compromising decisions and bend the rules for particular individuals. It should be noted that one study is not adequate evidence for specific conclusions about the role of n = Aff in managing. Furthermore, n = Aff is an important human need and must be recognized as a possible supporting factor in managing people.

Power. The need for power (n = Pow) is more important for understanding managers than is n = Aff.[15] N = Pow refers to the desire to have impact, to be influential, and to control others.[16] Individuals high in n = Pow enjoy being in charge, strive for influence over others, prefer to be placed into competitive and status oriented situations, and tend to be more concerned with gaining influence over others and prestige than with effective performance.

McClelland has identified "two faces of power"—a positive face and a negative face.[17] The negative face of power is aimed purely at personal gain; it is manipulative and characterized by dominance-submission relationships. The negative face of power is "personalized power" and is not very effective in organizations in which group goals and interdependent relationships are important. The positive face of power, or "socialized power," which combines a desire to influence others with concern for group goals and helping others to achieve those goals, is associated with effective management and good leadership. "Good" managers are not motivated by a need for personal aggrandizement, or by a need

TABLE 3–2
Work preferences of persons high in need for achievement, affiliation, and power

Individual Need	Work Preferences	Example
High need for achievement	Individual responsibility Challenging but achievable goals Feedback on performance	Field sales person with challenging quota and opportunity to earn individual bonus
High need for affiliation	Interpersonal relationships Opportunities to communicate	Customer service representative; member of work unit subject to group wage bonus plan
High need for power	Control over other persons Attention Recognition	Formal position of supervisory responsibility; appointment as head of special task force or committee

Source: John Schemerhorn, Jr., James G. Hunt, and Richard N. Osborn, *Managing Organizational Behavior*, p. 113. Copyright © 1982, John Wiley & Sons, Inc. Reprinted by permission.

to get along with subordinates, but rather by a need to influence others' behavior for the good of the whole organization.[18]

McClelland's research suggests that these needs have important implications for organizational selection and placement. For example, a person who has a high $n = Aff$ and a low $n = Pow$ and who is placed into a job requiring a strong $n = Pow$ will have the wrong motivational forces to be successful in the job. The theory is especially useful because each need is directly associated with a set of individual work preferences, as summarized in Table 3–2. Furthermore, it may be possible for people to acquire the need profiles required to be successful in various types of jobs. Success has been reported in stimulating people's needs for achievement and helping them adopt need profiles found to be associated with successful executives.[19]

Process Theories

In contrast to content theories, "process" theories focus on the internal choice that an individual makes about a particular work behavior—"will I finish the extra paperwork today before I go home or will I relax and start on it the first thing in the morning?" The matter of choice is central to what we have termed process theories.

Equity Theory   To understand equity theory let us look at the following situation: John Carlson has been working at design engineering since he graduated from college last year. He was at the top of his class in chemical engineering and received $1,800 a month starting salary. He has been ambitious and has proven very capable with his job responsibilities. His employer, after a year, was extremely pleased with John's performance and gave John a $200 a month raise. Since the raise John's attitude seems to have changed and his performance is down considerably. Why? John's employer has just hired a college graduate from his own alma mater to perform the same type of job at $2,050 a month—$50 more than John now makes.

This brief description illustrates the role equity theory plays in motivation. Equity can mean several things; we use it here as the equivalent of words such as fairness and justice. Individuals in organizations want equitable treatment, not only for themselves, but for others. This is not saying that all people should be treated equally. Pure equality would not take into account various levels of contribution to productivity and other factors that may enter into compensation decisions.

The equity theory involves a social comparison of existing conditions against some standard.[20] The most common illustration of this is when we compare ourself with another person and make a judgement about the equity or inequity of our present condition. Equity theory uses the relationship between two variables: inputs and outcomes. Inputs represent what an individual gives or contributes to an exchange; outcomes are what an individual receives from the exchange. Table 3-3 presents some typical inputs and outcomes.

According to equity theory, individuals assign weights to the various inputs and outcomes according to their own view of relative importance. After considering their own situation of inputs and outcomes, a person may reach three possible conclusions: (1) there is a perceived equity; (2) there is perceived positive inequity; or (3) there is perceived negative inequity. A perceived positive inequity exists when an individual feels he or she has received relatively more

TABLE 3-3
Possible inputs and outcomes regarding jobs

Inputs	Outcomes
Attendance	Pay
Age	Promotion
Level of education	Challenging job assignments
Past experience	Fringe benefits
Ability	Working conditions
Social status	Status symbols
Job effort (long hours, physical exertion)	Job perquisites (office location, parking space)
Personality traits	Job security
Seniority	Responsibility
Performance	

Source: Adapted from D. Belchner and T. Atchinson, "Equity Theory and Compensation Policy," *Personnel Administrator*, vol. 33, no. 3, (1970): 28. Copyright ©1970, The American Society for Personnel Administration, 606 North Washington Street, Alexandria, VA 22314

than others. A perceived negative inequity exists when an individual feels he or she has received relatively less than others in proportion to work inputs.

Returning to John's situation, how does he view the equity or inequity? Figure 3–5 summarizes the possible perceived inequity to which John is responding. As John views the situation, he may feel that his one year of experience is worth more than no experience, yet the new employee is receiving $50 a month more. What might have been John's reaction if both were hired at the same time and yet the other employee was still receiving $50 a month more? John could rationalize the difference as a result of performance and thus justify it. Either positive or negative inequity has motivational consequences because individuals wish to restore a sense of equity. To accomplish this, an individual may engage in any one of the following behaviors:[21]

1. Change work inputs (reduce or increase amount of work)
2. Change rewards received (seek recognition for work accomplished)
3. Leave the situation (leave job or ask for transfer)
4. Change the comparison points (re-evaluate the worth of the inputs or outcomes)
5. Psychologically distort the comparison (rationalize that the boss doesn't know quality work)

The consequences for managing under the equity theory are fairly clear, yet it is difficult to implement. The conceptual view of comparing inputs and outputs with other situations is easily understood by both the manager and the employee. The real difficulty results because the feelings of equity or inequity are determined solely by the individual's interpretation of the situation. Thus a manager must not assume that his or her view of the equity will be the same as the

John		New Hire
Job duties	=	Job duties
College degree	=	College degree
Experience (1 year)	>	Experience (None)
Salary ($2,000 a month)	<	Salary ($2,050 a month)
Person 1: Outcomes (Pay, status) / Input (Job duties)	? = ?	Person 2: Outcomes (Pay, status) / Input (Job duties)
John: $2,000 / Degree + 1 year experience	<	New Hire: $2,050 / Degree + no experience

FIGURE 3–5

John's view of his situation according to equity theory

employee's. The following guidelines can help maintain some control of the equity issue.

1. Recognize that one equity comparison will likely be made by each subordinate whenever visible rewards (pay, promotions, job responsibilities) are being allocated.
2. Anticipate employees' perceiving negative inequities. Carefully communicate to each individual the evaluation of the reward, an appraisal of the performance upon which it is based, and any comparison points used to make the decisions.

Most research of the equity theory has centered around pay levels as the outcome, with performance level as the input.[22] In addition, the studies tend to focus on the issue of underpayment and not the condition of overpayment. Underpayment (negative inequity) seems to lead to absenteeism and turnover.[23] It must be noted, however, that overreliance on pay as the primary motivator of human behavior isn't consistent with recent theories of motivation.

Expectancy Theory   Victor Vroom developed the basis for an expectancy theory of work motivation.[24] The theory's central question is what determines the willingness of an individual to exert effort to work at specific tasks? In other words, how does an individual choose to do what? The theory argues that motivation is determined by an individual's beliefs regarding effort—performance relationships and the probabilities of various possible work outcomes associated with different levels of effort or performance. Simply put, the theory is based on the logic that people will do what they can do when they want to.[25]

There are several versions of expectancy theory but they share certain assumptions. First, they assume that behavior is voluntary. That is, people are free to choose those behaviors suggested by their own expectancy calculations. Second, expectancy theories assume that people will choose in a rational manner so as to optimize actual or perceived outcomes. In other words, they will try to behave in ways that optimize their own gain.

Figure 3–6, as well as the following discussion of outcomes, expectancy, instrumentality, and valence should help us understand expectancy.

Outcomes are the end results of particular behaviors and are classified as first- or second-level outcomes. First-level outcomes are the direct result of expending some effort on the job or task—in other words, some level of performance. The performance could be more units per hour or fewer errors on paper work filled out. Second-level outcomes are viewed as consequences to which first-level outcomes are expected to lead. To put it another way, the end result of performance (first-level) is some kind of reward (second-level) for meeting that performance. A second-level outcome could be a raise, a promotion, leaving early, recognition from the supervisor, or feeling good about one's job.

Expectancy is the level of belief that a particular individual effort will result in a certain performance level. Specifically this means a self-assessment by the

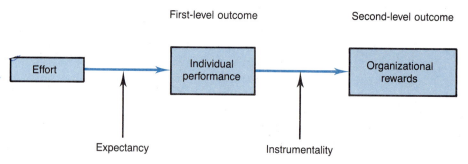

FIGURE 3–6
The expectancy theory model

employee about whether he or she can actually do the assigned work. Expectancy is based on probabilities and can vary from 1.0 ("I should have little trouble getting work done") to 0 ("No matter what I do, I'll never get the work finished").

Instrumentality is the relationship between performance (first-level outcome) and the performance's consequences (second-level outcome). As with expectancy, this variable is an expression of belief that performing a certain task successfully will lead to some rewards that the individual values (valence).

Valence is the strength of a person's preference for a particular outcome or reward. It is the value a person places on rewards, such as pay increases, promotion, recognition, and so on. Valences can have positive or negative values (+1 to −1). In the work setting a supervisory reprimand may have a negative valence for an individual.

The expectancy theory has been extended by Porter and Lawler to examine the factors that influence job performance and satisfaction.[26] Using their model, satisfaction is seen as a function of performance or the outcome of performance. Satisfaction in doing work is the real reward. This has implications for performance evaluation and organization rewards, discussed in chapter 10.

How can managers use expectancy theory while thinking about motivation? While managers do not go around calculating values for instrumentality, expectancy, and valence to arrive at a measure of employee motivation, it can be useful to help understand the complexity of motivation. Overly simplified conceptions of what motivates employees and how to motivate them can be detrimental to effective managing. Motivating human beings is a serious and complex undertaking.

Furthermore, valence helps managers reflect on the multiple outcomes of behavior. The employee's behavior can have positive, negative, or neutral outcomes. In general, outcomes most useful in motivating individual behavior are those that are "positively valent" to the individual. Outcomes the organization's managers think are positively valent are not necessarily the same as those the employees view as positively valent.

Finally, the concept of expectancy suggests some managerial behavior. Managers can positively influence employees' motivation by identifying the type and amount of behavior that will be judged good performance; classifying the performance criteria that will be evaluated; assuring that employees have appropriate job skills; actually making consequences contingent on good performance; and communicating those contingencies.

Goal-setting Theory   Like expectancy theory, goal setting is another way to energize and direct an employee's effort toward results desirable for the individual and the organization. A simplified view of this theory is shown in Figure 3–7. The basis of this theory is the belief that individuals have desires and aspirations. Locke uses the term value in place of desire or aspiration: "It is that which one regards as conducive to one's welfare."[27] These desires and aspirations result in intentions or goals. The goal then directs and results in behavior. Accomplishing the goal can lead to satisfaction and further motivation. Not accomplishing the goal can lead to frustration and low motivation.

Consider the following example. An employee values a challenge and new tasks. In a meeting, the supervisor proposes that the work unit has been missing

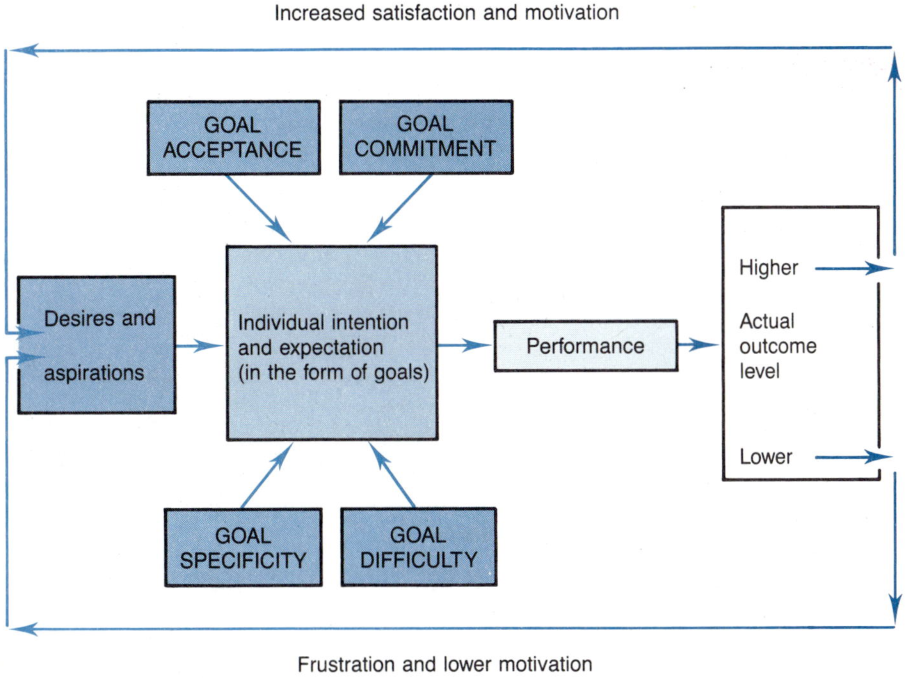

Increased satisfaction and motivation

Frustration and lower motivation

FIGURE 3–7
Model for goal-setting theory

some critical dates; there is concern about future performance. The employee asks whether some systematic study might prevent this in the future and volunteers to conduct such a study. The goal is the study and its report to the supervisor. Finishing the report becomes the outcome that reinforces the individual to accept future challenges. The following four aspects of goal setting can help us more fully understand this theory and its application.

Goal difficulty. There appears to be a direct positive relationship between goal difficulty and task performance. In a review of fifty-seven studies done by Locke et al., forty-eight of the studies supported the impact of goal difficulty.[28] In fact, it was found that the higher level of intention (the goal), the higher the level of performance. Even unrealistically high goals were positively related to performance, although not any more so than difficult but realistic goals.[29]

Goal specificity. Goal specificity also influences goal setting. Locke et al. also found support that specific goals lead to higher performance than general goals.[30] In fact, the correlation between a general goal and task performance results was almost identical to that between no goal and task performance. Rather than setting a general goal, such as "I'll do my best on the test," one might better set a more specific goal, such as "I'll get 10 more points on the motivation section of the test than I got on the quiz."

Goal acceptance. Goal acceptance is the degree to which you accept the goal as your own. It is obvious that one can set specific and difficult goals for employees, but will the employees accept the goals as their own and strive to attain them? Goal acceptance is determined prior to actually working on goal-related tasks. It is a manager's job to ensure that employees perceive a goal as their own.[31]

How does a manager accomplish this? First, the employee needs to perceive some personal benefit from accomplishing the goal—perhaps recognition, promotion, or compensation. Second, the employee must feel capable of reaching the goal. The employee must have the knowledge, confidence, and ability to work on the goal.[32]

Goal commitment. Finally, goal commitment is the degree to which you are dedicated to accomplishing the goal you have accepted. Why is this important? Goal commitment can increase or decrease after the work on goal-related tasks has started. This means that one's commitment can change as time progresses. The manager needs to continually pay attention to maintaining commitment, in terms of support, help, recognition, and reinforcement. The factors that ensure continual commitment are the same as those for goal acceptance.

The result of this goal-setting process for practicing managers has been the much publicized and criticized management by objectives (MBO). A possible reason for the divergent views of its usefulness and effectiveness may be that "MBO, like ice cream, comes in 29 flavors."[33] With such a variety of possible formats it is easy to see why the results will vary as well.

However, an MBO program should contain the following statements as a minimum:

- A series of goals (objectives) set jointly by the supervisor and the subordinate
- A continual dialogue between the supervisor and the employee to provide the needed support and redirection as conditions change
- A specific review session of the effort and accomplishment to date and a resetting of the goals if needed

While there is some general agreement that MBO is effective in many cases,[34] remember that any program may be used merely as a technique without the true support of other management systems, including management philosophy and organizational culture. Therefore, the goal-setting process in the form of MBO must have an organizational basis to be used effectively. It must be an extension of the management's concern for employee involvement and not just another management tool.[35]

Reinforcement Theory

So far we have discussed motivation from the content and process perspective, which both try to explain and predict a person's behavior by considering what is happening *inside* the individual. That is, they are concerned with explaining "why" people do things, such as to satisfy needs, pursue positive valences, or resolve felt inequities. In contrast, reinforcement theory is "acognitive." It avoids the necessity of looking within the individual and examining thought processes. Instead reinforcement theory focuses attention on the environment of the individual and its consequences for the person. Consider the following situation.[36] While walking down a street a person finds a $5 bill. Thereafter this person is observed to spend more time looking down when out walking. Why is this?

A cognitive explanation would suggest that this person looks down because of the high value held for money. The person reasons that more money may be found by looking down, so he or she decides to look down more frequently in the future. The individual makes a conscious decision and the observed behavior of looking down is the result.

Reinforcement theory gives a different explanation. When the initial behavior of looking down occurred, it was reinforced by the presence of a $5 bill. Having once been reinforced by this environmental consequence, the behavior becomes more likely to occur in the future.

Thus, reinforcement theory can be considered a motivation theory if we use our previous definition. A manager may use reinforcements to direct and especially sustain employee behavior. To understand reinforcement theory we next discuss operant conditioning, types of reinforcements, and schedules of reinforcement. Finally, we look at the application of reinforcement theory in behavior modification.

Operant Conditioning   Operant conditioning means that behavior is a function/result of its own consequences. Individuals learn to behave so they get something they want or avoid something they don't want. Operant behavior means voluntary or learned behavior in contrast to reflexive or unrelated behavior (looking for a $5 bill on sidewalks) and is influenced by the reinforcement or lack of reinforcement brought about by the consequences (finding a $5 bill) of the behavior. Reinforcement, therefore, increases the likelihood that the behavior (looking down at the sidewalk) will be repeated.

Behavior is assumed to be determined from outside (from the environment)—that is, learned—rather than from within (reflexive or unlearned). Skinner, credited with expanding our knowledge of operant conditioning, argues that by creating pleasing consequences to follow desired forms of behavior, the frequency of that behavior will increase. Individuals will most likely engage in desired behaviors if they are positively reinforced for doing so. Rewards, or positive reinforcement, are the most effective if they *immediately* follow the desired response. Likewise, behavior that is not rewarded, or is punished, is less likely to be repeated.

Types of reinforcement.   When we use reinforcement to obtain some specific desired behavior, we are shaping behavior. Suppose an employee's behavior is considered very inappropriate by management. If management only reinforced the individual when he or she happened to show desired responses, there might be very little reinforcement taking place. Management might thus apply shaping for better results.

We can shape behavior by systematically reinforcing each successive step that moves an individual closer to the desired response. If an employee has been habitually taking an hour for lunch that is supposed to last only a half-hour, and that employee comes back after fifty minutes, we can reinforce this improvement. Reinforcement increases as responses more closely approximate the desired behavior.

There are three ways to reinforce behavior or to shape behavior: through positive reinforcement, negative reinforcement, or punishment. *Positive reinforcement* occurs when a desired response is followed by something pleasant, for instance, when the boss praises an employee for a job well done. *Negative reinforcement* occurs when a desired response is followed by the termination or withdrawal of something unpleasant. If your classroom instructor asks a question and you don't know the answer, looking through your lecture notes is likely to avoid your being called on. This is a negative reinforcement because you have learned that looking busily through your notes avoids being called on by the instructor. *Punishment* is producing an unpleasant condition in an attempt to eliminate an undesirable behavior. An employee who receives a disciplinary letter for his or her file because of too many quality problems has received a form of punishment.

Extinction.   Another type of conditioning used to reduce or eliminate undesirable behavior is extinction. Extinction is the withholding of any reinforcement (positive or negative) for a behavior to be changed. Over time the nonreinforcement should eliminate or reduce this behavior. For example, coworkers may laugh at the disruptive behavior of another worker. This laughing at the disruptive behavior acts as reinforcement. If the group stops laughing, the group member will probably eventually stop the disruptive behavior.

The following example may help distinguish extinction from punishment. If a boss angrily tells an employee that a certain tone of voice isn't appropriate and won't be tolerated in the future, this is a form of punishment. Ignoring or not paying any attention to the tone of voice as the subordinate responds to the supervisor's instructions is a form of extinction. Generally, extinction takes longer to eliminate the undesirable behavior than does punishment, but may be more permanent when accomplished. Remember, however, that the elimination of an undesirable behavior will not necessarily be replaced with a desirable one. Therefore, the extinction process should be followed by some form of positive reinforcement for development of appropriate desirable behavior.

Schedules of Reinforcement   There are two types of schedules of reinforcement that are of interest—continuous and partial.[37] Continuous schedules provide rewards each time desired behavior occurs. In work organizations, there are almost no examples of continuous schedules. It would be extremely difficult to design and administer such a schedule.

A partial reinforcement schedule provides rewards on some intermittent basis. There are four types of partial reinforcement schedules: fixed ratio, variable ratio, fixed interval, and variable interval. A ratio schedule refers to the ratio of performances to reinforcement. The interval schedule refers to the time between reinforcements.

Fixed ratio schedule.   A reward is given after a fixed or constant number of responses. A piece-rate incentive plan is an example of a fixed ratio schedule—the employees receive rewards based on the number of work pieces generated. If the piece rate for a transistor installer in an electronics factory is $10 per 100, the reinforcement (money) is fixed to the number of transistors installed into the electronic equipment.

Fixed interval schedule.   The reinforcement schedule is on a fixed interval basis when rewards are spaced at uniform time intervals. The critical variable is time, and it is held constant. This is the common schedule for almost all salaried workers. When you get your paycheck on a weekly, semimonthly, or monthly basis, you are rewarded on a fixed interval reinforcement schedule.

Variable ratio schedule.   When the reward varies relative to the behavior of the individual, he or she is said to be reinforced on a variable ratio schedule. Sales people on commission represent an example of such a reinforcement schedule. In some situations, they may make a sale only after two calls on potential customers. On other occasions, they might need to make ten or more calls to secure a sale.

BOX 3–2

Creativity in Old Age: The Key to Productivity Is to Change the Environment

One problem [of aging] is often called a lack of motivation. Aging scholars lose interest; they find it hard to get to work; they work slowly. It is easy to attribute this to a change in *them,* but we should not overlook a change in their world. For *motivation* read *reinforcement*. In old age, behavior is not so strongly reinforced. Biological aging weakens reinforcing consequences. Behavior is more and more likely to be followed by aches and pains and quick fatigue. Things tend to become "not worth doing" in the sense that the aversive consequences exact too high a price. Positive reinforcers become less common and less powerful. Poor vision closes off the world of art, faulty hearing the enjoyment of highly fidelitous music. Foods do not taste as good, and erogenous tissues grow less sensitive. Social reinforcers are attenuated. Interests and tastes are shared with a smaller number of people.

Source: B. F. Skinner, "Intellectual Self-Management in Old Age," *American Psychologist,* vol. 38 no. 3, 239–244. Copyright 1983 by the American Psychological Association. Reprinted by permission of the publisher and author.

In a world in which our behavior is not generously reinforced we are said to lack zest, joie de vivre, interest, ambition, aspirations, and a hundred other desirable "states of mind" and "feelings." These are really the by-products of changed contingencies of reinforcement. When the occasion for strong behavior is lacking or when reinforcing consequences no longer follow, we are bored, discouraged, and depressed. But it is a mistake to say that we suffer from such feelings. We suffer from the defective contingencies of reinforcement responsible for the feelings. Our environment is no longer maintaining strong behavior.

Our culture does not generously reinforce the behavior of old people. Both affluence and welfare destroy reinforcing contingencies, and so does retirement. . . . Reinforcers need not occur too frequently if we are fortunate enough to have been reinforced on a good schedule. A "stretched variable-ratio schedule" refers to a process you have all experienced as you acquired a taste for good literature, in which the reinforcing moments occur much less often than in cheap literature. In

The reward, then, is variable in relation to the number of successful calls the salesperson makes.

Variable interval schedule. The schedule of reinforcements is of the variable interval type if rewards are distributed in time so that reinforcements are unpredictable. When an instructor advises a class that there will be a number of pop quizzes given during the course (the exact number of which is unknown to the students) and the quizzes will account for 30 percent of the grade, the instructor is using a variable interval schedule.

a comic strip you laugh at the end of every four frames, and in cheap literature something interesting happens every page. Learning to enjoy good literature is essentially learning to read for longer and longer periods of time before coming upon a moving passage—a passage all the more moving for having required a long preparation. Gambling is reinforced on a variable-ratio schedule, and pathological gamblers show the effect of a history in which they began with reasonable success and only later exhausted their resources. Many of the reinforcers in old age tend to be on a stretched variable-ratio schedule. If your achievements as a thinker have been spaced on a favorable schedule, you will have no difficulty in remaining active even though current achievements are spaced far apart. . . .

Old people find themselves spending time with others who are not interested in their fields. They may receive fewer invitations to speak or find it harder to accept them. . . . An appropriate measure of intellectual self-management is to organize discussions, if only in groups of two. Find someone with similar interests. Two heads together are better than both apart. In talking with another person we have ideas that do not occur when we are alone at our desks. . . .

In searching for an audience, beware of those who are trying to be helpful and too readily flatter you . . . those who help those who can help themselves work a sinister kind of destruction by making the good things in life no longer properly contingent on behavior. If you have been very successful, the most sententious stupidities will be received as pearls of wisdom, and your standards will instantly fall. If you are still struggling to be successful, flattery will more often than not put you on the wrong track by reinforcing useless behavior.

I have reported some of the ways in which I have tried to avoid growing old as a thinker, and in addition I have given you a sample of the result. You may wish to turn to another comparison with a different species and conclude, if I may so paraphrase Dr. Johnson, "Sir, an aged lecturer is like a dog walking in his hinder legs. It is not well done; but you are surprised to find it done at all."

Questions

1. What are the various aspects of old age that receive reinforcements from children? Governmental agencies? Society at large?
2. Do you agree with Skinner that you merely change some of the reinforcements? Discuss.
3. What implications do Skinner's ideas have for organizations and those people who are nearing retirement?

In general, variable schedules tend to lead to higher performance than do fixed schedules. In a fixed interval schedule such as weekly pay, the reinforcement is given for the time spent on the job rather than the performance. In contrast, the variable interval schedule generates higher rates of response and more stable and consistent behavior because of the close relationship between performance and reinforcement, and because of the uncertainty involved ("When will I receive the next visit from the boss?"). The employee tends to be more alert because of the surprise factor. A summary of the effects of various reinforcement schedules on behavior is presented in Table 3–4.

TABLE 3–4
Schedules of reinforcement

Schedule	Description	Example	Effects on Behavior
Continuous	Reinforcer follows every response.	A manager watches an employee learning to use a new machine; praise is given each time the process is done perfectly.	Rapid and positive influence on behavior; behavior weakens rapidly when reinforcement is stopped.
Intermittent	Reinforcer does not follow every response.		Slow in establishing a desired behavior; but behavior is more permanent when reinforcement stops.
Fixed interval	The first response after a specific period of time has elapsed is reinforced.	A paycheck is received at the end of a week's work; a grade is received at the end of a semester.	Produces an uneven response pattern varying from a very slow, unenergetic response immediately following reinforcement to a very fast, vigorous response immediately preceding reinforcement.
Fixed ratio	A fixed number of responses must be emitted before reinforcement occurs.	A person is paid on a "piece-rate," for example, for every 10 units produced a certain amount of pay is received; "commission" sales.	Tends to produce a high rate of response that is vigorous and steady.
Variable interval	The first response after varying or random periods of time have elapsed is reinforced.	A manager takes periodic but unscheduled walks around the unit; compliments are given to employees displaying desirable work behaviors.	Tends to produce a high rate of response that is vigorous, steady, and durable.
Variable ratio	A varying or random number of responses must be emitted before reinforcement occurs.	A worker's output is checked at random according to the number of units produced; when quality is 100%, a small monetary bonus is paid.	Capable of producing a high rate of response that is vigorous, steady, and durable.

Source: Adapted from Fred Luthans and Robert Kreitner, *Organizational Behavior Modification and Beyond*, p. 58. Copyright ©1985 by Scott, Foresman and Company. Reprinted by permission.

Behavior Modification   In organizations, behavior modification is the systematic application of operant conditioning principles to worker behavior. Behavior modification focuses on observable behavior, careful analysis and measurement of the behavior to be changed, application of operant conditioning for behavior change, and evaluation of the effect of behavior change.

We present a production case of a medium-sized industrial plant engaged in light manufacturing to illustrate the application of organizational behavior modification.[38] The plant manager felt the need to increase the plant's performance while maintaining employee morale. The approach used follows the basic procedures illustrated in Figure 3–8. Two groups of nine first-level production supervisors participated. One group underwent training in behavioral modification while the other, the control group, did not undergo any training. The plant manager described both groups of supervisors as having gone through the "school of hard knocks" to reach their present positions of management.

First, identify the goals and target behaviors of the program. The plant manager and the production supervisors described and carefully identified the changes they wished to make. The analysis included identification of observable and measurable target behaviors. The identification process may be done by the job holder or by the supervisor. In the production case, supervisors of the work groups were trained to identify behaviors for which reinforcement techniques could be used.

Second, measure target behaviors. To provide a baseline for future comparison and feedback, the frequency of the desired target behavior is counted or measured. In the production case, work-assignment completions, absences, rejects,

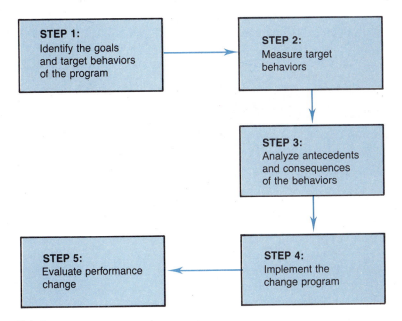

FIGURE 3–8
Major steps in behavior modification

quality-control problems, complaints, excessive breaks, leaving the work area, and scrap rates were selected for assessment. A preliminary three-month period of assessment was used to establish a baseline.

Third, analyze the antecedents and consequences of the behaviors. The behavior to be changed is often influenced by prior occurrences (antecedents) and has some identifiable consequences. A particularly disruptive machine operator was one case for whom the supervisor decided to study the application of antecedents and consequences. The individual often complained bitterly about the production standards to the supervisor (antecedent). In addition, the worker adversely affected the production of coworkers. In analyzing the situation, the supervisor concluded that he was probably serving as a reinforcing consequence by paying attention to the complaints. Such antecedents and consequences need to be identified. Effective behavior change requires replacement or removal of these reinforcing consequences.

Fourth, implement the change program. Positive reinforcement, negative reinforcement, punishment, and extinction may be used to change target behavior. Positive reinforcements are either intrinsic or extrinsic. We may introduce positive intrinsic reinforcement by structuring the job so that effective performance is challenging and interesting and provides self-worth. Extrinsic reinforcement includes performance-related financial incentives, supervisory recognition, and promotion. In the production case, supervisors used extrinsic reinforcements by thanking or sincerely praising a worker for good work. Special assignments to preferred tasks were also occasionally used. The extinction strategy involved eliminating any reinforcement associated with unwanted performance. A worker who enjoys creating rage in the boss by doing a task sloppily will experience extinction of that behavior if the boss does not become angry. In the production case, punishment was particularly avoided to prevent undesired and unintended responses such as poor morale, absenteeism, and turnover. In the previously described instance of a disruptive, complaining employee, the supervisor ignored the complaints (extinction) and listened very attentively when the employee offered constructive ideas for improvement.

Fifth, evaluate performance change. Effectiveness of behavior modification is evaluated in four areas: (1) reaction of the participants to the approach, (2) learning of the concepts and practices involved, (3) degree of behavior change that occurs, and (4) impact of behavior change in terms of actual performance results. Needless to say, the last item is the most important. To evaluate the success or failure, the original baseline is compared with the present measurements of behavior. In the production case, measurement comparison of behavior showed favorable results. Although initially the supervisors had misgivings, they came to favor the approach and, as a consequence, production performance was improved. After six months, the control group and the experimental groups were compared. The overall performance of the experimental group had significantly improved—complaints had declined, scrap rates had decreased, errors had been reduced, and number of rejects had dropped.

Summary of Key Concepts

1. The content theories, process theories, and reinforcement theory of motivation are aimed at energizing, directing, and sustaining desired behavior. Content theories concern themselves with what arouses behavior or what specific things motivate individuals. Process theories focus on the choice individuals face as they either perform a task or choose to not perform a task. Reinforcement theory, on the other hand, centers its attention on the environment of the individual and not the internal dynamics.

2. Maslow's and Alderfer's theories are based on the concept of relative satisfaction of one area or need, before individuals are motivated by other needs.

3. Herzberg theorizes that two distinct factors influence motivation—hygiene, which merely prevents dissatisfaction, and motivators, which are the real source of satisfaction and positive motivation for the individual.

4. McClelland identifies three needs that help us understand human motivation—achievement, affiliation, and power. With this concept of motivation it is possible to match through selection, placement, and training individual needs with job requirements.

5. Equity theory shows us how individuals may balance what they put into the job with what they get out of the performance and compare that with what they perceive others are contributing and receiving as rewards.

6. Expectancy theory views motivation as a relationship between effort on the individual's part and the associated accomplishments that receive rewards. The theory portrays the complexity involved in providing an environment conducive to motivating employees.

7. Goal setting involves matching employee aspirations with acceptable goals. Selecting somewhat difficult but specific goals is more motivating in terms of performance than setting goals that are too easy. Being committed to attaining a goal is a constant effort for both the employee and the manager.

8. Reinforcement theory does not concern itself with the internal conditions of the employee but, rather, attempts to structure the environment through reinforcements to get desirable behavior. The theory suggests that variable schedules of reinforcement lead to higher performance than do ratio schedules.

Key Terms

Achievement motivation	Hygiene factors
Behavior modification	Instrumentality
Equity theory	Motivation
Expectancy theory	Need hierarchy
Goal acceptance	Negative reinforcement
Goal commitment	Operant conditioning
Goal difficulty	Positive reinforcement
Goal specificity	Valence

MANAGERIAL APPLICATIONS

The motivational theories we have been dealing with thus far seem to make a great deal of sense. But what happens when these theories are applied in the real world? As a manager faced with bottom line responsibilities, how do you decide which motivation theory to use in attempting to get greater output from your employees? How much time do you have to review the theoretical procedures with which you are familiar when the pressure of the moment requires action?

In this section of the chapter, we deal with some of these very practical issues, referring to information taken from the popular press and examples of practices from a variety of organizations. We cover a case that was successful in applying some techniques of motivation and a case that clearly failed. We also look at what happens when workers become owners of the operation. In addition, we take a look at one motivator that has caused considerable debate—money. Finally, we consider some applications of reinforcement theory and look at future issues regarding motivation.

Since "real world" occurrences don't often fit neatly into preconceived packages, we probably raise more questions than we answer, but it should cause us to do some meaningful thinking about the processes of motivation in organizations.

A Case of Success

Let's start by looking at an organization that has had some real success in motivating people.

In the 1970s, Arthur Friedman ran an appliance store in Oakland, California, with his brother Morris.[39] To say that Mr. Friedman's approach to employee motivation is unusual is to understate. Consider that Friedman's 15 employees could set their own wages, determine their work hours, determine vacation time and schedule, select their own work tasks, and take money from the cash drawer.

Friedman did not "phase" the plan in or prepare his employees in any way for the change. He simply announced the new plan at a staff meeting, with immediate implementation.

The idea for the unusual scheme came from Arthur Friedman's approach to his own life. On weekends he taught seminars in such subjects as communications, sensuality, and hexing. The seminars all dealt with trust in other people to be adult and responsible in their behavior. It occurred to Mr. Friedman that he was teaching one thing on the weekend, but practicing something different in his business. He concluded that his employees should be made entirely responsible for decisions about their employment.

Reaction to the plan was stunned silence. By Friedman's own account, he had to chase the employees down one by one at the end of the first month and demand that they tell him what they wanted to be paid. Most of the employees said that they wanted to be paid what the other employees were being paid, but

Friedman forced them to name a figure (Could this be a form of equity theory?). None of the employees took an increase in pay, and one serviceman actually settled on a *lower* pay scale since he did not want to work as hard as the other repairman. Friedman also extended his novel pay plan to part-time and occasional workers.

No employees changed their work hours or their vacation time. Friedman actually encouraged employees to take extra time off if they were not feeling well, or even if they didn't feel like working. Without exception, the employees refused to take the extra time off.

Friedman insisted that all employees belong to the union, primarily because of the union health and welfare plans. He also insisted that all employees take at least the union scale in wages.

Once the plan was well underway, Friedman reported that employee morale was higher, and employees had a better understanding of the way the business worked, as well as a new appreciation of an employer's problems. Although sales levels stayed about the same, net profit increased each year, despite inflation, indicating that productivity and efficiency also increased.

Oh yes, Friedman extended his approach to customers as well: If bills were not paid, he wrote to the customer saying that the bill would be cancelled if it were not paid! If no payment was forthcoming the bill *was* cancelled, and the customer was asked to write a letter explaining why he or she chose not to pay. The number of delinquent accounts did not increase, and the store no longer had need for a collection agency.

There is no question that Friedman's was a successful operation, but there ought to be some questions going through your mind. Would an approach like that work in a larger organization? What happens if people take advantage of this approach? What happens if internal jealousies start to arise? Would this work over a longer period of time? These are interesting questions to which we don't know the answers. Equally interesting are the questions that deal with the reasons for success of the plan. If you examine the plan using the two-factor theory of motivation, it shouldn't work, for it is dealing mostly with satisfiers or hygiene factors. Or is it? The need theories would say that although the rewards were primarily monetary, the real rewards were at the esteem, self-actualization, or growth levels. Just the fact of dealing with people as individuals is enough to satisfy some of the ego needs. And to let employees set their own salaries! That's powerful stuff.

A Case of Failure?

Here's another item that intrigued us. Look at the system that was used to motivate teachers in the Penn Manor School District.[40] How could a system to provide additional merit pay for outstanding teachers go wrong?

Penn Manor School District, in Millersville, Pennsylvania, adopted a merit pay plan for its teachers and, at the end of a recent school year, paid $1,000 bonuses to 25 of its 233 teachers. District salaries average about $20,000 per year.

The bonus winners' names were published in the community newspaper, and a district official stated that the winners would serve as role models for other teachers. If we use Maslow's theory, not only are the lower level needs being met with money, but the recognition afforded the recipients through the newspaper satisfies some higher level needs.

The bonus recipients were of course pleased to get the awards, but some were skeptical of the overall value of the program. Teachers who competed for bonuses and did not win were even more skeptical.

Many teachers failed to qualify for a bonus, even though their principals regarded them worthy of it. One high school, for example, was allotted only ten awards to distribute among ninety-four teachers. Some of the teachers who did not receive awards regarded their failure as a personal rejection. No one seemed to know what the precise criteria for selection were. Some school administrators advised losers to sit in on bonus winners' classes, presumably to learn desirable techniques and behaviors.

How could you relate this to expectancy theory? If teachers knew exactly what activities led to excellence in teaching but also knew that there were only a relatively few merit rewards for that kind of performance, then their instrumentality rating would be extremely low. They would be less likely to strive for high performance because the chance that it would lead to a reward would be perceived as not worth the effort. The article also notes that school administrators could not state what the criteria for selection were. Therefore, the linkage between the effort and individual performance is unclear (refer to Figure 3–6) and expectancy by the individual is rated towards zero. Finally, it is assumed that money is highly valued by the teachers. That is, the valence approximates $+1$. But what if the act of teaching itself has the highest valence of possible individual rewards. What impact does that have on rethinking how to motivate teachers to be more effective?

Here we see a motivational system, set up with the best of intentions, that didn't work out. According to at least some of the theory, the officials of the school district went about it right in that they had some participation by the teachers in implementing the plan. That should work, shouldn't it? But think how you would react if your instructor told you that because of some financial pressures, enrollment would have to be cut, and each class would have to be reduced by 10 percent. The administration had decided that the easiest and fastest way to do this would be to flunk 10 percent of each class. Your instructor didn't like it, but had no alternative. To make the decision more fair the class should decide who should flunk. Participation? Of course. Motivation to accept the goals of the organization?

Money as a Motivator

Let's turn now to the issue of financial reward as a motivating force. Some theories (and surveys) indicate that money does not rank highly on a list of motivating factors, but consider the case of the Lincoln Electric Company.[41]

The Lincoln Electric Company of Cleveland, Ohio, is well known for its innovations in the area of employee motivation. The company relies heavily on incentives at all levels of the organization and pays most of its 2,000-plus employees on a piecework basis, with performance bonuses. It is not uncommon for bonuses to exceed regular pay. In mid-1983, the market for the firm's products (electric motors and welding equipment) was very soft and employees were working only thirty hours per week. Even with the reduced week, workers would *average* $30,000 to $35,000 for the year. In 1981, a good year, employees averaged $45,000, including the bonus. Contrast that with the average manufacturing wage in the U.S. of just over $18,000 per year.

How does the company do it? Each employee is responsible for the quality of his or her work. Careful records are kept of who works on each piece of equipment; defects that get past the worker, to be discovered by the company quality control inspectors or by customers, result in a lower merit rating, bonus, and pay.

Employees are allowed to buy stock in the company at book value, and now own about 50 percent of the shares. An employee must resell stock at book value on leaving the company.

The employees naturally are fond of the high wages, but there is a price that goes with the good pay—hard work. Older employees sometimes want to move to a job with no piecework. Since the company has no seniority system, the employee must compete on a merit basis with all other employees who want the new job.

Each department is allotted a specific number of merit points, thus a very high rating for one person may result in a lower rating for another. Under some conditions, this could result in an unhealthy form of competition. Still, turnover is less than 4 percent per year.

Which theory would help to explain Lincoln's success? Reinforcement might explain the piecework and quality aspects. What type of schedule is represented here? Piecework is a form of fixed ratio. Quality reports may be a variation of variable ratio but are negatively oriented. Or could you term the quality reports either negative reinforcement or punishment? If the quality reports are eliminated after the employee has no rejects for a period of time, we could say that quality reports are negative reinforcement. On the other hand, if the supervisor personally presents the report to the employee after a reject or problem, it is considered a form of punishment.

Would goal setting better explain the success? It would if workers keep setting incremental and increasingly higher levels of performance and decreasingly lower levels of rejects. The goal specificity would be relatively easy to establish. What about goal acceptance?

When did this state-of-the-art motivation system begin? In 1907.

Pay seems to be an important factor in this situation. We've also found pay to be important in other situations. For several years we have been having our students do the "Motivation at Work" exercise found later in this chapter. Invariably the results of these interviews indicated that pay was a very strong motivator.

As we examined these results more completely, we noticed that many of our students had interviewed other students who were working while attending school. For many of these individuals their jobs were a way of attaining enough financial support to pay tuition and other college expenses. For them, pay was extremely important, and they were willing to put up with some terrible working conditions and requirements to acquire the necessary finances.

A key factor in these situations was that they were short term, and the students involved could see an end to their unpleasant job situations. When we later required that our students interview people from other categories, for instance, career workers or workers who had been on a particular job for more than twenty years, we found that the results were much more in line with the findings of some of the theorists, especially Herzberg.

What we seem to be finding in the examples that we've looked at is that applying motivational theory is tricky business. Theory seems to be very useful in analyzing behavior after it has transpired but is less useful in predicting what will happen in organizations.

Do Worker-Owners Perform Better?

Another issue that often arises in discussions about motivation concerns whether individuals have a real interest in a situation. If one has a "piece of the action" does that mean more commitment and involvement in the organization's activities? Let's take a look at what happened in a couple of organizations in which the employees are also owners.

Worker ownership is not a new phenomenon, but it has never been widely practiced in the United States. The social changes experienced in the U.S. during the 1960s and 1970s may have created more interest in the concept. Unions are also expressing interest in worker ownership, perhaps as a way of saving members' jobs during economic downturns.

When Great Atlantic & Pacific Tea Co. closed all of its Philadelphia area supermarkets, the local food workers union helped twenty-four employees buy one of the stores.[42] Each employee invested $5,000 in the venture, and they opened what is probably the first employee owned and operated supermarket in the country.

The store has been a financial success from the start, with sales approximately 40 percent higher than those of the old A & P. Problems have been relatively minor, and attributable to inexperience. At first the new owners did not know how to order goods, and the store was frequently overstocked. Substitution of wholesale prices for retail prices in an advertisement cost the store some money. Management of employees has also created some problems. The owners hired sixteen additional workers, but had to lay off two of them during a sales slump. Learning to delegate responsibility has been hard for some, and contract talks have been difficult, since the owners are still union members. The owners do not pay themselves overtime when they work long hours.

There is a spirit of cooperation and support, with the owners performing tasks throughout the store rather than only within their own department. Shoplifting and employee pilferage is running at about 17 percent of the usual rate for supermarkets. The union has set up another worker-owned store and is interested in developing others.

Owning stock in a corporation is of course a very common form of ownership in the U.S., but most would agree that this form of ownership does not create the *feeling* of ownership, and certainly not the decision-making role experienced by the ex-A & P employees. A small airline headquartered in Phoenix, Arizona, seems to have at least partly overcome the lack of ownership felt by many employee-stockholders.[43]

Employees of America West Airlines are required to own company shares equal to 20 percent of their starting salary. The company finances the purchase at reduced prices through a payroll deduction plan. A profit-sharing plan distributes 15 percent of any net earnings to the employee shareholders. Employees currently own only about 6 percent of the company's stock. Base pay for the company's employees is considerably lower than the industry average. Pilots for example, are paid $32,500 per year, contrasted with an industry average of over $75,000. Customer service representatives, who also have duties as reservation agents, baggage handlers, and flight attendants, start at $12,600 per year. Rather than resenting the multiple roles, employees report that the job is made more interesting by the opportunity to do different things. Employees also maintain that they understand the company and the industry better through doing several jobs, resulting in better service for the airline's customers.

Again, which motivational theory helps explain the motivation and involvement experienced by these employees? In the worker-owner situation it is easy to see that higher level needs are being activated. Owning the supermarket means making many decisions and coming into contact with the other owners. Thus social and esteem needs are being met. In addition, this situation exemplifies one of the criticisms of need theory—lower level needs not being met doesn't mean that the individual is stuck on that level. Although safety needs seemed to be threatened because of initial inexperience, that didn't prevent the owners from continuing the store. In the airline situation, the multiple jobs held by the workers could easily be satisfying growth needs (Alderfer) or self-actualization (Maslow). Even Herzberg's motivators are being activated in this situation. Certainly money is not the primary motivator, as evident from the salary comparisons.

These two examples would seem to strongly support that real involvement in a situation has a very positive effect on behavior, from the viewpoint of the total organization as well as the individual.

What About Reinforcement Theory?

Any discussion about the application of motivational theories would be incomplete without some mention of those firms that have tried this approach.

What is interesting is that despite the promise and apparent simplicity of reinforcement theory, comparatively few organizations have implemented the techniques, although their numbers are increasing every year. Those organizations that have installed programs based on reinforcement theory have generally had good results.

A review by Hamner and Hamner lists stages common to most reinforcement programs in industry today:[44]

Table 3–5
Results of positive reinforcement programs in selected organizations

Organization	Participants	Program Goals	Reinforcers Used	Results
Michigan Bell— Operator Services	2,000 of 5,500: Employees at all levels in operator services	a. Decrease turnover and absenteeism b. Increase productivity c. Improve union-management relations	a. Praise and recognition b. Opportunity to see oneself become better	a. Attendance performance improved by 50% b. Productivity and efficiency has continued to be above standard
Michigan Bell— Maintenance Services	220 of 5,500: Maintenance workers, mechanics, first- and second-level supervisors	Improve a. Productivity b. Quality c. Safety d. Customer-employee relations	a. Self-feedback b. Supervisory feedback	a. Cost efficiency increase b. Safety improved c. Service improved d. No change in absenteeim e. Satisfaction with superior and co-workers improved f. Satisfaction with pay increased
B. F. Goodrich Chemical Co.	100 of 420: Manufacturing employees at all levels	a. Better meeting of schedules b. Increase productivity	a. Praise and recognition b. Freedom to choose one's own activity	Production has increased over 300%
General Electric	1,000: Employees at all levels	a. Meet EEO objectives b. Decrease absenteeism and turnover c. Improve training d. Increase productivity	Social reinforcers (praise, rewards, and constructive feedback)	a. Cost savings can be directly attributed to the program b. Productivity has increased c. Worked extremely well in training minority groups and raising their self-esteem d. Direct labor cost decreased

Source: Adapted, by permission of the publisher, from "Behavior Modification on the Bottom Line," by W. C. Hamner and E. P. Hamner, *Organizational Dynamics*, vol. 4 (Spring 1976): 12–14 © 1976 AMACOM, a division of American Management Associations, New York. All rights reserved.

- The first stage is to define the behavioral aspects of performance and do a performance audit.
- The second stage develops and sets specific goals for each worker. These goals are stated in concrete, behavioral terms. The goals, of course, relate to areas of concern discovered in the performance audit.
- The third stage involves employees in maintaining records of their own work. The self-feedback inherent in the record-keeping process provides a continuous schedule of reinforcement.
- The fourth and final stage is perhaps the most important. The supervisor reiews the employee's self-feedback report, as well as other indicators of performance, and praises the positive aspects of the performance. Good performance is thus reinforced. Withholding of praise for low performance should give the employee incentive to improve. Note that the employee already knows the areas of performance deficiencies through the self-audit.

Some results obtained by businesses are shown in Table 3–5. Needless to say, the results are impressive and seem to apply even in very large organizations.

What Does the Future Hold?

The noted opinion researcher Yankelovitch stated that, based on his findings, the kind of motivational tools we are now using in organizations are no longer effective for approximately 50 percent of the current work force.[45] About half of the people for whom the incentives no longer work are those who have chosen to drop out of organization life and make their living in some more independent manner. The number of people in this category seems to be steadily increasing. The other group for whom the current programs are no longer effective are the well-educated, younger, highly motivated individuals that are moving into middle and upper managerial positions in many organizations. While willing to use their considerable talents, they find the reward structure in many instances to be unsatisfactory for their situation and are asking for more individualized consideration. Yankelovitch feels that the kind of arrangement noted in the previously cited examples may be required in the future to create the kind of interest in the goals of the organization that are necessary for its success.

DISCUSSION QUESTIONS

1. Which type(s) of motivational theories (content, process, or reinforcement) do you find most useful to explain human behavior? Why? Which would best predict human behavior? Is it the same theory which merely explained behavior?
2. Suppose you had been asked to come up with a complete package for a motivational program for the entire organization. Which approaches would you include? Why?

3. If high achievers tend to be superior performers, why can't a manager increase organizational performance simply by hiring only high achievers?

4. Can an individual be *too* motivated, so that performance declines as a result of excessive effort? Discuss.

5. Discuss the advantages and disadvantages of operant conditioning as a motivational tool.

6. What words of caution would you give to a manager who was considering the use of behavior modification to improve the motivation of unionized machine shop workers?

EXERCISE: MOTIVATION AT WORK

One of the content theories discussed in this chapter was Herzberg's two-factor theory of motivation. Herzberg found one set of factors, called "motivators," that were very important in determining people's positive feelings about their jobs. Another set of factors, "dissatisfiers," helped to prevent dissatisfaction if they were in line with people's expectations but did little to induce positive motivation. Herzberg's research showed that the following factors were determined to be either dissatisfiers or motivators.

Dissatisfiers (Job Environment)	Motivators (Job Content)
Company policy and administration	Challenging job
Lighting	Feeling of achievement
Salary	Growth
Fringe benefits	Responsibility
Status	Advancement
Job security	Enjoyment of work
Supervisor	Earned recognition

In this exercise you will interview some people to determine what motivates them on the job—what causes satisfaction or dissatisfaction.

1. Interview at least three individuals who are currently employed. They can hold any position in any kind of organization. If possible, attempt to interview individuals at different levels in their respective organizations.

2. In your interview, be certain to ask the following questions of each person: (a) What are the things that give you the greatest feelings of satisfaction about your job? (b) How do you rank these satisfying things (from a.) in order of importance? (c) What are the things that give you the greatest feelings of dissatisfaction about your job? (d) How do you rank these (from c.) in order of importance? In the course of your interviews you will probably ask many other questions about how your interviewees feel about their jobs, but be *certain to ask these very specific questions*, and record the responses on forms similar to the one shown in Figure A.

3. Another area to cover in your interview is the importance of money as a motivator. Consider the following statement: "Evidence indicates that money, in itself, does not usually serve as a motivator to work harder or better. However, in the absence of what is perceived by the recipient as adequate or fair compensation, money is a source of

RECORDING FORM

Interview # 1 _____

Person interviewed: _____

Type of job: _____

Level in organization: _____

Length of time in job: _____

Length of time with the organization: _____

Factors Causing Greatest Feelings of Dissatisfaction	Factors Causing Greatest Feelings of Satisfaction
1.	1.
2.	2.
3.	3.
4.	4.
5.	5.
6.	6.
7.	7.
8.	8.
9.	9.

Summarize feelings about importance of money as a motivator.

FIGURE A

dissatisfaction."[46] Ask your interviewees to rank money in their list as compared to other motivators.

4. After you have completed your interviews, form groups of four to five persons and compare the results of interviews. Compile a list of motivators and dissatisfiers as determined by your interviews. Discuss what trends, if any, are apparent. Can you rank the factors in each category in order of importance? That is, what are the most important motivators? Satisfiers? Dissatisfiers? Do the results of your interviews tend to support or refute the findings from Herzberg's research? How do you explain this?

NOTES

1. Based on an article appearing in TIME (4 July 1983).

2. R. M. Steers and L. W. Porter, *Motivation and Work Behavior*, 3rd ed. (New York: McGraw-Hill, 1983).

3. D. Yankelovich, "New Rules in American Life: Searching for Self-fulfillment in a World Turned Upside Down." *Psychology Today*, (April 1981): 35–91.

4. Abraham Maslow, *Motivation and Personality* (New York: Harper & Row, 1954).

5. Edward E. Lawler, III, and J. L. Suttle, "A Causal Correlation Test of the Need Hierarchy Concept," *Organizational Behavior and Human Performance*, vol. 4 (1972): 265–87.

6. Lyman W. Porter, "Job Attitudes in Management: IV, Perceived Deficiencies in Need Fulfillment as a Function of Size of the Company," *Journal of Applied Psychology* (December 1963): 386–97; and John M. Ivancevich, "Perceived Need Satisfaction of Domestic Versus Overseas Managers," *Journal of Applied Psychology* (August 1969): 274–78.

7. F. Herzberg, B. Mausner, and B. Snyderman, *The Motivation to Work*, 2nd ed. (New York: Wiley, 1959); and F. Herzberg, *Work and the Nature of Man* (Cleveland, OH: World Press, 1966).

8. D. A. Whitsett and E. K. Winslow, "An Analysis of Studies Critical of the Motivation-Hygiene Theory," *Personnel Psychology* (Winter 1967): 391–416.

9. John P. Campbell et al., *Managerial Behavior, Performance, and Effectiveness* (New York: McGraw-Hill, 1970): 354.

10. C. P. Alderfer, *Existence, Relatedness, and Growth: Human Needs in Organizational Setting* (New York: The Free Press, 1972).

11. C. P. Alderfer, "A Critique of Salancik and Pfeffer's Examination of Need Satisfaction Theories," *Administrative Science Quarterly* (December 1977): 658–69.

12. George Harris, "To Know Why Men Do What They Do: A Conversation with David C. McClelland," *Psychology Today*, vol. 4 (January 1971): 35–41, 78–79.

13. Campbell, *Managerial Behavior*.

14. D. C. McClelland and D. H. Burnham, "Good Guys Make Bum Bosses," *Psychology Today*, vol. 9 (December 1975): 69–70.

15. D. G. Winter, *The Power Motive* (New York: The Free Press, 1973).

16. D. C. McClelland and D. H. Burnham, "Power Is the Great Motivator," *Harvard Business Review*, vol. 54 (March–April 1976): 100–110.

17. D. C. McClelland, *Power: The Inner Experience* (Boston: Irvington Publishers, 1975).

18. McClelland and Burnham, "Power is the Great Motivator," p. 100.

19. D. C. McClelland and D. Winter, *Motivating Economic Achievement* (Glencoe, IL: Free Press, 1971).

20. J. S. Adams, "Toward an Understanding of Inequity," *Journal of Abnormal and Social Psychology*, vol. 67 (1963): 422–436; and J. S. Adams, "Inequity on Social Exchange," in L. Berkowitz, ed., *Advances in Experimental Social Psychology* (New York: Academic Press, 1965): 267–299.

21. Ibid.

22. J. S. Adams and S. Freedman, "Equity Theory Revisited: Comments and Annotated Bibliography," in L. Berkowitz, ed., *Advances in Experimental and Social Psychology* (New York: Academic Press, 1976).

23. M. R. Carrell and J. E. Dettrich, "Employee Perceptions of Fair Treatment," *Personnel Journal* (October 1976): 523–24.

24. Victor H. Vroom, *Work and Motivation* (New York: Wiley, 1964).

25. Gerald P. Salancik and Jeffrey Pfeffer, "A Social Information Processing Approach to Job Attitudes and Task Design," *Administrative Science Quarterly*, vol. 23 (June 1978): 224–225.

26. L.W. Porter and E. E. Lawler, III, *Managerial Attitudes and Performance* (Homewood, IL: Irwin, 1968).

27. N. Branden, "Emotions and Values," *Objectivist*, vol. 5 (1966): 1–9.

28. E. A. Locke, K. N. Shaw, L. M. Saari, and G. P. Latham, "Goal Setting and Task Performance: 1969–1980," *Psychological Bulletin*, vol. 90 (1981): 125–152.

29. E. A. Locke, "Relation of Goal Performance with a Short Work Period and Multiple Goal Levels," *Journal of Applied Psychology*, vol. 67 (1982): 512–514.

30. Ibid.

31. Jay S. Kim, "Effect of Behavior Plus Outcome, Goal Setting and Feedback on Employee Satisfaction and Performance," *Academy of Management Journal*, vol. 27, no. 1 (1984): 139–149.

32. E. A. Locke and G. P. Latham, *Goal Setting: A Motivational Technique That Works!* (Englewood Cliffs, NJ: Prentice-Hall, 1984).

33. J. S. Hodgson, "Management by Objectives: The Experience of a Federal Government Department," *Canadian Public Administration*, vol. 16 (1973): 422–431.

34. J. N. Kondrasuk, "Studies in MBO Effectiveness," *Academy of Management Review*, vol. 6 (1981): 419–430.

35. M. A. Covaleski and M. W. Dirsmith, "MBO and Goal Directedness in a Hospital Context," *Academy of Management Review*, vol. 6 (1981): 406–418.

36. Edward L. Deci, *Intrinsic Motivation* (New York: Plenum Press, 1975): 7–8.

37. J. B. Miner, *Theories of Organizational Behavior* (Hinsdale, IL: Dryden Press, 1980): 205.

38. F. Luthans and R. Kreitner, *Organizational Behavior Modification*, 2nd ed. (Glenview, IL: Scott, Foresman and Company, 1984).

39. Summarized from "Theory Y or Unvarnished Charisma?" Stanford Business School *Alumni Bulletin*, vol. 45, no. 1, 13–16, 33–36. Copyright 1976 by the Board of Trustees of the Leland Stanford Junior University. All rights reserved.

40. "School's Merit-Pay Program Draws Gripes From Losers—and Winners," by Burt Schorr, *The Wall Street Journal* (16 June 1983): 31. Reprinted by permission of *The Wall Street Journal*, © Dow Jones & Company, Inc. 1983. All rights reserved.

41. "Ohio Firm Relies on Incentive-Pay System to Motivate Workers and Maintain Profits," *The Wall Street Journal* (12 August 1983): 19. Reprinted by permission of *The Wall Street Journal*, © Dow Jones & Company, Inc. 1983. All rights reserved.

42. "Worker Owned and Operated Supermarket Yields Financial Success, Personal Rewards," by Paul Engelmayer, *The Wall Street Journal* (18 August 1983): 27. Reprinted by permission of *The Wall Street Journal*, © Dow Jones & Company, Inc. 1983. All rights reserved.

43. "New Airline Surmounting Labor Dilemma," *The Wall Street Journal* (12 September 1983): 31. Reprinted by permission of *The Wall Street Journal*, © Dow Jones & Company, Inc. 1983. All rights reserved.

44. W. C. Hamner and E. P. Hamner, "Behavior Modification on the Bottom Line," *Organizational Dynamics*, vol. 4 (Spring 1976): 3–21.

45. Yankelovitch, "New Rules in American Life."

46. Robert E. Coffey, Anthony G. Athos, and Peter A. Raynolds, *Behavior in Organizations: A Multidimensional View*, 2nd ed. (Englewood Cliffs, NJ: Prentice-Hall, 1975): 220.

RECOMMENDED READINGS

E. E. Lawler, III, *Pay and Organizational Effectiveness: A Psychological View* (New York: McGraw-Hill, 1971).

This book analyzes the research and theories of motivation as they apply to pay issues.

R. D. Middlemist and R. B. Peterson, "Test of Equity by Controlling for Comparison Co-workers' Efforts," *Organization Behavior and Human Performance*, vol. 15 (1976): 335–354.

The article examines the utility of the equity theory for explaining employee performance in the organizational setting.

K. H. Chung, *Motivational Theories and Practices* (Columbus, OH: Grid, 1977).

This book reviews the major theories of motivation and integrates them into a theoretical framework. It finally translates theory into specific motivational programs applicable to organizations.

Gary P. Latham, and Edwin A. Locke, "Goal Setting—A Motivational Technique That Works," *Organizational Dynamics* (Autumn 1979): 68–80.

This article describes several studies using goals set by either the supervisor or the employee. The material shows that either method reduced absenteeism and injuries while increasing the level of productivity by 19 percent.

Paine's Department Store

Paine's Department Store is one of the largest members of a nationwide chain of department stores. It is located in an outlying shopping center near Starville, a university town of 100,000.[1] It has enjoyed 35 years of goodwill and community service. The store has enjoyed a good reputation in the immediate geographic area and is known as a fine place to buy quality products from friendly and courteous clerks. The store also is known for its after-the-sale service. During its 35 years in Starville, the store had experienced no major problems from customers or employees.

Timothy Jones, the General Manager, is now facing a problem, however, that is causing him a great deal of concern. During the last 6 to 8 months the store has experienced a high turnover rate among its sales personnel. The problem is considered to be a critical one because of the extra expense of training new personnel periodically and the loss of sales revenue which can be attributed to the inexperience of the new sales force.

To help solve the problem, Mr. Jones asked Jim Smith, his Personnel Manager, to review with him the personnel records of all employees who had worked for Paine's during the last 5 years. Jim Smith, a graduate of Middle States University, was in his early thirties and had just been promoted to the position of Personnel Manager at Paine's about 3 months ago. He had previously

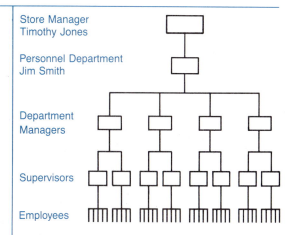

FIGURE A
Paine's Department Store organization chart

been a department buyer at another store in the national chain. His position at Paine's was second in importance only to that of Mr. Jones, (Figure A) and his duties as Personnel Manager included everything that one normally associated with the personnel function.

As Jim entered Mr. Jones's office, he found him sitting by the window staring out across the valley at Middle States University. Jones invited Jim to be seated and said, "Jim, I'll get right to the point. We have a very serious problem here at Paine's, and I hope that you can help me find a solution to it very quickly. Suppose we begin with your explaining the store's hiring policy to me."

Jim explained that it was the store's practice to hire two part-time employees for every full-time employee. The reasons for this were that the store was located in a university town; the

1. The University is a fully supported state institution with a full-time enrollment of 15,000 and a faculty and staff numbering 2,300.

Source: B. J. Hodge, Herbert J. Johnson, and Raymond L. Read, *Organizational Behavior Cases and Situations* (New York: Intext Educational Publishers, 1974): 178-185.

supply of part-time help was greater than its demand; and, by hiring part-time help, the department store was saving on company benefits such as pension and hospitalization plans, which the full-time employees received. Jim added that all the full-time employees were residents of the local community and the majority of them were male.

After looking over his charts and records for a moment, Jim reported that the number of part-time employees who had quit in the last year was almost six times greater than the number of full-time employees that had quit. (See Figure B.) Jones then suggested that perhaps the large turnover among sales personnel was caused by the hiring of college students and that the problem could be solved by hiring only local residents. Jim, however, disagreed with this conclusion for two reasons. He pointed out that one third of the part-time employees were young women from the surrounding areas and they were quitting as often as the students, and second, the other department stores in the area were not having the turnover problem with their part-time employees from the university.

Jones then asked Jim about the store's salary plan for part-time employees. Jim answered that all part-time help started at the hourly rate of $3.50. He added that this was the standard beginning rate in the community and that it was equal to, if not more than, the starting salary rate for other local department stores. With regard to raises, Jim reported that it was Paine's policy that all part-time employees receive a 50-cents-an-hour raise after the first 6 months of employment. They were also guaranteed a 15-cents-an-hour raise twice a year for the following 2 years. Other department stores in the area also give raises to their part-time employees after 6 months on the job. However, these raises are given on a merit system and are not guaranteed to all part-time help. Jim felt that the guaranteed raise system that Paine's used was superior to the merit system being used by other stores because it offered the part-time help more security. Jones agreed. Jones then suggested that perhaps the problem was traceable to the fact that an extensive work load was being assigned to part-time employees. Jim disagreed with this position because he maintained that the only duties that were required of part-time help that were not required of full-time help were clean-up and night duty. Jim indicated that he did not think that this could be a major problem because clean-up and night duty were standard assignments for all part-time employees at the other local department stores. Jones commented that perhaps full-time employees should share clean-up duties along with the part-time employees. Jim agreed that this was probably a good idea.

Jones then asked about the number and type of suggestions that the personnel office had received from the part-time employees. Jim's reply was that he had not received any suggestions since he had assumed his new position. He reported, however, that the previous personnel manager had told him of a few suggestions that he had received, but that he had discarded them as being unrealistic. At this point Jim mentioned that the supply room was out of suggestion forms and that he would need Mr. Jones's signature for the requisition in order to secure more. Jones said that he would gladly approve of the re-order of suggestion forms.

Jones then asked Jim what the main grievances of the part-time employees were. Jim said that as far as he could find out, they did not have any real grievances. He said that he had talked to

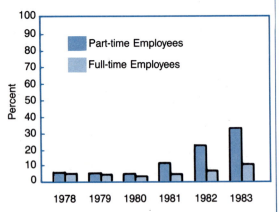

FIGURE B
Five-year comparison of turnover rates

several of the department managers and supervisors recently and that they had assured him that the part-time employees had no complaints. "That's interesting," Jones mused.

Jone then inquired about how the part-time employees got along with the store personnel. Jim said that from what he had been able to observe there were no "bad feelings" among the part-time employees. However, the part-time employees tend to form their own group and not socialize with full-time employees. Jim indicated that it was only on rare occasions that the part-time group mingled with the full-time employees.

Jones then asked Jim how the part-time employees felt about the store's management team. Jim replied that although he could not be sure, there were a few instances in the past in which part-time employees had requested transfers from one department to another because of personality conflicts with their immediate supervisors. He also said that they displayed a little resentment toward him and a few of the other members of the personnel department. Jones dismissed this by saying that employees always show some resentment toward management and personnel staffs because of their positions of authority. Then, after a few moments, Jones added that perhaps they had better hold a storewide

meeting of all personnel to make sure the part-time employees were not being treated too rough. Jim said he thought this might help the situation.

Jones got up, thanked Jim for his help, and told him not to forget to assign the full-time employees to clean-up and night duties. Jim left Jones's office. On the way to his desk he passed a break room where he saw a part-time employee sitting at one table and two full-time employees talking together at another table.

Questions

1. Of what value are fringe benefits (retirement, hospitalization, insurance, etc.) to building a sound base for employee motivation?
2. Do you feel Smith understands the importance of employee participation? What does participation have to do with employee motivation?
3. Do you feel that Smith understands the social implications of excluding the part-time workers from the store meetings?
4. What does Figure B really tell you about the situation?
5. What advice would you give Smith to improve the motivation of his employees?

CHAPTER FOUR
Communication

OUTLINE

FUNDAMENTALS OF COMMUNICATION

Communication and Its Importance
Communication Processes
Implications for Effective Communications
Summary of Key Concepts

MANAGERIAL APPLICATIONS

Information Overload
Effective Listening
Face-to-face Communication
An Unsuccessful Attempt
The Environment of Communication
Nonverbal Communication

OBJECTIVES

- Identify the essential elements of the communication process

- Explain the barriers to effective communication

- List six methods of reducing the communication barriers

- Describe how organizational networks affect the communication process

- Recognize the impact nonverbal behavior has on communication

- Describe the major managerial applications aimed at improving the communication process

Games to Help Managers Communicate?

While many "pop psychologies" (including the human-potential movement) are popular among individuals who want to grow and develop, many organizations consider them to be unprofessional and too "gamey" for corporate involvement. One example of popular psychology applied is Werner Erhard's organization called "est" (after the latin verb 'to be'). Human-potential firms such as est attempt to improve individuals' self-esteem, assertiveness, and communication with others.

Est and other human-potential organizations, however, are persuading business leaders that their theories can apply to corporations as well as individuals by increasing communication and constructive action and thus improving the company's performance.

One firm successful at getting businesses to use human-potential techniques is Laser Leadership Programs, whose clients include Grubb & Ellis, the nation's second largest real-estate firm; Joseph Magin Company, a chain of high-fashion clothing stores; and Walden Book Company.

The Laser program is geared toward breaking down business formalities that can hamper communication in organizations. To accomplish this, the sessions involve participants in seemingly nonsensical games. In one game, executives are given slips of paper with song titles printed on them. The executives identify and then form their work groups by humming the melody and locating others humming the same tune. Such games prevent executives from hiding behind formal corporate roles because they are forced to do things that are not part of those roles. Another example of breaking down communication barriers occurs in a workshop for May Department Stores Co. Managers take turns walking across a room as their colleagues watch, each manager taking a different path. The antics involved in trying to find a completely different route from a couple dozen others cause all pretenses of formality to be dropped. Laser also employs confidence-building techniques to get participants to take greater risks. One exercise has managers sit inside a circle of their peers while each peer makes some positive statement about the person.

The impact of such methods on the "bottom-line" is difficult to measure because of the intangible nature of communication problems. Nevertheless, after Walden Book sent close to 600 managers to such sessions, the company reported a "significant" drop in complaints to headquarters from its more than 500 stores. The sessions "cleared up a lot of the we/they feelings between the home office and the stores," says Jewell C. Roth, director of training.[1]

FUNDAMENTALS OF COMMUNICATION

Communication and Its Importance

Communication, like leadership and motivation, is one of the most discussed subjects in organizational behavior. Everyone favors improving communication, and no one doubts the importance of good communication to an effective and satisfying work and personal life. But because communications is an intangible factor in organizational life, how do we measure its impact on corporate profits? How do we really know when communications are good or effective?

What are other barriers that exist in organizations and that prevent effective communication, besides corporate roles and formality? How do we deal with these barriers?

What Is Communication?   To attempt to define the term *communication*, it may be helpful to look at some consequences of the communication process. The following example illustrates the consequences—and humor—of poor communication.

> A plumber wrote to the Bureau of Standards to ask about using hydrochloric acid for cleaning pipes. The Bureau replied, "The efficacy of hydrochloric acid is indisputable, but the chlorine residue is incompatible with metallic permanence." The plumber sent a brief note of thanks to the Bureau for their agreement with him. The Bureau hastily wrote him, "We cannot assume responsibility for the production of toxic and non-toxic residues with hydrochloric acid, and suggest that you use an alternative procedure." Again, the plumber sent a brief note of thanks for the confirmation of his opinion. Finally, the Bureau wrote the plumber, "Don't use hydrochloric acid, it eats the hell out of pipes." He understood.[2]

Communication is one of those words in the English language that is difficult to define. Everyone "knows" what communication is, and yet there is no generally acceptable definition of the term. Some communication researchers equate communication with "interaction." Thus, communication occurs whenever two or more individuals interact. Given such a broad meaning of communication, it makes sense to say, "one cannot *not* communicate."[3] Even strangers on a plane communicate by body movements—facing away from each other in their close seats when they wish to be left alone. It may be impolite to start the conversation by saying, "Please leave me alone." But it is okay to face the other direction in your seat if you wish to not talk to your fellow passenger.

Most definitions of communication are more limited in scope. One review of attempts to define communication found over ninety suggested definitions.[4] In spite of the lack of general agreement, it is possible to define communication in a way that is useful for our purposes. Effective communication is the information flow that results in a *shared meaning* and a *common understanding* for both the information sender and the information receiver.[5] Communication is more than simply the transmission of information between human beings. Remember the Bureau of Standards and the plumber! The essence of communication is that it is the conveyance of the *meaning* of information. Yet, we must go even further than merely transmitting meaning. If the Bureau of Standards had not continued to communicate, the results might have been disastrous for the home owner. Therefore, we must define communication in terms of effectiveness. The last correspondence from the Bureau to the plumber resulted in a common understanding for both. Note that "common understanding" and "shared meaning" do not necessarily mean agreement between the two parties about the subject being discussed but merely an understanding of what the other party is trying to say.

Importance to Management   Poor communication is often identified as the cause of problems in organizations. This is because the communication process provides the information used by managers in making decisions that affect the organization. When poor decisions occur, ineffective communication is frequently to blame. Recall the "we/they" feelings that were inhibiting effective communication between Walden Company stores and headquarters. We can speculate that without an effective flow of information inventories might be too high or too low for certain types of books or that the wrong types of books might be purchased in the first place.

Managers depend on their communication skills to get the information required to make decisions and to transmit the results and intention of these decisions to other people. Research indicates managers spend as much as 80 percent of their time in verbal interactions with other people.[6] Figure 4–1 shows how the time of five chief executives was distributed among various types of communications: telephone calls, scheduled and unscheduled meetings, plant tours, and desk work. Obviously, these executives spent a large majority of their work days in communication with other people.

A similar study of supervisors at DuPont showed the distribution of time spent in communicating as follows: meetings (administrative and technical), 53 percent; writing, 15.5 percent; reading, 14.9 percent; telephoning, 8 percent; and other, 7.7 percent.[7]

The responsibilities of a manager's role as an information-processing system are summarized in Figure 4–2. We can see that the manager is the center hub

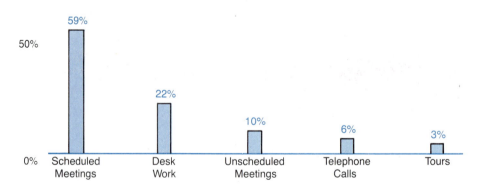

FIGURE 4–1
Distribution of managers' time among various communication media (Source: Adaptation of Figure 4 (p. 39) from *The Nature of Managerial Work* by Henry Mintzberg. Copyright © 1973 by Henry Mintzberg. Reprinted by permission of Harper & Row, Publishers, Inc.)

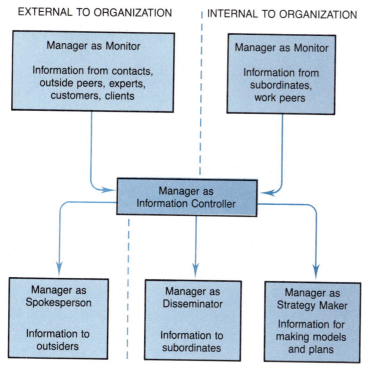

EXTERNAL TO ORGANIZATION | INTERNAL TO ORGANIZATION

FIGURE 4–2

The manager as an information-processing system (Source: Adaptation of Figure 10 (p. 72) from *The Nature of Managerial Work* by Henry Mintzberg. Copyright © 1973 by Henry Mintzberg. Reprinted by permission of Harper & Row, Publishers, Inc.)

of control of information flow. He or she stands at the intersection of information that flows upward, downward, and laterally in the organization's hierarchy of authority. The effectiveness of the communication involved can help or hinder the manager's attempts to promote high levels of job performance in the organization.

In downward communications, the manager transmits to subordinates job instructions, organizational goals, and performance feedback, along with a variety of other information. Laterally, the manager seeks to keep the activities of the work group coordinated with other work groups in the organization as well as with clients, customers, or suppliers. Upward communications provides opportunities for the manager to transmit to higher management levels information on work group activities, problems, and opportunities. Scott and Mitchell have specifically identified and described the major functions served by this communication within organizations.[8] They have specified four major functions of communication—emotive, motivation, information, and control—and classified them further by identifying (1) the orientation of the communication, (2) the objectives served by

TABLE 4–1
Purpose of communication

Function	Orientation	Objectives	Theoretical and Research Focus
1. Emotive	Feeling	Increasing acceptance of organizational role	Satisfaction; conflict resolution; tension reduction; role definition
2. Motivation	Influence	Commitment to organizational objective	Power, authority, compliance; reinforcement and expectancy theory; behavioral modification; learning
3. Information	Technological	Providing data necessary for decisions	Decision making; information processing; decision theory
4. Control	Structure	Clarifying duties, authority, accountability	Organizational design

Source: William G. Scott and Terrence R. Mitchell, *Organization Theory: A Structural and Behavioral Analysis* (Homewood, IL: Irwin, 1976): 193. Copyright © 1976, Richard D. Irwin, Inc. Reprinted by permission.

the communication, and (3) theoretical and research issues emphasized by those who studied that particular aspect of communication. Table 4–1 summarizes their findings. For example, if the major purpose of the communication to a subordinate from a superior is to motivate, then the orientation of the interaction and words is to influence the subordinate. This influence has as its objective gaining commitment to the superior's goals. Therefore, understanding the communication process can enhance the manager's use of the motivational theories that were discussed in chapter 3.

Communication Processes

Interpersonal Model   Let us examine the communication process involved in an interpersonal exchange between two people. The key components of the communication process are diagrammed in Figure 4–3. They include a source or sender, who is responsible for encoding an intended meaning into a message, and a receiver, who decodes the message into a perceived meaning. Feedback involves the receiver taking the role of sender and forming and encoding a response based on the *perceived* meaning of the previous message.

Encoding involves transferring the thoughts, motives, and emotions into symbols that convey meaning. For example, in writing this book we need to organize what is important for this chapter. We need to anticipate who will read

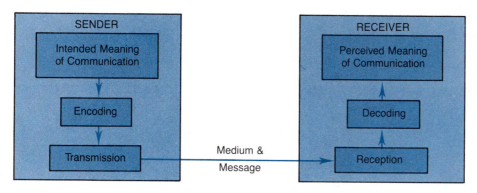

FIGURE 4–3
Components of the communication process

this book, how much experience they will have to which they can relate the concepts, and where in the course this subject will be covered. These questions and our guesses about the answers help us to write (encode) the content so that the reader learns about communication.

Some messages are unintentional or subconscious to the sender. For instance, if we met someone in the hallway and we were deep in thought, the encoding (our facial expression and body posture) and therefore the message sent might read "Don't bother me!" The encoding choices vary in appropriateness and understandability. Influencing the effectiveness of encoding are sender openness, trust, self-confidence, and fluency.

Transmission is a physical action by some part of the body. The vocal system (oral messages), hands (written messages), or body parts (nonverbal messages) may transmit messages. An actual message usually includes multiple transmittals, such as voice, voice inflection, facial expressions, and body movements.

The medium is the means by which messages travel from the sender to the receiver. Commonly used media include face-to-face conversation, telephones, letters, memos, speeches, and televideo conferences. This book, and in particular this sentence, is the medium. What is important to remember is that the sender's selection of a medium can be as important as the selection of symbols (encoding) to the receiver's understanding. For example, the Laser firm's game of humming a tune (medium) to locate other group members might have more significance to managers about the restrictiveness of one's corporate position on the communication process than would a lecture about the same subject.

Decoding is the translation of received messages into interpreted or perceived messages. If the communication has been effective, the meaning encoded by the sender is the same as that decoded by the receiver. In decoding a message the receiver takes into account not only the symbols received from the sender's message but also personal and situational factors surrounding the sender and

BOX 4–1

Firms Are Cool to Meetings by Television

A chief executive officer of a large company was practicing his speech prior to a live video conference. He was so engrossed that he failed to notice that technicians were beaming his voice to all locations to test the system. Later, when the video conference began and the executive announced he would make an impromptu speech; people around the country knew better and laughed.

Most business executives aren't comfortable with video conferencing, although it has potential to save them millions of dollars in travel time and expense. "The technology is impressive, and the executives like the concept," says A. Michael Noll, an expert at the University of Southern Cal-

ifornia. "Unfortunately, they are reluctant to use it."

International Resource Development, Inc., a consulting firm, recently concluded that the industry hasn't lived up to its promise because many executives who use it come across as "nerds." "People who have watched television for 20 years have built up all kinds of cultural expectations about people they see on the screen," says David Ledecky, a researcher with the firm. "They expect to see a Dan Rather or a Jessica Savitch, polished performers reading a script without a hair out of place. In contrast, executives or managers on a video conference tend to have their ties askew, don't always look at the cameras, may pick their noses, and seem unsure what to say."

Bruce Jelly, a researcher at Transfer Technology, Inc., says, "Television is a cold medium,

receiver. A statement such as "I'd like you to help me by writing a progress report for tomorrow's meeting" is interpreted quite differently when made by a peer in a participatory organization than when made by a boss in a highly authoritarian organization.

The decoding of the message is also influenced by the motives, emotions, and perceptual tendencies of the receiver. For the decoded message to completely match the coded one, the receiver must be able to align with the sender regarding symbols, motives, emotions, and perceptual processes. For example, the possibility of encoding and decoding the same intended message is more likely between two seasoned sales people discussing a sales forecast than the messages between an instructor and student arguing about an ambiguous test question.

Finally, the manner in which a responding message or an action is initiated is a form of feedback. Feedback occurs when the receiver becomes the sender and the original sender becomes the receiver. In this way the roles are reversed, and so

and it just doesn't transmit the body language, chemistry, and electricity of a personal meeting. Executives are often perceived as incompetent in video conferencing because television magnifies every gesture, facial tic, and universal motion."

Even companies that have won plaudits for their use of the new medium have a lot of learning to do. Tandem Computers Inc. of Cupertino, California, produces the monthly "Tandem Talk" for its employees. The show used to feature Tandem President James Treybig and other executives soberly discussing company matters in a fashion of a presentation to the stockholders. But employees grew tired of the format. After a couple of months, Tandem made the show less technical and added guests and videotaped segments, which brought back the viewers.

At another company, an executive who was supposed to be at a meeting stayed out of camera range for awhile talking to [someone]. Employees at the other end of the video conference didn't know he was there and made comments like: 'Where is that so and so?' 'He's late again, as usual.' 'Why that old SOB!'

Suddenly, the executive piped up in a booming voice: "Don't worry boys, I've been here all the time." The employees at the other end of the video conference apparently scattered. The camera showed an empty room.

Questions

1. Explain how body language can help the communication process under "normal" conditions. Why does it seem that body language produces the opposite effect in video conferences?
2. Why did the changes in format at Tandem "bring back the viewers"?
3. How should the executive in the last situation view the comments by the employees? Is there a way to capitalize on that situation for everyone's benefit?
4. Based on this chapter's material, under what conditions or situations would video conferencing be effective for an organization's communication process?

are the components of the communication process. Thus the total communication process involves constant feeding forward and backward, with adjustments continually being made and messages continually being sent and re-sent to try to achieve a greater understanding between both parties.

Organizational Communication   Up to this point we have been discussing the communication process between two individuals (or very small groups). When communication occurs within large groups, the channels by which information flows become critical. The way a group or organization structures itself determines the ease and effectiveness with which members can communicate. The actual pattern and flow of written or verbal messages between individuals is a communication network.

Many studies of communication networks have taken place in groups created in a laboratory setting. As a result, the research conclusions tend to be constrained by artificial settings and limited to small groups. Yet the application of the research to real organizational situations makes sense from a pragmatic point of view. Therefore, let us think in an organizational context while talking about a subject that has been researched only in laboratory settings.

Five common information networks are shown in Figure 4–4. The chain would represent a five level hierarchy where communication cannot move laterally, only upward or downward. A typical chain would be one in which the assembly-line worker reports to the first-line supervisor, who in turn reports to the general supervisor, who reports to the plant manager, who reports to the divisional manager. Another example is the organizational grapevine that passes information throughout the organization between different departments and organizational levels. The reason for comparing the grapevine to the chain is because the information usually travels in one direction and, being an unofficial system, it doesn't check out the accuracy of its messages after they are sent.

CENTRALIZED NETWORKS
All communications are controlled by manager (individual in circle)

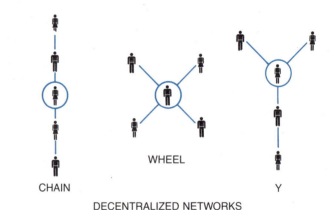

CHAIN　　　　　　　　　WHEEL　　　　　　　　　Y

DECENTRALIZED NETWORKS
No one individual controls the communication

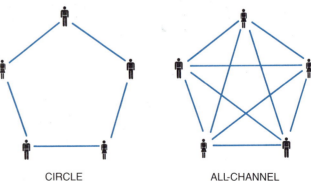

CIRCLE　　　　　　　　ALL-CHANNEL

FIGURE 4–4
Communication networks

When we look at the wheel, we can visualize a manager with four supervisors. However, there is no interaction between the supervisors. All communication and information is channeled through the manager.

The Y network when turned upside down is a hierarchy with two subordinates reporting to a supervisor. This supervisor, in turn, reports to another manager, who reports to one more level of supervision.

All three forms of organizational network (the chain, the wheel, and the Y) are centralized. They contain members (marked by circles in Figure 4–4 through which messages *must* pass to reach others.

The circle network allows members to interact with *adjoining* members directly but not with the other members of the same group. It is very difficult to find such a network in an organization or in other areas of one's life.

Finally, the all-channel network allows each member to communicate freely with all the others. The all-channel network has no central position, nor are there restrictions about who talks to whom; all members are equal. This network is best illustrated by a committee where no one member either formally or informally assumes a dominant, or leadership, position. All members are free to share their ideas, opinions, and feelings.

The circle and the all-channel networks are decentralized. There is no central person through whom communications flow. The all-channel network is more decentralized than the circle because the members in the circle can only communicate with two other people.

Effectiveness of Different Networks The importance of a communication network lies in its potential effects on such variables as member satisfaction, accuracy of solutions, and speed of task completion. Just how well centralized and decentralized networks perform depends on the complexity of the tasks.[9] Different results have been obtained when groups perform simple tasks (e.g., identifying a symbol common to all cards given to participants) and complex tasks (e.g., solving word problems). In typical communication network research, groups are given general problems to solve, one at a time, and the researcher measures how long it takes the network to solve them, how many errors are made, and how satisfied members are with their work.

The following conclusions have been reached on the basis of such research.[10] See Table 4–2 for a summary. First, while decentralized networks reached solutions faster and made fewer errors on complex problems, centralized networks reached solutions faster and made fewer errors on simple problems. A possible explanation of this is that the more information any one group member has to deal with at any one time, the more that person can become saturated. A person who is saturated is overloaded with information, and performance suffers. This is apparently what happened when a centralized network performed a complex task. The central person became so saturated with information that the group was slowed down and many errors were made. But the central person could easily solve a *simple* problem alone, having received the information from all other members of the network. On the other hand, because the group members in

TABLE 4–2
Effectiveness of communication networks

Performance Variable	Centralized Networks	Decentralized Networks
Speed (Number of problems solved)		
Simple Problems	Faster	Slower
Complex Problems	Slower	Faster
Accuracy (Number of errors made)		
Simple problems	More accurate	Less accurate
Complex problems	Less accurate	More accurate
Job satisfaction	Less satisfied	More satisfied

Source: Marvin E. Shaw, "Communication Networks," in L. Berkowitz, ed., *Advances in Experimental Social Psychology,* vol. 1 (New York: Academic Press), 1964. Reprinted by permission.

decentralized networks had several different options concerning where to send their messages, it naturally took longer for a solution to be reached; but the tendency for saturation is minimized.

A second conclusion from network research is that members of centralized networks are less satisfied with their work than members of decentralized networks. It appears that members enjoy having an equal say in decisions made in circle networks and do not like having decisions made for them by the central person in the wheel. This explanation makes sense in view of a great deal of subsequent research showing that workers are most satisfied with their jobs when they have participated in making decisions about them.[11] Refer to chapter 14 for specific organizational examples using this decentralized form of communication.

Implications for Effective Communications

We have defined effective communication as the transmission of information that results in a shared meaning and a common understanding for both the sender and the receiver. To understand some of the factors that can reduce the effectiveness of our communication and to realize how we might increase our effectiveness as communicators, we turn to the effects of nonverbal behavior on communications, some of the barriers to effective communications, and some ways of overcoming these barriers.

Nonverbal Behavior   Watch a busy executive going about his or her business; note the speed of movement, facial expressions, and posture. It doesn't take much to interpret a rapid pace, furrowed brow, and thrust-out chin as, "I am harassed and under pressure; don't bother me with trivial matters." Most people communicate something of the sort when feeling overworked. But when the individual is stopped by a concerned friend, who asks what's wrong, the harassed executive replies, "Nothing is wrong, I'll see you later." The verbal message says everything's okay, but the conflicting nonverbal message says things are not okay. Sometimes such nonverbal behavior can creep into a person's everyday style to the point where that person appears harassed even when not. If one is unaware of delivering the unintended message, one can be puzzled by the reactions of others. In the example just given, the person who is busy all the time may wonder why people don't come around to talk over problems even when they would be welcome.

One researcher studied the importance of nonverbal communication as contrasted with verbal communication in producing an attitude change.[12] He found that only 7 percent of attitude change is produced by the verbal content of messages. Thirty-eight percent was accounted for by paralanguage approaches, such as rate of speech, inflection, and voice quality. Facial expressions accounted for 55 percent.

Managers who use strong nonverbal communication tend to be seen differently than those who do not. Communicators who use many nonverbal messages are described as exciting, bold, strong, and hard. On the other hand, managers who use little nonverbal communication are seen as warm, informal, impressionable, and pleasant. Being able to give nonverbal messages that are *consistent* with verbal messages is important for functioning within organizations.[13]

It is easy to see how communication involves more than words. We convey hidden messages by the way we stand, by the distance we stand from another person, and by the expressions in our voice. These three forms of conveying messages—body movements and position (kinesics), space and proximity (proxemics), and vocal sounds other than words (paralanguage)—are the major forms of nonverbal communication.

Proxemics refers to the physical environment of communication. It deals with space, including location. How close do you stand to someone in normal conversation, for instance? Research indicates that in some cultures people stand very close together while in others they stand rather far apart.[14] You can get an idea of the accepted distance in your situation simply by gradually moving closer to someone as you're conversing. As soon as they start to back away from you, measure the distance—that is the distance for normal social interaction in your situation.

Other aspects of proxemics include physical arrangements.[15] When individuals from two different cultures communicate, there is the possibility that each may misread the jockeying for the proper distance to carry on the conversation. If one is a South American who continually moves closer, a North American may feel uncomfortable and continually move back to increase the distance between them. This moving away may be interpreted by the South American as an insult. Where is the guest chair relative to the office holder's desk? Is it positioned beside the desk, directly in front of the desk, or across the room? Each position conveys a subtle message. Figure 4–5 portrays this concept.

Kinesics applies to ways in which facial expressions and body positions affect communication.[16] What is your facial expression as you talk to others?

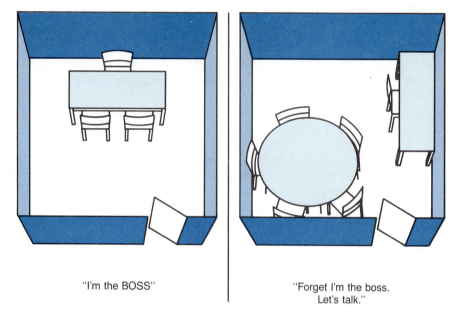

"I'm the BOSS"　　　　　　"Forget I'm the boss.
　　　　　　　　　　　　　　Let's talk."

FIGURE 4–5
Physical location of furniture as nonverbal message

What are your body gestures? What message is conveyed by an executive at a meeting who asks "Are there any questions?" as she raises her arm and looks at her watch? Even though the spoken statement appears to solicit questions, the gesture implies little or no remaining time, and tends to kill them. If you notice someone in the hall and he turns and suddenly walks away just as his eyes meet yours, you receive a kinetic message, whether intentionally sent or not.

Paralanguage refers to sounds—grunts, whistles, shouts, bells, horns, and so on.[17] In an organizational context, a great many of these are used as warning devices and as signals for shift changes, lunch time, and the like. Significant sounds could also include rattling of paper, shifting of chairs, coughing during a lecture, and other forms of nonlanguage or near-language communication.

Barriers to Effective Communication　During the following discussion it must be noted that we are looking at the overdoing of certain communication practices and resultant barriers to the communication process. But the practices themselves are not inherently bad. It can be argued that the proper application of the following practices can be effective means of handling communication in organizations. For instance, filtering can be a constructive means of uncertainty absorption.[18] Managers may purposely leave out information that they deem might create anxiety in employees and thus might prevent the employees from doing their jobs effectively.

Organizations cannot help but create some barriers to effective communications, simply because they have formal structures. The very existence of a hierarchy creates organizational and perhaps physical distance among people. In addition, the reliance upon having clear lines of authority in an organization requires that communication be more formal and follow prescribed channels. As a result, messages must pass through many levels before reaching their ultimate destination. Remember the parlor game "rumor," in which one person makes up a story that is passed around the group until it reaches the final member, who relates the message as received. This is an excellent example of the wheel network. Anyone who has played the game knows how much distortion can occur as information is passed from person to person. The same phenomenon can occur when information is passed through levels in an organization.

Human limitation also acts as a hindrance to effective communication. Instead of listening in a rational, objective manner to what is being said, one tends to become emotionally involved. Personal judgements are imposed in place of facts. As we noted in chapter 2, people can inject their own values into what they hear or read and, too often, can lose objectivity in the decoding process as a result.

Some of the most common barriers to effective communication are different frames of reference, filtering, in-group language, information overload, semantic differences, status differences, and time pressures.

Frame of reference. A frequent cause of communication problems is the different perceptions that the sender and the receiver have of the same message. Differing perceptions can be due to the sender and the receiver not having the same frame of reference; they may have very dissimilar bases of experience by which they read the situation in which communication takes place. For example, people raised in different cultures may react quite diversely to the same political message. An individual raised in a country such as Japan may take the statement of an elected official very seriously, whereas a person from another country, for instance, the United States, may have been encouraged to be critical of politicians and to put little faith in their words. Other examples of different frames of reference may be those of boss and subordinate, parent and child, line and staff, and instructor and student.

Filtering. Another barrier is the process of filtering that occurs as information is passed from one level to another in the organization. Filtering is the passing of partial information by the sender. The reasons for sending only some of the information are as various as the individual senders. Filtering can occur when information is transmitted either downward or upward in organizations.

Downward communication probably receives the greatest amount of attention from managers as they pass job instructions, procedures, practices, and goals to subordinates. Unintentional filtering can occur because of errors in receiving and decoding messages or in encoding a message for the next transmittal.

Differences in experiences, values, and unconscious motives account for much unintentional filtering. Deliberate filtering occurs because a manager disagrees with the message or for some reason does not want subordinates to receive it in the form in which it was sent. One researcher found that the vice president levels in organizations received only 63 percent of the information content communicated by the corporation board; plant managers received only 40 percent; and workers received just 20 percent of this information.[19] Messages are often simplified or summarized at various levels to speed the flow of messages or to add emphasis or clarity. However, the meaning of the message usually changes in the filtering process.

Upward communication suffers even greater problems of filtering than does downward communication. Greater intentional filtering occurs because of the desire of subordinates to withhold information or to change messages that reflect unfavorably on them and may threaten their promotion, pay, or other rewards. Subordinates who distrust their bosses, lack security, or have a strong desire for promotion are especially prone to filtering their messages.[20]

In-group language.   Another barrier to effective communication results from specialized words or vocabularies prevalent among occupational groups, particularly those with a professional status—doctors, lawyers, nurses, accountants, psychologists, or computer specialists. The development of a jargon can also occur in other common experience groups, such as electricians, actors, or police. The special language developed by these groups enhances communication among members but can pose problems for individuals who are not part of the group and do not share that common language. Remember the subculture and its language that developed around CB radios being used by truckers and then by the general public—"10-4, good buddy."

Overload.   This problem describes a condition in which any unit in the organization (e.g., a person, a committee, a department) becomes bogged down with too much information. Just like a college student who has two midterms and a quiz on the same day, people in organizations become overloaded by having too many things to do at once. Managers can feel overloaded when they arrive back at the office Monday morning after a two-week vacation and face an in-basket full of telephone messages, correspondence, reports, and a request to attend four meetings and make presentations by noon.

Seven categories of response to communication overload can be identified: (1) *omitting*—failing to process some of the information (for example, discarding "junk" or "occupant" mail), (2) *erroring*—processing information incorrectly; (3) *queuing*—leveling the peak loads by delaying until a lull occurs; (4) *filtering*—separating out less significant and less relevant information; (5) *approximating*—categorizing input and using a blanket or general response for each category; (6) *employing multiple channels*—introducing alternative channels for information flows; and (7) *escaping*—avoiding the information and going on another two-week vacation.[21]

Semantic differences. "Semantic" relates to the meaning of language. "Bear" (to carry) and "bear" (animal) mean different things; although the spelling and sound of the words are the same, the words are semantically different. In oral communication the perceived meaning of each must be derived from its context in a sentence or in a situation—grocery store versus Arctic wilderness.

Semantic problems are common in organizations. The terms "profit" and "efficiency" roll off the tongues of managers with warmth and affection, but in the language of the line workers the terms may carry a cold, impersonal message of "rip-off," "inflation," and "speed-ups" on the assembly line. Rationally, the two groups may agree upon a dictionary meaning, but in real-life communication, the words carry different emotional overtones for labor and for management.

Because of relatively common background experiences of managers, they tend to communicate better with one another than with line workers. To communicate effectively with the workers, managers must be sensitive to semantic problems and use words whose intended meaning will be understood. Fortunately, first-line supervisors, many of whom have been promoted from the ranks, typically have less difficulty communicating directly with employees. Higher-level managers are most likely to show their insensitivity in newsletters, bulletins, statements of rules, and in other written messages by the language they use.

Status differences. Significant differences in status tend to inhibit upward communication. Organizations can create status differences through titles, offices, and the amount of support resources distributed. But it is the individual who attributes meaning to the status difference. When a factory employee with dirty clothes and shoes enters the white-carpeted, walnut-paneled office of a well-dressed executive seated behind a massive desk, it is not surprising that some degree of intimidation occurs. This is especially true if the walls are embellished with diplomas, awards, or other evidence of high status. After all, the symbols were carefully selected to show that the office holder is important and powerful.

Time pressures. Managers often reflect that their scarcest commodity is time. Most organizations have many deadlines, which create time pressures that constrain an individual's ability to communicate. When people are under time pressures, the sender may not fully develop the message before sending it or may short-circuit the normal channels in hopes of getting a quick response. In addition, the time constraints may not allow the sender to receive feedback on whether the receiver captures the intended meaning of the communication.

Overcoming the Barriers How can we improve our communication skills? How can we improve the possibilities that the information flowing between ourselves and others will qualify as effective communication—the transfer of shared meaning and common understanding? How can we bridge the "communications gap" that exists in most organizations?

BOX 4–2

The Old Grapevine Is Doing Fine

Chicago—In the communications department of one of Chicago's largest banks, a staff member and supervisor have successfully avoided speaking to each other for 18 months. Any necessary correspondence is done by memo. They keep unofficial tabs on each other through the office grapevine.

A Loyola University professor often tests the waters with superiors for a plan in the offing by first leaking part of it through the grapevine.

At First Federal Savings and Loan Association of Chicago, the grapevine nearly had a senior executive resigned and out the door before it buzzed across a correction. It was the same first name, wrong last one and a much lower position on the management ladder.

Every company, every organization, every industry has a grapevine.

It's the unofficial source of information for everyone from the lowliest clerk to the chief executive officer and the chief executive's spouse. It hums loudest at a company that is autocratically managed or in a state of turmoil.

While it nearly always carries negative connotations, the office grapevine can be put to good use. In fact, in some instances, it is absolutely essential to the survival of an organization.

"Despite the stigma of the company grapevine, it can be used to supplement formal communications," wrote Vanessa Dean Arnold in a recent issue of "Management World," a trade publication. She is an assistant professor of business communications at the University of Mississippi.

She added, "In a healthy organization, there will be both formal and informal channels of communications. Managers should listen to and study the grapevine to learn who its leaders are, how it operates and what information it carries."

By being plugged in that way, management can frequently defuse potentially explosive situations by "feeding" the grapevine accurate or positive information, Arnold wrote. Failure to do so means the fear and insecurity that frequently set the grapevine humming will result in decreased productivity.

Despite the best efforts, however, defusing bad situations is difficult when an organization is in turmoil.

For example, International Harvester Co., always a formal company where lines of communication were rigidly defined, had the busiest grapevine in Chicago even before it began skirting Chapter 11 bankruptcy in 1981.

An executive with another Chicago institution that has an uncertain future sighs over the problems of keeping one step ahead of what he considers the frequently inaccurate company and industry grapevines.

"I try to keep one ear to the ground, so I can act with official communications (in response to the rumors)," he said.

He recalls being in a company elevator recently, carrying a file bearing the name of a firm that, with much publicity, had earlier considered buying his. Inside the file was a marketing backgrounder that he thought might be of use to a new employee.

On the elevator was a passenger, however, who couldn't have known that. "The guy practically bent over backwards trying to read what was on the cover of the file," the executive said with a laugh. "I told him what it was, and he got off the elevator kind of embarrassed, but I can imagine what the grapevine would have made of that if I hadn't told him."

More executives than one might think depend on the grapevine's tidbits. Frank Corrado, head of

Source: Article by Sally Saville Hodge, the *Chicago Tribune*, 28 August 1983, B6. Reprinted by permission.

Communications for Management in Chicago who also works with Hay Associates, well-known management consulting firm, said, "A senior manager who is not assigned a secretary who is always wired in is at a tremendous disadvantage."

Gloria Lewis, head of the department of counseling psychology and higher education at Loyola University, said she frequently plugged into the grapevine to test ideas on superiors.

"It's a way of gradually exposing part of a master plan ahead of time, so that by the time something happens, no one is surprised," she said. "But I only use it going up; that's not the way I would deal with colleagues, or students, or my support section."

Despite the fact that studies indicate many executives make as much use of the grapevine as Lewis does, Corrado insisted, "I'd much rather see (my clients) open up their formal lines of communication.

"Research on employee communications shows that the grapevine is the least desirable way of communicating with employees, but in some instances it is a survival mechanism that has to be used."

A classic case is the Environmental Protection Agency, until recently operating in a near-state of siege when top-level officials were accused of conflicts of interest.

Corrado said, "The lower-level managers kept the agency running, and it was the grapevine that kept everything glued together, because they weren't being told anything from the top.

"They got their information from car pools, from old friends networks, from field offices. The grapevine was absolutely critical to (the agency's) survival." Now, under new Director William Ruckelshaus, who has retained Corrado to revitalize official lines of communication, the grapevine is less necessary and not quite as active, Corrado said.

"He is trying to better establish the vertical lines of communication over the lateral lines, and a big turnaround in morale is built into it," Corrado added.

Educator Arnold points to a couple of other aspects of the maligned grapevine:

—Some studies have indicated the grapevine to be 80 to 85 percent accurate, with inaccuracies in the form of incompleteness rather than wrong information. Arnold writes that many researchers, in fact, believe much of the grapevine's information may be more accurate than information relayed by formal channels, particularly where managers are less frank and honest than they should be.

—Despite the generally held idea that women participate more actively in grapevine activity than men, other studies indicate men and women are equally active.

The grapevine does not necessarily follow the organizational hierarchy. It can go from secretary to president or from vice president to clerk. Arnold writes that in one firm an executive bypassed in the formal channels learned grapevine information from supervisors who were given news by their superior.

"The vice president of a large firm was surprised at both the speed and range of the grapevine when learning that his wife knew of a proposed relocation that had only been finalized that day," Arnold wrote. "It seems she heard it from their maid, whose husband was a custodian at the plant."

Questions

1. What is a grapevine? Under what conditions does the grapevine seem to flourish in an organization?
2. Do you agree with Corrado's statement that the "grapevine is the least desirable way of communicating with employees"? Why?
3. If you had to communicate some critical information about the organization's business and if you had a choice of using the formal communication system, which you knew to be slow and inaccurate, or the grapevine, which you knew was faster and more accurate, which would you use? Why?
4. What barriers are inherent in using the grapevine?

Overcoming the barriers to effective communication involves two tasks—improving our encoding of the message and improving our understanding of how others will receive, or decode, the message.

Effective timing. We have already said that managers may ignore a message or request simply because other problems are more pressing at the time. Time pressures can reduce a message's impact. Thus you can improve communication through effective timing. Standardize the timing of specific messages. For example, information about a critical project can be distributed every Monday for the duration of the activity. Organizational members affected by the information can then expect and be attentive to that particular report. Set key staff meetings during periods in the day or week when they will have the attention of the staff members. Some organizations use retreats for planning and problem solving. This time away from normal job pressures allows for the undivided attention of the participants to be focused on the ideas and information at hand.

Regulated information flow. One of the most obvious communication barriers in any organization concerns the flow of information. For example, the accounting department becomes busier and busier as the April 15 deadline approaches for filing corporate income taxes. Other duties become secondary to getting the tax return completed.

One solution for management is to employ certain individuals to control the flow of information, thus keeping others from getting overloaded with information. Such a person is known as a gatekeeper. The assistant to the president serves as a gatekeeper, deciding who will see the president, when, and for how long. The assistant may also read reports and other critical information and prepare a weekly summary for the president to review. Another solution to the problem of overload is to rank the information, deciding what takes priority and should be acted on first.

Parallel channels. When it is very important that a message be fully understood by both the sender and the receiver, it may be necessary to provide parallel and reinforcing channels of communication. For instance, a verbal message might be followed up with a memo or letter. The sender not only has gotten the attention of the receiver (through a face-to-face verbal exchange) but also has ensured that the sender and receiver will have records for reference (the memo or letter) in case they forget any details of the message. Likewise, sending minutes of meetings to the participants the next day is using repetition and parallel channels of communication to ensure understanding.

Empathy. Empathy is an awareness of the needs and motives of others. Speakers who use words or phrases that the audience feels are derogatory and offensive are not being empathetic to the audience.

Try to know your audience, even though it may comprise only one person, and to be sensitive to the needs and feelings of your listeners when you speak. Try to place yourself in their shoes and ask yourself, "How would I like to be addressed?"

Feedback. Individuals give feedback to make sure the message received was the message sent and to encourage further communication between the parties. When someone says, "What did you hear me say?" or "This is what I heard you say," the person is trying to make sure both parties understand what was communicated.

Managers frequently give feedback to other people, sometimes in the form of performance appraisals. Feedback poorly given can be threatening and become the basis for resentment and alienation between a manager and an employee.

Feedback is the process of telling someone else how you feel about something they did or said, or about the situation in general. Given that the intent is to give constructive feedback, consider the following suggestions when offering feedback:

- Feedback should be specific rather than general, with clear and recent examples. Statements like "you have good ideas" are less helpful than saying "your ideas for solving yesterday's customer complaint worked well."
- Feedback should be given at the earliest opportunity that the receiver appears ready to accept it. Thus, when a person is angry, upset, or defensive is probably not the time.
- Feedback should not include more than the receiver can accommodate at any particular time. For example, the receiver may become defensive if the feedback includes everything the receiver does that annoys the sender.
- Feedback should include only those things the receiver may be capable of doing something about.
- Feedback should be checked with the receiver to ensure that it is clear and seems valid.[22]

Effective listening. The ability to listen with understanding is necessary for effective communication. It has been estimated that as much as 40 percent of a white-collar worker's day is devoted to listening. Yet tests of listening comprehension suggest that these individuals listen at only 25 percent effectiveness.[23] Listening skills affect the quality of peer and superior-subordinate relationships. Perhaps the strongest advocate of effective listening is Carl Rogers.[24] He emphasizes that listening is an active process that demands careful attention and laborious thought. Instead of evaluating the message and its sender or preparing a response, the effective listener attempts to understand both the direct and subtle meanings contained in the message. To understand the total meaning requires attention to underlying feelings of the sender as well as to the verbal content of the message.

Can listening skills be developed? Some companies that believe they can have developed listening programs for their personnel.[25] Their programs explore techniques and rules for improving listening. An example of such rules are the "Ten Commandments for Good Listening."[26]

1. *Stop talking*
2. Put the talker at ease
3. Show the talker you want to listen
4. Remove distractions
5. Empathize with the talker
6. Be patient
7. Hold your temper
8. Go easy on argument and criticism
9. Ask questions
10. *Stop talking*

Notice that "Stop talking" is the first and last commandment. You can learn better listening skills. But no "commandments" or guides can help unless you *choose* to listen. Unfortunately, the failure to listen is not as much a function of inadequate listening skills as it is a function of the choice not to listen.

Communication and Management   Interest in identifying the communication behavior of effective managers has probably existed since the early days of civilization when people first tried to increase their proficiency by organizing themselves. This interest has been and probably will continue to be one of the most investigated areas of organizational communication.

But what have we learned that may help us understand some of the differences between effective and ineffective managerial communicators? Redding has summarized the results of much research and suggests the following general conclusions:

- The better managers tend to be more "communication minded," e.g., they enjoy talking and speaking up in meetings; they are able to explain instruction and policy; they *enjoy* conversing with employees.
- The better managers tend to be willing, empathic listeners. They respond understandingly to so-called silly questions from employees; they are approachable; they will listen to suggestions and complaints with the attitude of fair consideration and willingness to take appropriate action.
- The better managers tend to "ask" or "persuade," in preference to "telling" or "demanding."
- The better managers tend to be sensitive to the feelings and ego-defense needs of their subordinates; e.g., they are careful to reprimand in private rather than in public.
- The better managers tend to be more open in passing along information; they are in favor of giving advance notice of impending changes, and of explaining the reasons behind policies and regulations.[27]

Summary of Key Concepts

1. Effective communication is the information flow that results in a shared meaning and a common understanding for both the sender and the receiver. Since managers spend at least 80 percent of their time in some form of communication, effective managers need to develop effective communication skills.

2. A model of the process of communication contains sender, intention, encoding, transmission, medium, reception, decoding, perception, and receiver.

3. There are five basic information networks: chain, wheel, Y, circle, and all-channel. Some research shows that the centralized networks can be more easily overloaded but are faster and more accurate for simple tasks. Decentralized networks are more satisfying to the members and more accurate and faster when working on complex problems.

4. Nonverbal behavior that is consistent with verbal behavior enhances the communication process. Forms of nonverbal behavior include body movement and position (kinesics), space and proximity (proxemics), and vocal sounds other than words (paralanguage).

5. When certain organizational practices aren't managed, they can become barriers to the communication process. Possible barriers include different frames of reference, filtering, in-group language, overload, semantic differences, status differences, and time pressures. These can be addressed and minimized by effective timing, regulated information flow, parallel channels, empathy, feedback, and effective listening.

6. Some research shows that effective managerial communicators see the communication process as much a task to be managed and perfected as the other managerial responsibilities. And they seemed to enjoy the act of communicating.

Key Terms

Communication network

Decoding

Downward communication

Effective communication

Empathy

Encoding

Feedback

Filtering

Frame of reference

Kinesics

Lateral communication

Overload

Paralanguage

Proxemics

Semantic differences

Transmission

Upward communication

MANAGERIAL APPLICATIONS

As usual, our sources for this section of the chapter are the popular press, information from practicing managers, and our own experiences in the organizational world. We have selected only some of the concepts discussed in the preceding section to explore in this section. Our choices are mainly based on what we feel are the more important parts of the communication process for the practicing manager. We cover information overload, effective listening, face-to-face communication, one example of an unsuccessful face-to-face attempt, an example of how the environment can affect communication (proxemics), and nonverbal communication.

Information Overload

One of the most striking notions from the current literature is that, with all of the emphasis upon communication in organizations, it is easy to overload an individual's ability to process the information directed to him or her by the organization. This tendency is becoming more acute as we move into the information/technology revolution discussed in chapter 1 and further explored in chapter 13.

In a recent article in *Business Horizons*, Reed Sanderlin deals with this issue: "One cause of anxiety so many psychologists and social analysts have observed as a persuasive trait of modern culture is the overwhelming sense of confusion and disorientation many people experience in their lives and on their jobs. Such confusion and disorientation can result from too much information, from what has been called information overload."[28]

Sanderlin quotes a psychologist who specialized in treating victims of burnout, who stated that their foremost complaint about their jobs was too much paperwork. It wasn't the quantity or quality of work that they were required to produce that was causing difficulty but simply the amount of written material they were required to read and digest. This kind of overload causes difficulties in interpreting the information in a meaningful way and making it relevant to taking action and making decisions. Remember Miller's seven responses to overload listed earlier (omitting, erroring, queuing, filtering, approximating, employing multiple channels, and escaping).

Indeed, we have seen some unique ways that individual managers handle information overload. Some managers refuse to read any material that reaches them in any reproduced form. If they recognize that they have received a copy of a memo, they simply refuse to read it. Their assumption is that if it is not important enough for them to receive an original message it is not important enough for them to waste time reading it. One manager carries this attitude a step farther by refusing to read anything that is in writing. He feels that if an issue is really important, someone will call him, and if it is of critical importance, some living person will talk to him on a face-to-face basis! These managers to whom we refer work in a medium-sized organization that generates a great deal of paperwork. They might find it a good deal riskier to ignore written memos in an environment in which there were very few being circulated. Of course, someone just starting out in an organization would want to pay more attention to all the various information flows, including memos, until learning to make informed choices about which ones to give attention to.

An equally intriguing situation is that of a computer manufacturer with which we are acquainted.[29] In this organization of about 2,000 employees, every employee has a computer terminal. In fact, the CEO notes with pride that the company has more computer terminals than employees! The company uses the concept of electronic mail, the transmission of messages, memos, and reports by computer rather than by paper. This system has become so overloaded with information that managers perceive to be unimportant, that many of the managers are refusing to call up the messages available on their computer screens. Instead they wait for "hard copy" messages—messages on paper—to arrive. They simply ignore the new technological advances in information transmission. Again, we find the perception that if a message is really important it will somehow be delivered outside of the normal communication system—in this instance in some kind of paper form.

It is obvious from these brief examples that the individuals involved feel that the medium is an indication of the relative importance of the message being sent. Original copy, face-to-face, and hard copy have more significance for the receiver and for the decoding process.

Noting the differences between information and communication, Sanderlin makes several observations concerning the two that might be useful to practicing managers:

1. More information or better information directed at employees does not in itself constitute or ensure communication.
2. Too much information, in whatever form it is transmitted, may actually prevent effective communication with employees.
3. Employees vary considerably in their abilities and willingness to process information. Different employees are receptive to different types of information at different times and under different circumstances.
4. Employees can understand and act upon only what they can perceive, and what they can perceive is determined by their past experiences, their felt needs, their ambitions, and their views of what is real and what is not real.
5. Information is valuable only to the extent that it permits communication involving decision making and constructive action.
6. Employees need to be trained how to perceive and use the information that they receive. They must be provided with a useful frame of reference within which to process the information they receive.
7. Information overload cannot only make an employee experience a sense of personal inadequacy and despair, it can also cause a deeply felt cynicism about all efforts to communicate (remember the managers who will accept information only in certain forms!).[30]

Sanderlin also notes that the increasing use of computer graphics will help to focus the mass of information flowing in many organizations, but that other technological and organizational advances to reduce the sheer bulk of information will be needed before the situation can be considered to be under control.

Effective Listening

The concept of active listening has been receiving a good deal of attention in the organizational world as a means of improving communication. The Sperry Corporation is one of several organizations that has taken a very active approach toward improving listening skills in its organization. Motivated by an advertising campaign that featured the slogan, "We understand how important it is to listen," Sperry instituted a major training program in active listening that included literally all of the organization's 90,000 employees. Sperry officials have indicated that the program resulted in an operational definition of listening that was much broader than that usually used. In Sperry, "listening" is more than the mechanical act of hearing: ". . . listening is more than that. It's understanding, evaluating, interpreting—and ultimately responding to what you've heard. That total is our definition of listening."[31]

As a result of this extensive training Sperry managers feel that they have a much greater understanding of what is really going on in the organization and that the effectiveness of the activities has greatly increased.

In an article entitled "The Business of Listening," John L. DiGaetani goes beyond some generalizations about the importance of good listening and outlines some profiles of good and bad listeners.[32] He notes that the careful listener is not passive, but has a great deal of power in a situation, being able to direct and sway the conversation while observing minutely the other individuals involved. He identifies several types of poor listeners:

1. The Fidgeter uses body gestures or language clearly indicating that the fidgeter is not interested in the conversation and, in fact, is interested in few things that don't immediately relate to himself or herself.
2. The Aggressive Listener tries so hard to be a good listener that he or she intimidates people with stares and intensity.
3. The Pseudo-intellectual listens only for ideas and not the emotions behind them. This person is often bored by people's conversations because he or she misses a great deal of what is said.
4. The Overly Passive Listener has nothing to contribute to the conversation and will nod agreement with anything the other person says, perhaps out of a sense of fear.
5. The Inaccurate Listener hears "communism" if someone mentions "federally funded medical insurance." If someone mentions being busy, the inaccurate listener fears rejection. He or she can't hear what people are actually saying because of this kind of distorted listening.[33]

If these are the listening pitfalls that should be avoided, what are the keys to being a good listener? DiGaetani offers some ideas:

1. Learn to tolerate silence. Many people have a fear of silence, so they either

chatter or encourage other people to do so to kill the awful sound of silence. An ability to live with periods of silence in a conversation is helpful in achieving a more complete understanding of what is really taking place.

2. *Look and listen hard.* To observe other people while they speak is a real opportunity for understanding them. Look hard, and listen hard, for facial expressions, gestures, bodily movements, eye contact, and body language in general. This will help you to understand the real content of the communication.

3. *Know your power as a listener.* The listener has real power. A poor listener can destroy the speaker's desire and ability to communicate. Know your power as a listener and use it to your advantage.

4. *Ask questions.* Don't ask questions to be polite but to clarify what's going on. Don't be afraid to admit you don't know something. If you're not sure you understand directions, ask for them again.

5. *Reflect feelings.* Indicate through your responses what your feelings are. Similarly, show that you understand the feelings of others in the conversation—that you are aware of more than just the words that they are saying.

6. *Give positive and reinforcing nonverbal messages.* Make certain that your body reflects an interest and understanding in the problem.

7. *Know your own emotional biases and try to correct them.* Some of the biggest barriers to effective listening are emotional biases, attitudes, and prejudices within us that distort what we hear. It is impossible to be free of such biases, but if we know what our biases are, we will be aware that they may be affecting our ability to understand properly.

8. *Avoid judging.* Probably the single most important key to good listening is to avoid judging. If you are continually making judgements about what the speaker is saying as it is being said, you will strongly affect the willingness of the speaker to be open and honest with you, whether or not you agree with his or her comments.[34]

While the preceding suggestions are not a magic list to ensure good communication, they do deserve consideration. Poor listening is certainly one of the largest obstacles to good communication in any setting, and our awareness of factors that make us good or poor listeners should help us to overcome bad listening habits. We have found that it is relatively simple to train people to be good listeners, and it is a low-cost activity that more organizations should probably consider. The increase in listening skills and effective communication should more than justify the financial cost.

Face-to-Face Communication

Another aspect of good communication that has received a good deal of attention in the literature recently has been the desirability of returning to face-to-face, one-to-one communication. Professor Edgar H. Schein, one of the acknowledged leaders in the field of organization theory and behavior, states that the key element to successful implementation of solutions to management problems lies in the improvement of face-to-face relationships.[35]

Schein notes that face-to-face relationships are " . . . a basic element of any social action. Whatever else we need in the way of procedures, systems, and mechanisms, the process of social action always starts with face-to-face relationships among people. Face-to-face relationships can be thought of as the glue that holds organizations together, and such relationships are the links in the implementation chain."[36]

The advantage of a face-to-face relationship in communication is easily understood in light of the difficulties of implementing changes in organizations by using memos or written procedures. Anytime we try to influence the behavior of another we can run into questions such as "What was really meant?" or "Are you really serious about doing that?" Having some form of a relationship, such as that of a boss and subordinate, can affect the resulting communication. Open, trusting relations usually lead to more effective communications and fairly accurate assumptions about "what was really meant."

The concept of "repair strategies" deals with the skill and abilities required to maintain effective face-to-face relationships. For this to happen there must be a desire on the part of the people involved to maintain the relationship as well as an ability to see new elements in the situation, concerning either oneself or other people. Recognizing when changes have taken place and being able to incorporate these into an existing relationship is crucial to maintaining the effectiveness of that relationship. Schein also places great emphasis on disengaging our critical faculties in these communication relationships, to increase our ability to understand what is being said.

This notion of improving face-to-face relationships to improve effective communication is not confined to the literature. Many organizations are designing their physical structure and their operating policies to increase the frequency of face-to-face relationships. For example, in one high-technology organization with which the authors are familiar, the offices are constructed so that those working on a particular project have ample opportunity to communicate directly with each other.[37] Instead of a traditional office setup, groups of engineers are clustered in working areas in which all have direct visual contact with others on the same project. These areas are especially designed so that all of the resources necessary for the project are available within the area, further increasing the incidence of face-to-face relationships. This concept was not adopted to save space and should not be confused with the "bull pen" approach sometimes seen in orgnizations that are short of physical facilities. Rather, it is a conscious effort on the part of management to create an environment in which more effective communications can take place.

Top management in this firm has also adopted the same approach for itself. The president of the company shares a large work space with three other managers, those with whom he interacts on a variety of issues. They have thus eliminated many of the barriers to effective communication that can arise in organizations, including artificial, dysfunctional status barriers that often attach themselves to such things as office assignments. To assure privacy when dealing with customers or sensitive issues, the managers have access to several conference rooms close to their working areas.

An Unsuccessful Attempt

Another firm tried a similar approach in an effort to increase direct, face-to-face communications, but its activities were not as successful.[38] The company adopted an open office policy that resulted in the top management group of officers being located on one floor of the office building in a nicely decorated but open area. None of the area was enclosed by walls to form traditional offices. The firm also provided a series of conference rooms to handle those situations in which privacy was important.

After the system had been in operation for a few months, two interesting things began to happen. First, individual managers surrounded their areas with large, imposing displays of plants, in effect creating a "wall of jungle" that was impossible to see through and in a few instances almost impossible to penetrate. They constructed their own office walls, although with unconventional building materials, to attain a degree of privacy and status they felt they deserved.

The second event was that individual managers started to reserve the conference rooms for very long periods of time—in some instances for several months. Their rationale was that they were working on very important projects that required this kind of privacy. In some instances individual executives had special phone lines put into the conference rooms, moved in special furniture, and installed all of the equipment necessary to create a private office. As this practice became widely adopted among the highest ranking managers, it was evident that the open office concept had not worked. Over time, almost every manager had created his or her own private office in addition to having a space in the open office area.

We can see from the two examples just cited that what works for one organization does not necessarily work for another, even if they both have the same intentions.

The Environment of Communication

Face-to-face communication can also have its problems. Much depends upon where that communication takes place. A key step in selecting prospective employees is the interview. It is often the deciding point in the hiring process. But the physical environment of the interview can influence the effectiveness of the communication process and, therefore, the interview process.

How about a hotel room? It is common practice in staffing for sales positions to hold initial interviews in hotel or motel rooms. Such a practice gives traveling sales managers an opportunity to use interview time efficiently. They are not bothered by routine office tasks, and the interviewing site may be convenient to a large number of applicants. In spite of all these advantages, there are some problems. In a recent issue of the *Sloan Management Review*, the results of a survey of college students invited to be interviewed in such settings revealed that many individuals feel anxiety concerning such interviews and that some individuals refused to be interviewed in hotel or motel rooms.[39] Using identically worded advertisements, the researchers indicated different interview sites on different ads, including a suite in a hotel, a room in a local hotel, a room in a national chain hotel, and a room in a local office building. The least popular site was the local hotel, and the best received was the room in the local office building. While these findings held for both men and women, the responses of women were especially striking. While 98 percent indicated that they would appear for an interview in the office building, only 62 percent accepted the local hotel room as a suitable interview site.

The survey also found that interviewing in a hotel room was stressful to both men and women, but interviewing in an office produced far less anxiety. Not surprisingly, the environment in which face-to-face communication takes place has an important impact on the effectiveness of that communication, in some situations even precluding it from occurring.

Nonverbal Communication

Much has been written recently about nonverbal communication—gestures, body language, and patterns of movement that may reinforce or contradict what you say—and examples of effective and ineffective nonverbal communication abound. Observation of what is not being said in any particular classroom may tell more about what is really happening than the words being spoken. Just for fun, look carefully at the nonverbal communication in one of your next classes or meetings. Is it consistent with what is being said? What are the unspoken messages that are being transmitted? How do they change over time? Is there a consistent pattern of nonverbal communication? Often the answers to questions like these will tell more about communication effectiveness than looking at the announced agenda.

These notions about body language are much more than a matter of cursory interest, however. Nonverbal communications have practical ramifications as well. For example, body language is a very important consideration for lawyers when presenting cases in court.

Lawyers must look credible, according to Constance Bernstein of the Synchronics Group in San Francisco, an expert on courtroom body language.[40] No matter how much jurors try to focus only on evidence when deciding a case, they are influenced by the postures and gestures of lawyers and witnesses.

"If you take up a lot of space, that looks important to the jurors and the judge. They give that person importance," says Bernstein. Attorneys should also think about holding their heads straight, leaning forward, and not slouching. These postures have positive connotations.

"Crossing arms is a sure sign of trouble, as our abdomen is the first place we try to protect when we feel threatened. It's a protective gesture. But if an attorney wants the jurors to be open to persuasion, he has to show the jurors that he's open to them." An attorney must watch jurors and the judge to see how his or her performance is being received. "If a judge shows you an open palm, that's an open gesture," Bernstein said. "When you flash your palm, from a very primitive point of view, you're showing that you are not hiding anything. In the courtroom, you see a lot of closed fists."

While these examples are drawn from courtroom situations, the same kind of awareness of body language can be invaluable to a manager. For example, if a manager can "read" the audience while making a presentation, that is, interpret the body language of the listeners, the manager can determine how well the intended message is being received and whether or not some modifications should be made in the style of presentation. When talking with a subordinate during a performance appraisal session, a manager should be able to tell by reading the body language how well the person being evaluated is hearing what is being said and how well the appraisal is being acccepted.

DISCUSSION QUESTIONS

1. Explain the statement, "Words do not substitute for action."
2. How would you respond if someone said to you: "It's up to you to get me to understand you!"
3. Think of a person who you feel is a good communicator. What personal characteristics make that person a good communicator?
4. Why is it so difficult to obtain accurate information from upward or downward communication?
5. How should communication networks be designed?
6. If you were a manager of a plant where 300 employees worked and you wanted to communicate to them a sizable change in their fringe benefits package, how would you go about this task?

EXERCISE: COMMUNICATION

This exercise illustrates how difficult it is to communicate using one-way communication.

Instructions:

1. Study the following arrangement of the boxes. With your back to another person, instruct the person how to draw the boxes. Begin with the top square and describe each in succession, paying particular note to its relationship to the preceding one. No questions are allowed. Compare the following arrangement with that drawn by the information receiver.

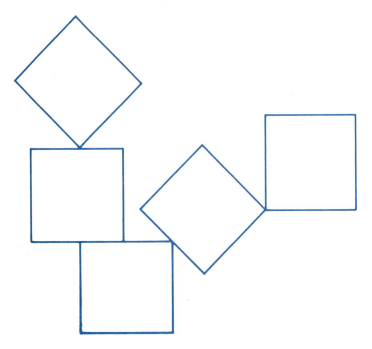

2. Try this same exercise using a two-way communication process that allows face-to-face contact and allows the receiver to ask questions. The results are usually much closer to the original set of boxes.

A very common result of this exercise is a far-from-perfect correspondence between the squares as shown here and the squares as drawn by the information receivers in one-way communication. The lack of opportunity to ask questions of the person giving the instructions and the absence of face-to-face contact makes it difficult for the information receiver to draw the squares accurately.

Source: Adapted from J. William Pfeiffer and John E. Jones, eds., A *Handbook of Structured Experiences for Human Relations Training*, vol. I (rev.) (San Diego, CA: University Associates, Inc., 1974): 13–18. Used with permission.

NOTES

1. "Game-Playing to Help Managers Communicate," *Business Week* (9 April 1979): 78–79.

2. S. Chase, *Power of Words* (New York: Harcourt, Brace & Company, 1954): 259.

3. B. A. Fisher, *Small Group Decision Making: Communication and the Group Process*, 2nd ed. (New York: McGraw-Hill, 1979): 93–99.

4. F. E. Dance, "The 'Concept' of Communication," *Journal of Communication*, vol. 20 (1970): 201–210.

5. L. W. Porter and K. L. Roberts, "Communication in Organization," in M. D. Dunnett, ed., *Handbook of Industrial and Organizational Psychology* (Chicago: Rand McNally, 1976): 1554.

6. H. Mintzberg, *The Nature of Managerial Work* (New York: Harper & Row, 1973): 38. These findings were supported by Lance B. Kurke and Howard E. Adrich, "Mintzberg Was Right!: A Replication and

Extension of the Nature of Managerial Work," *Management Science*, vol. 29, no. 8 (August 1983): 975–984.

7. R. A. Roth, "Control of the Technical Function," *Advanced Managemet Office Executive*, vol. 2, no. 4 (April 1963): 20–24.

8. William G. Scott and Terrence R. Mitchell, *Organization Theory: A Structural and Behavioral Analysis* (Homewood, IL: Irwin, 1976).

9. M. E. Roloff, *Interpersonal Communication: The Social Exchange Approach* (Beverly Hills, CA: Sage, 1981).

10. M. E. Shaw, "Communication Networks," in L. Bertowitz, ed., *Advances in Experimental Social Psychology*, vol. 1 (New York: Academic Press, 1964).

11. E. A. Locke and D. M. Schweiger, "Participation in Decision-Making: One More Look," in B. M. Staun, ed., *Research in Organization Behavior*, vol. 1 (Greenwich, CN: JAI Press, 1979).

12. A. Mehrabian, *Tactics of Social Influence* (Englewood Cliffs, NJ: Prentice-Hall, 1970).

13. A. G. Gitten, N. Black, and J. Walkey, "Non-verbal Communication and the Judgement of Leadership," *Psychological Reports*, 39 (1976): 1117–1118; and A. S. Imeda and M. D. Hakel, "Influence of Non-verbal Communication and Rater Proximity on Impressions and Decisions in Simulated Employment Interviews," *Journal of Applied Psychology*, 62 (1977): 295–300.

14. E. T. Hall, *The Hidden Dimension* (New York: Doubleday, 1966).

15. R. Sommer, *Personal Space* (Englewood Cliffs, NJ: Prentice-Hall, 1969).

16. A. E. Scheffen, *Body Language and Social Order* (Englewood Cliffs, NJ: Prentice-Hall, 1972).

17. A. D. Shulman, "A Multi-channel Transactional Model Social Influence Process" in W. R. Nord, ed., *Concepts and Controversies in Organizational Behavior* (Pacific Palisades, CA: Goodyear, 1976).

18. James G. March and Herbert A. Simon, *Organizations* (New York: Wiley, 1958).

19. R. G. Nichols, "Listening Is a Ten-part Skill," *Nation's Business*, 45 (1957): 58–60.

20. J. C. Athanassaide, "The Distortion of Upward Communication in Hierarchical Organizations," *Academy of Management Journal*, 16, (1973): 207–225.

21. J. G. Miller, "Informaton Input Overload and Psychopathology," *American Journal of Psychiatry*, 116, (1960): 695–704.

22. J. Anderson, "Giving and Receiving Feedback," in P. R. Lawrence, L. B. Barnes, and J. W. Lorsch, *Organizational Behavior and Administration*, 3rd ed. (Homewood, IL: Irwin, 1976): 109.

23. Nichols, "Listening Is a Ten-part Skill."

24. C. R. Rogers and F. J. Roethlisberger, "Barriers and Gateways to Communication," *Harvard Business Review* (July–August 1952): 28–35.

25. *Wall Street Journal*, vol. 64 (16 October 1979): 15.

26. K. Dans, *Human Behavior at Work* (New York: McGraw-Hill, 1972): 369.

27. W. C. Redding, *Communication with Organization: An Interpretive Review of Theory and Research* (New York: Industrial Communication Council, 1972): 436–446.

28. R. Sanderlin, "Information is not Communication," *Business Horizons* (March–April 1982): 41.

29. Author's personal communications.

30. Sanderlin, pp. 40–42.

31. J. L. DiGaetani, "The Sperry Corporation and Listening: An Interview," *Business Horizons* (March–April 1982).

32. J. L. DiGaetani, "The Business of Listening," *Business Horizons* (September–October 1980).

33. Ibid.

34. Ibid.

35. E. H. Schein, "Improving Face-To-Face Relationships," *Sloan Magazine* (October 1981).

36. Ibid., p. 46.

37. Author's personal communications.

38. Author's personal communications.

39. L. Kaufman and J. B. Wolf, "Hotel Room Interviewing—Anxiety and Suspicion," *Sloan Management Review* (Spring 1982).

40. The following quotes by Bernstein are from the author's personal communication.

RECOMMENDED READINGS

J. C. Wofford, E. A. Gerloff, and R. C. Cummins, *Organizational Communication: The Keystone to Managerial Effectiveness* (New York: McGraw-Hill, 1977).

This book discusses communication at three levels of analysis: interpersonal communication, group communication, and total organizational communication.

T. T. Allen and D. I. Cohen, "Information Flow in Research and Development Laboratories," *Administrative Science Quarterly*, 14, (1969): 12–19.

This paper discusses a study of communication patterns in two research and development laboratories. The study showed that gatekeepers were those persons who made the greater use of individuals outside the organization or who were more frequent readers of the literature.

M. B. McCaskey, "The Hidden Messages Managers Send," *Harvard Business Review* (November–December 1979): 135–147.

This paper describes how managers convey messages about themselves in three ways: through their metaphors, office settings, and body language.

Acme Aircraft Corporation

George Bruster took an engineering job with the Acme Aircraft Corporation soon after his graduation from State Engineering College. He was initially assigned the responsibility of supervising a group of engineers and engineering aides involved in conducting experimental test programs on various models of airplanes and airplane components.

Prior to his graduation, Bruster had spent several summers working for Acme Aircraft and had worked part-time for this organization for a period while attending school. At the time of his permanent employment he had held every position in the testing group other than that of crew chief. Because of his previous experience he was assigned the position of crew chief—an unusual assignment for a "new" engineer.

The average size of a testing crew was seven to ten individuals, of whom five were usually graduate engineers and the remainder engineering aides and technical assistants. The responsibilities of the crew chief included the over-all planning and coordinating of the test programs with which his group was involved. Approximately half of the crew chief's responsibilities were administrative rather than technical; and because of the nature of his responsibilities, the crew chief often was not the engineer on the crew who had the most experience or the greatest technical knowledge. Often older engineers, specialists in electronics or design, for example, would be working on crews headed by younger,

less experienced engineers. This type of arrangement had rarely created friction in the past—especially as the older specialists were usually not interested in accepting responsibility for anything but their particular part of a testing series. In addition, crew membership was constantly changing as crews were disbanded and reformed as tests were completed and new tests undertaken.

Figure A is an example of the organization of a typical testing unit.

On November 1, about four months after he had taken the full time job with Acme, George Bruster's group was assigned the project of testing a new model component for an experimental aircraft which Acme was developing. It was only the second major assignment that George's group had had since he took over as crew chief. This particular test series was of prime importance, for the results of the tests would be instrumental in providing data upon which Acme would base its design proposal to government representatives. If the company would provide an acceptable design, it would be in a favorable position eventually to gain a large—and profitable—production contract.

The unit supervisor stressed the importance of this particular series of tests to George and informed him that the entire testing group was under considerable pressure from top management to get quick and accurate results. Top men from the model design and instrumentation groups had been assigned to the tests, as well as one of the best report writers in the coordinating group.

Because of scheduling problems regarding the test facilities available at the Bristol plant of

Source: Adapted from *Organizational Behavior: A Management Approach*, by Harry R. Knudson and C. Patrick Fleenor (Winthrop Publishing Co., 1978). Copyright 1976 by Professor Harry R. Knudson, Graduate School of Business, University of Washington.

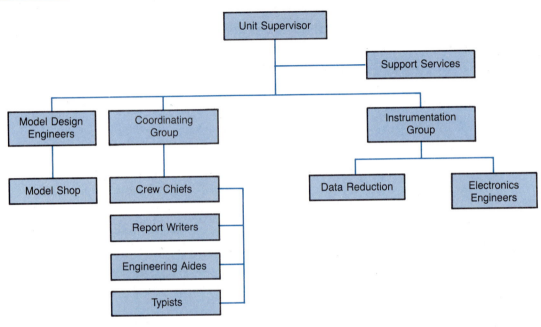

FIGURE A

Organization chart of a testing unit

Acme—the "home" office of the test group headed by Bruster—arrangements were made for the current series of tests to be conducted at the Culver City facilities of Acme. Culver City was located approximately 900 miles from Bristol; and while the Culver City operations were organized in the same manner as those at Bristol, the operations were run autonomously because of the physical distance between the two facilities. Thus, while Bruster and his crew would actually conduct the tests, they would be using the equipment and facilities of the Culver City operation.

George Bruster arrived at the Culver City test facility on November 7 to coordinate with the people there and make final test arrangements. After determining that the test was scheduled for December 1 and that his crew would receive the full cooperation of the local facility, he went to the data reduction group to arrange for the computer processing of data that would result from the test. The head of the data reduction unit, Gil Harmon, introduced George to the chief program-

mer, Dick Jones, with whom he was to work throughout the data reduction process.

George explained the importance of the test and showed Dick the type of information that would be required as final data from the digital computers.

After studying the information for a few minutes, Dick said, "I'll have to write a new program in order to give you the information you want. None of our present standard programs are capable of handling this job."

"How long will it take to write a new program?" George asked. "Oh, I could probably have it finished by the fifth of December. That's the last day of your test, so it will be done in time to reduce your data."

"That won't do!" George exclaimed. "We must have data from day to day all during the test. This proposal is red hot, and we must analyze our data on a day-by-day basis. That's the only way we can be sure we are taking the right approach in our test program. Each day's testing will be dependent on the data from the day before.

"So, what do you think? Can you have your program finished by the first?"

"Well, I dunno," mumbled Dick. "I might be able to finish by the first if there are no hitches in the program, but things seldom go that smoothly."

"But it is possible to finish by the first?" insisted George.

"It's possible, but I have other important programs to work on. Everything would have to work properly the first time."

"This project is so important it just has to be done on time. We don't have any choice but to plan it for the first of the month."

"Okay, I'll give it all the effort I can. With a little luck it will probably be ready for the first."

"Swell," concluded George. "I'll count on it."

After concluding all pretest arrangements, George returned to Bristol. During the remainder of November he was in frequent telephone communication with Culver City. All preparations were progressing satisfactorily and Dick Jones assured George that the program would be finished by the last day of November.

On November 30 George and his crew arrived at Culver City. The test was to begin the next day.

George found everything in readiness for his test, except that the data program was not quite finished. He went to Dick Jones and asked what the holdup was.

"No holdup," Dick replied. "The program will be completed by the end of the day, and we can check it out on the computer first thing in the morning. If everything checks out okay, we will be able to run your data from the first day's testing sometime tomorrow night. So you'll have your data the next day, just as you requested."

"What happens if everything doesn't check out?" asked George.

"It'll take a little while to iron out any bugs that may show up. But it shouldn't hold us up much; a few hours maybe."

"Will you be able to work overtime on this if it becomes necessary?"

"I think so. We should be able to get your data

for you one way or another, so don't worry. We'll let you know if we run into any major problems."

George was reassured and returned to his hotel satisfied that all was in readiness for the start of his test the following day.

The testing groups existed as staff units. As such, they conducted tests at the request of line and project groups who were in need of the particular information. It was the usual practice for the group requesting a test to send along a representative to make whatever decisions regarding the test program that might come under the jurisdiction of the line organization.

The requesting group for this test had sent along their senior project engineer, Richard Wallen, because of the importance of the test. Wallen was a fairly new supervisor but was well qualified technically. He was a "driver," worked his subordinates hard during rush programs such as this, and had a reputation of sometimes "rubbing people the wrong way" in order to achieve an immediate goal.

Wallen was directly responsible to the division general manager for the success of the program. One of his major concerns was whether or not the final data would be ready on a day-to-day basis. He asked George about it the night before the test.

George replied, "Dick Jones told me everything would be ready on time. The odds are real slim that anything would go wrong; and if something went wrong, it would only slow us down a couple of hours."

The following day the data from the first shift of testing was turned over to Jones for processing. However, the program did not check out properly and Jones was unable to give George his data the following day.

The same situation occurred the next two days of testing, with Jones unable to make his program work despite working several hours overtime each day.

On the fourth day the results were no better. Three hours after the testing shift was completed Wallen and Bruster went to see Jones. When they found that Jones had gone home, Wallen "blew his top" and told George Bruster to telephone Jones at his home and demand to know why he wasn't at the office working on the programming problem.

A few minutes later Gil Harmon, head of the data reduction unit, received a worried phone call from Jones, who quoted George as saying "If you don't get down here and start working on this program, it may cost you your job!"

Harmon passed on this information to Conners Simpson, who was instrumentation supervisor at Culver City. Simpson was shocked and angered at the attitude the visiting group was taking toward one of his men. He immediately phoned Wallen and demanded an explanation. He told him in no uncertain terms to "lay off" his men and also told Wallen to follow the proper chain of command and notify him first next time there was a problem. In addition, Simpson stated that he "had no intention of letting Jones come down and work on your damn program. Jones has been working twelve hours a day for the past week and has several other problems to deal with also. Besides, it's too late to salvage much of the data."

Before he hung up the phone, Simpson told Wallen, "This thing has gone too far. I'm going to take it to the boss and get it ironed our first thing in the morning. I want you and your crew chief to meet me, Jones, and Harmon in the boss's office at eight o'clock tomorrow morning."

The meeting was held, but the test series was considered unsatisfactory by all involved. The group had failed to get the desired information, and additional tests would have to be rescheduled at considerable cost in time and money.

The meeting proved to be a unique experience for George Bruster. Wallen denied outright that he had told George to use the strong language in speaking to Jones that had upset everyone so badly.

George could only reply that he thought that such language was Wallen's intent. George subsequently left the meeting shaking his head unhappily and trying to understand how the whole affair had deteriorated into such a mess.

Questions

1. Using the barriers described in this chapter, identify examples from the case that may explain some of the problems Bruster encountered.
2. Describe the communication process that occurred between Bruster and Jones as they discussed obtaining a data reduction program.
3. Describe the communication process that occurred between Wallen, Bruster, Jones, Harmon, and Simpson. What methods might have reduced the resulting conflict?
4. Identify what communication networks best describe this case. What suggestions for change might prevent this from happening again?

CHAPTER FIVE
Leadership and Power

OUTLINE

CONCEPTS OF LEADERSHIP AND POWER

Leadership or Managership?
Theories of Leadership
Power and Its Usage
Organizational Politics
Summary of Key Concepts

MANAGERIAL APPLICATIONS

Management by Wandering Around
Management by Walking Away
Working with the Best
Traits That Make a Great Boss

OBJECTIVES

- Discuss the differences between a manager and a leader

- List and describe the various aspects of trait theories

- Identify and define the major behavioral theories

- Descibe the three main situational theories

- Discuss the chief sources of power and their uses

- List and define the methods of influence

- Identify and discuss the major managerial applications

Basic Training Camp for Leaders

It is 5 A.M., and the 140 recruits are already in formation, beginning another day that will not end until 9 P.M. The recruits begin a spirited round of calisthenics, as instructors with stop watches search for slackers. During their time in camp, the recruits must pass rigorous tests in sixteen subjects, plus complete a forty kilometer night hike over mountain trails marked on maps that are not entirely accurate. Less than 30 percent of the class will pass all of the tests in the allotted time.

Another day in the life of an aspiring Special Forces recruit? Hardly, even though the camp is known by its inhabitants as "Hell camp." The Kanrisha management training camp is located in the foothills of Mount Fuji. The recruits are all executives, temporarily divested of the trappings associated with rank. For thirteen days, the trainees work to rid themselves of sixteen "ribbons of shame" pinned to their uniforms at the beginning of the training. The ribbons denote shortcomings in such things as reading, writing, speech, pronunciation, dealing with others, and good manners. In its first five years of operation, about 24,000 Japanese managers have gone through the school.[1]

CONCEPTS OF LEADERSHIP AND POWER

The Japanese are very serious indeed about leadership in the corporate sector. One can infer several things from the approach taken by the Kanrisha camp: First, the Japanese apparently believe that leaders should be very good at fundamentals such as the "three r's." Second, one way to teach trainees the importance of fundamentals is to deprive them of the trappings of power and publicly deem them inadequate in the skills they are supposed to possess. Finally, since more than 24,000 managers have experienced the camp, the clientele apparently accept the approach as valid and useful.

Leadership or Managership?

Leadership has long been considered one of the most important influences on organizational performance. For the manager, leadership is the means by which the goals and objectives of the organization are accomplished. Leadership has been a focus of attention for those who study organizational behavior because the leader significantly affects the attitudes, behavior, and ultimate performance of individual workers.

Leadership has been studied and researched for many years, resulting in numerous theories and models. As is true for motivation, no universally accepted theory of leadership has been developed. But each attempt at explaining leadership helps us to appreciate its complexity as well as its dynamic nature. In this chapter, we examine the development of leadership theory from early studies to current situational approaches. We first examine the concept of managerial functions and their relation to leadership, and then look at influence as one of the fundamental aspects of leadership. Next, we discuss the three main theoretical approaches to leadership—the trait, behavioral, and situational theories.

Managerial Functions   A manager has three major functions in an organizational setting. One function, *managing interpersonal relationships*, involves building and maintaining relationships with a variety of people both inside and outside of the organization. A second function, *managing information*, involves gathering and disseminating information that originates both inside and outside of the organization. The third function, *decision making*, involves making a range of decisions pertaining both to internal operating practices and to exchanges with other units of the organization and with the outside world.[2]

Each of these functions is associated with several specific roles (see Table 5–1). The role of symbolic figurehead, for example, is associated with the interpersonal function. This role entails carrying out certain social, legal, inspirational, and ceremonial duties that simply go with being the head of an organization. The higher a manager's position, the greater will be the time spent in the symbolic figurehead role. Closely related to this role is that of liaison, in which the manager gives and receives information and favors to learn what is going on elsewhere. The third interpersonal role is that of supervisor. A supervisor hires, trains, motivates, evaluates, and rewards subordinates.

One role associated with the informational function is that of monitor. By serving as a monitor of information from sources within and outside the unit, the manager keeps up-to-date on operations surrounding the unit. In turn, the manager has the role of disseminator, passing relevant information on to subordinates. In addition, the manager is a spokesperson, transmitting information to other units or the external environment.

As a consequence of their formal position and responsibilities, managers perform several roles that involve making decisions for the unit. The innovator role calls for initiating and designing changes in the way the unit operates. A related decision-making role is that of disturbance handler: the manager takes charge and makes decisions when nonroutine disturbances or interpersonal

TABLE 5–1

Roles associated with the three managerial functions

Function	Role
Interpersonal	Symbolic figurehead
	Liaison
	Supervisor
Informational	Monitor
	Disseminator
	Spokesperson
Decision Making	Innovator
	Disturbance handler
	Resource allocator
	Negotiator

Source: Adaptation of Figure 8, p. 59 from *The Nature of Managerial Work* by Henry Mintzberg. Copyright © 1973, by Henry Mintzberg. Reprinted by permission of Harper & Row, Publishers, Inc.

conflicts call for responses that individual subordinates cannot devise and/or implement. Another decision-making role is that of resource allocator, in which the manager parcels out the unit's resources through a series of decisions on how members will spend time, materials, and funds. Finally, the manager serves as negotiator for important decisions involving persons inside and outside the organization.

Each of the three managerial functions is important; however, it is not imperative that only the manager carry them out. Within an organization there may be individuals who can handle certain roles as well as, or more effectively than, the manager. For example, a manager who is not an effective public speaker (the spokesperson role) may delegate some of the necessary speaking activities to someone on the staff who is a good speaker.

Differences Between Managers and Leaders   Up to this point in our discussion of leadership, we have been talking about the functions of a manager. Does this mean that all leaders are managers? In certain respects, yes; but management and leadership are not synonymous: a person can be a leader without being a manager. For example, Henry Kissinger was President Nixon's national security advisor. Since his was a staff position, Kissinger had little direct line and supervisory responsibility. When he spoke at meetings, however, people were influenced by his ideas and arguments. Thus his leadership took the form of influencing others' ideas but not controlling them because of his organizational position.

Conversely, a person can be a manager without being a leader. People are managers by virture of the authority of their positions within an organization. They have the right to exercise authority because of their positions, but they may not choose to exercise their influence—or their subordinates may be influenced by other individuals or considerations. For example, the head nurse in a hospital is the designated manager of the staff nurses. Yet frequently the behavior of the staff nurses is influenced to a greater degree by directives of physicians.

Another way to sharpen the differences between managers and leaders is to consider the amount of time spent in traditional leadership activities, such as setting direction for others and communicating that direction for others to act upon.[3] This will usually vary according to characteristics of the leader, the followers, and the situation. As just noted, individuals sometimes choose to not exercise leadership. The director of a medical research laboratory will likely be required to spend less effort in leadership activity than the drill sergeant in a basic training camp, at least partly due to differences in the skill and background of the followers. Also, the more uncertain a situation or environment is, the more a manager may be compelled to exercise leadership. As much as 40 percent of a marketing vice president's time may be spent in leadership activities, whereas an assembly line supervisor would be likely to spend less than half as much time in similar activities.

Zaleznik described the distinction between leadership and managership as follows:

Leaders and managers differ in their conceptions. Managers tend to view work as an enabling process involving some combination of people and ideas interacting to establish strategies and make decisions. Managers help the process along by a range of skills, including calculating the interests in opposition, staging, and timing the surfacing of controversial issues, and reducing tensions. In this enabling process, managers appear flexible in the use of tactics: they negotiate and bargain, on the one hand, and use rewards and punishments, and other forms of coercion, on the other. Machiavelli wrote for managers and not necessarily for leaders. . . . Where managers act to limit choices, leaders work in the opposite direction, to develop fresh approaches to long-standing problems and to open issues for new opinions.[4]

A typical textbook on principles of management will denote the management functions as being planning, organizing, directing, staffing, and controlling, with leadership included in the directing function. Management is, then, a much broader concept than leadership, with the importance of leadership varying in response to conditions.

Definition of Leadership   If being a manager does not necessarily mean being a leader, what is leadership? When groups of people are asked to give a one- or two-word definition of what leadership means to them, words such as direction, example, powerful, motivator, control, authority, boss, and delegator are mentioned. Leadership involves all of these concepts. The one word that seems to pinpoint the major element of leadership, however, is influence. Using this word, we can define leadership as a process involving two or more persons in which one party attempts to influence the other's behavior with respect to accomplishing some goal(s).

There are three important implications of this definition. The first is that leadership is a *process*—a dynamic phenomenon. One researcher while defining a transformational leader spotlights this process as "a relationship of mutual stimulation and elevation that converts followers into leaders. . . ."[5] Second, leadership involves other people, who may be subordinates, peers, or superiors. Third, the outcome of the leadership process is "more concerned with getting results and achieving goals than with procedure and policy."[6]

Theories of Leadership

In the study of leadership, both early theories and those currently in vogue have focused on the same objective—identifying the factors that result in leader effectiveness. Is it, in fact, possible to identify certain characteristics, behaviors, or situations that make some leaders or some types of leadership more effective than others?

To answer this question, we summarize the concepts of three major theories of leadership: trait theory, behavioral theory, and situational theory. Early research examined leadership by asking questions about personal traits: "In terms of their individual characteristics, what kinds of people are the most effective leaders?" or "Is there a finite set of individual characteristics of traits that can distinguish successful from unsuccessful leaders?" Researchers later switched their attention from leaders' personal traits to their behavioral style. The key question became "Is one leadership style more effective than any other?" Put another way, attention shifted from *who the leader is* to *what the leader does.*

When both the trait and behavioral theories failed to offer a satisfactory explanation of leadership, researchers developed situational models of leadership. These models assume leadership to be a complex process that involves the leader, the subordinates, and the situation. The research question asked is "What set of situational determinants explain why certain leaders are more effective than others?"

Trait Theory   Many of the studies of leadership in the 1940s and 1950s focused on the traits of leaders. Researchers attempted to identify a set of biographical, emotional, physical, intellectual, and other personal traits that could differentiate successful from unsuccessful leaders.

In a review of the literature on leadership, Stogdill examined 124 research projects carried out between 1904 and 1947, and another 163 projects carried out between 1948 and 1970. Table 5–2 lists certain traits that these studies reported as being important for success in leadership.

Stogdill developed a leadership classification system based on six categories: (1) physical characteristics, (2) social background, (3) intelligence, (4) personality, (5) task-related characteristics, and (6) social characteristics.[7]

Physical characteristics.   Age, appearance, height, and weight were among the physical characteristics studied in some of the early leadership research. As might be expected, the findings were somewhat contradictory. Known leaders came in all sizes and shapes; researchers had to acknowledge that the correspondences between physical traits and leadership were tenuous at best.

TABLE 5–2
Studies of leader characteristics

Characteristics	Number of Studies
Social ability, interpersonal skills	49
Self-confidence	45
Ascendance, dominance	42
Drive for responsibility	29
Participation in social exchange	29
Achievement drive, desire to excel	28
Fluency of speech	28
Emotional balance, control	25
Knowledge	23
Originality, creativity	20
Task orientation (interest in work)	19

Source: Adapted with permission of The Free Press, a Division of Macmillan, Inc. from *Handbook of Leadership: A Survey of Theory and Research* by Ralph M. Stogdill. Copyright © 1974 by The Free Press.

Social background. A number of studies investigating the socioeconomic background of leaders have focused on such factors as education, social status, social mobility, and the leadership position attained.[8] In general, the findings have been that (1) high socioeconomic status is an advantage in attaining leadership positions; yet (2) more persons from lower socioeconomic levels are able to rise to positions of leadership today than formerly. This second finding suggests that in our maturing society social status is losing its significance as a determinant of leadership. In addition, no consistent links between leadership effectiveness and social background factors have been found.

Intelligence. Numerous studies have investigated the relationship between intelligence and being a leader, using a variety of measures of intelligence. Generally, leaders are characterized by superior judgement, decisiveness, knowledge, and fluency of speech. But the relationship between intelligence and leadership has been found to be weak—perhaps because researchers have had such difficulty in deciding what intelligence is.

One finding of interest from this research is that if the leader's verbal fluency far surpasses that of the subordinates, the leader's effectiveness is weakened. This may be because the leader uses vocabulary that the subordinates cannot understand, so communication from leader to subordinates is poor; and there may be resentment on the part of the subordinates about the leader's unknown language.

Personality. The findings of research investigating personality suggest that effective leaders are characterized by such traits as alertness, self-confidence, personal integrity, and the need to dominate. Although these findings have not been entirely consistent for all groups and industries, they do suggest that individual personality traits should be a component of any theory of leadership. The major problem in leader-personality research is finding valid ways to measure personality traits and to apply the findings to actual situations.

Task-related characteristics. Studies of task-related characteristics have produced uniform positive results suggesting that leaders have a high need for achievement, responsibility, and initiative, and are highly work oriented. In general, leaders have a high need for task accomplishment.

Social characteristics. Research examining social characteristics has found that most leaders participate in activities both inside and outside of the organization, interact well with a wide range of people, and work harmoniously with others. These interpersonal skills are valued by others because they tend to reduce conflicts and encourage trust.

Summary. Many studies on leader traits produced equivocal findings. In other instances, a study would lead to a clear-cut finding that a certain trait characterizes all leaders, but another researcher, using the same method of investigation, would fail to replicate that finding. In still other instances, researchers found that traits associated with effective leadership in some contexts could be dysfunctional in other contexts.

Behavioral Theory Because of the inadequacies of trait theory, social scientists in the early 1950s began to concentrate on leader behavior—what leaders do and how they do it. The underlying assumption in style-of-leadership research was that effective leaders use a specific style to lead others in achieving goals that result in high productivity and morale. Like the trait theorists who were looking for one set of distinguishing characteristics, the behavior theorists looked for the one best style of leadership that characterizes effective leaders.

Theory X and Theory Y. One popular explanation for leader behavior was developed by McGregor, who postulated that leaders act according to one of two sets of assumptions about subordinates.[9] One set of assumptions, called Theory X, is found in association with the traditional directive style of leadership. Leaders who subscribe to Theory X assume the following:

1. Most people have an inherent dislike of work and will avoid it if they can.
2. Because they dislike work, most people must be coerced, controlled, directed, and threatened or they will not put forth adequate effort toward the achievement of organizational objectives.
3. Most people prefer to be directed, wish to avoid responsibility, have relatively little ambition, and want job security above all.

In contrast, leaders who subscribe to Theory Y assume the following:

1. The expenditure of physical and mental effort is as natural in work as in play.
2. External control and the threat of punishment are not the only means for bringing about effort towards organizational objectives. People will exercise self-direction and self-control in the service of objectives to which they are committed.
3. Commitment to objectives is a function of the rewards associated with their achievement.
4. Most people learn, under proper conditions, not only to accept but to seek responsibility.
5. The ability to exercise a high degree of imagination, ingenuity, and creativity in the solution of organizational problems is widely, not narrowly, distributed in the population.

Theory Y leaders emphasize integration of subordinates' goals with those of the organization. But this is not to say that Theory Y leaders are never directive. As originally introduced by McGregor, this Theory X / Theory Y view of leader behavior describes a continuum. Even at the extremes of the continuum, some behaviors typical of the other extreme will be observed. For example, in basic military training, where the leadership style is highly directive, efforts are regularly made to instill a sense of commitment to the organization, from the unit level up to the organizational level (Army, Navy, etc.) and beyond to the nation served by the organization.

Until the recent advent of introspection about leadership style, it is unlikely that many leaders were aware of the assumptions underlying their behavior. McGregor maintains, however, that the assumptions encompassed in Theory X and Theory Y have always been at the heart of leader behavior.

The Michigan studies. In 1940, the Institute for Social Research at the University of Michigan began a large-scale program of research on the human problems of administration, part of which was concerned with discovering "the principles and methods of leadership and management which result in the best performance."[10] The research was conducted in a variety of organizations, including automotive, insurance, electronics, food, railroad, and paper companies. The research compared the style of leadership and other performance variables in the best and worst units in the organization. The best and worst units were identified according to such criteria as productivity, job satisfaction, employee turnover, absenteeism, waste, and costs. The studies identified two basic leadership styles used by managers and supervisors. The *job-centered style* is characterized by close supervision, coercive use of power, emphasis on schedules, and critical evaluation of work performance. The *employee-centered style* emphasizes delegation of responsibility and a concern for employee welfare, needs, advancement, and personal growth. Some researchers have called this the "human relations" approach.

One of the Michigan studies, conducted by Rensis Likert, involved comparing the productivity of various company sections in relation to management style.[11] Of seven high-productivity sections, six were managed in an employee-centered manner; only one was run by a job-centered supervisor. Among ten low-productivity sections, seven were managed in a job-centered manner. At first glance, these data would lead one to conclude that employee-centered management is the preferred style if high productivity is desired. Yet how do we account for the many exceptions to this "rule," in just this small sample? Other f ctors must also influence productivity.

Robert Tannenbaum and Warren Schmidt elaborated on the two styles identified in the Michigan studies.[12] Their model, using a continuum, specifies five stages between the two extremes of boss- and subordinate-centered leadership (see Figure 5–1). Tannenbaum and Schmidt hold that a wide range of factors determines whether directive leadership, participative leadership, or something in between is best. These factors fall into three groups:

- Factors relating to the *manager* (value system, confidence in subordinates, personal leadership inclinations, feelings of security in an uncertain situation)
- Factors relating to the *subordinates* (need for independence, readiness to assume responsibility for decision making, tolerance for ambiguity, inter-

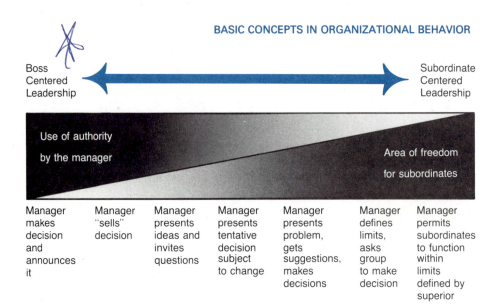

Boss Centered Leadership ←——————————————→ Subordinate Centered Leadership

Use of authority by the manager

Area of freedom for subordinates

| Manager makes decision and announces it | Manager "sells" decision | Manager presents ideas and invites questions | Manager presents tentative decision subject to change | Manager presents problem, gets suggestions, makes decisions | Manager defines limits, asks group to make decision | Manager permits subordinates to function within limits defined by superior |

FIGURE 5-1

A leadership style continuum (Source: Robert Tannenbaum and Warren H. Schmidt, "How to Choose a Leadership Pattern," *Harvard Business Review* (May–June 1973): 164. Copyright © 1973 by the President and Fellows of Harvard College; all rights reserved.)

est in the problem, understanding of and identification with organizational goals, knowledge and experience pertinent to the problem, expectations about sharing in decision making)

■ Factors relating to the *situation* (type of organization, the group's effectiveness, nature of the problem itself, time constraints).

These factors constitute a checklist that a manager can use to diagnose a situation to determine which style of leadership will work best. Consider, for example, time constraints as a determiner of leadership style. During a crisis period—say, during a strike at an important plant—centralized decision making about schedules and supplies is appropriate. But in a period of stability, a more democratic approach might be in order.

The Ohio State studies.   While the Michigan studies were going on, Ohio State University investigators were also studying the determinants of leader behavior and the effects of leadership style on work-group performance and satisfaction.[13]
The Ohio State researchers identified two leadership styles, analogous to those identified in the Michigan studies and by Tannenbaum and Schmidt. The Ohio State term for directive behaviors such as organizing and defining group activities and tasks, defining roles within the work group, establishing communications networks, and evaluating work group performance, is *initiating structure*—meaning the leader initiates the structure of the group and its activities. *Consideration* is the term the Ohio State investigators applied to behaviors associated with

employee-centered leadership: developing trust and respect between manager and subordinates.

One of the most important findings of the Ohio State research was that initiating structure and consideration were independent of one another. That is, the amount of "structure" manifested in a leader's behavior did not predict the amount of "consideration" that might be shown by the leader. A leader can simultaneously show a high degree of both structure and consideration. It is also possible to show a low degree of both, or a high degree of one and a low degree of the other. The independence of these two factors is shown in Figure 5–2.

Numerous investigations were conducted to determine the effects of initiating structure and consideration on group performance and morale. The results revealed that no one leadership style was best. In some studies, the combination of high structure and high consideration was associated with high performance and worker satisfaction. But other studies revealed that this combination produced some dysfunctional effects, such as absences, low performance ratings of the group leaders by their superiors, and low worker satisfaction.[14]

Other studies of the Ohio research showed discrepancies in how leadership styles were identified: leaders would identify their own style one way, and their subordinates would identify it another way.[15]

Summary.   In view of the complexities of human behavior, it is not surprising that the behavior theorists failed to identify one leadership style that is superior to all others in all situations. Nevertheless, leadership theory was considerably enriched by the more complex approach taken by these groups of researchers. Common sense tells us that a model of leadership claiming that, for example,

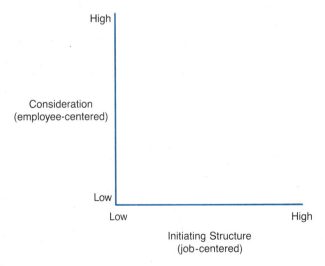

FIGURE 5–2
Two dimensions of leadership style

BOX 5-1

The Old Foreman Is on the Way Out, and the New One Will Be More Important

At Ford Motor Co.'s Edison (NJ) plant, workers on the trim-assembly line move back and forth between storage bins and the conveyor, picking up parts and installing them on freshly painted body shells that soon will become Escorts and Lynxes. Each worker has about a minute to do his job, putting on headlights, door locks, or headliners (ceiling fabric) before starting the cycle again. Repetition dulls the senses, and the setting is perfect for the old, bull-of-the-woods foreman who stalks up and down the line, berating workers for omitting a bolt or failing to tighten a screw.

Foreman Donald R. Hennion used to do just that: He was a "hard-nosed, loudmouthed disciplinarian," he says of himself. But now he chats with the workers, solicits their ideas, and even encourages them to use recently installed buttons to stop the line if a defect prevents them from correctly doing their jobs. The thought of an hourly worker stopping the line would have made old Henry Ford apoplectic. But the "stop concept" is one aspect of a worker participation program that has improved quality, reduced absenteeism, and lessened hostility between bosses and workers at Ford's Edison plant. Its success depends on first-line supervisors. They must listen to what workers have to say, use the workers' ideas, and focus on problem-solving rather than meting out discipline.

'ENABLING FUNCTION' These qualities very likely were important aspects of the foreman's role a century ago, before corporate growth made the supervisor a low-level, authoritarian bureaucrat. These days, the old-style foremen of a few decades ago have difficulty adapting to the participatory style. Computer-based technology poses other problems. It often takes the control and monitoring of production flow and quality out of the foreman's hands. Increasingly, younger workers come on the job with computer literacy and a better understanding of electronics than their supervisors have.

Experts agree that the first-line supervisor's role will change radically. Says Barry A. Stein, president of Goodmeasure Inc., a Cambridge (Mass.) consulting firm: "They [foremen] aren't going to control people anymore. They have to coach them, help do the planning, approve organizational direction, and make sure the directions are clear. It will be an enabling function rather than a control function."

Some foremen, like Hennion, changed relatively easily. Now 48, he started with Ford 26 years ago as an assembly-line worker and has been a supervisor at various levels since 1959. "The way I was taught," he says, "when your boss says, 'Do this, do this,' you do it, and you don't get a chance to ask why." Hennion began to change his management style about five years ago, when he was assigned to an unfamiliar job and had to rely on the workers' knowledge.

LEARNING TO LISTEN. Meanwhile, Ford and the United Auto Workers jointly began a worker participation program called Employee Involvement (EI). Edison management and the UAW have set up 13 problem-solving groups. Once every two weeks, Hennion meets for an hour with nine rank-and-filers in his department to analyze and solve production and quality problems.

Source: Reprinted from the April 25, 1983 issue of *Business Week*, pp. 74–75, by special permission, © 1983 by McGraw-Hill, Inc.

Edison is the first Ford plant where assembly-line workers can stop the line. Hennion's 30 assemblers frequently halt their line long enough (usually less than a minute) for Hennion to identify the problem and decide how to handle it. This puts pressure on the foreman but also results in many fewer defective cars reaching the street.

Hennion has accepted one of the more difficult concepts of worker participation—that hourly workers may know more than he does. "If an hourly guy brings something to me, I'll go and try it out," Hennion says. "It's surprising how much an employee can see that's wrong with a job."

Ford is only one of many companies that have trained first-line supervisors for the new role. But there are about 1.2 million foremen in manufacturing, according to an American Management Assns. estimate, and the majority still boss people around in the old, authoritarian way. Stein and other authorities on participatory management say the idea has not spread widely enough. "Only a relatively small fraction of the American economy is actively moving in this direction," Stein says.

LOST POWER. The first-line supervisor always had a crucial role in production and always came under intense pressure from above and below. In the early years of industrialization, the foreman was the most skilled and knowledgeable in a group of workers. As companies grew, he was absorbed into management as the person who "controlled" workers with the power to hire, fire, and mete out discipline.

But the foreman's power began to wane as early as the 1920s, when management became increasingly remote from the shop floor and relied on the staff specialists in production planning and quality control for information on operations rather than the people who were intimately involved with production, the workers and the foremen.

When unionism came to the mass-production industries in the 1930s, foremen lost the power to hire and fire. A major unionization campaign among foremen in the 1940s collapsed with the passage of the 1947 Taft-Hartley Act, which defined supervisors as essentially managerial. Caught between labor and management, the foreman is often called "the man in the middle."

Leonard A. Schlesinger, of Harvard University's business school, has recently conducted studies of how foremen react to the new environment. He says many of the pressures that drove supervisors into the union in the 1940s are at work today. Their pay has not risen as rapidly as that of union members. Their job security is shaky. Their ability to control the work force is being undermined—or so the foremen feel—by the use of computers on the shop floor and worker participation.

Furthermore, the use of self-managing work teams reduces the need for production supervisors. But Stein thinks it "inconceivable" that most corporations will be able to do without them in the forseeable future. "The first-line supervisor will become more important rather than less in the movement toward flatter and more flexible organizational structures," Stein says. "The old-fashioned foreman may not have a cheerful future, but the role of foreman does."

Hennion, a tall, slim man, often smiled and joked with workers as he walked up and down the trim-assembly line on a recent workday. "They even smile back now," he says. Constantly checking for defects, Hennion poked his head through the window of an Escort and asked an assembler whether the headliners were fitting correctly. Made at Ford's Utica (Mich.) plant, the headliners recently had been arriving at Edison with minor defects that hamper installation. Only the week before, Hennion and two hourly workers went to Utica and met with some 20 workers and supervisors who make the headliners. In the end, the Utica workers made several suggestions for improving production methods at their plant.

An interplant meeting of hourly workers to solve production problems is a rare event in the U.S. industry. The EI program has produced other dramatic changes in worker-boss relationships. In the past, Hennion says, foremen had a standard response to sloppy assembly work: They would summon the worker to a disciplinary hearing that usually ended in a reprimand, suspension, or even discharge for the worker. But little effort was made to investigate the reasons for the poor job. "Maybe he didn't have parts or was overworked, but we didn't have time to ask," says Hennion. "If you didn't discipline an hourly worker, your manhood was challenged. There were so many hearings, you had to stand in line to get into the office."

'ONE FAMILY.' There has not been a disciplinary hearing at the Edison plant for more than a year. Instead of yelling at a worker who fouls up, the supervisors try to analyze what went wrong. In turn, the workers have gradually replaced their hostile feelings toward foremen with trust. Before, they would keep quiet when they spotted a defect; now, they call the foreman or stop the line and volunteer ideas for improving quality. "Ford has discovered that to build a good car, they've got to have harmony," declares Earl Nail, president of UAW Local 980 at Edison. "Now, it's like we're all one family."

The participatory style allows a foreman to concentrate on improving production and quality rather than "always looking over my shoulder,"

as Hennion puts it. He has considerably more time to work with maintenance people, draw up better plans for the flow of material, and make minor engineering changes without calling the plant engineers. "You're more productive in the long run," Hennion declares. "People on the line seem happier. You still have the same boredom, but the attitude is changing. We're working as a team."

Questions

1. Describe Hennion's leadership style today and in the past.
2. What situational factors contributed to the changes in leadership styles?
3. Fiedler contends that it's better to change the job than the individual to get a better match. Is that what happened to Mr. Hennion? Or did Hennion change his style?
4. Using Fiedler's model for viewing power (see Figure 5-3), describe the changes that have taken place in the foreman's job since the 1930s. What impact will the continual introduction of technology have on the foreman's job and influence methods?
5. Why are the changes in leadership style portrayed in the article so slow in coming to other companies or industries?

production will be higher if the manager is concerned about both production and employee welfare, is more valid than a model claiming that production will be higher if the manager is a certain height, weight, and age.

Situational Theory In the late 1960s, researchers recognized that behavior theory was inadequate and began to develop other approaches to the study of leadership. Again, the subsequent research was influenced by the contradictory and equivocal findings of earlier research. The findings of trait and behavioral research strongly suggested that the most effective leaders are dynamic and flexible, addressing the uniqueness of each situation. The language used to describe the inadequacy of behavioral theory, in fact, pointed the direction of subsequent research: behavioral theory failed to identify a leadership style that is superior to all others *in all situations.*

Recent developments in leadership theory were foreshadowed by the model of Tannenbaum and Schmidt, previously summarized. Recall that they included situational factors in their "checklist" for choosing a leadership style. Although their model focused on the continuum of styles, the inclusion of situational considerations gave their model a richness that others lacked.

A contingency model. An extensive research program conducted by Fred Fiedler of the University of Washington resulted in the development of a contingency model of leadership effectiveness, a model that bears some similarities to that of Tannenbaum and Schmidt. Fiedler argued that the effectiveness of any leadership style is contingent on the characteristics of the situation.[16] An important feature of Fiedler's model is the leader's influence, which is determined by the situational factors of leader/member relations, task structure, and leader's positional power. According to Fiedler, if the leader's influence is either strong or weak, the preferred style is task-centered; only if the leader has moderate influence should the employee-centered style be adopted. These relationships are shown in Figure 5–3.

Let us consider the elements of this model in greater detail. Leader/member relations refers to the degree of confidence, trust, and respect subordinates have in the leader. This characteristic is evaluated as either good or poor. The assumption is that if they respect and trust the leader, it will be easier for the leader to exercise influence. If they do not, the leader may have to resort to special behaviors or favors to get good performance from the subordinates. Task structure refers to the nature of the subordinate's task—whether it is routine (structured) or complex (unstructured). An accounts payable clerk may work on a fairly structured task, whereas the corporate planner for an electronics firm probably works on an unstructured task. Leader position power refers to the extent of the leader's power base—the degree to which the leader can reward, punish, promote, and demote employees. According to Fiedler, position power is either strong (e.g., an operations manager) or weak (e.g., the leader of a volunteer group).

These three factors together determine the leader's influence, which Fiedler calls "situational favorableness" (the more influence a leader has, the more favorable the situation is for the leader). The greatest leader influence derives from a situation characterized by good leader/member relations, a highly structured task, and strong leader position power.

According to the model, the owner/manager of a large automotive retail store who is liked and respected by the employees should choose a task-oriented style. The situation would fall into Cell 1, because the tasks are highly structured for the sales clerks and stock personnel, the position power is strong, and the leader/member relations are good. Under these conditions, says Fiedler, a task-oriented leadership style can be expected to enhance organizational performance.

An employee-oriented style is more appropriate when leader influence is moderate. For example, in many research laboratories, the tasks of the scientists

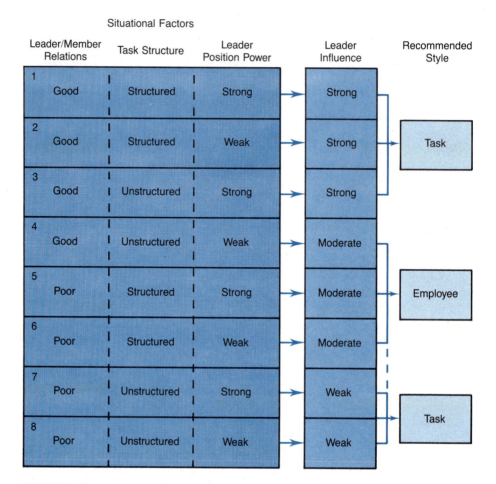

FIGURE 5–3

Fiedler's contingency model of leadership style (Source: Adapted from Fred E. Fiedler, *A Theory of Leadership Effectiveness* (New York: McGraw-Hill, 1967): 37. Used by permission.)

are quite unstructured, the leader may have weak position power, but leader/member relations are usually good. This situation is captured in Cell 4 of the model. Because research scientists prefer following their own creative tendencies to being told what to do by the research manager, an employee-oriented leadership style would contribute to high performance by the team of scientists.

A task-oriented style is again preferred when leader influence is weak (see Cell 8). A scenario for Cell 8 would be this: a volunteer committee meets to plan a picnic for a large company (unstructured task), the leader is not well liked by the other members of the committee (poor leader/member relations), and the leader cannot reward or punish other committee members for lack of participation (weak position power). Fiedler is of the opinion that a directive leadership style (task-oriented) is appropriate for this situation.

The Fiedler model has been tested in a number of settings, and has received some support,[17] but several groups of authors have criticized the model on various counts.[18] One problem is that the prescriptions for leadership style are based on empirical findings that Fiedler obtained using a questionable measure. Fiedler inferred leadership style in his studies from evaluations by leaders of their least-preferred coworker (LPC). The LPC is defined as the person with whom the leader has worked least effectively in a recent task. The LPC measure has been criticized from perspectives ranging from its psychometric properties[19] to its practical application in an organizational setting.[20]

Another problem with Fiedler's model is that the either/or classification of situational factors and leader influence is too simplistic. One need not be an authority on the subtleties of leadership to know, for example, that position power has gradations, as does leader influence. The same may be said of the other components of the model. Moreover, earlier research at Ohio State had shown that leaders can be both task-oriented and employee-oriented.

Fiedler's preference for a task-oriented style (in 5 of 8 situations) stands in marked contrast to the findings of Likert. At least one study has shown that middle LPC leaders perform effectively over the entire situational control range.[21] Such discrepancies need to be resolved before one model can be chosen over the others.

There is also evidence that the contingency model is not applicable in nonwestern societies,[22] a reservation that is not exclusive to this model. It is conceivable that *most* of our managerial theories are culture bound.

Despite these shortcomings, Fiedler's contingency model remains a dominant approach and provides a manager with the first attempt to combine classification of leadership style with classification of the situation. With this approach a manager has a framework to consider some of the situational characteristics and the corresponding leadership style that might be appropriate. Fiedler remains spirited in his defense of the model,[23] and continues to conduct and supervise research related to it.

Path-goal theory. The path-goal theory of leadership is based on the expectancy theory of motivation. As you remember, expectancy theory holds that motivation is the product of the value (valence) of goal achievement and the expectation (expectancy) that the goal will be achieved. Path-goal theory is also based on the concepts of initiating structure and consideration.[24] According to this theory, originally developed by Evans, leaders are effective depending on their ability to motivate subordinates to reach organizational goals and to find satisfaction in their work.[25] In other words, an effective leader is perceived by subordinates as helping the subordinates reach their goals (promotion, raise, recognition) and as a result become satisfied with that accomplishment while performing activities that help the organization accomplish its goals.

Path-goal is continually being developed; at present, it includes the following basic tenets:

1. A leader can increase the motivation of subordinates by making the rewards for productivity more attractive to them (that is, by increasing the valence of goal accomplishment). For example, a manager can reward high productivity with raises, promotions, and praise, thereby increasing the attractiveness of high productivity.

2. When the task of subordinates is poorly defined, a leader can increase motivation by clarifying the goal, or by giving structure to the path that leads to the goal (e.g., by providing supervision or instruction). Defining the task increases the expectancy of goal achievement and, consequently, motivation.

3. When the task of subordinates is well defined (e.g., assembly-line work), instead of initiating structure the leader should show consideration for the personal needs of the individual subordinates. Should the leader attempt to introduce structure when the task is already structured, the result could be a decrease in motivation, because the subordinates would probably feel insulted and resentful.

These tenets are logically consistent, and empirical support for them has been found,[26] though the support has not been consistent.[27] The inconsistent support may be partially due to inadequate measurement of leader behavior.[28] Many of the leadership scales used in tests of the path-goal theory may have contained items extraneous to the measurement of the leadership constructs.[29] Other empirical evidence points to the need to incorporate other factors in the theory, including aspects of the environment that may exert substantial impact on leader-follower interaction.[30] Some individuals do not react favorably when a leader provides structure in an unstructured situation: they prefer to operate without structure, or they prefer to create structure on their own (research scientists). One set of research studies found that whether employees had an internal or external *locus of control* affected their response to structuring leadership.[31] People with an internal locus of control believe that what happens to them is a result of their own behavior; those with an external locus of control believe it's a matter of luck—good or bad. "Internals" were found to be more satisfied working under an employee-centered supervisor; "externals" prefer to have their environment structured by a supervisor.

Other personal characteristics of subordinates that appear to affect their reactions to structuring leadership include education, need for achievement, perceived ability, willingness to accept responsibility, and need for independence. The message from recent research, then, is that leaders should not assume that providing structure when tasks are unstructured will invariably increase the motivation of subordinates—and thus, presumably, their own effectiveness. Once again we see that those who seek a leadership approach that will always be successful will probably be disappointed, because human beings are highly variable.

Situational leadership. Paul Hersey and Kenneth H. Blanchard, while at Ohio University, developed a model of leadership that incorporates concepts similar to those of consideration and initiating structure, identified in the earlier Ohio State studies.[32] In "situational leadership," the key concepts are *relationship* behavior and *task* behavior. Relationship behavior refers to a leader's engaging in two-way communication by providing socioemotional support, "psychological strokes," and "facilitating" behaviors. Task behavior refers to a leader's engaging in one-way communication by explaining *what* each follower is to do, as well as *when*, *where*, and *how* tasks are to be accomplished.

Hersey and Blanchard consider these two behaviors to be independent, which makes it possible to model their possible combinations two-dimensionallly (see Figure 5-4). The possible combinations are high task/low relationship, high task/high relationship, low task/high relationship, and low task/low relationship. These combinations constitute four basic leadership styles. Which style is appropriate in a given situation is determined by the "maturity level" of the subordinates.

"Maturity" is defined as the capacity to set high but attainable goals (achievement motivation), willingness and ability to take responsibility, and the education and experience of the individual or group. This maturity variable is considered for each specific task, function, or objective that the leader wishes to accomplish through the individual or group. For example, a sales representative might have a high maturity rating for sales call technique, but a low rating

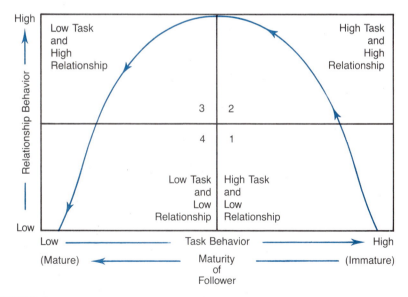

FIGURE 5-4

A model of situational leadership (Source: Paul Hersey and Kenneth Blanchard, *Management of Organizational Behavior: Utilizing Human Resources,* 4th ed., © 1982, p. 152. Adapted by permission of Prentice-Hall, Inc., Englewood Cliffs, NJ.)

BOX 5-2

There's an Art to Managing the Maverick

Not all employees have equal skills, so they shouldn't be treated equally.

Mavericks—employees who produce, but not always according to corporate rules—deserve special handling, said James Seitz, partner in charge of the New York office of accountants Touche Ross & Co.

True mavericks make things happen and tend to differ from the pack. They pursue an idea or a dream, and their purpose obviously is greater than other people's purposes, Seitz said.

"Mavericks also feel inhibited by too much structure," he said. "They feel the system designed to make things happen often gets in the way of making things happen."

How does a manager decide whom to support?

"Support goes to those who've sold you on their thought process of their ideas. When in doubt, you also support those who've been around awhile and have been successful, those who have a proven track record.

"With any maverick, I'd want to know what his motivation is. Is he simply experimenting for the sake of experimenting? You want to be sure that the common corporate good in some way is going to be served, but you have to have a lot of leeway in that process.

"You have to separate the dreamers from the realists. The job of management is to insert a mind-set of objectivity and practicality as it relates to running the business. You foster certain people's ideas and squelch others."

Productive mavericks should be supported, but a maverick doesn't have the right to abuse other people in the organization, Seitz said.

"I think you have to establish a corporate culture that says, 'We're all different and some of us are more equal than others in certain ways, but your rights end where your nose begins.'"

Mavericks pursuing new ideas are optimistic that they can get something accomplished in a short period of time for a reasonable amount of money.

"Then as they pursue the idea, reality strikes and more effort is needed, more money is needed. You have to somehow make a management decision between creeping commitment and cost that has not produced any result. That's the art of management."

Managers have to guide mavericks ("You have to know when you're dealing with a high roller") and nurture them.

Source: *USA TODAY*, (13 September 1983): 7B.

(perhaps owing to lack of experience) for developing and writing customer proposals. The manager could appropriately provide little or no direction to this subordinate with respect to sales calls but a great deal of counsel and supervision with respect to proposal writing.

An important aspect of situational leadership is that it calls for change in style as the situation—the subordinate's maturity level—changes. Thus, as the sales representative acquires proposal-writing skills, the manager should reduce task behavior and increase relationship behavior. This shift should continue until

"You have to take time to understand their idea or dream, and understand their motivation."

Management is the bookend for the highs and lows and ups and downs of a maverick's behavioral pattern. "You reinforce them when they're down and put a lid on them when they're getting too unrealistically enthusiastic."

A maverick, or any high performer, has to have a sense of how management will behave under certain situations. "You can't let them run amok," he said. "But you can have tolerance bands within which people can operate without worrying about management interference."

Mavericks should know that beyond those bands they must tell management before surprises of great magnitude take place, surprises that would preclude future support.

"What you really want to do is keep making a maverick's next move better by not letting them hurt themselves by violating too many rules of propriety in the early stages of the project," Seitz said.

To help mavericks avoid alienating others, "You have to be honest with them and let them know when they've done something extraordinarily good and something extraordinarily bad. You remind them how they like to be treated and cause them to think about how they might treat others.

"I know that sounds kindergartenish, but we've all experienced high-charging people so wrapped up in what they're doing that they, at times, lose their people sensitivity. Once you bring back to their realization that people are important, most I've dealt with are understanding," Seitz said.

Are other workers jealous of the special treatment the maverick receives? "I think most people respect, revere, and honor talent, even if they don't have it," he said.

"You don't have resentment if that talent is working for the organization and not being abusive to the organization. You might have a little bit of envy, but that is not destructive to the organization."

"But if we bent the rules for people who do not have talent," he warned, "I think people within the organization would see that immediately, and management would not be doing its job."

Questions

1. Do you agree with Speitz about treating mavericks with kid gloves?
2. What leadership style do you think would work with mavericks? Could you manage mavericks and nonmavericks in the same work group? Why? Why not?
3. How would Fiedler's theory of leadership fit the management of mavericks?
4. What power sources would you use with mavericks and what methods of influencing them would you use?.

the employee has reached a high level of maturity in the given task. Then the leader should reduce not only task behavior but relationship behavior as well. This sequence is illustrated by the maturity curve superimposed on the four leadership style quadrants in Figure 5–4.

While this theory has received criticism about its consistency,[33] and has not yet received empirical support, the model is appealing to practicing managers because it provides specific yet flexible guidelines for dealing with each subordinate in different situations. Hersey and Blanchard have developed instruments for self-assessment of leadership style and for identification of subordinate maturity levels. Though it might be difficult for a leader to determine whether an employee has an internal or external locus of control, for example, it is relatively easy to determine an employee's maturity level for a given task.

The model also allows the manager to select a leadership style according to observable abilities of subordinates; however, it does not address the question of how managers with a strong preference for one of the four leadership styles can achieve flexibility.

Power and Its Usage

> The power of the chief executive is hard to achieve, balky to manage, and incredibly difficult to exercise. . . . Many new Presidents, attempting to exert executive power, have felt it slip from their fingers and have faced a rebellious Congress and an adamant civil service, a respectfully half-obedient military, a suspicious Supreme Court, a derisive press, and a sullen electorate.[34]

The concept of power has been around for some time. Many times the terms *power* and *influence* are used interchangeably; however, in our discussion we distinguish their meaning. Influence is the process of affecting the thoughts, feelings, or behaviors of others. Influence as a process only exists during the conduct of interpersonal relations. Power is the capacity to influence others to get things done. Therefore, influence is the application of power. By virtue of position, managers hold power.

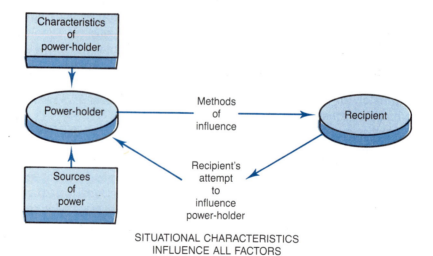

SITUATIONAL CHARACTERISTICS
INFLUENCE ALL FACTORS

FIGURE 5–5
The concept of power: An interaction

Power may be used or withheld, depending on the situation or the person who holds the power. For example, the office of President of the United States has power, the ability to influence. But the application may be different depending on who is occupying the office and the specific situation being considered by the office-holder. President Carter tended to withhold the use of power even during the Iranian crisis, while President Reagan used his power to get Congress to agree and act upon his economic measures during the recession of the early 1980s.

As with communication, power can be a two-way process. The power-holder can be influenced by the recipient's performance. For example, leaders show more consideration to subordinates who perform at a higher level. This often leads to higher satisfaction among the subordinates.

Figure 5–5 shows the interaction of basic concepts that are presented in this section. We consider the factors surrounding the power-holder and the methods used to influence.

Sources of Power   French and Raven have identified five fundamental sources of power: reward power, coercive power, legitimate power, referent power, and expert power.[35] These sources of power are not equally available to everyone in the organization, and the sources of power for managers and staff personnel are different.

Reward power.   Managers usually hold power in organizations by virtue of their ability to reward. This power is one aspect of motivation. The strength of the power differs upon the amount of reward that the manager controls and the strength of the subordinate's desire for the reward. Examples of reward power include pay increases, bonuses, and promotions.

Coercive power.   Coercive power is a force held by those who can cause others to have unpleasant experiences. It is usually conceived of as a form of punishment for not complying with the power-holder. Examples include discharge, demotion, and other disciplinary actions as well as threats to act. Managers need to exercise caution because the use of coercive power may bring about the opposite result that the power-holder intends. One study found that the use of coercive power actually decreased productivity as it was applied.[36]

Legitimate power.   Legitimate power is held by individuals because their position, role, or status provides an organizationally or culturally afforded right to direct the action of others. Legitimate power is based upon a mutually accepted perception that the power-holder has the right to influence the recipient. For instance, in an organization the manager has the right to expect certain tasks of the unit to be completed by subordinates. As a complementary right the subordinate expects to receive certain fair compensation for doing those tasks. This process has been termed ''psychological contracts.''[37]

Referent power. The recipient's identification with the power-holder is the basis of referent power. The recipient desires to be like the power-holder and therefore may act, perceive, feel, or think like the power-holder. In a sense, this is a form of charisma that draws respect and attracts others to the power-holder. In an organization, certain top managers may have referent power with young managers who aspire to reach those positions by emulating their success.

Expert power. Expert power is based on the special ability and/or knowledge that the power-holder has and is needed by the recipient. Accountants, engineers, and computer specialists gain organizational power as a result of information they collect and the knowledge they obtained from their professional training. A major problem with expert power as a power base is that it depends on the perceptions of others.[38] As we know from chapter 2, perceptions are often inaccurate. Furthermore, expert knowledge can quickly be used up as the problem is solved.

The preceding five sources of power are not completely independent. The person with legitimate power often has reward and coercive power. The person with reward power usually has coercive power.[39] The use of expert power can increase one's referent power.

One study showed that expert power is perceived as most effective in inducing workers' acceptance of change, whereas coercive and legitimate power were least effective. In addition, individuals were more likely to attribute compliance to their own will if referent, expert, or reward power was used, and less so if coercive or legitimate power was used.[40] Another study showed that the greater the coercive power—punitive behavior of supervisors—the greater the reported prevalence of fear, anxiety, anger, and depression among subordinates.[41]

The implications for a manager to have power are to (1) have a position with clear legitimate power, (2) have ability to reward compliance, (3) establish respect and attractiveness, and (4) develop expertise.

Characteristics of the Power-holder We do need to say a few things about the characteristics of the power-holder that may alter the influence attempts. Earlier in this chapter we focused on a number of leadership styles and their effects on subordinate behavior. If the leadership style is perceived by the subordinate as appropriate for the present conditions, then the influence attempt will be more successful. For example, using situational theories, certain conditions of task uncertainty are conducive to the manager's being very task-oriented with subordinates.[42]

Trust, credibility, prestige, and self-confidence are important power-holder characteristics. These qualities are not only significant for the manager who is attempting to persuade subordinates to follow a policy or decision, but also for the participative manager whose subordinates must believe that their involvement is not a guise for manipulating them to adopt a predetermined decision. A person who feels confident that an attempt to use power will be successful will use power more effectively. This self-confidence is based on the power-holder's perception of personal power and the amount of supervisory experience he or she has had.[43]

Methods of Influence   While there are a multitude of means to influence the recipient, they can be classified into two categories—direct and indirect. Table 5–3 shows the methods of influence derived by Kotter in a study of twenty-six organizations. He classified tactics according to whether they involved face-to-face (direct) or indirect influence. He concluded that successful managers are able to and do use all the influence methods.[44] While the research is fragmented and incomplete, some conclusions about the methods of influence are justified.

Clearly, choice of methods is constrained by the power-holder's base of power. Methods based on formal authority are not usable unless the appropriate authority is granted. Giving or withholding information is not possible unless the power-holder has control of the information. Indirect influence is difficult if one has no network of contacts or no control over structural aspects concerning the recipient. In addition, the choice of methods is situationally dependent. Two researchers have observed that effective use of power was contingent on the user's sensitivity to the particular situation, to the methods, and to the people involved.[45] There is some agreement that effective users of power begin with subtle methods, evolving to harsher methods only as required.

Organizational Politics

No discussion of power would be complete without some mention of organizational politics. By organizational politics we mean the ability to mobilize resources, energy, and information on behalf of a preferred goal or objective by an individual or group.[46] It is important to recognize that politics need not be "bad," although the term within an organizational setting is usually pejorative. One researcher states: "The survival of an organization may depend on the success of a unit or coalition in overturning a traditional but outdated formal organizational objective or policy."[47]

Yet part of our acceptance or rejection of political acts may hinge on our concept of the "means and ends." Consider the following situation. Mary is a project leader for a production start-up group responsible for meeting a certain deadline that requires coordination among the group members. However, her group is not very cohesive and Mary decides to create a little competition, which is supposed to stimulate work group cohesion (chapter 6 discusses this issue). Mary gives the group the impression that sales wants them to fail to meet the deadline so sales will be able to get some additional funds when both groups submit their new budgets in a couple of weeks.[48]

How do you evaluate this situation? You might feel that Mary's plan was justified, especially if the group did pull together and met its deadline. However, another argument might develop that although the group met its deadline, the side effects may mean that the production and sales groups will lose a cooperative relationship for future efforts and dealings.

TABLE 5-3
Methods of influence

Face-to-face Methods	What They Can Influence	Advantages	Drawbacks
Exercise obligation-based power.	Behavior within zone that the other perceives as legitimate in light of the obligation.	Quick. Requires no outlay of tangible resources.	If the request is outside the acceptable zone, it will fail; if it is too far outside, others might see it as illegitimate.
Exercise power based on perceived expertise.	Attitudes and behavior within the zone of perceived expertise.	Quick. Requires no outlay of tangible resources.	If the request is outside the acceptable zone, it will fail; if it is too far outside, others might see it as illegitimate.
Exercise power based on identification with a manager.	Attitudes and behavior that are not in conflict with the ideals that underlie the identification.	Quick. Requires no expenditure of limited resources.	Restricted to influence attempts that are not in conflict with the ideals that underlie the identification.
Exercise power based on perceived dependence.	Wide range of behavior that can be monitored.	Quick. Can often succeed when other methods fail.	Repeated influence attempts encourage the other to gain power over the influencer.
Coercively exercise power based on perceived dependence.	Wide range of behavior that can be easily monitored.	Quick. Can often succeed when other methods fail.	Invites retaliation. Very risky.
Use persuasion.	Very wide range of attitudes and behavior.	Can produce internalized motivation that does not require monitoring. Requires no power or outlay of scarce material resources.	Can be very time-consuming. Requires other person to listen.
Combine these methods.	Depends on the exact combination.	Can be more potent and less risky than using a single method.	More costly than using a single method.

Indirect Methods	What They Can Influence	Advantages	Drawbacks
Manipulate the other's environment by using any or all of the face-to-face methods.	Wide range of behavior and attitudes.	Can succeed when face-to-face methods fail.	Can be time-consuming. Is complex to implement. Is very risky, especially if used frequently.
Change the forces that continuously act on the individual: Formal organizational arrangements, informal social arrangements, technology, resources available, statement of organizational goals.	Wide range of behavior and attitudes on a continuous basis.	Has continuous influence, not just a one-shot effect. Can have a very powerful impact.	Often requires a considerable power outlay to achieve.

Source: J. P. Kotter, "Power, Dependence, and Effective Management," *Harvard Business Review* (July–August 1977): 133.

Possible Tactics Is this an isolated case? Probably not if we consider some research done to identify the tactics used by organizational members.[49] The major tactics included

Blaming or attacking others. One form of blaming is to minimize or avoid association with an undesirable situation by "scapegoating" or "getting off the hook." This is seen as a reactive tactic. Another form of blaming, which is proactive, involves making a rival look bad in the eyes of other influential organizational members.

Use of information. A key tactic in the political process is using information to better one's position. A variety of information uses were suggested, including withholding information when it might be detrimental to self-interest, avoidance of situations or individuals that might require explanation of undesirable information, distortion of information to create an impression or innuendo, or "objective" speculation about individuals or events.

Creating and maintaining a favorable image. This tactic includes general appearance, dress and hair style, sensitivity to organizational norms, drawing attention to successes (including those for which the individual may not be responsible), and creating the appearance of being on the inside of important activities.

Developing a base of support. Methods can include getting others to understand one's ideas before a decision is made, setting up the decision before the meeting is called, and getting others to contribute to the idea (making them feel that the decision is theirs) to assure commitment.

Other tactics. Other, less used but still important, tactics include ingratiation (praising others when normal circumstances do not warrant it), developing strong allies and forming coalitions, performing services or favors to create obligations, and using rewards, coercion, and threats to influence others.

Ethical Guidelines How do we as individual organizational members and managers judge the ethics of our political acts or tactics? One set of theorists proposes a conceptual scheme to judge the actual behaviors from a positive and negative perspective.[50] Table 5–4 shows the good and bad aspects of the three major ethical theories used to judge behavior. Utilitarian theory holds that actions should be judged by their consequences. Theory of moral rights asserts that human beings have certain fundamental rights to be respected in all decisions. Theory of justice requires that behavior be guided by equity, fairness, and impartiality.

Referring again to Mary and her work group, we can speculate about her "creating an impression" using the utilitarian theory. The more competitive atmosphere and resulting internal cooperation could lead to efficiency and productivity for Mary's group in the short run. But the sales group's rights (the right

TABLE 5–4
Ethical theories for judging political behavior

Theory	Positive Aspects	Negative Aspects
UTILITARIANISM The greatest good for the greatest number	1. Encourages efficiency and productivity 2. Parallels profit maximization and auditing methods; thus is easiest for business person to understand. 3. Encourages looking beyond the individual to assess impact of decisions on all constituencies	1. Makes quantifying all important variables virtually impossible 2. Can result in unjust allocation of resources, particularly when some individuals or groups lack representation or ''voice'' 3. Can result in abridging personal rights of some to achieve desired outcome
RIGHTS Individual's personal rights not to be violated	1. Protects the individual from injury and establishes spheres of freedom and privacy 2. Establishes standards of social behavior that are independent of outcomes	1. Can encourage individualistic, selfish behavior that, taken to an extreme, may result in anarchy 2. Establishes personal prerogatives that may set obstacles to productivity and efficiency
JUSTICE Fair distribution of benefits and burdens	1. Assures that allocation of resources are determined fairly 2. Is the ''democratic'' principle; does not allow a society to become status- or class-dominated 3. Protects the interests of those who may be underrepresented in organizations	1. Can encourage a sense of entitlement that reduces risk, innovation, and productivity 2. Can result in abridging some people's rights to accommodate the canons of justice

Source: Adapted, by permission of the publisher, from ''Organizational Statesmanship and Dirty Politics: Ethical Guidelines for the Organizational Politician,'' by M. Velasquez et al., *Organizational Dynamics* (Autumn 1983): 72 © 1983 Periodicals Division, American Management Association, New York. All rights reserved.

to expect correct information when requesting data from others) might be abridged in the future if Mary's group develops an antagonistic attitude and withholds information or other critical resources when requested by the sales group.

The outline of the three ethical theories in Table 5-4 may not provide positive, simple answers as to what actions are ethical and what are unethical. But rather, it provides a framework to consider one's actions before creating the act. It allows a manager to balance and weigh possible consequences when the need for immediate results clouds what those outcomes might be for all involved.

Summary of Key Concepts

1. Leadership and management are not synonymous. Leadership is an activity of management, but varies in importance with the management job and situations encountered.
2. Leadership theories can be classified as primarily trait, behavioral, or situational.
3. Trait theories have little empirical support, but interest in leader traits continues.
4. There is strong evidence that leadership behavior can be described along two dimensions: job centered and employee centered (University of Michigan), or initiating structure and consideration (Ohio State University).
5. Situational theories add moderator variables to the process of leadership, e.g., leader-member relations, task structure, leader position power, subordinate maturity, path-goal clarity.
6. Characteristics of subordinates is a relatively unresearched area of leadership.
7. Flexibility in adopting different leadership styles may be an important management skill.
8. Power is the capacity to influence, while influence is the application of power.
9. Fundamental sources of power are: reward power, coercive power, legitimate power, referent power, and expert power.
10. The major tactics of organizational politics include: blaming or attacking others, using information, creating and maintaining a favorable image, and developing a base of support. One can assess the ethics of certain political behavior by applying three theories—utilitarianism, rights, and justice.

Key Terms

Coercive power	Legitimate power
Consideration	Maturity
Expert power	Organizational politics
Influence	Power
Initiating structure	Referent power
Leadership	Relationship behavior

Reward power	Theory X
Situational leadership	Theory Y
Task behavior	Trait theory

MANAGERIAL APPLICATIONS

In this section of the chapter we look at some of the things that are going on in the real world in terms of leadership, as usual drawing from some of the current writings in the field, the experiences of practicing managers, and our own experiences as professors and consultants.

One of the trends that quickly emerges from the nontechnical literature is that there are a number of different styles of leadership being recommended by a variety of practicing managers. Some of these styles are related to those discussed in the first part of the chapter, but others have not yet been noted.

Management by Wandering Around

In their book *In Search of Excellence*, Peters and Waterman talk a great deal about successful leaders who seem to have a managerial style of "wandering around."[51] By this they mean that the managers seem to spend a considerable amount of their time visiting various parts of the operation, usually on an irregular timetable. There is no particular agenda for this wandering, but simply a desire on the part of the manager to see firsthand what is happening in different parts of the organization.

During the wanderings, the manager asks questions, makes observations, and, according to traditional organization theorists, violates the chain of command many, many times a day. When asked about the objectives of this kind of style, managers who practice it tend to use phrases like "keeping in touch," and "establishing a presence." Having a firsthand acquaintance with operations and establishing a model of managerial behavior are evidently strong motivators in these instances. The concept of closer control is not part of the wandering style; managers who wander do not do so as a means of attaining tighter control over operations. In fact, they go to great measures to keep from invalidating the control systems in operation. Although the chain of command is violated by the manager's having a great deal of contact with employees without regard for rank and organizational level, many of those who wander go to unusual lengths not to undercut the position of the on-line supervisors.

Sometimes this is a fine line to draw—providing an opportunity for the manager to keep in touch through personal observation while at the same time not usurping the authority of lower-level managers by solving problems on the spot, or by interfering with previously established plans and objectives. Indeed, it does not take much imagination to envision employees with complaints or "great ideas" that have not been fully rewarded, laying in wait for the big boss to wander by and hoping to get an on-the-spot hearing that might reverse an undesirable decision.

The wandering style has other inherent risks as well, illustrated by the following scenario involving the CEO of a widely geographically dispersed organization whose office happened to be located next to one of the company's plants. Times were difficult, and the industry was highly competitive. To provide a lift for the plant employees, show the flag, and get some firsthand information on what was going on during such a difficult period, the CEO started to wander through the plant. Without his realizing it, this practice became almost a daily habit.

The plant manager and his staff were frantic trying to determine what was wrong. This was not the CEO's usual style, and, given the disastrous conditions, something bad was surely on the horizon. Could the company be thinking of closing the plant? Fortunately, the plant manager had been with the company for a long time and had developed a friendly relationship with the CEO so that he was able—but only after some time—to ask the CEO directly what was going on, and why this sudden change of behavior had occurred. Didn't the CEO realize that he was giving strong impressions that there were serious problems in the plant and that the workers felt that he had lost confidence in them? Hearing this, the CEO immediately moderated the practice and made special efforts to assure the managers and workers that his intention was simply to be available in case they needed his help in this difficult period and to show by example that the organization was still very much alive and well.

One of the big problems in this instance, of course, was that the CEO altered his behavior too drastically without first giving the plant workers and managers an opportunity to change their expectations of his behavior. Those who practice the wandering style successfully provide lots of opportunity, over time, for expectations to develop that support this style of leadership. Note, too, that when the CEO found out that his wanderings were not having the intended effect, he did not cut them off altogether but merely reduced them sharply. The reason was that he had discovered that his wanderings were allowing him to get closer to the operations. While he realized the negative impact that his wanderings were currently having, he also knew that he had started to establish some expectations that wandering was acceptable CEO behavior, and he did not want to lose this.

Obviously, management by wandering around isn't suitable for all managers or for all situations, but it seems to be a style that is growing more and more prevalent with the current emphasis on staying in touch with both the customers and the operations. Managers who practice this approach seem to place emphasis on the interpersonal role (being a symbolic figurehead, liaison, supervisor).

Management by Walking Away

Management by walking away is a leadership style practiced by the president of Quad/Graphics of Pewaukee, Wisconsin. As described in *INC.* magazine, for one day each year, known as the Spring Fling, the entire management of Quad/Graphics walks away and leaves the operation of the organization in the hands of the employees.[52] The tradition began some ten years ago, as founder and President Harry V. Quadracci was looking for a way to get his managers out of the plant for a day of planning and socialization. The original plan was to shut down production for the day, but some unanticipated orders came in and, rather than pass them up, the company instructed the employees to run the plant themselves.

Quad/Graphics is recognized as a leader in the industry on two fronts, first for its technical excellence and second for its creativity and innovation in management and leadership. For example, Quad/Graphics employees work a three-day, thirty-six hour work week—three twelve-hour days—then get either three or four days off, depending upon whether it is their turn to work on Sunday. Productivity rose about 29 percent when this schedule was installed and seems to decrease by that much in those few instances when it was necessary temporarily to go back to the old five-day schedule. Quad/Graphics is also known for its employee stock ownership plan and profit-sharing program and an extensive range of employee benefits, including the opportunity to study toward a college degree on the company premises.

President Quadracci is known as a "fan" of management theory, and all of the currently popular buzzwords are a normal part of conversation in the company. More importantly, though, he has really created the kind of work force from which he can walk away—a company that will literally run itself.

A major part of his leadership philosophy is that responsibility should be assumed and shared. Anyone who sees something that needs to be done should assume the responsibility for doing it. According to Quadracci, neither he nor anyone else should have to point out what has to be done. In fact, Quadracci often refuses to tell his people what should be done. For instance, when the company needed greater backhaul revenue to finance expansion of its trucking fleet, Quadracci handed each of the drivers the keys to one of the company's large trucks and told them they were now owner-operators in a new division of the company and it was their responsibility to make the trucks profitable on their return trips. When the drivers asked what they should carry on the backhauls, Quadracci responded that he didn't know, and that they would have to find out themselves. The truckers rose to the challenge, went through some difficult times initially, but in a relatively short period had a profitable operation going.

It was the same procedure in many of the other expansion activities of the company. In each, Quadracci got the employees involved and then "walked away," leaving them to work out the strategies and the implementation of the expansions. Basically he treats his employees as entrepreneurs within the organization and asks them to assume responsibility for determining the nature of new activities, formulating appropriate goals, and developing implementation plans.

Quadracci notes that sometimes management by walking away is a difficult leadership style for him, as he has some opinions that he would like to express.[53] But he has found that to be consistent with his philosophy of sharing responsibility and encouraging employees to assume responsibility, often his best action is, in fact, to walk away. Quadracci's style seems to combine important elements of path-goal theory (increasing the valence of goal accomplishment, clarifying goals) and situational leadership (flexibility, developing subordinate maturity).

Working with the Best

One of the most intriguing articles concerning leadership that we've encountered recently appeared in "The Manager's Journal" section of *The Wall Street Journal.*[54] In this article, the author questions why managers should spend time dealing with people who are on the low end of performance efforts. What's wrong with the idea of spending the most time with the people who are performing well, rather then spending time working in areas of low percentage returns; that is, with people who are not performing as effectively? A leader can cause change in people, but rarely enough to justify the time invested in the process.

By concentrating managerial attention on those people who are doing well, the leader is able to focus on those areas where the highest productivity is potentially available. Unfortunately, one of the rewards for doing a job well in many organizations is to be ignored, as managers spend most of their time working in the problem areas, trying to get subpar performers to improve. The article suggests that giving attention to the high performers will increase productivity much more than attempting to shore up the lower performers.

One executive who adopted this style spent more and more time with his most successful salespeople, and less and less time with his "problem children." Essentially, he divided his people into three groups. He spent about 80 percent of his time with the top third. He listened to them, asked for details of their successes, rewarded them well financially, gave them extra assistance and, above all, lots of recognition and visibility. They responsed by doubling their efforts and productivity. Doubling effort is not useful in itself if productivity gains do not follow and last for a reasonable period. This group kept the new level of production over a period of several years.

This particular manager spent about 15 percent of his time with the bottom third of his people. This time was spent mostly in recruiting and selecting replacements, with the best source of replacements being recommendations from the top producers. He didn't spend time trying to develop these people to become high performers. Training became a self-help development program with some help from the top producers under a "buddy system." Under no circumstances were top performers permitted to function in training roles—their performance was too important to sacrifice to such activity.

The manager spent only about 5 or 6 percent of his time with the middle third of his people. They were always screaming for attention, but the only time that they received it was when they had results to contribute.

By strictly adhering to this pattern the manager was able to create the time to spend with the top group, thus making the strategy work. Incidentally, the manager worked regular hours and never took work home with him in the evenings or on the weekends. When he traveled, he visited only with his top producers. This approach, of course, flies in the face of leadership theories that support the concept of high people- and high task-oriented leadership.

Traits That Make a Great Boss

Dr. Warren Bennis, one of the most widely recognized scholars in the field of organizational behavior, completed a study in which he interviewed ninety "superleaders" in an attempt to determine if there were any traits that they had in common.[55] Among those interviewed were CEOs of some of the largest organizations, public officials, university presidents, newspaper pubishers, and the coaches of consistently successful athletic teams. On average, the superleaders were fifty-six years of age, male, college graduates, making about $300,000 per year, and still enthusiastically married to their first spouses.

Bennis identified five traits that the superleaders had in common:

- *Vision*—the capacity to create a compelling picture of the desired state of affairs, a picture that inspires people to perform in such a way that it is achieved
- *Communication*—the ability to portray the vision clearly and in a way that encourages the support of followers
- *Persistence*—the ability to stay on course regardless of the obstacles encountered
- *Empowerment*—the ability to create a structure that harnesses the energies of others to achieve the desired result
- *Organizational ability*—the capacity to monitor the activities of the organization, learn from mistakes, and use the resulting knowledge to improve organizational performance

The superleaders don't seem to pay much attention to popular theories on management and motivation, according to Bennis. During the interviews, he didn't hear them talking about innovative compensation schemes, new forms of Japanese management, or the latest theories of human development. According to the study, superleaders come in all sizes and shapes and evidence no common pattern of psychological background or makeup. They do seem to have a disregard for risk, in the sense that they do not think much about the possibility of failing. Once a project is undertaken, they assume that it will be successful. They also don't dwell much on their errors, striving to learn from them and then moving ahead quickly—but using the knowledge gained from the unsatisfactory experience.

Superleaders also don't seem to be so super once they are away from their area of expertise. Many of them are almost social misfits, don't like to make small talk, and rarely do anything without a specific purpose. For these reasons, most are happiest when they are at work. They get the most satisfaction when they are working in their areas of expertise in a situation over which they have a great deal of control. When they are unable to work under these conditions, they may become depressed.

This is an interesting study of the characteristics of those who are the leaders of some of our largest and most successful organizations. As noted in other studies such as this, successful leaders at this level seem to find their own satisfaction intertwined with that of the organization and may be unable to realize this satisfaction without using the organization as a vehicle for doing so. It would be interesting to take a look at our superleaders ten or fifteen years from now and see if the changing values that we see coming into the work environment have any effect on the satisfaction of these individuals, or even upon the way that we define a superleader. It would be interesting to think of successful leaders that you have known—even if they might not qualify to be "super"—and see if they have some of the characteristics found by Bennis. We suspect that the characteristic of vision would be among them. In fact, we can't think of a single instance in which a leader was successful without having a vision of how the situation should be and the ability to transmit that vision to followers.

Even though trait theory has received equivocal support at best, the search for meaningful leadership traits goes on.

DISCUSSION QUESTIONS

1. What is meant by effective leadership?
2. In what sense is a manager always a leader?
3. What problems are involved in using one leadership style? What advantages accrue from consistently using one style?
4. If you were to design a training session for managers about leadership, what would you include in the design?
5. In what ways are participatory methods superior to authoritarian leadership? Can you think of situations where you would have the opposite opinion?
6. Can a person have power without influence? In what situation would that be an advantage? A disadvantage?
7. Describe the most powerful person you know. Why is that person's power so strong? What methods of influence does he or she use?

EXERCISE: LEADERSHIP QUESTIONNAIRE

Please complete the following questionnaire. For each of the following 10 pairs of statements, divide 5 points between the two according to your beliefs and perceptions of yourself, or according to which of the two statements better characterizes you. The 5 points may be divided between the A and B statements in any one of the following ways: 5A 0B, 4A 1B, 3A 2B, 2A 3B, 1A 4B, 0A 5B, but not equally (2½) between the two. Weigh your choices between the two according to which one better characterizes you or your beliefs.

Source: W. Warner Burke, Teachers College, Columbia University. Used by permission of W. Warner Burke, 1984.

1. _____ A. As a leader I have a primary mission of maintaining stability.

   _____ B. As a leader I have a primary mission of change.

2. _____ A. As a leader I must cause events.

   _____ B. As a leader I must facilitate events.

3. _____ A. I am concerned that my followers are rewarded equitably for their work.

   _____ B. I am concerned about what my followers want in life.

4. _____ A. As a leader a primary task I have is to mobilize and provide focus for followers' needs.

   _____ B. As a leader a primary task I have is to ensure clarity of responsibilities and roles for my subordinates.

5. _____ A. A primary value I hold is honesty in all matters.

   _____ B. A primary value I hold is equal justice for all.

6. _____ A. I believe leadership to be a process of changing the conditions of people's lives.

   _____ B. I believe leadership to be a process of exchange between leader and follower.

7. _____ A. As a leader I spend considerable energy in managing separate but related goals.

   _____ B. As a leader, I spend considerable energy in arousing hopes, expectations, and aspirations among my followers.

8. _____ A. While not in a formal classroom sense, I believe that a significant part of my leadership is that of teacher.

   _____ B. I believe that a significant part of my leadership is that of facilitator.

9. _____ A. As a leader I must engage with followers at an equal level of morality.

   _____ B. As a leader I must represent a higher morality.

10. _____ A. What power I have to influence others comes primarily from my ability to get people to identify with me and my ideas.

   _____ B. What power I have to influence others comes primarily from my status and position.

James MacGregor Burns, in his book *Leadership* (1978), distinguishes between two kinds of leadership: *transformational* and *transactional*. A transformational leader "recognizes and exploits an existing need or demand of a follower. But, beyond that, the transforming leader looks for potential motives in followers, seeks to satisfy higher needs, and engages the full person of the follower" (p. 4). A transactional leader, on the other hand, is one who views the leader-follower relationship as a process of exchange—rewards for work, jobs for votes, favor for favor, and so on.

In a similar fashion, we can roughly expect the transactional leader to be more likely to initiate structure and be task-oriented; while a transformational leader would probably have higher regard for consideration and relationship-orientation. Which are you?

Scoring

The questionnaire is constructed according to Burns' two types of leaders—transactional and transformational. In other words, half of the A responses represent one type and half the other; the same is true for the B alternatives. The key is as follows:

Transformational	Transactional
1. B	1. A
2. A	2. B
3. B	3. A
4. A	4. B
5. B	5. A
6. A	6. B
7. B	7. A
8. A	8. B
9. B	9. A
10. A	10. B

By adding your responses for each of these two columns, you can determine what relative weight you are giving to one type of leadership as compared with the other. Burns contends that most of us are transactional rather than transformational. Compare your scores with your classmates and see if Burns is correct. Do you think that one or the other is more effective, given our changing work values (see chapter 1)?

NOTES

1. Adapted from R. Phalon, "Hell Camp," *Forbes*, (18 June 1984): 56–58. Used with permission.

2. H. Mintzberg, *The Nature of Managerial Work* (New York: Harper & Row, 1973).

3. Warren Bennis, "The Artform of Leadership," *International Management*, vol. 37, no. 5 (May 1982): 21.

4. A. Zaleznik, "Managers and Leaders: Are They Different?" *Harvard Business Review* (May–June 1977): 67–78.

5. J. M. Burns, *Leadership* (New York: Harper & Row, 1978): 4.

6. S. Donnell and J. Hall, "Men and Women as Managers: A Significant Case of No Significant Differences," *Organizational Dynamics*, vol. 8, no. 4 (1980): 60–77.

7. Bernard M. Bass, *Stogdill's Handbook of Leadership* (New York: Free Press, 1981).

8. R. M. Powell, *Race, Religion, and the Promotion of the American Executive* (Columbus, OH: Bureau of Business Research, Ohio State University, 1969).

9. D. McGregor, *The Human Side of Enterprise* (New York: McGraw-Hill, 1960).

10. Rensis Likert, *New Patterns of Management* (New York: McGraw-Hill, 1961).

11. Ibid.

12. Robert Tannenbaum and Warren H. Schmidt, "How to Choose a Leadership Pattern," *Harvard Business Review* (May–June 1973): 162–180.

13. Edwin A. Fleishman, "The Leadership Opinion Questionnaire," in Ralph M. Stogdill and A. E. Coons, eds., *Leader Behavior and Its Description and Measurement* (Columbus, OH: Bureau of Business Research, Ohio State University, 1957).

14. Edwin A. Fleishman, "Twenty Years of Consideration and Structure," in Edwin A. Fleishman and J. G. Hunt, eds., *Current Developments in the Study of Leadership* (Carbondale, IL: Southern Illinois University Press, 1973).

15. A. K. Korman, "Consideration, Initiating Structure, and Organizational Criteria: A Review," *Personnel Psychology* (Winter 1966): 349–361.

16. F. E. Fiedler, A *Theory of Leadership Effectiveness* (New York: McGraw-Hill, 1967).

17. M. J. Strube and J. E. Garcia, "A Meta-Analytic Investigation of Fiedler's Contingency Model of Leadership Effectiveness," *Psychological Bulletin*, 90, no. 2 (September 1981): 307–321.

18. See, for example, C. A. Schriesheim and S. Kerr, "Theories and Measures of Leadership: A Critical Appraisal of Current and Future Directions," in J. G. Hunt and L. L. Larson, eds., *Leadership: The Cutting Edge* (Carbondale, IL: Southern Illinois University Press, 1977).

19. R. W. Rice, "Psychometric Properties of the Esteem for Least Preferred Coworker (LPC Scale)," *Academy of Management Review* (January 1978): 106–118; and C. A. Schriesheim, B. D. Bannister, and W. H. Money, "Psychometric Properties of the LPC Scale: An Extension of Rice's Review," *Academy of Management Review*, 2 (1979): 287–290.

20. S. Shiflett, "Is There a Problem with the LPC Score in Leader Match?" *Personnel Psychology*, 34 (1981): 765–769.

21. J. K. Kennedy, Jr., "Middle LPC Leaders and Contingency Model of Leader Effectiveness," *Organizational Behavior and Human Performance* (August 1982): 1–14.

22. G. C. Theordory and H. Mafakhir, "Retesting Fiedler's Contingency Theory in Islamic Schools," *Journal of Psychology* (May 1982): 15–18.

23. F. E. Fiedler, "A Rejoinder to Schriesheim and Kerr's Premature Obituary of the Contingency Model," in J. G. Hunt and L. L. Larson, eds., *Leadership: The Cutting Edge* (Carbondale, IL: Southern Illinois University Press, 1977).

24. R. J. House and T. R. Mitchell, "A Path-Goal Theory of Leadership," *Journal of Contemporary Business*, vol. 3 (1974): 81–99.

25. M. G. Evans, "The Effects of Supervisory Behavior and the Path-Goal Relationship," *Organizational Behavior and Human Performance*, vol. 5 (1977): 277–298.

26. R. J. House and G. A. Dessler, "Path-Goal Theory of Leadership: Some post hoc and a priori Tests," in J. G. Hunt and L. L. Larson, eds., *Contingency Approaches to Leadership* (Carbondale, IL: Southern Illinois University Press, 1974).

27. C. N. Greene, "Questions of Causation in the Path-Goal Theory of Leadership," *Academy of Management Journal*, 22, no. 1 (1979): 22–41.

28. R. J. House and T. R. Mitchell, "Path-Goal Theory of Leadership," *Journal of Contemporary Business*, 3 (1974): 81–97.

29. C. A. Schriesheim and M. A. Von Glinow, "The Path-Goal Theory of Leadership: A Theoretical and Empirical Analysis," *Academy of Management Journal*, 20, no. 2 (1977): 398–405.

30. J. A. Schriesheim and C. A. Schriesheim, "A Test of the Path-Goal Theory of Leadership and Some Suggested Directions for Future Research," *Personnel Psychology*, 33 (1980): 349–370.

31. T. R. Mitchell, C. M. Symser, and S. E. Weed, "Locus on Control: Supervision and Work Satisfaction," *Academy of Management Journal*, vol. 18 (1975): 623–630.

32. P. H. and K. H. Blanchard, *Management of Organizational Behavior: Utilizing Human Resources*, 4th ed. (Englewood Cliffs, NJ: Prentice-Hall, 1982).

33. Claude L. Graeff, "The Situational Leadership Theory: A Critical View," *Academy of Management Review*, vol. 8, no. 2 (1983): 287.

34. Charles N. Greene, "The Reciprocal Nature of Influence Between Leader and Subordinates," *Journal of Applied Psychology*, vol. 60 (1975): 187–193.

35. J. R. P. French and B. Raven, "The Bases of Social Power," in D. Cartwright and A. F. Zander, eds., *Group Dynamics*, 3rd ed. (New York: Harper & Row, 1968): 259–269.

36. K. Sheley and M. E. Shaw, "Social Power: To Use or Not to Use?" *Bulletin of the Psychonomic Society*, vol. 13, no. 4 (April 1979): 257–260.

37. M. Mulder and H. Wilke, "Participation and Power Equalization," *Organizational Behavior and Human Performance*, vol. 5 (1970): 430–448.

38. R. E. Spekman, "Influence and Information: An Exploratory Investigation of the Boundary Role Person's Basis of Power," *Academy of Management Journal*, vol. 22 (1979): 104–117.

39. A. Litman, G. Fontaine, and B. H. Raven, "Consequences of Social Power and Causal Attribution for Compliance as Seen by Power-holder and Target," *Personality and Social Psychology*, vol. 14, no 1 (April 1978): 260–264.

40. R. J. Myers, "Fear, Anger, and Depression in Organizations: A Study of the Functional Consequences of Power" (dissertation, St. John's University, 1977), *Dissertation Abstracts International—The Humanities and Social Sciences*, vol. 39, no. 7, 4530 (January 1979).

41. J. Pfeffer, "Power and Resource Allocation in Organizations," in B. M. Staw and G. R. Salancik, eds., *New Directions in Organizational Behavior* (Chicago: St. Clair Press, 1977).

42. M. Patchen, "The Locus and Basis of Influence on Organizational Decisions," *Organizational Behavior and Human Performance*, vol. 11 (1974): 195–221.

43. J. P. Kotter, "Power, Dependence, and Effective Management," *Harvard Business Review* (July–August 1977): 125–136.

44. Kotter, ibid.; and G. Strauss, "Tactics of Lateral Relationship: The Purchasing Agent," *Administrative Science Quarterly*, vol. 7, no. 2 (1962): 166–167.

45. Gerald R. Salancik and Jeffrey Pfeffer, "The Bases and Use of Power in Organizational Decision Making: The Case of a University," *Administrative Science Quarterly* 19 (1974): 453–473.

46. Many possible definitions exist in the literature. See H. D. Lasswell, *The Analysis of Political Behavior: An Empirical Approach* (London: Routhedge & Kegan Raul, 1949): 7; and T. Burns, "Micropolitics: Mechanism of Institutional Change," *Administrative Science Quarterly*, vol. 6 (1961): 257–281.

47. R. H. Miles, *Macro Organizational Behavior* (Santa Monica, CA: Goodyear Publishing Company, 1980): 155.

48. Based on a case presented in G. Cavanagh, D. Moberg, and M. Velasquez, "The Ethics of Organizational Politics," *Academy of Management Review*, vol. 6, no. 3 (1981): 363–374.

49. R. W. Allen, D. L. Madison, L. W. Porter, P. A. Renwick, and B. T. Mayes, "Organizational Politics: Tactics and Characteristics of Its Actors," *California Management Review* (Fall 1979): 77–83.

50. M. Velasquez, D. J. Moberg, and G. F. Cavanagh, "Organizational Statesmanship and Dirty Politics: Ethical Guidelines for the Organizational Politician," *Organizational Dynamics* (Autumn 1983): 65–80.

51. T. J. Peters and R. H. Waterman, Jr., *In Search of Excellence* (New York: Harper & Row, 1982).

52. E. Wojahn, "Management by Walking Away," INC. (October 1983): 68–76.

53. Ibid.

54. Jack Falvey, "The Benefits of Working with the Best Workers," *The Wall Street Journal*, 11 May 1983.

55. Stephen Fox, "Professor Identifies Traits That Make Great Boss," *Associated Press*, 21 November 1982.

RECOMMENDED READINGS

John P. Kotter, "What Effective General Managers Really Do," *Harvard Business Review* (November–December 1982): 156–167.

This article is adapted from Kotter's book, *The General Manager*. It presents the results of actually watching general managers over an extended period of time. In contrast to what many theorists feel is a very systematic behavior pattern, Kotter found that effective managers are very unsystematic, very informal, and more reactive about running an organization.

Gary A. Yukl, *Leadership in Organizations* (Englewood Cliffs, NJ: Prentice-Hall, 1981).

This book presents various views of leadership from trait, behavioral, and situational research. It also covers other more pragmatic aspects of leadership, such as participation, delegation, and decision-making.

Fred E. Fiedler, "How Do You Make Leaders More Effective?" *Organizational Dynamics* (Autumn 1972): 2–8.

Fiedler argues that to improve leader effectiveness, the organization should change the job so that it matches the leader's style. He contends that a leader's style changes slowly, while the situation can be more quickly altered to produce the desired match.

Robert W. Allen and **Lyman W. Porter,** *Organizational Influence Processes* (Glenview, IL: Scott, Foresman, 1983).

This book presents a variety of articles focusing on the power and influence processes in an organization. The material looks at downward, lateral, and upward influence.

Hill Enterprises

When Hill Enterprises was founded ten years ago, its total assets consisted of one automatic lathe, one contract worth $2,200, and one employee. The employee was Robert Hill, president and sole owner, then twenty-one years old. He had one objective in forming Hill Enterprises—that of retiring with a million dollars in his personal bank account at the age of forty.

According to Robert Hill, the reasons Hill Enterprises was able to survive the first difficult years were his considerable abilities as a machinist, which he had developed during the nine years he was employed in the machine shop of a large manufacturing company, his willingness to work long and hard hours, and his knack for raising money for working capital. During the early years, he would customarily spend his evenings working at the plant and his days visiting banks, insurance companies, and personal friends in an attempt to acquire sufficient funds to continue operations. For the most part he was successful, and though he often had the feeling he was a bit overextended financially, his business continued to grow and show profits.

Potential employees who were willing to accept these conditions found that Mr. Hill meant what he said. Loyalty to the common cause was based on the number of hours of overtime a person put in. This high amount of overtime had two effects. First, Hill Enterprises was able to give its employees approximately double the take-home pay they could receive from other companies, thus reinforcing the promises Mr. Hill had made concerning financial rewards to individual employees. Second, even though the company was constantly growing and the work force was increasing in size, the large amount of overtime kept the number of employees to a minimum so that Mr. Hill had continuing face-to-face contact with them and could maintain a personal relationship with each of the employees.

As Hill Enterprises grew and progressed, Robert Hill continued his earlier pattern of operations. He set a grueling pace, continuing to work long hours late into the night and spending a large share of his time during the day attempting to raise additional working capital and financial support. He often held important conferences at 5:00 A.M. in order that supervisory personnel would be free to handle their regular work during the "normal" working hours. Mr. Hill seemed to enjoy the pace and pressure and seemed especially to like his frequent contact with the employees. His office consisted of a single beat-up desk in one corner of the production area. Thus he was immediately available to all to help with any problem, whether it was a production problem or a personal one. Many employees availed themselves of his accessibility and while he was in the plant he seemed to be constantly talking with one employee or another, either in his "office" or on the production floor. Often he would report on the progress of his personal bank account to the employees, a practice they enjoyed tremendously, as Mr. Hill would very vividly recount his financial manipulations.

The employees of Hill Enterprises responded to the situation by working long hours in poor en-

Source: Adapted from *Organizational Behavior: A Management Approach* by Harry R. Knudson and C. Patrick Fleenor (Winthrop Pub. Co., 1978): 263–268. Copyright 1976, Professor Harry R. Knudson, Graduate School of Business, University of Washington.

vironmental surroundings and under the constant pressure of schedules and production deadlines. Hill Enterprises at this stage had set up operations in a deserted store building, and physical working conditions were considerably less attractive than those of competing organizations.

Under the constant pressures to meet schedules, tempers were often short. The accepted way to reduce individual tension was to "fly off the handle." It was the privilege of the president as well as of any employee, and it was a privilege that was often used. Robert Hill had the reputation of being able to deliver the best "dressing-down" of anyone in the organization, and it was not unusual for an employee to comment on the skill with which Mr. Hill had "chewed him out." This give-and-take was not all one-sided, and employees regardless of their position felt free to talk back to Mr. Hill or the other supervisors, and often did. And because this was the accepted way to decrease tension and to achieve action, the incident over which an outburst occurred was immediately forgotten. The employees seemed to enjoy their existence with Hill Enterprises and underneath the tension and pressure each employee felt that he or she was capable and was contributing to the goals of the company.

But some nine years after the start of Hill Enterprises, as Robert Hill had often feared, his intricate financial dealings caught up with him. His considerably expanded enterprises were without adequate working capital and he was forced to bring in a new partner, Donald Robbins, who was willing to invest sufficient funds to keep the company going.

One faction of the work force thought that the arrival of Robbins was just another of Mr. Hill's seemingly endless manipulations for capital. The other faction believed that his arrival was the harbinger of the end of Hill Enterprises as they had known it. They sensed that it would be only a matter of time until Mr. Hill would lose control of the internal workings of his organization and that the high wages and overtime pay would be cut.

The immediate influence of the arrival of Robbins upon the operations of Hill Enterprises was negligible. Operations continued at the same hectic pace, and Mr. Hill's personal activities did not

appear to be appreciably different. He maintained his old "office" and was still available to help out on any particular problems that arose. However, as time passed, it became more and more obvious to the employees that Robbins demanded a great deal of Mr. Hill's time. Although he retained his desk in the corner of the shop for awhile, Mr. Hill soon set up new headquarters in the more plush surroundings of a new building that had been constructed adjacent to the shop facilities to house the sales and office activities of Hill Enterprises. Because of his new location and the demands made upon him by his new partner, Mr. Hill was unable to spend as much time with the employees in the shop as before. In addition, Robbins' apparent aloofness to the workings and problems of the production shop and its employees created resentment.

The employees noticed that shortly after Mr. Hill had moved his office, the time-honored method of "blowing off steam" as a prelude to constructive effort on a problem became more and more ineffectual. Mr. Hill was no longer around to arbitrate really serious disagreements and his customary "O.K., now that we've got that out of our system, let's get to work," was absent. While blowing off steam was still an accepted practice, an element of bitterness seemed to be apparent in such outbursts that occurred. This bitterness and a sense of resentment toward Robbins permeated the atmosphere of the shop, with the result that many employees adopted a fatalistic attitude both toward the future of Hill Enterprises and their own personal futures.

In this atmosphere a second major organizational change occurred. A new man with the title of "Works Manager" arrived to fill the vacuum created by Mr. Hill's forced attention to matters other than production. This man, Rod Bellows, was the son-in-law of Donald Robbins, the new partner. He was thirty-five years old, a graduate of Eastern State College, and had had ten years' experience as an industrial engineer with a large chemical company. He was hired by Hill Enterprises on the insistence of Donald Robbins, who felt that the production activities were inefficient and excessively costly. His appearance on the scene came as a surprise to the shop and production employees.

During his first few days with the company, employees often saw Bellows and Robbins in the production area. The men appeared to be conversing in earnest, and often pointed and gestured toward machines or individuals. Bellows continually took notes on a large clipboard. During this period, none of the employees was spoken to by either of the two men. The shop employees had not had official indication of Bellows' duties, responsibilities, or position in the company. They knew only by rumor that he was the new works manager.

Bellows made the following comments about his responsibilities at Hill Enterprises shortly after his arrival: "This company has a tremendous potential and an unlimited future. Robert Hill is a dynamic individual with great skills. He has certainly been successful to date. Mr. Robbins and I will complement these skills and make the company even more successful. Mr. Robbins has the ability and experience to do some long-range planning and get our financial affairs in order, and I have the responsibility and ability to make our production activities more effective. A major part of the problem as I see it is that we use our time inefficiently in production. We don't have any effective scheduling procedures or channels of responsibility and authority, with the result that the employees spend a lot of time bickering and conversing about things with which they should not really be concerned. Their job is to get out the production. Our job is to organize the production activities in such a way that this can be done at least cost. The whole basis for the situation is that in the past Hill Enterprises has been small enough to be controlled effectively by one man. Now, however, we are no longer really a small firm and we cannot continue to operate like one. I have some ideas and some techniques that I plan to initiate that I think will increase the effectiveness and efficiency of our production operations by 50 percent in very short order."

At the beginning of his third week as works manager, Bellows issued a series of changes in procedures to the production employees. Without exception these changes were made without con-sulting any of the workers in the shop. All of them were issued in typewritten memos, a new practice that many of the employees felt was unnecessary and undesirable because of the effectiveness with which they felt the existing informal channels of communications had been used. The extent of the changes requested by Bellows was significant, ranging from changes in production scheduling techniques to changes in working conditions for individual employees. One employee estimated that to carry out these written orders, hundreds of additional work-hours "which were just not available" would be required.

Bellows' personal contacts with individual employees were limited and consisted mostly of quick and forceful answers to any questions or problems that might be brought to his attention. Many of his decisions seemed to indicate a lack of awareness of the capacity of the tools used in the production processes. For example, because of his insistence on machine speedups for certain operations, several expensive tools were ruined and valuable production time was lost. After having received several memos from Bellows that they considered unreasonable, one small group of employees had christened him with the nickname "The Fool." As the number of written memos coming from Bellows' office increased, the resentment toward these memos became more apparent, and a strong adverse reaction to his presence was evident on the part of the production employees.

Some four months after Bellows' arrival, cooperation between the "oldtimers"—both the supervisors and the workers—hit a new high. Unfortunately, this "cooperation" was used to undermine any and all changes that the new works manager attempted to put into effect. As new orders and procedures originated from Bellows' office, the employees carried out the orders to the letter of the law because, in many cases, they afforded a justified means of wasting time and reducing production. Bellows gave no indication that he was aware of this situation.

Bellows also attempted to establish formal channels of communication within the production operations, for he felt that much needless discussion and confusion was in existence under the present system. He issued several organization charts that described the "approved" way in which communication was to be effected within the organization. These charts were uniformly ignored by the employees, who continued to rely on the previously accepted informal channels of action. It even became an unwritten policy that all information channeled to Bellows under the new system was censored and reviewed by the person or persons to be affected before it was sent to Bellows.

Yet in this new atmosphere the old loyalties to Robert Hill did not fade entirely. The office manager, the plant superintendent, and several foremen attempted to get his ear from time to time to inform him that things were not running smoothly. Mr. Hill was always surprised by such comments, and he attempted to reassure the employees by making remarks such as "It will take some time for us to get to know each other well, but I'm sure that everything will be straightened out in a little while." In addition, he made several trips to the production area, talking with employees individually and asking them to give Bellows a chance, as it was important for the success of Hill Enterprises.

Morale seemed to improve for a short while until Bellows issued a statement stating that no one in the plant was to bother the president with plant problems without consulting with him, Bellows, first. Shortly after this statement was issued by Bellows, Robert Hill again made several trips to the production area, talking to individual workers and attempting to explain that other problems prevented his spending as much time in the shop as he previously had. In several instances, he started to report on the status of his personal bank account. Noting that this was not too well received, however, he discontinued this practice.

As time passed, the situation continued to deteriorate. Many of Bellows' acts and orders seemed to be in direct contradiction to Mr. Hill's former policies and procedures. The individuals affected were confused as to which procedures to follow. Attempts to have Bellows clarify his orders either left the questioner more confused than before or were greeted with a curt, "We don't have time to discuss that. It is perfectly clear. Just read the memo." Within a few months, many of the personnel talked of leaving to look for other employment and a few did. Nine months after Bellows had taken the position of works manager approximately 25 percent of the production force had taken new jobs. The morale among those remaining was poor and a significant increase in product rejects was experienced. But during the same period both Robbins and Bellows felt that important advances had been made in "cleaning up" production activities and that the company was "looking better all the time."

Questions

1. Describe Mr. Hill's style of leadership. Mr. Robbins' style of leadership. Mr. Bellows' style of leadership.
2. Did Mr. Hill's style change over time? How do you explain the reasons for the change?
3. Would you use the theory of "walking around" or "walking away" to describe Mr. Hill's style initially?
4. How would you describe Mr. Hill's "chewing people out" in terms of leadership style?
5. What would you do if you were Mr. Bellows coming to work for this firm?

CHAPTER SIX
Group Dynamics

OUTLINE

FUNDAMENTALS OF GROUP DYNAMICS

Nature of a Group
Group Characteristics
Group Development
Summary of Key Concepts

MANAGERIAL APPLICATIONS

Groups for Creativity
Breaking the Chains of Command
Groups for Company Support
A Group Influence on a Member
A Good and a Bad Group
The Soul of a Group

OBJECTIVES

- Describe a group

- Identify several types of groups

- Define ambient and discretionary stimuli

- List the five characteristics of a group

- Discuss the various roles group members can play and the effect of these on the group

- Describe the issue of a two-edged sword for conformity

- Explain the stages of group development

- List the major characteristics of an effective group

- Identify and discuss the managerial applications of working with groups

Caught Napping: Secret Bedrooms on Factory's Night Shift

It seems that factory workers believe that night is for sleeping even when it's at work. At least that's what workers at an electronics factory believed, because for more than 16 years they slept through their night shifts in secret bedrooms built into the walls and ceilings.

A court hearing was told that outside contractors working in the factory found electrical cables they could not account for and traced them up through the ceiling and behind sliding hatches to their source—bedside reading lights. In hidden compartments they found fitted mattresses, blankets, pillows, sheets, bedside lamps, and an alarm clock. Yet no one was ever caught sleeping. It was guessed that some kind of alarm system warned the workers of approaching management.

As a result of the hearing, three foremen lost their jobs even though they appealed to the Bristol Industrial Tribunal to get their jobs back. "I thought if we admitted to the management that we knew about it we would have lost our jobs. There was nothing we could do," said one of the former foremen, George Cooper. "We just had to let it carry on." Sleeping on the job was already a 14-year-old tradition among nightshift maintenance crews when Mr. Cooper joined Plessey Semiconductor plant in western England two years ago.

Management did have some suspicions. An internal investigation was being conducted at the time of the discovery because it was noticed that tasks that should have been carried out at night were being left for the day shift. Management claimed that even if the foremen were not sleeping themselves, it was their responsibility to make it known to the management what was going on.[1]

FUNDAMENTALS OF GROUP DYNAMICS

In the preceding incident, we cannot help but wonder how such behavior was tolerated for so long by the foremen. What forces are acting in this situation that have such a powerful effect on the workers and the foremen? How can the night shift behave this way without the day shift complaining about the additional work? How could the workers control each other so that no one would mention the practice to outsiders and thereby risk exposing it?

Nature of a Group

An understanding of group processes is important in dealing with human behavior in an organization. Since we are all involved in groups, understanding group processes is also important in functioning effectively as individuals. All organizations involve interrelationships among groups within the organization and with groups in other organizations.

Individuals seldom, if ever, behave without being influenced by the groups to which they belong. Most people spend the majority of their lives involved with groups—family groups, social groups, professional groups, civic groups, and work groups. For many people, individual success depends on their ability to function effectively within groups. Yet, even though they are very important, the interpersonal relationships that develop in a group are extremely complex and are not completely understood.

Perhaps the most famous series of studies of group behavior began as quite something else. Roethlisberger and Dickson began a series of studies in the late 1920s at the Hawthorne assembly plant of the Western Electric Company.[2]

The experiments were designed to determine the effect of lighting on the efficiency of industrial workers. Experimental and control groups were identified, and illumination levels were varied for the experimental groups. Constant illumination levels were maintained for the control groups.

In one experiment a test group was submitted to increasing levels of illumination. Production increased in the test group—but it also increased in the control group! Another test group was subjected to decreasing light levels, finally to only three foot candles.[3]

Output went up! Output also increased in the control group. In another experiment illumination was decreased to .06 foot candles, approximately that of moonlight. Finally production began to fall off, perhaps because workers had difficulty seeing their work.

It became obvious to the researchers that something complex and unexpected had intervened in their lighting study. In an attempt to discover what this was, a study was designed that segregated a group of five workers in a room where the conditions of work could be carefully controlled. At specified intervals changes in working conditions were made and the group was studied for a full five years. Thorough records were kept of things like temperature and humidity, worker diets and sleeping habits. Output (the assembly of electrical relays) was also carefully measured. A thorough statistical analysis of literally tons of data found *no* significant relation between physical conditions of work and output.

But after the experiment had been underway for two years, the researchers knew that there were some other variables of interest. In making changes in the work arrangement the investigators often sought the advice and opinions of the workers. In this process, almost all of the common shop practices were altered. By the very act of designing the conditions for the test, the experimenters had changed the social situation in the room. It was those social changes that best explained the variations in productivity, not the level of illumination.

In Roethlisberger's words, "If one experiments on a stone, the stone does not know it is being experimented upon—all of which makes it simple for people experimenting on stones. But if a human being is being experimented upon, he is likely to know it. Therefore, his attitudes toward the experiment and toward the experimenters become very important factors in determining his responses to the situation."[4] The phenomenon described by Roethlisberger has come to be known as "the Hawthorne effect."

The importance of employee attitudes had been clearly established, thus the researchers changed their research focus and began interviewing employees about their likes and dislikes and what was important to them. Eventually, thousands of employees wre interviewed. These interviews established that the feelings of workers about their jobs have a strong impact upon their behavior.

The social aspects of work were demonstrated clearly in another part of the Hawthorne plant. A group of fourteen workers involved in three different jobs was observed and it was noted that the group set definite norms related to output, communication with supervisors, and certain acceptable modes of behavior toward other group members. As a result of these observations the researchers began to focus on the social functions performed by groups in the workplace. The following are some of the major conclusions developed from this later research:

1. Behavior of workers can not be understood apart from their feelings.
2. Manifestations of feelings takes different forms and is difficult to recognize or study.
3. Manifestation of feelings does not stand alone. It can only be understood in terms of the total situation.
4. The notion of the "rational economic human" is simplistic and of little value in explaining work behavior.

Roethlisberger summarized the Hawthorne studies: "What is meant is that the worker is not an isolated, atomic individual; he is a member of a group, or of groups. Within each of these groups the individuals have feelings and sentiments toward each other, which bind them together in collaborative effort. Moreover, these collective sentiments can, and do, become attached to every item and object in the industrial environment—even to output. Material goods, output, wages, hours of work, and so on, cannot be treated as things in themselves. Instead, they must be interpreted as carriers of social value."[5]

From our vantage point of this century's ninth decade, the observations of the Hawthorne researchers are "old hat." But at the time of the studies the results were revolutionary. People had never been studied in such fashion before, and the scope of the studies remains impressive to this day. The results of the studies inspired an enormous amount of subsequent research into the functioning of human groups, became the foundation of the "human relations" movement, and irrevocably changed the practice of management.

What Is a Group?   While appreciating some of the history behind the study of groups, we still need to develop some basic concepts to understand the dynamics of group behavior. Suppose you encounter a construction project that is tying up traffic and you get out of your car to join the other trapped motorists watching the mess. Or suppose you are in line for several hours waiting to purchase some concert tickets. Are these examples of groups? Not in the way behavioral scientists define the term. According to their definition, "a group is a collection of individuals who interact with each other on a regular basis and see themselves to be mutually dependent with respect to the attainment of one or more common goals.[6] Neither the individuals at the traffic jam nor those waiting in the line for concert tickets would meet all of the conditions of this definition. They would be considered aggregations or collections of individuals, but not groups.

The term *group* is generally restricted to that number of individuals who can be aware of and influence each other. There is no absolute restriction on the size of a group. Under the right set of circumstances, fifty individuals in a large drama class might perceive themselves as a group, but, as a general guide, twenty persons is commonly used as an upper limit for group size. The reason for this is that beyond this number, interaction, mutual influence, and coordination becomes more difficult, and the group breaks into smaller subgroups.

The behavioral science view of a group implies that the individual members of a group are psychologically aware of each other.[7] This psychological awareness extends the preceding definition one more step by imposing the additional criterion that group members must be aware of one another's needs and potential resource contributions.

Although the delayed motorists at the aforementioned construction site do not meet the definitional requirements of a group, what would happen if an accident occurred at the site, trapping some construction workers? A plausible scenario would have the observers organize themselves as a rescue team. A leader or leaders would emerge and activities would be assumed by or assigned to individuals. There would be interaction with other observers, mutual dependence to achieve the goal of freeing the trapped workers, and psychological awareness of the other rescue team members.

Thus a collection of individuals that is not a group can become a group to deal with an environmental change. At the end of the rescue operation, it is likely that the group would then dissolve, with members driving away pehaps not knowing the names of the compatriots with whom they had shared an intense experience. As the force of the change in the environment dissipates, the conditions that caused the group to form disappear, and it disbands.

Types of Groups   Within an organization the most important distinction regarding groups is whether a group is formal or informal. Employees become members of formal groups because they are assigned to them. Within these formal groups people are assigned positions such as foreman or chairperson. All members of a particular group share similar activities, skills, responsibilities, and assigned goals. They recognize that they are part of the work group, and the group exists as long as the task or goals exist. Examples of formal groups are a research team, a board of directors, a production committee, and a market research group. Some formal groups, such as a committee or a task force, are temporary in nature. They are created for a specific purpose and typically are disbanded with its accomplishment. Temporary work groups usually have a chairperson who is accountable for results.

Informal groups are groups that emerge naturally from the interaction of the members, who may or may not have purposes that are related to or congruent with the goals of the organization. Often the very nature of the organization has a significant influence on the formation of informal groups. The departmentalization, physical layout, type of production process, personal practices, or management climate of an organization may facilitate the formation of informal groups in a typical organization. Informal groups may emerge to fulfill friend and affiliation needs or to counteract some threat that group members have in common. An informal lunch group may discuss problems members share on the job and how they might resolve those problems. At coffee breaks, at lunch time, or after work, informal groups may also form to fulfill interests or friendship needs. Common characteristics, such as age, political beliefs, religious interests, or recreational interests, may result in the formation of interest or friendship groups. But groups may also form simply because people are located close to each other. At times the goals of informal groups may run counter to those of the formal organization. For example, a crew of young waiters and waitresses may be more interested in having a relaxed atmosphere at work than in providing good service to the customers.

If an individual feels thwarted by a company policy or supervisory practice, he or she may form or seek out an informal group for comfort or action to counter the practice. Thus, groups can provide an important support function.

Group Influence on Members   Groups can vary in the degree of impact on the attitudes and behavior of individual group members. In very highly cohesive work groups, for example, individuals place high value upon their group membership. In such cases, individuals conform to group norms in part simply to maintain their membership in the group. One way to understand how a group influences its members is to examine those aspects—stimuli—that a group controls in the work environment. Stimuli may include people, furniture, job assignments, equipment, financial resources, and promotional opportunities.

Hackman classified these stimuli as either ambient or discretionary.[8] Ambient stimuli are those conditions that are automatically present for group members and are available to individuals because of their membership in the group. For example, individuals may like their fellow group members and, consequenly, want to maintain group membership so they can interact with people they like. Other ambient stimuli relate to the various rewards that may accompany membership in a group—extra compensation, status and prestige, exposure to influential people, or the possibility of getting away from the day-to-day routine of one's regular job. Finally, the group's task itself can be an important ambient stimulus. If members find their task interesting or important, they will value being a part of and staying in the group in order to work on that task.

Discretionary stimuli are transmitted to individuals by group members on a selective basis. Just being a group member does not guarantee receiving discretionary stimuli; their receipt is contingent on the behavior of the group member. Examples of discretionary stimuli include a supportive environment, social acceptance, social rejection, and information possessed only by group members. For instance, a member may selectively distribute information to other members he or she likes or to those who can reciprocate with other information.

Groups utilize discretionary stimuli to educate and socialize members, to exert pressure for conformity to group norms, to facilitate task accomplishment, to satisfy different needs of individual members, to enhance the status of specific members, to create diversity, and also to encourage tolerance for deviance from group norms.[9]

Another method of understanding a group's influence on members was suggested by Kelman.[10] He has identified three processes of social influence in groups: compliance, identification, and internalization. The antecedents and consequences of the three processes differ.

Compliance occurs when an individual allows a group or another person to influence him or her in the hope there will be a favorable reaction from the influencer. The favorable reaction may take the form of a specific reward such as a compliment. Compliance does not result in changes in private beliefs. The individual complies because it results in a satisfying social effect, and will probably not engage in the same compliance behavior when out of sight of the influencing parties.

Identification occurs when one adopts a specific behavior because it is associated with a role relationship that forms part of one's self-image. To maintain self-definition as a group member, one must typically behave along certain lines that meet the expectations of fellow group members. Adolescent "in-groups" provide many examples of the identification process. Modes of dress, manner, and use of language tend to be specific and rigorously adhered to by group members even when they are not with the group. Identification differs from compliance in that the individual actually believes in the adopted opinions and actions. The influencing agent (the group) does not have to be present for the behavior to occur. Unlike compliance, the individual is not concerned primarily with pleasing the group, but is concerned with meeting the group's expectations for role performance, because such behavior is part of the individual's self-image.

Internalization occurs when one accepts influence because it is congruent with one's value system. Both compliance and identification behavior results in rewards. But internalization behavior is intrinsically rewarding and, in fact, may be provided by very specific behavior demanded in training by elite volunteer military strike forces, such as the Army Rangers or Navy Seals.

Note that the modes of socialization are not mutually exclusive. A group may exercise more than one process of influence upon a given individual.

Kelman hypothesized that the source of the influencing agent's power determined the mode of identification. If the group can supply or withhold means needed by the individual for achievement of goals, the influence will tend to take the form of compliance. To the extent that membership in the group is attractive and desirable, influence will tend toward identification. To the extent that the group is seen to represent creditability and "truth," influence will tend toward internalization.[11]

From this short discussion it becomes quite obvious that group dynamics has definite implications for management. A manager must understand that a group can either support or hinder the accomplishment of organizational objectives. For example, a positive work group could help a manager deal with an employee who has had some negative experiences with the organization gain a different perspective. A positively oriented work group can do a very effective job of training new employees. On the other hand, a manager may have to seriously consider disbanding a work group that becomes detrimental to the unit's work. But this act may not disband the informal group, which can still exist to frustrate the manager. In such an instance, the manager should consider helping the group solve the problems causing its dissatisfaction.

Group Characteristics

What other variables can influence the behavior or performance of a group member? We have already looked at the impact of ambient and discretionary stimuli on individual member attitudes and behavior. We now consider six other characteristics that influence groups and group members and therefore need to be understood by managers.

Size   As a group's size increases, the interaction between individuals becomes more difficult, and it may become harder for members to influence each other and to see how individual members contribute to the common purpose. In general, the research on group size shows the following:

- Very small groups (two to four members) show more tension, agreement, and asking of opinions, while larger groups show more tension release and giving of information. In smaller groups it is more important that everyone get along with one another, whereas in larger groups members can express more differences of opinion.
- Groups with an even number of members have a greater difficulty in obtaining a majority and, therefore, create a state of more tension.
- The relationship between group size and performance appears to be inconclusive and may depend more on the type of task being performed.
- Members of smaller groups report greater satisfaction than those in larger groups. Members of small groups apparently have more freedom from psychological restrictions and thus are more satisfied.
- Turnover and absenteeism increase as the group gets larger, especially for blue-collar workers. It seems that, as the group size increases, the tasks become more specialized, and communications between members and between members and supervisors become poorer, which may lead to less satisfaction of higher-level needs. This does not seem to hold for white-collar workers because such workers seem to have more opportunities available to them outside of the group to satisfy their needs.[12]

As groups grow in size, more communication and coordination are required to realize the collective potential of the membership. Although it is difficult to pinpoint an ideal group size, and a manager should not attempt to build a group around some ideal size, it has been shown that for groups formed to solve problems the following occur:

Fewer than five members results in

- Fewer people to share task responsibilities
- More personal discussions
- More participation

More than seven members results in

- Fewer opportunities to participate
- More members' inhibitions
- Domination by aggressive members
- Tendency to split into subgroups[13]

While these findings argue for some smaller ideal group size, this must be weighed against the fact that increasing group size offers more ideas and other human resources to achieve the task of the group. The impact of a group size on the resources available and the effectiveness of a group's communication/coordination is a tradeoff that must be considered when staffing a committee or work group.

Cohesiveness   Cohesiveness refers to the amount of attractiveness of group members towards each other. Cohesiveness means there is unity in the group and members pull in the same direction.

There are differences in cohesiveness among groups of friends, sports groups, and work groups. In some groups cohesiveness is described as a group spirit or a team spirit. In other groups, members not only seem to lack team spirit, but even seem to dislike one another. Contrast the Japanese style of management, where there is a strong identity between the workers and the firm, and much of American industry, with its 9-to-5 punch-the-time-clock culture. Group cohesiveness can be increased or decreased under certain conditions.[14] To increase group cohesiveness the attractiveness of the group to group members must increase. This can occur under the following conditions:

- Individuals have the opportunity to gain prestige or status within the group.
- Group members are in a cooperative relationship rather than in competition with one another.
- Group members can fulfill more needs through participation in the group.
- An increase occurs in the prestige or status of the group in an organization.
- The group is attacked from the outside, causing members to deal with the external threat.

To decrease the cohesiveness of a group, the level of attractiveness of the group towards members must decrease. This can occur under the following conditions:

- Interpersonal conflict results from members' disagreements over ways to achieve group goals or solve group problems. (Members of highly cohesive groups may often have disagreements, but they try to settle them quickly.)
- Participation in the group results in an unpleasant experience for an individual.
- Membership places limits on the individual's participation in other individual or group activities outside the group.
- The evaluation of the group by outsiders who are respected becomes negative.
- Conditions exist in the group that prevent or restrict effective communication. Reduced communications may result if one or two members dominate group activities and prevent other members from participating.

While a cohesive group is good for its members, does that mean it's good for the manager and the organization too? Research answers that it depends on the group's performance norm.[15] A basic rule of group dynamics is that the more cohesive the group, the greater the conformity of members to group norms. When the performance norm is positive, high conformity has a very beneficial effect; when the norm is negative, however, high conformity can mean substantial undesirable results.

Norms   A group norm is a standard of behavior that is expected by members of a group. Norms are often referred to as "rules" that apply to group members.[16] When violated, they may be enforced with reprimands and other group sanctions. In the extreme, violation of group norms can result in social ostracism or expulsion of a member from the group.

Norms are developed within a group over time and serve two purposes. First, they identify what behavior is considered appropriate. Exhibiting appropriate behavior leads to group approval and respect. Second, norms define the limits of behavior for group members. As members approach these limits, they are likely to receive signals from other members that they are close to violating group norms. For example, a production unit may have a performance standard set by the industrial engineers of 400 units per day. But the group may establish its own production norm of 325 to 345 units per day. This norm is the expected output for all its members. If a new group member attempts to show his or her "stuff" and increase the number of units above 345, the other members may begin to behave in ways that thwart the new member's action and prevent the new member from reaching a higher number of units.

The more important a norm is to a group the more likely the group is to enforce the norm. Very important norms are termed pivotal norms, and acceptance of them is an essential requirement for group membership.[17] An example of a pivotal norm from the opening story in this chapter might be keeping the hidden locations for napping a secret. Less important norms are called peripheral norms; their violation does not result in loss of group membership, although some lesser

BOX 6–1

Group Norms Are Sometimes Stressful

Mark Bentlage is a Continental Airlines flight attendant. Prior to a strike against his employer Mr. Bentlage lived a "nice, routine life." After the strike was declared, his life became filled with uncertainty and even fear. The uncertainty and fear did not come from lack of income or job prospects, for Mr. Bentlage did not join his striking coworkers. He elected to cross the picket lines. In other words, he became a "scab."

His reward from striking peers consisted of threats and obscene language. He parked his car in a secret lot provided by Continental and asked a neighbor to watch his home while he was away.

The pressures placed on nonstrikers became intense. Some examples:

- Ground communication with a Continental plane was jammed by a mystery radio operator broadcasting the word scab.
- A flight attendant was spat upon and shoved when she crossed a picket line.
- Strikers took pictures of employees reporting to work.

Source: "Continental Air Workers Crossing Picket Lines Face Rising Hostility," *The Wall Street Journal* (11 October 1983): 35.

- Someone temporarily took over the radio frequency of a Continental flight during a landing approach.
- At some airports, hoping to avoid confrontations, the company loaded workers onto police-escorted buses that delivered them to flights at the runways.

Other pressures were much more subtle but probably just as intense. Workers reported frequent telephone calls from striking friends entreating the worker to join the strike. Continued resistance would generally result in cessation of the telephone calls, but at a high price. In the words of one employee: "Some of these people are my best friends, and they won't even talk to me. That really hurts."

Questions

1. Using the theory of norms, explain the behavior of the striking employees.
2. What would be the consequences for those employees who go back to work during the strike?
3. If you were a manager at Continental, what would you do concerning your employees once the strike is over?

penalty may be imposed by the group. An example of a peripheral norm could be the type of language or dress used by the group.

Roles Roles are the behaviors expected of those in particular positions in a group. In formal groups there are usually job or position descriptions that define behavioral expectations for specific positions. For example, leader workers or holders of specific kinds of positions, such as bank tellers, are expected to behave in certain ways because of the role of that position. Organizations often spend large amounts of money and other resources to train people to behave in ways consistent with that organization's role expectations. In most informal group situations, that is, when the group has not been established by the organization, role expectations are developed by the group members themselves and may never be formalized. They develop as a result of experiences and interactions in the group.

Most role behavior in groups can be classified into three categories: task-related, maintenance-related, and self-related behavior.[18] The following task-related roles are directed toward establishing and accomplishing the goals of the group:

- *Idea Initiator* proposes tasks or goals, defines problems, and suggests procedures or ideas for solving problems.
- *Information Seeker* requests facts, seeks information about a group concern, asks for expression of feelings, requests statements or estimates, solicits expressions of value, and seeks suggestions and ideas.
- *Information Giver* offers facts, provides information about group concern, states beliefs about matters before the group, and gives suggestions and ideas.
- *Coordinator* pulls together related ideas, restates suggestions after the group has discussed them, and offers a decision or conclusion for the group to consider.
- *Evaluator* helps assess the group's functioning and evaluates or questions the practicality, logic, or facts concerning suggestions by other group members.

Maintenance-related roles are directed toward the well-being, continuity, and development of the group. The following are various roles in this category:

- *Encourager* exudes friendliness, warmth, and responsiveness to others and encourages, supports, acknowledges, and accepts others' contributions.
- *Gatekeeper* helps keep communication channels open, facilitates everyone's participation, and suggests procedures that permit sharing of what members have to say.
- *Standard Setter* tests whether the group is satisfied with the way it is proceeding and points out explicit or implicit operating norms to see if they are desired.
- *Harmonizer* attempts to reconcile disagreements, reduces tension, and gets members to explore differences.
- *Group Observer* stays out of the group's activities and gives feedback on the progress of the group.
- *Follower* goes along in a passive manner and provides a friendly audience.

Self-related roles are oriented only to the individual needs of the members, often at the expense of the group. The following are examples of this category:

- *Blocker* acts very negatively and resists most movement that the group proposes.
- *Avoider* maintains distance from the other members and resists interacting with other group members.
- *Recognition Seeker* calls attention to self, boasts about what he or she does or can do, and tries to prevent being placed in an inferior position.
- *Dominator* asserts authority by manipulatng the group or certain individuals, by using flattery or asserting a superior status or right to attention, and by interrupting others' contributions.

Effective group functioning rests on a group's ability to utilize and balance both the task-related and maintenance-related roles as the group accomplishes its tasks.

Conformity Conformity is the degree to which group members adhere to the rules and practices outlined for group members. Conformity in groups is a two-edged sword. Groups need to have a certain amount of conformity to function effectively, yet excessive pressure for conformity can undermine the group's ability to achieve individual or organizational objectives. Either too little or too much pressure for conformity can be harmful to a group's functioning.

The phenomenon of conformity is itself a neutral concept; the degree and type of conformity are the important considerations. On the one hand, it would be impossible to have an effective group without some behavioral norms, rules, and procedures. Imagine a newly formed project group that is told to produce a comprehensive plan to introduce a new product within a few days' time. This group would need time to figure out what the norms will be as well as what roles members will play. Unless these ground rules are defined there would be no pressure to conform, and the group would be unlikely to be able to perform its assigned task effectively.

On the other hand, pressure to conform can be excessive and the group can demand conformity in ways that have nothing to do with achieving individual or organizational objectives. For example, group pressure on members to socialize only with other group members or to dress in a certain way are not legitimate. Extreme pressures to conform can diminish individuality and ultimately the identity of those who compose the group, causing the group to become homogenous and lacking in a variety of skills and abilities.

A classic research study by Solomon Asch provides us with some insights about the nature of group conformity.[19] He gathered eight individuals in a room and showed them three lines of unequal length. He then showed them a fourth line and asked them to say which of the previous lines matched it in length (see Figure 6–1). Their answers were stated in the presence of the other participants. The experiment contained a series of these public judgements. In reality, the first seven participants were confederates of Asch and had been instructed to answer correctly several times in the beginning. In the last phase of the experiment, the answers given by the confederates were obviously wrong. But in about a third of

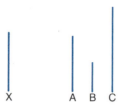

FIGURE 6-1
Asch's experiment: Confederates were instructed to make inaccurate statements
that line C was closest in length to line X.

the cases the unknowing participant agreed with the other group members. When
later explaining their choices, the individuals commented that they decided to go
along with the group even though they knew the answer was wrong.

Another classic study was conducted by Muzafer Sherif employing the
autokinetic effect.[20] It had been established in perceptual research that if a
subject looks at a fixed point of light in an otherwise dark room, the subject will
see the light "move." There are considerable individual differences in the amount
of perceived motion.

Sherif placed subjects separately in such a darkened room and had them
report an estimate of the fixed light's motion. Upon repeated tests each subject
established a narrow range or norm within which the estimates fell. Sherif
repeated the experiments but placed the subjects in the room in groups rather
than as individuals. He required the subjects to report aloud their estimates. The
individual ranges quickly converged to a group range that was peculiar to the
group. Sherif concluded, "The fact that the norm thus established is peculiar to
the group suggests that there is a factual psychological basis in the contentions of
social psychologists and sociologists who maintain that new and supra-individual
qualities arise in the group situations."[21]

In another variation of the study, members of a group were later placed in
the individual setting. As individuals these subjects carried the range and norm
set by the group in their prior setting to the new situation. These powerful
laboratory studies showed that individuals modify their perceptions to fit that of
the group, and that when a group norm has been set, it influences subsequent
individual perception.

Very little research has been done concerning the differences in performance or satisfaction as a function of the degree of conformity present in a group.
Some inferences, however, do seem justified. To start with, the relationship
between conformity and effectiveness would be moderated by the task and the
motivation of the members. A group whose members all conformed to one
opinion would probably not be able to effectively accomplish tasks requiring
diversity of opinions and ideas. Furthermore, the members might not be motivated to use their influence to further productivity. A manager must be keenly
aware of the effects of conformity and try to maintain a balance between some
individual initiative and group conformity.

Socialization   For our purposes, socialization is the process by which employees are transformed from outsiders to participating organizational and group members. As such, socialization is more than a group phenomenon, but much of the influence in the process is exerted by the work group. This concept is important to managers because the outcome of the socialization process can enhance or inhibit the attainment of organizational objectives. It is the same process by which organizational culture is established and passed from employee to employee and work group to work group.

One theorist sees the aim of socialization as inducing one to conform willingly to the ways of the groups to which one belongs.[22] Another states, "Organizational socialization is one such concept [by which people establish psychological contracts], referring to the fact that organizations have goals, norms, values, preferred ways of doing things which are usually taught systematically, though not necessarily overtly, to all new members."[23]

The actual process of socialization happens in stages. One researcher visualizes three stages: (1) getting in, (2) breaking in, and (3) settling in.[24] Getting in occurs before the prospective employee enters the organization. It involves the prospective employee acquiring information of what life in the organization is really like. Obviously, the organization can influence the results by the information it reveals to the individual. The second stage, breaking in, occurs when the individual enters the organization and becomes a member of a work group. The new employee is concerned with gaining acceptance, developing competence in doing the job, and establishing clear requirements for job and career performance. The organization can effectively influence this stage through a carefully designed orientation plan and structured training programs based on frequent performance evaluations. The final stage, settling in, concerns how the employee balances various conflicting demands—organizational life versus family life and work group expectations versus organizational expectations. The company can positively influence this stage through employee counseling, flexibility in scheduling and work assignments, and managing other conflicts that could stifle individual creativity and contribution to organizational objectives.

Socialization is a good example of an organizational behavior concept that spans several areas of study. It is included in this chapter because the socialization process is heavily influenced by the work group. But the results of socialization and the determination of what direction socialization takes have broader implications within the overall field of organizational behavior. The fact that the socialization process can be influenced by the supervisor and other organizational members outside the immediate work group means that areas such as communication and leadership are important to a full understanding of this phenomenon.

Group Development

Most of the research and interest in group processes has focused on what happens after the group has become an ongoing entity. This approach makes sense because the early developmental stage of most groups is short compared to the group's overall existence. A manager, however, must also be concerned about how the group develops because orderly development can mean later effectiveness. The manager must keep the group from getting caught in one phase of its development, which could prevent it from becoming as effective as it could be. Managers must therefore understand and appreciate the stages through which a group progresses.

Stages of Group Development   Most of us have been in some kind of group from its beginnings to its maturity. We have experienced the subtle influences that change the group from one in which we are at first uncomfortable to one in which we might seek comfort when the rest of our lives seem threatening. This is typical in the process of group development. Yet the changes are usually so subtle and the development so natural that we may be unaware of the process. We rarely try to understand or influence it.

To appreciate and understand this natural process we must identify the four stages a group encounters during its development.[25] They are orientation, differentiation, integration, and maturity. Table 6–1 summarizes the characteristics of each stage.

Stage 1—Orientation.   During the orientation stage individuals attempt to identify with the group in terms of a give-and-take relationship. They focus on identifying the task of the group, the ways the group will attempt to satisfy their individual needs, who is the leader, the initial ground rules for what is acceptable behavior, and how this group fits into the larger organization. During the orientation stage "the tone is often one of 'niceness' as members test boundaries and seek acceptance."[26] Members first introduce themselves and find out about the others in the group. They then start discussing the objectives of the group, how they will accomplish those objectives, who will do what and when, who the leader is, and what he or she is really like.

Stage 2—Differentiation.   The differentiation stage reflects the process of getting a better "feel" for the composition of the group and its task. It also is the point where members confront problems arising from the orientation stage and attempt to solve these problems. During this stage the group tries to nail down the means that will be used for accomplishing the group task and satisfying individual members' needs. The differentiation stage is also characterized by the increased potential for interpersonal conflict and competition because individuals bring to the group unresolved problems relating to different feelings toward authority, power, dependency, and leadership. For instance, group members who expect autonomy may rebel and become hostile if a leader attempts to exercise strong control. On the other hand, group members who prefer to have authoritarian leadership may be confused, anxious, and hostile if strong direction is not given. Coalitions of members may be formed to enhance the chances for need satisfaction. Unless these conflicts, issues, and problems are confronted and solved to

TABLE 6-1
Stages of group development

Stage	Group Activity
Orientation	Members get acquainted and size up the situation Initial task definition and identification of simple group processes First attempts to clarify member roles and authority/responsibility relationship Members try to determine how their skills will fit the group task and how the group activity will help group members Tentative decision on leadership and behavioral norms
Differentiation	Progress on identifying roles and norms Better feel for group task and for composition of group Formation of coalitions within the group to promote certain views and interests Emergence of interpersonal and subgroup conflicts Working through conflicts Emergence of competing values and norms for guiding behavior
Integration	Norms operating to obtain conformity Procedures established for coping with deviations from norms Work flow handled easily Development of cohesiveness among group members Danger of "groupthink," where loyalty to the group becomes a powerful group norm Members perceive themselves as a group
Maturity	Appreciation of group's need for stable norms, roles, goals, leadership, and work processes Appreciation of group's need to be flexible about changing demands on group Members' awareness of each other's strengths and weaknesses Acceptance of individual differences Tolerance of conflict over task-related issues, positive approach to conflict management Minimal interpersonal conflict

Source: From *Organizational Behavior: A Managerial Viewpoint* by Robert Albanese and David D. Van Fleet (1983): 259. Copyright © by CBS College Publishing. Reprinted by permission of the Dryden Press, CBS College Publishing.

the satisfaction of individual members, the group may never advance beyond this stage.

Stage 3—Integration. The integration stage benefits from the groping and conflict of the prior stage. During integration, problems are resolved as members are able to evaluate the issues involved with their tasks and the frustrations they experience in performing the tasks. Open discussions provide the mechanism for understanding the problems and working out solutions. The interpersonal relationships within the group are marked by increasing cohesion, sharing of ideas, providing and getting feedback, and exploring ideas and actions related to the task at hand. One danger of the integration stage is that members can become enchanted by the group's cohesiveness, which can encourage "groupthink" and discourage those constructive variations from group norms that are essential to creative and effective behavior in the group. See Table 6–2 for a description of groupthink and how to prevent it.

Stage 4—Maturity. The final stage of group development is maturity. Maturity in the life of a group refers to the group members' integration of the needs for both flexibility and stability. A mature group recognizes the necessary role of a stable system of norms, standards, and other consistencies in regulating the behavior of individual members. At the same time, a mature group remains flexible enough that it can adapt to changing tasks and other contingencies it must face as it completes its objectives. One sign of a mature group is its ability to accept ideas and even individuals from outside the original group and to integrate both into its ongoing activities.

Groups vary in their ability to progress through the stages of development due to their own characteristics and situational factors. Rapid progress can be expected for groups with mature and competent members who are well motivated toward group objectives. Vice versa, members who have strong internal conflicts about authority, status, power, or relationships with others tend to retard group

TABLE 6–2
Groupthink

Symptoms	Prevention Actions
1. Illusions of the group as invulnerable	1. Leader encourages open expression of doubt
2. Rationalizing away data that disconfirms assumptions and beliefs	2. Leader accepts criticism of his or her opinions
3. Unquestioned belief in group's inherent morality	3. Higher status members offer opinions last
4. Stereotyping competitors as weak, evil, stupid, and so on.	4. Get recommendations from similar group
5. Direct pressure on deviants to conform	5. Periodically divide into subgroups
6. Self-censorship by members	6. Members to get reaction from outsiders
7. Illusion of unanimity (silence equals consent)	7. Invite outsiders to join discussion periodically
8. Self-appointed "mindguards"—protecting group from disconfirming data	8. Assign someone the role of "Devil's Advocate"

Source: Adapted from Irving L. Janis, *Groupthink,* Second edition, copyright © 1982 Houghton Mifflin Company. Adapted with permission.

growth. Members whose personal anxieties inhibit their open communication and trust of others may also retard growth. Leaders who practice tight group control will encounter conflict as the group moves beyond the orientation stage. If these leaders persist in demanding tight control, the group will be unable to progress further. Research studying the effects of leadership style on the rate of development of training groups found that groups developed more rapidly with nondirective leaders than with directive leaders.[27]

To develop, groups must maintain a stable membership for a period of time. The environment of the group must provide stability and security for its members. Insecurity because of threatening managerial, organizational, or economic conditions creates anxieties that inhibit growth. The prevailing managerial philosophy of the organization is important. If top management emphasizes strong authoritarian control, groups, even at the lowest level in the organization, will tend to follow this model and remain in the first stages of development.

For these reasons, management must recognize the complexity involved as groups develop and realize that it is a process to manage in the same sense as managing the development of an individual.

Characteristics of Effective Groups   We determined in the last two sections that groups usually face some difficult issues as they develop into mature and effective work groups. In this section, we focus more on some of the characteristics of those groups that reach a sufficient level of maturity to warrant being called effective—those that have met the social and task needs of group members and completed the organizational tasks assigned. Remember that the following characteristics are not mutually exclusive in nature. Effective groups not only exhibit most of these characteristics, but the characteristics are additive and complementary in nature.

Clarity of focus.   Effective groups are clear on the broad purposes for which the group was formed. This may be the development of a new product application or a restructuring of a nonprofitable division. The group knows why it exists and what it is trying to do. This characteristic can be termed as "purposing—that continuous stream of actions by an organization's formal leadership that has the effect of inducing clarity, consensus, and commitment regarding the organization's basic purposes."[28] The key element is that the group's purpose has a direct relationship to the organization's mission or goals. This is in contrast with a group whose purpose is more tangential, for example, a group responsible for designing the program to collect contributions for the United Way. Purposing allows a clearer commitment to accomplishing the stated group goals, resulting in a higher level of motivation and energy. When members are highly motivated, each wishes to be valued by the group and will communicate fully and frankly all information that seems relevant.

Supportive atmosphere.   An effective work group provides emotional support to its members. Support can take the form of encouraging ideas expressed, listening to

BOX 6–2

Thinking Small: Large Computer Firms Create Little Groups

Recently Matt Sanders was kicked out of his office. His belongings and two new workers moved into space at Convergent Technologies Inc., a computer manufacturer. He had to borrow desks and phones. His boss, Allen Michels, said, "If you get into trouble, call me, and if you get some good news, call me too. But I ain't calling you." Needless to say, Mr. Sanders was scared.

Mr. Sanders was not being fired but in reality was named the new leader of a "strike force" to build a new computer that would allow Convergent to enter the market of low-priced personal computers in a short time. The concept was to create an entrepreneurial force that had so often in the past been the beginnings of many Silicon Valley firms. In essence, this approach, which is being used by other large or maturing technology companies, is allowing Mr. Sanders to

form his own "company-within-a-company."

Companies in a similar situation believe that small work groups, when given enough freedom, can react better and more quickly to the abrupt changes that constantly confront them. Several examples follow this approach of "small is better." Apple Computer Inc. turned to a small group to help develop its Lisa, an easy-to-use machine for business people. Timex Corp. did likewise to get into the computer business quickly with its Timex Sinclair 1000. Daniel Ross, the vice president, says one of the virtues of the small-group approach is that responsibility gets pushed to lower-level employees. Also, he says, small groups can better focus their energies on a single goal—"Creativity is fostered in this kind of organization."

Mr. Michels of Convergent feels that this approach is the only way to compete with the Japanese. He argues that the use of small work groups is more productive for Americans than trying to adopt the Japanese style of management, which depends on the Japanese worker's intense

Source: Adapted from *The Wall Street Journal*, Friday, 19 August 1983, p. 1.

a group member's problems, or even providing help with a knotty technical problem. Group members offer suggestions, comments, ideas, information, and even criticisms in a helpful manner. Just as importantly, these contributions are received in the same spirit. This does not imply that there are no differences of opinion about a subject; in fact, there may be more expressions of differing ideas about a problem because the members feel safe and not too ego-involved to contribute their ideas.[29] In particular, members are able to accept criticism and make constructive use of it. The criticisms may deal with any relevant topic— decisions, interpersonal relations, group processes, or supervisory actions.

loyalty to the firm. "You keep things small so you can create a culture, the right culture," says Mr. Michels. "You inject a harmonious attitude. You give them the right amount of freedom so that there is no sense of futility."

Mr. Sanders had to find his own location for the group, which ended up being a one-story shabby building. The only help he would get from Convergent was money. He wasn't allowed to take any employees with him. Most of the new staff were raided from other computer firms, such as Hewlett-Packard, Texas Instruments, and Atari. Most were given stock when they signed on. Convergent and the working group kept in close touch with certain Convergent managers acting as "kind of an informal board of directors." The group even assumed a code name, "Ultra," and swore all to keep secret the doings within the group.

The machine that they have been working on was presented to the marketplace about nine months after the group started. Karen Toland, the marketing director, says, "I don't have to go through two department heads and write six memos if something needs to be changed. I walk across and say, 'Hey, Charlie, this space bar feels like . . .' and he fixes it." She says that producing the product was an intense process of give and take, made easier because everyone knew each other. She recalls "lots of arguments" with the engineers when she wanted to call a button on a computer a "Do It" key instead of the more standard, computer-jargon "Execute." "They thought I was nuts," she says. The matter was thoroughly thrashed out, and the machine now has a "Do It" key.

Questions

1. Can you use the characteristics of an effective work group to describe the group formed by Mr. Sanders?
2. What were some the reasons for not using the established organization to develop the new product? Use the material from the chapter to defend your position.
3. What group norms and roles are exemplified by Ms. Toland's statements about the "Do It" key?
4. What advice would you give Mr. Sanders about the possibility of 'groupthink' occurring in his organization? How can he prevent it from happening?
5. What stage of development do you think this group has attained? What is the next issue it will face?

Blending of task and maintenance roles. In previous sections, we talked about group behaviors as being task-related, maintenance-related, or self-related. In an effective group, the distinction between "task functions" and "maintenance functions" tends to dissolve. The group members discover that the task requirements demand integrative actions and they have developed behaviors and attitudes that fulfill these requirements. Much of this blending is a result of the group members' having experimented with various behaviors over a period of time. This is similar to an individual learning to play tennis. At first one makes a whole series of seemingly unrelated and conflicting moves. But as one continues to practice, the moves become natural and flowing. In a similar fashion, group members are able to mix task and maintenance roles in the same communication. What may be a suggestion for a new direction to solve a problem is viewed as a supportive comment by other group members.

Group composition.   Another aspect of an effective work group is the composition of membership over time. If one were to examine the individuals, especially their skills and personalities, one might conclude that they don't seem to fit. One might even say that the group is composed of castoffs and misfits. This is not to say that certain groups with members of similar backgrounds aren't effective, but rather that their effectiveness is contained to situations where group cooperation is important. For example, this kind of homogeneity might be critical for a group in the public view whose main purpose is to exhibit a cooperative attitude. In contrast, certain situations call for a high degree of creativity and problem-solving ability, which can only be generated in a heterogeneous group. People with different backgrounds—technical, educational, or cultural—help to bring fresh perspectives to the problem or issue at hand. A case in point might be the creation and introduction of a new product, as presented in Box 6–2. A group responsible for this complex task must have skills and abilities spanning many technical and operational areas. In addition, the mix of requirements changes over time as the new product reaches the stage of public introduction, creating a need for the group composition to change to reflect the new tasks. The actual membership must change and new members must be added and oriented. Effective groups not only allow but may demand group membership changes as the group encounters new technical problems. In effective groups these new members are carefully introduced to the group to give them a chance to become psychologically a part of the work unit.[30]

Resisting control.   A final characteristic of effective work groups is the seeming paradox of the group fulfilling the organization's need for high performance, but at the price of being a relatively hard subunit to manage.[31] This characteristic seems to be particularly evident in more technical firms. One case involved the introduction of computerized axial tomography (CAT Scan) during the mid-1970s. The organization established a special group to design and introduce this technology to the medical community. The group itself resisted most attempts to control its behavior. It had a pay scale (when it hired from the outside) higher than the other parts of the firm; it appropriated human and technical resources as it felt appropriate, even to the outcry of other top managers from whom the resources were taken; and it communicated with whomever it felt would further its goals without using the normal channels or formalities required of other units. When the product was introduced, the group was quickly disbanded.[32] The resistance of effective work groups to management control may frustrate the larger system, but this behavior may be tolerated by management so the group can do what the organization itself can not do through normal methods.

Summary of Key Concepts

1. Groups have very important consequences for organizational performance and effectiveness. Much of what we know about groups started with the Hawthorne study.
2. Groups are usually limited in size and may be informal as well as formal in nature.
3. Groups influence their members through rewards associated with membership. Primary means of influence include compliance, identification, and internalization.
4. A group's size can affect individual behavior. Larger groups tend to be less satisfying and can lead to more turnover. Smaller groups seem to allow greater participation and satisfaction.
5. Cohesiveness tends to increase as members are attracted to other group members and if the group is threatened by outside pressures. Cohesiveness may, however, be detrimental to organization effectiveness if the group's norms are counterproductive.
6. Norms and roles are the group's expectations about individual members' behaviors. Norms are general expectations about all group members' behaviors while roles are usually related to particular positions individuals hold in a group. Roles are task- or maintenance-related.
7. Conformity is a powerful influence on group members' behavior. While conformity is needed to get group members to work together, research has shown that conformity can also have negative consequences in the form of blind obedience.
8. Socialization is a process whereby an employee becomes a participating member of the work group and the organization. The process includes (1) getting in, (2) breaking in, and (3) settling in.
9. Groups develop through predictable stages, much like individuals, from dependence to interdependence. Each stage has its own issues to be resolved before the group can move on to the next stage.
10. When a group becomes mature and effective, it exhibits certain characteristics: clarity of focus, supportive atmosphere, blending of task and maintenance roles, appropriate group composition, and resisting control.

Key Terms

Ambient stimuli	Groupthink
Cohesiveness	Identification
Compliance	Informal group
Conformity	Internalization
Discretionary stimuli	Norms
Effective group	Roles
Group development	Socialization

MANAGERIAL APPLICATIONS

There are a great number of examples of the functioning of groups in the real world from which we could draw, and one of the problems we had in writing this section was choosing from among the many, often dramatic, examples of group activity.

We chose to look at several issues a manager may encounter when either using or being a part of a group. One situation concerns how an organization uses groups for creativity. Another looks at how group composition must match technical and organizational knowledge to perform effectively. This is followed by a case in which the organization's employees created their own group for accomplishing a very large task—how to buy a gift. We also look at an example of the amount of control groups exert on members. The next example contrasts the experience of members in a "good" and "bad" group. Finally, we present some excerpts of a fascinating story of how a technical group designed and developed a new computer system.

Groups for Creativity

Sometimes organizations create groups for specific purposes. The Arthur D. Little Company (ADL), a well-known consulting firm, creates groups to provide an element of cross-fertilization that has proven to be very effective with clients.

As reported in *The Wall Street Journal*, ADL's "unstructured approach" has projected the company into the position of one of the nation's largest, most successful consulting organizations.[33] For an organization full of management experts, ADL is managed along very loose lines. The 1,052 consultants nominally are divided into thirty-six sections. But nobody ever assigns anyone else to work on anything.

About fifty "leads" or potential cases come in each week for review by a lead management committee. In most instances, assuming ADL agrees to undertake a project, the person who brought in the lead is designated as "case team leader" if he or she is interested in heading up the project. Then, no matter how junior the leader, he or she can ask anyone in the firm to join the case team, including the chairman or the president of ADL.

No one has to work on a particular case team just because an invitation to do so is extended. An invitation may be declined for any reason—a consultant may be too busy, doesn't feel qualified, or just isn't interested in the project.

The object of the system is cross-fertilization, and ADL states that because of the system it has a broader range of experts from more different kinds of disciplines than firms that specialize in just management or engineering or science. ADL likes to say that it is "problem oriented" while other consulting firms are "client oriented." ADL brings a team of appropriate specialists to the problem while other firms simply assign the problem to whoever is in charge of developing business for that company.

People who enjoy working at ADL praise the free-wheeling style. According to one satisfied consultant, "Good people have the opportunity to work on a wide range of projects over time and don't fall into the rut of concentrating on only one area of specialization."[34]

The object of any consultant at ADL, new or old, is to achieve forty hours of work each week that is billable to clients. As a consultant advances in the firm, his or her billing rate increases, so a team leader concerned about completing a project within the allocated budget might have some incentive to use a newer person because that person is cheaper. But even with this advantage, a new person must still initiate enough contacts within the firm to be offered assignments on project teams.

One new hire spent his first few days phoning his new colleagues saying "Hi, I'm new on board. Can I come talk with you for a while?" The objective, of course, is to be assigned to a case. Often a new person has trouble filling his or her time, and this can be frustrating. As competence and skills become known, however, this problem disappears.

By using this system, ADL feels that it achieves an exceptionally high level of creativity and is able to provide its clients with an unusually high quality of service. The informal atmosphere provides the opportunity for individual employees to grow and develop their skills, and, by furnishing the opportunity for individuals to interact with others outside of their field of specialization on projects in which they are sincerely interested, everyone benefits.

Certainly the record of ADL over many years indicates that it has discovered some of the very positive kinds of emergent group behavior that can occur in a receptive environment and has been able to use this knowledge for the benefit of both the organization and its clients.

Breaking the Chains of Command

In a recent essay in *Newsweek*, Andrew S. Grove, a founder and president of Intel Corporation, comments upon the way Intel establishes groups of engineers to deal with certain situations.[35] Groups are important, according to Grove, because in today's high-tech environment things are changing so rapidly that it is necessary to bring the newest, most sophisticated technical expertise to a problem. Yet the people who possess this level of knowledge may not have the maturity and wisdom to make decisions effectively.

Grove differentiates between power based on *knowledge* and power based on *position*. A person recently graduated with a technical degree will possess, presumably, the latest technical information. The power this person has because of that knowledge will last until the next round of technical advances occurs. But if this person does well in the organization, promotions will follow, and the power that the person has based on position will increase, as will the ability to see situations from a broader, more managerial perspective. This is very similar to the need to balance task roles with maintenance roles in a group.

If the person who was once at the cutting edge of technology is permitted to make decisions for which his or her level of technical expertise is no longer appropriate, poor decisions will result. Conversely, if a person with very high levels of technical knowledge but little knowledge of the organization's operations and reason for success is permitted to make decisions, poor decisions will also result. In general, the faster the change in the technology on which the business depends, the greater the divergence is likely to be between knowledge and position power.

To avoid this problem, Intel mixes "knowledge-power people" and "position-power people" so that they together make the important decisions for the organization. Groups are devised that contain both kinds of people. Very junior members of the organization participate with very senior members in making decisions of critical importance.

According to Grove, this approach works only if the people on these decision teams feel that they participate in the decisions as equals, forgetting or ignoring status differentials. To promote this condition, Intel dispenses with many of the perks that typically separate junior and senior people in organizations. Private dining rooms, plush offices, and limousines don't exist at Intel. There are no reserved parking places or corporate jets. In fact, the company doesn't even have offices. Instead it has a maze of cubicles separated by soundproofed partitions five feet high—for the chairman of the board and the president on down. Symbols of status do not promote the flow of ideas and information necessary for the decision teams to function effectively, thus Intel has tried to eliminate them from the company environment. (Remember the discussion about status and obstacles to effective communication.)

The process of mixing knowledge-power people with position-power people is becoming more common both at Intel and throughout all of industry. We see it, for example, in many of the quality circle efforts discussed in chapter 14. While the nature of high-tech industry may have given organizations in the field little choice but to adopt new forms of organization, the success of many high-tech firms suggests that organizations in more traditional industries might find group decision techniques such as those used at Intel to be effective.

Groups for Company Support

The following is one example of a group that has reached a high level of maturity and effectiveness. See if you can use its description to identify key characteristics such as clarity of focus, supportive atmosphere, blending of task and maintenance roles, group composition, and resisting control.

A unique group was formed by employees of Delta Air Lines during the summer of 1982.[36] In the spring of that year, the airline industry was suffering the effects of a weak economy, high fuel prices, and the aftermath of the air controllers' strike. Profits were low or nonexistent, and for the first time in twenty-five years Delta Air Lines had shown a quarterly loss of $18.4 million. In spite of the loss, however, Delta management decided to give employees a healthy wage increase.

In response to this increase, several employees wondered what, if anything, they could do to thank the company for this unique gesture during a very unsettled time. They came up with the notion of buying Delta an airplane! After a great deal of discussion, a small group of flight attendants decided that it would be wonderful if the employees of Delta would buy the company its first Boeing 767, the flagship of a new fleet of mid-sized jets scheduled to start service later in the year. Would you consider this small group formal or informal?

After checking with top management to see if such a thing would be possible—taking advantage of Delta's "open door" policy of access to top officials—the group decided that they would "go for it!", confident that they could gain the support of 80 percent of the work force. The average gift per employee would have to be $810 if the goal was to be realized.

Delta President David Garrett told the flight attendants that such a gift would be magnificent, but that the program would have to be totally voluntary, no records on individual giving could be kept by the volunteers, and no divisive competitive fund-raising drives could be held. Management provided some office space for the group, access to the company's communication system, and use of the payroll department for voluntary payroll deductions. Appropriate technical and legal advice was also furnished. If the group was not formal before, it certainly became so when some of the organization's resources were committed to the project.

At first the campaign floundered. Many people in the company took the initial announcement as some kind of joke, and others were disconcerted because news of the project was acquired prematurely by the press and several employees learned of the project secondhand. But the campaign eventually began to grow rapidly. In addition to providing for contributions through payroll deductions, the group members decided to accept cash contributions as well. As a result, several other kinds of people were able to contribute to the campaign, including many of Delta's retired employees, passengers, and people completely outside of Delta's operation who were intrigued by the idea of employees giving an airplane to their company.

A key to the success of the project was to keep the lines of communication clear. As might be expected in a project of this nature, all sorts of rumors were floating around. The organizing group established a "Project 767 Hotline" to provide accurate information about the status of the project. This effort had real payoff and was credited with greatly increasing the flow of contributions from within the company, as people were assured of receiving prompt, accurate answers to any questions they might have about the project.

On December 15th, 7,000 Delta employees gathered at Atlanta's Hartsfield International Airport to christen the flagship of the Boeing 767 fleet. The name? *The Spirit of Delta*. Final figures showed that 77 percent of Delta's employees contributed to the fund.

This is a unique example of how a few people with an idea can become a force in an organization. Using their organization skills and their ability to get other people to buy into their dream, the flight attendants in the original group were able to provide their company with a new airplane costing about $33 million; but perhaps more importantly, they were able to imbue the organization with a spirit and purpose that greatly increased its ability to operate effectively.

A Group Influence on a Member

A typical pattern of a group's influence upon one of its members is reported by Farmer, Richman, and Ryan in their book *Incidents in Applying Management Theory*. [37] In this instance, a new worker is introduced to some of the production norms of the group to which he has been assigned. It is a good example of the group characteristic called conformity.

Frank Jackson deftly soldered the last wires in the interconnection. That was 18 for the morning—not bad he thought. He moved on to the next computer and began to string out cable for the next job.

"You're new here, aren't you?" The man was standing beside Frank, soldering iron in hand.

"Yeah. I came from Consumer Products Division—been with the company for ten years."

"I'm Jim Miller. Been working here in computer assembly for five years."

The men shook hands. Jim walked back to the last job that Frank had done and looked it over. "Pretty good, Frank, pretty good." He looked back down the assembly floor. "How many have you done this morning?"

"Eighteen."

"Hey, you're quite a rate-buster, aren't you?" Jim laughed. "Most of us here figure 15 interconnections a day is about par for the course."

"Well, these I'm doing are pretty easy."

Jim frowned. "Yeah, but look what happens. You do 20, maybe 25 easy ones, and the boys stuck with the hard jobs look bad. You wouldn't want that to happen, would you?"

"Well, no, of course not."

"That a boy!" Jim smiled. "You know, the boys here have a bowling team—kind of a company deal. Not everybody is on it—just the interconnection group. Even a few of them don't make it. You know, we like to keep it a friendly bunch." He paused. "Like to come next Wednesday?"

"Why, OK. Sure.

"Jim, what does the foreman think about the number of jobs a day?"

"Him? He don't know the difference, and if he did, what difference would it make? You can't find good interconnection men right off the street. He goes along—the boys upstairs don't know how fast the work should go, and they don't bother him. So he doesn't bother us."

Frank looked over the next job. He was doing the toughest kind of interconnection, and he knew that any reasonably skilled man should be able to do at least 40 jobs a day on most of the other interconnections. But this was going to be a relaxing job. He didn't like to goof off, but these people were going to be working with him every day—and he wasn't about to get off on the wrong foot with them. Besides, he liked to bowl.

"It's all cost plus anyhow," Jim said. "The company gets plenty from the government for the work. They got nothing to worry about. Hey, come with me—we can have a smoke. We've got plenty of time."

This example seems like a stereotype of group behavior. A new worker is persuaded to lower production to receive the friendship of the group. It is an excellent example of group norms and also illustrates compliance—the individual produces only the prescribed amount but continues to believe that he or she could produce more. If Frank believed the group's norm, the process would be identification.

Many of us have probably experienced something similar to this; we have gone into a new job and, eager to do well, produce a high output. Especially if it is a part-time job, the longer range implications and the influences of the group may seem unimportant. Our students who have part-time or temporary jobs often comment that it would be very easy to be the top producer; and sometimes they are. But if they stay on the job for any length of time, their production usually falls off to a level comparable with that of the permanent employees. Even when this occurs, students report that there is no question that they could retain the higher level of output indefinitely.

It might seem that the influence of a group upon an individual is always negative, but this is not necessarily the case. Individuals who would prefer not to work very hard are often influenced to do so by the group. Can you think of some examples from your own experience of the positive impact that groups can have on an individual's performance? Look to different kinds of athletic teams for examples, for it is often in these areas that group influence on individuals is most visible in terms of certain kinds of diet, training routines, codes of dress, and other behaviors.

A Good and a Bad Group

In one of our graduate courses on entrepreneurship, we regularly require that small teams of students work together in developing a business plan for an activity they might wish to start as a new venture after graduation. The first step in the process is to select a prospective business, after which the team develops a plan. This activity takes the major part of an academic quarter and requires a great deal of effort on the part of the student teams. The final reports are reviewed by a panel of "venture capitalists," in actuality a team of practicing executives who decide which, if any, of the teams deserve financial support. There is usually at least one real-life venture capitalist on the panel, as well as two or three other executives who have been successful entrepreneurs.

As a final activity of the course, we ask the members of each student team to evaluate the performance of their team. Here is the report of a student who was very satisfied with the way his team performed. Incidentally, his team was one of those selected to receive "funding."

This was one of the most enjoyable and 'synergistic' teams of which I have had the privilege to be a member. Some of the group attributes I especially noticed were the following:

Commitment. Each group member was dedicated to creating the best business plan possible. We really wanted to win! This involved meeting two or three times a week as a group, as well as pavement pounding, literature search, writing, and conceptualizing on an individual basis.

Enthusiasm. We were all eager to make the project as realistic as possible, and, if it turned out well, we were really willing to consider pursuing it as a career.

Attention to detail. No one wanted serious errors or gross assumptions in the business plan. We strived to gather enough data to make qualified statements rather than relying on 'armchair' generalities.

Ability to meet deadlines. Partly a function of our enthusiasm, we had established by the end of our first meeting a time-framed, task-oriented schedule for data gathering, writing, report preparation, discussing reviews, review/revision, and a great deal of preparation for the team presentation. In essence, we had conceptualized the areas that needed to be addressed and had delegated responsibilities to individual members. Every deadline was either attained on time or early.

Ability to reach consensus. Whenever an issue arose on which team members may have had different perspectives, the issue was discussed to the point of mutual agreement. Everyone was kept satisfied.

Resourcefulness. Team members demonstrated this characteristic very well in terms of identifying and contacting persons knowledgeable about a particular aspect of the venture, as well as identifying literature relevant to concept development. The team was also resourceful at the point in time when we were faced with a pricing policy problem that weakened the competitive positioning of the venture; the group members reassessed the collected data and were able to discover another, ultimately successful, positioning strategy.

Contrast the kind of comments in the preceding report with the following comments from a member of a team that did not do well in the seminar.

Our team had a lot of trouble. We spent a lot of time deciding which project to pursue, and several of the team members advocated projects to which they were very strongly emotionally attached. When it became apparent that their project was not the one that the group was going to work on, they immediately lost enthusiasm for our efforts.

We had a lot of trouble arranging times for our meetings, even though we were supposed to have uncommitted times in common when we could meet. Some people had decided to use these times for other purposes, and we just couldn't get them to come to some of the meetings.

One of our members was simply not interested in what we were doing. He planned to take the CPA exam the next quarter and was spending all of his time studying for that. He just wanted to pass this course. He didn't care how well he did as long as he passed.

Everyone had big ideas and good suggestions, but no one seemed to actually do the work. We spent a lot of time at our meetings arguing about who had agreed to do what at the previous meeting.

> I was embarrassed by our final presentation. Compared to those of the other teams, we were terrible. I wouldn't have given us any venture capital if I had been on the panel. I wouldn't want to be on a team with those people again!
>
> I keep asking myself what went wrong and what I might have done early on to get us working in a more productive manner. I think of myself as being a pretty effective person in group situations, and I'm surprised that I ended up on such a disaster.

It's easy to see the differences in the kinds of experiences the two teams had. One team was exceptional and everything seemed to go right for it. The other team never got started in a productive way and did a poor job on its project, even though the final presentation seemed to be okay because of the significant verbal skills of two of the members. Incidentally, in our judgement, the teams were approximately equal in basic abilities. One of our criteria in selecting the teams was to provide a reasonably even distribution of capabilities. The author of the latter student report raises an interesting question—what the student could have done early in the experience when it became clear that the group was not productive. You might ask which task-related or maintenance-related roles were missing in this last group?

The Soul of a Group

One of the most fascinating books we have read recently is *The Soul of a New Machine* by Tracy Kidder.[38] The book details the story of the development of a new computer by Data General Corporation. A great deal of the book chronicles the experiences of a team of engineers assigned to work on the "Eagle Project," the name given to the effort to develop a new state-of-the-art computer upon which would depend a great deal of the company's future.

Eagle was not the only project team in existence. In fact, Data General had several teams of engineers working on essentially the same project, even though the design of just one team would ultimately be chosen.

> [the company] liked to see a little competition stirred up among teams. Let them compete with their ideas for new products, and bad ideas, as well as the negative points of good ones, are likely to get identified inside the company and not out in the marketplace. That was the general strategy. . . . What it meant downstairs [for the Eagle team] was that they not only had to invent their new computer but also had to struggle for the resources to build it. Resources meant, among other things, the active cooperation of such so-called support groups as Software. You had to persuade such groups that your idea had merit and would get out the door, or else you wouldn't get much help—and then your machine almost certainly wouldn't get out the door.[39]

One of the fascinating events in the environment of the Eagle team was the process of "signing up," making a strong emotional commitment to do whatever was necessary to get the machine out on time. In a sense this corresponds to the social influence process of internalization—acceptance of the group's expectations as intrinsically rewarding and therefore observed even in the absence of the other group members. The managers of the Eagle team spent a great deal of time determining the best way to get individual team members to make that commitment. The following illustrates how one such member "signed up":

> You troop into a conference room with most of the other new hires, feeling a little nervous, and there waiting for you are the brass: the vice president of engineering, another lower-level but important executive, and West (the team manager). The speeches are brief. Listening intently, you hear all about the history of the 32-bit superminis. These have been around awhile, but sales are really starting to pick up. DEC's starting to turn out VAXes [a competitor and its computer] like jelly beans, and the word is that DEC will probably introduce a new model of VAX in about nine months. No one's saying it's your fault, but Eagle's late, very late. It really must be designed and brought to life and be ready to go by April. Really. In just six months. That won't be easy, but the brass think you can do it. That's why you were hired— you're the cream of the crop. Everything depends on you now, they say.[40]

During such a meeting one can conceptualize that the first stage of group development starts—orientation. In such a session the group's goal is clarified and, it is hoped, the members accept the objective as their own.

> You feel good about yourself and what you're doing when you leave that meeting. You go right back to your desk, of course, and pick up Booth's algorithm. In a little while, though, you feel you need a break. You look for someone to share coffee with you. But everyone is working, assiduously, peering into manuals and cathode-ray tubes. You go back to your reading. Then suddenly, you feel it, like a little trickle of sweat down your back. "I've gotta hurry," you say to yourself. "I've gotta get this reading done and write my code. This is just one detail. There's a hundred of these. I better get this little piece of code done today."
>
> Practically the next time you look up, it's midnight, but you've done what you set out to do. You leave the basement thinking: "This is life. Accomplishment. Challenges. I'm in control of a crucial part of this big machine." You look back from your car at the blank, brick, monolithic back of building 14A/B and say to yourself, "What a great place to work." Tomorrow you'll have to get to work on an instruction in the morning, however; FFAS is upon you. "Oh my God! FFAS! They need that code next week. I better hurry."
>
> The pressure . . . I felt it from inside of me.[41]

As the project progressed the teams bonded together very strongly, and this bonding often resulted in some abberations of language.

> To almost everything they touched, the Microteam attached their prefix. The office that the four of them shared, sitting virtually knee to knee, had a sign on the door that said "The Micropit"; the room in which they held their weekly meeting was the micro-conference room. They gave out microwords and one of the engineers had his microporch. One of them owned a van, which became the microbus. . . . Then,.in the

first warm days of spring, they created the outdoor microlounge, to which they repaired on Friday afternoons.[42]

Part of this need to establish a new language and define their own space is an example of resisting control by the formal organization—one characteristic of an effective work group. We can also easily see that such behavior could be counterproductive if the organization had not carefully matched the group's goals with the organization's.

The book goes on to describe the various activities of the team as it progressed through the victories and frustrations of building a new computer. It provides great insight into the ways that groups function in organizations, and we recommend it to you highly.

Toward the end of the book, after the machine has been successfully developed, some of the team members were reliving their experiences.

> They were building temples to God. It was the kind of work that gave meaning to life. That's what West and his team of engineers were looking for, I think. They themselves like to say they didn't work on their machine for money. In the aftermath, some of them felt they were receiving neither the loot nor the recognition they had earned, and some said they were bitter on that score. But when they talked about the project itself, their enthusiasm returned. It lit up their faces. . . . Many looked around for words to describe their true reward. They used phrases such as "self-fulfillment," "a feeling of accomplishment," "self-satisfaction.". . . [one engineer] struggled with those terms with growing impatience. Then he said: "Look, I don't have to get official recognition for anything I do. Ninety-eight percent of the thrill comes from knowing that the thing you designed works, and works almost the way you expected it would. If that happens part of *you* is in that machine."[43]

DISCUSSION QUESTIONS

1. Think of a group with which you have been involved. What type of group was it, according to the discussion in the chapter? What developmental stages did it encounter?

2. If a manager believes that his or her group has set performance standards well below what they are capable of attaining, what can the manager do? By what means can the manager raise the performance standards to a higher level?

3. Often a work group loses cohesiveness. Think of such a group. What was the cause? What were the effects? How can the manager increase the cohesiveness of such a group?

4. What are examples of group norms? How do groups get members to conform to norms? What implications do norms have for the manager of the group?

5. Why is the study of groups important to management?

6. Contrast the characteristics of an effective group with the description of the "Soul of a Group." What are the implications for a manager who is trying to set up a project group?

EXERCISE: GROUP NORMS

From reading the chapter, you are aware that groups develop norms to control individual members' behavior. Some of these norms can facilitate the group to accomplish its tasks and objectives. Other norms can hinder a group and keep it from developing. This exercise should help you understand how this happens.

Answer the following questions from your experience as a group member. Use a specific group you are (were) an active member of and whose membership is (was) important to you. For example, you can use the class in which you are now studying this chapter.

Questions

1. What were three behaviors expected by the group members that were communicated to you verbally?
2. What were three behaviors expected by the group members that you had to discover on your own?
3. Which expected behaviors were the most important to the group from your list of six (prioritize them)?
4. How did you participate in the communication of these norms to other group members?
5. What happened to group members who violated the group's norms by not behaving as expected?
6. Did you violate any of the group's norms? What happened?
7. Which of these norms are helpful to the group? Which hinder the group?

   Now take your list and share it with a small group of fellow students. If several of you used the class as the example, make a composite of your group norms and make a composite list in order of importance. Answer the following questions.

8. Did any of the listed norms appear as you worked in the small group?
9. How were they communicated during your discussion? Which were most influential? Which were most helpful? Which hindered you?
10. What conclusions can you make based on this exercise?

NOTES

1. "Caught Napping: Secret Bedrooms on Factory's Night Shift," *The Seattle Times* (UPI), Thursday (11 August 1983) A10. Reprinted with permission of United Press International, Inc.
2. F. J. Roethlisberger and W. J. Dickson, *Management and the Worker* (Cambridge, MA: Harvard University Press, 1939): 11.
3. F. J. Roethlisberger, *Management and Morale* (Cambridge, MA: Harvard University Press, 1939): 21.
4. Ibid.
5. Ibid.
6. K. N. Wexley and G. A. Yukl, *Organizational Behavior and Personnel Psychology* (Homewood, IL: Irwin, 1977).

7. See Edgar N. Schein, *Organizational Psychology*, 2nd. ed. (Englewood Cliffs, NJ: Prentice-Hall, 1970): 81.

8. J. R. Hackman, "Group Influence on Individuals," in M. D. Dunnette, ed., *Handbook of Industrial Organizational Psychology* (Chicago: Rand McNally, 1976): chap. 13.

9. L. W. Porter, E. F. Lawler, III, and J. R. Hackman, *Behavior in Organizations* (New York: McGraw-Hill, 1975): 371–374.

10. H. C. Kelman, "Processes of Opinion Change," *Public Opinion Quarterly*, 25 (1961): 57–78.

11. Ibid.

12. R. M. Steers, *Introduction to Organizational Behavior* (Glenview, IL: Scott, Foresman, 1981): 188–190.

13. E. J. Thomas and C. F. Fink, "Effects of Group Size," in L. L. Cummings and W. E. Scott, eds., *Readings in Organizational Behavior and Human Performance* (Homewood IL: Irwin, 1969).

14. Marvin E. Shaw, *Group Dynamics: The Psychology of Small Group Behavior*, 2nd ed. (New York: McGraw-Hill, 1976).

15. L. Berkowitz, "Group Standards, Cohesiveness, and Productivity," *Human Relations* (November 1954): 405–419.

16. D. Birenbaum and E. Sagarin, *Norms and Human Behavior* (New York: Holt, Rinehart & Winston, 1976): 10–11.

17. E. N. Schein, *Organizational Psychology*, 3rd ed. (Englewood Cliffs, NJ: Prentice-Hall, 1980): 100.

18. L. R. Hoffman, "Applying Experimental Research on Group Problem Solving to Organizations," *Journal of Applied Behavioral Science*, 15 (1979): 375–391.

19. S. E. Asch, "Effects of Group Pressure Upon the Modification and Distribution of Judgements," in H. P. Guetzkow, ed., *Group Leadership and Men* (Pittsburgh: Carnegie Press, 1952): 177–190.

20. M. Sherif, *The Psychology of Social Norms* (New York: Harper, 1936).

21. Ibid., p. 105.

22. L. Mann, *Social Psychology* (New York: Wiley, 1969).

23. E. Schein, *Organizational Psychology*, 2nd ed. (Englewood Cliffs, NJ: Prentice-Hall, 1970).

24. D. C. Feldman, "A Practical Program for Employee Socialization," *Organizational Dynamics* (Autumn 1976): 64–80.

25. J. S. Jacobson and E. Jacobson, "A Model of Task Group Development in Complex Organizations and a Strategy of Implementation," *Academy of Management Journal*, 1 (1976): 98–111; and W. G. Bennis and H. A. Sheperd, "A Theory of Group Development," *Human Relations*, 9 (1965): 415–445.

26. R. B. Caple, "The Sequential Stages of Group Development," *Small Group Behavior*, 9 (1978): 471.

27. D. C. Lungren, "Trainer Style and Patterns of Group Development," *Journal of Applied Behavioral Science*, 7 (1971): 689–709.

28. Peter B. Vaill, "The Purposing of High-Performing Systems," *Organizational Dynamics* (Autumn 1982): 23–39.

29. R. Likert, "The Nature of Highly Effective Groups," *New Patterns of Management* (New York: McGraw-Hill, 1961).

30. G. Strauss and L. R. Sayles, *Personnel: The Human Problems of Management*, 2nd ed. (Englewood Cliffs, NJ: Prentice-Hall, 1967): 200.

31. Vaill, "The Purposing of High-Performing Systems."

32. R. E. Callahan and P. Salipante, Jr., "Boundary Spanning Units: Organizational Implications for the Management of Innovation," *Human Resource Management* (Spring 1979): 26–31.

33. *The Wall Street Journal*, (7 November 1983): 27.

34. Ibid.

35. *Newsweek* (3 October 1983): 23.

36. L. Lawrence, "Thank You, Delta Air Lines," *Reader's Digest* (November 1983): 112–116.

37. Richard N. Farmer, Barry M. Richman, and William G. Ryan, *Incidents in Applying Management Theory* (Belmont, CA: Wadsworth Publishing Company, 1966): 123–124. Reprinted by permission.

38. Tracy Kidder, *The Soul of a New Machine* (New York: Avon Books, 1982).

39. Kidder, *The Soul of a New Machine*, 112. Copyright © 1981 by John Tracy Kidder. By permission of Little, Brown and Company in association with the Atlantic Monthly Press.

40. Ibid., 114–115.

41. Ibid., 115.

42. Ibid., 154.

43. Ibid., 273.

RECOMMENDED READINGS

Tracy Kidder, *The Soul of a New Machine* (New York: Avon Books, 1982).

This book describes a group development from inception to the final demise as it struggles to develop a new computer system. It is an in-depth analysis of the feelings and thoughts of the team members as the group develops.

Peter B. Vaill, "The Purposing of High Performing Systems," *Organizational Dynamics* (Autumn 1982): 23–39.

The article describes the leaders of high-performing systems as sharing three commitments—time, feeling, and focus—that enable them to project and maintain a clear and effective sense of purpose among the members.

Ex-Policeman Tells What Makes a "Bad Cop"

Denver, Nov. 4. (A.P.)—What makes a policeman go sour? I can tell you. I was a Denver policeman until not so long ago. Then I quit so I could hold my head up.

Don't get me wrong. I'm not trying to shift the burden of responsibility for the burglaries, break-ins, safe jobs and that sort of thing. That is bad, very bad. But I will leave it to the big shots and the newspapers and the courts to say and do what needs to be said and done about that.

My concern is about the individual officer, the ordinary, hard-working, basically honest but awfully hard-pressed guy who is really suffering now.

Young fellows don't put on those blue uniforms to be crooks. There are a lot of reasons, but for most of the guys it adds up to the fact they thought it was an honorable, decent way of making a living.

Somewhere along the line a guy's disillusioned. Along the way the pressures mount up. Somewhere along the way he may decide to quit fighting them and make the conscious decisions to try to "beat" society instead.

But long before he gets to that point, almost as soon as he dons the uniform in fact, he is taking the first little steps down the road that does, for some, eventually lead to the penitentiary.

Let me back up a little. I want to talk about how you get to be a policeman, because this is where the trouble really starts.

Source: Case copyright 1964 by Professor Harry R. Knudson, University of Washington. By a former Denver policeman as told to Mort Stern, the *Denver Post*, 2 May 1962. Copyright 1962 by the *Denver Post*. Reprinted by permission. "Addendum" from *The Wall Street Journal*, 2 May 1962. Copyright by Dow Jones & Company, Inc. Reprinted by permission.

Almost any able-bodied man can become a policeman in Denver. If he is within the age brackets, if he is a high-school graduate, if he has no criminal record, he is a cinch.

There isn't much to getting through the screening, and some bad ones do get through. There are the usual examinations and questionnaires. Then there is the interview. A few command officers ask questions. There is a representative of civil service and a psychiatrist present.

They ask the predictable questions and just about everybody gives the predictable answers: "Why do you want to become a policeman?" "I've always wanted to be a policeman. I want to help people." Five or ten minutes and it is over.

Five or ten minutes to spot the sadist, the psychopath—or the guy with an eye for an easy buck. I guess they weed some out. Some others they get at the Police Academy. But some get through.

Along with those few bad ones, there are more good ones, and a lot of average, ordinary human beings who have this in common: They want to be policemen.

The job has (or had) some glamour for the young man who likes authority, who finds appeal in making a career of public service, who is extroverted or aggressive.

Before you knock those qualities, remember two things: First, they are the same qualities we admire in a business executive. Second, if it weren't for men with these qualities, you wouldn't have any police protection.

The Police Academy is point No. 2 in my bill of particulars. It is a fine thing, in a way. You meet the cream of the Police Department. Your expectations soar. You know you are going to make the grade and be a good officer. But how well are you really prepared?

There are six weeks at the academy—four weeks in my time. Six hectic weeks in which to learn all about the criminal laws you have sworn to enforce, to assimilate the rules of evidence, methods of arbitration, use of fire-arms, mob and riot control, first aid (including, if you please, some basic obstetrics), public relations and so on.

There is an intangible something else that is not on the formal agenda. You begin to learn that this is a fraternity into which you are not automatically accepted by your fellows. You have to earn your way in; you have to establish that you are ''all right.''

And even this early there is a slight sour note. You knew, of course, that you had to provide your own uniforms, your own hat, shoes, shirts, pistol and bullets out of your $393 a month.

You knew the city would generously provide you with the cloth for two pair of trousers and a uniform blouse.

What you didn't know was that you don't just choose a tailor shop for price and get the job done.

You are sent to a place by the Police Department to get the tailoring done. You pay the price even though the work may be ill-fitting. It seems a little odd to you that it is always the same establishment. But it is a small point and you have other things on your mind.

So the rookie, full of pride and high spirit, his head full of partly learned information, is turned over to a more experienced man for breaking in. He is on ''probation'' for six months.

The rookie knows he is being watched by all the older hands around him. He is eager to be accepted. He accepts advice gratefully.

Then he gets little signs that he has been making a good impression. It may happen like this: The older man stops at a bar, comes out with some packages of cigarettes. He does this several times. He explains that this is part of the job, getting cigarettes free from proprietors to resell, and that as a part of the rookie's training it is his turn to ''make the butts.''

So he goes into a skid-row bar and stands un-

comfortably at the end waiting for the bartender to acknowledge his presence and disdainfully toss him two packages of butts.

The feeling of pride slips away and a hint of shame takes hold. But he tells himself this is unusual, that he will say nothing that will upset his probation standing. In six months, after he gets his commission, he will be the upright officer he meant to be.

One thing leads to another for the rookies. After six months they have been conditioned to accept free meals, a few packages of cigarettes, turkeys at Thanksgiving and liquor at Christmas from the respectable people in their district.

The rule book forbids all this. But it isn't enforced. It is winked at at all levels.

So the rookies say to themselves that this is O.K., that this is a far cry from stealing and they still can be good policemen. Besides, they are becoming accepted as ''good guys'' by their fellow officers.

This becomes more and more important as the young policeman begins to sense a hostility toward him in the community. This is fostered to a degree by some of the saltier old hands in the department. But the public plays its part.

Americans are funny. They have a resentment for authority. And the policeman is authority in person. The respectable person may soon forget that a policeman found his lost youngster in the park, but he remembers that a policeman gave him a traffic ticket.

The negative aspect of the job builds up. The majority of the people he comes in contact with during his working hours are thieves, con men, narcotics addicts and out and out nuts.

Off the job his associations narrow. Part of the time when he isn't working, he is sleeping. His waking, off-duty hours are such as to make him not much of a neighbor. And then he wants to spend as much time as he can with his family.

Sometimes, when he tries to mix with his neighbors, he senses a kind of strain. When he is introduced to someone, it is not likely to be, ''This is John Jones, my friend,'' or ''my neighbor''; it is more likely to be, This is John Jones. He's a policeman.''

And the other fellow, he takes it up, too. He is

likely to tell you that he has always supported pay increases for policemen, that he likes policemen as a whole, but that there are just a few guys in uniform he hates.

No wonder the officer begins to think of himself as a member of the smallest minority group in the community. The idea gradually sinks into him that the only people who understand him, that he can be close to, are his fellow officers.

It is in this kind of atmosphere that you can find the young policeman trying to make the grade in the fraternity. But that is not the whole story.

A policeman lives with tensions, and with fears.

Part of the tensions come from the incredible monotony. He is cooped up with another man, day after day, doing routine things over and over. The excitement that most people think of as the constant occupation of policemen is so infrequent as to come as a relief.

Part of the tensions come from the manifold fears. I don't mean that these men are cowards. This is no place for cowards. But they are human beings. And fears work on all human beings.

Paramount is the physical fear that he will get hurt to the point where he can't go on working, or the fear that he will be killed. The fear for his family.

There is the fear that he will make a wrong decision in a crucial moment, a life-and-death decision. A man has been in a fight. Should he call the paddy wagon or the ambulance? A man aims a pistol at him. Should he try to talk to him or shoot him?

But the biggest fear he has is that he will show fear to some of his fellow officers. This is the reason he will rush heedlessly in on a cornered burglar or armed maniac if a couple of officers are present—something he wouldn't do if he were alone. He is tormented by his fears and he doesn't dare show them. He knows he has to present a cool, calm front to the public.

As a group, policemen have a very high rate of ulcers, heart attacks, suicides and divorces. These things torment him, too. Divorce is a big problem to policemen. A man can't be a policeman for eight hours and then just turn it off and go home

and be a loving father and husband—particularly if he has just had somebody die in the back of his police car.

So once again, the pressure is on him to belong, to be accepted and welcomed into the only group that knows what is going on inside him.

If the influences aren't right, he can be hooked.

So he is at the stage where he wants to be one of the guys. And then this kind of thing may happen: One night his car is sent to check on a "Code 26"—a silent burglar alarm.

The officer and his partner go in to investigate. The burglar is gone. They call the proprietor. He comes down to look things over. And maybe he says, "Boys, this is covered by insurance, so why don't you take a jacket for your wife, or a pair of shoes?" And maybe he does, maybe just because his partner does, and he says to himself, "What the hell, who has been hurt?"

Or maybe the proprietor didn't come down. But after they get back in the car his partner pulls out four $10 bills and hands him two. "Burglar got careless," says the partner.

The young officer who isn't involved soon learns that this kind of thing goes on. He even may find himself checking on a burglary call, say to a drugstore, and see some officers there eyeing him peculiarly.

Maybe at this point the young officer feels the pressure to belong so strongly that he reaches over and picks up something, cigars perhaps. Then he is "in," and the others can do what they wish.

Mind you, not all officers will do this. Somewhere along the line all of them have to make a decision, and it is at that point where the stuff they are made of shows through. But the past experience of the handouts, the official indifference to them, and the pressures and tensions of the job don't make the decision any easier.

And neither he nor the department has had any advance warning, such as might come from thorough psychiatric screening, as to what his decision will be.

Some men may go this far and no farther. They might rationalize that they have not done anything that isn't really accepted by smart people in society.

This is no doubt where the hard-core guy, the one who is a thief already, steps in. A policeman is a trained observer and he is smart in back-alley psychology. This is especially true of the hard-core guy and he has been watching the young fellows come along.

When he and his cronies in a burglary ring spot a guy who may have what it takes to be one of them, they may approach him and try him out as a lookout. From then on it is just short steps to the actual participation in and planning of crimes.

Bear in mind that by this stage we have left all but a few policemen behind. But all of them figure in the story at one stage or another. And what has happened to a few could happen to others. I suppose that is the main point I am trying to make.

ADDENDUM

The following item appeared in the Tax Report column of the May 2, 1962, issue of The Wall Street Journal:

Denver police salaries would be raised out of a $2.7 million yearly hike in revenues from a proposed boost in the city's sales tax to 2% from 1%. The proposal comes before Denver voters June 5. Officers' low pay has been blamed in part for a recent scandal involving the arrest of 57 Denver policemen on burglary charges. A 2% retail sales tax is levied by the state.

Questions

1. What norms are existing for the new 'rookie' to deal with when he 'hits the streets'?
2. Describe how such norms may have come into existence and seem to be sanctioned by the larger organization.
3. How does the environment affect the strength or weakness of these norms?
4. What pressures exist to not conform to the norms?
5. Is this an example of 'groupthink'? Defend your answer with material from this chapter.
6. What can be done to change this situation? From where will this pressure for change come and how will it start?

CHAPTER SEVEN
Decision Making

OUTLINE

DECISION-MAKING CONCEPTS

Introduction
Decision-making Process
Decision-making Style
Techniques of Decision Making
Summary of Key Concepts

MANAGERIAL APPLICATIONS

A Realistic Look at Decision Making
Information Gathering
Decision Making in Japan—Consultative or
    Participative?
Computer-based Decisions

OBJECTIVES

- Describe major steps in the decision-making process

- Identify factors that influence the decision-making process

- Discuss ramifications of decision-making styles

- Know when others should be included in decisions

- Describe some strengths and weaknesses of group decision making

- Describe techniques for defining problems, generating alternatives, evaluating alternatives, and choosing an alternative for implementation

Great Business Decisions Through the Years

1897—The Remington Arms Company was offered rights to a patent on a typewriting machine owned by the Wagner Typewriting Machine Company. Remington refused the offer. Wagner was later taken over by the Underwood Company.

1948—British and American automobile experts were asked to consider taking over the Volkswagen factory in Germany as part of postwar rebuilding. The experts were blunt in their rejection, claiming the VW did not ". . . meet the fundamental technical requirements of a motorcar."

1962—A representative of Decca records was visited by a British piano-shop owner who was managing an unknown pop group. After listening to a demonstration record the Decca representative declined to take the group on, stating that groups with guitars were on their way out. The group was the Beatles.

1960s—General Motors suffered dismal sales of the Chevrolet Nova in the Mexican market. "No va" means "no go" in Spanish.[1]

DECISION-MAKING CONCEPTS

Introduction

The luxury of hindsight generally makes it easy to evaluate the quality of decisions, especially if they missed the mark spectacularly. After all, we know what really happened. Unfortunately, the decision maker does not have the ability to project through time to see how the decision will turn out. Decision making is one of the most difficult and least understood aspects of the manager's job. Decisions must be made with no foreknowledge, and most frequently with incomplete information even about the current state of affairs.

The Importance of Decision Making   Decision making has been described as the very core of the managerial process.[2] It has also been argued that there are two basic managerial functions: the sequential functions of planning, staffing, organizing and controlling, and the continuous functions of problem solving and decision making.[3]

Decision making is a pervasive activity, not in the least limited to the management realm. Anytime we choose among alternatives, we make a decision. We make a decision when we choose to see a movie rather than a baseball game. Airline executives make a decision by choosing to buy a Boeing 747 rather than a competing airliner. An entrepreneur makes a decision in electing to refuse a merger opportunity. Though the stakes are higher in the airline and merger decisions, all the situations have more in common than one might suppose. In each case there is a problem or opportunity. The environment is scanned and alternatives generated. The alternatives are judged by a set of criteria, and a choice is made that is consistent with the criteria.

We may never know if we made the "best" decision—after all, unless we experience both the movie and the ball game, how can we tell? And how about alternatives not considered—for example, ice skating, boating, or playing golf? But we can tell if we made a "good" decision by reviewing the results of that decision. If it was consistent with our objectives (reflected by the criteria used to assess the alternatives) and improved upon the previous situation, we have every reason to be satisfied with the decision.

Let us look at the decision-making process and investigate techniques used by managers in that critical management function.

Decision-making Process

The Rational Model   A decision model that specifies a logical sequence of decision-making steps may be termed a *rational model*. Scholars who propose such models, however, differ over the number of steps. Robertshaw, Mecca, and Rerick suggest an antecedent condition, three problem-solving steps, and the consequent condition:

1. Trouble, need, or problem
2. Definition of problem
3. Generation of alternatives
4. Evaluation of alternatives
5. Solution[4]

Simon describes the process in three stages:

1. Intelligence
2. Design
3. Choice[5]

Elbing identifies four steps:

1. Diagnose
2. Find alternative solutions
3. Analyze and compare alternatives
4. Select alternative to be followed[6]

Ansoff contends there are ten steps:

1. Problem recognition and identification
2. Diagnosis
3. Analysis and generation of alternatives
4. Strategic decision
5. Program analysis and step-by-step plan

6. Program decision
7. Communication and leadership of plan
8. Measurement of results
9. Assessment of trends
10. Prospects for the future[7]

There is more agreement than one might suppose at first glance. Simon's three stages are equivalent to Elbing's four steps, the five steps of Robertshaw et al., and the first four steps of Ansoff. Ansoff has gone beyond the immediate decision choice and included a second level of decision making, implementation of the decision and follow-up. Implementation and follow-up are often considered to be the difference between decision making and problem solving. That is, decision making is seen as a part of the problem-solving process. For our purposes, the terms *decision making* and *problem solving* are used interchangeably. Later in the chapter we examine techniques of problem solving/decision making, using a classification similar to Elbing's.

The decision models of Robertshaw, Simon, Elbing, and Ansoff share another characteristic: they are prescriptive, telling how people *should* make decisions. Other approaches have been descriptive in nature.

Satisficing   Simon has argued persuasively that decision makers cannot maximize, but rather they satisfice; that is, they seek alternative actions that are "good enough."[8] As we discussed earlier, it is unlikely that a best solution can be identified. For example, what do the terms "maximize profit," or "maximize cost saving" really mean?

Since people generally have multiple goals, elements of the various goals are likely to conflict. Maximum cost savings may be inconsistent with maximum profit. For example, delaying equipment maintenance will decrease cost and increase profit in the short run, but not in the long run. Therefore most managers would fund maintenance at a reasonable level even though costs are not reduced.

Incrementalism   Incrementalism builds upon the past and makes only marginal changes in the existing situation. Lindblom coined the term "muddling through" to describe this approach to decision making.[9] He has argued that ". . . no more than small or incremental steps—no more than muddling—is ordinarily possible".[10] In other words, the manager is constrained by events and circumstances, and can generally make only minor changes in the situation. The manager must ". . . learn to simplify complex problems systematically by (1) considering only those policies that differ slightly from current policies and by (2) ignoring important possible consequences and values of neglected policies."[11]

The Garbage Can Model   Cohen, March, and Olsen conceptualized the decision process as a garbage can.[12] As members of an organization generate problems and solutions, they dump them into the garbage can. The organization is seen as ". . . a collection of choices looking for problems, issues and feelings looking for decision situations in which they might be aired, solutions looking for issues to which they might be the answer, and decision makers looking for work".[13]

The four examples of the rational model differed only in number and specificity of the steps. Each of the examples assumes that the decision process proceeds in the sequence listed. By contrast, the garbage can model envisions problems, decision participants, choice opportunities, and solutions to be swirling around in a "decision space," combining in ways that frequently do not follow the rational model sequence. In other words, the garbage can model admits the possibility of decisions (results) in search of problems. For instance, more than one organization has embraced quality circles as an answer to an unclarified problem.

The garbage can model, unlike the rational model, includes decision participants. Thus, personal preferences, idiosyncracies, personality variables, etc., can be taken into account. The rational model would assume that, given the same "facts," two decision makers would arrive at similar solutions. The garbage can model admits that a surgeon is more likely to recommend surgery for a given ailment than is a general practicioner.

In short, the rational decision model emphasizes how decisions *should* be made, while the garbage can model attempts to describe how decisions frequently *are* made in organizations.

Though stated in humorous form, the garbage can model focuses on problems, decision participants, choice opportunities (decisions), and solutions. The model suspends the sequential requirements of the rational model of decision making, and asserts that the steps can be scrambled and, in some cases, reversed.[14]

Subjective Expected Utility   The Subjective Expected Utility (SEU) model of decision making has some similarity to both classic economic theory and the expectancy-valence models of motivation theorists. The SEU decision model, like expectancy-valence models of motivation, assigns probabilities (expectancies) and utility (valence) to outcomes. Like classic economic theory, SEU assumes that the decision maker will attempt to maximize utility.[15]

Probabilities are usually considered to be subjective, and utility is a measure of value, which may also be subjective. The decision maker lists alternatives and the consequences of those alternatives. The expected value of a consequence is the product of its worth and the probability of its occurrence. The worth of an alternative is the sum of the expected worth of all consequences associated with that alternative. From a group of alternatives the alternative with the greatest expected worth would be chosen for implementation.

Suppose, for example, that a florist wants to purchase a new delivery van and will choose between two equally priced models. The florist might assign probabilities and values to consequences, as in Table 7-1.

Delivery van number one will be the choice since it maximizes the utility of the available choices. Note that van number two has a greater probability of

TABLE 7–1
Example of SEU decision process

	Effect	Probability (P)	Worth (W)	P × W
Van #1	Low maintenance costs	.7	5	3.5
	Low operation cost	.2	3	.6
	High trade-in value	.3	2	.6
			Total Expected Utility	4.7
Van #2	Low maintenance costs	.5	5	2.5
	Low operation cost	.3	3	.9
	High trade-in value	.4	2	.8
			Total Expected Utility	4.2

economical operation and good trade-in value than van number one, but the weight given by the florist to low maintenance cost tips the balance toward van number one.

This admittedly simple example demonstrates the decision process as depicted by the SEU model. But does this simple model adequately represent more complicated decisions? Some research evidence suggests that it does.[16] The doubting observer would question human ability to use such a model in complex decisions involving many subtleties, yet there is ample evidence that great predictive success can be attained with simple models.[17]

Other Factors to Consider   Lest the reader believe that decision making involves only the dispassionate listing of alternatives and the logical assignment of preferences and probabilities, let us note some other considerations.

Values.   A great deal of research has shown a relationship between personal values and managerial decision making.[18] Values will be reflected in many parts of the decision process, including the choice of decision-making style. We examine decision style later in this chapter.

Experience.   Researchers have noted a puzzling phenomenon called preference reversal in certain decision settings. Individuals faced with a choice of situation A (high success probability and low maximum reward) and B (low success probability and high maximum reward) will indicate a preference for situation A but place a higher value on situation B.[19]

Regret theory suggests an explanation—when faced with new choice situations people recall previous experience and form expectations about the pain or pleasure the alternatives might entail.[20] Although the decision maker might actually value situation B more, past failure in risk taking might lead to a stated preference for situation A. Other research has shown that success-oriented and failure-oriented persons respond differently to risk.[21]

Propensity toward risk. The willingness to take risk has also been shown to be related to personal characteristics,[22] locus of control, sex,[23] and availability of information.[24] There is also evidence that groups experience "risky shift," that is, tend toward acceptance of more risk than individual decision makers.[25]

A Decision Process Model   Kast and Rosenzweig have proposed a decision process model that includes many of the situational and personal variables that we have described.[26] An adaptation of that model is shown in Figure 7–1.

The context of a problem is defined by factors both external and internal to the decision maker(s). The individual or group dealing with the problem generates plausible alternative actions. One lists presumed effects of the actions and estimates the probability of their occurence, as well as the impact or importance of the effect. If the impact is trivial, one would probably eliminate consideration of that effect. If the impact is great, it may weigh disproportionately in the final decision. A design change in the flap system of an airliner might improve fuel efficiency, but if there is even a small probability that it will be prone to structural failure, it becomes a major issue in the decision. After evaluating the implicit (or explicit) weights of projected effects, the decision maker balances the alternative with the other alternatives and makes a final choice.

The decision maker's values play a role in both the development of alternatives and in the determination of the impact and balance. Theoretically the number of alternatives may be nearly infinite, but the decision maker's value system screens many alternatives from consideration. For example, communist bureaucrats grappling with a problem of distributing goods to citizens would not consider the alternative of a free market approach. Values also influence the perception of decision impact; an environmentalist and a plant operations manager would very likely disagree as to the impact of a change at the plant from a low-sulphur fuel to a cheaper high-sulphur variety.

Describing effects and assigning probabilities are predictions by the decision maker. Experience and knowledge influence these predictions. Obviously, decision makers do not approach all decisions in so structured a manner. Some decisions are so repetitive and routine as to be programmed. In fact, more and more such decisions are being made by computers, such as automatic ordering for inventory at specific sales levels. Most organizational decisions are not programmed, and many are not routine. The more responsibility a manager has, the more nonroutine decisions there are. For those nonroutine decisions a manager often follows a framework much like that of Kast and Rosenzweig.

Decision-making Style

We have already noted that a number of factors influence the individual's approach to decision making. In the managerial context, an important early choice must be made about the level of participation to be allowed in the decision process. A most useful model was developed by Vroom and Yetton to help

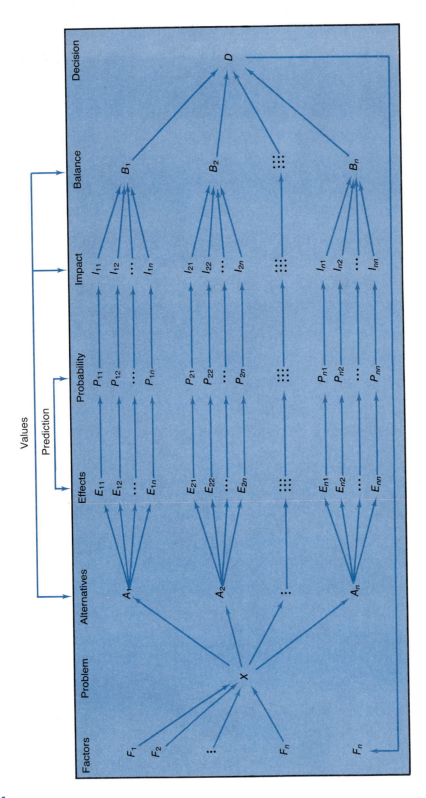

Ma Bell's Problem-Solving Guide

American Telephone and Telegraph provides a problem-solving guide to its managers. The guide consists of nine key questions, each with up to twelve additional support questions. The key questions follow:

1. What is the current situation?
2. What is the desired situation?
3. What are the restrictions (on action)?
4. What is causing the current situation?
5. What has to be changed to get what you want?
6. Is there a Standard Operating Procedure? What other solutions are possible? Pros? Cons?
7. Which solution seems best?
8. How will I prove the solution worked?
9. How will I implement the solution?

Questions one and two define the problem as a "gap." If there *is* a problem, the manager applies the company's "Five P's" to determine if it is worth solving.

- Prediction: If I don't do anything, will it go away? Stay the same? Worsen?
- Penalty: What does the problem cost me? The organization? What happens if I don't solve it?
- Payoff: What happens if I solve it? What are the benefits to the organization?
- Priority: How badly does it hurt? Which is more important, solving this or doing something else?
- Possibility: Will I be able to do something about it? Should I tackle it?

Questions

1. What are the greatest strengths of AT&T's problem-solving guide?
2. Is the guide specific enough? Is it too specific?
3. With all of the decision-making models available, why does managerial merry-go-round still occur?

Source: Adapted from "A Guide to Problem Solving," American Telephone and Telegraph Co. publication IL6MT2. Used with permission.

managers select an appropriate level of participation.[27] They described five alternative decision styles, shown in Figure 7–2.

The styles vary greatly in the amount of participation allowed. Style AI allows no participation at all. Style AII is slightly less autocratic, but uses subordinates only as information sources. Styles CI and CII are consultative in that subordinates provide ideas and opinions, not just information. Style GII is fully participative.

Vroom and Yetton proposed that the selection of a decision style should be based upon problem attributes, the need for quality in the decision, and the need for acceptance by people who will implement the decision. A decision tree was then constructed (Figure 7–3) for use by the decision maker. The decision maker

AI   You solve the problem or make the decision yourself, using information available to you at that time.

AII You obtain the necessary information from your subordinate(s), then decide on the solution to the problem yourself. You may or may not tell your subordinates what the problem is in getting the information from them. The role played by your subordinates in making the decision is clearly one of providing the necessary information to you, rather than generating or evaluating alternative solutions.

CI   You share the problem with relevant subordinates individually, getting their ideas and suggestions without bringing them together as a group. Then you make the decision that may or may not reflect your subordinates' influence.

CII You share the problem with your subordinates as a group, collectively obtaining their ideas and suggestions. Then you make the decision that may or may not reflect your subordinates' influence.

GII You share the problem with your subordinates as a group. Together you generate and evaluate alternatives and attempt to reach agreement (consensus) on a solution. Your role is much like that of chairman. You do not try to influence the group to adopt "your" solution, and you are willing to accept and implement any solution that has the support of the entire group.

FIGURE 7–2

Types of management decision styles (Source: Reprinted, by permission of the publisher, from "A New Look at Managerial Decision Making," by Victor H. Vroom, *Organizational Dynamics,* Spring 1973, p. 67. © 1973 AMACOM, a division of American Management Associations, New York. All rights reserved.)

answers the questions posed at the top of the model. Note that there are fourteen "problem types" or terminal nodes in the decision tree. Problem type 2, for example represents a situation where quality is not important but acceptance of the decision by subordinates is critical. On the other hand, the subordinates will likely accept the decision even if they are not consulted. Therefore the most autocratic style, AI, is appropriate.

The individual decision mode epitomized by Style AI flies in the face of the conventional prescription to practice participative decision making. Yet one can easily envision circumstances where the constraint of time or lack of access to people to consult makes individual decisions necessary. Decisions involving confidential data may also have to be taken alone. Furthermore, given an environment of trust and respect between manager and subordinates, there would be many situations where subordinates would actively support an individual decision.

From a managerial perspective the model's greatest value is that its use requires a decision maker to *think* about the problem, the people involved, and the organization's goals. By answering the questions in the model the manager is forced to develop a problem statement, determine the type of information needed, and consider the impact of alternatives.

DECISION MODEL

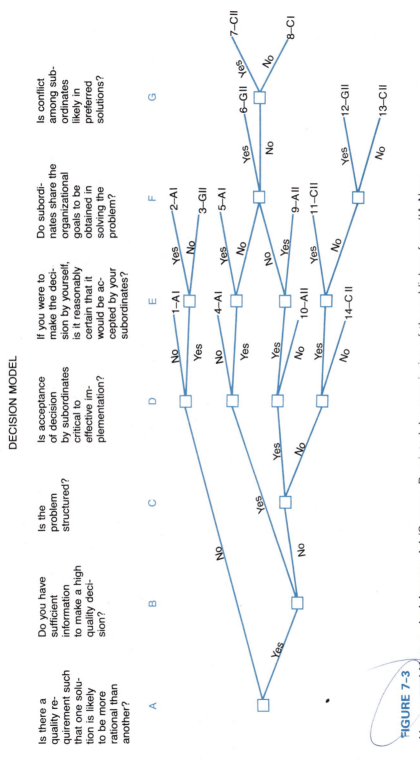

| A | B | C | D | E | F | G |

Is there a quality requirement such that one solution is likely to be more rational than another?

Do you have sufficient information to make a high quality decision?

Is the problem structured?

Is acceptance of decision by subordinates critical to effective implementation?

If you were to make the decision by yourself, is it reasonably certain that it would be accepted by your subordinates?

Do subordinates share the organizational goals to be obtained in solving the problem?

Is conflict among subordinates likely in preferred solutions?

FACTORS: DECISION QUALITY?
DECISION ACCEPTANCE
TIME REQUIRED TO MAKE DECISION

257

Strengths and Weaknesses of Group Decision Making The questions in the Vroom and Yetton model point to some of the strengths of including others in the decision process. If there is a quality requirement, evidence indicates that group performance is frequently better than that of the average group member.[28] When information is lacking, the group can generally bring more information resources to the decision. It has further been shown that degree of participation is positively associated with accuracy.[29] Participation is also positively related to satisfaction in the job and negatively related to job tension and career dissatisfaction.[30]

There are drawbacks to the use of groups. Groups take longer to make decisions than do individuals.[31] Not all employees want to participate.[32] Those with high authoritarianism traits and low independence needs are relatively unaffected by the participative experience.[33] As noted in an earlier section, groups tend toward more risky decisions than the average group member. This of course is not inherently a drawback, since creative solutions to problems may entail more risk than solutions derived incrementally. Other potential disadvantages include dominance by one individual, social pressure to conform, and destructive competition among group members. Despite potential drawbacks, however, group decision making has significant strengths that should appeal to the modern manager.

Techniques of Decision Making

For the remainder of this section we focus on techniques used in the decision process. We examine some approaches to problem definition, generation of alternatives, evaluation of alternatives, and selection of alternatives for action.

Problem Finding It is not always easy to recognize when a problem exists. Visit a bank on the last day of the month and observe the long lines at the teller windows. Do the lines signify a problem? If you ask the last person in the longest line, the answer will probably be yes. If you ask the bank manager, the answer may be no, since it is known that the bank will be extra busy when people deposit their monthly paychecks. The person in line might argue that the bank was understaffed. The bank manager might argue that hiring additional staff to handle peak loads would cost more than the benefits are worth. In some respects, then, a problem, like beauty, is in the eye of the beholder.

A manager must always be alert to the possibility that an apparent problem is only a symptom of a deeper problem. If a bank experienced long lines most days, the lines then might be symptomatic of an underlying problem of understaffing. If staffing levels seemed adequate, the lines might be caused by inefficient tellers, in which case the underlying problem could be related to poor training programs or outmoded procedures. Alternatively, the tellers could be new and inexperienced, in itself a possible symptom of excessive turnover. As we note in chapter 10, turnover can be caused by many factors.

It should be obvious that definition of the problem is a critical first step in the decision process. Many managers have spent large sums of money and great amounts of time and energy solving the wrong problems. An all too typical response is depicted in Figure 7–4.

In decision merry-go-round the manager intuitively reacts to the visible symptoms and hastily arrives at "the" cause, intuitively leaps to "the" solution, and quickly enforces the decision. Ignored in this intellectual blitzkrieg are potential problems created by the decision itself. If the problem is not solved, then the process begins again. Managers often plead the pressure of time in making a decision but somehow find the time to re-do the decision process to overcome errors.

Take the example of a small business suffering a sales decline. The owner/manager might leap to the conclusion that the firm is not spending enough on advertising. So the manager might reduce budgets in other areas to provide cash for additional advertising. Possible consequences: product development falls behind, quality control becomes more difficult, cash flow problems develop, sales fall even further. Sales decline can be caused by many factors. If the manager in our example guessed correctly, everything would be fine. But a wrong guess may start up the managerial merry-go-round. Wouldn't it be better to take time to do it right initially?

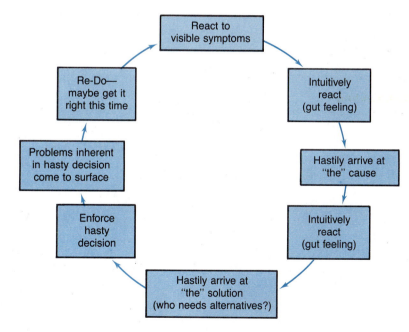

FIGURE 7–4
Managerial merry-go-round

Defining the Problem   To avoid decision merry-go-round it is very useful for the decision maker to put a "problem statement" in writing. This step provides at least two very real benefits. First, the manager must think about the problem in a disciplined way. Second, the problem statement can be shared with appropriate others, providing a focus for analysis and comment. Paradoxically, the critical first step of problem solving has been given less attention than the succeeding steps. Martin has suggested "A crisis is but a problem discovered or addressed too late. We seem to have become crisis addicts."[34]

Martin goes on to define four steps in problem identification: measuring results, comparing results to objectives, determining the significance of the difference, and communicating threshold differences to management. This implies that there *are* objectives, and that results will be measured. Churchman, Ackoff, and Arnoff acknowledge the frequent lack of explicit objectives and performance measures in their approach to problem formulation.

1. Identify decision maker(s)
2. Identify decision maker's objectives
3. Examine the system and its environment
4. Consider alternative courses of action and their consequences
5. Edit and condense the list of objectives and actions
6. Define a measure of effectiveness (objective function)[35]

Other writers have proposed similar steps for problem definition.[36] It is important to recognize that objectives are not always explicitly stated, so considering attributes of the decision makers can be a key aspect of problem definition.

A problem can be viewed as the gap between the current state and a desired state. Describing elements of the gap is a good first approximation of the problem. Unfortunately, the perceived problem (gap) may be different from the actual problem. Martin suggested that when the perceived problem is greater than the actual problem, the organization or decision maker responds in a panic mode: resources are deployed to solve a problem that has been overstated.[37] A crisis mode occurs when the perceived problem is less than the actual problem. The actual problem may have existed for some time without being perceived. Problem definition then may be the most important step in problem solving.

Generating Alternatives: The Need for Creativity   After the decision maker is satisfied with the definition of the problem, alternative approaches must be generated. This stage demands creativity, and it is clear that the level of creativity varies greatly between individuals. There has been in the last few years much investigation of the creative process and application to decision making.[38]

One of the landmark efforts was that of Adams.[39] He defined several areas in which creativity can be blocked: perceptual, cultural/environmental, emotional, and intellectual.

Perceptual blocks often occur when the decision maker is unable to classify the importance of information and lends too much importance to trivial information or too little importance to crucial data.

Cultural/environmental blocks occur as a consequence of who we are and where we are. In a true communist state, a problem of inefficient distribution of goods would be solved through almost any means other than a free market mechanism. In an organization that punishes failure, risk, even when desirable, would not be taken. Instead, most managers would make conservative decisions.

Emotional blocks may arise from personal fear of failure or ridicule, while intellectual blocks sometimes are caused by the blinders of specialization and the weight of "knowledge" that make it difficult to visualize a problem in an unorthodox manner.

The axiom that two heads are better than one holds merit here. Research generally supports the commonsense notion that the average number of ideas generated by groups will be greater than the average number generated by a similar number of individuals acting alone.[40] A technique that capitalizes on the creative potential of groups is brainstorming.

Brainstorming. Brainstorming was developed for use in an advertising agency to aid generating creative advertising ideas.[41] A problem is presented to a group, which proposes as many solutions to the problem as possible in a given amount of time. Four rules are followed in the first stage of brainstorming:

1. No evaluation or discussion of alternatives is allowed.
2. "Freewheeling" is encouraged. Ideas should be presented freely without regard for practicality.
3. Quantity is wanted.
4. Combination and "building" upon previously presented ideas is encouraged.[42]

As ideas are generated, the session leader or a designated member acts as recorder, listing the ideas on large sheets of paper. We have observed that the time consumed in recording sometimes hinders spontaneity, so we generally use two recorders.

Since spontaneity is encouraged in the brainstorming process, some attention must also be given to the composition of the group. It is generally not desirable to convene a group of experts on the topic, since their expertise may make it difficult for them to develop truly novel approaches. One can be so close to a problem that going beyond it for unusual solutions is difficult, an example of Adams' emotional blocks.

What about a single expert in a group of nonexperts? One argument holds that the expert will dominate the group and suppress innovative ideas from others. On the other hand, a true expert can help a decision-making group select alternatives. The group climate must also be at least moderately trusting and supportive. Participants are requested to offer "far-out" ideas, which would be unlikely if there is a chance that an idea would be exposed to ridicule later.[43]

The brainstorming group frequently "warms up" with an exercise unrelated to the focal issue. For example, the group might be asked to brainstorm possible uses for a dead car battery, ways to decrease congestion at O'Hare airport, or products that could be made from a wire coat hanger. The brainstorming session can be halted at the end of the idea generation phase or be extended to evaluate the alternatives.

A variation on brainstorming keeps all but the leader of the group uninformed of the problem under consideration. A key word is used to describe the problem area. For example, the word *security* might be used to start discussion on computer system security. It is assumed that more innovative ideas will emerge because the discussion is not narrowly limited.

Nominal Group Technique.   The Nominal Group Technique (NGT) is another technique for generating and evaluating alternatives. Developed by Delbecq and Van de Ven,[44] NGT has been widely applied in industry, government, health care, and educational environments. As in brainstorming, the first step involves presentation of a problem. From that point the two techniques have little in common.

In the second step of NGT, group members individually and silently put their ideas in writing. The term "nominal" refers to this part of the process. Though group members are in the same room, they are working independently; hence they are a group in name only.

After the group has stopped writing, ideas are voiced in round-robin fashion until all members have stated their ideas. The ideas are recorded in terse phrases on a flip chart. General discussion and clarification of the ideas follow. If desired, evaluation of alternatives and selection of one or more alternatives for implementation may follow.

Proponents argue that the early steps of Nominal Group Technique are superior to brainstorming because participants have adequate time for thinking and reflection, avoid interruptions, and avoid the problems of status pressure, pressure to conform, and competition.[45]

The Delphi survey technique.   The Delphi technique was developed at the Rand Corporation in the 1960s as a method for involving people in decision making who cannot come together physically.[46] Delphi thus allows the use of experts, clients, administrators, or other constituencies too numerous to handle in a small group setting or who are separated by distance or schedule difficulty.

Delphi is a series of questionnaires, the first of which poses a broad question. For example, a university posed the question "In what ways should this university be serving the community in the year 1995?" to selected members of the student body, alumni, faculty, staff, members of the business community, and city residents.

Responses to the first questionnaire form the basis for a follow-up questionnaire. The second questionnaire begins to forge consensus by asking respondents to select a subset of the ideas for further analysis and/or clarification. There may be several follow-up questionnaires in the Delphi process.

Unlike brainstorming or NGT, Delphi can provide anonymity to the respondents if desired. However, Delphi can be very time consuming due to mail delay and time involved in response and preparation of follow-up questionnaires.

BOX 7–2

Change in Decision Making at SAS

When Jan Carlzon was appointed president of Scandinavian Airlines System (SAS) in 1981, it had suffered its greatest loss ever. At the end of the next year SAS posted its greatest profit ever. How did Carlzon do it? By his own account the turnaround came from putting the airline through a cultural revolution. The main elements of the change were a new emphasis on customer service and pushing decision authority as far down the hierarchy as possible.

The corporate organization chart was symbolically changed from the traditional pyramidal shape to that of a wheel, with the president's office at the center. Carlzon likened the structure to that of a modern airport with a traffic controller in a centrally located tower.

Reversing the common practice of demanding more and more information for decision making, SAS in some cases actually reduced the amount available to headquarters. Many statistics previously supplied monthly were provided only quarterly. Statistics and research in some departments were eliminated entirely. Customer contact

personnel were granted authority to use personal initiative when dealing with passengers.

Carlzon's action orientation is exemplified by his statement, "It is much better to try, and make something that is not 100 percent correct, than not to do anything. We want to be one percent better in 100 details rather than 100 percent better in a single detail."

Lest it appear that Carlzon has adopted a laissez faire style, the reader should know about his emphasis on flight punctuality. After announcing that he wanted SAS to be the most punctual airline, he installed a terminal in his office so he could personally monitor arrival and departure times. Some months later the Association of European Airlines reported SAS to be number one in punctuality in Europe and the North and South Atlantic.

Questions

1. How would you characterize the decision style of SAS's Jan Carlzon?
2. What reasons might Carlzon have for reducing the amount of information available to some units (including headquarters)?
3. What are the most significant risks in Carlzon's granting of personal initiative to employees in customer service?

Source: Reprinted with special permission from "Personal Touch Pulls SAS out of Its Stall," *International Management* (December 1982): 19-22. Copyright © McGraw-Hill Publications Company. All rights reserved.

Evaluating Alternatives and Making the Decision   The brainstorming, NGT, and Delphi techniques may all be extended beyond generation of alternatives to evaluation and even the final choice. Each approach has something to recommend it.

The great strength of brainstorming lies in the rapidity with which large numbers of alternatives can be generated. The group may then discuss and evaluate all of the alternatives presented. Consensus may be forged, but it generally takes a substantial amount of time. As an interacting group, the brain-stormers can fall prey to the problems inherent in an unstructured meeting format. A strong group leader can keep discussion on track, but even then several meetings may be required before consensus is reached.

Both NGT and Delphi generally select alternatives through a voting process. In the case of NGT, discussion and evaluation of alternatives follow the initial listing. It is important that alternatives receive adequate clarification and discussion, so considerable time can be consumed. After discussion, participants individually vote by ranking or rating the alternatives. The preferred alternative is then derived mathematically.

For example, assume that an NGT group of six members was asked to evaluate five alternatives and select one for implementation. After discussion the group members individually ranked the alternatives by priority. The group leader then put the priorities on a blackboard, as in Table 7–2.

Alternative number three is preferred. Even though participants one and four did not strongly support alternative three in their voting, there is a good chance that they will support the group decision. NGT has allowed each group member to discuss and analyze the alternatives, and every participant has had a similar role in selection of the alternative.

Delphi has some strong similarities to NGT. Both techniques rely on individual effort to produce ideas, combine the ideas for evaluation, and use voting procedures to select an alternative. The major differences between the techniques lie in the extent of personal interaction. Delphi respondents are usually anonymous, and participation at each step is on an individual basis. NGT participants form an interacting group during the clarification and evaluation steps.

The advent of personal computers has opened fascinating possibilities for the application of the Delphi technique. Imagine participants separated by many miles and several time zones. The Delphi questionnaires could be "posted" in

TABLE 7–2

Example of NGT voting

| | Alternative Number | | | | |
Participant Number	1	2	3 Priorities	4	5
1	2	1	3	4	5
2	4	3	1	5	2
3	3	4	2	5	1
4	1	2	3	4	5
5	3	4	2	1	5
6	5	3	1	2	4
Sum	18	17	12	21	22
Mean Ranking	3.0	2.83	2.0	3.5	3.67

electronic bulletin boards, allowing respondents to participate as their schedules permit. Some of the delays in turnaround that seem inherent to the Delphi process could thus be significantly reduced. Respondents would also have the capability to seek clarification of alternatives. The new electronic Delphi might be viewed as a hybrid of Delphi and NGT. Some of NGT's immediacy could be combined with the Delphi advantage of tapping the knowledge of experts and the opinions of wide-spread constituencies. (In chapter 13 we explore that issue further, along with other facets of computers and their impact on the world of work.)

Important aspects of the decision approaches are summarized in Table 7–3.

It is important to recognize that the approaches discussed can be used in combination. We have on occasion used brainstorming to generate alternatives and NGT to evaluate and reduce that list to a smaller set (rather than to a single alternative). The reduced set of alternatives we then referred to a staff group for further analysis and recommendation. A single executive reviewed the analysis

TABLE 7–3
Comparison of decision approaches

	Time	Acceptance	Number of Alternatives	Analysis of Alternatives	When to Use the Techniques
Individual	Short	Very low to high	One to many	Superficial to thorough	When acceptance is not an issue When creativity and many options are not crucial When time is the overriding factor
Brainstorming	Moderate	Usually high	Many	Usually thorough	When many alternatives are wanted When participation is important
NGT	Moderate	Usually high	Many	Usually thorough	When many alternatives are wanted When participation is important When consensus is needed
Delphi	Long	Usually high	Many	Differs among the respondents	When many alternatives are wanted When participation is important When consensus is needed When participants cannot be in the same location

and recommendation and selected an alternative for implementation, using Vroom and Yettons decision style CII.

Computational Decision-making Techniques There are a number of algorithmic decision-making approaches available to the manager, such as payoff matrices, linear programming, and decision trees. We will not cover those approaches here since they are typically dealt with in finance, accounting, operations management, and decision theory courses, and our emphasis here is on the behavioral aspects of decision making.

The computational techniques are extremely useful in many decision situations, but they do suffer from some of the weaknesses of more heuristic approaches. Any decision approach is only as good as the data and the assumptions that fuel it. In some respects the computational techniques are particularly prone to this weakness. The nature of the techniques often create an illusion of specificity and scientific rigor. An example of this problem befell a colleague who teaches operations and logistics management.

He was shopping for a new automobile and used linear programming as an aid (and as an applied example for his class). He listed a number of "hard" criteria and constraints—such as price, EPA mileage rating, fuel capacity, trunk space in cubic feet, etc.—and "soft" criteria—such as seat comfort, instrument layout, etc. He analyzed and rank ordered fifteen automobile models (A through O) by their ability to fulfill the objective function. Models B, E, and G were ranked first, second, and third. Our colleague actually purchased model F, which was ranked fifth. When questioned about this unusual result our colleague said simply, "But I *like* model F!"

The moral of the story: no decision-making method is free of the values, perceptions, and assumptions of the decision maker. Our colleague left an important criterion out of the algorithm.

Summary of Key Concepts

1. Observation suggests that managers frequently adopt an incremental or "satisficing" approach to decision making rather than maximizing.

2. Decision theory is often prescriptive, complete with analytic steps, but the garbage can model suggests the steps can be scrambled or even reversed.

3. Many factors outside the immediate situation influence the decision process. Examples include the manager's values, experience, and propensity toward risk.

4. A decision maker should be able to use several different decision styles and know when it is important to include others in the decision.

5. Group decision making can enhance decision quality and acceptance, but it is more time consuming. In addition, not all employees favor participation.

6. Definition of the problem is probably the most important step in problem solving, but is the least researched.

7. Brainstorming, Nominal Group Technique, and the Delphi survey technique are useful tools for including others in problem solving and decision making.

Key Terms

Alternative generation

Brainstorming

Computational decision-making
    techniques

Delphi survey technique

Incrementalism

Nominal Group Technique

Problem finding

Satisficing

Subjective Expected Utility

MANAGERIAL APPLICATIONS

In the first part of the chapter, we address the broad areas of decision processes, decision styles, and decision-making techniques. In this section, we look at some of the issues involved in these areas from the viewpoint of a practicing, action-oriented manager.

A Realistic Look at Decision Making

One of the first things that practicing managers tell us is that decision making is not accomplished "according to the book." In theory, a manager sits alone in an office considering different courses of action, absorbing piles of data—much of which is computer-generated—discarding inappropriate alternatives, and finally choosing the one alternative that is most likely to achieve the organization's stated objectives. This decision is communicated throughout the organization and the various members then strive to implement it. That's what the theory says.

According to Robard Y. Hughes, that decision process has little relation to reality.[47] More likely is a picture that looks like this: a harried manager with ten other pressing matters on his or her mind, constantly interrupted by the telephone, tries to make sense out of stacks of almost unintelligible information that may or may not be relevant to the situation at hand. Trying to find a way out of this mess, the manager seeks information from subordinates who provide a carefully screened view of the situation, emphasizing their perception of it, their idea of resources available to deal with it, and the "best" solution to the problem. Finally, the manager makes a delaying, "time buying" decision that does not seem to be very forthright or decisive. And things go on pretty much as they have in the past.

Many organizational decisions are not clear cut; they are slippery and amorphous. Because of the information explosion we are confronted with reams of data—and an opportunity to collect about as much additional data as we want to pay for. Consequently, we tend to surround ourselves with so many "facts" that we are often unable to see any clear pattern that would help in making the decision. In fact, past a certain point, the more information we have available the less helpful it is in making a good decision.

Part of the reason for this is that the "facts" often are in conflict. A recent survey of chief executive officers found that one of the main obstacles they saw to increased productivity at the highest levels of organizations was the inability to get any real "facts."[48] According to one CEO surveyed, "Nobody knows anything, yet everybody knows everything." He related the difficulties that his organization had experienced in trying to obtain some information relating to the future trend of interest rates that would be very important to some significant decisions regarding resource allocation that he would soon have to make. He and his staff met with several of the most prominent experts in the country, each of whom had very impressive credentials, and found that their opinions were in direct conflict. One expert predicted a rise in future interest rates, another predicted a decline. Faced with this situation, the CEO was forced to use his own judgement in determining which of the experts was correct and to spend a large amount of resources based on this determination.

While this example was unique because of the financial implications, the CEO stated that this type of situation was not unusual. He was often forced to use his inexpert judgement to determine which of several conflicting expert opinions was correct—or at leaast would provide the most reasonable basis for the decision that had to be made. So one of the realities of decision making is that obtaining factual information to incorporate into the decision process may be difficult or even impossible. The chief executive's story seems to support the notion of incrementalism as a common decision method.

Much decision theory states that decisions are rational, but hunches have a great deal of value in decision making. A manager should not permit healthy instincts to be "educated out." We are not computers and shouldn't attempt to perform as they do. When a person has been working and managing in a field for some time, his or her hunches are more than just flights of fancy. They may be instantaneous efforts by the brain to riffle through multitudinous files, pull out the pertinent ideas and experiences, collate them, and provide a fast answer. Hunches are the product of instinct, experience, perceptiveness, and intelligence. It would be foolish to act on hunches all the time or without doing some checking, but it is wasteful to ignore the "flash" answer from the brain when it is confronted with a problem.[49]

Most decisions are probably made with the expectation that action will follow, yet often it does not. This can happen for a multitude of reasons—the decision is inappropriate, the people who will be affected by the decision don't agree with it, the resources to carry it out aren't available, the decision isn't understood—but it often happens. The CEO of a major international organization relates that a chief frustration is that "we sit here in our fancy offices at headquarters and make all sorts of decisions that we think will have an impact on what we do—and how we do it. We spend a lot of time and effort in doing this, for obvious reasons. Yet in one historic case—historic to us, at least—we made some major changes in several of our programs only to find that in our field offices, after a year had gone by, NOTHING HAD HAPPENED! In spite of the fact that we had done all the kinds of things we were supposed to do to get the program changes implemented."[50] Things often don't happen as the theory says they should!

Might the people at headquarters have neglected to include the field personnel in the decision process? Had they been included would implementation have occurred?

Information Gathering

We've just said that facts may be in conflict, that they may be difficult to obtain, and that too much information may get in the way of making an appropriate decision. Yet in the fast food industry, the acquisition of information on the probable success of potential new products is a major, expensive effort. According to the *Wall Street Journal*, the fast food industry is becoming increasingly sophisticated in deciding what foods to sell.[51] They are adopting exhaustive market research techniques and expanding their development staffs in an effort to make these decisions better. Four years ago, for example, Wendy's didn't even have a research and development staff. Now they have forty-two people in that area.

While using a series of sophisticated information gathering and testing techniques, there is still a portion of individual input in the decision process. Ray Kroc, founder of McDonald's Corporation, always insisted that franchises near his home be included in test market areas for new products. He wanted to personally sample each new proposed addition to the menu.

Even such seemingly trivial matters as which cola should be served now get major attention from fast food chains. Before switching to Pepsi from Coke, Burger King Corporation spent more than two years examining data from the soft drink industry and doing its own market research. At one point, it sent employees on an undercover mission to Jack-In-The-Box franchises to clock how much time was wasted informing customers who asked for Coke that the chain serves Pepsi instead.

While there is great secrecy regarding the introduction of new products in the industry, the basic procedures at the leading chains are essentially the same. Ideas for new products come from a variety of sources—with the notable exception of customers (the chains fear that taking ideas from this source would invite lawsuits demanding royalties). Successful ideas have come from franchise owners, company employees, and company chefs, and from monitoring grocery store shelves and scanning hundreds of cookbooks each year.

All the major chains spend hours timing how long it takes employees to put pickles on buns, spread ketchup, and flip hamburgers. Before McDonald's puts an item on its menu, it runs simulations in a test kitchen using register tapes from a busy period at one of its restaurants. As the tester reads from the tapes, he adds orders for the new food. The results help McDonald's judge the effect a new product might have on the restaurant's overall efficiency.

Obvious barriers to an item making it to the big time in the fast food field are problems inherent in providing a standard menu throughout the chain, and the logistics of lining up enough suppliers to provide the needed ingredients for such massive orders. For example, McDonald's had to line up enough chicken to sell five million pounds of McNuggets a week. And with 6,200 restaurants in the United States, the company can't afford to be involved in items whose price might fluctuate widely on the national market. "Just deciding to put three strips of bacon on a burger can have a tremendous effect on the supply of pork bellies," according to Burger King officials.[52]

Yet, in spite of all of this attention to detail and gathering of solid information on which to base a decision, new product failures do happen. McDonald's withdrew the McRib barbecue sandwich from the market. This brings us back to the issue of information in the decision process. When is too much information dysfunctional? How do you know when you have enough? How do you know if what you have is accurate? How do you know if your information is relevant? These are difficult questions with no easy answers. Look at your own experience and see what examples you can come up with that shed some light on the issue of information in decision making.

Decision Making in Japan—Consultative or Participative?

Japanese management systems have had great impact upon management thinking throughout the world. Much of the interest in Japanese management systems has focused on the ways in which decisions are made in Japanese organizations. Some observers have confused the Japanese system of consultative decision making with participative decision making. The two methods, however, are quite different.

The extensive face-to-face communication observed in Japanese companies is sometimes confused with participative decision making. However, data from several studies indicate that the extent of face-to-face communication bears no relationship to employees' perceptions of their level of participation in decision making. The usual procedure for decision making is that a proposal is initiated by a middle manager, most often under the directive of top management. This middle manager engages in informal discussion and consultation with peers and supervisors. When all are familiar with the proposal, a request for a decision is made formally and, because of the earlier discussions, it is almost inevitably ratified, often in a ceremonial group meeting. This does not indicate unanimous approval, but does imply consent to its implementation. The manager does not decide until others who will be affected have had sufficient time to offer their views, feel they have been fairly heard, and are willing to support the decision even though they may feel it is not the best one.[53]

This kind of decision making is not "participative" in the American sense of the word, which implies frequent group meetings and negotiation between manager and subordinates. Nor is it "bottom-up." Rather, it is a top-down, or interactive consultative, process, especially when long-term planning and strategy is involved. It is perhaps more akin to the Vroom-Yetton CI or CII styles than anything else. Although the locus of responsibility may appear ambiguous to outsiders, it is actually quite clear within the organization, especially at the upper levels.

Computer-based Decisions

One of the most intriguing things we have seen recently has been a series of brochures from a management consulting firm that advertises a decision-making service based on computer analysis of your managerial characteristics and the characteristics of your customer. Much of what we talk about in the decision-making process section of this chapter—values, willingness to take risk, leadership style—is placed into a computer that analyzes this data and then gives specific instructions on how to behave. It's almost like not making any decision at all!

In the sales-oriented brochure we saw, the sales manager answers eighty-six questions asked by the computer about himself or herself.[54] The same process is followed to gather data about the customer. The manager need not have any knowledge of computers to do this, according to the brochure. Then

> the computer searches through thousands of possible responses based on your answers. In seconds, you have a sales strategy report, on-line and printed. A winning sales strategy that is based on the personal characteristics of your customer, and you. Sales strategy reports give you specific facts. No punches pulled. You learn your customer's strengths and weaknesses. And your strengths and weaknesses. Each detailed 5–7 page strategy analysis is different, each specific to the unique situation. Each sales strategy report shows you how you have to be different with different customers.[55]

We have not personally used this service and cannot comment on its validity or effectiveness. The notion that a computer could assume such a large part of the decision process and assume the kind of components of that process that this software system purports to assume would not have been accepted by the managerial community five or ten years ago. But with the advances in computer technology that have been made in recent years and the continuing rapid advances that are currently being made, we expect to see more and more of the decision-making process be somehow oriented to computers. It will probably be oriented in ways in which the computer plays a part in the value and relationship issues, rather than in the relatively simple process of data crunching. As the salesperson enters your office, you might have to ask if you are really dealing with a person or with a computer—formulated strategy being communicated by a person!

DISCUSSION QUESTIONS

1. Does Subjective Expected Utility leave any critical variables out of the decision-making process? If so, what are they and why should they be included?

2. In what specific ways might values influence decision making?

3. A question in the Vroom and Yetton model asks: "Is acceptance of the decision by subordinates critical to effective implementation?" How could a manager, especially a new manager, determine the answer to that question?

4. Consider the following situation: You are a member of a fraternity/sorority that has extra budget funds and it has been decided the funds should be used for a group function. Only three ideas were offered at the meeting and none were satisfactory. The group is now splitting into factions and hostility is becoming apparent. What specific suggestions can you make to restore harmony and decide on a use for the funds?

5. Imagine two managers in similar jobs. One of the managers feels uncomfortable in making decisions alone. This manager involves others in virtually every decision, no matter how trivial. The second manager subscribes to the steely-eyed, granite-jawed philosophy of individual decision-making. This manager rarely asks others opinions, even in decisions that affect them directly. As an outside observer, what differences would you expect to see in the functioning of these managers' units?

EXERCISE: PERSONNEL ASSIGNMENT

You are supervising the work of 12 engineers. Their formal training and work experience are very similar, permitting you to use them interchangeably on projects. Yesterday your manager informed you that a request had been received from an overseas affiliate for four engineers to go abroad on extended loan for a period of six to eight months. For a number of reasons, he argued and you agreed that this request should be filled from your group.

All your engineers are capable of handling this assignment and, from the standpoint of present and future projects, there is no particular reason why any one engineer should be retained over any other. The problem is somewhat complicated by the fact that the overseas assignment is in what is generally regarded as an undesirable location.

Source: Reprinted, by permission of the publisher, from "A New Look at Managerial Decision Making," by Victor H. Vroom, *Organizational Dynamics*, Spring 1973, p. 73. © 1973 AMACOM, a division of American Management Associations, New York. All rights reserved.

Questions

1. Analyze this situation using the Vroom and Yetton model.

2. What process would you employ to select the engineer to go on loan? Outline the specific steps you would take.

NOTES

1. Reprinted from *David Frost's Book of The World's Worst Decisions*," by David Frost and Michael Deakin. Copyright © by David Paradine Productions Limited. Illustrations copyright © 1983 by Arnie Levin. Used by permission of Crown Publishers, Inc.

2. A. M. McDonough, *Information Economics and Management Systems* (New York: McGraw-Hill, 1963): 72.

3. R. A. MacKenzie, "The Management Process in 3-D," *Harvard Business Review* (November–December 1969): 80–87.

4. J. E. Robertshaw, S. J. Mecca, and M. N. Rerick, *Problem Solving: A Systems Approach* (New York: Petrocelli Books, 1978).

5. H. A. Simon, *The New Science of Management Decision* (New York: Harper & Row, 1960).

6. A. O. Elbing, *Behavioral Decisions in Organizations* (Glenview, IL: Scott, Foresman, 1970).

7. H. I. Ansoff, "Managerial Problem Solving," *Journal of Business Policy*, 1 (1971): 3–20.

8. H. A. Simon, *Administrative Behavior*, 3rd ed. (New York: Free Press, 1976).

9. C. E. Lindblom, "The Science of Muddling Through," *Public Administration Review* 19 (1959): 79–88.

10. C. E. Lindblom, "Still Muddling, Not Yet Through," *Public Administration Review* (November–December 1979): 517.

11. C. Cates, "Beyond Muddling: Creativity," *Public Administration Review* (November–December 1979): 528.

12. D. Cohen, J. G. March, and J. P. Olsen, "A Garbage Can Model of Organizational Choice," *Administrative Science Quarterly* 17 (1972): 1–25.

13. Ibid., p. 2.

14. J. Martin, "A Garbage Can Model of the Psychological Research Process," *American Behavioral Scientist* (November–December 1981): 131–151.

15. B. Fischoff, B. Goitein, and Z. Shapira, "Subjective Expected Utility: A Model of Decision-Making," *Journal of the American Society for Information Science* (September 1981): 391–399.

16. L. R. Goldberg, "Simple Models or Simple Processes? Some Research on Clinical Judgements," *American Psychologist*, vol. 23 (1968): 483–496; and L. R. Goldberg, "Man Versus Model of Man: A Rationale, Plus Some Evidence, for a Method of Improving on Clinical Inferences," *Psychological Bulletin*, vol. 73 (1970): 422–432.

17. R. M. Dawes, "The Robust Beauty of Improper Linear Models," *American Psychologist* (1979): 571–582; and R. M. Dawes and B. Corrigan, "Linear Models in Decision Making," *Psychological Bulletin*, 2 (1974): 95–106.

18. H. A. Gadr, E. R. Gray, and B. L. Kedia, "Personal Values and Managerial Decision Making: Evidence from Two Cultures," *Management International Review*, vol. 22 (1982): 65–68; and G. Hofstede, *Culture's Consequences: International Differences in Work Related Values* (Beverly Hills, CA: Sage Publications, 1980).

19. D. M. Grether and C. R. Plott, "Economic Theory of Choice and the Preference Reversal Phenomenon," *American Economic Review* (September 1979): 623–624.

20. G. Loomes and R. Sugden, "A Rationale for Preference Reversal," *American Economic Review* (June 1983): 428.

21. J. Kuhl, "Standard Setting and Risk Preference: An Elaboration of the Theory of Achievement Motivation and an Empirical Test," *Psychological Review*, vol. 85 (1978).

22. R. Libby and P. Fishburn, "Behavior Models of Risk Taking in Business Decisions: A Survey and Evaluation," *Journal of Accounting Research* (Autumn 1977).

23. S. A. Karagenick and M. M. Addy, "Locus of Control and Sex Differences in Skill and Chance Risk-Taking Conditions," *Journal of General Psychology* (April 1979).

24. A. Tversky and D. Kahneman, "Judgment under Uncertainty: Heuristics and Biases," *Science*, vol. 185 (1974): 1124–1131.

25. N. R. Johnson, J. G. Stander, and D. Hunter, "Crowd Behavior as 'Risky Shift': A Laboratory Experiment," *Sociometry* (June 1977): 183–187; J. P. Kahan, "A Subjective Probability Interpretation of the Risky Shift," *Journal of Personality and Social Psychology* (June 1975): 977–982; and D. G. Pruitt and C. Costentino, "The Role of Values in the Choice Shift," *Journal of Experimental Social Psychology* (July 1975): 301–316.

26. F. E. Kast and J. E. Rosenzweig, *Organization and Management: A Systems and Contingency Approach* (New York: McGraw-Hill, 1979).

27. V. H. Vroom and P. W. Yetton, *Leadership and Decision-Making*, (Pittsburgh: University of Pittsburgh Press, 1973).

28. I. Lorge et al., "A Survey of Studies Contrasting the Quality of Group Performance and Individual Performance, 1930–1957," *Psychological Bulletin* (November 1958): 337–372.

29. C. R. Holloman and H. W. Hendrick, "Adequacy of Group Decisions as a Function of the Decision-Making Process," *Academy of Management Journal*, 2 (1972): 175–184.

30. J. W. Driscoll, "Trust and Participation in Organizational Decision Making as Predictors of Satisfaction," *Academy of Management Journal*, 1 (1978): 44–56.

31. J. A. Alutto and D. J. Vrenenburgh, "Characteristics of Decisional Participation by Nurses," *Academy of Management Journal*, 2 (1977): 341–347.

32. V. H. Vroom, "Some Personality Determinants of the Effects of Participation," *Journal of Abnormal and Social Psychology*, 59 (1959): 322–327.

33. K. Lewin, "Frontiers in Group Dynamics: Concept, Method and Reality in Social Science; Social Equilibria and Social Change," *Human Relations*, 1 (1947): 5–41.

34. M. P. Martin, "Problem Identification", *Journal of Systems Management* (December 1977): 10.

35. C. W. Churchman, R. L. Ackoff, and E. L. Arnoff, *Introduction to Operations Research*, (New York: Wiley, 1960).

36. G. Mosard, "Problem Definition: Tasks and Techniques," *Journal of Systems Management* (June 1983): 16–21; and C. S. White, "Problem Solving: The Neglected First Step," *Management Review* (January 1983): 52–55.

37. Martin, "Problem Identification."

38. S. Baker, *Systematic Approach to Advertising Creativity* (New York: McGraw-Hill, 1979); J. P. Guilford, *The Nature of Human Intelligence* (New York: McGraw-Hill, 1976); and G. M. Prince, *The Practice of Creativity* (New York: Collier, 1973).

39. J. L. Adams, *Conceptual Blockbusting: A Guide to Better Ideas* (San Francisco: W. H. Freeman, 1974).

40. E. J. Hall, J. Mouton, and R. R. Blake, "Group Problem Solving Effectiveness Under Conditions of Pooling Versus Interaction," *Journal of Social Psychology*, 59 (1963): 147–157; and R. A. Weber, "The Relation of Group Performance to the Age of Members in Homogeneous Groups," *Academy of Management Journal*, 3 (1974): 570–574.

41. A. F. Osborn, *Applied Imagination* (New York: Scribners, 1957).

42. Ibid.

43. W. A. Frederickson and G. Kizziar, "Accurate, Deceptive, and No Prior Feedback about Decision-making Acumen as an Influencer of Group Decisionmaking," *Journal of Applied Social Psychology*, 3 (1973): 232–239.

44. A. L. Delbecq and A. H. Van de Ven, "A Group Process Model for Problem Identification and Program Planning," *Journal of Applied Behavioral Science* (July–August 1971).

45. A. L. Delbecq, A. H. Van de Ven, and D. H. Gustafson, *Group Techniques for Program Planning* (Glenview, IL: Scott, Foresman, 1975).

46. N. D. Dalkey, *Delphi* (Rand Corporation, 1967).

47. R. Y. Hughes, "A Realistic Look at Decision Making," *Supervisory Management* (January 1980): 2–8.

48. H. R. Knudson, "Productivity—A Dilemma for the 1980's," paper presented at the Western Division, American Institute of Decision Sciences, December 1982.

49. Hughes, "A Realistic Look at Decision Making."

50. Knudson, "Productivity."

51. "Fast-food Firms' New Items Undergo Exhaustive Testing," *The Wall Street Journal*, (5 January 1984): 19.

52. Ibid.

53. N. Hatvany and V. Puciok, "An Integrated Management System: Lessons from the Japanese Experience," *Academy of Management Review*, vol. 6, no. 3 (1961): 473.

54. "The Sales Edge," brochure from The Human Edge Software Corporation, Palo Alto, CA, February 1984.

55. Ibid.

RECOMMENDED READINGS

J. E. Robertshaw, S. J. Mecca, and M. N. Rerick, *Problem Solving: A Systems Approach* (New York: Petrocelli Books, 1978).

This book views problem solving from a systems perspective. The sections on systems model construction and problem definition are particularly useful.

A. L. Delbecq, A. H. Van de Ven, and D. H. Gustafson, *Group Techniques for Program Planning* (Glenview, IL: Scott, Foresman, 1975).

This is a step-by-step analysis of the NGT and Delphi techniques, extremely useful for the practitioner.

J. L. Adams, *Conceptual Blockbusting: A Guide to Better Ideas* (San Francisco: W. H. Freeman, 1974).

This book is interesting reading, with many examples and unique suggestions for fostering creativity.

Getting Out of the Army

Jay Abbott is confident that his future will be secure and financially rewarding should he decide to remain in the army. He entered the army more than 10 years ago as a commissioned officer after completing his college education on an ROTC scholarship. Jay, who is 31 years old, has progressed to the grade of captain and is currently being considered for promotion to major. He has no reason to believe he will not be promoted to the grade of major. He has been successful in all of his appointments, is well liked by everyone—his peers, superiors, and subordinates—and has an unblemished record.

However, upon reaching the 10-year mark, Jay had second thoughts regarding whether he should stay in or leave the army, and has been thinking about leaving ever since. He has felt increasingly resentful that the army has affected a large part of his personal life. Although he had always preferred to wear his hair shorter than that of most young men, he resented the fact that even if he wanted to let it grow out or have sideburns, he couldn't do it. It was the principle of the whole idea—the intrusion of the army into his personal life. The fact that this intrusion extended beyond himself, to the behavior of his wife and children, bothered him even more.

Jay's wife, Ellen, was finishing up her master's thesis. This took up a substantial portion of her free time; yet her lack of involvement in the officers' clubs was inevitably frowned upon. There was just no such thing as a private family life in his position. He didn't even have much time to spend with the family. His job required long hours of work, including weekend duty, which left little time for his wife and two daughters, aged seven and nine. Another problem constantly on his mind was the fact that Ellen, holding a degree in design engineering, was unable to pursue any kind of real career—something that was important to both of them.

These thoughts raced through Jay's mind over and over again as he tried to decide what would be best for him and his family. There were a lot of positive factors about the army, he kept reminding himself: he was already earning $21,000 a year, and with his near-certain promotion, this would be raised to $25,000. He could not forget the fact that he was being recommended for the Army's Command and General Staff College. There was little chance he would not be approved and, upon completing the program, his future would be even brighter. If he stayed, he'd be able to retire in just 10 more years (at age 41) with a permanent retirement income of half his final salary plus free medical and dental coverage. By then, he figured he would probably be a lieutenant colonel with a base pay of around $37,000; at worst he would retire a major. At 41, there would be plenty of time to devote to a second career should he so desire.

But then, Jay could argue that regardless of how attractive the benefits seemed, it was a fact that salaries in the armed services had not kept pace with the rising rate of inflation; Congress had held the lid on raises at five percent. Furthermore, he did not anticipate any change in their posture in the next few years. In fact, Jay had read several newspaper articles indicating that Congress was considering reducing benefits for

Source: Leslie Rue and Lloyd Byars, *Management: Theory and Application*, 3rd ed., pp. 82–83. Copyright © 1983 by Richard D. Irwin, Inc. Reprinted with permission.

the armed services—the 20-year retirement specifically.

Jay had done some checking around and learned that the training and experience received in the army was valuable to civilian employers. Having been commissioned in the signal corps, he had vast experience in the area of telecommunications. He had recently completed a tour as an instructor in a service school. He had also been in many positions of leadership during his term in the army. At 31, he probably had more firsthand managerial experience than most civilian managers. He knew that large organizations were currently hiring young ex-military officers at salaries of $5,000 higher than recent college graduates.

Jay knew he had to make a decision soon. The closer he got to the 20-year mark, the more he stood to lose by leaving the army. He knew that if he was going to make a change, it had to be soon.

Questions

1. What should Jay do?
2. What factors should be considered in Jay's decision?
3. What role would values play in Jay's decision?

PART THREE
Organizational Aspects of Organizational Behavior

CHAPTER EIGHT
Conflict Management

OBJECTIVES

- Describe major conflict models
- Identify conditions when conflict is desirable
- Describe the effects of intergroup conflict
- Discuss major conflict resolution modes
- Describe techniques for stimulating conflict

All My Police Chiefs

Four Algona (Washington) City Council members yesterday staged an early morning coup and physically reinstated Dave Norton as the town's police chief. The move deposed Chief Al Lee, whom Mayor Bud Larson had installed when he fired Norton in January.

The embattled Larson fumed and fidgeted as the day passed, planning his revenge on the plotters.

"I don't know what they're up to," Larson said angrily as he paced about the small town's City Hall. "They're getting involved with things they have no control over. This is ridiculous."

The City Council's swift action apparently took Larson by surprise. He didn't admit defeat though, until his troops deserted him. When all three of the town's police officers supported Norton, Larson knew he'd lost.

But another chapter in the soap opera was expected to unfold today because of a directive Larson issued to Norton yesterday afternoon. In it, Larson, in a shrewd maneuver, ordered Norton to work "under the supervision and direction" of Lee.

Norton said he would not comply with the order. Algona has only one police chief, he says: Dave Norton. "We can't allow one man to rule in the way that has been in effect—a Gestapo manner," Norton said. "Here you have one man defying the whole world. You can't have that—it's reminiscent of Hitler's Germany."

Norton said he would go to court if Larson followed through with his threat to fire him for disobeying the directive. He sees that as the final remedy to the problem. "I refuse to recognize the legality of this order," he said.

It wouldn't be Norton's first time in court over the issue. The town's Civil Service Commission has ruled twice that Larson improperly fired Norton, and a King County Superior Court ruled the same way. But Larson, increasingly alienated from many of the town's residents who have launched a recall drive, won't give up.

Meanwhile, confusion reigns in the Algona Police Department. Although Lee still wore his chief's badge and answered the phone as "Chief Lee," it was apparent who was in charge yesterday, at least in the police department. Algona's police force was taking orders from its former boss—Norton.

Lee promised not to do anything to "adversely affect" Norton's orders. He said he didn't want to add to the confusion of the situation. He also said he has hired a lawyer, and hinted he might sue the town if he gets fired.[1]

THE STUDY OF CONFLICT

Introduction

The opening story demonstrates clearly some problems that destructive conflict can create: frustration, hostility, and disruption of organizational processes. The citizens of Algona could surely be forgiven if they wanted to start afresh with a new police chief, mayor, *and* city council.

Though the Algona situation is unusual in both its severity and its impact on an entire community, organizational conflict is not unusual. A survey of executives and middle managers by the American Management Association revealed that the managers spent about 24 percent of their time dealing with conflict. They considered conflict management equal to or slightly higher in importance than planning, communication, motivation, and decision making.[2]

Considering the time expended dealing with conflict, it seems reasonable that managers should learn the causes of conflict, ways to diagnose the type of conflict confronting them, and methods or techniques for managing the conflict.

Conflict Defined

The term *conflict* has been used at times to describe the antecedent conditions to the conflict episode (for example, scarcity of resources), affective states of individuals such as hostility or anxiety, cognitive states of individuals relative to their awareness of conflict situations, and conflict behavior states ranging from passive resistance to overt aggression.[3]

As we will use the term, conflict refers to all types of opposition or antagonistic interaction.[4] It is not certain whether competition should be considered conflict. In American folklore, competition is indisputably a good thing, while conflict is usually a bad thing. In terms of our simple definition of conflict, it is hard to treat competition as a separate category. Competition implies opposition and, as NFL football players will attest, frequently involves antagonistic interaction.

Rather than attempt a definitional separation, let us simply note that there is constructive conflict and destructive conflict. Constructive conflict can cause individuals and organizations to become more creative and productive by rising to a challenge. Destructive conflict consumes personal and organizational resources in hostility, spitefulness, and bitterness.

Models of Conflict

A number of scholars have proposed theoretical models of conflict. Thomas has categorized the models as oriented to either the process or the structure of a conflict situation.[5] Process models identify the events within a conflict episode and trace the relationship of each event to succeeding events. Structural models define underlying conditions and describe how those conditions shape events and influence conflict behavior.

Another group of academicians has developed what we will call organizational conflict models. We briefly review examples of each model type.

Pondy's Process Conflict Model   Pondy proposed the process conflict model in Figure 8–1.[6] The aftermath of preceding conflict episodes sets the stage for those that follow. Past experience with the antagonistic party sets expectations and to a certain extent determines the response to a new episode.

Latent conflict refers to the underlying conditions for conflict. Scarcity of resources, the drive for autonomy versus the need for control, and divergence of personal or unit goals are examples of such underlying conditions. Environmental effects also influence latent conflict. For example, an organization in a declining

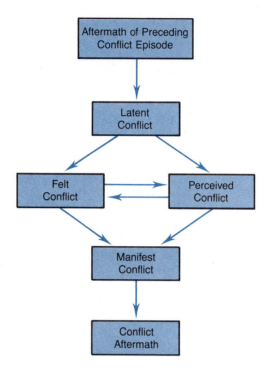

FIGURE 8–1
Pondy's conflict model (Source: Adapted from L. R. Pondy, "Organizational Conflict: Concepts and Models." *Administrative Science Quarterly,* vol. 12 (1967): 306, Figure 1. Used by permission.)

industry faces more stressful conditions than an organization in a stable or growing industry.

Perceived conflict occurs with awareness of the existence of the latent conditions. Divergent goals do not create conflict until someone notices that they are divergent. Perceived conflict is still incipient; the parties have not yet responded affectively. Two mechanisms operate to keep latent conflict from being perceived. First, suppression occurs when conflict is only mildly threatening and not "worth" dealing with. Second, the attention-focus mechanism represents organizational and individual priorities. There may be more conflicts than can be dealt with easily, so attention is focused on only a few.

Perceived conflict does not always become felt conflict. People may disagree over an issue but feel no anxiety or animosity. Felt conflict reaches the level of experience. At least some of the parties respond affectively, perhaps through anxiety, frustration, or feelings of hostility.

Manifest conflict is expressed through behavior. The expression may be as low key as apathy or as dramatic as overt hostility or aggression. Whether perceived conflict and felt conflict become manifest conflict depends partly on the availability of resolution mechanisms such as administrative review procedures or appeal processes. If the disagreement is strategic in nature, especially involving unit goals, then conflict is likely.

The conflict aftermath then becomes an environmental factor for the next conflict episode. If the conflict is resolved, the parties may move toward a cooperative relationship; if not, the conflict may expand to previously uninvolved parties or issues.

Pondy suggests that the origins of organizational conflict are informational, political, functional, and social. Conflict can occur in any of the subsets while affecting and being affected by conflict in the other subsets.

An example of a conflict situation may help clarify the Pondy model. The athletic department at a university had "tolerated" the existence of intramural sports for some time. There had been periodic conflict over scheduling of practice fields and gymnasia among intramural squads, and between intramural and collegiate teams. The collegiate teams, of course, had established priority for all facilities. The cause of the latent conflict—lack of athletic resources—showed no sign of change.

The aftermath of preceding episodes was a residue of mistrust between intramural organizers and the athletic department. In fact, current students knew of conflict episodes going back more than ten years—when they were still in junior high school. Thus, perceived conflict was handed down from one student generation to another.

Conflict was also felt by the student groups, since there was recurring anxiety about the schedules, which were adjusted several times during a season. One spring, particularly bad weather had made the outdoor fields vulnerable to damage from overuse. Rather than attempt a compromise, the athletic department ruled that all fields were closed to intramural activity. The manifest conflict that followed began with petitions to the university administration, but quickly escalated to vandalism of athletic facilities and verbal abuse of athletic department staff members. Security personnel were soon posted at the collegiate practice sessions.

The conflict aftermath was a heightened level of mistrust between the parties, and yet another athletic department horror story was added to student folklore.

Thomas' Structural Conflict Model   Thomas developed the structural model of conflict shown in Figure 8–2.[7] The circles represent the interacting parties. Each party acts within certain pressures and constraints, which shape the conflict episode.

Each party brings certain behavioral predispositions into an episode. For example, highly competitive people may tend to place interaction in a competitive context more frequently than their less competitive peers. A party's behavior may also be influenced by social pressure. The union shop steward may not wish to appear too cooperative with a management request. Cultural norms can also exert social pressure on a party. For instance, assertive conflict behavior

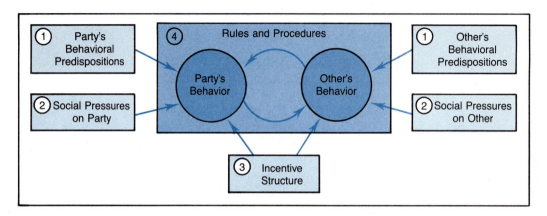

FIGURE 8–2

Thomas' structural conflict model (Source: K. Thomas, "Conflict and Conflict Management," in M. Dunnette, ed., *Handbook of Industrial and Organizational Psychology* (Chicago: Rand McNally, 1976): Copyright © 1976. Reprinted by permission of John Wiley & Sons, Inc.)

is less acceptable, and less likely to occur, between Japanese protagonists than American.

Another source of influence is the incentive structure, or the manner in which the satisfaction of one party is linked to the satisfaction of the other party. Two issues are involved: the stakes, or importance, to each party, and the extent to which there is conflict of interest. High stakes could lead to either competition or collaboration, depending upon the level of conflict of interest. Conflict of interest would probably not induce competition if the stakes were trivial. Two managers competing for a promotion would undoubtedly perceive both high stakes and significant conflict of interest.

The final source of influence is the rules and procedures governing the negotiations of the parties. These may be formal agreements, such as a rule stating that the production department must have five days lead time for new orders, or informal agreements, for example, that employees who travel are not required to travel on weekend days.

Robbins' Organizational Conflict Model   Robbins proposed the conflict model shown in Figure 8–3.[8] Conflict is seen to originate from three sources: communication, the organization structure, and personal-behavioral factors.

Communication.   Although the conflict sources are not necessarily listed in order of importance, we do know that much conflict is attributable to problems in communication. Some scholars refer to communication conflict as "pseudo conflict," to distinguish it from conflict over substantive issues.[9] The effect of communication conflict can, however, be anything *but* pseudo.

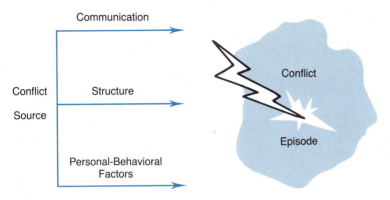

FIGURE 8–3
Robbins' conflict model (Source: Adapted from Stephen P. Robbins, *Managing Organizational Conflict: A Nontraditional Approach*, © 1974, p. 99. Adapted by permission of Prentice-Hall, Inc., Englewood Cliffs, NJ.)

Semantic difficulties may cause different interpretations of a message. This is especially likely to occur when individuals or groups have very dissimilar backgrounds. Each party interprets the message via their experience and training. The message understood may be entirely different from the message intended.

Communication is also altered by its route through the organization. As information passes vertically through the organization, each level may stress and interpret it differently. Something deemed critical by one organizational level may be considered superfluous at another level.

Structure. Structural variables such as bureaucratic qualities, reward systems, task interdependence, and heterogeneity of staff can lead to conflict between both individuals and groups. A high level of bureaucracy can lead to frustration and the search for methods outside the formal structure for accomplishment of tasks. The resulting "rule breaking" may lead to conflict. If parties are being evaluated and rewarded on factors that conflict with one another, conflict is likely as each tries to improve position. An example is the classic strain between sales and manufacturing. Sales may be rewarded for adapting to client needs, including rush orders and special designs. As a cost center, manufacturing may be rewarded for maintaining long production runs and minimizing special runs.

The more interdependent tasks and job roles are, the greater the need for cooperation and quality communication, and the greater the potential for conflict.[10] The more heterogeneous the staff, the more likely that conflict will result from communication or differing values and priorities.

Personal-behavioral factors. These factors include personality, role satisfaction, status, and goals; and Robbins suggests that management has little control over them.[11] It is clear that personal styles of leadership and decision making differ.

There is obvious potential for conflict when different styles collide. Role satisfaction, role status, and goals have been shown to be related to conflict,[12] but not always causally or significantly.[13]

Brown's Organizational Conflict Model   Another theorist has directed attention to the potential for conflict at organizational interfaces, which he defines as "the meeting grounds where social units come face to face and parties interact."[14] Brown proposed that four types of interface are particularly likely to experience conflict: department interface, level interface, culture interface, and organization interface.

Department interfaces are the meeting points of units that need coordinated action to achieve some organizational goal. For example, university admissions and registrar departments must cooperate in the review of new student files for admission and registration.

Level interfaces are transaction points for different levels of an organization. Corporate headquarters and divisional headquarters or union representatives and management personnel are examples of parties at different levels that must interact.

Culture interface brings together parties who are different in some relevant aspect. Obvious examples are racial minorities interacting with a dominant race, or men and women interacting. Somewhat less obvious are young workers and older workers, or union members and nonunion workers. An interface may be cultural when the parties hold somewhat different values about ingredients of the interchange.

Organization interfaces bring together organizations that depend upon one another for information or resources. Regulatory agencies and the regulated organizations, or business firms and their suppliers are examples.

Intergroup Conflict

Conflict between groups can be described via the conflict models just discussed, but there are some unique aspects worth noting. Conflict between groups is often more visible than conflict between individuals, if only because there are more people involved. Group dynamics play a very interesting part in conflict between groups.

Walton, Dutton, and Cafferty state that relationships between departments in a formal organization could be characterized by the responsiveness of one department to the needs of another, the accuracy of information exchange, and the attitudes of department members toward other departments and their members.[15] Indices of intergroup conflict include interference with the performance of another group (the greater the interdependence between the groups the easier interference becomes), distortion or withholding of information, overstatement of needs in order to influence the other department, annoyance, and distrust.

BOX 8–1

Who Are Those Masked Men?

Conflict Clinic, Inc. is a group of experts on negotiation from three universities. Like the Lone Ranger, the experts are ready to ride to the scene of a conflict, lend assistance, and then trot off. The masked men include professors of business, psychology, law, urban planning, and anthropology.

Conflict Clinic concentrates on finding what each party really wants and needs, which may differ greatly from its stated position. Though the clinic has had at least one major case, involving a labor dispute, not everyone thinks such help can be useful. The clinic was interested in an international territorial dispute, but one of the sides said of the situation: "The problem hasn't been a lack of efficient negotiators. The problem has been (the other side's) intransigence."

Source: B. Davis, "Negotiations Faltering? You Might Try These Masked Men of Academe," *The Wall Street Journal* (26 July 1983): 25.

Questions

1. For what types of conflict would Conflict Clinic's services be most appropriate?
2. What are the advantages of seeking outside help in conflict resolution? Are there any disadvantages?

Sherif conducted a landmark field experiment in intergroup conflict when he and his associates organized a boys' summer camp in a way that two groups would form and compete with each other.[16] The study has been replicated with so many other groups, and the responses have been so predictable, that the effects have been described in four distinct categories:[17]

Effects Within Each Competing Group

1. Each group becomes more closely knit and elicits greater loyalty from its members; members close ranks and bury some of their internal differences.
2. Group climate changes from informal, casual, and playful to work and task oriented; concern for members' psychological needs declines while concern for task accomplishment increases.
3. Leadership patterns tend to change from more democratic toward more autocratic; the group becomes more willing to tolerate autocratic leadership.
4. Each group becomes more highly structured and organized.
5. Each group demands more loyalty and conformity from its members to be able to present a "solid front."

Effects Between Competing Groups

1. Each group begins to see the other group as the enemy, rather than merely a neutral object.
2. Each group begins to experience distortions of perception—it tends to perceive only the best parts of itself, denying its weaknesses, and tends to perceive only the worst parts of the other group, denying its strengths; each group is likely to develop a negative stereotype of the other ("they don't play fair like we do").
3. Hostility toward the other group increases while interaction and communication with the other group decrease; thus it becomes easier to maintain negative stereotypes and more difficult to correct perceptual distortions.
4. If the groups are forced into interaction—for example, if they are forced to listen to representatives plead their own and the others' cause in reference to some task—each group is likely to listen more closely to their own representative and not to listen to the other group's representative except to find fault with the presentation; in other words, group members tend to listen only for that which supports their own position and stereotype.

Effects On the Winning Group

1. The winning group retains its cohesion and may become even more cohesive.
2. The winner tends to release tension, lose its fighting spirit, and become complacent, casual, and playful (the "fat and happy" state).
3. The winner tends toward high intragroup cooperation and concern for members' needs, and low concern for work and task accomplishment.
4. The winner tends to be complacent and to feel that winning has confirmed the positive stereotype of itself and the negative stereotype of the "enemy" group; there is little basis for reevaluating perceptions, or reexamining group operations to learn how to improve them.

Effects On the Losing Group

1. If the situation permits because of some ambiguity in the decision (say, if judges have rendered it or if the game was close), there is a strong tendency for the loser to deny or distort the reality of losing; instead, the loser will find psychological escapes, such as "the judges were biased," "the judges didn't really understand our solution," "the rules of the game were not clearly explained to us," or "if luck had not been against us at the one key point, we would have won."
2. If loss is accepted, the losing group tends to splinter, unresolved conflicts come to the surface, and fights break out, all in the effort to find the cause for the loss.

3. The loser is more tense, ready to work harder, and desperate to find someone or something to blame—the leader, itself, the judges who decided against it, the rules of the game (the "lean and hungry" state).
4. The loser tends toward low intragroup cooperation, low concern for members' needs, and high concern for recouping by working harder.
5. The loser tends to learn a lot about itself as a group because positive stereotype of itself and negative stereotype of the other group are upset by the loss, forcing a reevaluation of perceptions; as a consequence, the loser is likely to reorganize and become more cohesive and effective, once the loss has been accepted realistically.

Note that many of Schein's results support your learning from chapter 6. How might group cohesiveness, norms, and conformity influence what happens within each competing group and what happens to the winning and losing groups?

We can see the conflict between groups when we consider the relationship between line and staff of many organizations. Many of the interactions and feelings described above are common to line and staff conflict. In a recent consulting project for a major corporation, we found the following complaints and stereotypes operating:

Line managers felt that

- Staff people are "meddlers" who overstep their authority
- Staff suffers from limited perspective; their specialization keeps them from seeing the broad picture
- Staff advice is frequently naive or unworkable
- Staff frequently complicates inherently simple concepts and procedures

Staff managers felt that

- Line managers resist anything new
- Line people call for staff help only when situations become hopeless, then blame failure on staff advice
- Line treats staff as second-class citizens
- Line ignores staff advice and won't give staff authority to implement solutions

These perceptions may fall into the "nothing ever seems to change" category. Dalton was reporting similar results in 1950.[18]

Desirable Conflict

Early management theory as well as practice considered conflict to be dysfunctional by definition—an evil to be dispatched as quickly as possible. In recent years, significant rethinking has occurred, and a number of people are arguing that a certain amount of conflict is not only desirable, but necessary in an effective organization.

The perspective that conflict is frequently helpful has been termed the interactionist view.[19] This view holds that conflict is inevitable, and the task of management is to manage that conflict and its resolution in ways that contribute to organizational performance. A moderate level of conflict is probably necessary to spur evaluation of organizational processes and to prepare groundwork for change. Conflict can arouse motivation to solve a problem that might otherwise go unattended and can lead to creative behavior in pursuit of a solution.

Individuals and groups who are satisfied with the status quo may be aroused to recognize problems and address them only when opposition is felt. For example, racial minorities in the United States made great strides in the human rights area only after the white majority was shocked out of apathy by the civil rights movements of the 1960s and 1970s.

In the terms of labor negotiators, parties engage in bargaining when their interests primarily conflict, and in problem solving when their interests are common.[20] Examples of the first situation are the ubiquitous wage and salary negotiation, or the bargaining between production and sales departments over delivery schedules. The latter might be represented by a union/management task force on health care cost containment. In each example, groups or individuals protect their interests, but the inherent tension need not be dysfunctional, nor even reach the level of felt conflict. Indeed, these conflicts may well lead to a more effective distribution of resources than if either party had sole discretion.

Brown describes bargaining and problem solving as productive conflict.[21] Problem solving exchanges tend to be open and undistorted. While bargaining exchanges are more inhibited, the interaction continues in a common direction. Brown suggests that too little conflict occurs when issues are suppressed or if parties withdraw from confronting issues.

As noted in a previous section, intergroup conflict can create increased cohesion and loyalty within competing groups. The groups become more highly organized and increase their task orientation as well. There are even some positive elements involved in losing the conflict: the losing group tends to learn about itself as a group; it is likely to reorganize and become more cohesive and effective.

Summary of Key Concepts

1. A working definition of conflict includes all types of opposition or antagonistic interaction—thus including competition in the definition.
2. Models of conflict tend to focus upon either the process or the structure of a conflict situation. Structural models take environmental variables more explicitly into account.
3. Dynamics of intergroup conflict are remarkably predictable. Effects within and between competing groups, as well as effects on both winning and losing groups, can be accurately forecast.
4. Conflict is not always undesirable. A certain level of conflict may be necessary for organizational effectiveness.

Key Terms

Conflict

Felt conflict

Intergroup conflict

Latent conflict

Manifest conflict

Organizational interfaces

Perceived conflict

Productive conflict

Structural conflict model

MANAGERIAL APPLICATIONS

In this section we look at the spectrum of dealing with or managing conflict that occurs in organizations. We discuss how managers may avoid conflict or actually stimulate conflict in certain situations.

A manager of our acquaintance states his approach to conflict succinctly: "I don't get mad—I get even." This wonderfully simple philosophy suffers the bane of many wonderfully simple philosophies—it creates more problems than it solves. As Schelling points out, threat is costly when it fails.[22] If it has to be carried out, punitive action is usually painful or costly to both sides. Brinkmanship involves getting onto a slope where one may fall in spite of efforts to save oneself, dragging the adversary over the edge as company. As we have seen in our review of some conflict models, we are dealing with complex dynamics.

Sheane suggests three elements to intervention: strategic—choosing the right aim; tactical—choosing the right method; and common sense—not mixing strategic and tactical elements.[23]

In chapter 7 we discussed decision making and problem solving, stressing the importance of defining the problem and selecting appropriate methods of resolution. Undesirable conflict virtually always becomes a serious problem if it is left unresolved. Conflict models are useful in diagnosing the type of conflict, but once conflict is diagnosed, a resolution technique must be chosen.

How Managers Resolve Conflict

Thomas developed one of the more useful classifications of conflict handling modes, based upon the *intentions* of parties in resolving conflict. The classification is shown in Figure 8–4.[24] Two underlying dimensions are cooperativeness (attempting to satisfy the other party's concerns), and assertiveness (attempting to satisfy one's own concerns). Five behaviors are described in the two-dimensional space. Competing behavior (assertive, uncooperative) values one's concerns at the other party's expense. The opposite behavior is accomodating (unassertive, cooperative), which satisfies the other party's concerns at the expense of one's

FIGURE 8–4

Modes of conflict behavior (Source: Adapted from Thomas Ruble and Kenneth Thomas, "Support for a Two-Dimensional Model of Conflict Behavior," *Organizational Behavior and Human Performance,* 1976, 16, Fig. 1, p. 145. Used by permission.)

own. Avoiding (unassertive, uncooperative) neglects all concerns by ignoring the issue or delaying a response. Collaborating (assertive, cooperative) is an attempt to fully satisfy the needs of both parties. Compromising is moderate in both cooperativeness and assertiveness. Compromise implies that both parties have some concerns left unsatisfied. Research has supported the existence and documented the use of these behaviors.[25]

TABLE 8–1

Attribution of conflict handling modes to self and to other party

	Attributed to	
	Self (%)	Other (%)
Collaboration	41	4
Compromise	25	6
Accommodation	8	2
Avoidance	5	16
Competition	21	73

Source: Adapted from K. W. Thomas and L. R. Pondy, "Toward an 'Intent' Model of Conflict Management among Principal Parties," *Human Relations,* 30 (1977): 1094. Used by permission.

BOX 8–2

Conflict Issues

Schmidt and Tannenbaum suggested that the nature of a conflict will vary depending upon the kind of issue on which people disagree. They said the differences were over the following:

Facts. Sometimes the disagreement occurs because individuals have different definitions of a problem, are aware of different pieces of relevant information, accept or reject different information as factual, or have differing impressions of their respective power and authority.

Goals. Sometimes the disagreement is about what should be accomplished—the desirable ob-jectives of a department, division, or section, or of a specific position within the organization.

Methods. Sometimes individuals differ about the procedures, strategies, or tactics that would most likely achieve a mutually desired goal.

Values. Sometimes the disagreement is over ethics—the way power should be exercised, or moral considerations, or assumptions about justice, fairness, and so on. Such differences may affect the choice of either goals or methods.

Questions

1. Which conflict is generally easiest to resolve: conflict over facts, methods, values, or goals? Which is most difficult? Why?
2. Which resolution techniques might work best for conflict over facts? Over methods? Goals? Values?

Unfortunately, there may be a tendency for parties in conflict to ascribe purer motives to themselves than to the other side.[26] As shown in Table 8–1, managers tended to see themselves as much more collaborative and less competitive than their antagonists. They also viewed themselves as avoiding conflict much less frequently than the other party.

Avoiding Conflict

There are situations when conflict avoidance makes sense, and we mention those presently, in Table 8–2. Frequently, though, avoiding issues simply makes the problem worse. We observed an organization experiencing an ownership change. The original owner had built the company from its inception and had become quite close to the original employees. He involved them in a great many decisions and valued their input. Without this involvement, it is doubtful that the company would have made the progress that it did.

In time, the owner had to take in some new partners for financial reasons. The newcomers were more concerned about "systems" than they were about

TABLE 8-2
Uses of the five conflict modes, as reported by a group of chief executives

Conflict-handling Modes	Appropriate Situations
Competing	1. When quick, decision action is vital—e.g., emergencies 2. On important issues where unpopular actions need implementing—e.g., cost cutting, enforcing unpopular rules, discipline 3. On issues vital to company welfare when you know you're right 4. Against people who take advantage of noncompetitive behavior
Collaborating	1. To find an integrative solution when both sets of concerns are too important to be compromised 2. When your objective is to learn 3. To merge insights from people with different perspectives 4. To gain commitment by incorporating concerns into a consensus 5. To work through feelings that have interfered with a relationship
Compromising	1. When goals are important, but not worth the effort or potential disruption of more assertive modes 2. When opponents with equal power are committed to mutually exclusive goals 3. To achieve temporary settlements to complex issues 4. To arrive at expedient solutions under time pressure 5. As a backup when collaboration or competition is unsuccessful

participation in decision making, and they established a great many procedures to be followed "without question." Many of the original employees objected strongly to the new procedures, which greatly diluted employee influence over operations and restricted their independence.

Many of the old employees disliked the change so much that they tried to convince the original owner to return the operation to the old practices. He was unwilling to bring the issue up for fear of destroying harmony with the new partners. Many of the old employees quit; a year after the new partners had joined the firm, about 50 percent of the employees had been recently hired. Productivity had been badly affected. By avoiding the situation, the owner reaped high employee turnover and reduced productivity. There were also the significant though less tangible costs of employee frustration, stress, and bitterness.

TABLE 8–2
continued

Conflict-handling Modes	Appropriate Situations
Avoiding	1. When an issue is trivial, or more important issues are pressing 2. When you perceive no chance of satisfying your concerns 3. When potential disruption outweighs the benefits of resolution 4. To let people cool down and regain perspective 5. When gathering information supersedes immediate decision 6. When others can resolve the conflict more effectively 7. When issues seem tangential or symptomatic of other issues
Accommodating	1. When you find you are wrong—to allow a better position to be heard, to learn, and to show your reasonableness 2. When issues are more important to others than yourself—to satisfy others and maintain cooperation 3. To build social credits for later issues 4. To minimize loss when you are outmatched and losing 5. When harmony and stability are especially important 6. To allow subordinates to develop by learning from

Source: Kenneth W. Thomas, "Toward Multi-Dimensional Values in Teaching: The Example of Conflict Behaviors," *Academy of Management Review,* 2 (1977): 487, Table 1. Reprinted by permission.

Choosing Conflict Modes

A survey of chief executives produced guidelines for using the five conflict handling modes.[27] Careful review of Table 8–2 shows that the executives had given substantial thought to the question of conflict resolution. We advise the aspiring young manager to benefit from the obvious experience and wisdom summarized in the table.

Stimulating Conflict

We noted earlier that conflict has some functional aspects. Robbins is one of the foremost proponents of conflict as a management tool.[28] He suggests that conflict can be stimulated via three vehicles: communication, organization structure, and personal-behavioral factors.

Bypassing usual communication channels, repressing information, transmitting ambiguous or threatening information, or transmitting too much information can stimulate conflict. Changes in structure can stimulate conflict through creation of uncertainty, redistribution of power, changes in job design, and changing dependencies.

Personal-behavioral factors are the most difficult to manage, but status incongruence, creation of role conflict, and placement of individuals with incompatible goals can increase unit conflict.

Sharpening Conflict

We have observed some very skillful managers purposely bring an existing conflict into high focus and thrust the burden of resolution upon those who are involved in it. For example, the vice-president of a large organization was promoted to president. He was aware that serious conflict had been developing among several executives at the vice-presidential level. He felt that if he was to be effective as the new top executive, the conflict would have to be dealt with as quickly as possible. Taking advantage of his new position—for no one yet knew how he would act—he told the five vice-presidents involved in the conflict that he had made reservations for them at a resort hotel far from the company, that they should all go to the resort the next day and that they should come back in no more than five days with the conflict resolved. If they couldn't do this, they shouldn't come back at all!

Obviously this is a very direct—and risky—way to manage conflict. It worked well in this case, perhaps because of the shock value, but also because the new president took steps on a longer range basis to eliminate some of the reasons for the conflict. Had he not done that, the vice-presidents might have grudgingly buried the conflict for awhile, but it probably would have risen again at a later date, perhaps in a different form.

Sharpening is a very special technique of conflict management. If a manager is unsure of his or her ability to function in a situation of high tension and volatility, the approach should be adopted only after very careful analysis. Sharpening may not be considered by some as a resolution technique, if resolving means to come to a disposition satisfactory to all concerned. The vice-presidents noted above may not have been satisfied with the outcome, but from the viewpoint of the new president, the conflict had been resolved.

Conflict and Performance Appraisal

Appraising employee performance is a managerial activity that frequently creates interpersonal conflict. As noted in this chapter, conflict is not always dysfunctional. Unfortunately, much conflict stemming from the appraisal process *is* dysfunctional, because it often stems from unclear goals, expectations, and standards of performance.[29] The manager generally must assume a large share of the blame when such issues remain unclarified. We look in some detail at the appraisal process in chapter 10.

DISCUSSION QUESTIONS

1. At what point in the conflict episode (latent-perceived-felt-manifest) should a manager generally become involved? Why?
2. In organizations you are familiar with, does conflict come primarily from communication, structure, or personal-behavioral factors?
3. Of Brown's "interface" conflicts (department, level, culture, organization), which would be most difficult to resolve? Why?
4. Under what circumstances might a manager *want* to create conflict between his or her group and another group?
5. Which of the conflict resolution techniques discussed do you believe to be most useful? Which is least useful? Why?
6. Under what circumstances is conflict useful to the manager? To an individual?

EXERCISE: SPORTSWEAR, INCORPORATED

Sportswear, Incorporated, is an example of a typical conflict situation found in organizations. In this particular instance, problems of production, shipping, and inventory have reached the point that the manager in charge has called a meeting of those involved. Many of these people hold viewpoints that are in conflict. The manager is under great pressure to achieve some sort of resolution of the situation.

PROCEDURE: Your instructor will give you specific instructions for this exercise. Do not proceed further until you have received these instructions.

Sportswear, Incorporated is a manufacturer of several types of outdoor clothing for men and women, including ski jackets and parkas, special jackets and coats for hunting and fishing, and a line of casual coats and jackets designed to appeal to the high school and college student. The activities of Sportswear are fairly well confined to the western part of the United States, although the company does have one sales representative in the midwestern states.

Although Sportswear has been in business for over forty-five years, it wasn't until the end of World War II that it really began to do well and its line of jackets and coats began to receive popular acceptance. Until the mid-1960s manufacture of coats and jackets was fairly routine. At that time, however, fashion and style became increasingly important in outer wear, especially in ski clothing and casual coats and jackets. Somewhat to its surprise, the company found that it had people on its staff with definite skills in fashion and design, and, building on these skills, Sportswear has enjoyed great success and has grown and expanded considerably.

With growth, however, has come a certain amount of difficulty. One of the current problems bothering Jess Robinson, executive vice president, concerns delivery of merchandise to customers. The current situation involves ski jackets, but the same kind of problem has arisen before with other lines.

Because many of the items in the Sportswear line are fashion items, the company is very cautious regarding production and inventory levels for each one. If, for example, quilted ski jackets with a mosaic pattern do not become popular and production on these jackets has been high, Sportswear may find itself in the undesirable position of having a large inventory of these jackets on hand for which there is little market demand. Such inventory would probably have to be sold at a loss. On the other hand, if an item becomes "hot" on the market, Sportswear may find itself unable to meet promptly the demands of its customers for this item, even though production of the items is immediately increased.

Most of the 1,300 stores and shops who handle Sportswear products customarily order a few of each item in the line. If an item does become popular, they immediately reorder—often by telephone or wire—to meet their demand. As many of the items are seasonal, speed in filling these orders is imperative. Often, however, a waiting period of four to five weeks is involved before delivery on reorders can be made. During this period pressure for quick delivery becomes intense. Customers call anyone and everyone at Sportswear who they think can help their cause. The nine sales representatives of Sportswear, who are paid partially on a commission basis, attempt to have their orders filled as soon as possible and go to great lengths to achieve speedy delivery, even to the point of resubmitting orders with the notation "RUSH" or "URGENT," or when they are in town visiting the factory to attempt to put pressure on the production people to work on their orders first.

The result of such pressure is confusion and even more delay. With duplicate orders on hand, no one knows what the level of demand for an item really is. The production people become incensed at the activities of the salespersons attempting to push their orders through the factory, and customers become irritable and complain because they cannot meet the demands of their own customers.

In an attempt to resolve this problem, Jess Robinson has called a meeting of the following individuals: Ross Bennett, production manager; Willis Patten, sales manager; Warren Harte, shipping and inventory control manager; and Douglas Kraft, credit manager.

This exercise concerns these individuals and Mike Hodgson, midwestern sales representative of Sportswear.

Role for Jess Robinson, Executive Vice President

You have called a meeting of several of your people to discuss the problem of delivery on customer reorders and are now on your way to the conference room, where the meeting will be held. You have been tied up on the phone and are a few minutes late, so you expect that everyone will already be there.

The problem, in a nutshell, is that there seems to be no system or priorities for receiving, producing, and shipping reorders—especially on "hot" items. The customer may order a few of several items in the line, find one or two which go over big, order more, and then have to wait four or five weeks for delivery. Because of the seasonal factor, a time lag of four or five weeks can affect total sales significantly.

To compound the problem, your sales staff puts pressure on the production people and resubmits the same order several times in an attempt to get its orders filled first. Then, too, customers complain. You have had five calls today from nervous customers concerning their orders.

The easy way to resolve the problem, of course, would be to increase production on all items, but that would involve too large an investment in inventory and too large a risk on those items which didn't sell well.

Something has to be worked out today, for the situation can't continue as it is.

Role for Ross Bennett, Production Manager

You're glad that this meeting has been called because the problem of pressure from salespersons has plagued you for a long time. What they don't realize is that you are six to seven months ahead of them. They're worried about ski jackets now, but you've already started production on the spring line of jackets and fishing stuff.

You're willing to help in any way that you can, but people have to realize that if you really go to work on ski jackets now, the spring line won't be ready on time. You've got to take your instructions for additional production of current stuff from the inventory control people.

One thing you will insist on, though, is that all salespersons are barred from the factory—permanently. As you've told Jess Robinson, things have just gotten out of hand. Why, the salesman from the midwest was in the factory for several hours today, trying to get his orders pushed through first.

Role for Douglas Kraft, Credit Manager

You're glad that Mr. Robinson has called this meeting, for with the confusion that exists, your work is made all the more difficult. One of your main jobs is to see that all incoming orders are checked to determine if the credit status of the customer is O.K. Bad debts have been a problem in the past, but you can control them if you check each order. If a customer's record is not good, you can refuse to ship the order to him or demand full payment before the order leaves the plant.

When the pressure in on, however, you sometimes find that your people are having to go through the process of checking credit several times on what appears to be the same order. And salesreps are not above taking an order right to the factory if they think they can get away with it by bypassing your operation entirely.

Every order must be checked to see that the customer's credit standing is satisfactory.

Role for Warren Harte, Shipping and Inventory Control Manager

Well, perhaps this meeting will result in getting some of the pressure off your department. During the past week you bet that your people have received over two hundred calls wanting to know if a certain order has been shipped yet.

What people don't realize is that you can't just ship orders without a certain amount of processing. You are responsible for control of an inventory valued at $450,000 and you can't run an operation that size without some kind of system. Each order must be checked against paper inventory and physical inventory before it is shipped. If you are low on an item, or completely out, you've got to tell the production people to get to work on it. But you can't do this until the necessary paperwork is completed. The duplicate orders you have been receiving lately confuse things terribly.

Your people in shipping are all good people who work hard. Maybe this meeting will be a chance to press for those two new fork-lift trucks they have been wanting. They won't solve the problem, but they should help a great deal in getting orders out once the paper work has been done. You estimate that the new fork-lift trucks will cost about $10,000.

Role for Willis Patten, Sales Manager

Well, you suppose Jess Robinson is going to jump down your throat at this meeting. Every time you get under pressure, everyone blames the Sales Department. They don't realize that sales are the only thing that keep the company going.

You're proud of the sales growth the company has experienced and feel that it is due in large measure to the enthusiasm of your sales staff. Sure, they might get a little out of hand at times, but salesreps who didn't press for their orders wouldn't be worth having. And you can appreciate that your people are paid on commission, too.

People don't realize that repeat orders and customer service are the foundation of the business. Anything and everything should be done to keep the customers happy.

Mike Hodgson, your man who handles midwestern sales, happens to be in town today. You have asked him to attend the meeting because you feel that he can present a picture of what really happens in the field. You're not sure that he knows everyone who will be there.

Role for Mike Hodgson, Midwestern Sales Representative

Will Patten, your boss, has asked you to attend a meeting to discuss the problem of delivery on customer orders. You're not sure who will be there, but as you understand it, he hopes that you will be able to provide a picture of what happens in the field as the result of late delivery to customers.

You will be glad to do that. This problem of late delivery on reorders is especially difficult for you, because you don't get a chance to get back to the factory to push for your orders as often as the other salesreps who are located closer to the home office. And it really burns you up when you have a good customer like, for example, The Campus Shop at the state university, which is waiting and waiting for orders to arrive. Then you find that some little clothing store on the West Coast got delivery in two weeks. You realize that everyone can't get their orders at the same time, but something should be done to make sure that the big, steady customers get prompt service. You can tell a little guy that he won't get delivery for a while and he has to take it. A big customer won't. You try to see your big customers about every three weeks and it's embarrassing if their orders haven't come in.

It's more than embarrassing, for if a big customer cancels an order, you may lose a fat commission and the chance to sell your other lines. Right now you have three big orders waiting for delivery and you have spent a good deal of time over in the factory today trying to get them speeded up. You've got to take advantage of your infrequent visits to the home office to do what you can for your customers.

You'll be glad to tell them what it's like in the field!

Source: Reprinted with permission from H. R. Knudson and C. P. Fleenor. *Organizational Behavior: A Management Approach* (Cambridge, MA: Winthrop Publishers, 1978): 411–414. Copyright 1976 Professor Harry R. Knudson, Graduate School of Business, University of Washington.

NOTES

1. L. Jones, "All My Police Chiefs," *The Seattle Times* (30 June 1983): C1.

2. G. L. Lippitt, "Managing Conflict in Today's Organizations," *Training and Development Journal* (July 1982): 67–72.

3. S. M. Schmidt and T. A. Kochan, "Conflict: Toward Conceptual Clarity," *Administrative Science Quarterly*, 13 (1972): 359–370.

4. S. P. Robbins, *Managing Organizational Conflict* (Englewood Cliffs, NJ: Prentice-Hall, 1974).

5. K. W. Thomas, "Conflict and Conflict Management," in M. D. Dunnette, ed., *Handbook of Industrial and Organizational Psychology* (Chicago: Rand McNally, 1976): 889–935.

6. L. R. Pondy, "Organizational Conflict: Concepts and Models," *Administrative Science Quarterly*, 12 (1967): 296–320.

7. Thomas, *Conflict and Conflict Management*, p. 912.

8. Robbins, *Managing Organizational Conflict*.

9. E. Rhenman, L. Stromberg, and G. Westerlund, *Conflict and Cooperation in Business Organizations* (London: Wiley-Interscience, 1970).

10. J. J. Molnar and D. L. Roger, "A Comparative Model of Interorganizational Conflict," *Administrative Science Quarterly* (September 1979).

11. Robbins, *Managing Organizational Conflict*, p. 51.

12. J. D. Hunger and L. W. Stern, "An Assessment of the Functionality of the Superordinate Goal in Reducing Conflict," *Academy of Management Journal* (December 1976); A. C. Szilagyi, "An Empirical Test of Causal Inference Between Role Perception, Satisfaction With Work, Performance and Organization Level," *Personnel Psychology* (Autumn 1977); and K. W. Mossholder, A. G. Bedeian, and A. A. Armenakis, "Role Perceptions, Satisfaction and Performance: Moderating Effects of Self-Esteem and Organizational Level," *Organizational Behavior and Human Performance* (October 1981): 224–234.

13. R. S. Schuler, "A Role Perception Transactional Process Model for Organizational Communication-Outcome Relationship," *Organizational Behavior and Human Performance* (April 1979).

14. L. D. Brown, *Managing Conflict at Organizational Interfaces* (Reading, MA: Addison-Wesley, 1983).

15. R. E. Walton, J. M. Dutton, and T. P. Cafferty, "Organizational Context and Interdepartmental Conflict," *Administrative Science Quarterly* (December 1969): 522–543.

16. M. Sherif, O. J. Harvey, B. J. White, W. R. Hood, and C. Sherif, *Intergroup Conflict and Cooperation: The Robbers Cave Experiment* (Norman, OK:) University Book Exchange, 1961).

17. Edgar H. Schein, *Organizational Psychology*, 3rd ed., © 1980, pp. 173, 174–175. Reprinted by permission of Prentice-Hall, Inc., Englewood Cliffs, NJ.

18. M. Dalton, "Conflicts Between Staff and Line Managerial Officers," *American Sociological Review* (June 1950): 342–351.

19. Robbins, *Managing Organizational Conflict*.

20. R. E. Walton and R. B. McKersie, A *Behavioral Theory of Labor Negotiations: An Analysis of a Social Interaction System* (New York: McGraw-Hill, 1965).

21. Brown, *Managing Conflict*, p. 41.

22. T. C. Schelling, *The Strategy of Conflict* (Cambridge, MA: Harvard University Press, 1960).

23. D. Sheane, "When and How to Intervene in Conflict," *Personnel Journal* (June 1980): 515.

24. Thomas, *Conflict and Conflict Management*.

25. M. A. Rahim, "A Measure of Styles of Handling Interpersonal Conflict," *Academy of Management Journal*, 26 (2) (1983): 368–376; R. A. Cosier and T. L. Ruble, "Research on Conflict-Handling Behavior: An Experimental Approach," *Academy of Management Journal*, 24 (4) (1981): 816–831; and G. L. Lippitt, "Managing Conflict in Today's Organizations," *Training and Development Journal* (July 1982): 67–74.

26. K. W. Thomas and L. R. Pondy, "Toward An 'Intent' Model of Conflict Management among Principal Parties," *Human Relations* 30 (1977): 1094.

27. K. W. Thomas, "Toward Multi-Dimensional Values in Teaching: The Example of Conflict Behaviors," *Academy of Management Review*, 2 (1977): 487.

28. Robbins, Managing Organizational Conflict.

29. C. P. Fleenor and M. P. Scontrino, *Performance Appraisal: A Manager's Guide* (Dubuque, IA: Kendall/Hunt, 1982).

RECOMMENDED READINGS

S. P. **Robbins,** *Managing Organizational Conflict: A Nontraditional Approach* (Englewood Cliffs, NJ: Prentice-Hall, 1974).

This book presents a well-stated case for the need to initiate conflict in certain circumstances, and describes methods for doing so.

P. J. Nicholson and S. C. Goh, "The Relationship of Organization Structure and Interpersonal Attitudes to Role Conflict and Ambiguity in Different Work Environments," *Academy of Mannagement Journal,* 26 (1) (1983): 148–155.

This article ties together some relationships between organization structure and role conflict.

D. Robey and D. Farrow, "User Involvement in Information System Development: A Conflict Model and Empirical Test," *Management Science,* 28 (1) (1982): 73–85.

The conflict between information system designers and users is classic. This article presents a model of that conflict.

J. Sullivan, R. B. Peterson, N. Kameds, and J. Shimada, "The Relationship Between Conflict Resolution Approaches and Trust—A Cross-Cultural Study," *Academy of Management Journal,* 24 (4) (1981): 803–815.

The article presents an interesting view of cultural differences in the resolution of conflict.

L. D. Brown, *Managing Conflict at Organizational Interfaces* (Reading, MA: Addison-Wesley, 1983).

This is one of the better sources for learning about conflict from a systems perspective.

The Production Department

KCDE-TV is one of two television stations in Tuttle, a city of 100,000 population, with a metropolitan area of 175,000.

KCDE-TV (and radio) for some time had serious morale problems, especially in the television production department. KCDE employed 85 people in six departments: general office; data processing; news; engineering; radio; and television production. The television production group formed the single largest department, about 20 people. The functional areas of the production department are announcing; directing; switching; camera operating; and videotape operating. See Exhibit A for description of these functions.

As is the case with many small to medium-sized stations, KCDE was looked upon as a training ground by many members of both management and staff. This was a reason offered by management on occasion for not granting a raise to an employee. It was suggested to the employee that if he wished to remain at KCDE he had better accept his present wage as the maximum for the foreseeable future. He then would find it necessary to move on to a bigger city if he expected to be paid more for the same job. The turnover, especially in the radio and production departments, was high.

Each employee negotiated his own salary with management since there was no union representation. There were no published salary ranges, but staff members knew that approximate ranges in 1970 were as follows:

Source: Reprinted with permission from H. R. Knudson and C. P. Fleenor, *Organizational Behavior: A Management Approach* (Cambridge, MA: Winthrop Publishers, 1978): 403–407. Copyright 1976 C. Patrick Fleenor.

Announcers	$850–950/mo.
Directors	850–925
Switchers	775–825
Video tape operators	750–825
Camera operators	700–750

The salaries were based on a 48-hour, six-day week. Much conversation among the crew members centered around what they all agreed was a low pay scale. As one of the crew members put it regularly in conversation: "No where else can you work a six-day week, a night shift, and virtually every holiday for such lousy money."

Benefits were another sore point. The company made group insurance available, but there was no retirement program. Though providing paid vacations, the company paid the vacationing employee for two 40-hour weeks. The two-week paycheck then was less by sixteen hours of overtime what the employee was accustomed to.

Working conditions with regard to physical comfort and safety were adequate and about average for the industry.

It was a common feeling among the crew members that they were being "used" to one degree or another by management. The men knew that many general office workers for the city's major private employers and the state government were making more money than they, working better hours and shorter weeks. Adding salt to the wound was the feeling that the television job required infinitely more creative ability than the general office worker needed or had. At the same time, most felt their jobs were intrinsically interesting, and far more challenging than office or administrative work.

Great animosity was directed toward the as-

Announcers are responsible for performing live commercials and programs, and for providing audio recordings for locally produced slide, film and videotape commercials. Since the work load is variable, they typically have other duties, e.g., writing commercial copy, or reading news for the radio station.

The director is ostensibly the most creative member of the crew. He is responsible for the "on-air" presentation. He either recommends a set for a commercial or program, or approves an idea presented by some other member of the crew. During the actual broadcast or recording session, the director is in charge of all activities.

The switcher, sometimes referred to as the technical director, performs the physical operations at the control board required to put various video sources on the air, and to mix the sources at the director's command. He also is responsible for loading slides and film on the various projectors.

The video-tape operator loads and "cues" video tapes on the video tape machines for the playback of commercials and programs on the air. He also sets up the machines for the recording of commercials and programs. The video tape machines are extremely complicated and quite difficult to operate, requiring a practiced touch for trouble-free operation.

The camera crew operate the large studio cameras, moving them on the director's cue and selecting the shots the director asks for. The camera operators do the actual construction of the sets, and do most of the lighting, sometimes under the direct supervision of the director.

An additional member of the operating crew is an engineer, who is not a member of the production department but is expected to provide technical advice to the director. The engineer's primary responsibility, however, is the maintenance of the expensive, complicated electronic gear.

EXHIBIT A

sistant general manager of the station. His previous post was chief engineer of the station, where he was tagged with the nickname "Overkill" by some members of the engineering department. This name was inspired by his tendency to over-react to situations. On one occasion he had fired an employee for smoking in the television control room. Though parts of the studio and control areas were posted against smoking, members of the staff looked upon this regulation as trivial. Care was taken not to smoke only when the assistant general manager was in the immediate area.

More than once, Overkill threatened to have a vital piece of equipment removed, ". . . unless you guys take better care of it." The threats were obviously hollow, since the station couldn't operate without the equipment. He had been heard to refer to the operating crew and the engineering department, or various members as "coolies."

The leader of the production department itself was not spared the crew's wrath. Every member of the crew looked upon Gary Brown, the production supervisor, as, as one of the switchers put it, "a miserable, two-timing s.o.b." More than one of the crew had had the experience of making a request for a raise, only to find some weeks later that the production supervisor had "forgotten to take it up," or to be counseled that "this just isn't the right time to ask." It had been observed by everyone in the production staff that Gary often delivered different versions of a story to upper management than he gave to his subordinates. It was generally felt that he always sided with management, especially Overkill, rather than backing his subordinates.

The general manager of the station, Gordon Frederick, was a retired military officer and an ex-mayor of the city. He was active in political causes and was out of town frequently, leaving the day-to-day operation of the station to the assistant general manager. Most of the staff members looked upon Frederick as being a slightly befuddled autocrat since he conducted regular "inspections" when in the building, and indulged a fetish for small detail, such as seeing that the flags were removed from the flagpole in front of the building promptly at sunset. He was responsible for, and for the most part the author of, a booklet of company rules and regulations called the Blue Book. In the Blue Book were voluminous descriptions of each job title within the organization, and page upon page of rules pertaining to coffee breaks, use of company telephones, and virtually every other activity within the building.

The Blue Book was treated with varying degrees of contempt by most staff members, and with utter contempt by the production department. Those who had been in the military service insisted parts of the Blue Book text were lifted wholesale from military manuals. It was felt that the book's only value was to management, in that some obscure regulation could be used to chastise an employee, while other rules were totally ignored. For example, the Blue Book stated that the company had a policy against members of the same family being employed. However, Overkill's son Steve worked as a full-time cameraman, one of the director's wives worked in the office, and the husband of the TV program director served as a technician.

The Blue Book also contained rules for communication between departments, the management feeling being that the rank and file of one department should not communicate directly with their counterparts in other departments in matters of operations. For example, if a newscaster became upset at a camera operator, director, or any other member of the production staff in connection with a newscast, he or she was to inform the news director, who would then take the matter up with the production supervisor. This rule was totally ignored.

Though the Blue Book delineated a very rigid chain of command, it was fairly common for orders to the production crew to come from Overkill, the program director, or Brown, the pro-

duction supervisor. On occasion, in the case of an equipment failure or similar emergency, these orders would conflict, resulting in confusion until the three decided upon a common plan.

Job security was felt to be nonexistent. Many of the workers felt directly threatened by Overkill and verbally expressed their fear of his capricious behavior.

Seemingly arbitrary changes of shift upset some of the crew. In early Spring of 1970, one of the directors was moved to the position of video tape operator. Though his salary was left at its old level, this move involved a real loss of prestige. No explanation was given to members of the crew. A cameraman was promoted directly to the position of director, by-passing several switchers. Again, there was no explanation.

Sabotage, in the name of "games," became quite common among the operating crew. It was not too unusual for a film projector to be misthreaded, causing the film to be torn to ribbons when the projector was started, resulting in program down-time. Program sets would occasionally topple over during a video taping session, or microphones would refuse to work. One favorite trick was the tripping of master light breakers for the control room areas. Another was pounding on the wall of an area where an announcer was on the air. One of the more ingenious acts involved the wiring of a prop telephone on the TV news set. The phone was then rung during a newscast, causing the newscaster to "break up." Though members of management never appeared to suspect sabotage, its occurrence was by no means rare.

Also in the Spring of 1970, Ron E., an announcer, came to work for KCDE radio. The television and radio control areas were adjacent to one another, and some of the announcers worked both radio and television. There was a great deal of social contact between employees of both sides.

At the end of his first pay period, Ron became tremendously upset. His check totaled about $50 less for the two week period than he thought it would be. According to Ron, the radio station manager had hired him at $900 a month, but his first check was paid at the rate of $800 a month.

Ron promptly complained to his supervisor, and the matter was taken to the general manager. He informed Ron that the radio station manager did not have the authority to hire an announcer at such a salary as Ron had been promised. There was no offer to compromise on the salary. Frederick offered to pay Ron's moving expenses back to the city he had left just weeks before. Ron's answer was; "And what the hell am I supposed to do for a job if I do return?" Feeling he had no choice, Ron accepted the lower salary.

In May, about a month after the salary episode, Ron began questioning other employees about the possibility of unionizing the station. His idea was met with great enthusiasm by the members of the production department. More than one of them indicated that though they did not like unions, they liked the management of KCDE even less. The few holdouts expressed fear for their jobs, but no one expressed any promanagement thoughts.

Several meetings were held with union representatives and the union formally notified Mr. Frederick of their intention to organize the production department. This action was met with disbelief on the part of Frederick, followed soon by a meeting to stress to employees that "the door is always open, and you know we're inter-

ested in your problems." Union "horror" stories soon followed, accompanied by a frigid atmosphere and veiled threats by both sides. Rumor generation reached very high levels.

In early August, Ron E. was fired for "inattention to duties." He filed an unfair labor practices suit against the station management with the National Labor Relations Board. The filing of the suit served to freeze the unionization proceedings until the suit was resolved.

In the meantime, Frederick, Brown, and Overkill turned to a well-known management consulting firm for help in analysis of the organizational and personnel problems.

Questions

1. What is the basic nature of the conflict between management and workers?
2. Is the conflict based on (a) facts, (b) methods, (c) goals, or (d) values? What makes you think so?
3. If you were a member of the consulting firm, what would you do? Be specific.
4. How can you explain the disbelief on the part of management when the union announced its organizational drive?

CHAPTER NINE
Organization and Job Design

OUTLINE

UNDERSTANDING ORGANIZATION AND JOB DESIGN

MANAGERIAL APPLICATIONS

OBJECTIVES

- Identify key elements of the organizational environment

- Describe dynamic attributes of the external environment

- Define organization structure and describe major structural dimensions

- Know the differences between mechanistic and organic organizations

- Describe the processes of differentiation and integration

- Identify and describe the main types of organization structure

- Describe major approaches to job design and identify their similarities and differences

- Address the issues involved in integrating organization design, job design, and individual employee differences

Curse of Cairo: The Bureaucracy Is Alive and Well!

In Cairo, Egypt, there is a stone building, called *Mogamma* or "complex" which houses the Egyptian governmental services. The first floor, alone, has 42 windows to process applications for residence permits. The building's 11 stories contain the records of many agencies. Throughout the complex, files and paperwork are scattered haphazardly on shelves, desk tops, floors, window sills, and corridors.

There seems to be endless movement but little work. In a typical office on one of the upper floors, 10 women are jammed together at tiny desks. There are four battered typewriters in the room, but no one is typing. Some of the women are reading newspapers; others are gossiping; several are drinking tea; one is knitting.

Yet, the red tape is awesome. It takes two days and 11 different approvals to transfer a car registration; it takes four days and 12 signatures to clear a shipment of books at the post office.

The bureaucrats' watch word is *fut aleina bukra*, an Arabic expression that means "pass by tomorrow." While some are looking for bribes to speed up the process, often they simply can't be bothered. A 1974 study found that only 15 percent of Egyptian government employees regularly come to work on time and that the average civil servant works solidly only 20 minutes to two hours per day.

Sometimes, people get tired of waiting for their requests or petitions to be handled. There are occasional suicides at the Mogamma, as frustrated petitioners hurl themselves from the 11th floor balcony, and an ambulance is permanently parked outside the building.

But from where does all of this bureaucracy originate? Many analysts argue that the bureaucratic mentality dates back over 4,000 years to the centralized administration developed by the Pharaohs. The German sociologist Max Weber described Pharaonic Egypt as a "purely bureaucratic state." One theory holds that such a culture was a result of the "hydropolitics" of the Nile: that in a river society, rigid rules were necessary to harness the annual flooding.

While there may be a reason for this form of government, it still doesn't help those who have to use its services. One individual who lost his residence due to another's carelessness and is suing through the court system (another unique Egyptian bureaucracy) has been waiting six years for a legal decision. His last court appearance was simply to prove to the judge that he was still alive.[1]

UNDERSTANDING ORGANIZATION AND JOB DESIGN

Introduction

From the preceding story, we can begin to understand the complexity of organizational design and its impact not only on its inhabitants but on those who depend on it for services. But without some structure, even a bureaucracy, can we have a workable system (to provide service to the public)? While we may all quickly agree that even a bureaucracy is a lesser evil than anarchy, which form of organizational design would better serve the designers as well as the users? What are the major forms to choose from? Under what conditions might one form be preferred over another? How can individual jobs be designed? What influences those kinds of decisions? These are just a few of the questions that will help us as we explore both organization design and individual job design.

To understand organization design, let us begin with a side-trip to the *Oxford English Dictionary*. The definition we want is not that of organization, but of the word tangible. The first two meanings of the word relate to the sense of touch: Something is tangible if it can be discriminated or discerned through the sense of touch. Organizations are obviously not tangible in that sense. It is the third meaning of tangible we are after: ". . . that can be laid hold of or grasped by the mind, or dealt with as a fact."[2]

Organization structure is not tangible in the first two senses of the word. It is certainly not the bricks and mortar of buildings. It is not the job titles or even the people in the organization. Organization structure is defined by the patterning of relationships and activities.[3] Organization structure is neither permanent nor unchanging. It can be changed in anticipation of environmental change or in response to environmental change. It also changes in unplanned, often minor ways. It is a rare organization that has a two-year-old organization chart that is still accurate.

It is useful to distinguish between formal organization and informal organization. The formal organization represents the relationships desired by those who command the enterprise. The ubiquitous organizational chart, an attempt to capture important elements of those relationships, can provide a pictorial representation of at least gross features of the organization structure. The informal organization is characterized by those personal contacts, interactions, and groupings that form among people working within the formal organization.

We examine some common types of formal organization, but first we consider elements outside of the organization that must be acknowledged in the design of the structure.

Organization and Environment

Organizations are generally viewed as subsystems of a larger (supra) system.[4] The organization is in a symbiotic relationship to its environment and takes from it inputs necessary for its operation. The organization's outputs are then transported back to the environment.[5]

The organization and its relationship to the environment might be pictured as in Figure 9–1. The formal organization is represented by the partial organization chart within the traditional pyramid shape. The informal organization is represented by the arrows of contrasting color. Outside the organization lies the environment, composed of dynamic elements that affect the organization's processes.

Environmental Dimensions In one sense, the environment is everything external to the organization. In the introductory story what was the environment? Part of the environment was the present culture of Egypt and the Middle East. But, as the story indicates, it is possible that history and the physical need to

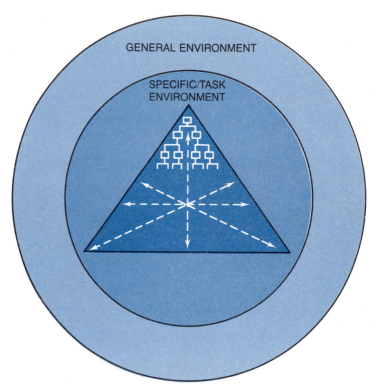

FIGURE 9-1
The organization and its environment

harness the river were part of the environment for the present form of a bureaucratic government.

For use in analysis and decision making, the environment must be defined in meaningful parts. A common way to visualize the environment is in two levels: the societal or general environment, and the task or specific environment.[6] A number of classification schemes that have been offered for the general environment are summarized in Figure 9-2.

General environment.   The general environment is considered to affect all organizations similarly within a given society. For example, regional airlines operate in different parts of the country, but the business traveler will find more similarities than differences between Alaska Airlines and Air Florida. Major airports are operated variously by cities, counties, transportation authorities, and port authorities, but organizationally there is little difference among them. University systems in Texas, California, and Michigan have many organizational similarities, but they are very different from universities in Germany, Singapore, and the Soviet Union.

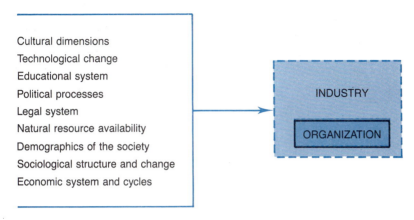

Cultural dimensions
Technological change
Educational system
Political processes
Legal system
Natural resource availability
Demographics of the society
Sociological structure and change
Economic system and cycles

INDUSTRY

ORGANIZATION

FIGURE 9–2
Components of the general environment

The general environment has significant but often subtle influence on the inputs available to the organization, methods for transforming the inputs to outputs, and acceptable form of outputs. Consider for example possible effects of the changing demographics of American society. The number and proportion of senior citizens will increase substantially over the next two decades. This will have substantial implications for virtually every industry, from banking to real estate development.

Specific environment. The specific, or task, environment is the sum of forces directly relevant to the particular organization. While the general environment is the same for all organizations within a society, the specific environment is different for each organization. Components of the specific environment for a hypothetical industrial firm are shown in Figure 9–3.[7]

The proximity of the task environment means that organizational decision makers must consider its elements consciously and specifically. Potentially, the elements of the specific environment are more volatile than those of the general environment. Yet changes in the general environment will affect aspects of the task environment. Take our example of a shift in demographics. Some likely effects on the task environment for an organization serving an older client base would be an increase in the size of the customer component, as well as an increase in the competitor component. Regulatory control over the industry might increase (senior citizens vote regularly).

An organization serving the youth market would expect a shrinking customer component, and might search for new ways to compete for a bigger share of that component. We can see now that though the general environment is the same for all organizations, a change in that environment will affect task environments differently.

Customer Component
  Distributors of product or service
  Actual users of product or service
Suppliers Component
  New materials suppliers
  Equipment suppliers
  Product parts suppliers
  Labor supply
Competitor Component
  Competitors for suppliers
  Competitors for customers
Sociopolitical Component
  Government regulatory control over the industry
  Public political attitude towards the industry and its particular product
  Relationship with trade unions with jurisdiction in the organization
Technological Component
  Meeting new technological requirements of own industry and related industries in production of product or service
  Improving and developing new products by implementing new technological advances in the industry

FIGURE 9-3

Some components of the specific environment for an industrial firm (Source: R. B. Duncan, "Characteristic of Organizational Environments and Perceived Environmental Uncertainty," *Administrative Science Quarterly* (September 1972): 315. Reprinted with permission.)

Dynamics of the Environment   Since the elements of both the general and specific environments exhibit change, organization designers must be concerned about both direction and intensity of such change. Some important dynamics of the environment have been suggested by Khandwalla.[8]

Five attributes of the external environment are proposed to have impact on both strategic and structural variables. The attributes are turbulence, hostility, diversity, technical complexity, and restrictiveness.

A turbulent environment is one marked by dramatic change. Information quickly becomes obsolete in this type of environment and the organization must build quality methods for sensing the environment (intelligence capability). Many environmental elements faced by electronics companies can be characterized as turbulent. The opposite of a turbulent environment is a placid environment.

An environment that is hostile is one that is stressful and potentially damaging or destructive to the organization. Many environmental elements for the nuclear power industry in the United States would fit this description. The opposite of a hostile environment is one that is benign.

A diverse environment is one that is heterogeneous. The marketing environment for a department store is much more diverse than that of a tax accountant. The department store has a wide variety of clients with many different needs. The tax accountant has a more homogeneous set of clients, all with similar needs.

An environment is technically complex if information needed for making decisions is technically sophisticated. Aspects of the aerospace industry's environment are technically complex, and managers must be able to interpret technical information while forming decisions. By comparison, the environment of a mobile home manufacturer is much less technically complex.

A restrictive environment places constraints on how the organization operates. Airlines face a fairly restrictive environment since there are numerous constraints upon how they may operate. Many of the constraints are of a legal nature, such as safety standards and limitations on the type of cargo the airlines can carry. Constraints can also be political. For example, major cities often limit the number of late evening and early morning flights, and they direct take-off and landing approaches away from areas of high population density (or high political clout).

Figure 9–4 depicts the relationships between the concepts we have discussed so far and the organization itself. It is important to note that for a given

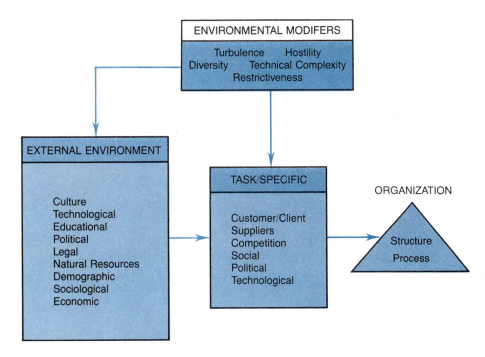

FIGURE 9–4
The dynamic environment

organization, one environmental element may be turbulent while another is placid. For example, the external political environment of American universities is relatively placid, while the demographic environment is not. Changes in the birth rate beginning a couple of decades ago continue to deplete the ranks of the late teenage component, the traditional "raw material" of universities in this country. Universities are responding to this environmental change in a number of ways, including placing more emphasis on continuing education and developing innovative programs to attract new clientele.

Response to environmental change frequently entails a structural change in the organization. A common organizational response to increased environmental diversity is the creation of new units ("departmentation") to cope with the change. For example, many universities have developed departments of continuing education. These departments are frequently autonomous units that draw upon the faculty of several schools within the university. The "product" is instruction that takes forms different from that in the traditional degree programs. Another example might be a manufacturing firm that develops new markets in a foreign country. If the firm enjoys early success it will likely find that the old organization structure is inadequate to cope with both the domestic and foreign markets. A reasonable and usual response is the development of a specialized department to deal with the foreign market.

Organization Design

The design of an organization is the result of actions by authorities in the organization to coordinate the activities of "positional incumbents" (people holding various roles or jobs in the organization). These actions include the specification of reporting relationships and formal communication channels, methods for coordinating the factors of production, and definition of positions and units. The object of the organization design, at least implicitly, is efficient operation in pursuit of organizational goals.[9]

As noted earlier, organization structure involves relationships, and attempts at defining elements of structure can be placed in that context. There is a vast literature in organization theory about organization structure and design. Here we describe only some major aspects of the topic.

Structural Dimensions   Four structural dimensions have appeared frequently in the literature: complexity/specialization, formalization, centralization, and configuration.[10] These dimensions are most effectively used in a comparative sense. For example, we can confidently claim that organization A is more centralized than organization B and less specialized than organization C. We can also compare units within a single organization and perhaps find that the financial function in organization A is more centralized than the sales function.

Complexity/specialization.   This dimension refers to the number of specialized components or units within the organization. If we compared the research and development components of two companies and found one to have separate units for fundamental and applied research while the other had only an undifferentiated research and development department, the first firm would, of course, be the more complex.

Complexity can also be assessed by the amount of vertical differentiation. An organization with six management levels is more complex (vertically) than one with four levels.

Formalization. This is measured by the extent of explicit requirements for operations—the degree to which regulations are spelled out. Elaborate systems of rules and procedures are good indicators of formalization. The space shuttle program is a good example of high formalization. Rules and procedures mind-boggling in both number and complexity must be followed by everyone from contractors who build the shuttle components to the launch crew and the flight crew.

Relatively low formalization can be found in academic units of your university. The faculty members are quite free to select the sequence of tasks they perform. Rules that do exist are sometimes not rigorously enforced (maintaining office hours, for instance).

Centralization. This dimension refers primarily to the location and level where recurring decisions are made. The department store where clerks are allowed to accept returned merchandise is less centralized (in that function) than the competing store where supervisors must accept returns. A firm that allows employees to select among several procedures for accomplishing a task is less centralized than one that requires an employee to request deviation from the standard procedure.

Configuration. The organization chart is a gross representation of configuration. The "height," or number of vertical levels, and "width," or number of units at each level, are common measures of configuration, as are managerial span of control and ratios of direct to indirect workers. The terms *tall* and *flat* are often used to describe configuration. A tall organization has several hierarchical levels and correspondingly narrow spans of control. A flat organization has fewer managerial levels and wide spans of control at those levels.

As we indicated earlier, the dimensions of structure have to do with the patterning of relationships. There are some other major features of organizational design, and we turn to these next.

Mechanistic and Organic Organizations   A major study in the 1950s provided a new way to describe organizations.[11] Organizations that are relatively adaptable and flexible are termed organic while those that are relatively rigid and inflexible are termed mechanistic. Mechanistic organizations are further characterized by high specialization, relatively narrow spans of control, and many rules and procedures. Organic forms tend to have wider spans of control, less specialization of roles, and fewer rules and procedures. Because of these characteristics mechanistic organizations are best suited to stable, slowly changing environments. Organic forms are best suited to dynamic environments.

Returning to the beginning story of Egyptian government, which form is most descriptive of their system? Organic? Mechanistic? Does it correspond to the environment in which it exists? Is culture part of that environment? RESTRICTIV ENVIRONMEN

The drivers' license bureau in your state is a good example of a mechanistic organization. The environment is very stable and the workload predictable. Rules and procedures are carefully followed, sometimes maddeningly so. The registrar's office in your university is probably mechanistic also. That office must maintain complete records for every student, both present and past, and must be able to retrieve those records no matter how old they are. The registrar's office also reviews files of prospective graduates and is the final authority on whether a student has fulfilled graduation requirements. Many rules and procedures are applied in the process.

Examples of organic organizations would include most research and development units, professional sports teams, and the trauma ward of a major hospital. Organicism does not imply complete lack of rules, procedures, and supervision. It simply implies the ability of the organization and its inhabitants to react to environmental change quickly and without panic or serious resistance. That is accomplished through a structure less rigid than that of the mechanistic organization.

Differentiation and Integration   Differentiation and integration describe structural configuration in response to complexity both within the organization and outside it.

Differentiation.   Differentiation is the degree to which the organization is segmented into identifiable components. An organization is differentiated both vertically (number of levels) and horizontally (number of clearly distinct units).

Organizational size is correlated with both types of differentiation. A small business is usually "flat," perhaps with only one manager. Employees perform several functions, thus horizontal differentiation is low. As the company grows, layers of management are added and the benefits of specialization among employees are exploited.

The environment is also an important factor in determining differentiation.[12] Generally, the more complex the external environment the more horizontally differentiated should be the organization. In essence the units manage relationships with environmental sectors. For example, a computer company might form separate marketing and sales units for large business use, small business use, and home use. By contrast, a construction equipment manufacturer might have a single department to handle all marketing and sales.

Integration.   Integration refers to the degree of coordination and control. The more differentiated the organization the greater the need for integration. The benefits of specialization come at some cost of reduced communication and difficulty of coordination.

Typical devices of integration include the management system itself. Reporting relationships, meetings, memos, and plans are all instruments of integration. Complexity also begets complexity. The more differentiated the organization is the more complex and numerous the integration devices tend to be.[13] Job titles like "production coordinator" and "customer liaison" indicate roles that are heavily integrative. Many staff functions are integrative in nature.

Structural Types

On the one hand it is encouraging to know that there are very few classifications of organization structure. On the other hand the permutations appear endless. The classic forms of organization structure are the functional and the divisional. A more recent type is the matrix form. Each is described in turn.

Functional Organization The functional organization is characterized by the grouping of activities by specialization. Many of the organizations we deal with on a day-to-day basis as consumers are organized by function. The supermarket has checkers, produce people, butchers, and perhaps bakers among its functional specialists. The local department store has sales clerks, security people, accountants, and perhaps tailors and elevator operators on staff.

The obvious major advantage of functional organization is that of specialization. Employees can focus upon a limited number of specialized activities and theoretically become more proficient at those activities. The other side of the coin is that functional specialization can lead to coordination problems, communication difficulty, and suboptimization. If the credit department emphasizes its function by too rigorous screening of credit applicants, potential customers may be driven away. High specialization sometimes leads to the creation of professional jargon that is incomprehensible to people outside that function, as many who deal with computing departments will attest.

Functional structure also places a great deal of responsibility on the person at the top of the pyramid. Since no position below the top has an overall view of the organization, development of general management talent is limited. When succession inevitably becomes necessary, there may be no one in the organization capable of assuming the top post.

Divisional Organization Typically, as the organization enjoys success, new products or services are added in an attempt to better serve current clients and to attract new clients. The addition of products or services and resulting growth tends to exacerbate the problem of coordination among functions, as well as within functions. The typical response is to reorganize to a divisional structure.

The most common divisional structure is by product or service, though many retail firms are divided geographically and some service organizations are divided by time or process stage. The divisional structure has several potential advantages. Organizing around products or product lines allows employees to identify with specific outputs and to focus energy on a smaller set of output than in the old functional structure. Each division in essence becomes a separate business. The division general manager has responsibility for profit for the division. This arrangement simplifies assignment of responsibility for success or failure of major organizational components and also provides the larger organization with a talent pool of general managers.

Major disadvantages include duplication of resources and potential destructive conflict between divisions. If division A has need for an electrical engineer one-third of the time and division B has need for an electrical engineer one-half time, the company will almost certainly hire two electrical engineers or pay high overtime costs to engineers on staff. Most budgeting and scheduling systems do not encourage the sharing of resources between divisions. While competition between divisions can provoke desirable increases in efficiency, that competition must be kept within reasonable limits. General Motors is delighted when Chevrolet takes sales away from Ford, but not so pleased with the idea of Chevrolet taking sales away from Pontiac.

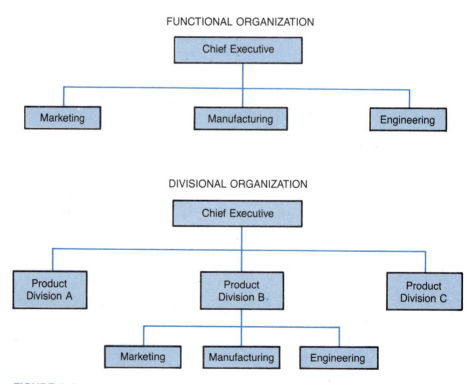

FIGURE 9-5
Examples of functional and divisional organizations

Simple functional and divisional structures are shown in Figure 9–5. Observe that the divisions in Figure 9–5 are organized functionally. It is conventional to describe an organization as functional or divisional based upon the structure at the highest level of aggregation.

Matrix Organization   The matrix organization is a product of the aerospace industry, but is now used rather widely, especially in high-technology industries. The employee in a matrix has two "homes"—in a function such as engineering, design, or manufacturing, and in a project or product organization. The employee may work in more than one project or product team at the same time, and can be reassigned quickly if the need arises.

Matrix places a premium on lateral relations. The matrix tends to change membership and fluctuate in size. Each member is likely to have two superiors: the matrix/product manager and a functional manager. The matrix concept consciously violates one of the old "principles" of management, that every employee should have only one supervisor. Figure 9–6 depicts a matrix organizational chart.

The great advantage of the matrix organization is its flexibility. People and resources can be added or removed quickly to meet changing demands. The added flexibility can come at relatively high cost to some participants. The following are just a few of many questions that must be addressed:

■ What happens to people no longer needed by the matrix?

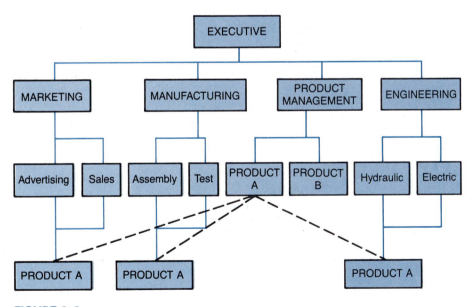

FIGURE 9–6
The matrix organization

- Who appraises employee performance, functional manager or matrix manager?
- Who determines salary increments?
- How is employee time "charged out"?
- How is employee time scheduled between matrix groups—which has priority?

Uncertainty for participants is generally high in the matrix form. The potential of great organizational flexibility is balanced somewhat by the inherent coordination problems. Lack of clarity about responsibilities can lead to inefficiency and to conflict over "turf." Clearly, a company should not adopt matrix organization merely because it is a glamorous concept.

Choosing the Right Structure   At the beginning of this chapter we emphasized the importance of environmental factors in organization design. Here we apply one of the decision-making approaches described in chapter 7—the decision tree. Duncan proposed the decision tree reproduced in Figure 9–7.[14] The organizational designer must consider the goals of the organization and the nature of the environment. The latter can be accomplished by analyzing components of the general and task environments described earlier.

One must determine whether the environments are simple or complex, static or dynamic. The simple environment has a small number of factors that are somewhat similar to one another. A complex environment has many factors that are dissimilar. If the environment is static, the factors remain basically the same. If the environment is dynamic, the factors are changing continually.[15]

The decision tree acknowledges that in a complex environment some components of the organization can face static conditions while other components face dynamic ones. Thus we may have mixed structures with varying degrees of lateral relations, including matrix. Like any decision device, this decision tree will not make the choice for the organization designer. But it will force the designer to ask important questions and to adopt a rigorous analytical approach.

It should be obvious by now that important aspects of jobs are heavily influenced by organization structure and design. Keeping that in mind, we move to the topic of job design.

Job Design – DEGREE OF SPECIALIZATION

That organization design affects job design is clear when we remember some differences between organic and mechanistic organizations. The mechanistic organization specifies required activities more clearly than the organic. The degree of decentralization in decision making is low and the span of control narrow in the mechanistic organization. The organic organization has a higher degree of decision decentralization and wide spans of control. Employee interactions in the mechanistic system are vertical and oriented toward instructions and decisions,

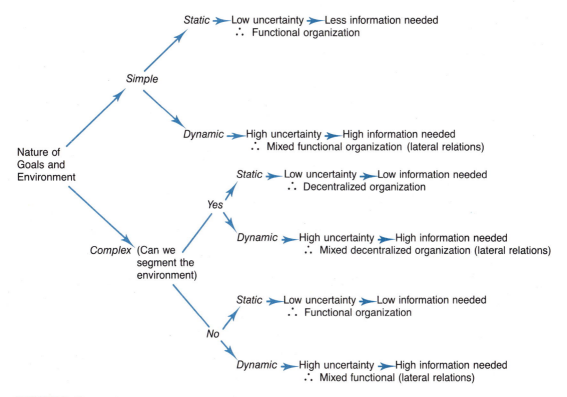

FIGURE 9–7
Organizational design decision tree (Source: Reprinted by permission of the publisher, from "What Is the Right Organization Structure?" by R. Duncan, *Organizational Dynamics* (Winter 1979): 72. © 1979 by AMACOM, a division of American Management Associations, New York. All rights reserved.)

while the organic system relies more on lateral communications emphasizing advice and information.

Job, or task, design has become increasingly important to both managers and researchers in the last few years. There are both economic and human reasons to be concerned about the subject. Properly designed jobs can have positive impact on productivity.[16] A positive relationship has been shown between job design and the performance of individuals with high need for achievement.[17]

From the purely humanistic perspective, we would argue that organizations and their management have an obligation to provide jobs that do not demean or psychologically punish the individual. The employee who dislikes his or her manager can generally find ways to avoid that person, but the employee who dislikes the job is trapped. The employee is likely to quit eventually, but may go through a period of increased absenteeism first. A substantial amount of research has linked task design to job satisfaction and to employee absenteeism and turnover rates.[18]

Approaches to Job Design The topic of job design has frequented economic literature for at least two centuries. Adam Smith, in *The Wealth of Nations*, provided the first industrial example of the benefits of specialization.[19] In observing the manufacture of pins Smith noted that eighteen distinct subtasks could be defined. One worker performing all eighteen subtasks could produce a relatively small number of pins in a workday. By specializing in just one or a few of the tasks, a group of workers could produce many times the number of pins that could be produced if each worker performed all of the tasks. Engineers soon took up the issue,[20] and specialization of labor became the foundation for job design. It has been a mixed blessing.

Scientific management. Frederick W. Taylor had enormous impact upon the design of industrial jobs, an impact that continues to this day.[21] Taylor, an engineer by training, felt that the practice of management should be as analytically based and scientifically grounded as the practice of engineering. For Taylor, the problem was quite simply one of discovering the scientific principles that underlay the practice of management.

Scientific management emphasized the analysis of jobs and the simplification and standardization of the tasks performed. As a consultant to the Bethlehem Steel Corporation and other firms, Taylor was able to implement many of his ideas about job design. He and his colleagues developed the process of time and motion study, variations of which are still used by industrial engineers. Through time and motion study followed by task simplification and standardization, plus the introduction of piecework incentive systems, Taylor was able to demonstrate large increases in worker productivity.

The thrust was to simplify jobs as an economic benefit to the organization. Specialization would result in the greater productivity described by Adam Smith. In addition, the simpler the job the less skill the worker needed. Therefore selection and training procedures would be less elaborate and expensive.

Useful as Taylor's techniques were and are, there has been a tendency to ignore the human element in their application. The results have not always been anticipated, as you can see in Box 9–1. There are at least two lessons to be learned from the misapplication of Taylor's principles: first, people resist being treated as if they were pieces of machinery. Second, highly specialized tasks are often boring, leading to job dissatisfaction and its attendant problems.

Perceived overspecialization has led to a reaction by both workers and theorists. A substantial amount of effort has been expended in the past three decades to undo some of the simplification championed by Taylor and his colleagues.

Job enlargement. Job enlargement was the first concerted attempt to redesign tasks away from the religion of simplification and standardization. Job enlarge-

(handwritten margin notes:)
1. MACHINE PACING
2. REPETITIVENESS
3. LOW SKILL REQUIREMENT
4. TASK SPECIALIZATION
5. LIMITED SOCIAL INTERACTION
6. TOOL AND TECHNIQUES SPECIFIC

BOX 9–1

Job Design Resisted

In 1978 the Safeway grocery chain conducted a large-scale time and motion study in its Richmond, California distribution center. The project led to a new Work Rate System. Supervisors and consultants armed with stopwatches roved through the distribution center and timed workers at every activity. For purposes of analysis body movements are measured in Time Motion Units, or TMUs. One hundred thousand TMUs equals one hour. Typical movements are "walk," "reach," "grasp," "transport," etc. Eye focus and eye travel are also measured.

Safeway created a computer data base from the time and motion study, and also included information on the size and weight of all inventory items, a blueprint of each warehouse with the location of every rack and slot, the temperature of the air and the coefficient of friction when boxes are slid across each other. These data were used to develop work standards for the center's employees. The process was not entirely smooth. In the words of one worker

The company tried to figure in everything you could imagine. Roving supervisors followed us everywhere with stopwatches. At first they said to take as long as we wanted for each job. But then they set averages, keying on the faster workers.

When the system came in last April, each job order had a certain time limit stamped at the bottom. You had

maybe 27 minutes to stack 110 items on a pallet and get it to a certain truck bay. You had 30 minutes to eat, 10 minutes for break and 4.8 minutes to go to the men's room. A day's work is 420 to 430 minutes. Everything comes out of that. You have to meet the time standard on each order or out you go.

Certain orders were literally impossible to do in the time they gave, while others you could do with 10 minutes to spare for a smoke. It was crazy. When there was a slowdown on the floor, you'd actually bargain over minutes with the supervisor. They'd say, 'I'll give you four minutes off,' and I'd be arguing for six minutes.

At least 90 percent of the workers were disciplined under the system. At one point Safeway had to stagger the suspensions (10-day disciplinary layoffs) they handed out because they were running short of workers on the floor!

Finally, 3,500 workers from eight union locals walked out of the plant, charging a work speedup in violation of the contract. Safeway responded that the change was not a speedup, but rather a "productivity recovery."

Questions

1. Is the scientific management model useless in today's organizations? Why or why not?
2. Might the time and motion study have been implemented in a less threatening way? If so, how?
3. Regardless of justification, how wise was it for Safeway to discipline so many workers?

Source: Adapted from T. Brom, "Workers Rebel Against 'Scientific Supervision,'" *Pacific News Service*, 1978. Used with permission.

ment generally involves expanding the job horizontally by adding related activities. Consider an assembly line worker who plugs electronic boards into slots on a TV chassis, then passes the unit on to the next station, where another worker attaches the housing and control knobs. Both workers' jobs could be enlarged by allowing them to do all of the operations mentioned. Ultimately each worker might assemble an entire receiver and do the quality inspection as well.

Note that this is analogous to allowing Adam Smith's pin makers to re-complicate their jobs. Some of the benefits of specialization are given up in job enlargement, but to what purpose? Much of the literature on job enlargement is from the 1950s and 1960s and is somewhat equivocal. On the one hand, job enlargement yielded positive results, especially in terms of job satisfaction.[22] On the other hand, some scholars questioned the certainty of positive reaction by employees to job enlargement.[23]

Job rotation has been another attempt to mitigate effects of job specialization. Job rotation involves changing the task assignments rather than the task itself.[24] In the TV assembly example above, the two workers would exchange work stations on a pre-arranged basis, thus switching activities. Probably the primary use of job rotation at the rank and file level is for training purposes. Job rotation has been used extensively at the managerial level also, to groom talented managers for advancement to upper management. In this case, however, the rotation is not repeated over time, as on the assembly line.

Job enrichment. Job enrichment is distinguished from job enlargement by the elements of decision making and control granted to the worker. Here the job is expanded vertically, not just horizontally.

Unlike most managerial concepts, job enrichment can be traced back to a single theory: Herzberg's two-factor theory of motivation.[25] As you recall from chapter 3, Herzberg argued that elements of job content—achievement, recognition, the work itself, responsibility, advancement, and personal growth and development—were motivating factors. Proponents of job enrichment use those elements as target concepts in job design. The concepts were put into operation by Herzberg as shown in Table 9–1.

Herzberg and his associates directed a job enrichment program at a US Air Force base involving more than 1,000 workers in distribution, material management, personnel, civil engineering, transportation, data processing, procurement, and maintenance.[26] Herzberg reported that at the end of two years $1.75 million had been saved in the form of reduced sick leave, lower turnover, less overtime and rework, and material savings. The implementation cost of the project was approximately $500,000.

Sweden has long been accepting of employee participation in decision making, and in recent years the Riksdag has mandated certain kinds of participation by legislation.[27] The Volvo plant located near Kalmar, Sweden, has been the site of some of the most famous job design experiments. The Kalmar plant, built in the 1970s, was designed for the operations of semi-autonomous work teams. Instead of a traditional assembly line, teams of about fifteen workers are gathered in bays. Each team is responsible for assembling one or more automobile subsystems, for example, the electrical system, hydraulic system, or instrumentation. Buffer inventories allow groups to work at their own pace, change job assignments within the group, and even take time off as long as production

① CONTROL OVER RESOURCES
② ACCOUNTABILITY
③ FEEDBACK
④ WORK PLACE
⑤ ACHIEVEMENT OPPORTUNITIES
⑥ PERSONAL GROWTH AND DEVELOPMENT

TABLE 9–1
Herzberg's two-factor theory made operational

Principles of Vertical Job Loading	
Principle	Motivators Involved
A. Removing some controls while retaining accountability	Responsibility and personal achievement
B. Increasing the accountability of individuals for own work	Responsibility and recognition
C. Giving a person a complete natural unit of work (module, division, area, and so on)	Responsibility, achievement, and recognition
D. Granting additional authority to employees in their activities; job freedom	Responsibiilty, achievement, and recognition
E. Making periodic reports directly to the worker rather than to the supervisor	Internal recognition
F. Introducing new and more difficult tasks not previously handled	Growth and learning
G. Assigning individuals specific or specialized tasks, enabling them to become experts	Responsibility, growth, and advancement

schedules are met. Each group is responsible for inspecting the work and receives immediate feedback about productivity and quality.[28]

Quality at the Kalmar plant appears to be higher than at other plants, and absenteeism is lower. On the other hand, despite the fact that the land for the plant was contributed by the Swedish government, construction costs were about 10 percent higher than for a conventional assembly line facility, and operating costs are higher than in a conventional plant.[29]

Individual Differences and Job Design A significant contribution to job design methodology came from a study by Turner and Lawrence in the mid 1960s.[30] The researchers identified six task dimensions present to a greater or lesser degree in jobs: variety, autonomy, required social interaction, opportunities for social interaction, required knowledge and skill, and responsibility. The dimensions are known collectively as requisite task attributes.

Job characteristics theory. Hackman and Oldham extended the pioneering work of Turner and Lawrence and created a comprehensive framework for task design.[31] In the model, core job dimensions affect critical psychological states of the worker, which in turn relate to personal and work outcomes (see Figure 9–8). The core job dimensions are similar to the requisite task attributes of Turner and Lawrence:

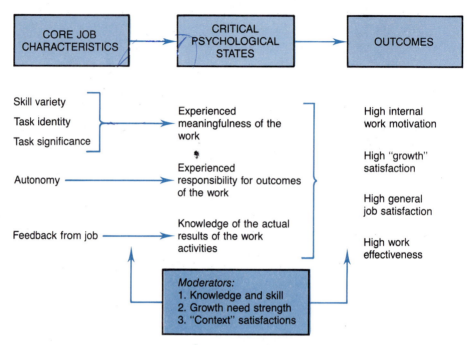

FIGURE 9–8

The job characteristics model (Source: J. R. Hackman and G. R. Oldham, *Work Redesign* © 1980, Addison-Wesley, Reading, MA., p. 90, Figure 4.6. Reprinted with permission.)

1. *Skill variety*—the degree to which a job requires a variety of different activities in carrying out the work, involving the use of a number of different skills and talents of the person.
2. *Task identity*—the degree to which the job requires completion of a "whole" and identifiable piece or work; that is, doing a job from beginning to end with a visible outcome.
3. *Task significance*—the degree to which the job has a substantial impact on the lives or work of other people, whether in the immediate organization or in the external environment.
4. *Autonomy*—the degree to which the job provides substantial freedom, independence, and discretion to the individual in scheduling the work and in determining the procedures to be used in carrying it out.
5. *Feedback*—the degree to which carrying out the work activities required by the job results in the individual obtaining direct and clear information about the effectiveness of performance.[32]

The critical psychological states of the job characteristics theory are viewed as primary determinants of employee motivation and satisfaction. They are defined as follows:

1. *Experienced meaningfulness of the work*—the degree to which the individual experiences the job as generally meaningful, valuable, and worthwhile.
2. *Experienced responsibility of work outcomes*—the degree to which the individual feels personally accountable and responsible for the work he or she does.
3. *Knowledge of results*—the degree to which the individual understands, on a continuous basis, how effectively he or she is performing the job.[33]

As shown in Figure 9–8, the core job dimensions—skill variety, task identity, and task significance—are related to the critical psychological state of experienced meaningfulness of the work. Assuming no intervening variables, one could conclude that the more variety, the greater the task identity, and the greater the task significance, the more meaningful the work would appear. Similarly, the greater the autonomy, the more responsibility would be experienced, and the greater the feedback, the higher the knowledge of results. When energized, the critical psychological states will lead to high internal work motivation, high quality work performance, high work satisfaction, and low absenteeism and turnover.

The model proposes three moderating variables—knowledge and skill, growth need strength, and "context" satisfactions—that intervene between the core job dimensions and critical psychological states, and between the critical psychological states and personal and work outcomes. Even a job with high motivating potential can turn off an employee who lacks the knowledge and skill to perform effectively. The theory proposes that when jobs are high in all of the core job dimensions people with high growth needs experience the psychological states and will react more favorably to them than workers with low growth needs. "Context" satisfactions include workers' feelings about pay, job security, peer relations, and other work-related aspects.

Job Design, Organization Structure, and Individual Growth Needs Porter, Lawler, and Hackman proposed a schema for relating job design and organization design to the growth need strength of individuals.[34] A brief study of Figure 9–9 shows that only cells two and seven provide the necessary congruence of the design elements with growth need strength. In cell two, low growth need employees with simple routine jobs within a mechanistic organization structure will perform effectively and have adequate levels of attendance and job satisfaction.

If we apply this model to the beginning story, we can see that certain assumptions were made by the original designers of the Egyptian system. They assumed that the workers had low growth needs and therefore could effectively perform simple, routine clerical functions, such as checking files and signatures and filling out more forms. All of these tasks could take place within a rigidly controlled structure. Some aspects of the assumptions must have been invalid, however, since the workers were only contributing twenty minutes to two hours work per day. Which assumptions need to be reexamined?

In cell seven, high growth need employees in enlarged (or enriched) jobs are located in an organic organization structure. It is predicted that high-quality performance, high job satisfaction, good attendance, and low turnover will result.

Predicted Relationships

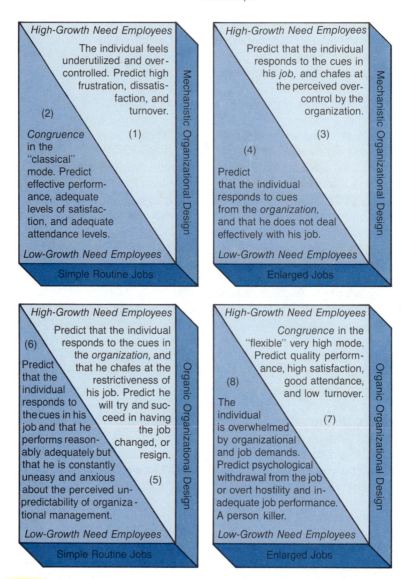

FIGURE 9–9

Organizational design, job design, and employee characteristics (Source: L. W. Porter, E. E. Lawler, III, and J. R. Hackman, *Behavior in Organizations*, p. 310. Copyright © 1975 by McGraw-Hill Book Company. Reprinted with permission.)

All other combinations in the matrix will result in lowered effectiveness and/or increased job stress and alienation.

The model emphasizes the importance of a multivariate approach to organi-

BOX 9–2

A Dream Job?

This job has everything going for it: work ten minutes and be paid for 12 hours, free airline tickets, per diem expense account, special drink allowance. The job does not require a college degree, or even a high school diploma. Past work history is unimportant. Ready to sign up?

Before signing on the dotted line, you should know that the job is in a nuclear power station. And we mean IN. The work takes place deep within a steam generator, in an atmosphere so radioactive that exposure must be severely limited.

The people in this job are called jumpers, and they perform repairs inside the steam generators, frequently on rusted or corroded pipes. Sometimes they must climb several stories up a narrow passageway to reach the repair site. The jumpers are elaborately clothed, down to full helmets, air hoses and plastic boots.

The Nuclear Regulatory Commission does not allow any nuclear plant worker to get more than 3,000 millirems of radiation in three months or 5,000 millirems in a year. Jumpers sometimes work in areas where the three-month limit is reached in five minutes.

Jumpers are not usually employees of the nuclear plant. Instead they are provided by temporary help firms that specialize in the industry. They have no union, job security, or health plan.

Questions

1. The areas where the jumpers work could be decontaminated, but it would take weeks or months and be very expensive. Is the nuclear industry exploiting the unskilled workers who become jumpers?
2. How would the jumper's job rate in the Hackman-Oldham job characteristics model (Figure 9–8)?
3. For what reasons would the power plants not want jumpers as fulltime, or even permanent part-time employees?

Source: "Ten Minutes' Work for Twelve Hours' Pay? What's the Catch?" *The Wall Street Journal* (12 October 1983): 1. Reprinted by permission of *The Wall Street Journal*, © Dow Jones & Company, Inc., 1983. All rights reserved.

zation and job design. The two are interdependent, and singly and jointly interdependent with characteristics of people in the work roles. It is useful to note here that the terms mechanistic and organic do not necessarily refer to the entire organization. Departments, divisions, and other units can be more or less organic than other components of the organization.

A review by Gavin and Fleenor on the locus of control suggests that some aspects of job design should reflect differences in employee locus of control.[35] If the work force consisted largely of employees high on internal locus of control, management would be advised to consider enriched jobs and participative management techniques. In a work force dominated by high externals, management should provide relatively structured tasks within a mechanistic structure.

In recent years organizations and their managers have necessarily become more concerned with the rights of employees in the workplace. As progress is made in the more visible areas of employee rights, such as equal opportunity and job safety, managers will inevitably become more sensitive to some of the subtle issues in job design. It is at least plausible that in the future employees will come to expect a job that fits their needs as individuals, not just the economic needs of the organization.

The Role of Job Satisfaction

It is not clear that job satisfaction always or even usually leads to increased productivity or effectiveness. Despite that, it is possible to argue that job satisfaction is a worthy social goal. Why *not* design jobs in ways that will enhance satisfaction?

Job satisfaction has been well researched, and reviews of that literature appear periodically. Some interesting findings suggest that there is a positive relationship between occupation prestige and job satisfaction. A study conducted by the National Opinion Research Center showed that when effects of job prestige are removed, professional-technical workers have low job satisfaction.[36] This seemingly contradicts the popular belief that professional work is intrinsically more rewarding than other work, and suggests that prestige is a major factor in professional occupation satisfaction.

Other studies have shown that role conflict and ambiguity are negatively correlated with job satisfaction,[37] while goal clarity and participation are positively related to job satisfaction.[38] Although role ambiguity may decrease satisfaction, there is evidence that high internal-locus-of-control workers are less affected by the ambiguity.[39]

Organization structure correlates of job satisfaction were summarized in one literature review as follows:

- As one moves up in the organization hierarchy, satisfaction increases.
- There seem to be important differences between satisfaction levels of persons in line and staff positions.
- Manager job satisfaction tends to increase as the number of subordinates supervised increases.
- In tall organizations, high-level executives are most satisfied, while in flat organizations lower-level executives are most satisfied.[40]

Variables that are unrelated to the work environment (for example, economic conditions in the community or relationship with family) may also affect job satisfaction. It appears that demographic variables such as age, race, and sex also moderate job satisfaction.[41]

These results render the Porter-Lawler-Hackman model of Figure 9–9 less precise than one might wish, but by no means detract from the overall value. It is clear that we do not yet know enough about job satisfaction despite considerable research in the area. The major research question to be answered: What five, ten, or fifteen variables explain the most variance of the job satisfaction construct?

The major philosophical question to be answered: Must job satisfaction contribute to performance, or is it a social good to be pursued for its own sake?

Summary of Key Concepts

1. Organizations have formal and informal aspects. The formal relationships between people and departments are officially designed and sanctioned by the organizational hierarchy. The informal organization develops through personal contacts between people.

2. Since organizations are dependent on their environment, the environment will influence the organization's design and structure.

3. The structure of an organization may be described using various dimensions: complexity/specialization, formalization, centralization, and configuration.

4. Mechanistic organizations tend to be more rigid and inflexible, have narrower spans of control, and have more rules and regulations than organic organizations.

5. While there are many forms of organizational structures, most can be described as functional, divisional, or matrix. Part of the decision about which structure is most appropriate concerns the complexity and dynamics of the environment in which the organization exists.

6. While job design is primarily concerned with getting a set of tasks done effectively, recent pressures for more involvement in one's job has made the design of jobs more difficult and complex.

7. Scientific management emphasizes the simplification and standardization of jobs. Job enlargement involves expanding one's job horizontally to add related tasks. Job enrichment concerns the addition of elements of decision making and control to one's job (vertically adding elements).

8. As employees become more vocal about their needs, job design will undertake the complex task of matching individual needs with organizational efficiencies.

9. Job satisfaction is negatively correlated with role conflict and ambiguity while positively correlated with goal clarity and participation. Many other aspects of one's situation aren't clearly associated with job satisfaction or dissatisfaction. Much more research needs to be done in this area to identify the variables and test their responsiveness to job satisfaction and job performance.

Key Terms

Centralization	Integration
Complexity/specialization	Job design
Configuration	Job enlargement
Differentiation	Job enrichment
Divisional organization	Matrix organization
Environment	Mechanistic organization
Formalization	Organic organization
Functional organization	Organizational structure

MANAGERIAL APPLICATIONS

In this section we discuss how environment influenced the structure of the phone company. Next we examine the issue of recentralization and a successful matrix structure. Finally, we explore several areas of job design: the Topeka experiment, boredom on the job, alternative work schedules, and job sharing.

A Change in Environment

A dramatic change in corporate environment occurred to the American Telephone and Telegraph Company in the early 1980s, when the company was ordered to divest its operating divisions. Several new companies were formed and perhaps the most famous company in the world, "Ma Bell," was no more.

AT&T, newly free of the operating divisions, immediately began developing a new corporate culture. The old culture, rooted deeply in a service ethic, had for years influenced the organizational structure and the kind of people the company hired.[42] Engineering and manufacturing had traditionally been the routes to top management, but with divestiture, a recognition of the need for marketing expertise developed. Unfortunately, marketing had never assumed the importance of engineering and manufacturing when the company was a protected monopoly, and there were few marketing executives at senior management levels. The Bell tradition of developing people from within would be too slow to accommodate the rapidly changing environment, so the company was faced with the need to search for outside talent.

The change also presented the company with new opportunities. For years Bell had manufactured computers for its own use, but it was not allowed to compete in the open market with computer companies. Divestiture and deregulation changed all of that. The company's immense financial and technical resources should allow it to become a formidable competitor, though its relative weakness in marketing makes combat with IBM a daunting prospect.

Though an organization must react to external forces, it needn't wait for the forces to act. A division of Honeywell (Honeywell Defense and Marine Systems Group) spent several years creating what they call the "energetic organization."[43] The program attempted to encourage and nurture entrepreneurial activity in the heart of a large corporation. Divisional task teams were formed and engaged in participative problem solving. A need for improved communication was a predictable problem, but the solution was not. It was recommended that status reports be sent both directions, not just upward. Managers are now expected to report on the status of their units to the employees as well as to upper management.

Many other changes were made in the company, but for us, the most interesting question is *why*? In the words of one company spokesman, "Recognizing that these times of rapid shifts in technology and consumer demand require that an organization be quick on its feet, we aimed to improve the group's ability to respond quickly to the changes that might be needed in whatever realm they arise."[44] In other words, if you think the environment is going to change, you should be ready to change with it.

Organization Design

As employees, most of us feel that our organization is a model of permanence—never changing, rarely affected by outside events. While it is true that few organizations face the turbulence encountered by AT&T, organizations do change over time. Ask anyone who has been on extended leave (a year or more) if the organization was the same when that person returned. The answer will almost certainly be no.

Some structural changes can be classified as "tinkering." For example, a medical center created a new management position called Patient Accounts Manager to oversee both the billing and credit departments. The change was a good one since coordination of activity in the departments was lacking, but from an overall organizational perspective the change was minor.

Contrast that minor change with the immense upheaval of American Telephone and Telegraph. Business units with annual sales in billions of dollars were spun off, and the remaining corporation was dramatically restructured. Western Electric, a gigantic enterprise in its own right, became only a trade name, with its manufacturing plants assigned to various business lines. Much of the old Western Electric is now part of AT&T Consumer Products. For over 100 years the Bell System had been a largely domestic operation. Within a period of months in 1983 and 1984 the company had either gained equity positions in or entered into projects with organizations in South Korea, Ireland, The Netherlands, Italy, the United Kingdom, and other countries.[45]

Recentralization The casual reader of management literature would conclude that decentralization is necessary to achieve the organizational flexibility required of these parlous times. Maybe.

Beatrice Foods is a company with over $10 billion in annual sales. In the 1960s and 1970s Beatrice grew rapidly through acquisitions and by 1980 was selling 9,000 products produced by over 400 businesses in its corporate shell. The company also faced competitors that were consolidating business lines and brand names. By 1982 Beatrice was experiencing an earnings decline.

A new chief executive began a two-year program that would reorganize the firm into six business units, divest fifty companies, consolidate units in similar businesses, essentially eliminate two layers of management, and centralize many purchasing functions, as well as advertising.[46]

A Matrix Success Earlier in the chapter we pointed out strengths and weaknesses of the matrix organization. One company that has faced the problems of converting to the matrix form is Ebasco Services, Inc., an engineering and consulting firm.

Ebasco has been involved in a number of nuclear power plant projects, which have a sorrowful history of missed deadlines, cost overruns, and changing government regulations, all adding to the predictable stress of the matrix organization. Disputes over conflicting priorities, mistrust between functional specialties, and misunderstanding of the company became too serious to ignore. Line management turned to the human resources department for help.

Specific problems were identified through a study, and then an organizational development program was designed to address them. Elements of the program included a forty-five-hour supervisory development course, formal seminars to explain the matrix structure to employees, a career tracking program, and team-building interventions for groups in conflict. A dual performance evaluation system began, so that employees reporting to two bosses are evaluated by both.[47]

The program was so successful that top executives of the firm began using organizational development facilitators in their meetings, and facilitators have become frequent participants and leaders of project group meetings. The nature of Ebasco's business creates need for the flexible matrix form. Unlike many firms, Ebasco faced matrix-associated problems head-on. A classic problem-solving process was used: problems were identified through a study; alternatives were evaluated, selected and implemented; then a follow-up assessed the usefulness of the programs.

Job Design

In the late 1970s, Hackman discussed two approaches to job design.[48] The first he called a Route One approach, fitting jobs to people. The second approach, Route Two, involves fitting people to jobs. The difference is enormous. The Route One approach changes elements of the job to create more challenge and autonomy for the worker. Route Two designs work for maximum economic and technological efficiency. Individual needs are subordinated to the requirements of the job, though efforts may be made to help workers adjust to those requirements. Hackman argued that a discernable trend toward Route Two is apparent.

Let's look at a few examples of job design and working arrangements of the near past to help us decide for ourselves.

The Topeka Experiment   A famous example of innovation in job and organization design took place at General Foods' Gaines Pet Food plant near Topeka, Kansas. The plant opened in 1971 amid much publicity about its innovative management practices.

A rigorous selection process was used in hiring workers and supervisors (called "team leaders"). The organization was set up in teams for processing, office functions, and warehousing/packaging. Teams had a large number of activities to perform, and assignment of team members to tasks was subject to team consensus.

The plant had a single job classification and starting pay rate for all workers. Pay increases were based upon skill in a number of jobs. The more quickly workers learned all of the team jobs, the more quickly they could advance in pay.

While early reports of the project glowed with praise,[49] later reports have been more cautious. Whitsett and Yorks argued that the design was cosmetic rather than innovative.[50] They held that the technology of the plant was not designed to accommodate autonomous work groups. Instead, work teams were traditionally built around the existing technology, a sharp contrast to radical innovation such as at the Volvo Kalmar plant.

Whitsett and Yorks went on to argue that the plant reflected little more than good human relations practices, and that evidence of worker tension and other problems were ignored by many writers.

Some of the early results were impressive. Turnover and absenteeism were greatly reduced, product quality was high, and the plant went almost four years without a lost time accident.[51] However, the cause of these results was questioned by Fein, who suggested that the early success was due to the quality of the work force, not organization or task design: "Writers who extoll the GF-Topeka case do not understand, or refuse to see, that this plant is unique not because of the management style, but because of the workers themselves, who were hand picked."[52]

If the critics are correct, the Topeka plant is a sophisticated example of the Route Two approach: selection of employees to fit the job, attempts to help workers adjust to the requirements, and emphasis upon the technical requirements of the job. What is your opinion? Is it possible that the Topeka plant was successful in matching employees and jobs as in the Porter et al. schema in Figure 9–9?

Is Boredom Dangerous?   Airline flight has become one of the safest modes of travel, thanks in large measure to jet propulsion and electronic technology. But there is concern among pilots, the airline industry, and the government that these advances have been a mixed blessing.[53] Cockpits of newer aircraft are so automated that crews run the risk of inattention caused by boredom. Increasingly, long distance flights have been found to be as much as several hundred miles off course. The reason? Misprogramming of on-board computers, neglecting to switch back to automatic pilot, and failure to double-check coordinates. In one case, the cockpit crew of a freighter had dozed off and passed over their destination at more than 30,000 feet.

It has been noted for years that increasing automation in industrial jobs increased worker boredom, leading to inattention and even accidents. Now it appears that sophisticated electronics has introduced the same problems to more glamorous jobs.

Alternative Work Schedules—The New Wave?   In recent years there has been significant interest in alternative work schedules, for example flexitime, staggered starts, and the compressed work week. Flexitime allows the employee a certain amount of discretion in work schedule. In some cases flexibility is very great. One organization we know of allows employees each Thursday to submit a proposed work schedule for the following week. The supervisors then must review the work schedules and make adjustments necessary for work coordination. Other organizations require a "core time," a time span during the day when employees must be present, for example from 10 AM until 2 PM. It is then the employees' choice whether to arrive early (and leave as early as 2 PM), or to arrive at work as late as 10 AM.

Staggered starting times allow less discretion than flexitime, but still allow employees some alternative. Staggered starting times were briefly popular during the fuel crises of the 1970s as part of a program to cut down on freeway congestion, and thus fuel consumption. The new schedules were popular with many employees and are still used to some extent.

The compressed work week allows employees to accomplish their work in fewer days. The most common arrangement is the 4/40—four ten-hour days followed by three days off. Although the three-day weekend is attractive to most people, some organizations have found worker fatigue to be a problem inherent in the ten-hour shifts.

Each of the alternative schedules has its champions, but none have become as widespread as anticipated. Reactions to flexitime have been the most thoroughly researched, and the results have generally shown increased satisfaction with the work schedule, with supervision, and with interactions with family and friends. Transportation coordination has generally been an area of increased dissatisfaction.[54]

Job Sharing   Job sharing is another work arrangement that has gained favor in the last few years. Many companies split jobs among part-time workers, with two or more workers dividing responsibilities of a single job. This activity tends to increase when the economy is troubled, and it gives the organization several advantages. For example, the costs of retirement benefits, insurance, and other benefits can be reduced or eliminated completely.

Although part-time job sharing is not necessarily sought out by the employees, there has been an increasing trend for people to do just that. It has long been common for people in family businesses to share jobs, perhaps alternating days at work, etc., but now other organizations are allowing the practice. Several universities have allowed two professors to share the same faculty position. Stanford University has a wife and husband team who serve jointly as financial aid officer in the medical school.[55] An insurance agent of our acquaintance splits his practice with a partner, each working on alternate months.

Whether any of the new approaches to work will become a significant factor cannot be predicted, but it is clear that the potential for flexibility is greater than in the past. With some effort, individuals interested in custom-fitted work arrangements should be able to find a congenial situation.

DISCUSSION QUESTIONS

1. Given that an organization has a general and a specific environment, should all managers be concerned equally with the two environments, or should concern differ according to management level?
2. If you were the chief executive of a functionally organized firm and you felt the organization structure was inefficient, what information would you seek to determine if your feeling was accurate?
3. The project/matrix form of organization has been used for decades in large construction projects. What reasons are there for this?
4. Consider the job of an elevator operator. How might the job be enlarged? How might it be enriched?
5. Some managers argue that the only responsibility of the organization is to provide a safe working environment, not interesting and personally rewarding jobs. Do you agree?

EXERCISE: THE DENVER PROJECT

Ken Mayhew was deep in thought as he gazed across his desk and through the glass partition to the busy machine room. He felt pleased and a bit flattered that he'd been chosen to supervise the new operations decentralization project, an installation and shakedown assignment that would last several months.

In April of the preceding year, Canada and Associates, a systems design consulting firm, had studied the company's existing DP activities in great detail. They reported favorably on the general systems design, hardware, and the software currently in use. They had also complimented the Vice President of Data Processing on the quality of maintenance of programs and the level of qualifications and training for personnel in both the Systems Department and the DP Operations Department.

The consultants expressed a deep concern, however, about back-up capability and the current high operating cost and suggested that an appropriate approach for building capacity as well as providing capability for breakdown or overload problems would be to duplicate the existing configuration of equipment rather than replace it with a larger system. Thus, a separate, intact unit located in the second largest division (Denver) would provide additional capacity and back-up capability instead of the major expenditure for radically increasing system power in a single central unit.

The current hardware configuration consists of an IBM 370/168 (2 MB) CPU, eight (50 MB) disk units, twenty (1600 BPI) tape drives, four (2000 LPM) printers, and a stand-alone data entry system with 24 terminals. The operation is currently manned 24 hours per day, seven days a week. Breakdown time has been minimized by having carefully trained operators and by good service support from vendors. Capacity utilization has ranged in the high 80 to low 90 percent figures (over 3 shifts), and a lengthy list of new applications is backlogged. The existing backlog of new applications is forecast to require approximately 50 percent additional capacity, if entirely implemented.

Current physical facilities are strained. Equipment, supplies, and working space for staff are severely limited, as is space for all departments in the company's headquarter office building.

An alternative to locating the duplicate operation in Denver is that of locating a satellite DP site in New York, the headquarter city. Site costs, problems in securing adequately trained staff, security of equipment, and safety of operations staff working around the clock all mitigate against a second location in New York City.

The Wheeled Products Division, located in Denver, had expressed considerable interest in locating DP Operations in its administrative building. Several sound reasons had been advanced in support of this idea. Space was available, the Denver employment situation was strong, and the Division's own DP activity utilized nearly 30 percent of capacity of the central computing facility. Data transmission costs could be saved and labor costs reduced. Finally, vendor support in Denver was considered to be exceptionally good.

Ken's concern focused on the staff he must select to install and shake down equipment, to start up the systems to be run at Denver, and to build the operations staff that will assume responsibility for the Denver operation once it is operating satisfactorily. Early estimates anticipated that the Denver operation could be running in approximately 8 to 10 months. Ken's key operations supervisors are

(1) Ed Snedecor—age 46. Worked 15 years at IBM, has worked with the 360 series equipment since its introduction, prefers shiftwork, likes to recruit his own assistants. He grumbles frequently about lack of adequately trained or motivated workers in the labor market today. Dislikes interruptions in his operating schedules, and is intensely interested in minimizing machine time on his shift. He competes with the other shift supervisors in achieving operating rate goals. Has not expressed much interest in participating in vendor training on new equipment, particularly configurations involving scientific applications or units of significantly greater power. High school plus 1 year college.

(2) Nancy Jacobs—age 33. College graduate. Started with the company 10 years ago. Began as programmer, but found operations more to her liking. Has worked in all phases of operations. Excellent trouble shooter. Finds new applications interesting, and frequently requests permission to attend vendor seminars or new equipment and management seminars offered through a local university. Nancy is well liked by her subordinates, but is sometimes seen as too willing to interrupt established routines and schedules to accommodate the requests of users with problems.

(3) Carole Larkin—age 47. High school plus 2 years of business college. Carole began her work in operations 25 years ago as a key punch/verifier operator. Carole's performance over the years has been steady and dependable. She has risen from her entry level job through data entry until 7 years ago, when at her supervisor's request she attended, over a 12-month period, vendor training programs in operating mainframe and I/O equipment. Her performance in the program was quite acceptable. She has commented that she found schooling to be quite demanding, often involving study well into the night time hours. After completing her training, she worked as an assistant shift supervisor for 2 years, then acted as "fill in" supervisor (covering vacations, illnesses, and leaves of absence) for 3 years, then was made shift supervisor 2 years ago. She has performed quite well in her present job. Her subordinates seem to like Carole, particularly her desire to establish and maintain a clear and well-understood work schedule that is followed rigorously. Carole has said, "I'd like to be able to know—even if I'm 20 miles away—exactly what we are currently working on when I get a question on our operation from topside (top management)."

(4) Edward Leonard—age 32. Business graduate (UCLA) plus MBA from Pepperdine. Ed was a management trainee with the corporate training program. He has been with the company 4 years and with DP Operations 3 years. His ability to recruit and train new

employees is considered to be a great strength. Technically, Ed is still learning about data processing equipment and systems. He has attended numerous vendor training programs and has performed well. When tricky technical issues arise, Ed is inclined to look to vendor representatives or an experienced operator or supervisor for help. Ed has said that he'd like to see the company move toward more sophisticated equipment, and sees his future tied to an ability to learn the new equipment from the moment it is installed. Ed's long-term aspiration is to reach executive level, either through DP, or through the Systems/Controller routes.

Ken's specific problem is as follows: He is expected to choose persons to install the equipment, train and/or recruit the needed staff for operations, and begin the implementation of existing routines.

Ray Johnson, Assistant Vice President for Computer Operations, has been very specific about applications to be run at the Denver facility. They will include

First: All operations that affect only the Wheeled Vehicle Division.

Next: Routine operations for the corporation that can be accommodated by mail or messenger delivered I/O (i.e., card decks or paper/magnetic tape and mailed or messenger delivered checks, documents, and reports).

Next: Backup operations for the corporation during central facility peak loads or downtime. This requires telecommunication linkage to meet time deadlines, for batched daily runs.

Interactive (real time) operations are explicitly excluded (to hold data transition costs down). Debugging and testing of programs will be confined to the central facility.

Source: J. E. Dittrich, University of Colorado. Reprinted with permission.

Directions

1. Break into an even number of groups, with six to ten people per group.

2. Review the biographical profiles of the DP Operations Department employees.

3. Make judgements regarding the growth need strengths of the employees, then examine the tasks to be performed.

4. One-half of the groups in the room will use the judgements made in Step 3 to select a team to be sent to Denver to install and manage the initial year or two of operation of the "Denver Project." The other groups will use their judgements to select the team to be left in New York.

NOTES

1. By David Ignatius, *The Wall Street Journal* (Thursday, 24 March 1983): 1. Reprinted by permission of *The Wall Street Journal*, © Dow Jones & Company, Inc., 1983. All rights reserved.

2. *The Oxford English Dictionary*, Compact Edition (Oxford, England: University Press, 1977): 32–33.

3. J. D. Thompson, *Organizations in Action* (New York: McGraw-Hill, 1967): 51.

4. F. E. Kast and J. R. Rosenzweig, *Organization and Management: A Systems and Contingency Approach*, 3rd ed. (New York: McGraw-Hill, 1979).

5. P. N. Khandwalla, *The Design of Organizations* (New York: Harcourt Brace Jovanovich, 1977).

6. R. H. Hall, *Organizations: Structure and Process* ((Englewood Cliffs, NJ: Prentice-Hall, 1972): 297–324; and R. N. Osborn and J. G. Hunt, "Environment and Organization Effectiveness," *Administrative Science Quarterly* (June 1974): 231–246.

7. R. B. Duncan, "Characteristics of Organizational Environments and Perceived Environmental Uncertainty," *Administrative Science Quarterly* (September 1972): 315.

8. P. N. Khandwalla, *The Design of Organizations*, pp. 333–340.

9. R. H. Miles, *Macro Organizational Behavior* (Glenview, IL: Scott, Foresman, 1980): 23–25.

10. T. Burns and G. M. Stalker, *The Management of Innovation* (London: Tavistock, 1961).

11. P. R. Lawrence and J. W. Lorsch, *Organization and Environment: Managing Differentiation and Integration* (Homewood, IL: Irwin, 1967).

12. P. R. Lawrence and J. W. Lorsch, "Differentiation and Integration in Complex Organizations," *Administrative Science Quarterly*, 12 (1967): 1–47.

13. R. Duncan, "What Is the Right Organization Structure?" *Organizational Dynamics* (Winter 1979): 59–80.

14. Ibid., p. 63.

15. J. R. Hackman, "Work Design," in J. R. Hackman and J. L. Suttle, eds., *Improving Life at Work: Behavioral Science Approaches to Organizational Change* (Santa Monica, CA: Goodyear, 1977).

16. R. Steers, and D. Spencer, "The Role of Achievement Motivation in Job Design," *Journal of Applied Psychology*, 62 (1977): 472–479.

17. J. R. Hackman and G. R. Oldham, "Motivation Through the Design of Work: Test of a Theory," *Organizational Behavior and Human Performance*, 16 (1976): 250–279; and P. H. Mirvis, and E. E. Lawler III, "Measuring the Financial Impact of Employee Attitudes," *Journal of Applied Psychology*, 62 (1977): 1–8.

18. Ibid.

19. A. Smith, *The Wealth of Nations*, 1776 (London: Routledge, 1890).

20. C. Babbage, *On the Economy of Machinery and Manufacturers* (London: Charles Knight, 1832).

21. F. M. Taylor, *The Principles of Scientific Management* (New York: Harper, 1947).

22. R. H. Guest, "Job Enlargement: A Revolution in Job Design," *Personnel Administration*, 20 (1957): 9–16; A. K. Rice, "Productivity and Social Organization in an Indian Weaving Shed," *Human Relations*, 6 (1953): 297–329; E. L. Trist, and K. W. Bamforth, "Some Social and Psychological Consequences of the Longwall Method of Coal-Getting," *Human Relations*, 4 (1951): 3–38; and C. R. Walker, "The Problem of the Repetitive Job," *Harvard Business Review*, 28 (1950): 54–58.

23. C. L. Hulin and M. R. Blood, "Job Enlargement, Individual Differences, and Worker Responses," *Psychological Bulletin*, 69 (1968): 41–55.

24. R. W. Griffin, *Task Design: An Integrative Approach* (Glenview, IL: Scott, Foresman, 1982).

25. F. Herzberg, B. Mausner, and B. Snyderman, *The Motivation to Work* (New York: Wiley, 1959).

26. F. Herzberg, "Orthodox Job Enrichment," *Defense Management Journal*, 2 (1977): 21–27.

27. R. J. Aldag and A. P. Brief, *Task Design and Employee Motivation* (Glenview, IL: Scott, Foresman, 1979): 133.

28. P. G. Gyllenhammar, "How Volvo Adapts Work to People," *Harvard Business Review* (July–August 1977): 105–113.

29. R. J. Aldag, and A. P. Brief, *Task Design*, p. 134.

30. A. N. Turner and P. R. Lawrence, *Industrial Jobs and the Worker* (Boston: Harvard Graduate School of Business Administration, 1965).

31. J. R. Hackman, and G. Oldham, *Work Redesign* (Reading, MA: Addison-Wesley, 1980); and J. R. Hackman and G. R. Oldham, "Motivation Through the Design of Work."

32. J. R. Hackman and G. R. Oldham, "Motivation Through the Design of Work: Test of a Theory," *Organizational Behavior and Human Performance*, 16 (1976): 257–258.

33. Ibid., p. 256–257.

34. L. W. Porter, E. E. Lawler, III, and J. R. Hackman, *Behavior in Organizations* (New York: McGraw-Hill, 1975).

35. W. B. Gavin and C. P. Fleenor, "The Relationship of the Locus of Control Construct in an Industrial

Environment to the Expectancy-Valence Model of Behavior." Unpublished research paper, Albers School of Business, Seattle University.

36. C. N. Beaver, "Occupational Prestige as a Factor in the Relationship between Occupation and Job Satisfaction," *Personnel Psychology* (Winter 1977): 607.

37. R. T. Keller, "Role Conflict and Ambiguity: Correlates with Job Satisfaction and Values," *Personnel Psychology* (Spring 1975): 57–64.

38. R. D. Harvey, "Relationships between Goal Clarity and Participation in Goal Setting," *Journal of Applied Psychology* (April 1976): 103–105.

39. C. J. Berger, and L. L. Cummings, "Organization Structure: How Does It Influence Attitudes and Performance?" *Management Review* (February 1977): 40–43.

40. P. D. Peretti, "Effects of Community, Family, and Home Variables on Job Satisfaction," *Australian Journal of Social Issues* (August 1976): 222–229.

41. R. N. Taylor and M. Thompson, "Work Value Systems of Young Workers," *Academy of Management Journal* (December 1976): 522–535; C. A. O'Reilly, "Job Satisfaction among Whites and Nonwhites: A Cross Culture Approach," *Journal of Applied Psychology* (June 1973): 295–299; and C. N. Weaver, "Age and Job Satisfaction among Males and Females: A Multivariate, Multisurvey Study," *Personnel Psychology* (April 1978): 105–109.

42. M. Langley, "AT&T Has Call for a New Corporate Culture," *The Wall Street Journal*, (28 February 1974): 24.

43. R. J. Boyle, "Designing the Energetic Organization," *Management Review* (August 1983): 21.

44. Ibid.

45. K. K. Wiegner, "Prometheus Unbound, and Seeking His Footing," *Forbes* (12 March 1984): 141–148.

46. S. Shellenbarger, "Beatrice Foods Moves to Centralize Business to Reverse Its Decline," *The Wall Street Journal* (27 September 1983): 1.

47. "How Ebasco Makes the Matrix Method Work," *Business Week* (15 June 1981): 126.

48. J. R. Hackman, "The Design of Work in the 1980s," *Organizational Dynamics* (Summer 1978): 3–17.

49. R. E. Walton, "How to Counter Alienation in the Plant," *Harvard Business Review* (November–December 1972): 70–81.

50. D. A. Whitsett and L. Yorks, "Looking Back at Topeka: General Foods and the Quality-of-Work-Life Experiment," *California Management Review*, 25 (4) (Summer 1983): 93–109.

51. R. E. Walton, "Work Innovations at Topeka: After Six Years," *Journal of Applied Behavioral Sciences*, 13 (1977): 423.

52. M. Fein, "Job Enrichment Does Not Work," *Atlanta Economic Review*, 25 (1975): 52.

53. M. Toner, "Cockpit Complacency," *The Seattle Times/Seattle Post Intelligencer* (16 October 1983): A5.

54. R. B. Dunham, and J. L. Pierce, "The Design and Evaluation of Alternative Work Schedules," *Personnel Administrator* (April 1983): 67–75.

55. J. F. Diggs, "Job Sharing: For Many, a Perfect Answer," *U.S. News and World Report* (23 August 1982): 66–68.

RECOMMENDED READINGS

J. R. Hackman, "The Design of Work in the 1980s," *Organizational Dynamics* (Summer 1978): 3–17.

> The author discusses the decision that must be made between fitting jobs to people and fitting people to jobs.

J. R. Hackman and G. R. Oldham, *Work Redesign* (Reading, MA: Addison-Wesley, 1980).

> This volume addresses the design of work for individuals and for groups. It includes the Job Diagnostic Survey and its scoring key.

A. C. **Hax** and N. S. **Majluf,** "Organizational Design: A Survey and an Approach," *Operations Research*, 29 (3) (1981): 417–447.

This article reviews the major forms of organization structure and steps in the design of structure.

H. **Mintzberg,** "Organization Design: Fashion or Fit?" *Harvard Business Review* (January–February 1981): 103–116.

The author gives suggestions for managers on how to fit elements of structure to elements of the situation, including the environment.

The Treadfree Keypunchers

All keypunching for the Treadfree Manufacturing Corporation is performed in one organizational unit, headed by a Manager of Keypunching Services. This manager is responsible for two supervisors, two clerks, and about twenty keypunch and verifying machine operators. Most of the operators are young, on their first or second fulltime job, and have high school diplomas.

As seen in Figure A, most work to be keypunched comes from five departments: accounting (30 percent), engineering (10 percent),

Source: J. R. Hackman and G. R. Oldham, *Work Redesign* Copyright © 1980, Addison-Wesley, Reading, MA. pp. 131–135. Reprinted with permission.

sales (20 percent), personnel (20 percent), and production staff (10 percent). Another 10 percent of the work comes from miscellaneous departments throughout Treadfree.

Representatives of client departments bring work to be done to a receiving clerk, who has a desk at a corridor window in the keypunch room. The clerk accepts the work, completes a work order form that indicates job specifications (such as special cards or codes) and the date the cards are needed. The data and work order form are then given to Supervisor I, who checks the materials to make sure that they are clear and legible, and that the due date is realistic given other work in progress. If there is any problem with the work

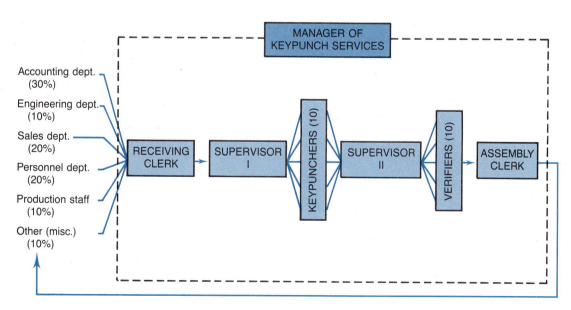

FIGURE A

as submitted, Supervisor I returns it to the receiving clerk, who calls the client and resolves the difficulties. Problems having to do with due dates are negotiated directly between Supervisor I and the client.

Supervisor I keeps a queue of jobs to be done on the shelves by her desk, and when a keypuncher becomes free, gives the next job to be done to that individual. For especially large or especially urgent jobs, the supervisor may break the work into several parts and give the parts to several operators. Occasionally it is necessary to have a keypuncher set aside work in progress to do part of a rush job.

When a job (or portion of a job, if the work was broken up when assigned) is completed, it is given by the keypuncher to Supervisor II. This supervisor makes a quick check for accuracy of codes, formats, and card types, and notes the due date for the work to be completed. He then places the work in a queue on his shelves and gives the next highest priority job to the next available verifier. Because of a history of errors in keypunched work, all jobs are verified, which es-

sentially involves repunching the data, except that the verifying machine merely confirms that the right punches already have been made on completed cards. Verifiers correct any mispunches they find.

After a job (or portion of a job) has been verified, it goes to the assembly clerk. The assembly clerk compiles the completed cards and, when all portions of the job are finished, prints the cards on a line printer. The assembly clerk then calls the client to say that the job may be picked up at the assembly clerk's corridor window.

Supervisor I is responsible for the receiving clerk, the ten keypunchers, and any problems having to do with scheduling or due dates. When work is especially heavy, she may obtain permission from the manager to bring on some part-time help. Supervisor II is responsible for the assembly clerk, the ten verifiers, and any problems having to do with quality and accuracy. If clients discover problems in the work after picking it up, they contact Supervisor II, who will have someone who is free (or can be made so) among the verifying staff do the corrections. Since it takes

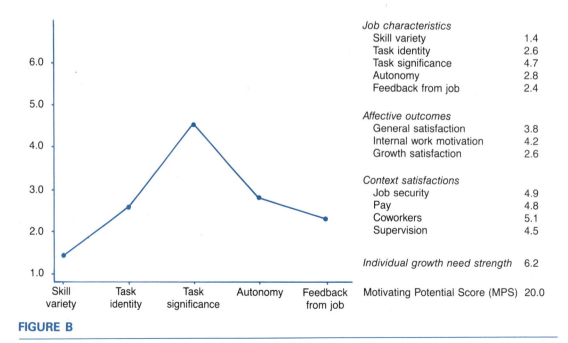

Job characteristics	
Skill variety	1.4
Task identity	2.6
Task significance	4.7
Autonomy	2.8
Feedback from job	2.4
Affective outcomes	
General satisfaction	3.8
Internal work motivation	4.2
Growth satisfaction	2.6
Context satisfactions	
Job security	4.9
Pay	4.8
Coworkers	5.1
Supervision	4.5
Individual growth need strength	6.2
Motivating Potential Score (MPS)	20.0

FIGURE B

somewhat longer to initially punch the cards than it does to verify them, having the verifiers do any corrections or repunching tends to "balance" the workloads of the keypunchers and verifiers. Nevertheless, on occasion it is necessary for Supervisors I and II to move someone from keypunching to verifying or vice versa to deal with a "lump" in the workflow.

An evaluation of the job using the Job Diagnostic Survey (JDS) reveals the diagnostic profile shown in Figure B. The job characteristic scores have been confirmed using multiple observers (in this case supervisors and outside researchers) and multiple methods (interviews in addition to the JDS).

Questions

1. Given the results of the diagnosis, how would you change this job?
2. What specific steps would you take to improve the standing of the core job characteristics?

CHAPTER TEN
Organizational Rewards and Performance Appraisal

OUTLINE

CONCEPTS OF REWARDS AND EVALUATION

Basic Types of Rewards
The Role of Money
Linking Rewards to Performance
Performance Appraisal Systems
Methods of Performance Appraisal
Performance Planning
Summary of Key Concepts

MANAGERIAL APPLICATIONS

Factors to Consider
A Method for Categorizing Incentive Plans
One Sample Incentive Plan from Each Cell

OBJECTIVES

- Differentiate between intrinsic and extrinsic rewards

- Discuss the role of money, and the impact of rewards on absenteeism and turnover

- Describe potential benefits of performance appraisal, and pitfalls to successful implementation

- Know the strengths and weaknesses of major methods of performance appraisal

- Know why employee participation is necessary and how participation is accomplished

- Evaluate the quality of performance objectives

- Understand the process of performance planning

Herbie the Waiter

Herbert Pischler is unique in the world of restaurant waiters. His faithful customers, gluttons for exasperation, know him better as "Herbie-the-World's-Worst-Waiter," a title bestowed on Pischler many years ago by the *New York Daily News* and a distinction that Herbie proudly accepts.

Herbie has been around for a long time, and he's been in and then quickly out of the best hostelries in town. Herbie and his current headquarters, Costello's, are a natural match.

Situated conveniently for many of New York's more curmudgeonly and card-in-the-hatband sort of newspapermen, Costello's has played host to people such as the late Ernest Hemingway, who used to enjoy fist fights as much as the food and drinks. Herbie-the-World's-Worst-Waiter is a legend still around for us to enjoy, though at his age he explains, "I'm just barely navigatin', but the boss wants me to hang around since I'm still good for the business, I guess."

Legend has it that Herbie first laid claim to his title as worst waiter by spilling a large bowl of soup in the lap of the Prince of Wales many years ago and at someplace other than Costello's, where it is highly unlikely that royalty will ever drop by for a few jars on the way home to the castle. Herbie claims that this historic event has been exaggerated over the years.

"This I did not do," he says. "I did not spill soup in the lap of the Prince of Wales. Mostly, it went all over the colonel sitting beside him."

Herbie is cherubic and always well-intentioned, but he is also rather absent-minded and prone to sudden naps. Many is the time when a customer in his station, wondering why so much time had passed since asking for the bill, found Herbie sitting at the bar, head in hands and fast asleep.

There was the time, too, when a table full of wagering reporters sent Herbie out to a newsstand at nearby Third Avenue and East 42nd Street for the racing form. When the world's worst waiter failed to return after an hour's time, the reporters formed a posse and went searching for Herbie. They found him curled up on a bench near the newsstand, sound asleep, snoring peacefully beneath the racing form with the latest results from Aqueduct.

Eddie Fitzpatrick, co-owner of Costello's, says, "Everybody loves Herbie. He's an asset."

Indeed, it is sometimes difficult to get a table at Herbie's station, even knowing that your meal is sure to come with an imprint of Herbie's right thumb. "Accidents always got to happen," Herbie explains.

It is rumored that Fitzpatrick used to threaten Herbie with dismissal if the world's worst waiter should ever improve.[1]

CONCEPTS OF REWARDS AND EVALUATION

How would you like to be Herbie's manager? Would you apply all of the best business school management techniques to get him whipped into shape, or

The authors wish to thank Dr. Peter Scontrino for his contribution to this chapter.

would you fear that customers would complain if Herbie began doing things right? The perspective of the person doing the evaluation would color it. For instance, would the customer and the manager evaluate Herbie the same? Probably not. How might his fellow employees view Herbie's performance?

We discovered in chapter 3 that people are motivated by different things, and that they respond to cues in the environment that are reinforcing to them. We now move beyond the general issue of motivation to the more specific issue of rewards in the workplace, how they work, and how to use them to change performance. Later in the chapter we examine methods for evaluating performance and describe the process of performance planning.

Basic Types of Rewards

It is useful to view rewards or outcomes as being of two basic types: intrinsic or extrinsic. Intrinsic rewards are those that occur directly as a result of performing an activity and are outcomes that an individual grants to himself or herself. A feeling of accomplishment upon completing a task is an example of an intrinsic reward, as is a feeling of creativity, pleasure at being ahead of schedule on a project, or anticipation of an interesting task to be performed. Think about Herbie-the-World's-Worst-Waiter. What intrinsic rewards might he gain from his job?

Extrinsic rewards are those that are mediated or granted by external agents such as the organization, supervisor, friends, and so on. Obvious examples are compliments, salary increases, and promotions. Less obvious extrinsic rewards might be appealing to Herbie: Can you describe any?

The problem faced by both an organization and by the managers within is two-fold. First, what kinds of rewards appeal to people, and second, how should those rewards be delivered?

On the surface it would seem simple to find out what people value. After all, one could simply ask them. It is not as simple as it sounds, though. Some theorists argue that money is the most important extrinsic reward, while others think interesting work is more important. Both groups are able to cite research supporting their argument.[2] Pay has been rated first in importance in some surveys but rated much lower in others.[3] Something as subtle as question wording can influence the rating. For example, "high" pay will usually be rated lower than "adequate" or "fair" pay when placed with otherwise identical groups of rewards. Desire for intrinsic rewards varies at least as much as for extrinsic rewards. The background of people and their experience in work influences the importance of rewards. The amount of reward received influences the importance attached to it. At least for extrinsic rewards, individuals who receive a small amount tend to value it the most.[4]

The Role of Money

Vroom states that individuals develop conceptions of proper or equitable levels of reward at least partly from information about the rewards received by others.[5]

Dissatisfaction occurs when one's level of reward falls below the proper or equitable level.

It seems obvious that a person does not compare the level of rewards received with those of all other persons. It has been demonstrated, though, that comparison is sometimes made with people outside the immediate organization and that outside comparison is more typical of managers than of nonmanagers.[6]

Pay Secrecy   Information about the level of rewards must be either available or *assumed* before comparison can take place. In the absence of real data, people make their own estimates of what others are receiving. Lawler has shown that managers generally overestimate the pay of other managers around them, and in fact the larger a manager's raise the larger the manager believed other managers' raises were.[7] Lawler's research also showed that the greater the overestimation of others' pay, the greater the dissatisfaction. This would seem to place in question the value of pay secrecy, a common policy among organizations.

Although there seem to be good reasons for making pay "public," so employees may have real data for comparison, there seems to be only qualified enthusiasm on the part of people in organizations to change the practice of secrecy. Table 10–1 shows the results from a survey of more than 1,200 managers in a large corporation.

Interestingly, where pay is already public, as in many government organizations, employees generally support the practice.[8] Pay secrecy almost certainly makes the administration of pay easier since decisions need not be explained in detail. Still, since employees will make equity comparisons with or without actual data, less secrecy in pay administration makes sense.

Linking Rewards to Performance

Motivation theory teaches us that people will act in ways that lead to reward or that avoid punishment. Therefore "all" an organization or manager need do is

TABLE 10–1
Attitudes toward communicating pay information

Item	Individuals Agreeing (%)
Each individual's salary should be communicated to all employees	8.1
Having more information on pay levels would help me know where I stand	55.1
Persons should be told the ranking of their salary within their pay grade	85.7
Salary information should be more confidential	18.5
Staff members should be told the range of merit pay in their pay grade	93.2

Source: Edward E. Lawler, *Pay and Organization Development,* © 1981, Addison-Wesley, Reading, MA. P. 45, Figure 4.1. Reprinted with permission.

provide incentives for desired behavior and/or sanctions for undesired behavior. This is easier said than done, for reasons that we explore when we discuss performance appraisal.

Absenteeism This type of behavior is relatively well documented in most organizations. It should be noted that voluntary absenteeism is the main focus of this section. In contrast, involuntary absenteeism may be caused by illness or a disabled car. Voluntary absenteeism is an undesirable behavior and one that costs a great deal of money in sick pay, overtime for other workers, and administrative cost. Since the "performance" (absenteeism) is quite easily measurable, the effect of incentive plans for reduction of absenteeism should be discernible.

Wallin and Johnson tested the effect of a lottery reward system designed to reduce employee absenteeism.[9] A program was initiated under which employees could qualify for a monthly drawing, provided they had perfect attendance records for the month. Names of those with perfect attendance were posted on the company bulletin board. The drawing resulted in the winner receiving a cash reward. A measure of sick leave costs was calculated monthly for the year preceding the lottery. Monthly sick leave costs were also calculated for a year after starting the lottery. Sick leave costs for the lottery year were more than 30 percent lower than in the prelottery year.

Luthans and Maris tested the effect of application, withdrawal, and reapplication of an incentive program for reducing absenteeism.[10] The incentives for attendance consisted of the extrinsic rewards of congratulatory notes from supervisors and letters in personnel files. Absenteeism fell from the historical baseline rate of 8.94 percent to 3.91 percent. After a period of time the incentive program was withdrawn and absenteeism rose to 12.99 percent. When the incentive program was reintroduced, absenteeism fell to 5.37 percent.

Stephens and Burroughs compared two reward systems used to reduce absenteeism among hospital nurses, ward clerks, and nursing assistants.[11] System A awarded $20 to employees without absenteeism during a three-week period, while System B awarded $20 to employees not absent on eight randomly selected days during a three-week period.

Five of six units showed a decrease in absenteeism while the contingency was in effect. System B was slightly more effective than System A, though not statistically significant. In the postcontingency period absenteeism increased to a level higher than the precontingency baseline period, which is consistent with the findings of Luthans and Maris.[12]

It should be noted that the preceding incentive schemes appeal to the employee's motivation to attend, and have demonstrable effect. We should not let that delude us into believing that absenteeism is a simple phenomenon. Steers and Rhodes surveyed more than 100 empirical studies and developed the process model of employee attendance in Figure 10–1.[13]

Obviously, incentive schemes for improved attendance will address only some of the influences proposed by the model. Incentives might even serve to "mask" certain effects. For example, if aspects of the job situation (Box 1) were

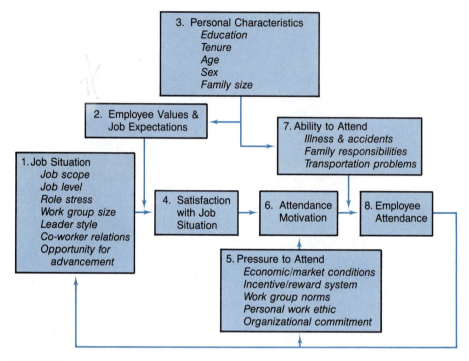

FIGURE 10–1

Major influences on employee attendance (Source: R. M. Steers and S. R. Rhodes, "Major Influences on Employee Attendance: A Process Model," *Journal of Applied Psychology,* 4 (1978): 393. Copyright © 1978 by the American Psychological Association. Reprinted by permission of the authors.)

leading to unacceptable absenteeism levels, better attendance might be bought via an incentive program. The incentive approach would not deal with the cause of the problem, and overtime might in fact cost more than dealing directly with the job situation or changing selection procedures to hire employees more suited to the job situation. Another concern is that in focusing upon reducing absenteeism rather than dealing with job design, turnover might increase as absenteeism decreases. Paying people more to spend more time in a situation they dislike may well cause them to leave the organization sooner than they might have otherwise, since absenteeism no longer serves as a convenient "safety valve."

Turnover The question of turnover raises some difficult yet interesting issues. Clearly, zero turnover is not desirable. For one thing, all employees would retire at the same time! The introduction of new ideas and new personalities is important to keep any organization in touch with the outside world.

Turnover varies substantially by type of employer. In 1977, the median monthly turnover rate for manufacturing firms was 1.5 percent, but was 2.4

percent for health care organizations. In other words, the median health care organization could expect to lose almost one-third of its employees per year.[14]

Employee turnover can be classified as voluntary or involuntary in origin. Voluntary turnover is initiated by the employee, while involuntary turnover is initiated by the organization. Involuntary turnover means, of course, that the employee is terminated, but not always for reasons of poor performance. Many people are terminated in bad economic times; their jobs literally disappear.

From the organization's perspective, turnover can be classified as desirable or undesirable. Undesirable turnover would include the employees lost through layoff and those lured away by competitors. Desirable turnover occurs when low performers or surplus employees leave the firm. The task faced by the organization and its management is to minimize undesirable turnover and facilitate desirable turnover. The general approach would, of course, entail creating a work environment and reward structure that encourages and motivates high-performing employees to remain in the organization. This assumes that methods are in place to identify high performers and reward them appropriately. Thus we turn to the topic of performance appraisal.

Performance Appraisal Systems

We address the reasons for conducting performance appraisal first and then describe and evaluate some of the most common approaches.

In recent years accountability and productivity have become bywords. The challenge for many organizations lies in maintaining a high quality of product or service at an effective cost ratio. A greater emphasis on accountability means a greater emphasis on developing standards for performance that accurately reflect the efficiency and output of employees. Performance appraisal when properly administered can provide these very essential standards.

Performance appraisal should not be viewed as an isolated exercise, but as an integral part of the management process. It is an essential management tool. With everyone—employees, supervisors, and managers—cooperating, a sound appraisal system can set the framework for a cohesive organization-wide management philosophy.

Any realization of organizational purposes is contingent upon employee motivation and support. Workers are motivated to perform their jobs well when they have some sense of their employer's expectations or performance standards.[15] Their motivation is further improved when they can participate in setting these standards and then receive regular feedback relative to them. The main thrust in establishing a formal performance appraisal system is to spell out those standards. Once this is done, the organization will find easier access to all of the system's potential benefits and uses.

Potential Benefits of Performance Appraisal   For top management, performance appraisal can demonstrate a concern for effective utilization of resources and can help analyze program results. It can also provide information for changes in the organizational structure and act as a check on the effectiveness of personnel selection procedures, by comparing scores on selection tests, interviews, etc., with later performance. Appraisal can also be linked to various budgeting procedures and serve as a basis for merit pay increases.

For mid-level managers, performance appraisal can be used to evaluate potential of employees at all levels and to identify training needs. A good appraisal system can improve performance by assuring that supervisors and employees understand the key functions and responsibilities of the employees' jobs. This allows identification of operational problem areas and can facilitate communication between supervisors and subordinates, frequently resulting in improved morale. Performance appraisal is also an important source of documentation for personnel decisions.

For first-level supervisors, performance appraisal can provide the basis for effective feedback to the employee, help to identify problems and training needs as they develop, strengthen the supervisor's management role by making the supervisor a critical link in the organization's personnel process, and improve communication between supervisor and subordinate.

For employees, appraisal can provide detailed feedback on their strengths and weaknesses, provide positive reinforcement for good performance, and spell out supervisory concerns about poor performance. A carefully planned appraisal system will also provide an opportunity for counseling and for career development.

The crucial question for the organization and its managers is whether they are willing to invest the time to develop a good performance appraisal system. The rewards are substantial, but so are the time and effort required to develop and implement a performance system. No appraisal system is worth much unless enough time and energy are invested to assure a properly job-related, reasonably objective result.

Historic Pitfalls Performance appraisal has historically encountered deep-rooted resistance. One reason is that traditional approaches have usually tried to measure personal attributes of the individual rather than focusing on the achievements and the behaviors related to the job. In the past, evaluation has been informal, often quite subjective, and based on "standards" such as appearance, mannerisms, and personal habits.[16]

Assessments of an employee's personal attributes that are not job-related are inappropriate means on which to base personnel decisions. The challenge lies in moving from this type of system, which is potentially unfair, prejudicial, and secretive, to a system that is fair and equitable to all employees.

The focus must be on what employees do and how well they do it. An appraisal system will be effective if an employee's performance is measured against a set of job-related standards understood by all parties. It should be noted, however, that a system that emphasizes results rather than personal traits requires a greater expenditure of management's time and effort. There is no quick and simple means to accomplish this results-oriented approach.

BOX 10–1

The High Cost of Unfair Appraisal

In the last few years thousands of employees have filed suits claiming wrongful discharge, and many of the suits were related to employers' methods of performance appraisal. Employees successful in their litigation can collect sizable punitive and compensatory damages:

- A manufacturing executive was passed over for promotion and his performance began to fall. Though receiving vague signals of dissatisfaction from upper management, the executive received no dismissal warnings and was given no opportunity to improve before his firing. A court awarded the fired manager $360,906 additionally but then reduced the award to $61,000 since he had in fact displayed poor performance in the job.
- An IBM sales manager claimed her resignation was forced because the company was unhappy that she was dating a manager from a competing firm. She was awarded $300,000.
- Three former executives of I. Magnin were awarded $1.9 million in a suit that claimed unfair dismissal and age bias.
- An analysis of forty California jury verdicts showed that the terminated employees won 75 percent of the cases, and the median award was $548,000.
- The risk of unfair appraisal reaches beyond the organization itself. According to at least one lawyer, supervisors "may have *personal* liability if they don't give honest appraisals." [emphasis added]

Questions

1. Should organizations be liable for sizable judgements for unfair dismissal?
2. Should managers have personal liability for such dismissal?
3. What should a manager do to protect against such a charge? Be specific in your recommendation.

Source: Adapted from "Firing Line: Legal Challenges Force Firms to Revamp Ways They Dismiss Workers," by Joan S. Lublin, *The Wall Street Journal* (13 September 1983): 1.

An appraisal system's success is contingent on the careful delineation of individual responsibilities as they relate to the organization's objectives, as well as an explanation of how performance factors relate to specific jobs. There is a built-in risk of establishing too rigid or unrealistic objectives for employees.[17] There is also the tendency to highlight those areas that lend themselves more readily to quantification and to ignore those areas that require qualitative assessment. The consequences of either can be damaging to employee morale. Strategies for developing proper performance objectives get prime attention here.

Evaluation of performance has also been subject to serious legal and social criticism.[18] One difficulty has been whether or not job performance factors *can* be quantified into measurable standards. In practice, appraisal systems have also lacked consistency in evaluation of different employees. There is often inadequate training of raters, and evaluations have sometimes been used inappropriately in personnel decisions. In some cases organizations have been enjoined by the courts to cease unfair practices because the evaluation used showed no significant relationship to the job performance.[19]

Many organizations profess to advocate merit pay plans and are interested in linking performance appraisal with merit pay. Many attempt to attach an employee "incentive" component to their five- or six-step plan, wherein the employees advance a step each year according to "merit." But what happens all too often is that the employees receive the step increase in their paychecks with no substantial evaluation ever occurring. Thus, "merit" pay turns into an automatic longevity increase. Implementing merit pay as an accessory to performance appraisal is complicated by the changing legal atmosphere and by budgetary constraints. Merit pay in the strictest sense—that is, adjusting the levels of pay to levels of work behavior—is therefore not the simple practice it appears to be. Probably one should first develop an appraisal mechanism that can prove its worth on other levels, such as improving communication or promoting more balanced workloads. The decision to tie appraisal to a merit pay plan should be made only after the entire organization is comfortable with an established and trusted evaluation system.

Those who are not convinced that the appraisal system is in their best interest will create roadblocks to its success. In some cases the pressure of the civil service bureaucracy or union trepidation have made it nearly impossible to use evaluation results in making key personnel decisions. The whole process is therefore deemed by some managers to be a meaningless exercise.

Employee Participation　The person who knows a particular job best is usually the person performing that job. Therefore employees should be involved in designing the system that will evaluate their job performance. This involvement should familiarize employees with the intent of the system and thus lessen feelings of suspicion and fear that often develop. If employees do not support the appraisal system, it ultimately will fail.

The decision to use a formal appraisal system is a management decision. But once management makes the choice to develop and implement a system, they should contact employee unions, guilds, and professional organizations and invite them to participate. Participation allows management to explain the purpose of evaluation and to identify union, guild, or employee organization concerns about the evaluation process. This early stage is also the appropriate point to solicit additional input, to obtain union, guild, or professional support for the system and to bargain over anticipated impact with regard to merit pay, disciplinary procedures, employee rights and protection, and other conditions of employment.

Management Support　Top administrators must be solidly committed to any performance appraisal system for it to be fully effective. If possible they should be

BOX 10–2

Evaluation Failure

It is tempting to explain the failure of evaluation systems solely in terms of employee or employee union resistance. Unfortunately, it is not that simple. True, employees are people and few people look forward to being evaluated.

Yet despite this human trepidation, my experience suggests that employees at all organizational levels—from agency head to entry level positions—want to be evaluated. Employees want to know what is required of them and how well they are doing it. They want to be more productive—to achieve.

It is management's responsibility to make this happen. The failure to make employee evaluation systems work, therefore, is fundamentally a management problem.

Questions

1. Do you believe it true that employees want to be evaluated?
2. Rapp lays the failure of evaluation systems squarely upon management. Do you agree? Do nonmanagerial employees have responsibility as well? If so, does their responsibility differ from that of management? How?

Source: Brian Rapp, "You Asked for It—But Did You Get It?" Reprinted from *Public Management Magazine*, May 1978, p. 9, by special permission. © 1978, the International City Management Association, Washington, D.C.

---

actively involved in the evaluation of their own subordinates. An effective way for them to demonstrate support is to install the performance system first for themselves. Such action clearly states to all concerned that top management is committed to the program. It also makes clear that it will be used for all employees rather than just rank and file.

Methods of Performance Appraisal

As in other management decisions, the selection of an appraisal system involves many trade-offs. In this section we discuss some major approaches to appraisal: essay, ranking, management by objectives/results/accountabilities, criteria only, and criteria and standards.

Descriptions and examples of these appraisal systems are provided, and then we critique each system using technical, personal, and organizational considerations. Each system has something substantial to offer, and each has its own drawbacks. Eight criteria are used in critiquing the systems:

1. Usefulness in providing feedback to the employee
2. Possibility of using numerical scoring for comparisons and other administrative purposes

FIGURE 10–2
Sample essay appraisal form (Source: C. P. Fleenor and M. P. Scontrino, *Performance Appraisal: A Manager's Guide* (Dubuque, IA: Kendall/Hunt, 1982): 24–25. Reprinted with permission.)

EMPLOYEE PERFORMANCE APPRAISAL

NAME OF EMPLOYEE		OFFICE	
SOCIAL SECURITY NUMBER	JOB TITLE	SECTION	
TIME PERIOD COVERED	TYPE OF APPRAISAL ANNUAL ☐ SPECIAL ☐		DATE OF REVIEW

I. APPRAISAL OF PERFORMANCE:

A. WAS THE REGULAR DAY TO DAY WORK DONE AS EXPECTED?
   YES ☐   NO ☐   PARTIALLY ☐

B. WERE THE MAJOR RESULTS REQUIRED OF THIS POSITION ACHIEVED?
   YES ☐   NO ☐   PARTIALLY ☐

C. TO WHAT EXTENT AND HOW WELL WERE THEY ACHIEVED?

D. IF THERE WERE PROBLEMS WHAT ACTIONS WERE TAKEN?

E. WHAT IMPROVEMENT IS NEEDED IN THIS AREA?

II. APPRAISAL OF WORKING RELATIONSHIPS:

A. HOW WELL DID THE EMPLOYEE ESTABLISH AND MAINTAIN RELATIONSHIPS WITH OTHER PEOPLE THAT WERE NECESSARY TO GETTING RESULTS IN THIS JOB?

B. IF THERE WERE PROBLEMS WHAT ACTION WAS TAKEN?

C. WHAT IMPROVEMENT IS NEEDED IN THIS AREA?

III. EMPLOYEE DEVELOPMENT:
  A. LIST DEVELOPMENTAL OPPORTUNITIES PLANNED WITH THIS EMPLOYEE
    1. FOR IMPROVEMENT ON PRESENT JOB:

    2. FOR ADVANCEMENT:

IV. SUMMARY APPRAISAL:

V. EMPLOYEE COMMENTS:
  A. WHAT STEPS CAN YOU TAKE TO IMPROVE YOUR PERFORMANCE?

  B. WHAT ASSISTANCE DO YOU NEED FROM YOUR SUPERVISOR TO IMPROVE YOUR PERFORMANCE?

  C. WHAT ADDITIONAL TRAINING WILL ASSIST YOU IN IMPROVING YOUR JOB PERFORMANCE?

3. Reliability, or consistency in measurement
4. Validity, or job relatedness
5. Time/cost of development
6. Time/cost of use
7. Rater acceptance
8. Ratee acceptance

Essay Approach As its name suggests, the essay approach to appraisal requires the rater to respond to one or more open-ended essay-type questions concerning the performance of the person being rated. The typical essay appraisal includes five or six questions and is two or three pages in length. Figure 10–2 shows a sample essay appraisal form. All of the appraisal forms presented in this chapter have been or are currently being used in organizations.

When we evaluate the essay approach, we find the following:

1. Usefulness in providing feedback to the employee—essay may or may not be useful depending on the amount of detail provided by the rater. The quality of the feedback is entirely dependent on the rater.

FIGURE 10–3
Sample ranking appraisal form (Source: C. P. Fleenor and M. P. Scontrino, *Performance Appraisal: A Manager's Guide* (Dubuque, IA: Kendall/Hunt, 1982): 26–27. Reprinted with permission.)

Instructions

Please read these instructions all the way through before ranking anyone.

There are _____ Unipolar Alternation Ranking Forms following these instructions. You are to complete each form before going on to the next form, and you are to fill them out in the order in which they are presented. All of the directions below apply to each form.

1. Write your name on the top of the rating form.
2. Read the list of names on the left hand side of the ranking form.
3. Look over the list of names and decide which one individual is *best* described by the rating characteristic. Draw a line through that individual's name and number and write both the name and number in the blank space on the right side of the words "1 most descriptive of."
4. Look over the remaining names and decide which one individual is *least* well described by the rating characteristic. Draw a line through the individual's name and number and write both the name and number in the blank space on the right side of the words "2 least descriptive of."
5. Next, out of those names remaining on your list, select the individual you think is *best* described by the rating characteristic. As before draw a line through his name and number and write both the name and number in the blank space on the right side of the words "3 next most descriptive of."
6. Next, out of the names remaining on your list, select the individual you think is *least* well described by the rating characteristic. As before, draw a line through this individual's name and number, and write down the name and number in the blank space to the right of the words "4 next least descriptive of."
7. Continue this ranking procedure (selecting the individual for whom the rating characteristic is most descriptive and then the one for whom the rating characteristic is least descriptive) until you have drawn a line through each name and number on the list.

RANKING FORM

Your Name: _____ Department: _____ Date: _____

Rating characteristic: Effective written communications

Definition: This rating factor involves composition of reports, directives, letters, memos, proposals, and other documents and the use of good principles of writing such as clarity, brevity, appropriate format, sufficient documentation, etc.

Individuals to be ranked. Cross off each name after you rank it.		rank-ing order	Individuals whom you have ranked		
Individual names	number		The above rating characteristic is	Individual's name	number
		1	most descriptive of		
Martin Rand	2078				
Mary Bennett	2079	3	next most descriptive of		
Joe Bjordal	2081				
Howard Nichols	2083	5	next most descriptive of		
Jerry O'Brien	2089				
David Nakamoto	2091				
Charlene Neves	2092	7	next most descriptive of		
Robert Telson	2093				
Harry Turner	2095	9	next most descriptive of		
Sylvia Vasks	2099				
Shirley Rice	3002	11	next most descriptive of		
Helen Rodriguez	3003				
		13	next most descriptive of		
		15	next most descriptive of		
		17	next most descriptive of		
		19	next most descriptive of		
		20	next least descriptive of		
		18	next least descriptive of		
		16	next least descriptive of		
		14	next least descriptive of		
		12	next least descriptive of		
		10	next least descriptive of		
		8	next least descriptive of		
		6	next least descriptive of		
		4	next least descriptive of		
		2	least descriptive of		

2. Numerical rating—not possible with an essay. There is no satisfactory method of assigning numerical values to essays.
3. Reliability—quite difficult to assess. Attempts to assign numerical values to essay appraisals suggest that they are not reliable. This is due in large part to the highly subjective nature of essay appraisal. Reliability increases as the content of the appraisal becomes more objective.
4. Validity—essays are valid to the extent that they emphasize job-related criteria. Validity is difficult to establish for the same reasons that reliability is difficult to establish.
5. Time/cost of development—the essay is very easy to develop.
6. Time/cost of use—properly done, the essay takes a lot of time.
7. Rater acceptance—may be high or low, depending on the rater.
8. Ratee acceptance—may be high or low, depending on the quality of the feedback provided.

Ranking The ranking approach requires the rater to "line-up" employees from best to worst. Ranking is used most frequently in conjunction with salary decisions to determine how much of a merit increase each employee will receive.

Employees might be ranked according to one global criterion, such as overall performance, or according to a number of different criteria, such as quality of work, leadership ability, or coordination skills. These more specific rankings would then be averaged to arrive at an overall ranking. A sample of a ranking appraisal form is presented in Figure 10-3.

Evaluation of the ranking approach shows the following:

1. Usefulness in providing feedback to the employee—little meaningful feedback comes from ranking. The reasons for the ranking are left to the imagination.
2. Numerical ranking for administrative purposes—though a numerical rating does result from ranking, the scale is of ordinal type. The relative difference between the ranks is unknown. Ranks one and two may be very close, with a large gap between two and three.
3. Reliability—better than for essay, but frequently the only reliable ranks are the very top and bottom. Those ranked in the middle tend to shift ranks as reranking occurs.
4. Validity—while the criteria may be job related, the lack of reliability indicates that validity is not high. One cannot have validity without reliability.
5. Time/cost of development—ranking forms and criteria can be developed quickly.
6. Time/cost of use—of all evaluation techniques, ranking requires the least amount of the rater's time.
7. Rater acceptance—if rankings are not communicated to employees,

raters will generally have little resistance. If rankings must be shared with employees, there will be significant rater resistance since rankings are difficult to explain satisfactorily. Raters may also complain that there is no fair way to compare ranks across departments. The second-ranked employee in department X may not be as good as the fifth-ranked employee in department Y.

8. Ratee acceptance—employees generally view the approach as being out of their control and the feedback they receive as minimal.

Management by Objectives/Results/Accountabilities   We use this phrase broadly, encompassing all approaches that include two major elements. First, at some point in the appraisal process superior and subordinate meet to discuss goals and jointly to establish goals for the subordinate. Second, the superior and subordinate meet to appraise the subordinate's performance in terms of the previously established goals. Individual employee objectives evolve at least in part from the total organization objectives as represented by department or unit objectives. Figure 10–4 depicts a typical management by objectives (MBO) appraisal form.

When we evaluate the MBO format, we conclude the following:

1. Usefulness in providing feedback to the employee—if objectives include specific performance standards as in Figure 10–4, feedback potential is high. If only five or six objectives are developed, however, there may be important aspects of the job for which no feedback is given.
2. Numerical rating for administrative purposes—difficult or impossible. It is nearly impossible to compare different objectives in terms of level of difficulty. Cuthbert may have four easy objectives and accomplish all of them, while Farnsworth may have four difficult objectives and complete two of them. Which is the better performer?
3. Reliability—high if performance standards are developed for each objective, as in Figure 10–4. Without performance standards, reliability will probably be low.
4. Validity—Objectives *should* be job related, of course, so validity can be high if performance standards are created.
5. Time/cost of development—there are many models available in the MBO literature, so design time can be modest.
6. Time/cost of use—development of objectives and standards is sometimes difficult. Five to ten hours per employee is not uncommon.
7. Rater acceptance—the lengthy time demands often lead to resistance by raters.
8. Ratee acceptance—employees generally like the MBO approach *if* they are meaningfully involved in development of both objectives and standards.

PRINCIPAL ACCOUNTABILITIES	SPECIFIC OBJECTIVES	STANDARDS	TARGET DATES	
			Planned	Actual
List in order of importance, the key accountabilities of your job—those specific areas within which you are held accountable for producing results.	For each accountability, state specifically the end results you plan to accomplish during the time period covered.	For each Specific Objective, list the measures such as cost or quality indicators that must be considered in accomplishing the objective. Indicate when the objective must be achieved, i.e., weekly, monthly or a specific date.		

SIGNATURES
Employee _____ Date_____
Supervisor _____ Date_____
Reviewed by:_____ Date_____

FIGURE 10–4

Sample management by objectives appraisal form (Source: C. P. Fleenor and M. P. Scontrino, *Performance Appraisal: A Manager's Guide* (Dubuque, IA: Kendall/Hunt, 1982): 30–31. Reprinted with permission.)

PERFORMANCE REVIEWS

6 MONTHS based on completion of objectives to date					1 YEAR based on achievement of entire objective				
ACHIEVEMENT LEVEL				COMMENTS FOR REVIEW	ACHIEVEMENT LEVEL				COMMENTS FOR REVIEW
Exceeded	Achieved	Partially met	Little or no action	Use this column to support the achievement level indicated. If revisions are made on the original objectives and standards, state the reason and adjustment here.	Exceeded	Achieved	Partially met	Little or no action	Use this column to support the achievement level indicated. If revisions are made on the original objectives and standards, state the reason and adjustment here.

UNPLANNED ACCOMPLISHMENTS

List other accomplishments achieved by this employee not listed above.

BOX 10–3

Resistance to Evaluation

Any changes in policies, procedures, and systems within an organization create losses to the people within these organizations. Such changes are losses in that they take away what is known and familiar. These losses, no matter how logical or beneficial the change may ultimately be, produce anger in employees who are affected by the change—which is just about everyone, since nearly everyone is involved in employee evaluation policies and procedures.

There are several important things which can be done to overcome many of the resistances to evaluation. The loss and the resulting anger which results from change can be ameliorated by (1) imposing the change very slowly, over a period of months rather than days, and (2) involving the people who will be affected by the change in the planning process.

Questions

1. Johnson suggests that change in performance appraisal methods take place over several months. Why? Are there reasons for making the change more quickly? What are they?
2. Does change always produce anger, as asserted?

Source: Jerry W. Johnson, "Some Psychological Aspects of Employee Evaluation." Reprinted from *Public Management* magazine, May 1978, pp. 3-4, by special permission. © 1978, the International City Management Association, Washington, DC.

Criteria Only   A list of rating criteria without accompanying performance standards is called a criteria-only rating format. The list is accompanied by a rating scale giving definitions for various levels of performance. As you can see in Figure 10–5, however, the definitions are not specific to each criterion. The criteria-only approach is the most widely used by organizations.

Applying the eight evaluation factors to the criteria-only approach, we note the following:

1. Usefulness in providing feedback to the employee—feedback tends to be too vague or generalized since the performance standards are not specific to a particular criterion. In addition, the performance standard definitions do not tell the employee what must be done to achieve a particular performance rating.
2. Numerical rating for administrative purposes—an integral part of this approach to appraisal.
3. Reliability—since criteria-only systems lack performance standards, reliability suffers.
4. Validity—if criteria are specific to a particular job, the appraisal is job related. But without any definition of performance standards, the degree to

FIGURE 10-5

Sample criteria-only appraisal form (Source: C. P. Fleenor and M.P. Scontrino, *Performance Appraisal: A Manager's Guide* (Dubuque, IA: Kendall/Hunt, 1982): 33–35. Reprinted with permission.)

This section evaluates the skills, knowledge, and techniques an employee applies in achieving the desired job objective. Using the standards indicated below, rate the employee's performance in the evaluation.

STANDARDS FOR REVIEW

CODE

1. Distinguished: Clearly outstanding—Performance far exceeds the job's requirements in all respects. Only the best belong at this level.

2. Commendable: Above acceptable—Performance is noticeably better than required by the job. Long seasoned and highly proficient employees belong here.

3. Competent: Satisfactory—Performance meets the job's requirements, overall. This is the level of performance expected of most seasoned employees. It implies that the employee achieved all that is expected of the position. A majority of employees belong at this level.

4. Provisional: Improvement needed—Performance falls short of meeting the job's requirements in one or more significant areas. This is normally reserved for inexperienced new incumbents and others who are performing at less than the job's expectations. At this level, there is a demonstrable need for improvement.

A. Work Management Skills

Regardless of whether an employee is in a management position, responsible for securing results through the efforts of others, or is in a professional/technical position and is responsible primarily for his or her own results, there are basic work management skills that must be applied in achieving job objectives. Consider the abilities the employee has demonstrated in the following areas.

Planning

—Forecasts and anticipates future conditions and events that will affect work objectives.
—Sets or recommends realistic, measurable, results-oriented objectives.
—Establishes and sequences logical action steps and time schedules for achievement of objectives.
—Determines accurately the necessary manpower, equipment, and financial resources to achieve objectives.
—Analyzes the cost of achieving an objective in relation to the return its accomplishment will bring before making recommendations.
—As required, formulates clear and concise policies and procedures for achievement of objectives.

Comments:

RATING
1   2   3   4

Organization

—Arranges and relates work assignments so that objectives are accomplished effectively, involving the fewest people necessary at the least cost.
—Eliminates or minimizes overlap and duplication of effort.
—Effectively utilizes time available.
—Understands and works within limits of designated authority and responsibility.
—Delegates work as appropriate.
—Demonstrates understanding of line/staff relationships and responsibilities in working with superiors, peers, and subordinates.

Comments:

RATING
1   2   3   4

Leadership

—Makes decisions based on rational analysis of related factors and consequences rather than on spontaneous reaction.
—Creates understanding and acceptance in both oral and written communications.
—Contributes to team efforts and is effective in motivating others to work toward accomplishment of common objectives.
—As required, selects qualified people to perform the work to be done.
—As required, works with subordinates to improve knowledge, skills, and attributes required to achieve objectives.

Comments:

1   2   3   4

Controlling

—Develops and/or utilizes specific criteria or standards through which results can be measured.
—Records and reports work being done and results accomplished.
—Analyzes and evaluates the quality of the work done and the results secured in relation to the standard set.
—Takes corrective action to meet specified standards and secure the results desired.

Comments:

1   2   3   4

B. Technical Skills and Knowledge

Describe below the specific technical skills and knowledge required to perform this position. Evaluate the degree of proficiency the employee demonstrates in applying these to the job objectives.

	RATING
Skill:	1 2 3 4
Skill:	1 2 3 4
Skill:	1 2 3 4
Skill:	1 2 3 4
Comments:	

C. Additional Performance Criteria

List here and comment on any other factors you believe to be relevant in evaluating this employee's performance.

which a performance rating actually represents a particular level of performance may vary from rater to rater.

5. Time/cost of development—criteria for a particular job family can be developed by a small group of employees in a half day or less.
6. Time/cost of use—depends upon the amount of comments required by the organization to support the ratings. If no justification is required, the criteria-only approach is very easy to use.
7. Rater acceptance—generally high since it is viewed as being relatively easy and straightforward.
8. Ratee acceptance—high if justification for the ratings is required (feedback), but only moderate if justification is not required.

Criteria and Standards The criteria-and-standards approach goes one step beyond the criteria-only approach, since performance standards are developed for each of the criteria. The process involves three steps:

1. Identify groups of similar jobs (job families)
2. Develop performance criteria
3. Develop standards of performance for each of the criteria

CRITERION ONE—PLANNING

This aspect of the job involves designing, scheduling, and implementing short and long range plans; scheduling workload within plan; anticipating deviations from the plan.

These statements describe persons who are usually rated *outstanding* on planning by most raters.

5. _____ Develops several clear alternative action plans to achieve objectives

_____ Initiates alternative plans when original objectives are not being met

_____ Questions current plans against lost or developing opportunities

These statements describe persons who are usually rated *exceeding job standards* on planning by most raters.

4. _____ Anticipates arising problems with prepared contingency plans

_____ Keeps goals and objectives clearly and frequently in front of subordinates

_____ Meets with those concerned to review the work situation, asking for inputs in developing problems/opportunities

These statements describe persons who are usually rated *meeting job standards* on planning by most raters.

3. _____ Reviews action plans with superior

_____ Has plan objectives which fit the needs of other departments

_____ Completes status reports on time

_____ Maintains planning process without attempting to improve it

_____ Has "stretch" in plan but does not indicate how it will be done

These statements describe persons who are usually rated as *needing improvement* on planning by most raters.

2. _____ Completes plan late

_____ Holds planning meetings only when requested by superior or peers

_____ Plans do not contain alternatives

These statements describe persons who are usually rated *unsatisfactory* on planning by most raters.

1. _____ Plans only when forced to plan by superior

_____ Does not involve subordinates in the planning process

_____ Plans do not include objectives

_____ Plans contain unrealistic assumptions

0. _____ This criterion is not applicable or I have not had the opportunity to observe performance on this criterion.

FIGURE 10–6

Example of a criteria and standards appraisal form (Source: C. P. Fleenor and M. P. Scontrino, *Performance Appraisal: A Manager's Guide* (Dubuque, IA: Kendall/ Hunt, 1982): 37–38. Reprinted with permission.)

CRITERION TWO—ACCEPTING RESPONSIBILITY AND INITIATING ACTION

This aspect of the job involves the amount of personal responsibility taken for the completion of work, the amount of work progress made without complete supervisory direction, the willingness to think through work barriers and to keep working toward priority goals, to follow up on work that seems necessary to achieve priority job or unit goals.

These statements describe persons who are usually rated *outstanding* on accepting responsibility and initiating action by most raters.

These statements describe persons who are usually rated as *exceeding job standards* on accepting responsibility and initiating action by most raters.

These statements describe persons who are usually rated as *meeting job standards* on accepting responsibility and initiating action by most raters.

These statements describe persons who are usually rated *below job standards* on accepting responsibility and initiating action by most raters.

These statements describe persons who are usually rated as *unacceptable* on accepting responsibility and initiating action by most raters.

5. _____ Anticipates problems and tries to eliminate them.

_____ Advances unit goals in ways others overlook.

_____ Assumes responsibility for making his/her job or unit the best.

_____ Stays informed on "higher level" needs.

4. _____ Not afraid of making mistakes and accepting the blame.

_____ Accepts additional responsibility.

_____ Takes action on problems even when supervisor is out.

_____ Conceives and carries through jobs on own initiative.

3. _____ Takes action on all tasks which are due to be completed.

_____ Completes job even without specific instructions.

2. _____ Doesn't want to do work.

_____ Takes "own time" to get work done.

_____ Neglects the work s/he is not interested in.

_____ Won't initiate action on own.

1. _____ Fills time by doing personal things.

_____ Completes task only under direct supervision.

_____ Requires 100% guidance to get things done.

_____ Cannot be left to work without supervison.

0. _____ This criterion is not applicable or I have not had the opportunity to observe performance on this criterion.

The performance standards answer the questions of "how good is good?" or "how bad is bad?" for each of the criteria. Satisfactory performance for planning ability is defined differently from satisfactory performance for employee counseling ability. Two criteria with performance standards are shown in Figure 10–6.

Evaluating the criteria-and-standards approach to appraisal provides the following conclusions:

1. Usefulness in providing feedback to the employee—high if the criteria are job related and the standards are clearly defined.
2. Numerical rating for administrative purposes—an integral part of this approach to evaluation.
3. Reliability—generally high, since performance standards give raters a consistent frame of reference.
4. Validity—generally high because criteria are job related and the standards reflect different degrees of performance for the criteria.
5. Time/cost of development—high; two hours or more may be required to define performance standards for a single criterion.
6. Time/cost of use—low, since the standards provide much of the justification for the rating.
7. Rater acceptance—raters dislike the developmental effort required, but they like the final product.
8. Ratee acceptance—high, since many of the questions that go unanswered in other approaches to appraisal are an integral part of the criteria-and-standards approach.

Table 10–2 summarizes the advantages and disadvantages of the five approaches. It is important to remember that success or failure of any appraisal system is dependent on a number of factors involving the people, the organization, and the environment.

TABLE 10–2

A comparison of the advantages and disadvantages of five major approaches to appraisal

	Essay	Ranking	MBO	Criteria Only	Criteria and Standards
Feedback	Rater-dependent	Little	Usually high	Usually vague	Usually high
Numerical rating	No	No	No	Yes	Yes
Reliability	Low	Low	Low	Moderate	High
Validity	Low	Low	Low	Moderate	High
Time/cost of development	Little	Little	Little	Moderate	High
Time/cost of use	High	Little	High	Moderate	Moderate
Rater acceptance	*	Low	*	High	High
Ratee acceptance	*	Low	*	Moderate	High

* May be high, medium, or low depending on how the procedure is implemented and used.

Source: C. P. Fleenor and M. P. Scontrino, *Performance Appraisal: A Manager's Guide* (Dubuque, IA: Kendall/Hunt, 1982): 40. Reprinted with permission.

Performance Planning

Performance appraisal in many organizations tends to focus only upon the past. But we propose that the appraisal process should also be directed at the future. While feedback on past performance is vital, that performance cannot be changed. Something can be done about performance in the future. Discussion of future performance can motivate employees to perform better by specifying goals for performance and standards for measuring progress. Finally, discussing future performance orients both manager and employee to the possibilities for improved communication and unit effectiveness.

The extent and nature of performance planning depends upon the level of commitment to performance improvement held by the manager, the subordinate, and the organization. If performance improvement is a matter of indifference beyond ritual lip service, planning will merely be an exercise. If improvement of performance is important, planning is greatly facilitated by sound appraisal and thoughtful feedback to the employee by the manager.

The planning element may be a small part of the performance appraisal interview (PAI) for most employees, but can be of particular importance for some employees. It is clearly critical for the deficient employee, yet planning is important for the "star" employee as well. Performance objectives and career objectives stated in terms of training, education, job assignments, etc., can be results of the planning session.

The traditional appraisal process might be depicted as in Figure 10–7, with emphasis placed on activities from the date of appraisal to some period in the past, usually one year. We suggest the process shown in Figure 10–8 instead, in which emphasis is placed upon "what's next" as well as on the past. Performance goals provide both supervisor and employees with periodic checkpoints for assessing employee progress.

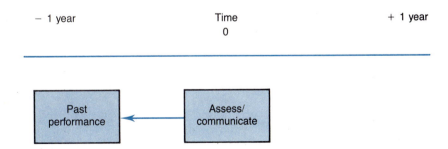

FIGURE 10–7
Appraisal of the past (Source: Adapted from C. P. Fleenor and M. P. Scontrino, *Performance Appraisal: A Manager's Guide* (Dubuque, IA: Kendall/Hunt, 1982): 103. Reprinted with permission.)

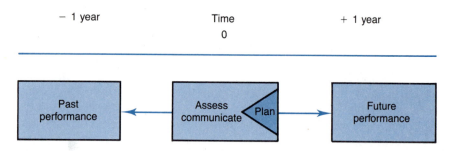

FIGURE 10–8
Evaluating the past and shaping the future (Source: Adapted from C. P. Fleenor and M. P. Scontrino, *Performance Appraisal: A Manager's Guide* (Dubuque, IA: Kendall/Hunt, 1982): 104. Reprinted with permission.)

Planning Possibilities   Planning possibilities stem from a variety of decisions. Little or no planning is required if both manager and employee are satisfied with the performance level and if previously established objectives are seen as appropriate for the next review period. This situation occurs when the significant characteristics of acceptable job performance have been well defined for some period of time, and where the character of the job has changed little and is not expected to change significantly during the next review period. It also occurs when the employee—for valid reasons, such as proximity to retirement—is not interested in establishing more challenging objectives, such as preparation for other jobs or promotion.

A second possibility for planning is shown in Figure 10–9. In this case the supervisor perceived a discrepancy between the employee's actual performance and desired performance. The supervisor has communicated these concerns during the performance review period and has provided the employee with an indication of the standards being used to assess performance. Given these benchmarks, the employee is well aware of the performance discrepancy. When the employee and the supervisor meet, it is clear that one task will be to develop an approach to solving this performance problem. Before real progress can be made, both supervisor and employee must agree that a problem does exist. By providing feedback on a continuing and timely basis throughout the performance review period, the supervisor lays the groundwork for indicating that there is, in fact, a problem.

Supervisor and employee must also agree that the source of the problem has been defined. The supervisor who believes that the match between the job and the employee is the source of the problem is likely to find little agreement from the employee who believes that the problem is in the job itself.

In defining the problem the manager may want to consider the following questions initially:

1. Can the job itself be altered in some way to improve performance? Performance problems can be caused by a poorly designed workflow.

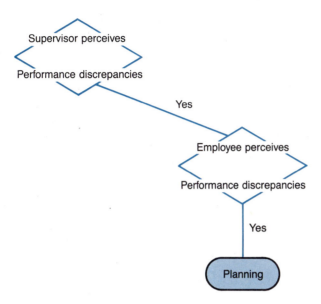

FIGURE 10–9
Planning where performance discrepancy exists (Source: C. P. Fleenor and M. P. Scontrino, *Performance Appraisal: A Manager's Guide* (Dubuque, IA: Kendall/Hunt, 1982): 105. Reprinted with permission.)

Environmental factors such as poor lighting or cramped work areas can also cause lower performance.

2. Does the job provide feedback to the employee? Does the employee know how well or poorly he or she is doing without having to be told?

3. Is some aspect of the job distasteful? Is the job dirty or unrewarding or is the work environment physically uncomfortable? Is the job performed at a time of day that disrupts the employee's personal life?

4. Is the employee the problem? Does the employee have the skills necessary to perform? This kind of problem is more likely to occur when some aspect of the job has changed during the review period so that new or unpracticed skills are required.

5. Will training or retraining improve performance? For example, a supervisor may have received some training in conducting appraisal reviews two years ago but could now use a refresher course.

6. Will additional practice improve performance? The employee who types or files only infrequently may indeed be a poor performer when pressed into emergency service.

7. Is the match between job and employee the problem? For example, the best performer may be promoted to a supervisory position with no preparation for the promotion. The organization may have gained a low-performing supervisor while losing a top-performing employee.

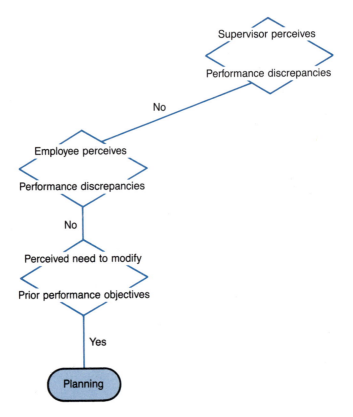

FIGURE 10–10
Planning in the absence of performance discrepancy (Source: C. P. Fleenor and
M. P. Scontrino, *Performance Appraisal: A Manager's Guide* (Dubuque, IA: Kendall/
Hunt, 1982): 107. Reprinted with permission.)

8. Are external factors the problem? Personal problems may create stress
   that in turn affects performance.

A third kind of planning situation is described in Figure 10–10. In this setting
both employee and manager agree that employee performance during the review
period met or exceeded established standards, yet both agree on the need to
establish new performance objectives. This situation often occurs with relatively
new employees or employees new to a particular job. Standards appropriate for a
trainee may become inappropriate as the person gains experience and expertise.
Or perhaps a long-term employee is seeking additional responsibility as a basis
for transfer or promotion. This kind of planning is also necessary when the job
itself will be changed during the next review period. Performance objectives must
be changed to accommodate modifications in the job itself.

Writing Performance Objectives   Creating specific performance objectives is always a good idea. The general urging to "do better" is usually not enough to cause noticeable improvement.[20] Just as one creates a plan for capital investment, a plan for building a home, or a plan for a personal vacation, the supervisor and employee can create a plan for performance improvement.

Performance objectives are a logical outcome of the appraisal sequence. Defining them forces employee and supervisor to focus on issues of past performance and guarantees that the PAI helps the employee plan for future progress.

Raters often find it difficult to write performance goals and objectives that convey to the ratee exactly what must be done to improve performance. Affirmative answers to the following questions confirm that the performance objectives are complete.

1. Does the objective spell out the who, what, when, where, and how of performance improvement? Is the standard of performance in writing? Is it *specific*?
2. Is the objective clearly related to job performance? Does it allow the supervisor and subordinate to focus on the issues of greatest importance? Is it *pertinent*?
3. Is it possible to perform at the level being set as the standard? In other words, is the objective *obtainable*?
4. How will accomplishment be measured—by quality, quantity, frequency, efficiency? Is the objective *measurable*?
5. Will improvement in performance be visible? Is it *observable*?

Readers with military experience are familiar with the all-purpose meat product Spam. To help you remember the requirements of good performance objectives we offer the mnemonic device "SPAMO"—Specific, Pertinent, Attainable, Measurable, Observable. The more closely the objective meets the SPAMO criteria the less likely either supervisor or employee is to neglect clarification of what was to be done when and by whom.

Both manager and employee should give some thought to objectives in advance of the PAI. The manager should consider having employees frame their own objectives. These can be reviewed by the supervisor and clarified or adjusted.

It is crucial that performance objectives be stated in writing. The human memory is an extremely fallible record, but written objectives can always be reviewed. Though writing objectives is time consuming, it can be a significant step toward improving job performance.

Summary of Key Concepts

1. Rewards are either intrinsic or extrinsic and money is usually considered extrinsic. Pay secrecy seems not to be beneficial for organizational purposes of motivation.
2. Both absenteeism and turnover can be modified by various reward programs sponsored by the organization. However, care must be taken to make sure that the real causes of both problems are not masked by the incentive programs.

3. Performance appraisals can be used effectively to check selection procedures, identify training needs, and facilitate the communication process between boss and subordinate.

4. To maximize the benefits of appraisal programs, the employee should participate in their design and usage.

5. There are several approaches to the performance appraisal process: essay, ranking, management by objectives, criteria only, and criteria and standards. Each has its own set of advantages and disadvantages.

6. The appraisal process can be expanded by focusing on the future as well as the past through performance planning.

Key Terms

Criteria and standards approach	Incentive plan
Criteria only approach	Individual productivity incentive
Criterion	Intrinsic reward
Essay approach	Management by objectives (MBO)
Extrinsic reward	Performance planning
Group productivity incentive	Ranking

MANAGERIAL APPLICATIONS

The raison d'être for reward systems is productivity. If reward systems, performance appraisal, and other management tools discussed in the text do not ultimately have an impact on the productivity of the organization, they are wasted, or at least misdirected, effort.

The authors observed the following situation in a small manufacturing plant. The plant had met an exceptionally heavy production schedule by working all hourly employees an average of sixty-six hours per week over a five-week period. At the end of the five weeks, the plant manager was so appreciative of the effort from all of the employees that he gave each of the employees a $300 bonus. The hourly employees, who averaged over $4,000 in pay during the five-week period, thought it was nice to get a few extra dollars. The office staff, who had worked limited overtime, thought the bonus was wonderful. The supervisors, who were salaried employees and were not eligible for any additional pay for working overtime, were furious. They saw the $300 not as a bonus but as an insult. One supervisor commented that the bonus amounted to $2.50 an hour for all of the extra hours worked.

On hearing of the supervisors' grumblings, the plant manager vowed never to "waste his money on ungrateful employees again." The plant manager spent over $30,000 to upset a very key group of employees!

Factors to Consider

Before turning to a variety of methods for linking rewards to performance, let's first identify some factors to consider when exploring the usefulness of any reward.

What Performance Can Be Measured?   Linking rewards to performance definitely implies that performance can, in fact, be measured. If performance is too difficult or too expensive to measure, then linking rewards to unmeasurable performance makes the decision extremely subjective. If employees do not perceive a good linkage between their performance and the reward, then the reward will have little motivating value.[21]

What Performance Is Important to the Organization?   If a manager is interested in some aspect of productivity but ends up measuring attendance because attendance records are available and productivity records are not, the manager is emphasizing the wrong behavior. This is not meant to imply that attendance is unimportant. Attendance, however, may not be linked to productivity.

If the manager then goes one step further and ties rewards to attendance, then the message is very clear—attendance is more important than productivity. This message is probably not intended by the manager. Unfortunately, when we link an incentive to some behavior, that behavior receives attention.

The authors were working with the manager of an animal control department in a large city who conveyed the following story. One of the senior managers felt that the animal control officers were spending too much time drinking coffee and not enough time catching strays. To get the officers out of the coffee shops and into their trucks, this senior manager informed all officers that the number of miles driven per day (as measured by the odometers in the trucks) would be recorded daily and used for employee appraisals. Overnight the number of miles driven tripled . . . and the number of strays collected decreased dramatically. The behavior of the officers changed; unfortunately, the attention was focused on the wrong behavior.

Do Employees Have Line-of-sight?   Can employees see a linkage between their performance and the performance leading to the incentive? If employees perceive that their performance will have little or no impact on their department's performance and if the incentive is contingent on the department's performance, then the incentive will have little motivational value. An example of poor line-of-sight is the typical organization-wide profit sharing plan. Many employees perceive that they personally can have little impact on profit. For them the profit sharing plan has little incentive value.

Are the Rewards Seen as Fair?   In chapter 3 we discussed equity theory. Equity becomes of prime importance whenever rewards are considered. Rarely are the rewards too large, but frequently the rewards are too small. Many organizations allocate a very small salary percentage (often only 1 or 2 percent) to reward outstanding performers. When a 1 percent "bonus" is divided into twenty-six pay periods, the amount received each pay period does not appear to represent the value of "outstanding performance".

Expectancy-valence theory from chapter 3 suggests that we explore the question of whether or not we have incentives that will capture our employees' attention.

Is the Incentive Plan Understandable?   Is the incentive system one that can be understood by the employees involved? If the incentive scheme is based on "asset turns" and employees do not understand what an "asset turn" is, then the incentive is of limited value. Incentive plans may be complex as long as the employees can still understand them.

Is There a Short Time Interval Between the Desired Performance and the Incentive?   As we saw in our discussion of reinforcement theory, the most effective reinforcers, that is, incentives, follow the desired behavior closely in time. The absenteeism plans discussed earlier exemplify the importance of short time intervals between the performance and the reward.

Is the Incentive System Compatible with Organization and Individual Values?   If an organization is emphasizing the development of employee teams, an incentive scheme that rewards individual behavior may prove to be dysfunctional. If managers or other employees are opposed to a particular incentive plan, it is doubtful that the incentive plan will have any impact on the desired behaviors.

A Method for Categorizing Incentive Plans

There are literally hundreds of different approaches that have been developed to have an impact on employees' performance. These approaches run the gamut from the behavior modification plans for improved attendance (mentioned earlier in this chapter) to organization wide productivity improvement plans. To discuss such a heterogeneous array of incentives, some method of organizing these plans is required. We have found it helpful to use the matrix presented in Figure 10–11 to categorize productivity incentive plans.

Three dimensions are included in this matrix. The first dimension addresses the question of the incentive plan's probable impact on productivity. Some plans are designed to have a very direct and immediate effect on productivity; others are created with the hope that they will affect productivity through their effect on some intervening variable such as employee morale.

		Impact on Productivity	
		Direct	*Indirect*
Financial Incentive	Individual Incentive	1	2
	Group Incentive	3	4
Nonfinancial Incentive	Individual Incentive	5	6
	Group Incentive	7	8

FIGURE 10–11
A matrix for categorizing productivity incentive plans

The second dimension considers the financial aspects of the plan. Financial incentives involve cold, hard cash paid in one of two ways—either directly to the employee, that is, as a bonus, or indirectly to the employee, that is, in fringe benefits.

Dimension three focuses on the recipient of the incentive. Is the incentive plan directed toward individual performance, as in a sales commission, or does it reward group performance, for example, a profit-sharing plan?

The combination of these three dimensions produces a matrix with eight cells. Figure 10–12 presents the matrix with examples of the actual productivity incentive plans that could be included in each cell.

One Sample Incentive Plan from Each Cell

In this section we briefly describe one incentive plan from each cell in the matrix. We have selected plans that are either typically found in many organizations or currently growing in popularity.

Individual Productivity Incentive

A *financial-direct impact: Merit pay.*   Merit pay, or pay-for-performance, plans include all of those approaches to compensation that involve two components: (1) some method of assessing individual performance and (2) some reward, typically an increase in salary or a bonus. Merit pay is deceptively simple. From this chapter it should be clear that it can be quite difficult to assess an individual's performance. And it can be even more difficult to compare different employees' performance to

Impact on Productivity

		Direct	Indirect
Financial Incentive	Individual Incentive	Piece rates Commissions Bonus plans Suggestion awards	"Cafeteria" fringe benefits Perquisites Tuition programs
	Group Incentive	Gainsharing plans Group bonuses	Profit sharing Fringe benefits
Nonfinancial Incentive	Individual Incentive	Job enrichment Earned time off	Flexitime Recognition programs
	Group Incentive	Quality circles Zero defects	Quality of work life programs Safety programs Survey feedback

FIGURE 10–12
Examples of productivity incentive plans for each cell of matrix

determine who is deserving of merit pay. Last, but by no means least, is the problem of having enough money available to give all of the meritorious performers a significant reward.

A financial-indirect impact: Cafeteria fringe benefits.   A "cafeteria" approach to fringe benefits allows employees to tailor their fringe benefit package to their own needs at that point in their lives. For example, many working couples both have medical insurance that covers the worker and the spouse. A cafeteria approach would allow one of the spouses to substitute some other benefit for medical insurance.

Cafeteria fringe benefit plans are usually not linked directly to productivity or performance. Rather they are viewed as a general reward to recruit new employees and to reduce turnover, which does have a long term, though indirect, impact on productivity.

A *nonfinancial-direct impact*: *Earned time off*. Earned time off programs allow an employee to leave the work site once having completed a certain amount of work. The employee is paid only for the actual hours that he or she works. In some organizations the earned time off may be used for educational programs offered by the organization. In other organizations the employees are allowed to go home once their work is completed.

A *nonfinancial-indirect impact*: *Flexitime*. Flexitime, or flex time, is a system of scheduling work that allows each employee to select a starting time and quitting time that best meets personal needs and preferences. Usually all employees are required to be present for certain "core" hours, perhaps from 10 AM to 2 PM. Some organizations allow employees to "bank" hours during the week so that they may leave early on Friday.

Group Productivity Incentive

A *financial-direct impact*: *Gainsharing*. Gainsharing includes a variety of group incentive plans that have the following characteristics: (a) a management style that encourages employee involvement and teamwork, (b) a system that facilitates employee involvement so that all employees have a method for making their ideas and suggestions known, and (c) a plant-wide bonus system that shares productivity improvements with all employees on a monthly basis. The major gainsharing plans include the Scanlon Plan, the Rucker Plan, and Improshare.[23]

A *financial-indirect impact*: *Profit sharing*. Profit-sharing plans typically involve a once-a-year sharing of profits with all employees. Usually profits must exceed a specified minimum level before any sharing occurs. The method of payment ranges from full cash payouts to completely deferred payouts, which are typically used to fund a pension plan.

Often profit-sharing plans involve a special effort to communicate with all employees to encourage productivity improvement so that there will be more profit to share.

A *nonfinancial-direct impact*: *Zero defects*. A zero defects program is defined as a systematic and ongoing process of involving small groups of employees in formal problem-solving meetings. Employees are grouped by work team, by department, or by product line, and identify quality or productivity problems for analysis and solution that will result in zero defects. What makes this an incentive is the inherent pride in their work that such a program may instill in employees and the possible competition between groups that can be generated.

A nonfinancial-indirect impact: Survey feedback.　The survey feedback process entails collecting data systematically from the various work groups and feeding back the results. With this data, work groups can begin to solve various issues identified by the survey that may be limiting the work group's effectiveness. Having this control may lead to satisfaction and, therefore, be an indirect incentive to improve the work group's performance.

DISCUSSION QUESTIONS

1. Do you feel that people at work respond more to intrinsic rewards than to extrinsic rewards? Why or why not?
2. What intrinsic and extrinsic rewards might Herbie the waiter get from his job?
3. Which method of performance appraisal would you like to use as a manager? Why?
4. Which method of performance appraisal would you like as an employee? Why?
5. Would you prefer a policy of pay secrecy? Why or why not?
6. Is it more important for the rater to accept the system than for the ratee? Why or why not?

EXERCISE

Write two personal performance objectives. One of them should be short term, perhaps related to this course or some other. The other objective should be longer term, perhaps related to your job or personal life.

Exchange your objectives with those of a classmate. Read that person's objectives and evaluate them with the SPAMO* criteria. Make suggestions on "improving" the objectives, especially in terms of specificity, measurability, and observability.

Rewrite your own objectives based upon the critique you have been given. Use the benchmarks in your objectives to keep track of your progress.

* Specific, Pertinent, Attainable, Measurable, Observable

NOTES

1. T. L. Adcock, "They Also Wait Who Only Stand and Serve." *Northwest Orient Magazine* (October 1983): 65. Reprinted with permission.
2. *Work in America* (Cambridge, MA: M.I.T. Press, 1973).
3. E. E. Lawler, *Pay and Organizational Effectiveness: A Psychological View* (New York: McGraw-Hill, 1971).
4. C. P. Alderfer, "An Empirical Test of a New Theory of Human Needs," *Organizational Behavior and Human Performance* (4): 142–175.
5. V. H. Vroom, "Industrial Social Psychology," in G. Lindzey and E. Aronson, eds., *The Handbook of Social Psychology*, 2nd ed., vol. 5 (Reading, MA: Addison-Wesley, 1970): 200–208.

6. M. Patchen, *The Choice of Wage Comparisons* (Englewood Cliffs, NJ: Prentice-Hall, 1961).

7. E. E. Lawler, "Secrecy and the Need to Know," in M. Dunnette, R. House, and H. Tosi, eds., *Readings in Managerial Motivation and Compensation* (East Lansing, MI: Michigan State University Press, 1972): 362–371.

8. E. E. Lawler, *Pay and Organization Development* (Reading, MA: Addison-Wesley, 1981): 45.

9. J. A. Wallin and R. D. Johnson, "The Positive Reinforcement Approach to Controlling Employee Absenteeism," *Personnel Journal* (August 1976): 390–392.

10. F. Luthans and T. Maris, "Evaluating Personnel Programs Through the Reversal Techniques," *Personnel Journal* (October 1979): 692–698.

11. T. A. Stephens and W. A. Burroughs, "An Application of Operant Conditioning to Absenteeism in a Hospital Setting," *Journal of Applied Psychology*, vol. 4 (1978): 518–521.

12. Luthans and Maris, "Evaluating Personnel Programs."

13. R. M. Steers and S. R. Rhodes, "Major Influences on Employee Attendance: A Process Model," *Journal of Applied Psychology*, 4 (1978): 391–407.

14. Bureau of National Affairs, "Quarterly Report on the Employment Outlook: Job Absence and Turnover," *Bulletin to Management* (9 March 1978): 3.

15. J. Kim and W. Hamner, "Effect of Performance Feedback and Goal Setting on Productivity and Satisfaction in an Organizational Setting," *Journal of Applied Psychology*, 61 (1976): 48–57.

16. G. Latham, K. Wexley, and E. Pursell, "Training Managers to Minimize Rating Errors in the Observation of Behavior," *Journal of Applied Psychology*, vol. 60 (1975): 550–555; and A. Pizam, "Social Differentiation—A New Psychological Barrier to Performance Appraisal," *Public Personnel Journal*, vol. 4 (1975): 244–247.

17. J. Ivancevich, "Differing Goal Setting Treatments and Their Effects on Performance and Job Satisfaction," *Academy of Management Journal*, vol. 20 (1977): 406–419.

18. S. Johnson and L. Ronan, "Exploratory Study of Bias in Job Performance Evaluation," *Public Personnel Management*, vol. 8 (1975): 315–323; and R. Lazer, "The Discrimination Danger in Performance Appraisal," *The Conference Board Record*, vol. 8 (1976): 60–64.

19. G. Lubben, "Performance Appraisal: The Legal Implications of Title VII," *Personnel*, vol. 57 (1980): 11–21.

20. Ivancevich, "Differing Goal Setting Treatments."

21. Lawler, *Pay and Organization Development.*

22. R. J. Doyle, *Gainsharing and Productivity* (New York: American Management Association, 1983).

RECOMMENDED READINGS

D. D. Ely, "The Fable of the Farmer's Folly." *Personnel Journal* (August 1974): 579–582.

This delightful parable stresses the motivational aspect of performance appraisal.

C. P. Fleenor and **M. P. Scontrino,** *Performance Appraisal: A Manager's Guide* (Dubuque, IA: Kendall/Hunt, 1982).

Much of the material in this chapter comes from this book. The entire performance cycle, from the choice of an appraisal system to the conduct of the performance appraisal interview, is covered.

M. London and **G. Oldham,** "Effects of Varying Goal Types and Incentive Systems on Performance and Satisfaction," *Academy of Management Journal*, 21 (1978): 537–546.

This article reviews the importance of goal setting and describes different types of goals.

The Seabrook Manufacturing Company

"All we need now is a strong man to complete the side show!" exclaimed Joe Larson, purchasing manager of the Seabrook Manufacturing Company, as he entered the office of Dale Wolff, personnel representative for the Purchasing Department.

"What do you mean, Joe?" asked Dale.

"You know that we have a lot of visitors and suppliers through here, and that old bag isn't doing much to doll up the area. These secretaries have a good deal to do with the impressions people get of our outfit, and they should be at least presentable! We spend thousands of dollars for carpeting and pictures and now this!"

"Whom are you talking about?"

"I don't know what her name is, but you know damn well whom I'm talking about! The Blimp! Take care of it, will you?"

The Purchasing Department of Seabrook Manufacturing Company occupied the major portion of the third floor of the headquarters building of the company. The main working force was located in a large open area at several rows of desks. Executives of the division, all of whom were under the control of Larson, were located in private offices that extended along the outer edge of the general working area.[1] The secretary for each executive was situated at a desk directly in front of the office of the executive for whom she worked, but was separated from the rest of the workers by a wide aisle. This aisle was the main passage used by visitors and personnel from other divisions of the company to get from the reception lobby to the executives' offices. The secretaries' desks were finished with a walnut stain as contrasted with the lighter-colored finishes used on other desks in the open area, and the space between secretaries' desks was significantly greater than the space between other desks on the floor. The office layout of the Purchasing Department is shown in Figure A.

Mary Lampson, the secretary in question, had just been promoted to her new position as Jack Henderson's secretary and had moved to her new location while Larson had been away on a business trip. After his former secretary had submitted her resignation, Jack Henderson had selected Mary Lampson as his new secretary after reviewing the personnel files and talking with several individuals currently employed in the department whom Dale Wolff had recommended as candidates for the position.

Mary Lampson was forty-eight years old and had been with the Seabrook Manufacturing Company for seventeen years, ten in the Purchasing

Source: Reprinted with permission from *Organizational Behavior: A Management Approach* by Harry R. Knudson and C. Patrick Fleenor (Winthrop Publishing, 1978): 43–45. Copyright 1976 by Professor Harry R. Knudson, Graduate School of Business, University of Washington.

[1] Dale Wolff reported directly to Joe Larson.

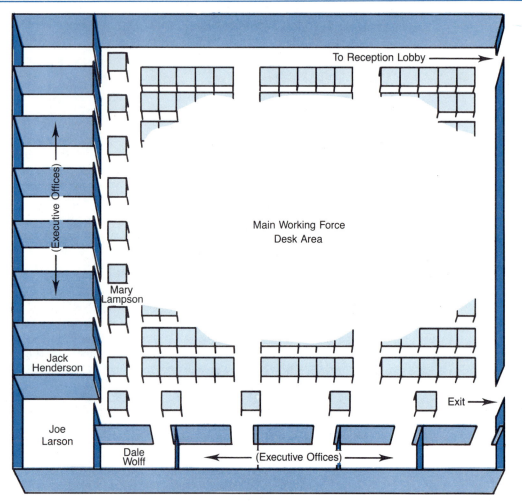

To Reception Lobby →

(Executive Offices)

Main Working Force
Desk Area

Mary
Lampson

Jack
Henderson

Joe
Larson

Dale
Wolff

Exit →

← (Executive Offices) →

FIGURE A
Purchasing Department office layout

Department. She had started work at Seabrook shortly after her husband died. Prior to her assignment as Henderson's secretary, she had performed secretarial duties for several units in the department, but had always been located in the open area with the general employees of the division. She had two grown sons who had completed college and had moved to other parts of the country and one other son, twenty years old, who was a sophomore at Eastern State University. Her record at Seabrook was unblemished. She had created favorable impressions wherever she had worked, and her former supervisors were unanimous in their praise of her abilities.

Mary Lampson was five feet, four inches tall and weighed two hundred and twenty-five pounds. Although her weight had been a continuing problem for her, she was very pleased with her recent progress on a weight control program, and had lost sixty pounds in the last two years by following her doctor's orders very closely. She was enthusiastic about her new job, for she could use the increase in salary to help put her youngest son through college and, as she put it, "keep the creditors a little farther from my door."

While not knowing quite how to "take care of it," Dale Wolff decided that his first step should be to talk with Jack Henderson, Mary's boss.

After Wolff related his conversation with Larson, Jack Henderson replied: "What a hell of a way to run a railroad! You do what you want to, Dale, but things are in pretty miserable shape when looks are more important than ability. I'm certainly not going to mention this to Mary!"

Questions

1. To what do you attribute Joe Larson's comments?
2. What did he mean when he told Dale Wolff to "take care of it"?
3. What do you think of Jack Henderson's comments? Why did he react as he did?
4. What, if anything, should Wolff do? Why?
5. What, if anything, should Henderson do? Why?
6. What, if anything, should be said to Mary Lampson? Who should say it? Precisely, what words should be used?

CHAPTER ELEVEN
Management of Change

OUTLINE

CONCEPTS OF CHANGE

Pressures for Change
Model for Understanding Change
Diagnosing the Situation
Dealing with Resistance to Change
Implementing Change
Summary of Key Concepts

MANAGERIAL APPLICATIONS

Problem Definition and Diagnosis
Alternative Selection
Applications of Force Field Analysis
Evolution or Revolution?

OBJECTIVES

- Identify the major pressures for change facing organizations

- Describe the steps involved in the change process

- List the six methods of collecting data about the organization

- Identify the main sources of resistance to change and how to reduce them

- Explain the various approaches and differences between the four types of change agents

- List and describe the change strategies for the individual, work group, intergroup, and organizational levels

- Discuss the major managerial applications of the change process

How Difficult Is It to Change an Organization's Culture?

While hard times, such as a recession, force companies to pursue back-to-basics strategies, Emerson Electric Company has taken that approach all along—through the good and the bad times. Its main strategies include reinvesting in basic businesses, relentless cost-cutting, and continual product improvement. Its products range from appliances, pump motors, and heating elements to consumer products such as tools, fans, chain saws, hot-water dispensers, and garbage disposals. In the last twenty-five years, it has consistently outperformed most U.S. manufacturers.

Ironically, though, Emerson's very success in building a corporate culture that focuses so thoroughly on year-by-year returns may hamper its quest to deliver the new technology its markets demand. A culture that was built on cost-cutting and total dedication to the bottom line must be made flexible enough to encourage the development of technologies and products whose payoff may be years down the road.

Chairman Charles Knight shares this concern, even though under his leadership tight management controls were developed. During the '80s, Knight is discarding some of his caution. Knowing that Emerson must change, he is spending money where he once conserved it. In contrast to the recessions of the '70s, Emerson is not reducing its research and development expenditures for new products to improve short-term earnings.

But so deeply embedded is Emerson's old culture that some company officials still question whether top management will stick to its new policy if success does not come quickly. For example, managers at one division worry that an important new product might be dropped if profits suffer for any extended period. Their concern is generated from the compensation system that affects division management. While 10 percent to 15 percent of the bonuses awarded is tied to their development of new products, some 50 percent of their bonuses still rides on their bottom-line results.

Another facet of management's concern about Emerson's ability to change is the tradition of being highly decentralized. Emerson must now build a new structure that fosters the sharing of scarce human and financial resources. Emerson had consistently encouraged personnel to identify with their divisions. In fact, divisions kept their own names, and employees' loyalty was to their divisions, not Emerson. Now staff are being asked to contribute their engineering, marketing, and manufacturing expertise and resources to interdivisional goals and programs.[1]

CONCEPTS OF CHANGE

The preceding story raises some questions concerning the management of change. How can managers become more effective in coping with and managing change? What are some of the reasons Emerson feels the need to change how it conducts its business? What areas should Emerson consider changing to become more "flexible"? What might be some problems that could prevent Emerson from implementing its new direction? Are there methods or procedures that might facilitate Emerson's changing its culture? Is there a model that can help managers plan and understand the process of change?

The first point to consider is what some of the reasons are for change or what pressures are creating a need for Emerson (or any other business in a similar situation) to consider doing things differently. After we consider the pressures for change, we review a model for planned change. This model leads us through the steps of diagnosis, alternative generation, implementation concerns, and evaluation of the results.

Pressures for Change

In the case of Emerson, one force creating a need for change is the market competition. But, as we shall see, at any period of time, firms, groups, and individuals face a multitude of pressures.

It is easy to begin appreciating the enormity of the forces for change when we review literature such as Naisbitt's *Megatrends*.[2] Naisbitt sees American society evolving and feels that through this restructuring both organizations and individuals will need to cope differently in the future, if not today.

He outlines several trends that have relevance for organizations:

1. Although we continue to think we live in an industrially based society, we have in fact changed to an economy based on the creation and distribution of information. "The new source of power is not money in the hands of a few but information in the hands of many." (p. 16)
2. We are moving in the dual direction of high tech/high touch, matching each new technology with a compensatory human response. "We must learn to balance the material wonders of technology with the spiritual demands of our human nature." (p. 40)
3. No longer do we have the luxury of operating within an isolated, self-sufficient, national economic system; we now must acknowledge that we are part of a global economy. "Business is replacing politics as the world's gossip." (p. 70)
4. We are redirecting our attention from merely short-term time frames and corresponding rewards to dealing from much longer-term time frames. "Strategic planning is worthless—unless there is first strategic vision." (p. 94)
5. In private as well as professional lives, we have rediscovered the need and ability to act innovatively and to work from the bottom up as well as from the traditional approaches. "The big-business mergers and the big-labor mergers have all the appearances of dinosaurs mating." (p. 87)
6. We are shifting from mainly institutional help to more self-reliance in all facets of our lives. "We are shifting from a managerial society to an entrepreneurial society." (p. 149)
7. We are giving up our dependence on hierarchical structures in favor of informal networks. "The failure of hierarchies to solve society's problems forced people to talk to one another—and that was the beginning of networks." (p. 191)
8. From a black/white society with limited choices, we are exploring the need to have multiple options to create our futures. "In today's Baskin-Robbins society, everything comes in at least 31 flavors." (p. 232)

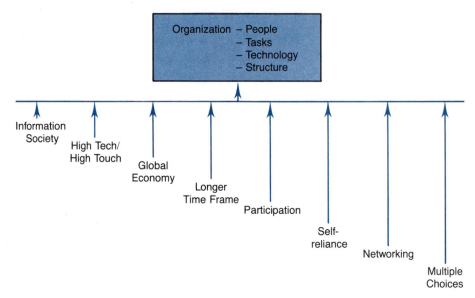

FIGURE 11-1
Pressures causing change in organizations

It is easy to see from this list that the only conclusion we can have is that change is not a periodic evil organizations must face before things return to "normal." Rather, change itself has become the norm. Figure 11-1 provides a framework to explain some of the pressures for change that will face organizations in the near future.

Managing change and coping with the consequences of change has become a primary managerial function. It should have the same status afforded the typical managerial responsibilities such as planning, controlling, staffing, and measuring.

Model for Understanding Change

To understand how change affects the organization and how managers need to manage the process of change, we propose the model in Figure 11-2 as a guide. This model will also help us understand how Emerson is responding to some of its pressures to change.

Forces for Change   Let us first focus our attention on pressures for change. At any point in time organizations face a multitude of forces that have consequences for the firm if not addressed. One force for change that Emerson experienced was increased competition from the market place. Figure 11-1 shows other pressures that are influencing organizations and will cause them to change over time. Which might influence Emerson?

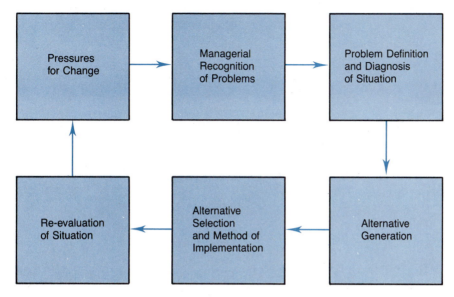

FIGURE 11–2
Model for managing change

Managerial Recognition of Problem It is the manager's job to recognize these forces, as Mr. Knight did, and decide whether the magnitude of the resulting problem is significant enough to consider making changes in either structure, technology, task, or management processes.

Diagnosis of the Situation If the manager decides that the problem warrants attention, the next step is to diagnose the situation. The result of the diagnosis should be a clearer statement of the problem, which entails the establishment of specific change goals. Part of the diagnosis of Emerson's situation might include the fact that their compensation system does not support the development of new products. If Mr. Knight defines his problem as a need to create new products, he must address some of the internal managerial processes, such as compensation, to attain his goal.

During the planning phase of this model, managers must identify constraints that might affect the selection of alternatives in the next phase. For example, a firm may only have $50,000 available to solve any particular problem, such as a technical or equipment problem. In the case of Emerson, the historical tradition of being highly decentralized might act as a constraint as Mr. Knight tries to get the various units to share resources for new product development.

Alternative Generation After identifying the problems and the limiting conditions, the manager can focus attention on considering alternative approaches and techniques to solve the problem. Researchers have proposed a useful framework

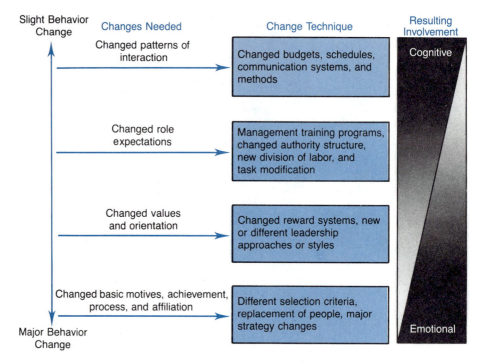

FIGURE 11–3

Matching change techniques with changes needed (Source: Adapted from P. Lawrence and J. Lorsch, *Developing Organizations: Diagnosis and Actions* © 1969, Addison-Wesley, Reading, MA: p. 87, Fig. 6. Reprinted by permission.)

for considering various alternatives and their method of introduction.[3] They stress the importance of carefully diagnosing the organization and its environment and considering the mismatch, if any, between the two. Then the manager should consider what type of behaviors need to be changed and the techniques available to bring about the changes. According to Figure 11–3, on what level of change would Emerson need to focus if it wanted to have its divisional managers develop new products?

Alternative Selection and Method of Implementation   Having developed a set of alternatives to consider, a manager must decide which technique or combination of techniques to use and what approach to follow while implementing the solution. Unfortunately, managers are too often very subjective when making this important decision. Managers have favorite techniques or ideas that may place additional constraints on the decision-making process (review chapter 7 for some examples). Returning to the Emerson problem, we might wonder which alternatives would receive serious consideration knowing that Mr. Knight's previous strategies centered around "relentless cost-cutting." If you were a manager in this organization, what types of alternatives would you suggest? Why?

A complementary issue for the manager to consider is what approach to use while implementing the alternative. In other words, which form of power should a manager apply when implementing an alternative? One researcher categorized three approaches to implementing change.[4] Figure 11–4 summarizes these approaches.

When the manager uses a unilateral approach to change, the subordinate makes little or no contribution. The supervisor relies on position power and authority to unilaterally implement change. The actual process of implementing change is usually by decree. The management tells the employees what the change is and how to implement it. The subordinate's responsibility is to follow the manager's directions.

Another approach recognizes that authority is present in an organization, but that it must be carefully used and shared with subordinates. If the organization has capable subordinates, there can be a sharing of power in reaching important change decisions and implementing those changes. The chief method employed with a shared approach is group decision making and problem solving. The manager and the subordinates equally share responsibility and power to arrive at a method of introducing the needed changes.

A final approach is to delegate power. Under this method, subordinates actively participate in the change program from the onset to the implementation. The subordinates diagnose, analyze, and consider various solutions to the prob-

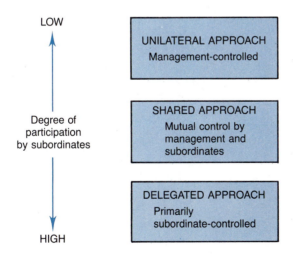

FIGURE 11–4

Three approaches to implementing change (Source: Larry E. Greiner, "Patterns of Organizational Change," *Harvard Business Review* (May–June 1967): 122. Copyright © 1967 by the President and Fellows of Harvard College; all rights reserved.)

lems. The delegated approach is based on the assumption that the subordinates know more about the technological and task aspects of their jobs than does management. Therefore, they should have the most say about the types and methods of change.

Which approach should Emerson apply? Unilateral? Shared? Delegated? Which form would be acceptable to the subordinate? Which method would symbolize the philosophy Mr. Knight is trying to establish?

Evaluation of Change   The final step in any change process should be to evaluate its effectiveness. Did the change indeed result in a more effective organization and more effective employees? In one sense this is the bottom line for the organization to survive. Emerson is trying to change its management's orientation from the short term to a longer time frame. It wants managers to share resources between divisions and become less competitive with each other. But will Mr. Knight know when this has happened? How will he evaluate the programs implemented to bring about these changes? When will he know, in two months, two years, or ever, if the change is effective? The difficulty of this very question has frustrated managers and researchers alike; the result has been few attempts to measure change efforts on any systematic basis.

Having presented a conceptual framework to understand the manager's role in the change process, we now consider how to deal with change, including methods to diagnose the situation, understanding and dealing with change, some strategies for implementing change, and the managerial applications.

Diagnosing the Situation

Throughout this book, we have stressed how important it is for the manager to understand the uniqueness of each situation. This orientation is especially critical when a manager is considering changes within the organization. Diagnosis is the first step to understanding a situation.

For example, a manager might complain that first-line supervision needs to be more sensitive to the line workers. A quick suggestion to correct this situation might be to institute communication training. But what is really meant by being "more sensitive" to the line workers? Does this mean that supervisors need to listen more to their workers? Does it mean the number of grievances submitted is too high? Or does it mean that management wants more worker suggestions about how to improve operations? The manager must first diagnose the specific problem before applying a solution. We have found that most situations require more complex solutions than that offered by a simple communications program.

Traditional versus "Action Research"   One issue with which a manager is confronted initially is what approach to use in diagnosing the situation. The traditional approach and the "action research" approach utilize the same steps to define the problem and arrive at a solution, but the methods to collect the data and analyze it are different. Figure 11–5 summarizes these differences.

	Traditional Approach	**Action Research Approach**
Data collected from:	Workers and supervisors	Everyone in the organization within work groups under study
Data reported to:	Top management, department managers, and employees through written reports	Everyone who participated in study
Focus:	Problem finding	Problem finding, feedback, problem solving
Implications of data are worked on by:	Top management (mainly)	Everyone in work teams, with workshops starting at the top and working down the organization
Outsiders employed to:	Design & administer questionnaire, develop report & solutions	Help management design & administer questionnaires, help facilitate feedback of data, & help work teams problem solve
Action done by:	Top management (mainly)	Work teams at all levels

FIGURE 11–5
Diagnosis: Traditional approach versus action research (Source: Adapted from
A. D. Szilagyi and M. J. Wallace, *Organizational Behavior and Performance*, 3d ed.,
p. 572. Copyright © 1983 by Scott, Foresman and Company. Reprinted by
permission.)

The fundamental concept of "action research" is that it involves those from
whom data is collected in the interpretation of that data and in problem solving.
The idea was first conceived by Dr. Kurt Lewin. He was interested mainly in social

BOX 11–1

Fighting in a Tough Market

Honeywell, Inc. has had a reputation for being a leading manufacturer of control systems for commercial as well as residential markets. In addition, they are a primary defense contractor. But Honeywell also wants to be a computer giant.

This isn't easy, and has caused more grief and problems for Honeywell than profits. International Business Machines Corporation has outflanked Honeywell's information-systems division in hardware, and Honeywell is unknown in the software business. As if this isn't enough, there are internal conflicts and morale problems to compound the issues facing Honeywell as they struggle to expand this division.

Mr. Spencer, Honeywell's chief executive officer, sees little choice since defense spending is slowing down and residential markets are shrinking for the foreseeable future. If Honeywell can

tie together their expertise in control systems, such as heating and cooling, with general data-processing functions, Mr. Spencer promises continued growth and profits for the information-systems division.

However, the job of obtaining record earnings in a new area won't be that easy. First, the heir apparent, Mr. Renier, has a reputation for getting action. Mr. Renier's predecessor had eliminated 1,200 jobs to cut costs, and Mr. Renier has continued that task during his tenure by eliminating 2,300 more. This has earned him the title, "Neutron Jim," a reference to the neutron bomb. "All the buildings were still here. It's just the people who were gone," says a survivor.

But his actions helped reverse the two-year decline in earnings and actually increased pretax profit by 64 percent to $131 million. It must be noted that this turn-around came from cost-cutting and not growth; revenues fell 1 percent.

Another problem facing Honeywell is its customer relations. Many customers complain that they don't have useful software for their expensive hardware. In some cases, they have felt that

Source: From "Hanging Tough, Honeywell is Pushing Its Computer Business Despite Past Problems," by Claudia Waterloo, *The Wall Street Journal* (Monday, 25 June 1984): 1. Reprinted by permission of *The Wall Street Journal*, © Dow Jones & Company, Inc., 1984. All rights reserved.

change and felt that the process of action and evaluation, as well as feedback, was critical in determining the direction and intensity of the social change he was working on. He felt that the data would have greater meaning if the data was interpreted by those who supplied it. In addition, the interpretation coming from the members of the group being surveyed might also expose other areas for study that were not originally conceived by the researchers. Finally, he felt it would help the participants in the research to understand the nature of the problem they faced and would lead them toward solving the problem and developing action steps that they could work on as a total group.

Action research differs from the traditional approach in terms of who works with the data collected during the diagnosis. Action research involves the col-

the company doesn't indicate future product developments and causes them needless problems and expense as they develop their own software. "We'll tell you when it's ready to ship out the door," complains the former president of Honeywell Large Systems Users Association. "That doesn't facilitate long-range planning."

Part of the issue of customer relations stems from the internal problems facing Honeywell. In one instance a group of military-product engineers developed a commercial software program that made it easier for remote terminals to communicate with each other. However, this product wasn't developed along normal company channels and the funds were actually subverted from normal military programs instead of budgeted from the commercial side. The company preferred to wait until another development group (which was company sanctioned with approvals and funds) finished its own slower project.

Not to be dissuaded, one of the frustrated developers showed the program to some of Honeywell's customers on his own. Because of its unique features and popular demand, it has been added to the product catalogue and installed in more than 1,000 locations.

To address these internal problems more directly, Mr. Renier has had bickering managers undergo some training off-site to develop more teamwork between the various functional areas. One such program has the managers help each other scale 12-foot walls and trust one another by falling backward off a ladder into the arms of colleagues. Mr. Renier has also addressed various employee meetings about the large layoffs in the form of a lecture called "tough love," which focused on the tough measures needed to save a company.

While there are some signs of a turn-around (shipments of large computers are expected to increase 20 percent this year), many analysts feel that Honeywell won't know for years if it has really solved its problems or if the revival is a result of a booming economy.

Questions

1. Which pressures for change are present in this story? Which are being addressed by Mr. Renier?
2. Which management systems need to be changed for Honeywell to become more competitive in the computer market? What advice would you offer Mr. Renier to accomplish these changes?
3. What issues are the off-site training addressing? What issues are addressed by the "tough love" talk? Do you agree with the analysts about the turn-around?

lected data being analyzed and fed back to the work group for analysis, interpretation, solution generation, and corrective action. In contrast, the traditional approach usually has an outside "expert" or top management work with the data. In both approaches the data are collected from the organization or specific work groups, but the traditional approach has the analysis and solution generation handled by other than the group studied.

To summarize, the major difference between action research and traditional research is the involvement of those studied in the analysis and interpretation of the data. It is based on the assumption that this involvement will elicit more personal commitment to the needed recommendations and changes, which the traditional approach may not provide.

Force Field Analysis Having chosen either action research or a traditional approach, the manager needs a method to conceptualize the complexities inherent in the change process. One method is the force field analysis, also developed by Kurt Lewin.[5] The framework in Figure 11–6 shows that there are two types of forces that pressure an organization. "Driving forces" are those that encourage change, growth, and development. "Restraining forces" are those that resist change and encourage stability and the status quo. Both driving and restraining forces can be external or internal to the organization. The framework shows the organization in terms of people, tasks, technology, and structure.

Structure refers to the relatively stable set of formally defined working relationships among members of an organization. Examples of structural changes are changing the number of individuals reporting to a manager, changing the level to which a department reports, and adding units or work groups to the organization itself. Technology refers to the equipment and materials, methods of production or operation, and specialized knowledge or experience used to perform tasks. An example of technology change might be the introduction of computerized automation to an organization. Tasks refer to the actual jobs performed in an

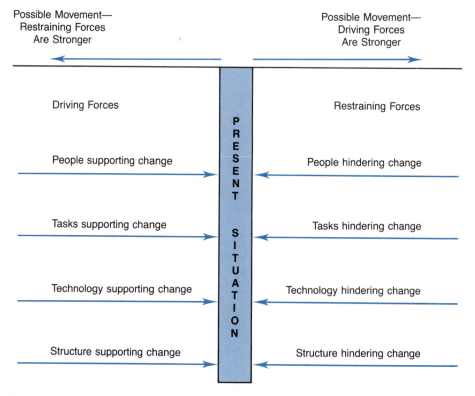

FIGURE 11–6
Forces acting on organizations

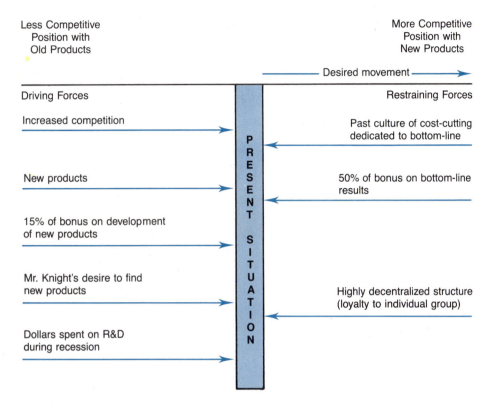

FIGURE 11-7
Force field analysis of Emerson Electric Company

organization, which vary in scope and depth. Change efforts directed at tasks are attempts to alter scope and depth of the activities performed by individuals. People refers, of course, to those individuals in an organization.

We can use the force field analysis to understand the situation facing Mr. Knight of the Emerson Electric Company as he tries to change the organization. Figure 11-7 illustrates the forces acting on Emerson. What advice would you give Mr. Knight based on this analysis?

Data Collection Approaches The approaches that can be used in data collection include interviewing, questionnaires, sensing, polling, collages and drawings, and observations. The best procedure is to use multiple methods to validate each other.

Interviewing. In the interview, the interviewer asks questions directly of the participant. Interviews can be highly structured, using a set of predetermined questions, or highly unstructured, starting with broad, general questions and allowing the participant to lead the way. Interviewing is a direct, personal way to get private views and feelings from the interviewee.

Questionnaires. This is probably the most widely used approach for gathering information. There are a number of predesigned questionnaires available that have been validated and tested for reliability.[6] While traditional questionnaires have the inherent limitation of only finding out what the researcher wants to know, they can be improved if jointly developed by the manager and the respondents. This allows the resulting questionnaire to be broader and reflect the participant's own concerns as a subject of study.

Sensing. Sensing is not an approach commonly used to collect data but is a method by which managers can inform themselves of issues, concerns, needs, and resources of individuals within the organization. It entails an unstructured group interview. The manager selects, usually on a random basis, employees with whom the manager has little or no contact and interviews them. The types of groups can vary from a unit that works together to members from various levels and functions within the organization. Sensing can allow the manager to gather rich information and ideas, to learn how the organizational goals and objectives are understood within the organization, to report on pertinent information that employees should know, and to test proposed courses of action for impact on different groups within the organization.

Polling. Data can be collected through a variation of voting, which can help a group evaluate its current state and diagnose corrective action, if appropriate. A group of coworkers might feel tense, frustrated, and anxious about working together. Such feelings of conflict are usually a symptom of a buried or unresolved issue. Polling can cause that issue to surface for the group to resolve. A manager may suggest that members assign a number to their degree of optimism about whether they will successfully achieve a goal. They are to use a scale of one to ten, with one representing none, five meaning moderate, and ten representing complete. A resulting low average would indicate to the manager that there is an unresolved problem in the group.

Collages and drawings. Collages and drawings are simply artistic expressions of problems. For example, one client of the authors had an organization undergoing internal conflict between departments. Representing the problem graphically clearly showed the conflict between two departments and some of the issues causing the conflict (different goals and styles of managing). Collages may require large sheets of paper, magazines from which pictures and words may be cut, and other materials. Drawings may be in color or in pencil. Both techniques may be prepared by individuals, by subgroups working together, or by the total group. Organizational members are often suspicious of what seems to be a child's game, but the approach easily involves everyone at a level of experiencing that they normally do not obtain in a working situation. One of the authors used this approach with an MBA class that seemed to have lost its motivation. The resulting drawing created tremendous energy among the students and allowed the problem—conflicting needs concerning testing—to be explored. One MBA student said: "I thought you were crazy to ask us to draw pictures. But I'm going to use this with my workers. It helps reduce the barriers between people."

Observations. One can gather information by watching the actual behavior of people at work or interacting with each other. Observation can be very casual (noticing things while walking through a work area) or highly structured (doing a time and motion study). Observation can also range from complete participant observation, where the researcher is also a member of the group being studied, to more detached observation, where the researcher is clearly not part of the group and uses audio-tape and other obvious methods of observation. Casual observation allows the manager to collect data that can be compared with data collected through other techniques. The difference between observation and sensing is that sensing allows the manager to interact with the employees while observation doesn't.

Dealing with Resistance to Change

Change forces are always present and continually demand some response from organizational members. But, as we all know, people do not often readily embrace change initiated by others. Forms of resistance include staying away from work, filing fictitious grievances, sabotaging equipment or performance, and reducing output or productivity. Resistance can be overt, such as slowing down production, or covert, such as not clearly hearing how to operate the new machine and continually not meeting quality standards.[7]

Causes of Resistance An organization proposes change to become more effective; but the individuals whose jobs or tasks are affected by the change may not see that. They see the change from their own perspective, which may be quite different from that of the organization in which they work. To understand this inherent conflict in perspective, let's look at some of the common causes of resistance.

Economic loss. Any change that creates the feeling that certain positions will be eliminated and workers will be laid off or demoted to lesser jobs will probably meet with resistance. Employees fear partial or entire loss of earnings. Even the promise of retraining may not lessen this fear for the worker. Consider the reactions created by the introduction of computers to most work areas—"I wonder how many jobs they can do away with now?"

Knowledge and skill obsolescence. Some organizational changes make individual workers' knowledge and skills, acquired over long periods of time, obsolete. Computers have an image of making past expertise routine. Therefore, a bookkeeper whose security and identity is the mastery of a complex accounting system is understandably threatened by the change to a computerized system.

Fear of unknowns.   Most people become anxious when confronting a new situation for the first time. The anxiety stems from the unknown factors that may call for a new response from the individual. Employees working on a day-to-day basis have some idea about the routine problems that may surface and the reactions of their supervisor to most situations. There is a comfort in that knowledge. When a change occurs, such as an office move, the normal pattern is disrupted and the individual must begin to recreate a normal pattern—"Will I find new friends? Will I have new responsibilities? Who will be my new boss?"

Group resistance.   In chapter 6, we discussed how groups develop norms for individual behavior within the group setting and how this affects task performance. The more attractive or cohesive the group is to its members, the greater the influence that the group can exert on the members. If management initiates new procedures that are viewed as threatening to a group, the group will likely resist the new procedures. This may partially explain what causes "wild cat" strikes by workers when firms introduce changes without proper notification and preparation.

Threats to social system.   Most individuals work because of social as well as economic needs. The social relationships that develop in the workplace are often more important to employees than commonly realized. While a firm may be able to clearly demonstrate that the employees will not suffer any financial loss because of a change, there may still be substantial resistance due to the disruption in social relations and friendships. An example of this type of resistance is the introduction of a new office layout that has people face new walls or new coworkers.

Threats to power and influence.   Resistance can also occur because the proposed changes will restructure and potentially reduce one's power and influence. From chapter 5 we know that one source of power for an individual is the control of something that other people need, such as information or other resources. Yet a force acting on today's organization is the trend toward Management Information Systems (MIS), making more information available to more organizational members. For instance, many management personnel could have access to key performance data through the use of computers, instead of the data being available to only a few upper-level managers. Those managers who would lose this source of influence and power would probably find ways to slow down the introduction of MIS.[8]

Reducing Resistance   Once a manager has identified potential resistance to changes being planned, how can he or she attempt to reduce or avoid that

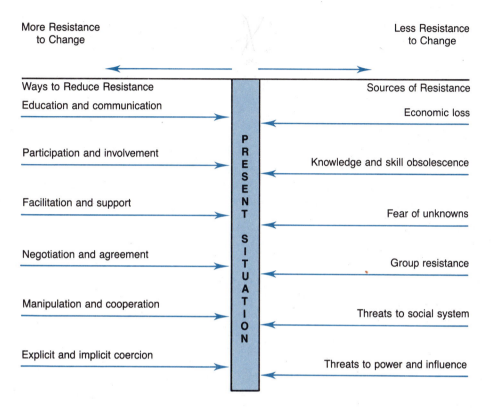

More Resistance to Change ← → Less Resistance to Change

Ways to Reduce Resistance	PRESENT SITUATION	Sources of Resistance
Education and communication		Economic loss
Participation and involvement		Knowledge and skill obsolescence
Facilitation and support		Fear of unknowns
Negotiation and agreement		Group resistance
Manipulation and cooperation		Threats to social system
Explicit and implicit coercion		Threats to power and influence

FIGURE 11–8
Force field analysis: Methods to reduce resistance

resistance? Figure 11–8 applies force field analysis to show both the sources of resistance and some approaches to reducing resistance.

The most popular approaches to deal with resistance to change include the following:[9]

Education and communication. This method deals with the lack of information or inaccurate information about the proposed changes. It suggests educating employees before introducing the change itself. It further suggests openly discussing ideas and issues to help employees see the logic and the need for a change.[10]

Participation and involvement. Using this approach, the initiators of change are able to increase their information level to create a more effective change while allowing those who might resist to get involved. As those affected by the change discuss its design and implementation, new ideas and information can be generated. At the same time, this process allows others to develop a sense of "ownership."[11]

BOX 11–2

Wrong Number: AT&T Manager Meets Resistance

When William F. Buehler's bosses at AT&T gave him permission to establish his own methods of operation with a new marketing department, Mr. Buehler took them literally. Instead of using Bell's standard practice of reams of paperwork, endless meetings, and a strict chain of reporting relationships to get approvals, Mr. Buehler discarded the planning manuals and employee tests and put the salespeople on a compensation plan that was unmatched at Bell. Besides using a commission-based reward system, Mr. Buehler fired those who couldn't meet the sales goals.

Did it work? Only too well! Sales of this unit outperformed other units selling larger, more expensive information systems. The term used to describe the energy level of the salesforce was "Buehler Fever."

However, Mr. Buehler is no longer head of this group. He still is a vice president, but of some planning position. Many of his former subordinates are worried about what's going to happen next to the unit. "We're all upset and worried that we'll lose our new culture," says James Lewis, an account executive.

What happened? Isn't this the kind of innovation that AT&T needs to enter the competitive marketing world that divestiture brought?

The story is complicated, but some comments by various interested parties help clarify it. Mr. Robert Casale, who ran the rival but more traditional sales program and who became the new boss of Mr. Buehler's group, states that the change was designed to "integrate the two discrete sales staffs in order to eliminate duplication in central support services." Mr. Lewis speculated that "Bill Buehler ruffled some feathers at the top. I wouldn't rule out that his different style of leadership caused him to be pushed out of a line position." David Nadler of a New York consulting firm said, "Frequently in entrenched organizations where something new and entrepreneurial is tried, the experiment may not survive because it's too threatening to the old line."

What was Mr. Buehler's approach? To set up his sales group, Mr. Buehler used the book *In Search Of Excellence* as a guide. He would use phrases from the book in memos and meetings—

Source: Adapted from "Wrong Number: AT&T Manager Finds His Effort to Galvanize Sales Meets Resistance," by Monica Langley, *The Wall Street Journal* (16 December 1983): 1. Reprinted by permission of *The Wall Street Journal*, © Dow Jones & Company, Inc. 1983. All rights reserved.

Facilitation and support. In a situation where workers are resisting because of problems of adjustment, a simple method is to be supportive. This can include providing emotional support, simply listening, giving time off the job, or providing training for acquiring new skills.

Negotiation and agreement. Certain changes clearly restructure the amount of influence and power that a group may have after the change. Because of this

"Keep it simple," "reward results, not process," "customer is king." "That little list of points was the only guide I gave my new work force in January—no detailed plans or directives. I wanted the team to know from the start that this was an entrepreneurial venture, and they were to abide by these points in a way that worked best for them," says Mr. Buehler.

He also visited his various branches across the nation rather than having the personnel come to him in New York. "The staffers in my branch have been with Bell for years, but this was the very first time any of them had ever seen an AT&T vice president. . . . And then he actually sat down with the billing staff and ate hoagie sandwiches," stated Mr. Focazio, one of those managers he visited.

He also used peer pressure to get results, besides his own authority. Sales results were posted on boards located for everyone to see. "As hokey as it may sound, when a person comes to work every day and sees his red tab isn't the highest one up there, he will work that much harder."

While the initial attempts to change the work methods of his own group weren't smooth, the group eventually got the hang of it and began to make demands on Mr. Buehler. As the orders for more products increased, the managers wanted assurances that the products would be available on time from other units responsible for production. When they wanted less paperwork, Mr.

Buehler reduced the contract from four pages to one. When they wanted quicker approvals of customer designs and bids, Mr. Buehler had a committee respond in days rather than the normal months of Bell System deliberation. "Decisions that would have taken two years in the Bell System were made in days by Bill Buehler," states another account executive.

But with Mr. Buehler leaving his group, the traditional way of doing things—"The Bell Way"— seems to have won this battle. However, we may not have heard the last of Mr. Buehler—"I'm meeting with my new planning staff, and . . . we are having a difference of opinion on how we view the world, but I'm used to this kind of resistance. Hey, it's not stopped me before, and it won't now."

Questions

1. If the programs which Mr. Buehler is implementing will help AT&T become competitive, why is he meeting resistance from the very people who placed him in that position?
2. What resistances are present in this story? How would you go about dealing with them?
3. Describe the "old AT&T culture" and the "new Buehler culture." Will Mr. Buehler be able to implement his ideas in his new job? What advice would you give him?

threat of loss, resistance may only be reduced if the firm provides some incentives to employees for compliance with the change. For example, in a labor-management situation, incentives might involve the trade-offs for instituting a new job classification system with increased future job security or financial benefits. For example, the Communication Workers of America negotiated for U.S. West, a holding company of regional telephone companies, to set aside $10 million to retrain workers displaced by computers.[12]

Manipulation and cooptation. When the previously mentioned approaches do not work or seem too costly, managers may resort to some covert methods of influencing employees to accept change. They may choose to be selective about who gets what information and how much information, how accurate the information is, and when to disseminate the information. Another technique would be giving key roles to certain individuals or groups during the design or implementation of the change to gain their cooperation.[13]

Explicit and implicit coercion. Some changes demand swift implementation to take advantage of benefits. In addition, change initiators might possess considerable power. Both situations lend themselves to managers threatening employees with a loss of jobs, decreased promotional opportunities, or job changes to gain compliance with change.

Implementing Change

Once an organization or a manager decides that changes are needed and has established the change objectives, several other issues need to be addressed before implementation is initiated. This section explores some of these issues, including what type of change agent is appropriate, what type of interventions should be considered, and how to approach evaluation.

Types of Change Agent A change agent is an individual or team of individuals whose responsibility is to design and introduce a change. Organizational change efforts frequently require an outsider or someone from inside the organization with an outsider's perspective, such as a new manager, a manager from another unit, or a manager who doesn't seem bound by the firm's culture, politics, or traditions. While very little research has explored what type of change agent is most effective, some research has been done to identify different types of change agents, according to their characteristics and methods of implementing change.

One researcher, Noel Tichy, identified four basic types of change agents: "Outside Pressure" type (OP), "People-Change-Technology" type (PCT), "Analysis-For-The-Top" type (AFT), and "Organization Development" type (OD).[14] These types differ in certain areas: personal characteristics, values relative to change, conceptualizations about what mediates change, change techniques employed, and the setting in which change work is carried out.

Outside pressure type. OPs work to change systems from outside the organization. They are not members of the system they are trying to change and use such tactics as mass demonstrations, civil disobedience, and violence to accomplish their objectives. One such agent related, "I go into communities where I am invited and help create a strategy to meet whatever problem the group has. Often my role is in offering options that are more radical than the community might accept. This is done to encourage the group to consider other alternatives."[15]

People-change-technology type. This type of change agent works for management to change the way people behave through various behavioral science technologies. PCTs may be concerned with worker motivation and morale, including absenteeism, quality and quantity of work, and turnover. The methods used by PCTs include job enrichment, management by objectives, and behavior modification. The major assumption underlying this orientation is that if individuals change their behavior, the organization will also change, especially if enough individuals change. They "help individuals . . . focus on definition of goals, obstacles, . . . individual motivational patterns . . . and individual self-development."[16]

Analysis-for-the-top type. The focus of an AFT is on changing the organizational structure or technology so as to improve output and efficiency. This approach relies primarily on the rationality of individuals. The AFT change agent generally has an operations research or similar technical background. Specific approaches might include introducing computerized information-processing systems and developing new task groups to operate the innovations. An AFT might consult mainly with corporations to make strategy decisions and to make operating decisions and control management processes, such as investing and production control."[17]

Organization development type. OD change agents focus their attention on internal processes such as intergroup relations, communication, and decision making. Their diagnosis includes a strong focus on organizational culture, and their intervention strategy is often referred to as a cultural change approach. Says one such agent, "I work on the human side of the enterprise. That is, I help people . . . work out their problems of interpersonal relationships and communications, conflicts of interest, etc. . . . In this way I help an organization develop and modify its governmental and problem-solving mechanisms."[18] This approach to the change process grew out of such areas as sensitivity training, survey data feedback, and team building.

Tichy also looked at how each type of change agent implements decisions for change (see Table 11–1). The most striking difference is that over half of the OPs reported that they had to develop power to implement change. Since they work outside the organization, this is to be expected. OD change agents work more with the entire system so their response indicates that they provide information to others who will make the decisions about change. Both the PCTs and AFTs tend to use the influence mode to implement change in the organization. A distinction that we can assume is that the AFT change agent is an expert, so the target of influence is top management; whereas the PCT tries to influence whichever group of individuals he or she is trying to change (for example, using behavior modification with first-line supervisors).

As a manager, what type of change agent is appropriate for your organization? Which change agent would be most effective for the changes you are considering? The answer will be influenced by the amount of involvement re-

TABLE 11-1
Which types use which means to implement change

Implementation Means	Types of Change Agents			
	Outside Pressure	People Change Technology	Organization Development	Anlaysis for Top
Develop the power to implement change	52%	0%	0%	0%
Influence individuals within the system to implement change	36%	67%	30%	56%
Provide information for decision-makers to make own decision	12%	33%	69%	44%
Total (number per category)	100% (43)	100% (18)	100% (33)	100% (39)

Source: Noel Tichy and Harvey Hornstein, "Stand When Your Number Is Called: An Empirical Attempt to Classify Types of Social Change Agents," *Human Relations,* vol. 29, no. 10 (1976): 963. Used with permission of Plenum Publishing Corporation.

quired to successfully gain commitment to the changes. Figure 11-9 depicts the relationship between the amount of involvement needed from the organization and from the type of change agent.

If a manager does not want to be involved in the change process, then the "expert" used to plan and implement the change would probably be the Analysis-For-the-Top change agent. On the other hand, if the manager wants to be intimately involved in all aspects of the change process, the Organization Development change agent would be more appropriate because of the system-wide methods that OD change agents utilize. While it is harder to classify exactly where the People-Change-Technology change agents fit, it seems likely that their methods fall more in the middle of the continuum. The manager becomes somewhat involved when calling the PCT into the organization and outlining some of the problems to be addressed. The change agent and the manager may together collect data to help pick which specific methods to use. After that the PCT usually designs and implements the changes required without the manager's direct involvement. Finally, the Outside Pressure change agent is external to the organization; therefore, managerial involvement is usually limited to responding to the various tactics used by the OP.

Types of Intervention Intervention describes a method or means to manage change more successfully. These means may include either responding to forces for change or creating forces to help prepare organizational members to accept the change.

As we know from the discussion so far, the organizational change is a complex and comprehensive process. Table 11-2 categorizes the various types of interventions that can address the many aspects of the change process. Interventions can focus on the individual, the work group, several groups, or the total

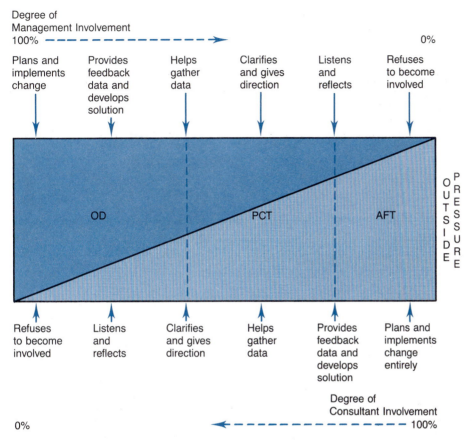

Degree of
Management Involvement
100% - - - - - - - - - - - - → 0%

Plans and implements change

Provides feedback data and develops solution

Helps gather data

Clarifies and gives direction

Listens and reflects

Refuses to become involved

OD PCT AFT

OUTSIDE PRESSURE

Refuses to become involved

Listens and reflects

Clarifies and gives direction

Helps gather data

Provides feedback data and develops solution

Plans and implements change entirely

Degree of
Consultant Involvement
0% ← - - - - - - - - - - - - 100%

FIGURE 11–9
Management versus consultant involvement

TABLE 11–2
Types of interventions

Individual	Work Group	Intergroup	Total Organization
Laboratory training	Team building	Conflict resolution	Survey feedback
Life planning	Conflict resolution	Third party facilitating	Management by
Training programs	Process consultation	Organizational	objectives
Job design		mirroring	Technostructural
Role analysis			activities
Coaching and			Confrontation
counseling			meetings
			Quality of Work Life
			(Sociotechnical)
			programs

organization. Before reviewing several of the most widely used intervention methods, we must emphasize that these interventions are aimed at specific change objectives, which should be identified during the planning and diagnostic phases of the change process.

Laboratory training.   Laboratory training is an intensive workshop for an individual or work group whose major goals include (1) the development of a spirit of inquiry and willingness to experiment with one's role in the organization and the world; (2) an increased awareness of other people and expanded interpersonal awareness; (3) improved sincerity in relationships with others; (4) greater ability to collaborate with superiors, peers, and subordinates rather than to use authoritative approaches; and (5) greater ability to resolve conflict through developing alternatives and problem-solving techniques, as opposed to manipulating, coercing, or compromising. This approach is also referred to as sensitivity training. Ranging from a few days to a week, it focuses on giving participants a better understanding of themselves and how groups function. Individuals learn how they act in interpersonal and group situations, how others perceive their actions, and how others react to them.

The laboratory training can involve a stranger t-group or a variant t-group.[19] The stranger t-group is composed of members who do not work together and may not know each other. The variant t-group is composed of individuals who do work together. The learning focuses on improving the working relationships within the group. In this situation, the change intervention is geared to the work group level and could be classified accordingly (see Table 11–2).

Life planning.   This intervention consists of a series of activities to help individuals look at their values, life experiences, goals, and action-steps to prepare them to achieve their objectives. It can be used very effectively in conjunction with other interventions, such as job redesign, role analysis, and counseling.

The intervention attempts to help individuals take more control over their work and life choices.[20] It is based on the assumption that as people more actively plan to achieve their future goals, they can see how to better perform in their present position and prepare themselves for future opportunities. The result is more satisfied and realistic employees who are continually improving their skills.

Job design.   This approach entails changing the type or number of tasks an individual performs.[21] It has become increasingly popular in recent years (see chapter 9). The most discussed form of job design is job enrichment. Other forms include work simplification, job enlargement, job rotation, and autonomous work groups.

The impetus for looking at specific jobs centers around the popular notion that reducing job routine will relieve worker boredom and result in a more satisfied and productive worker. The job design intervention involves examining the current structure of the worker's activities for the purpose of restructuring them for performance improvement.

Team building.   Team building is a series of sessions to improve the effectiveness and performance of individuals who work together on a continuing basis.[22] A team building session is not a typical staff meeting; it may last from two to five days, usually away from the facility. The focus of the sessions are on group goals, work distribution, and how the group functions to more effectively reach its objectives. In many cases, an outsider (this can be an internal change agent) facilitates the process.

Process consultation.   A variation of the team-building approach is process consultation.[23] Process consulting is a set of activities on the part of a consultant to help the manager and the work group understand and act upon their own processes to become more effective. Instead of trying to accomplish the team improvement over several concentrated days, the process consultant attends normal work group meetings over several months to help the group develop more effective interactions. Typical activities include stressing communication patterns in meetings, clarifying roles and responsibilities, and resolving conflicts among work group members. Ideally, the work group intervention would be a combination of a team-building session followed by periodic process consultation to reinforce or clarify the improved working relationships back on the job.

Conflict resolution.   Conflict resolution focuses on getting conflicting groups to bring to the surface the real and imaginary sources of tension occurring between them. They then test to see which issues lend themselves to being resolved and propose various solutions to find one acceptable to both groups.

While conflict can and does occur *within* groups, this intervention is focused on the conflict *between* work groups or units because of their different needs.[24] For example, manufacturing wants to run its production lines as fast as possible and is usually willing to accept a certain amount of below-standard output. On the other hand, sales wants its customers satisfied so repeat sales occur. Below-standard products may cause customers to buy elsewhere. This situation can easily lead to conflict between production and sales.

During a conflict resolution session, which can last several days, the groups explore how they can make their respective goals more compatible and therefore eliminate possible future dysfunctional conflicts. (Remember that certain organizational conflict is healthy and a source of creativity—see chapter 8.)

Organizational mirroring.   A variation of conflict resolution is organizational mirroring.[25] This technique requires that each group indicate how it views its own behavior and the behavior of the other groups involved, and how it thinks the other groups view their behavior. This data is then exchanged, and a given group can see two main discrepancies: the difference between how it sees other groups and how those other groups see themselves, and the difference between how it sees itself and how the other groups see it.

Once the groups have shared data, they can view each other more realistically and identify issues that are preventing them from working together more closely toward certain organizational goals. This intervention differs from conflict resolution in terms of intensity with which the groups regard one another. If, historically, the groups haven't worked together very well, then conflict can become a form of company mythology, rather than real issues that lend themselves to accommodation. For example, union-management relations could be very emotional, with each side having built a negative image of the other. "We've never been able to work with them, not since the 1970 strike." In this case, the most effective method of changing the history might be to use the organizational mirroring first and follow up with conflict resolution, once the emotional barriers have been reduced to the point that the real issues can be identified.

Survey feedback.   This approach involves systematically collecting data about the organization, primarily through questionnaires.[26] Occasionally, interviews are used to supplement the questionnaires. The collected data are analyzed and fed back to the various work groups for analysis, interpretation, and corrective action, if needed. The two major components of this process are the attitude survey and small discussion groups. During the small group discussion, an outside person (again, this may be an internal change agent) helps the group work together to pinpoint the findings, problems, and solutions. The survey feedback acts as both the diagnostic process and the change intervention.

Management by objectives.   The MBO process integrates goals at various levels through the goal-setting process. Goal setting requires not only determining clear, concise objectives, but also developing realistic action plans and systematically measuring the resulting performance. Finally, there are built-in corrective measures to deal with problems of goal changes.

   MBO is both a management philosophy and a well-defined process.[27] Its managerial philosophy centers around the concept of being proactive and participatory rather than reactive and autocratic in management approach.

Sociotechnical.   This approach is really a series of various interventions aimed at changing the relationship between social and technical aspects of one's job. A popular title used by companies and union organizations is "Quality of Work Life."[28] This method looks at several questions. What are the major elements inherent in employees' jobs that cause dissatisfaction and lower performance? How is employee well-being affected by the workplace and changes in the work environment? To what extent are job conditions determined by the technology used and the structure in which the jobs exist? Can the organization's performance be positively affected by improving the quality of work life of the individual worker? Answers to these questions provide the information needed to design tasks and jobs so that the resulting work is more efficient for the company and more satisfying for the worker.

   While this list of questions is not exhaustive, it does indicate the direction of the intervention. An example of this approach is the autonomous work group, which has its foundations in the British coal mining industry.[29] The autonomous work group evolved to replace the traditional assembly line with work teams. Instead of each individual doing one or two separate tasks over and over again, the team is responsible for a whole unit of production. The traditional approach to coal mining was specialization, with each individual performing only one task. By contrast, the autonomous work group concept requires individuals to be cross-trained to handle any job within their shift's work schedule. They would also perform some of the supervisor's tasks, such as training new members, scheduling work, and keeping track of who performed which tasks during the shift.

One application of this intervention is used by the Saab auto company in Sweden.[30] The automobile engine is assembled by a small group of five to ten workers. They all have related duties, and they decide among themselves how to assign tasks and distribute their effort. They rotate jobs—each team member learns how to do all the assembly tasks. The group has broadened responsibilities to include inspection, quality control, housekeeping, and maintenance. Each group puts together the cylinder block, heads, rods, and crankshaft. They work at their own pace and they determine the time they will spend on breaks. The results have been encouraging; there is evidence of higher satisfaction, lower turnover and absenteeism, and improved quality of work.[31]

Evaluation of the Change Process   A final step in the change process is evaluating the progress or lack of progress that has been made. This is also the most difficult step. First, it is difficult to measure change over an extended period of time because of other major, often uncontrollable changes that influence the effects of the original change effort. For example, the elimination of a major competitor would have a significant impact upon an organization undergoing some internal changes to become more effective. It would be difficult to say definitively whether the change effort caused the positive results or the elimination of competition made organizational inefficiencies less noticeable.

Second, it is difficult for researchers to gain entry into organizations to perform systematic evaluations. Management is usually concerned about the disruption of normal operations as the researcher tries to interview or get questionnaires filled out. In addition, the very act of collecting evaluation data may affect the results of the evaluation.

Finally, the evaluation process is affected by the clarity of the originally stated change goals. Management is often concerned about correcting a problem immediately, which can result in an abbreviated diagnosis with unclear or partially accurate goals. As the change intervention is implemented, the diagnosis may change and so should the original goals. If this redirection does not occur, the resulting evaluation will be affected.

While these problems adversely affect evaluation and make it the weakest link in the change process, it is also the greatest source of reinforcement for management to continue its efforts to make the organization more effective. The only alternative to systematic measurement procedures is the "gut feel" of top management—hardly a strong support or guide during difficult times.

Therefore, it is important to try to measure in some way whether or not the intervention is working. The following are general guidelines:

1. Do not establish just one measurement that only occurs at the conclusion of the change. Instead, conduct a series of measurements over an extended period of time. This is important because change does not always take place immediately after the intervention. In some cases there is a lag time, which reflects people learning how to really use the new system.

2. Recognize how complex the change process is—cause-and-effect relationships are rarely very direct in nature, much less completely understood by researchers. An intervention may not have a direct cause-effect relationship to other factors. For example, implementing an MBO system may not improve coordination between departments immediately. Other factors may hinder the interdepartment cooperation, and the MBO system may only address some of the issues.

3. Don't be overly dependent on quantitative measures to the exclusion of some qualitative ones. Most managers are more comfortable with numerical signs of progress, such as profits, costs, down-time, turnover, and accidents. Yet many interventions will first affect employee feelings and reactions to the intervention itself. These qualitative measures can be an effective guide to the depth, speed, and even initial success of a particular change intervention. If people are reporting positive results, this may provide additional incentive to continue the process even though the quantitative measures haven't responded yet. An example of qualitative measurement is an attitude survey or even testimonials about the change progress.

Summary of Key Concepts

1. Organizations face many pressures for change, including need for more information, higher technology, longer time frame, more self-reliance, and multiple choices.

2. Our model for the change process includes pressures for change, recognition of problems, diagnosis of situation, generation and selection of alternatives, and evaluation of the change.

3. During the diagnosis stage, a manager can use the traditional approach with little employee involvement or the "action-research" approach with more employee involvement. Data collection can include interviewing, questionnaires, sensing, polling, collages and drawing, and observations.

4. The change process may meet with resistance caused by the effects of the change. Resistance can stem from several sources—economic loss, knowledge and skill obsolescence, fear of the unknown, group resistance, threats to social system, and threats to power and influence.

5. The most effective methods to reduce resistance include education and communication, participation and involvement, facilitation and support, and negotiation and agreement.

If these do not produce results, management may resort to manipulation, cooptation, and forms of coercion.

6. There are four basic types of change agents, who vary in change goals, tactics for implementation, and values associated with their change methodology. These are the outside pressure (OP) type, analysis-for-the-top (AFT) type, people change technology (PCT) type, and organization development (OD) type.

7. Interventions are the means to manage the change. The major interventions can be classified by levels—individual, group, intergroup, and organization. The proper method can be chosen after a thorough diagnosis.

8. While evaluation is difficult because of other, uncontrollable events and the potential disruption caused by the evaluation, it should be attempted to help support the change effort and, if necessary, redirect it.

Key Terms

Action research	Intervention
Change agent	Planned change
Data collection approaches	Resistance
Force field analysis	Traditional research

MANAGERIAL APPLICATIONS

In this section of the chapter, we look at some of the ways in which managers actually deal with change in organizations. We see how the technical and social aspects affect the implementation of change. We also compare how one manager reduced resistance to change by simply doing some conscious thinking about the social consequences of the change. We explore how to apply force field analysis to the conditions surrounding the change. Finally, we see how a very divergent style of leadership—revolution—can be effective in managing change.

Management of change is one of the areas in which a manager's skill is very visible, for initiating change in an organization or managing a change that has been initiated by someone else—usually someone higher in the organization—necessitates taking *action*. A leader's action is apparent and can not be hidden, as can, for example, a discussion of leadership philosophy.

It is useful to refer again to the model of the change process that we talked about earlier, for many of the application examples can be directly related to that model (see Figure 11–2).

Problem Definition and Diagnosis

One of the most common patterns that we see effective managers using in the area of problem definition and diagnosis really has its base in some of the more classic writings about managing change. In the early 1950s, Paul Lawrence of the

Harvard Business School developed some concepts concerning change that seem to be particularly useful to practicing managers.[32] Lawrence notes that there are really two components to any organizational change, a *technical* part of the change, and a *social* part of the change. The technical part deals with those actions that will increase efficiency, lower costs, move the organization to the forefront of technology, or other desirable technical objectives. Social components of the change are those that deal with the social disruptions that will occur in accomplishing the technical goals.

For example, in instituting a new procedure to increase efficiency, it may be that interactions required of the people involved will be significant, and will negatively, from their point of view, change the satisfying ways they have developed to relate to coworkers. Under the "old" system, Charlie may have been at the center of a communications network and received all of the status rewards that go with that position. Under the new system, Charlie may no longer be in that desirable (to him) position. He may even feel that he has been demoted, though nothing like that has taken place officially. In the view of those initiating the change such disruptions of relationships are secondary in importance to the desire to achieve the technical objectives of the change.

Lawrence took his analysis a step further when he declared that, based on his observations and research, the often heard statement "people resist change" was not as universally applicable as it seemed. Certainly people resisted some changes, but they also enthusiastically accepted many others. How would you feel about a decrease in tuition, for instance? Or a new rule limiting the number of term papers that could be assigned in any academic period? People tend to resist changes that disrupt satisfying social relationships. People tend to resist changes that have been imposed without their having had a chance to participate in the planning of the change. People tend to resist changes designed by specialists far from the scene of the action and imposed by organizational edict. Looking at your own experience, identify three or four changes that you strongly resisted and three or four that you enthusiastically accepted. Do you see a pattern that relates to the social and technical aspects of change that we have been discussing?

Alternative Selection

Knudson, Woodworth, and Bell take this concept several steps further as they talk about the process of selecting an alternative that will most likely prevent resistance to change.[33] They state that it is easier to plan a change in such a way that resistance to that change is reduced rather than to let the resistance develop and have to overcome it later. The key is to pay adequate attention to the social aspects of the change in the planning stage, thus reducing the possibilities of later resistance. The "best" change is one that accomplishes the technical goals with as little disruption of social factors as possible. The phrase *no change-change* describes that ideal situation in which changes have been made in the technical aspects of the situation while keeping the social aspects constant.

We often use this approach in management seminars when dealing with the topic of managing change. Our first step is to ask the participants to analyze a change situation in which they are presently involved or will soon be involved, by identifying the social factors and the technical factors in the situation. Next, we ask them to develop two or three alternative plans of action that would permit them to achieve the technical aspects of the change while keeping the social factors as close to unchanged as possible. The following example indicates how this can be done.

A U.S. Army colonel in charge of the financing and budgeting for a military organization in Germany was faced with the need for a change in the budgeting process. The budgeting process covered five operating units, and, because of the way these units were involved in the process, important value judgements about what was best for these operating units were being made by the finance and budgeting unit.

The existing system and the proposed change are as follows:

- *Existing System*. Finance and budget section gathers necessary information from each of the units and develops a budget for the entire command, including decisions on which projects in each operating units are most important.
- *Proposed System*. Operating units would prepare their own budgets—a process designed by the budget and finance group starting at the lowest operating unit and involving all operating units. (Estimated time for the change—two years)

The colonel listed the following expected sources of resistance to the proposed system:

- Existing people at all levels would have to be retrained in budgeting skills.
- Additional budget people would have to be hired by the operating units.
- Operating units know very little about budgeting.
- Combat officers know that their soldiers regard "paper pushing" as low status.
- It would take time away from combat duties, which the officers like much better.
- Personnel would be worried that they could not do this new task.
- Personnel would see the new task as interfering with more important duties.

The colonel was asked how he was going to successfully implement this change in light of all of the anticipated resistance. He replied that he was close to the general and the general would order the new change instituted, even though it would take a lot of time and effort and pressure to get it successfully accomplished.

He was asked to re-examine his proposal in light of the information we have been discussing and see if he couldn't devise an alternative plan that would accomplish the important technical aspects while reducing the amount of social change required by the original alternative. After working *only fifteen minutes* he came up with the following revision in his proposal.

Revised Proposal. The budget and finance office would continue to develop the budget in the existing way up to the point at the end of the process where a value judgement decision on program priorities had to be made (that is, deciding the relative importance of programs). At this point, commanding officers of the operating units would be asked to assign budget priorities to their own programs. The budget process would then proceed according to current practices.

The colonel in charge of budget and finance activities felt that the officers in the operating units would be glad to set priorities for their own projects and did not anticipate any resistance to the new plan. He estimated that it would take about two days to implement the new change! Note that in both proposals the technical aspects of the change were handled well, but in the revised proposal the possibilities of resistance to the change were reduced considerably by paying attention to the social aspects of the change and keeping them as stable as possible. Note that the only changes made in the social aspects of the change were positive ones from the point of view of the operating commanders, for they were permitted to play an important, high-status role in the budget process without losing any of the advantages (to them) of the old system. Note, too, that the time required to come up with a new plan with significant potential to reduce resistance to the change was extremely small. A very good investment!

Remember, it is much easier to plan a change in such a way that you reduce potential resistance to change than to devote efforts and resources later on to overcoming resistance that might have been prevented. The example of the colonel is not unusual. Typically, managers can develop better plans—ones that in their judgement are very likely to reduce resistance to change—by spending just a small amount of time developing alternatives that consider the importance of the social aspects of change.

Applications of Force Field Analysis

We talked quite a bit about force field analysis as an analytical tool in the first part of the chapter. Does it really work? Do managers actually use this kind of theoretical approach in analyzing change situations. Based on our experience, the answer is an unequivocal "*yes!*"

One of the best systematic explanations of force field we have seen from a manager's point of view is contained in the book *Management: An Experiential Approach.*[34] The concept is described much as we have described it, but the manager is then given a structured approach to help put the concept into action. The manager briefly describes the situation as it now exists, and the desired situation. Having done this in just a few words, the manager then identifies those forces that are tending to keep the situation as it is, and those that are tending to change the situation in the desired direction. Managers should look in four broad areas for either driving or restraining forces, for although forces may not stem from each of these areas, they are too important to overlook.

- *Technological forces*—forces that relate to the technology of the change. For example, a manager may desire to increase productivity by 10 percent, but the equipment now available can't do this. The fact that the technology doesn't exist is a restraining force. But if the technology did exist, it would be a driving force pushing toward the desired change.
- *Organizational forces*—forces that relate to the particular organization involved (its culture, management practices, norms, and history). These include any factor peculiar to the organization, from which a driving or a restraining force might come.
- *Individual forces*—forces related to any of the individuals involved in the situation. For instance, the proposed change may be in an area of great interest to the organization's CEO. The fact that the CEO is interested in the change becomes a driving force. But perhaps members of a work group to be affected by the change don't want to break up their group. This desire becomes a restraining force. Charlie wants the change to go through because he thinks that if it does he will be promoted. Grace doesn't want the change implemented because if it is she may have to move to another city. Any of these personal considerations can be the source of driving or restraining forces.
- *External forces*—any forces outside the organization that relate to the change. For example, a competitor may initiate a new, bold, extensive advertising campaign. This campaign may be the basis of a driving force to change our current advertising campaign. Government regulations can be driving or restraining forces pushing for or against change in the organization.

After identifying the driving and restraining forces in the situation, the manager then evaluates the forces according to how strong they are. This is not a sophisticated evaluation, merely an indication of whether a force is strong, mid-level, or weak. In fact, attempting to categorize the strengths of the forces too finely would probably cause more problems than it was worth.

The next step is to evaluate the forces in terms of the ability to control or influence them. Again, this evaluation can be quite general, as it is probably impossible to evaluate the forces with great precision. The purpose of this step is to determine the most effective places to apply the resources availale to implement the change. For example, a restraining force may be very strong but there may be nothing that a manager can do now to influence or control that force. It would thus be a misuse of resources to attempt to work on that force. The manager might better deal with a force over which he or she has a great deal of influence, for the possibility of positive payoff is much higher.

Thus far, the entire process has been one of analysis, but the next step is to develop an action plan (or plans) to effectively deal with the strongest forces over which the manager has the most control. Ideally, the manager should develop several alternate plans of dealing with these forces so that the best one can be chosen. Too often managers develop only one action plan without giving adequate thought to possible alternates.

The final step is to implement the desired action plan.

Our experience with a number of managers indicates that they develop great skill in working with force field analysis in a very short period of time, and it is not unusual for a manager to make significant progress with a real "back-home" problem in just a few hours.

But it is important to recognize that force field is not a panacea. Simply because the manager does some analysis does not mean that effective action plans automatically pop into existence. It is not objective. The entire process is based on the managers *perception* of the situation. That perception may have little relation to reality. But at least the process is systematic and helps to prevent some important factor being overlooked. It also helps to get a "handle" on what may be a complex situation.

So while there are some problems with the concept, practicing managers usually find that it is one of the most practical and useful of all of the management tools in the area of change.

Two final thoughts about force field are based on the experiences of managers. While it is primarily an analytical tool, some managers use it also as a communications tool. They instruct their staffs in how to do a force field analysis and then require that everyone bring their analysis of a certain situation to a staff meeting. These analyses are shared, providing an opportunity to ascertain how close the staff's perception of the situation is, and providing a natural jumping off place for further discussion that should result in more complete understanding and more effective changes.

Some managers have found it very effective to think of taking action in stages. Many managers have told us that one of the strongest driving forces in a particular situation is their desire to have a change implemented. They can put either positive or negative pressures on their subordinates until the change is made, if they choose to do so. Because they have this opportunity, managers feel that if a change is desired relatively quickly, the most effective approach is to increase the driving forces, that is, the attention that the manager pays to the situation. Recognizing, however, that an organization has a limited capacity to deal with pressure, they take some long-term actions to relieve some of the restraining forces so that their organization will retain its ability to accommodate pressure. Thus, their action pattern is to increase driving forces, getting a relatively quick change but then later to take actions to reduce restraining forces over the longer term, thus keeping the continuous infusion of pressure from damaging the organization.

Evolution or Revolution?

A word or two on how changes are made in organizations is in order. Some managers advocate a slow, deliberate process of change, with a great deal of participation and discussion by all involved before the change is finally initiated. Another approach advocates making a change very quickly, even though there might be significant resistance, then dealing with that resistance when it arises. Managers who adopt this approach usually say things such as "we had to do something quickly, and I didn't want to spend all of my time in meetings talking about it," or "lots of discussions would have caused more trouble than they were worth. I just decided to do it and deal with the flack later."

As we noted in our discussion of choosing strategies for changes, there are trade-offs in using any of the strategies noted, and the manager must make that trade-off according to his or her objectives in a particular situation. But we do find tendencies in the literature to downgrade the "power" kinds of strategies. We recognize that they are alternatives, but we also tend to think that no really good manager would use such a strategy. But managers do use power strategies, and some managers use them very effectively.

For example, one manager we know has made a career of using power strategies to bring about unpopular changes in potentially volatile situations. He has been brought in to initiate significant changes and has done so very quickly, riding over all opposition. He is the target of all kinds of protests, invectives, and sometimes personal threats. But the changes do get made. He takes a lot of heat for a year or two but then is replaced by a manager more concerned with feelings, participation, and the social implications of change. This new manager then deals with all the resistance to the change that has developed, but reverting to the old system is not an option. The resistance is dealt with in terms of the new system. Grumbling continues but eventually the opposition dies out or at least is reduced to a tolerable level.

This particular manager has developed a reputation for being greatly skilled in implementing change in this fashion. Over the past fifteen years he has done this using power strategies in the same industry in five separate organizations in five different locations. In essence, he has made a career of implementing change using power strategies.

This is a unique situation, but it should cause us to think about different styles that a change agent could use. We must recognize that any style can be effective if the change agent is skillful in using that style. Think about this in terms of your own experience and see if you can find examples of change agents that have successfully implemented changes using very different styles.

DISCUSSION QUESTIONS

1. What are some sources of pressures for change within this course of study? Within the college or university you are attending?
2. Using the force field analysis, diagnose Emerson Electric Company's situation. Which forces would lend themselves to being changed to make Emerson more effective?
3. How might you implement change processes in some student organization on campus?

What type of change agent would be most effective in helping you implement those change processes?

4. Identify which change interventions you would suggest to Mr. Knight. Describe how each would alter the organization of Emerson in a positive manner.

EXERCISE: ANALYZING CHANGE IN ORGANIZATIONS

Change is necessary—yet change is resisted. In this exercise you will be asked to describe some change in an organization of your choice. You will also be asked to determine the reasons for the change and the types of resistance encountered.

The necessity for change is often based on technical factors, while resistance to change is often social in character.

Specific reasons for change may include

1. Need for increased efficiency
2. Changes in the economic picture
3. Growth (or the desire for growth)
4. New technology (machines, processes)
5. Appointment of new management
6. New markets or clients
7. Legal changes, new regulations

Reasons for resistance to change are often based on

1. Fear of economic loss (more work for same pay, loss of overtime)
2. Change in perceived security (possible layoffs, difficulty in learning new routines)
3. Conditions of work (change in hours, procedures)
4. Job satisfaction (less challenge, closer supervision, reduction in authority)
5. Social dynamics (loss of status, group pressure to resist change, requirement to change workmates)
6. Irritation with the way change was handled (misunderstood reasons for change, change made too quickly, not being asked for opinion)
7. Cultural beliefs (change not consistent with tradition, deep mistrust of management)

Instructions:

Interview a manager about an organizational change he or she has knowledge of. Review the material in this chapter before conducting the interview. Take notes as the manager describes the change, the conditions that precipitated it, and the manner in which the change was accepted or resisted. If possible, also interview a worker who participated in the change and elicit his or her description on the change. Then, using the preceding categories, determine the reasons for the change and the reasons for the resistance. Prepare a report containing your findings, along with recommendations for methods management might have used for avoiding resistance. If no resistance occurred, specify the action of management and workers that made smooth change possible. Compare your findings with other classmates.

NOTES

1. "Emerson Electric: High Profits from Low Tech," *Business Week* (4 April 1983): 58–62.

2. John Naisbitt, *Megatrends* (New York: Warner, 1982).

3. Paul R. Lawrence and Jay W. Lorsch, *Developing Organizations: Diagnosis and Actions* (Reading, MA: Addison-Wesley, 1969): 87.

4. Larry E. Greiner, "Patterns of Organization Change." *Harvard Business Review* (May–June, 1967): 119–130.

5. Kurt Lewin, "Quasi-Stationary Social Equilibria and the Problems of Permanent Change," in N. Margulies and A. P. Raia, eds., *Organizational Development: Values, Process and Technology* (New York: McGraw-Hill, 1972): 65–70.

6. J. W. Pfeiffer and R. Heslin, *Instrumentation in Human Relation Training*, published in 1973 by University Associates, Box 615, Iowa City, IA, 52240; and D. A. Lake, M. B. Miles, and R. B. Earle, Jr., *Measuring Human Behavior*, published in 1973 by Teachers College Press, Columbia University, 1234 Amsterdam Ave., New York, NY, 10027.

7. Wendell L. French, Cecil H. Bell, Jr., and R. A. Zawacki, *Organizational Development: Theory, Practice and Research* (Dallas: Business Publications, 1978).

8. See M. Lynne Markus, *Systems in Organizations: Bugs and Features* (Marshfield, MA: Pitman Publishing, 1984).

9. J. P. Kotter and L. A. Schesinger, "Choosing Strategies for Change," *Harvard Business Review* (March–April 1979): 111.

10. Vincent E. Giuliano, "Communication Levels Involved in Change," *Financial Executives* (August 1967): 12–26; and Richard C. Huseman, Elmore R. Alexander, III, Charles L. Henry, Jr., and Fred A. Denson, "Managing Change through Communications," *Personnel Journal* (January 1978): 20–25.

11. L. W. Grunenfeld and F. F. Foltman, "Relationship among Supervisors' Integration, Satisfaction, and Acceptance of a Technological Change," *Journal of Applied Psychology*, vol. 51, no. 1 (1967): 74–77; and Peter Vanderwicken, "Collegial Management Works at Jim Walter Corp.," *Fortune* (March 1973): 115.

12. *Seattle Times* (21 October 1984).

13. "Seiscom Runs into Difficulties, and Some Blame Chairman's Ambitious Expansion," *Wall Street Journal* (5 April 1983).

14. Noel Tichy, "Agents of Planned Social Change: Congruence of Values, Cognitions, and Actions," *Administrative Science Quarterly*, vol. 19, no. 2 (June 1974): 164–182; and Noel Tichy, "How Different Types of Change Agents Diagnose Organizations," *Human Relations*, vol. 28, no. 9 (1975): 771–779.

15. Tichy, "Agents of Planned Social Change," p. 169.

16. Ibid., p. 170.

17. Ibid., p. 169.

18. Ibid.

19. R. T. Golembiewski, "The Laboratory Approach to Organization Change: Schema of a Method," *Public Administration Review*, vol. 27 (1967): 211–221.

20. W. L. French and C. H. Bell, Jr., *Organization Development: Behavioral Science Interventions for Organization Improvement* (Englewood Cliffs, NJ: Prentice-Hall, 1978), 147.

21. J. R. Hackman and G. R. Oldham, *Work Redesign* (Reading, MA: Addison-Wesley, 1980).

22. R. Beckhard, "Optimizing Team Building Efforts," *Journal of Contemporary Business*, vol. 1, no. 3 (1972): 23–32.

23. E. H. Schein, *Process Consultation: Its Role in Organization Development* (Reading, MA: Addison-Wesley, 1969).

24. M. Dalton, "Conflict between Staff and Line Managerial Officers," *American Sociological Review*, vol. 15 (1966): 3–5.

25. Glenn H. Vaney, *Organization Development for Managers* (Reading, MA: Addison-Wesley, 1977): 139.

26. J. L. Franklin, "Improving the Effectiveness of Survey Feedback," *Personnel* (May–June 1978): 11–17.

27. Stephen J. Carroll and Henry L. Tosi, *Management by Objectives: Applications and Research* (New York: Macmillan, 1973).

28. J. O'Toole, ed., *Work and the Quality of Life* (Cambridge, MA: MIT Press, 1974).

29. E. L.Trist and K. W. Bamforth, "Some Social and Psychological Consequences of the Longwall Method of Coal-Getting," *Human Relations,* vol. 4 (1951): 3–38.

30. Noel Tichy, "Organizational Innovations in Sweden," *Columbia Journal of World Business* (Summer 1974): 18–22.

31. Noel Tichy, "Job Redesign on the Assembly Line: Farewell to Blue-collar Blues," *Organizational Dynamics* (Autumn 1973): 55–60; and W. A. Pasmore and J. J. Sherwood, eds., *Sociotechnical Systems: A Source Book* (La Jolla, CA: University Associates, 1978).

32. Paul R. Lawrence, "How to Deal with Resistance to Change," *Harvard Business Review,* vol. 32, no. 3 (May–June 1954): 45–57.

33. H. R. Knudson, R. T. Woodworth, and C. H. Bell, *Management: An Experiential Approach,* 3d ed. (New York: McGraw-Hill, 1979): 207.

34. Ibid., p. 209–210.

RECOMMENDED READINGS

Lester Coch and **John R. P. French, Jr.,** "Overcoming Resistance to Change," *Human Relations* (August 1948): 512–532.

This is a classic article about the research conducted in a textile plant that needed continually to change the workers' jobs. It outlines the research comparing various methods of implementing change and the results. Resistance is explored, from the reasons why to ways to reduce it.

M. Beer, *Organization Change and Development* (Santa Monica, CA: Goodyear Publishing Company, 1980).

This book provides a comprehensive analysis of the field of OD. It describes the process of change and discusses the basic intervention methods. A selection of cases is also included.

Edgar F. Huse, *Organization Development and Change,* 2d ed. (St. Paul, MN: West Publishing, 1980).

Huse describes the approaches to organizational development and change, including methods geared to process and structural changes. Each section includes several cases.

David A. Nadler, "Managing Transitions to Uncertain Future States," *Organizational Dynamics* (Summer 1982): 37–45.

This article draws upon the views of AT&T Chairman Charles Brown. The focus of the discussion is how to manage a major organizational transition even though the end state is unstable and uncertain. It presents a model to conceptualize the complexity and suggests some managerial implications.

The Fairford Library

The City of Fairford is a relatively small "old mill town" city of 15,000 people. Most of the families in the area have lived there for many generations. The only new people in the area are those whose families have been transferred there by one of the major local manufacturers. In fact, most of the people in the city departments have worked there for most of their lives.

At the city's library, Miss Clark had been the librarian for 37 years, until her retirement in 1965, and had worked at the library for a total of 58 years. Mrs. Foster, the assistant librarian, had worked at the library ever since she had graduated from high school. She was planning on retiring within the next year or two. Mrs. Little, in her early 50s, had worked at the library for almost 15 years, and Mrs. Arnold, about 55 years old, had worked at the library for almost as long.

All of these ladies had worked together for many years and virtually all decisions were made with joint consultation. Even the hiring and firing decisions were made by all. They chose their hours, their preferred days off, and whenever they decided that they would like a special day off, they immediately arranged their schedules to make it possible. During this period the work load and atmosphere was very relaxed and friendly. It was so friendly that during off hours the ladies would telephone one another to chat. If they arrived late for opening the library, no one really cared. If they had errands to do, they were free to attend to them.

Source: A. Cohen, S. Fink, H. Gadon, and R. Willits, *Effective Behavior in Organizations*, rev. ed. Copyright © 1980 by Richard D. Irwin, Inc. Reprinted by permission.

The board of trustees and the city manager made all of the important decisions, and the ladies were not given the official responsibility for decision making although they often took it upon themselves to make day-to-day decisions.

After Miss Clark retired, the library was renovated and expanded to include the basement as a part of the library. A new librarian was hired by the trustees and given the decision-making responsibilities. He took the office upstairs. Mrs. Foster, the assistant librarian, acquired a newly created basement office in which she could take charge of ordering and cataloging books (see Figure A for floor layout).

She liked this office very much because she was out from under the "eye" of the librarian and not visible to the public. Mrs. Foster liked her job and often enjoyed reading some of the more interesting books that she cataloged. She had worked here for so many years and felt that she had the most power in the library personnel structure. After all, she knew many people and knew just where every book was to be found. She said that while she would like to be the librarian she did not want the tension that would surely go along with it. She felt very secure where she was and did not see any reason to change. She enjoyed the way of life which the work provided her.

Mrs. Arnold, the children's librarian, had a nice room adjoining Mrs. Foster's office. The desk in the children's room was placed so that patrons could be seen at the desk by Mrs. Foster if Mrs. Arnold was not in the room. This arrangement also provided the two ladies with a better opportunity for chatting back and forth. Mrs. Arnold always seemed busy even though the children's

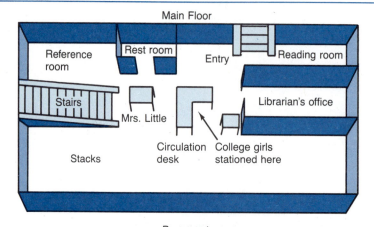

Main Floor

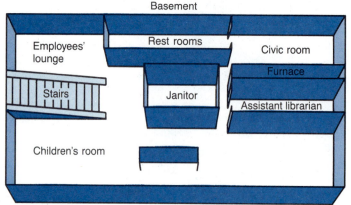

Basement

FIGURE A
Library floor plan

room was usually in disorder with uncharged books on the desk and scattered around. It would have taken only an hour a day to keep it neat. Mrs. Foster always was reprimanding Mrs. Arnold about the state of messiness, but Mrs. Arnold ignored Mrs. Foster's complaints.

Mrs. Little, the reference librarian and circulation overseer, worked upstairs. Although she was supposed to assist people in finding books and reference materials and do minor bookkeeping, she spent most of her time keeping an eye on the other employees and reporting back to Mrs. Foster.

A Mrs. Hoffe worked at the circulation desk.

She was about 35 years old and new to the area. She was very easy to get along with, and everyone in the library enjoyed working with her.

Two college girls, who had started while still in high school, also worked there. Their work varied, but they interacted with all of the library personnel. They were well liked by the other employees, worked quickly and efficiently, and were given much responsibility.

After they had completed all of their work plus any other work that anyone else had that needed to be done, they would chat and joke with Mrs. Hoffe, read magazines, or send someone downstairs to get refreshments. The college girls and

Mrs. Hoffe knew what they were doing and could handle almost any situation. They knew that they were valuable staff.

The group of older ladies consumed time by working at a slow pace and chatting throughout the day, often leaving work undone until the next day. The group of younger women worked efficiently and joked around only after getting the work done. Much friction developed between the two groups.

During the five years after Miss Clark retired, three librarians were hired. In each case, there was so much conflict between the librarian's objectives and those of the trustees and older staff that the librarian soon decided to find employment elsewhere. For example, Mr. B's policy was to run the library on a military basis, exert tyrannical rule over employees, and override decisions made by trustees. Because of the great turnover in librarians, the assistant librarian (with the trustees behind her) virtually ran the place.

When the trustees selected the fourth librarian, Mr. Fischer, everyone felt that he would stay longer than others since he had brought his family with him to the area. He was about 35 years old, had a master's degree in history and one in library science, and several years' experience in actual library work. However, he immediately found that many of his progressive objectives were not in harmony with the objectives of the older staff. Two of these objectives were to reorganize the library so that it became an information center for the whole community and to have the employees of the library be more involved in getting the community interested in the library. Rather than back off, he pushed his objectives more strongly and sought to determine why the conflict existed.

Ever since he first started work, Fischer had shown more interest in and friendliness to Mrs. Hoffe and the college girls. He soon established a favorable relationship with them. During the time that he was trying to find out why his ideas, based upon his experience in large city libraries, were rejected, he found that he was supported by Mrs. Hoffe and the college girls. Soon he began to use the three of them as a liaison between the "old guard" and himself rather than

going directly to the older ladies. He found that whenever he mentioned a change in the system, the older ladies rejected his ideas immediately, often talking behind his back and poking fun at him.

For example, when he suggested that they get out into the community to find ways to give greater service, they would accuse him among themselves of just wanting to socialize instead of working. Similarly, when he would be at meetings with school personnel or town officials, the ladies would attack him for not being "at work." In talking to their friends and the public they claimed he "goofed off" a lot.

Mr. Fischer judged productivity by how quickly the employees completed their assigned tasks, how neatly the tasks were done, how closely they followed his instructions, and whether or not they were easily distracted from their duties. The lack of respect on the part of the older women became so great that he found that whenever he mentioned the disorder that the children's librarian had created or the general lack of productivity of the older ladies they were resentful. He soon began avoiding them.

The not-so-permanent personnel and Mrs. Hoffe respected his authority and his person to a high degree. Mr. Fischer found that he only had to mention something that he would like done and either Mrs. Hoffe or one of the two college girls would drop everything else and do it. It got so that he would discuss any changes that he would like with them, getting their opinions and suggestions as to how they would go about it.

Business communication between the groups declined. The older ladies' productivity level fell even lower as they spent more and more time complaining amongst themselves.

Although the library's written policy gave Mr. Fischer the final say in hiring and firing decisions, he had to move with caution because the trustees had the final power. He considered firing the assistant librarian, Mrs. Foster, moving the children's librarian upstairs to work on circulation, and giving the job of children's librarian to Mrs. Hoffe. He believed this would help since when she had to replace Mrs. Arnold in the children's room, Mrs. Hoffe had proved herself by doing a better job. She kept the room neater and kept un-charged books off the desk and put away.

Mr. Fischer believed all of his ideas were plausible, but he was beginning to be perplexed as to how to go about applying them.

Questions

1. Using the force field analysis methodology, diagnose the situation facing Mr. Fischer at the end of the case. Which forces would you suggest that he address? Which method of data collection would you recommend to Mr. Fischer? Why?

2. Pick one type of change agent and define how you would intervene in this case to bring about change. Remember to clearly define your change objectives. Why did you choose the change agent you did? Choose the one least like you and suggest what might be your new strategy. What were the differences?

3. Which resistances are likely to be present in this case? Which level of interventions might Mr. Fischer use to make the library more effective?

PART FOUR
Issues in Organizational Behavior

CHAPTER TWELVE
Stress

OBJECTIVES

- Define the concept of stress and how it affects the body

- Describe the major personal and organizational life stresses

- Identify and discuss the consequences of stress

- Explain methods of handling stress more effectively

- Describe some managerial implications of dealing with stress

Stress: A Personal Subject

Joe Stuart, an aggressive and successful attorney, was feeling frightened and angry as he drove home through the heavy rush hour traffic. The doctor's report that afternoon had scared Joe. Either he slowed down, stopped smoking, lost weight, drank less, got more exercise and—above all—stopped driving himself so hard, or the chest pain would turn into a heart attack before he was 40.

The traffic light turned green, and Joe's car charged into the intersection, narrowly missing a blue sedan. "Idiot!" Joe exploded at the driver. "How can I slow down? I've got four new cases coming to trial next month. Relax! How can I relax when I'm responsible for those briefs? What am I supposed to do, retire at age 36?"

Soberly Joe recalled the doctor's final words: "Joe, right now you have a choice. But if you keep pushing yourself and neglecting your health, you won't live to see your kids grow up."

"Damn it all!" The light changed. "Hey you!" Joe yelled at the driver of the car ahead. "Get moving! I don't have time to waste!"[1]

UNDERSTANDING STRESS

We all experience stress at some point in our daily lives. Sometimes stress can have positive effects, and sometimes it can be harmful. Joe Stuart was experiencing stress while driving home, but so have most of us as we have fought traffic. Joe seems more upset by his predicament than he should be. What other factors contributed to Joe's stress?

Since stress can be positive or negative, understanding stress and our reactions to it is critical. On the one hand, having enough stress to live or work at an effective level can create satisfaction, a sense of well-being and accomplishment, and other rewards. On the other hand, excessive stress can result in loss of efficiency, failure to perform well, and negative effects on mental and physical health. While it is clear that we need a balance in the amount of stress to work and live, it is not clear how to achieve that balance.

In Joe's case, his doctor is suggesting that the stress is excessive and Joe should begin to slow down. Joe seems to be experiencing stress both on his job and in the manner in which he lives his daily life. In some sense, we can't separate our private lives from our work or professional lives. What should Joe do? Where does he start to change how he manages his stress? Does the organization have any responsibility to help Joe manage his stress? Are there any payoffs for the organization to be concerned about Joe's level of stress?

These questions should help us explore stress from a personal perspective and an organizational perspective. In this chapter, we try to understand how we are affected by stress mentally and physically. We then look at some sources of stress both in our daily lives and at work. Next we review some methods of coping with stress to make it more manageable. Finally, we discuss some of the managerial implications of dealing with stress in organizations.

Nature of Stress

What Is Stress?   Stress involves the interaction of an individual and the environment. Stress is a consequence of or a response to an action, situation, or force that places special physical demands, psychological demands, or both on an individual.[2] Stressors are the antecedents of the individual's reaction of stress. Stressors can take a variety of forms, from job requirements, demands from coworkers, friends, and family to self-imposed demands. While the sources are many, the result is individual stress.

Stress can be viewed as an adaptive response to demands. How adaptive and, therefore, how manageable for the individual is an important question but a difficult one to answer because our individual responses (our personal stress level) are mediated by individual characteristics and/or psychological processes (see Figure 12–1). The characteristics may include age, sex, race, health status, and heredity. The psychological processes might include attitudes, beliefs, values, motivation, and other personality dimensions, such as tolerance for uncertainty.

Returning to Joe Stuart, we can see that Joe's four critical cases, the doctor's report, and his own need to be successful influence how he responds to the traffic—very differently than if he were beginning a vacation with a clean bill of health and a new promotion. As Figure 12–1 suggests, the mediating individual characteristics are critical to our understanding of what is "excessive" stress.

How Does Stress Work?   What is stress from a physical standpoint, and why should you be concerned about stress if it is so natural? The answers to these two questions should motivate us to try to manage our individual stress reactions.

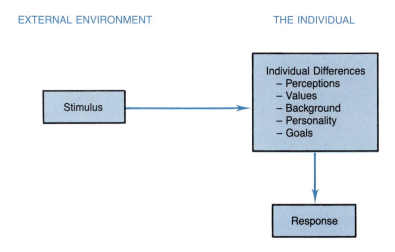

FIGURE 12–1
A simplified view of stress

When an individual faces stressors, the reaction is a "fight or flight" response, which includes biochemical and bodily changes. While this alternative of fight or flight resulted from our early beginnings (kill for food or be killed), our human nervous system still responds the same way to modern stressors. While the saber-toothed tiger is gone, our imaginary saber-toothed boss or traffic congestion can elicit the same response—fight or flight.

While it is beyond the scope of this book to explain the complex physiochemical bodily reactions to stress, it must be remembered that these responses are the same whether we are fighting for our lives in an auto accident or feeling stress because we have quarreled with our boss. In the physically urgent situation—the auto accident—we would probably relax and turn off the stress reaction once we found out that we were not hurt. But could we as quickly not continue to think about the argument for days after the incident with the boss? If we are still brooding about what it may mean to our future pay raises and promotions, we are most likely still being stressed bodily with strong chemicals keeping us in a state of readiness. Continual readiness can wear out the body quickly if no periods of rest occur to restore energy.

Sources of Stress

Since stress can have destructive as well as positive consequences for an individual and indirectly for the organization, it is important to identify the major sources of stress both in our personal lives and at work.

Life Stressors   In the early 1950s, University of Washington psychiatrist Thomas Holmes determined that the single common denominator for stress is "the necessity of significant change in the life pattern of the individual."[3] Holmes found that among tuberculosis patients, for example, the onset of the disease had generally followed a cluster of disruptive events: a death in the family, a new job, or a marriage. Stress did not cause the illness, Holmes emphasized—"It takes a germ"—but tension did seem to promote the disease process. Holmes found that merely discussing upsetting events could produce physiological changes. An experiment in which sample biopsies were taken before and after discussions of certain subjects showed that tissue damage resulted from talking about a mother-in-law's coming visit.

In we think about Joe Stuart and his drive home, we can see this process at work. As Joe replays the conversation with the doctor and reviews the work that faces him in the next several weeks, he becomes more agitated. The additional stress makes him react in a stronger fashion to the traffic than would otherwise happen if he were listening to soothing music on the radio.

In an attempt to measure the impact of "life change events," Holmes and Richard Rahe developed a life events scale called the "Social Readjustment Rating Scale (SRRS)." (See Table 12–1 for the major classifications of life events and their equivalent stress values.) They studied the clinical effects of major life

TABLE 12–1

The social readjustment rating scale

Rank	Life Event	Mean Value
1	Death of spouse	100
2	Divorce	73
3	Marital separation	65
4	Jail term	63
5	Death of close family member	63
6	Personal injury or illness	53
7	Marriage	50
8	Fired at work	47
9	Marital reconciliation	45
10	Retirement	45
11	Change in health of family member	44
12	Pregnancy	40
13	Sex difficulties	39
14	Gain of new family member	39
15	Business readjustment	39
16	Change in financial state	38
17	Death of close friend	37
18	Change to different line of work	36
19	Change in number of arguments with spouse	35
20	Mortgage over $10,000	31
21	Foreclosure of mortgage or loan	30
22	Change in responsibilities at work	29
23	Son or daughter leaving home	29
24	Trouble with in-laws	29
25	Outstanding personal achievement	28
26	Wife begin or stop work	26
27	Begin or end school	26
28	Change in living conditions	25
29	Revision of personal habits	24
30	Trouble with boss	23
31	Change in work hours or conditions	20
32	Change in residence	20
33	Change in schools	20
34	Change in recreation	19
35	Change in church activities	19
36	Change in social activities	18
37	Mortgage or loan less than $10,000	17
38	Change in sleeping habits	16
39	Change in number of family get-togethers	15
40	Change in eating habits	15
41	Vacation	13
42	Christmas	12
43	Minor violations of the law	11

Source: Reprinted with permission from T. H. Holmes and R. H. Rahe, "The Social Readjustment Rating Scale," *Journal of Psychosomatic Medicine*, vol. 11 (1967): 213–218. Copyright 1967, Pergamon Press, Ltd.

changes of 5,000 people suffering from stress-related illnesses. After evaluating interviews and questionnaire responses, they were able to assign a numerical value to each life event, ranking them by the medical histories of patients examined. It was found that those who had a high score on the life change index were more likely to contract illness following the event. In research to validate the SRRS, it was found that 80 percent of the people with scores over 300 and 53 percent of the people with scores between 150 and 300 suffered some form of stress-related illness. However, the SRRS does not account for a person's capacity for meeting and dealing with stress.

One researcher studying two groups of middle- and upper-level executives suffering from high stress found that the group with little or no illness had some personal characteristics that allowed them to cope better with the large number of stressful life events.[4] Those individuals had a high sense of commitment to themselves in terms of a purpose in life, a high sense of control over what occurs in their daily lives, and a view of change as a challenge to be explored rather then a problem to overcome.

Despite the shortcoming of not always predicting stress for individuals based on life events, the Holmes-Rahe SRRS appears to be a more reliable and valid instrument than most of the popular press stress-oriented instruments available.[5]

Stressors at Work   We can see why managers need to understand and be sensitive to the issue of stress in organizations. In addition, organizations must recognize that stress is not a personal characteristic that employees leave on the coat rack in the morning and pick up again as they leave to go home.

Before we look at possible sources of stress in organizations, it is worthwhile to review a study that attempts to identify the linkages between stress and performance.[6] Figure 12–2 presents the model the researchers were using to look at stress and organizational performance. The study used a medium-sized food processing company with 86 percent of the personnel responding. The research viewed the following variables as possible sources of stress: shift changes; task characteristics (autonomy, complexity, interdependence, closeness of supervision, routinization); leadership attention to subordinate; job involvement; job level (position within hierarchy); and personal characteristics (sex, age, level of education, length of tenure in organization).

The results of this research provided some support for using a multidimensional model of stress. The data revealed that both the contextual and role-related variables contributed to the magnitude of job stressors. As one became more involved with the job (a form of ego involvement), work overload and low status became less stressful. With close supervision, one's options were less and caused role frustration. It could be explained that perceived lack of individual control might lead to more stressful reactions to work.

Personal characteristics can also influence the strength of felt stress. One finding concerned age: older employees felt less stressed than younger employ-

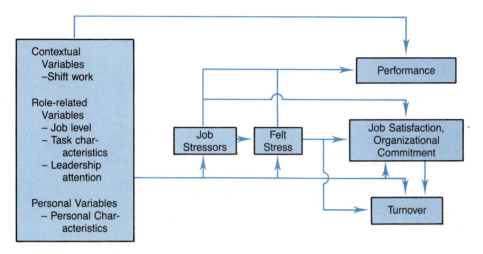

FIGURE 12-2

Stress and performance (Source: Saroj Parasuraman and Joseph A. Alutto, "Sources and Outcomes of Stress in Organizational Settings: Toward the Development of a Structural Model," *Academy of Management Journal,* vol. 27, no. 2 (1984): 330–350. Reprinted by permission.)

ees. A possible explanation is that increased maturity (generally associated with age) tends to enhance the stress-tolerance ability of individuals. This maturity is the ability to find different methods to cope with the stressful situation and more realistic expectations about what can be done in the organization. Another finding was that the amount of perceived autonomy also influenced the amount of felt stress. As the degree of role and behavior latitude increased, individuals dealt more effectively with the stressful work experience.

The significance of this latter set of findings is potentially great since certain characteristics may minimize a person's feeling stressed. It is this very issue that may allow organizations to help individuals cope with stress more effectively while performing jobs with inherent stress characteristics, such as law enforcement and social agency work.[7]

While we need to be careful in trying to generalize to all situations from this one study, it does suggest that managers need to appreciate potentially stressful conditions.

Ineffective communication. Stress can result from a lack of communication or from a lack of the right kind of communication at the right time. We each see the world differently and we interpret communication attempts differently. For example, there is nothing more stressful than discovering that you have arrived at an appointment with your boss at the wrong time. You misunderstood the appointed time, your boss is upset, and you are edgy.

BOX 12-1

Student Shock

Kate, 24 years old, graduated last month from University of Southern California as a business major but despised it. She switched majors four times and was so depressed that she would break out crying for no reason.

Brad, 20, dropped out of a small private university in rural California and now works at a hamburger stand. "I felt totally confused and isolated at college," he says. He considered suicide but decided he couldn't inflict that pain on his parents.

College students like these two are undergoing unusually severe stress these days brought on by a cross current of poor job prospects, weakening family support, and a bewildering array of choices. Counseling centers all around the country report that psychological problems of college students today are more numerous and more serious than in previous years.

"Student shock," says Mary Anne Rust, a clinical psychologist in Encino, CA, "increased enormously and neither students nor parents fully realize it." Mounting case-loads at campus psychological counseling centers reflect the pressures. More students than ever before are seeking help for a wide variety of stress-related problems such as depression, anxiety, migraine headaches, and eating and sleeping disorders.

Students not only are more troubled these days, they are also more indecisive. They take longer to get through school and often switch majors and schools several times. At Middlebury College in Vermont, more and more students are taking five to six years to complete their bachelor's degrees. Many students are switching majors as late as their senior year. And a growing number drop out for a year or more to get their bearings.

Robert Dye, a 22-year-old student at Memphis State University in Tennessee, began as a geology major, but the courses seemed dull. So he switched to business, which he thought would lead to a job, but he found accounting "pretty boring." He had always been interested in nu-

Information overload.   This is a frequent cause of stress among individuals. Information overload simply means that an individual is given too much data in a given period of time and is unable to deal with it. The person is unable to answer letters or return phone calls, must miss or cancel appointments, and experiences stress as a result.

Underutilization of abilities.   A job may be dull and boring, or the nature of the work does not require use of the individual's full abilities. The degreed engineer who must spend a majority of time doing routine office work and filling out forms may have stress from underutilization.

triton and athletics, so he thought the field of dietetics might offer a possibility. After talking to a dietician and deciding that wasn't for him, he took a battery of vocational tests, showing his interests were strongest in television or film production. Currently, after four years at Memphis State and no degree, he would like to get into the television business but he thinks that realistically he should try advertising or sales.

Dye says he is baffled by the huge number of courses and majors. "You can take courses ranging from Beatle mania to computer mania," he says. "You can make up your own major by combining several different fields. Then you go into a counselor and ask if the field you select will be good in five years. The answer I received was, 'It might be and it might not.' Do you wonder why I'm confused?"

Students' fears about their future have a basis in fact. "The job outlook for college graduates appears bleak for the rest of this decade," says Russell Rumberger, a Stanford University researcher who studies job prospects. Part of the problem is that these college students are members of the "baby boom," the largest population group in U.S. history. For the first time in American history, these students are facing the spectre of downward mobility, the probability that they will be worse off financially than their parents who graduated from college in the 1950s and early 1960s.

With divorces increasing, there is less family support at home for the college students today. Often parents are divorced and have their own financial and emotional problems. "Many students at 18, 19, or 20 need lots of guidance and support," says Grana Taylor-Hecht, a psychologist. "And in many cases the family is no longer there to provide that support."

Psychologist David Elkind believes that society is forcing children to grow up too fast, to achieve too much in school and sports, and to undertake adult responsibilities before they are ready. He calls the current situation "stress born of rapid, bewildering social change and constantly rising expectations."

Questions

1. What are Kate, Brad, and Robert expressing in their comments about college life? How would you describe your own college days?
2. Describe Mr. Dye's reaction to his present state of confusion. What might be some of his sources of stress? What advice would you give to Mr. Dye?
3. Do you agree with Mr. Elkind's statement about "stress born of rapid, bewildering social change and constantly rising expectations"? Defend your position.

Role conflict.   In this situation, stress results from conflicting job demands, expectations, and goals. To do a job both "faster" and "better" may not be possible. For example, the production manager may want units produced faster while the quality control manager wants better units. An employee caught between the two managers will experience the stress of role conflict.

Role ambiguity.   Without clear job objectives, the scope of responsibility is not understood. When individuals do not know what specific job performance is expected, they begin to experience stress. Role ambiguity can also result from not understanding what part a job plays in meeting organizational objectives.

Company policy, salary, and working conditions.   Employees can also experience stress when they feel that they should receive more money for their work, or if company policy restricts them from doing things they feel they must do to be effective in their job. For example, a manager wishes to assign a few extra duties to an individual for a specific project, but union regulations do not allow it. Stress can also result from physical conditions such as noise, heat, cold, safety hazards, air pollution, uncomfortable spatial arrangements, and shift work.

Job change.   Individuals and work undergo constant changes as organizations attempt to become more efficient or competitive by requiring different tasks and job responsibilities. These changes can cause stress for the job holder. For example, a firm may computerize its accounting function. As a result, a job that did require certain decisions and calculations may become merely a data collection and entry position for the computer. As with most changes, job change entails an element of uncertainty and risk that contributes to stress. Change can be especially stressful for individuals afraid of losing their jobs.

Stress carriers.   Many of us come in contact with people who generate stress within us. The angry boss, the dissatisfied customer, or the obnoxious coworker can increase on-the-job stress. Many stress carriers have no idea of the negative impact they have on others; other stress carriers seem to enjoy the stressful effect they have on others.

Consequences of Stress

At this point we have some understanding of what stress is and what some of the causes are. We need to review some of the potential consequences of stress that need to be addressed by the individual and the organization if they are to manage the level and amount of stress.

General Consequences   Recall the opening story of Stuart and Box 12–1, "Student Shock." Stress can have a multitude of consequences for people and the organization, many of which are potentially dysfunctional, disruptive, and dangerous. One researcher developed a taxonomy of stress consequences that includes the following:

1. Subjective effects: Anxiety, aggression, apathy, boredom, depression, fatigue, frustration, guilt and shame, irritability and bad temper, moodiness, low self-esteem, tension, nervousness, and loneliness
2. Behavioral effects: Accident proneness, drug use, emotional outbursts, excessive eating or loss of appetite, excessive drinking and smoking, excitability, impulsive behavior, impaired speech, nervous laughter, restlessness, and trembling
3. Cognitive effects: Inability to make decisions and concentrate, frequent forgetfulness, hypersensitivity to criticism, and mental blocks

4. Physiological effects: Increased blood and urine catecholamines and corticosteroids, increased blood glucose levels, increased heart rate and blood pressure, dryness of the mouth, sweating, dilation of the pupils, difficulty in breathing, hot and cold spells, lump in the throat, numbness and tingling in parts of the limbs
5. Organizational effects: Absenteeism, poor industrial relations and poor productivity, high accident and labor turnover rates, poor organizational climate, antagonism at work, and job dissatisfaction[8]

It must be noted that stress is not *always* a precursor to these consequences, yet sufficient "felt" stress may be a primary causative or a contributing agent.

Stress and Health   Health consequences of stress are probably more frequently experienced in the work world than any place else. This is due in part to the large amounts of time we spend on the job and on career-related activities. Organizations are becoming increasingly sensitive to quality-of-life issues and the impact these may have on the human costs of doing business.

A long list could be compiled of the possible health consequences of job stress. Cardiovascular disease, gastrointestinal disorders, respiratory problems, arthritis, headaches, bodily injuries, skin disorders, physical strain or fatigue, and death have been suggested to be responses to job stress. Medical researchers have also discovered possible links between stress and cancer.[9]

Two other researchers concluded from their review of work and health literature that the following stress-health linkages have been determined:

1. Four occupational categories (blue-collar unskilled, blue-collar skilled, white-collar nonprofessional, and white-collar professional) can be ordered from least to most with respect to the job characteristics of participation in decisions, social support, certainty about the future, complexity, and freedom from quantitative overload and unwanted overload.
2. Not having the above job characteristics is seen to be stressful. Thus, the occupational ordering can be taken to reflect relative stress levels.
3. Stressful working conditions are associated with boredom and dissatisfaction with work roles, which in turn are related to feelings of depression, irritation, and anxiety.[10]

The conclusion suggests that certain working conditions may lead to dysfunctional psychological states and that these negative states are ultimately detrimental to physical health. What is interesting in this review is that higher levels of job stressors are associated with lower status occupations, suggesting that stress and ulcers being the exclusive domain of executives is a myth.

While stress alone does not cause heart disease, considerable research does link stress and coronary disease.[11] Heart disease by itself accounts for 52 million lost work days annually, which represents almost $15 billion in wages.[12] Simply the cost of recruiting replacements for executives lost to heart disease is about $700 million annually. The total bill, just in terms of dollars, is estimated to be close to $30 billion per year in lost productivity, retraining costs, medical care, and premature retirement.

The following work sheet computes the replacement costs of individuals lost to heart disease.[13] To understand the example, consider a medium to large organization employing 4,000 people.

1. Number of employees	4,000
2. Men in age range 45–65 (.25 × line 1)	1,000
3. Estimated heart deaths per year (.006 × line 2)	6
4. Estimated premature retirement due to heart problems per year (.003 × line 2)	3
5. Company's annual personnel losses due to heart disorders (sum of lines 3 & 4)	9
6. Annual replacement cost (the averge cost of hiring and training replacements for experienced employees) (line 5 × $4,300)	$38,700
7. Number of employees who will eventually die of heart disease if present rates continue (.5 × line 1)	2,000

While this worksheet highlights some of the effects of heart disease, it does not include medical costs, lost wages to the families, and performance reductions.

Psychological Effects of Stress   In addition to recognizing and understanding stress-related physical illnesses, we must not underestimate the effects of mental or psychological discomfort resulting from stress. While 6 percent of the population are alcoholics, another 10 percent are estimated to be problem drinkers. Combine these facts with the 6 billion doses of prescription tranquilizers and 9 billion doses of amphetamines and barbiturates consumed annually, and there is strong evidence that people are experiencing high levels of tension, anxiety, and stress.[14] But what are the direct psychological consequences of stress? They can include depression, anxiety, nervous exhaustion, disorientation, feelings of inadequacy, loss of self-esteem, lowered tolerance for ambiguity, apathy, loss of achievement motivation, and increased irritability. The really deadly aspect of these outcomes is that they can form a closed loop of increasing higher levels of stress. Joe Stuart, to whom we were introduced in the beginning story, is an example. The more stress Joe experienced, the more irritated he became. The more irritated, the more he felt stressed.

While physical illnesses entail more obvious costs to the individual and the organization, mental health problems do have consequences for organizations. The United States Clearing House for mental health information reports that U.S. industry recently had a $17 billion annual decrease in its productive capacity due to stress-induced mental health problems.[15]

One other cost of stress not yet mentioned is the cost in reductions in the quality of life. It is impossible to place true dollar figures on mental or physical health, let alone on happiness; but if it were possible, we might find that the previously cited cost figures would seem insignificant.

Coping with Stress

So far we have explored what stress is and what some of its consequences are for the individual and the organization. We now examine some methods of coping more successfully with stress to reduce the felt, or perceived, level of stress suggested in Figure 12–2.

Any approach to stress management must begin with the individual employee taking some responsibility for wanting to reduce stress. Once this choice is made, then organizational or managerial approaches will have some definite benefits for the individual. Because of the authors' conviction that self-awareness and self-help are important, this section focuses on several areas that you may want to explore.

Exercise   Many physicians believe that the single most important indicator of health is cardiovascular endurance, and that is what regular exercise can develop, particularly activities such as jogging, walking, bicycling, and swimming, to mention only a few. Research tends to support this belief. In a study of the effects of exercise, middle-aged men were divided into two groups, exercisers who completed a jogging program and nonexercisers. Both groups were tested before and after experiencing three stress emotions: anxiety, depression, and hostility. The exercisers showed significantly greater reductions in all three stress emotions as compared to the nonexercise group.[16]

Exercise enthusiasts are even more adamant about the value of aerobic exercise, such as jogging, for stress reduction and general good health:

> An aerobic mode of exercise is one in which you exert yourself enough to breathe somewhat heavily, yet you do not consume oxygen faster than your heart and lungs can supply it to your muscles; that is, you don't get out of breath. For this reason, you can continue exercising aerobically for fairly extended periods without discomfort. This is the key to staying with a conditioning exercise such as jogging.[17]

The rationale for the stress reduction may be that a person who invests two or three hours per week running slowly and easily for long distances has a handy escape route from the pressures of working and living, at least during the time spent jogging.

Diet   Any nutritionist will quickly point out how inadequate the American diet is and also point to the need, therefore, for supplements and special approaches to

BOX 12-2

Wild Night at the Erawan

The recital last evening in the chamber music room of the Erawan Hotel by the United States pianist Myron Kropp, the first appearance of Mr. Kropp in Bangkok, can only be described by this reviewer and those who witnessed Mr. Kropp's performance as one of the most interesting experiences in a very long time.

There was a bit of disorder at the outset when the ushers, apparently brought in from the dining room, had some trouble placing late concertgoers in their proper seats.

The audience eventually was seated, and a hush fell over the room as Mr. Kropp appeared from the right of the stage attired in black formal evening wear with a small, white poppy in his lapel. With sparse, sandy hair, a sallow complexion, and a deceptively frail looking frame, the man who has popularized Johann Sebastian Bach approached the Baldwin concert grand, bowed to the audience, and placed himself upon the stool.

It might be appropriate to insert at this juncture that many pianists, including Mr. Kropp, prefer a bench, maintaining that on a screw-type stool they sometimes find themselves turning sidewise during a particularly expressive strain. There was a slight delay, in fact, as Mr. Kropp left the stage briefly, apparently in search of a bench, but returned when informed that there was none.

As I have mentioned on several other occasions, the Baldwin concert grand, while basically a fine instrument, needs constant attention, particulary in a climate such as Bangkok. This is even more true when the instrument is as old as the one provided in the chamber music room of the Erawan Hotel. In this humidity the felts that separate the white keys from the black tend to swell, causing an occasional key to stick, which apparently was the case last evening with the D in the second octave.

During the raging storm section of the D Minor Toccata and Fugue, Mr. Kropp must be complimented for putting up with the awkward D. However, by the time the storm was past and he had gotten into the Prelude and Fugue in D Major, in which the second-octave D plays a major role, Mr. Kropp's patience was wearing thin.

Some who attended the performance later questioned whether the awkward key justified some of the language which was heard coming from the stage.

However, one member of the audience, who had sent his children out of the room by the midway point of the fugue, had a valid point when he commented over the music and extemporaneous remarks of Mr. Kropp that the workman who greased the stool might have done better to use

Source: "Wild Night at the Erawan," by Kenneth Langbell, *Seattle Times* (20 December 1970): E1 (a satire reprinted from the *Bangkok Post*).

our diets.[18] Extremists tout black strap molasses, sprouted wheat, brewer's yeast, dolomite pills, and a host of vitamins, with little attention paid to the effects of stress or the benefits of exercise. We advocate a moderate approach.

One should view one's diet as the sum total of the substances introduced into one's body—drugs, tobacco, and drinks, as well as food. A good diet consists of a balanced combination of foods that supplement the basic ingredients of

some of the grease on the second-octave D key.

Indeed, Mr. Kropp's stool had more than enough grease, and during one passage in which the music and the lyrics both were particularly violent, Mr. Kropp was turned completely around. Whereas before his remarks had been aimed largely at the piano and were therefore somewhat muted, to his surprise and that of those in the chamber music room he found himself addressing himself directly to the audience.

But such things do happen, and the person who began to laugh deserves to be severely reprimanded for his undignified behavior. Unfortunately laughter is contagious, and by the time it had subsided and the audience had regained its composure, Mr. Kropp appeared to be somewhat shaken. Nevertheless, he swiveled himself back into position facing the piano and, leaving the D Major Fugue unfinished, commenced on the Fantasia and Fugue in G Minor.

Why the concert grand piano's G key in the third octave chose that particular time to begin sticking I hesitate to guess. However, it is certainly safe to say that Mr. Kropp himself did nothing to help matters when he began using his feet to kick the lower portion of the piano instead of operating the pedals.

Possibly it was this jarring or the un-Bach-like hammering to which the stuck keyboard was being subjected. Something caused the right front leg of the piano to buckle slightly inward, leaving the entire instrument listing at approximately a 35-degree angle from that which is normal. A gasp went up from the audience, for if the piano had actually fallen, several of Mr. Kropp's toes, if not his feet, would surely have been broken.

It was with a sigh of relief, therefore, that the audience saw Mr. Kropp slowly rise from his stool and leave the stage. A few men in the back of the room began clapping, and when Mr. Kropp reappeared a moment later, it seemed he was responding to the ovation. Apparently, however, he had left to get the red-handled fire axe which was hung backstage in case of fire, for that was what he had in his hand.

My first reaction at seeing Mr. Kropp begin to chop at the left leg of the grand piano was that he was attempting to make it tilt at the same angle as the right leg and thereby correct the list. However, when the weakened legs finally collapsed altogether with a great crash and Mr. Kropp continued to chop, it became obvious to all that he had no intention of going on with the concert.

The ushers, who had heard the snapping of piano wires and splintering of sounding board from the dining room, came rushing in, and, with the help of the hotel manager, two Indian watchmen, and a passing police corporal, finally succeeded in disarming Mr. Kropp and dragging him off the stage.

Questions

1. Identify Mr. Kropp's major sources of stress. Which do you feel he could have anticipated and therefore prevented?
2. Do you feel Mr. Kropp had other ways to cope with his stress? What advice would you give him for future concerts in distant places?

nutrition without an overbalance of fats, sugars, or calories; vitamin supplements taken in moderation (such as a concentrated multivitamin); minimal use of "junk" foods and those heavily laced with additives, colorings, and preservatives; moderate use of alcohol[19]; no use of tobacco;[20] no use of hard drugs; moderate use of caffeine; and rare use of patent medicines unless required for medical treatment of specific disorders.

Relaxation Techniques Deep relaxation is a highly specific neurological state of the body.[21] You cannot reach this state merely sitting or lying down quietly. It requires a specific mental approach. There are a multitude of avenues to reach this state—meditation,[22] progressive relaxation,[23] hypnosis, autogenic training,[24] and biofeedback.[25]

In the deep relaxation condition, one feels physically relaxed, somewhat detached from the immediate environment, and usually even detached from body sensations. It involves a feeling of voluntary and comfortable abandonment of one's conscious control and stewardship over major body functions. This abandonment requires a distinctly passive attitude in which one simply turns over control of the body to its own built-in "autopilot."

One's mental activity in the deep relaxation state can range from controlled concentration on positive images or messages, to drifting free association, to the "neutral silence" characteristic of meditation. Deep relaxation is a profoundly restful condition. People who enter this state for fifteen to twenty minutes open their eyes later feeling a pronounced sense of peacefulness and release from all tension. Most people also report feelings of optimistic cheerfulness, kindliness toward and acceptance of others, and general good humor. Physiologists also report dramatic changes in certain key body measurements such as heart rate, breathing rate, blood pressure, and skin temperature.

Organizational Approaches While the previous approaches are geared to help the individual reduce or manage perceived stress, organizations can also work to reduce the stress levels due to faulty organizational policies, procedures, and practices. Most of these approaches serve the dual objectives of reducing stresses for individuals and also making the organization more effective in its internal functioning. Some of the possible programs are inherent in the study of organizational behavior and are somewhat addressed throughout this book.

Some examples of areas that address those stressors identified as work related are improving communication (chapter 4), realistic performance and goal setting (chapter 10), improving the job design and structural relationships in the organization (chapter 9), designing better methods of implementing change programs (chapter 11), and managing the areas of organizational conflict (chapter 8).

In addition, organizations can more directly address the individual's handling of stress levels through training. For example, the New York Telephone Company has instituted a companywide stress management program designed to teach meditation and relaxation techniques to employees.[26] The employees feel that regular meditation helps them cope with the work stress and increases their efficiency in the job.

Rigorous research tends to support this method of stress management. One research study looked at a stress training program administered to public agency employees. An experimental group undertook eight weeks of training to help the participants recognize stressful situations and to reorient their personal reactions to the stressful events to make the events less stressful. This was combined with progressive relaxation techniques to help them manage their felt stress levels. A control group with similar characteristics was established. They were told that their program would start in three months.

The researchers did find that the participants who underwent the training experienced fewer physical indications (reduced levels of stress-related hormones in bloodstream) and fewer reported psychological indicators (less anxiety, depression, and irritation) of stress. While the authors were very cautious about their results because they couldn't get total replication from the control group (this group underwent the same training program three months after the initial group), they did indicate that some of the stress indicators of the new group were reduced.[27]

If we were to try to reach some conclusion of how to manage stress more effectively in organizations, the effort should probably be very systematic. First, if the excessive stress results from internal organizational practices, management should attempt to correct those situations. If the practices are more a response to external demands and cannot be readily changed—as is the case with tax preparers and the April 15 deadline, social workers who must deal with difficult human miseries, and law enforcement and medical agencies who have a simultaneously boring and dangerous occupation—then an appropriate approach might be to help those employees deal with the inherent stress more effectively. This can be accomplished through various stress reduction training programs with periodic reinforcements.

Summary of Key Concepts

1. Stress can have positive or negative consequences for the individual. A certain amount of stress is beneficial to one's performance.

2. Stress is one's attempt to adapt to demands whether self-imposed or imposed by others. The body's reactions prepare one to fight or flee from the stressful situation.

3. Life presents many situations that could be stressful for an individual. The Social Readjustment Rating Scale helps us look at various life events and the potential levels of stress they can cause.

4. Work has many potential stressors for an individual. Most are situations that also make the organization less effective.

5. While the consequences of stress on the mind and the body are well documented, we must remember that each individual reacts to stress according to his or her ability to cope; therefore, the consequences may be mediated by one's personality and/or outlook on life.

6. Individuals can cope with stress through a variety of approaches, including exercise, diet, and relaxation techniques. Organizations can help by reviewing their internal practices for effectiveness and by providing optional training where the working conditions cannot be changed.

Key Terms

Bodily reactions to stress	Relaxation techniques
Diet	Stress
Exercise	Stress consequences
Fight or flight response	Stressors

MANAGERIAL IMPLICATIONS

> I don't think that an incentive program is a day-to-day incentive—most people forget about it during the year. I think their pride, their desires, what's expected of them matter more. For instance, take a group of six product managers. They know that the way to get ahead is to be a better product manager than the other guy. And when that promotion finally comes, I'll tell you, it generates stress in the other five for sure.[28]

The above comment by Mr. Carroll, CEO for Lever Brothers, illustrates the major dilemma created by stress. Although an appropriate amount of stress can lead to better performance, excessive stress will likely lead to reduced performance and, ultimately, deteriorating health.

In this section we look at how stress manifests itself in the workplace, some occupations that are inherently stressful, organizations that have been identified as stressful, geographic areas of the U.S. in which living is stressful, what organizations are doing about stress, and, finally, you and your job as a source of stress.

Stress in the Workplace

Results of organizational stress can be heard by anecdote in any organization, and surveys have supported the notion that stress in the workplace is a serious problem. Zaleznik and colleagues studied 2,000 personnel in management, staff, and operations positions of a large Canadian firm, which had just undergone a major reorganization.[29] The researchers found a number of stress symptoms in five categories—emotional distress, medication use, cardiovascular illness, gastrointestinal disturbance, and allergy-respiratory problems. Table 12–2 shows some of the symptoms and their rate of occurrence.

The Zaleznik study listed some of the more common psychological and physiological responses to stress, but many of the responses are not visible to the outside observer. In an article on executive "burn out," Levinson listed several observable characteristics of the over-stressed individual:

1. Chronic fatigue
2. Anger at those making demands
3. Self-criticism for putting up with the demands
4. Cynicism, negativism, and irritability

TABLE 12–2
Stress symptoms and their frequency of occurrence

Symptom	Percent Reporting Symptom
1. Emotional distress:	
Insomnia	24.0
Restlessness and agitation	21.2
Fatigue	19.1
Irritability	13.2
Worry about a nervous breakdown	11.3
Moodiness	11.0
2. Medication use:	
Vitamin pills	1.4
Other prescriptions	6.9
Sleeping tablets	3.2
3. Cardiovascular illness:	
Rapid heart beat	7.8
High blood pressure	6.2
4. Gastrointestinal disturbance:	
Digestion problems	11.1
Colitis	5.9
Stomach-distress medication	4.5
5. Allergy-respiratory problems:	
Hay fever	8.5
Respiratory difficulties	3.5

Source: A. Zaleznik, M. F. R. Kets de Vries, and J. Howard, "Stress Reactions in Organizations: Syndromes, Causes and Consequences," *Behavioral Science*, vol. 22, no. 3 (1977): 4. Reprinted with permission.

5. A sense of being besieged
6. Hair-trigger display of emotions[30]

Lest anyone think that middle managers carry all of the stress while business owners are stress-free, a study by Boyd and Gumpert suggests otherwise. One thousand chief executives of small firms in New England were surveyed. Although the entrepreneurs were generally very satisfied with their choice of career and financial well-being, the survey also uncovered a high price for that satisfaction. The most frequently mentioned costs (in order of frequency) were as follows:

1. Personal sacrifices
2. Burden of responsibility
3. Dominance of professional life
4. Loss of psychological well-being
5. Lack of human resources
6. Uncontrollable forces
7. Isolation in problems

8. Friction with partners and employees
9. Commitment of personal finances for start-up
10. Difficulty of finding creative time[31]

To the minimum-wage, unskilled worker, the preceding list might be a less than convincing list of stressors. But stress is a consequence of factors *perceived* as stressful and cannot be judged qualitatively from a different perspective. After all, a snowstorm might be delightful to children and to skiers but might create terrific stress for the person who has a meeting on the other side of town.

Stressful Occupations

Every job has some stressful elements, but some occupations are inherently stressful, such as the police officer's job. Though incidence of *actual* physical danger is relatively rare, the officer faces many *potentially* dangerous situations. Firefighters' jobs contain episodes of extreme physical effort and hazardous working conditions, separated by periods of low activity and even boredom. Shift work can also create stress through requiring periodic adjustment in living habits. Police officers generally work rotating shifts, which adds another element of stress to their lives. Firefighters frequently work a full twenty-four hours (or more) on duty, followed by an equal time off.

Air traffic controllers have long been thought to have one of the most stressful occupations. The job tends to be very fast paced and requires split-second decision making; a mistake can literally cost hundreds of lives. Controllers are almost impossible to insure for disability. Early retirement caused by medical problems is very high for air traffic controllers. At least one estimate places such retirement at 95 percent.[32] Seeking relaxation from job stress through the use of alcohol and other drugs is relatively common, and there is concern in some quarters that many air traffic controllers are trying to cope with job stress by using drugs.[33]

Though one must sympathize with holders of stressful jobs, it is an error to assume that the greatest stress is experienced in such occupations as air traffic controller, police officer, and firefighter. A 1975 study by the National Institute for Occupational Safety and Health surveyed 22,000 workers in 130 occupations. The second highest incidence of stress was found among office workers! A 1980 study found that video-display terminal operators had the highest stress of all occupational groups.[34]

There are at least two implications. Mundane office jobs are occupied by literally millions of people. Thus, occupational stress is virtually pandemic rather than a serious matter only for certain high-profile occupations held by relatively few people.

Furthermore, as the economy continues its shift to a service basis, the number of people in office work will increase both absolutely and proportionally. Unless increasing attention is paid to occupational stress, the toll taken on human welfare may become intolerable.

Stressful Organizations

One may unknowingly choose a stressful organization. A new employee in the Canadian firm studied by Zaleznik would find himself or herself in the middle of stressed coworkers, hardly a low-anxiety situation. *Dun's Review* proposed several years ago that, from an employee's point of view, the ten most stressful companies in America were Revlon, ITT, Chrysler, Crane, Singer, Gallo Winery, W. R. Grace & Co., Wachovia, Procter & Gamble, and Johnson & Johnson.[35] Stress in the companies was attributed to causes as various as the personality of the chief executive, competitiveness of the industry, and financial losses leading to reorganization.

Stressful Living

As if stressful organizations were not enough, there is evidence that certain parts of the country are more stressful to live in than others. Professor Murray Strauss of the University of New Hampshire developed a stress index for states. The fifteen factors included such variables as divorce rate, personal bankruptcy, violent crime, mortgage foreclosures, infant mortality, and diseases related to smoking and drinking. The highest stress states, in descending order, are Nevada, Alaska, Georgia, Washington, Oregon, Alabama, and California. The state scoring least stress on the Strauss index was Nebraska.[36]

That stress is a major, and costly, factor in contemporary life is beyond dispute. Consider the following findings:

- The American Academy of Family Physicians estimates that two-thirds of office visits to family physicians are prompted by stress-related symptoms.
- Stress-related absenteeism, company medical expenses, and lost productivity are estimated to cost between $50 billion and $75 billion per year.
- The three best-selling drugs in the U.S. are Tagamet, an ulcer medication; Inderal, a hypertension drug; and Valium, a mild tranquilizer.[37]

What Organizations Are Doing

Corporations and other organizations have become increasingly aware of both the visible and hidden costs of stress and have developed programs to help employees cope with the problem. Approximately one-fifth of the Fortune 500 companies have some sort of stress-management program. Programs range from the very common alcoholism program to smoking reduction efforts, exercise facilities, biofeedback instruction, and meditation classes. Some companies have reported impressive results. The Equitable Life Assurance Society provided a biofeedback program for employees with frequent stress-related health complaints. The program reduced the employees' average number of visits to the company medical office by more than 75 percent, saving an estimated $5.52 in medical costs for every dollar invested.[38]

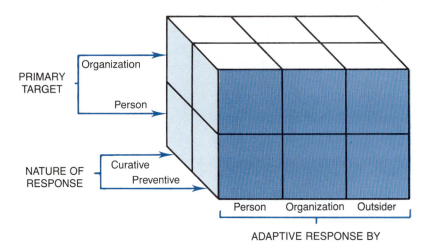

FIGURE 12-3

Responses to stress (Source: J. E. Newman and T. A. Beehr, "Personal and Organizational Strategies for Handling Job Stress: A Review of Research and Opinion," *Personnel Psychology*, vol. 32 (1979): 3. Used by permission.)

As previously cited, New York Telephone offered meditation lessons for employees with stress-related symptoms. The program reduced the diagnosed hypertension rate from 18 percent to about 9 percent and is saving $130,000 a year from reduced absenteeism alone.[39]

Newman and Beehr have provided a useful framework for organizations to use in approaching the problem of job stress (see Figure 12-3).[40] The nature of the response to stress can be either curative or preventive. Curative responses would typically take a form of the previously discussed programs. They are intended to reduce or control existing stress. Preventive responses would include analysis of organizational conditions, followed by measures to prevent stress from becoming more severe. The target of the response could be either the organization or the person (or both). Strategies could be devised by the individual, the organization, or could come from outside persons or institutions. Newman and Beehr provided the following examples of the three strategies.

Personal Strategies   These are strategies aimed at changing

1. the person's psychological condition
2. the person's physical condition
3. the person's behavior
4. the person's work environment

Organizational Strategies   These methods focus on changing

1. organizational characteristics or conditions

2. role characteristics or conditions
3. task/job characteristics or conditions

Outsider Strategies   These are strategies directed toward changing

1. the person
2. the environment[41]

You and Your Job

Aside from the social problem of stress, stressful occupations, and stressful organizations, how about your own job? How do you know when you have too much stress? Figure 12–4 provides a checklist to help you recognize whether you are using stress to your advantage.

If you checked seven to ten items in the figure, you are at a "comfortable" stress level that probably enhances your performance. If you checked five or six statements, you probably get the job done but are likely to feel tired afterward. If you checked four or fewer items, stress is likely to limit your effectiveness.

You can control stress, but you must first recognize it as a problem. Don't wait for someone you know to recognize it for you—by then it may be too late. Ultimately, it is your responsibility to monitor your well-being. It is a responsibility that cannot be delegated.

Check those statements that generally apply to you.

1. _____I feel exhilarated after completing an important business deal or project.
2. _____Stress helps me to be more alert and to think clearly and perceptively.
3. _____I am able to "come down" physically and emotionally just a few hours after the termination of a stressful situation.
4. _____The stress I experience is rarely prolonged or severe.
5. _____I am able to stay calm and work productively under pressure.
6. _____I can accept setbacks and interruptions without emotional letdowns.
7. _____I approach problems with flexibility and seek to generate several alternative solutions.
8. _____I generally view problems objectively and realistically.
9. _____Stress increases my motivation and drive.
10. _____I know how to channel stress into productive work.

FIGURE 12–4
Stress in your job (Source: Rosalind Forbes, *Corporate Stress* (New York: Forbes, Associates, 1979): 14. Used by permission.)

DISCUSSION QUESTIONS

1. Describe how individual differences (values, backgrounds, attitudes) can affect how the individual will experience stress.

2. Discuss how an organization might identify its stressors. What might be done to help employees cope with stress?

3. Identify one situation when the fight-or-flight response was particularly inappropriate for your behavior.

4. What actions or techniques do you or can you use to cope with stress in your personal life? In work?

5. As a manager, how do you know when your subordinate is experiencing appropriate levels of stress for performance? What, as a manager, seems most difficult to apply to help your subordinates cope with stress?

EXERCISE: MIND-CLEARING

Find a comfortable position in your chair or bed. Close your eyes and try to relax. Breathe deeply two or three times. Now, take another deep breath, hold it a few seconds, and then slowly let it out. Mentally say to yourself that you are becoming calm, you are relaxing, and you are at peace.

Let all your muscles go as loose and limp as you possibly can. Start with your right leg and gradually move to every other part of your body. First tighten your muscles, then deliberately relax them.

Eventually your arms and legs may start to feel heavy. Or they may instead feel unusually light. Whatever feeling you have, take time to experience the sensation of it fully.

Now pretend you are walking through a forest. As you visualize the setting, feel the grass beneath you getting softer and softer. Soon you reach the end of a long, cool trail and find it leads into a beautiful, room-sized opening. The opening is filled with scented wild flowers, and it is completely yours to enjoy. No other person knows about your forest room. Remember that you have this room available to you whenever you want to come to it. Spend at least two or three more minutes in your forest room.

While relaxing deeply in your special retreat, notice each breath you take. You will find that you become more comfortable and relaxed with each additional breath. Breathe slowly and deeply.

When you have had a while in which to experience fully the relaxation of your forest room, or whatever other refuge you visualize, make a suggestion to yourself of whatever you want to accomplish that day. Stay in your state of relaxation while you decide how you want to accomplish it. Then slowly visualize yourself walking back out of the forest. You will feel rested and refreshed, wide awake and calm.

Source: Rosalind Forbes, *Corporate Stress* (New York: Forbes Associates, 1979): 192–193. Used by permission.

NOTES

1. A. P. Brief, R. S. Schuler, and M. Van Sell, *Managing Job Stress* (Boston: Little, Brown, 1981): 64.
2. J. M. Ivancevich and M. T. Matteson, "Organizations and Coronary Heart Disease: The Stress Connection," *Academy of Management Review* (October 1978): 14–19.

3. T. H. Holmes and R. H. Rahe, "The Social Readjustment Rating Scale," *Journal of Psychosomatic Medicine*, vol. 2 (1967): 213–218.

4. S. C. Kobasa, "Stressful Life Events, Personality, and Health: An Inquiry Into Hardiness," *Journal of Personality and Social Psychology*, vol. 37, no. 1 (January 1979): 1–11.

5. B. S. Dohrenwend and B. P. Dohrenwend, eds., *Stressful Life Events: Their Nature and Effects* (New York: Wiley, 1974); and E. Gunderson and R. Rahe, eds., *Life Stress and Illness* (Springfield, IL: Charles C. Thomas, 1974).

6. S. Parasuraman and J. A. Alutto, "Sources and Outcomes of Stress in Organizational Settings: Towards the Development of a Structural Model," *Academy of Management Journal*, vol. 27, no. 2 (1984): 330–350.

7. J. Gaines and J. M. Jermier, "Emotional Exhaustion in a High Stress Organization," *Academy of Management Journal*, vol. 26, no. 4 (1983): 567–586.

8. T. Cox, *Stress* (Baltimore, MD: University Park Press, 1978).

9. K. Brammer and B. H. Newberry, eds., *Stress and Cancer* (Toronto: C. J. Hogrefe, 1982).

10. D. Katz and R. L. Kahn, *The Social Psychology of Organizations*, 2d ed. (New York: Wiley, 1978).

11. M. T. Matteson and J. M. Ivancevich, "Organizational Stressors and Heart Disease: A Research Model," *Academy of Management Review*, vol. 4 (1979): 347–357.

12. American Heart Association, *Heart Facts* (American Heart Association Communication Division, 1978).

13. Adapted from J. M. Ivancevich and M. T. Matteson, *Stress and Work*, p. 92. Copyright © 1980 by Scott, Foresman, and Company. Reprinted by permission.

14. J. Follman, *Alcoholism and Business* (New York: AMACOM, 1976).

15. A. Kornhauser, *Mental Health of the Industrial Worker* (New York: Wiley, 1965).

16. S. Lynch, C. H. Folkins, and J. W. Wilmore, "Relationships Between Three Mood Variables and Physical Exercise" (University of Pittsburgh, 1973, unpublished).

17. K. Cooper, *Aerobics* (New York: Bantam Books, 1968): 12.

18. D. Rubin, *The Save Your Life Diet* (New York: Ballantine, 1975).

19. M. E. Chafetz, H. T. Blane, and M. T. Hill, *Frontiers of Alcoholism* (New York: Science House, 1970).

20. R. D. Caplan, S. Cobb, and J. R. French, "Relationships of Cessation of Smoking with Job Stress, Personality, and Sound Support," *Journal of Applied Psychology*, vol. 60 (1975): 211–219.

21. H. Benson, *The Relaxation Response* (New York: Morrow, 1975): 49.

22. H. Benson, "Your Innate Asset for Combating Stress," *Harvard Business Review* (July–August 1974); and R. B. Kary, *The Transcendental Meditation Program for Business People* (New York: AMACOM, 1976).

23. E. Roskies, M. Spevack, A. Sukes, C. Cohen and S. Gilman, "Changing the Coronary-prone (Type A) Behavior Pattern in a Nonclinical Population," *Journal of Behavioral Medicine*, vol. 1 (1978): 201–216.

24. H. Lindemann, *Relieve Tension the Automatic Way* (New York: Wyden, 1973).

25. B. Brown, *Stress and the Art of Biofeedback* (New York: Harper & Row, 1977).

26. W. A. McGeveran, "Meditation at the Telephone Company," *Wharton Magazine*, vol. 6, no. 1 (1981): 29–32.

27. D. C. Ganster, B. T. Mages, W. E. Sime, and G. D. Tarp, "Managing Organizational Stress: A Field Experiment," *Journal of Applied Psychology*, vol. 67, no. 5 (1982): 533–542.

28. H. Benson and R. L. Allen, "How Much Stress Is Too Much?" *Harvard Business Review* (September–October 1980): 90.

29. A. Zaleznik, M. F. R. Kets de Vries, and J. Howard, "Stress Reactions in Organizations: Syndromes, Causes and Consequences," *Behavioral Science*, vol. 22, no. 3 (1977): 151–162.

30. Harry Levinson, "When Executives Burn Out," *Harvard Business Review* (May–June 1981): 76.

31. D. P. Boyd and D. E. Gumpert, "Coping with Entrepreneurial Stress," *Harvard Business Review* (March–April 1983): 44–64.

32. R. Forbes, *Corporate Stress* (Garden City, NY: Doubleday, 1979): 81.

33. "Sky High": Air-Traffic Controllers' Abuse of Drugs Alarms Many in the Profession," *The Wall Street Journal* (27 May 1983): 1.

34. "Hazards of the Workplace," *The Seattle Times* (13 March 1983): D50.

35. R. Forbes, *Corporate Stress,* p. 3.

36. "Regions: High Stress States," *The Wall Street Journal* (25 October 1983): 31.

37. "Stress: Can We Cope?" *Time* (6 June 1983): 48–54.

38. Ibid.

39. McGeveran, "Mediation at the Telephone Company."

40. J. E. Newman and T. A. Beehr, "Personal and Organizational Strategies for Handling Job Stress: A Review of Research and Opinion," *Personnel Psychology,* vol. 32 (1979): 1–43.

41. Ibid.

RECOMMENDED READINGS

J. C. **Quick** and J. D. **Quick.** "Reducing Stress through Preventive Management," *Human Resource Management* (Fall 1979): 15–22.

The authors analyze the nature and consequences of stress, discussing causes of stress in organizations and analyzing approaches the manager may take to reduce stress.

P. **Goldberg,** *Executive Health* (New York: McGraw-Hill, 1978).

The book gives an overview of the reasons for and consequences of executive stress as well as related health issues. It also focuses on plans and programs to manage the stressors causing psychological symptoms of stress.

B. B. **Brown,** *Stress and the Art of Biofeedback* (New York: Harper & Row, 1977).

Brown describes the various aspects of using biofeedback to manage the symptoms of stress, detailing numerous techniques to reduce stress.

The Eighth Floor

Tom, a bright engineer in his mid-thirties, has been working in a very large electronics and missile firm for over eight years. His present assignment as a project manager for a critical $2.5 million government project began two years ago. Approximately ten more months will be required for its final completion.

Tom is directly responsible for fifteen men (six are engineers and the remaining nine are classified as technicians). Some of his primary responsibilities include planning, coordinating, and meeting critical target dates, solving technical problems which might arise, and serving as a liaison between the production facilities and his project group, which is performing the necessary engineering work.

Tom's immediate superior is Harry, the chief engineer, who oversees all governmental projects encompassing a broad range of electronic and missile arms contracts. The company bids against other prime contractors in the industry. At any one time Harry's responsibilities include three or four projects similar to Tom's assignment.

The company has recently been the successful low bidder for a new government contract. Harry has been given the responsibility to select the project manager and he has asked Tom to stop by his office; their discussion follows:

HARRY: Tom, glad to see you; how's your project coming?

TOM: Fine, we're having no problems now. Matter of fact we're about sixty days ahead of our target completion date. We shouldn't experience any unexpected bottlenecks from now on.

Source: Dorothy N. Harlow and Jean J. Hanke, *Behavior in Organizations* (Boston: Little, Brown, 1975): 496–498.

HARRY: That's great. Glad to hear that we can bring one project in early. I called you in today because of a new project that we have to get started. We have just been awarded a prime contract for $6.1 million. It's not going to be an easy one. It has a mighty tight completion date in addition to some tough engineering problems. We want to get one of our best men on it, and, Tom, I think you're it. It's going to entail a lot more responsibility than your current project. But naturally, it's going to mean more dollars to you because we're going to give you a nice raise when you start the project.

TOM: Sounds great, but I don't know if I want to tackle something like that right now.

HARRY: What do you mean? What's the difficulty?

TOM: Well, let me explain. Right now I'm attending Army Reserve meetings Wednesday nights. I'm trying to maintain my officer status in the Army, so I have to attend these weekly meetings. You know the company has been stressing community involvement, so I joined the J.C.s about a year ago. We meet once a month and I chair a major committee. Also, I've been attending night graduate classes at the University. I'm working on my master's in engineering, and this takes two nights a week plus my studying time. It hasn't been easy. I've been carrying a pretty heavy load above the project responsibilities.

HARRY: Well, that doesn't sound like it's too much, Tom. I think you can handle this new project with no difficulty.

TOM: I don't know. Anyway, Jane, my wife—you know she's pregnant with our second child—she really doesn't like me being away so many nights. It seems I'm carrying my work home too many nights, and too many weekends tend to be shot with my work. Less than four weeks ago we moved into a new house. I'm kind of anticipating our addition to the family; we needed more room, and we have a lot of work to do in the house. Work I like to do. It's very relaxing to be doing some of the yard work and fixing up around the house. So I look forward to that. It does give me an opportunity to let down a little. So with the new project, if I tackle that with everything else, well, I really don't think I want to now.

HARRY: Tom, O.K. I appreciate your personal problems. I hear what you're saying; but why don't you think about it. Give it some thought and let me know.

A week later, Harry again called Tom into his office.

HARRY: Well Tom, what have you decided?

TOM: Harry, really, I've given it a lot of thought. I've talked it over with Jane, and I don't think I want to tackle something like this right now. Why don't you let me finish my project? It's going to take me about a year and by that time, hopefully, I'm going to be out of graduate school. Maybe I can reduce my participation in the Reserves in some way and not take on any more new responsibilities. I think I'll be in a lot better shape, time-wise, next year.

HARRY: We need this project started now! That's why I called you in. We can't wait and you're our man. You have to do it for us. If you refuse, as far as I'm concerned you might as well turn in your resignation. The company needs you. We're in a bind and here you're telling me you're not going to be able to deliver for us.

TOM: (After a long silence) Putting it that way, I guess I'll do it.

Two months have passed since Tom accepted responsibility for the new project. Things have not been going too smoothly for Tom since then. Tom walks into Harry's office one morning.

TOM: Harry, I need your help. I'm sinking. This load is killing me!

HARRY: Come on now, you're overwrought. Settle down, you're O.K. You're making it. I've been reading your reports and you're doing a fine job. Be patient, it's going to be all right.

TOM: I'm telling you, Harry, the pressure is getting to me. I sometimes break out in hives. I . . . get somebody else! Get Charley over here to take the project. Let me change places with him or put me back on my old project. *Please!*

HARRY: Tom, I'm telling you, we don't like quitters around here. You took this job, now you do it!

A month later Harry got a telephone call from the company's physician. The doctor told Harry that Tom had been rushed to the local hospital, was admitted, and was undergoing treatment. Tom was on the eighth floor—the psychiatric ward—he had a complete mental breakdown.

Tom was discharged from the hospital three months later and spent the next year at home, not really working one full day the entire time. The company has kept paying his salary but now is seriously considering discontinuing his employment with the company next month.

Questions

1. List and discuss the major sources of stress for Tom. Which stressors are common to most people in similar circumstances? How does this compare with the chapter's list of stressful occupations?
2. What impact does Tom's boss have on Tom's stress level? Is the approach typical of organizations that need employees' involvement? What other approach could have been utilized to get Tom's commitment?
3. What methods might this organization use to help its employees cope with stress?
4. What responsibilities does the organization have to Tom after his nervous breakdown?

CHAPTER THIRTEEN
Impact of Computer Technology

OBJECTIVES

- Describe how computer technology has affected the definition of work
- Identify the major consequences for the individual
- Explain how computer technology influences communication in organizations
- Discuss how leadership and organizational power will be affected by computers
- List the major structural implications of computer technology
- Identify and describe the managerial implications of these changes

Different Views of the Computer

Thomas Lindstrom is a commercial airline pilot. He was selected for the job because of his intelligence, physical strength, and mental stamina—characteristics that are critical for the complex and varied decisions a pilot must make during flight time. Lately, Lindstrom's job just isn't the same. He is now required to monitor a set of computer controls that automatically makes all flight decisions. On a good flight, he shouldn't have to do a thing. Lindstrom is bored and angry. Thousands of dollars were invested in his training, but he now is expected to baby-sit a control panel.

Gerry Alvarez is a bill collector working in the headquarters of a large discount store chain. He has been a collector for more than ten years and takes pride in his ability to recoup cash for the company. He has learned to master various techniques for cajoling people to pay up. But lately his job just isn't the same. The firm has adopted a computer system to distribute and organize collection activities. While the system allows for a greater volume of transactions, it takes most of the skill requirements out of the job. The computer randomly distributes accounts among the collectors, and the greater volume assures that "you can't get to know any account in depth. The computer tells you which account to work, and you can't keep an overview of your accounts because the file is automatically updated each day." Gerry wants to quit his job. He thinks the pressure is too great and the only way to get the supervisor off his back is to key in work he has not completed. He also feels that anyone can now do the job; being a "good collector" no longer makes a difference.

Linda Winthrop is a data analyst in the commercial planning department of a large bank. She spends her days accessing information from a central data bank and plugging it into various forecasting models that serve as the strategic basis for critical marketing and credit decisions. Linda does not let on but she has little or no trust in the system upon which she must depend for most of her information. There are the technical kinks—her data is sometimes mutilated or disappears entirely—yet even when things run smoothly she does not trust that all the proper calculations are performed. She keeps parallel records and often repeats calculations manually before she uses them for a report. It takes extra time, but this way she feels in control of the information.

Nellie Weymouth was a linotype operator until recently when her job was altered. Instead of working that big printing contraption and handling all the crafty judgements it required, she now works at a computer terminal where she types information into a visual display unit. As far as Nellie is concerned, the difference between hot and cold type is that "one has no blood and doesn't really need people at all." The main preoccupation she and her friends share each long night as the paper is printed is—"how can we make something go wrong? After all, the rest of the fun is mostly gone."[1]

Shirley McCall is a circuit designer for a communication firm. She was recently transferred from an outside job as a line worker and trained to use the new computer-assisted circuit design. Although Shirley has never used a computer terminal before this transfer, she and her fellow trainees wonder why the "old-timer circuit designers are complaining about using the computer." Listening to the old-timers, Shirley can't understand why using ten different books to design one circuit was so much fun for them. She and her new friends enjoy being able instantly to call up the information they need to design a circuit by pushing a few keys, and to complete a circuit design in one fifth the time it took before computers were used. Shirley willingly admits that sometimes it is frustrating to lose everything once in a while when the machine "goes down" but then that's the "time to go to coffee."[2]

Jim Colton, manufacturing manager at an x-ray equipment company, used to quarrel regularly with sales manager Patrick Sharp. "He was always coming down here because he was out of some piece of equipment he had promised a customer or a part to get a hospital's radiographic department up and running again," remembers Colton. But now that a computerized inventory and scheduling system has been installed at the firm, the two men joke about how boring life has become. "We don't yell at each other anymore," says Colton with a grin. "My job has changed drastically. The computerized system has eliminated 95 percent of our emergencies—I know what we need and when. Now I spend my time planning, not reacting."[3]

Dick Birge, professor of management, has just received some suggestions from his boss, the department chairman, to see if he can use the new computer lab in his Business Policy and Organizational Behavior courses. Replied Birge, "Where do I start? I'm having enough trouble keeping up with my research and literature in my own fields much less begin to understand how to apply computers to my classes. Most of my students know more about computers than I do. Besides, how do you computerize human behavior?" Several months after his conversation with his boss and after many sessions with some knowledgeable students who saw this as a challenge to educate the teacher, Birge is seen carrying four big boxes up to the airline counter and his wife complaining, "Can't you be without your computer for two weeks?"[4]

COMPUTERS ARE HERE TO STAY

Computer-mediated Work

What do these individuals have in common? It isn't the type of jobs or organizations in which they work. It isn't their feelings about their jobs.

The common experience is the introduction of computers and computer-based information technology to their jobs—which are at all levels of the organization, worker and managerial. A term to describe this phenomenon is *computer-mediated* work.[5]

Which aspects of organizational behavior covered in the previous chapters will help us understand the impact of information technology? What motivates these workers as they adjust to computer-mediated work? What leadership issues are raised as computers act as an interface between subordinates and managers? Will information systems have any effect on the distribution of power in organizations? How will communication and decision-making be handled with more rapid information systems replacing paperwork? How will employees respond to these changes?

The purpose of this chapter is to help sort out the various reactions to computer technology. It must be noted that the research concerning the impact of computers is extremely scarce at this time. Nevertheless, we believe it is important to utilize what knowledge is available to understand and appreciate what will be a major influence on how work is performed in organizations. Much of what is presented is based on what organizations are currently attempting as they struggle with the new revolution—the information society.

Information Society

In 1982 about one million computers or data terminals joined the four million already in use in offices in the United States. The number is expected to increase by some 25 percent each year for at least the next decade. By 1990, about half the American work force will be using video display terminals (VDTs).[6]

John Naisbitt, in his book *Megatrends*, has described ten major transformations that he sees taking place now in our society.[7] First on his list is the shift from an industrial society to an informational society. He uses the term *informational society* because the work performed has changed. In 1950, only about 17 percent of jobs were in information. Now more than 60 percent of us work with information as programmers, teachers, clerks, secretaries, accountants, managers, and technicians. Even in manufacturing firms most of the workers hold information jobs. Most employees spend their time creating, processing, or distributing information.

It is this informational aspect of most jobs that is being influenced by computer technology. Computers can speed up processing of information, increase the accuracy of it, and make it more readily available to individuals within and outside the organization.

However, computer technology is not limited to just information jobs. Robots, controlled by computers, do actual work. It is true that initially robots were used in jobs that were extremely dangerous. Now their usage has expanded into the unskilled and skilled labor market. At Ford Motor Company, robots test engines. General Motors uses robotic welders. And there are ten government agencies where robots pick up and deliver mail. Conservative estimates predict that by 1990 we will be producing 17,000 robots per year and that the total robot work force will reach 80,000. Most experts would double those figures.[8]

It is obvious that we have just begun to find applications for computer technology. If we only half believe the statistics about their impact on how we perform work, it still will mean that most of us will be directly or indirectly affected by these technological innovations during the next several years.

In the "pursuit of excellence," most organizations subject their employees to some form of computer-mediated work. The reasons for this pursuit include increasing productivity, enhancing services or products for customers, improving the management systems, and reducing organizational uncertainty.

Several things are certain about the machines already in place. They are all operated by humans, and the linkage between human and machine is not always smooth or effective. Reviewing the opening stories of computer-mediated jobs, we find that in four cases—the airline pilot, the bill collector, the data analyst, and the linotype operator—the results were not all positive from the individuals' point of view, and in certain instances they found ways to circumvent the system.

On the other hand, computer technology can not only increase individual productivity but also have unanticipated positive benefits for the organization. The circuit designer not only accepted the computer assistance but couldn't conceive of doing the job in its former state. The manager viewed the computer as a method of freeing up his time to plan and, more importantly, to establish a better working relationship with his colleague in sales. The professor, who was initially concerned about how he could possibly learn this new technology and teach others who know more about the technology than he did, couldn't be without his machine even on his vacation.

Impact on Individuals

A Shift in the Definition of Work   In chapter 1, we discussed how work has undergone various changes as a result of the Industrial Revolution and recently the information revolution. We also noted that organizations in their pursuit of effectiveness and efficiency have reduced jobs to their simplest components to allow specialization by the individual workers. While this has largely resulted in more effective organizations, the result for the individual worker is a reduction to a minimum of physical involvement with the job activities and the product or service.

Continuing this pursuit of increased productivity has led organizations to introduce computers in the office and on the production floor. As a result, computers have also influenced the definition of work.

One aspect of this new definition is the restriction of the work experience. Unlike traditional industrial work, which depended upon machines that were extensions of the human body, computer-mediated work involves little in the way of physical effort. For example, consider the typical secretary in an office. The secretary types various letters and reports, retrieves and files paperwork, opens and sorts mail, schedules appointments, answers telephones, among other activities. With the advent of a fully automated office system, the secretary has a single terminal with its video screen and keyboard. The boss has similar equipment. All of the previous activities can now be accomplished by interacting with the computer equipment instead of moving paper or dealing physically with other individuals.

As we can see from this example, computer-mediated work reorganizes the relationship between a person and that person's work. An individual must learn to accomplish the task through the medium of an information system rather than by working directly on the object of the task—product or paperwork. This means that the object of work is removed from direct sensual contact; that is, it can no longer be touched, seen, heard, smelled, or tasted. Information about that object is accessible only as symbols reflected back through the medium of the information system. What the airline pilot, circuit designer, bill collector, linotype operator, data analyst, and manufacturing manager have in common is that their work consists of reading and manipulating electronic symbols. Those symbols, the

BOX 13–1

A Robot and Liking It, Thanks

In August 1981, an exposé in the magazine *Mother Jones* portrayed Bell System telephone operators as a frenetic, anxiety-ridden lot, trapped in an inhuman occupation. But recent Bell System research has found that many of the operators actually enjoy their work. If they can initially adapt to being operators, psychic job satisfaction seems to follow, and they will probably be at Bell for a long time.

In the early 1950s, AT&T used about a quarter of a million operators. The majority of those jobs have disappeared with automation, but Bell claims that the remaining 88,000 operators will continue to be needed for the predictable future. In a computer age, they may be the last human relay stations. Yet theirs is perhaps the most automated work in the world. They are at the leading edge of human robotics in American labor.

Typical operators sit or stand in front of button-laden consoles for six and a half hours a day. Their ears are plugged into machines that feed them a constant stream of unknown voices and numbers—up to two calls a minute, or 800 per shift. Their hands punch in the numbers on their computer consoles faster than the eye can see. They handle people in calm or crisis, then instantly dispose of them.

"If there is as much as a ten-second lull between calls, they don't like it," says Edward Youngs, a Bell Labs psychologist who has studied 500 veteran operators. "They are extremely occupied by their work, but remember almost nothing of what has occurred afterwards. Oper-

Source: Reprinted from *Psychology Today* magazine (March 1983): 22. Copyright © 1983 American Psychological Association. Used by permission.

language of the computer, mediate between the workers and the work they once performed directly.

This abstraction of work routines, which is shared by many occupations, from nurses to bank tellers, shifts the individual's involvement from a physical dimension to a cerebral dimension. But this increased demand for a particular form of mental effort does not mean a correlative increase in the degree to which these jobs are interesting, varied, challenging, or promising. Instead, the increased cerebral attention is often experienced as boring, routine, and stressful.

Computer-Related Stress   From chapter 12 we saw that the greatest stress occurs where the individual faces psychological demands yet has little control over how to get the work done. These are often machine-paced jobs such as those of assembly-line worker, punch-press operator, and telephone operator.

A few early reports indicate that certain routine computer-mediated jobs have resulted in higher levels of stress. Swedish researchers are finding that office

ators have overlearned their jobs and can function at the level of peripheral awareness. The callers' information seems to pass from their ears to their hands without ever becoming part of a cognitive process. With time, their awareness of what they're doing just goes away."

"I never hear a word the callers say," says Chuck Bradley, a 28-year-old operator at Mountain Bell in Denver. Bradley has handled 650,000 long-distance calls in his two years on the job. "As the voices come into my mind, I just freeze the information in one part of my brain and hold it there. Then I pull it out whenever I need it. This allows me to distance myself from my work and ignore the fact that callers treat me like a rock. Who I am and what I do don't meet. My identity is separate from my job."

Like airline stewardesses, operators must suppress their own feelings and personalities, always be "up" and pleasant to customers, and make callers believe that they care. "Many operators like the sense of structure in their jobs," says Charles Thornton, director of operator services for AT&T. "There seems to be a sense of comfort in this, or perhaps a lack of discomfort. The job is unambiguous. Ambiguous situations make some people uncomfortable."

Chuck Bradley, for example, says that operators like having one part of their lives—their work—uncomplicated. "There will be no surprises at my job today. I have the complete freedom of doing only what is required. All I have to do is pick up the headset and plug in and the calls will come. My supervisor once told me, 'We want you to make the right decisions on the job without knowing why.' I'm on automatic."

Questions

1. What kind of personality do you feel would be most consistent with the modern-day telephone operator? What kinds of personalities would not be consistent? (See chapter 3.)
2. How do you explain that the operators are described as "extremely occupied by their work" and "I'm on automatic?" Can you think of other jobs requiring this type of worker involvement?

workers who spend most of their day at visual display units show significantly more physiological symptoms of stress, including high blood pressure and high stress-related hormone levels, when compared to employees who do not interact continuously with computers.[9] A similar finding resulted from a National Institute for Occupational Safety and Health study of workers in five organizations.[10]

The shift to mental work occurs even in factories. A researcher talked to workers in a machine plant ten weeks before and ten weeks after a robot was installed. Before the robot, a factory worker would pick up metal stock, place it on a milling machine, clamp it in, have the machine mill, stamp, or punch the metal, then unclamp it. Now the robot did all that; the worker ran the robot.

The mill job changed from handling metal to handling the robot control panel. The workers were unanimous in praising the robot for eliminating fatigue and physical strain from their work. But they complained of more subtle kinds of stress. Where once a worker could joke, sing, or daydream as he loaded the milling machine, the robot demands his full attention. As one worker said, "I don't have time to talk with anyone. I don't want them breaking my concentration."[11]

Individual versus Computer Control   What happens to workers' sense of control when computer technology is introduced to their jobs? Little direct research has been done in this area. We can, however, apply research that results from the introduction of technology to simplify jobs, which is a form of job design.

Imagine a job in an accounts receiveable department where the former clerical job included checking in new accounts, completing a brief credit check, reviewing the account for outstanding balances, and sending the final billing. This job becomes computerized. Now the job has no paper to review; all work is automatically logged in by sales; and the computer assigns the account for the clerk to work on, does a credit check, and fills out the billing with all appropriate discounts included. The clerk's job now merely entails reviewing and entering certain information on the screen.

Not only has the job become very routine and boring, but the computer now controls the process or flow of tasks. In certain jobs the computer also controls the speed of operation. In addition, numerical calculations of the clerk's speed and accuracy are readily available to management.

Problems of morale and motivation result. In many instances individuals desire to retain some control over the job and will search out ways to do so. For example, our clerk may utilize the exception subprogram to slow down the processing of accounts or may even put in "garbage" to see if the computer catches the mistake. Outsmarting the system becomes the most challenging aspect of the job. Recall a similar response from the linotype operator at the beginning of the chapter—"how can we make something go wrong . . . since the rest of the fun is mostly gone?"

In certain cases, the employee's creativity and energy is focused on providing diversions or problems. The lack of problems and uncertainty becomes boring, so one's motivation is to create uncertainty. According to some motivation theories, challenge and responsibility are motivating factors for workers. When the computer handles or reduces the challenge as well as the variety in one's job, one seeks out these factors.

Many managers' first response to this situation is to look for ways to increase control over the work process, but the more they attempt to control the process, the more the employees will search out ways to subvert that control and gain some personal sense of mastery.

For management this issue of control is even more complex and challenging. "It is much easier to envision how to exert managerial control over a set of people turning bolts and screws than it is to envision such control over people who must mentally attend to and process information. Nevertheless, this is likely to be the crux of the managerial challenge in the post-industrial society."[12]

Communication via Computer Technology   Another area affected by computer technology is the communication process between individuals, groups, and organizational units. "The auditor who once visited branches, where he worked with people and checked the books maintained by those people, is now limited to abstract information. The account officer who knows how to assess a loan by sizing up a company executive is increasingly being asked to go by the data. The bill collector who knows how to deal with people over the phone, establish relationships, and cajole them into paying, must now put less emphasis on the personal touch and pay more attention to the information in the computerized files."[13]

With computer technology there is less need for direct face-to-face contact. From the chapter on communications we know that nonverbal communication has an impact on the communication process, sometimes positive and sometimes negative. Managers can utilize nonverbal communications to influence subordinates, peers, or superiors to their point of view. Without this additional source of contact and information, the individual must rely solely upon computer-generated information.

Some interesting research gives us insight into this aspect of computer-mediated behavior. Researchers at Carnegie-Mellon University used computer terminals at various locations around the campus to study how electronic communications shape human communications. They asked eighteen groups of three students to grapple with a fictitious situation that called for a tough decision—for example, deciding between an exciting but chancy career in music or pursuing a safer job in sales, which the individual does not like. In one trial, the students talked anonymously, via the computer; in another they identified themselves as they corresponded over computer lines; and in a third trial they spoke in person. There was a time limit in all trials.

The computer sessions were stormy. It took the groups longer to come to a decision, arguments were common, and the students frequently swore, calling each other names and being abusive. On the other hand, the researchers saw that in person, a single, vocal participant sometimes swayed the group's decision. In the computer groups, the discussions were more equal, everyone getting their "air time," and having some weight in the outcome.[14]

Additional research at Stanford University confirms this unruly aspect of the communication process. While studying the computer culture through the eyes of students, researchers found several aspects of "normal" social etiquette to be missing. They found that the social niceties—who speaks to whom, when or whether to interrupt, how people are to be addressed—haven't been worked out yet. Communicating by computer breaks down social barriers that might otherwise stifle people. For example, students are less hesitant to ask questions of professors through computer networks than in person.[15] The computer network can also overcome status biases (remember the obstacles for effective communication). While discussing issues, people of lower status speak up more and are given more hearing. Obviously, on a computer network, it is often unclear what a speaker's social status is.[16]

A similar set of conclusions were arrived at in research at the Bell Laboratories. In a rather complex research design three communication alternatives were simulated: meeting face-to-face, speaking through an intercom or via teleconference, and communicating through a two-way television hook-up (videoconference). Individuals were asked to read some nonsense words, such as "lokanta" and "vahamet," and a classification system (how well the participant pronounced the nonsense words) indicated to what extent the individual was nervous. The results showed that the face-to-face meeting produced the most nervousness, the two-way television the next lesser level of nervousness, and the intercom situation the least nervousness.

The implication raised by this research is that certain behavior can be performed better face-to-face than through other forms of communication. However, novel tasks, requiring new learning or thinking, can be performed more successfully over a link such as a computer or teleconference. The relative lack of presence in some communication channels, then, may be advantageous for some tasks—learning, writing, or designing.[17]

While the direction of the discussion is pointing towards the positive aspects of using the computer to communicate, other research indicates that individuals have some reservations about using the computer and other electronic methods.

Telecommunicating is being used by some of the largest firms—Atlantic Richfield Company, Tandem Computers, Inc., Westinghouse, Bechtel Co., and Midland Ross Corporation—to reduce costs and travel for their executives around the country.

Still, a research group at MIT proposes that mere transmission of an image, voice, or words is a far cry from sending a sense of a person's presence—and it is in large part to have that sense that people want to meet in the first place. "Clearly, for purposes of notifying colleagues of bits of news, or circulating long tracts of information, the paper memo, or its electronic equivalent, will do. . . . However, there are times when a bona fide meeting is called for. There are complex issues to resolve, minds to persuade, actions to motivate, ideas to talk through.[18]

The drawbacks of a lack of face-to-face contact are especially applicable for top executives. The most important factor keeping the computer out of their offices is the realization that this technology has little to offer them directly. The nature of their work—in a word, unstructured—is such that it's not particularly susceptible to computerization.[19]

Academic studies of what managers actually do support this perception. According to the research, for example, executives typically much prefer the spoken word to the written. Kotter, who summarized his exhaustive observation of executive behavior in an article titled "What Effective General Managers Really Do," states: "Most executives don't spend much time dealing with routine, highly verifiable facts, but rather with ambiguities. How do you check out the validity of ambiguous information? By listening to the voice of the person relating it to you, probing away, looking for what's really soft."[20]

Similar results were found in other research conducted at Bell Labs, which uses computer networks that tie Bell Labs in New Jersey to researchers across the country.[21] It was found that people don't like to use their terminals for messages of importance. If they have weighty matters on their mind, they are most likely to send a message such as "I'm at extension 2600. Call me." Unless the individuals know each other well and have worked on other projects, they are reluctant to use the computer link for business.

Other researchers have proposed implications of computers that they feel warrant further study. First, they see the future automated office as increasing the volume of communication among all organizational linkages, including the upward communications. Most of this increase will be due to the fast and simple communications afforded by the use of computers. Reports and on-line data will be readily accessible by individuals who can quickly redo figures and conclusions. However, the authors point out the real possibility of information overload at the higher levels of management as managers receive a multitude of normally timed reports and many unscheduled reports by subordinates. Finally, the authors propose that the accessibility of data will tend to reduce the filtering associated with both upward and downward communication. With terminals, managers in headquarters can be in instant contact with distant operations and have the same data available to them about the unit's performance as the local management. There will simply be little that a manager can do to delay or change the information.[22]

Decision Making and the Computer Probably one of the biggest initial reasons for using computers was to eliminate the boredom, increase the speed, and improve the accuracy of routine decisions and calculations. Through algorithms and decision rules used by individuals, it is possible to incorporate much skill and knowledge intrinsic to many jobs into a computer program. Remember the airline pilot, bill collector, linotype operator, bank analyst, circuit designer, and manufacturing manager. As decision rules become more explicit, they are theoretically subject to more deliberate planning. Thus what was once a decision is not exactly a decision any more. Instead the rules for using information are specified and written in the form of a computer software program. Certain jobs now entail just monitoring the performance of the system, not making decisions directly.

Consequently individuals become insulated from the actual situational complexities that the computer program is designed to handle. Over time, it becomes accepted fact that the program and the accompanying technology are the final word about the "reality" of the situation. It is fear of this kind of dependency that has airline pilots concerned about the new generation of computer-driven planes. This may partially explain the incident of Korean Airlines Flight 007, shot down by a Soviet interceptor in September 1983. After various governmental probes into the reasons for KAL 007's being off course, some experts feel that the exclusive reliance on the plane's computerized navigational system, with no pilot checkup on its performance, may have contributed to the catastrophe.[23]

One set of research studies at the University of Minnesota focused on the decision maker, the decision environment, and the characteristics of the information system. It involved a series of experimental games in which various information systems characteristics (for example, computer-based output or certain paper-oriented aids) were evaluated as to their success with particular decision makers (categorized by quantitative aptitude and cognitive style) in different simulated environments (for example, production, procurement, inventory control).

One particular experiment was conducted in an inventory management setting, and the participants were given different types of outputs on which to base their decisions. The outputs included (1) tabular versus graphic format, (2) decision aids versus lack of decision aids, (3) exception versus full reporting, and (4) reports giving only "necessary" data versus reports containing "overload" information. Some of their conclusions were as follows:

- Participants receiving graphic output and decision aids had the lowest costs (the objective).
- Participants receiving decision aids took longer to make decisions.
- Participants receiving graphic output used the fewest reports.
- Participants receiving the "overload" information requested more reports than those receiving the "necessary" information.[24]

Another experiment focused on the impact of two different forms of information on operations management decision making. One group received their output in the form of "raw" data (meaning that there were no systematic summaries or tables), and the other group received the data in a statistically summarized format. Those with the summary data had the lower total production costs (made better decisions) but took longer to make decisions and had less confidence in the quality of their decisions.[25]

These experiments and others conducted at Minnesota reported the following as their key findings:

- Computer-system output can lead to faster decisions and the use of less data.
- Graphic output may have results similar to that of computer systems and may lead to "better" decision making.[26]

Turning from research to application, how is the computer actually influencing organizational decision making? *Business Week* found several trends regarding the use of personal computers, telecommunicating, and networking:

1. Individual managers now make decisions by combining information developed within their companies with outside data bases, including economic and industry statistics. Such data allow them to put together studies of their businesses, markets, competition, pricing, and forecasts in a few hours—studies that once took months of work.
2. New systems can turn reams of numbers into charts and colorful graphs that are easy for managers to understand. Printouts can thus be more quickly digested for faster action.

3. Electronic mail allows reports, memos, and drafts to be transmitted simultaneously to a number of people within the company. Such systems greatly speed in-house communications. Managers can get signoffs on memos rapidly, making for faster decisions.
4. Computerized scheduling systems make it possible to set dates for large meetings without consulting executives individually.
5. Telecommunicating cuts travel time and expense by enabling managers in distant spots to talk "face-to-face" via television linkups. New companies, such as VideoNet in California, are being formed to produce teleconferences, and even such hotel chains as Intercontinental Hotels Corporation and Hilton Hotels Corporation are establishing teleconferencing facilities to lure multiple business bookings.[27]

This is not to say that computer technology has total acceptance by individuals who could use it to make decisions. One researcher who has interviewed practicing managers from a variety of firms has seen resistance.

> For the manager who functions in the context of a continual flow of complete information, . . . the ambiguity is reduced. For example, in the marketing area of one bank, an information system was developed that could provide complete profiles of all accounts while assessing their profitability according to key corporate criteria. Top management and systems developers believed the system could serve as a constant source of feedback to account officers, helping them to manage their account activities and maximize fee-based revenues. But the marketing professionals steadily resisted utilizing the system. The flow of "perfect" information, in reducing ambiguity, was also seen as limiting their opportunities for creative decisions.
>
> The uncertainty of limited information may lend itself to errors of judgement, but it also provides a "free space" for actions that feel inspired. This free space is fundamental to the psychology of professional work—it is the reason that most people would prefer being professionals to assembly-line workers.[28]

Organizational Implications

The Art of Leadership versus the Science of Computers   The introduction of computers has often "improved" (from the manager's and the organization's viewpoint) performance evaluation and work monitoring through the collection of routine operational data. A superior is thus better able to evaluate personnel. For example, telecommunications, office automation, and integrated data bases provide and record simplified access to information that a manager may then use to evaluate subordinates.

One such system for improving the production quota and speed while providing individual performance data occurs in the insurance industry. "Automatic call distributors" are widely used where clericals "process" phone calls from customers. The device simultaneously tallies the number of calls each clerk handles, measures the average delay in answering calls, and counts the calls lost by the switchboard after thirty seconds of ringing. Time standards often set the pace for every clerical job within the insurance company: coding each A-type claim is allotted 4 minutes, a B-type claim 4.7 minutes. Each clerk keeps a running record of the work he or she does on a production sheet by task and day of the week. Computer terminals used by data entry operators record the number of key strokes per minute and lines processed per day. Many of these "input typists" are paid piecework rates rather than an hourly wage. For claim processors, each claim is coded with the employee's name. The computer rejects any inaccurate forms, keeping track of the number of mistakes along with volume and speed.[29]

As a result of this up-to-the-minute reporting system, supervisors need not spend hours collecting data and observing the employee or reviewing personnel files before conducting a performance review. Instead the supervisor only needs to access the computer and ask for printouts of various job criteria, such as speed or accuracy. Interpersonal relationship can thus become less important to the manager than access to information. In a sense, this can become a form of remote supervision.

At this point we do not have any research to indicate what the consequences of remote supervision would be, but we can list a few possibilities. First, remote supervision could lead to less face-to-face interaction between the employee and the supervisor. That relationship and its inherent control and connectedness to the larger organization would probably have less meaning for the employee, increasing worker alienation. Another possible consequence of remote supervision is an increased level of stress for the employee. With the possibility of consistent but remote surveillance, the employee is constantly aware of the computer's need for perfection in data entry and processing. The circuit designer, introduced earlier in the chapter, stated that she and others felt constant pressure to be "perfect." "We never know when the boss will come down and show us a computer printout on our progress. Quite frankly, I know my blood pressure is higher on this job."[30]

Remote supervision is not limited to blue-collar employees. A division manager or a plant manager can traditionally hold a certain amount of independence by maintaining control of key information, whether through timing of its release to top management or using various formats that might affect the "desirableness" of the results. With computer technology, however, top management can access day-to-day performance figures of even distant locations.

Business Week cites one such example—that of the president of Northwest Industries in Chicago, Ben Heineman. Previously Mr. Heineman had to rely upon the finance department to supply summary reports about divisional performance. "Now, with access to his company's data base, Heineman can instantly call up detailed information on current or past performance of Northwest subsidiaries, along with comparative industry and economic information from outside data bases. Often, by examining intricacies of his business he would not have seen in the past, Heineman spots something out of the ordinary—an aberration in inventory levels, for example, or an unusual pattern in production. He is thus prepared to ask searching questions of a subsidiary president."[31]

One researcher feels that this readily accessible data and its remote supervision raises several questions for a firm:

> First, some policy decisions must be confronted that address the kind of information appropriate to each level of management. Top managers can quickly find themselves inundated with raw data that they do not have the time to understand. It also creates a tendency for top managers to focus on the past and present when they should be planning the future.
>
> It would seem that this new access capability would expand top management's opportunities to monitor and direct and, therefore, improve the performance of subordinate managers. But as the on-line availability of such information reaches across management hierarchies (in some companies all the way to board chairpersons), reduced risk taking and its effects begin to take hold. Managers are reluctant to make decisions on the basis of information that their superiors receive simultaneously. As one plant manager said to his boss in division headquarters: "I'm telling you, Bob, if you're going to be hooked up to the data from the pumps, I'm not going to manage them anymore. You'll have to do it."[32]

But can management philosophy and leadership style affect or mediate how people feel and react to computer controlled work? A researcher studying the work system of bill collectors for a discount store chain did find some differences attributable to leadership style of the supervisors. Two back offices had identical automated systems that randomly distributed accounts between collectors on a continual basis throughout the work shift. The accounts were automatically queued so that the collectors had no say regarding the order in which they handled accounts. The offices were held accountable for specific production goals that kept the collectors working at a continuously fast pace.

One office was directed by managers who closely supervised their employees so that they remained glued to their visual display units and telephones. The supervisors prohibited interaction between the workers and continued to walk the floor reminding the employees of the production goals and the penalties for not meeting them. As a result of the pressure the collectors felt, they tried to sabotage the information system by keying in fictitious data or leaving account information incomplete. The turnover rate was almost 100 percent during the first year of automating this function.

The second office had supervisors who viewed their employees as adults who wanted to put in a full day's work. Supervisors saw their role as information resources who would help out with a difficult account or offer advice if requested by the employee. These managers were perceived as fair and the office atmosphere was relaxed and friendly. Employees were allowed to chat with one another as long as it didn't interfere with their work. The second office collected a quarter of a million dollars more than the other office during the first year. In addition, account information was more accurate and turnover figures were lower.[33]

One final instance of worker reaction to computer technology illustrates the importance of managerial sensitivity to the introduction of automation and the art of leading.

BOX 13–2

Terminal Tedium

Plymouth, MA—The building is in an industrial park three miles from the famous rock. And it is a factory of sorts, despite the burnt sienna carpeting and the indirect lighting.

The people who work here process health-insurance claims for Blue Shield of Massachusetts. The facility is highly automated, and the work is done with video display terminals (VDTs). Six hours a day, except for one 15-minute break, processors sit before their terminals transferring data from claims forms to a company computer system.

The computer revolution came to Plymouth a little more than a year ago, and a claims processor here offers counterrevolutionary criticism: "The girls at work call it a sweatshop. Most of them figure they won't last more than two years."

Over the past decade, computer-based automation has reached into many an American office, changing the nature of work and making the video display terminal nearly as ubiquitous as the typewriter. Sophisticated systems have helped to increase productivity and reduce employers' labor costs. At Blue Shield of Massachusetts, productivity has tripled in some areas since the company automated, according to Philip J. Gillette, the executive vice president.

A Throwback?   More and more, however, critics are beginning to question whether the new technology is improving the lot of office workers. Could it instead be producing new forms of tedium and certain of the abuses of nineteenth-century factory life, namely, piecework and exploitation of labor?

"Automation is being used to increase control over employees and to create a situation of constant pressure for productivity. It has created the electronic equivalent of the moving assembly line," charges Judith Gregory, research director of 9 to 5 National Association of Working Women, an office workers' group based in Cleveland.

The term "office automation" encompasses the use of computers by all types of white-collar workers, including managers. But the labor issue seems confined to the automation of the most routine office jobs. Most controversial of all are the high-volume data-processing centers such as Blue Shield's Plymouth production center. These electronic factories make use of the most sophisticated technology and, critics say, the most questionable labor practices.

Controlled by the Machine   A recent study by the U.S. Public Health Service offers some support for the criticism. The study looked at three types of workers: professionals who occasionally used video display terminals, clerical workers who did data-processing with video display terminals, and clerical workers who had comparable jobs but who did the work manually.

"The clerical workers using the VDTs reported by far the most physical and mental stress, says Barbara Cohen, a research psychologist who helped conduct the study. The terminal users had to follow rigid work procedures and didn't have any control over their work, Mrs. Cohen notes. "It was the machine that was controlling them."

The electronic factory is mostly a creature of banks, insurance companies, credit-card concerns, and other companies with particularly large data-processing requirements. In appearance, these places tend to be similar: a large, quiet room with video display terminals grouped in clusters or rows. The terminals are linked to a central computer. Data processors serve as electronic-age stevedores, loading and retrieving information.

The Comforts of Home At Blue Shield, there are roughly 40 processors on each of two, six-hour shifts. They sit in groups of six or so, and each cluster is supervised by a "team leader." The soft clicking of terminal keyboards is the most often heard sound.

It is a comfortable place, "like a home environment," says Mr. Gillette. Blue Shield designed its own lighting system and is especially proud of it. The light bounces softly off the ceiling from high-intensity bulbs recessed in custom desk fixtures. The effect is almost romantic, but its purpose is to reduce glare on the video screens.

As in many automated back offices, the computer system has been programmed to monitor workers' performance. To start, Blue Shield developed time standards for each of the tasks performed by processors, a technique that harks back to the concepts of scientific management developed by Frederick Taylor and others in the late 19th century. Mr. Taylor, one of the first management consultants, conducted elaborate time-and-motion studies in early factories and offices, concluding, for example, that a clerk should take $^{44}/_{100}$ of a second to make one snip with a pair of scissors.

The computer keeps track of how much work is done and prints out a production report for each employee every week. Every minute of working time is accounted for under such "computer-speak" headings as "positive direct time" and "negative indirect time."

The report shows the time a job should have taken along with the actual time it took. The computer compares the two figures to produce a productivity score calculated to the second deci-mal point. Wages are tied to productivity and are adjusted accordingly, up or down, every two months.

"You're paid on production. You know that if you stop to go to the ladies' room it's coming out of your paycheck," says a processor, who asks to remain anonymous. She compares the job to piecework, noting that processors don't get health insurance or other benefits—though Blue Shield, their employer, is itself a health-insurance company—because they're only part-time workers. And none are allowed to work more than 5¾-hour days.

The criticism "isn't fair at all," counters Mr. Gillette, who prefers to call the processors "flex-time" workers—housewives who don't want to work fulltime. He cites as a benefit of the job that processors are given paid time off from the terminals to take certain training courses. Mr. Gillette is incredulous that anyone would fault working conditions at Plymouth. "The last thing in the world it is is a sweatshop. A person can make a pretty damned good piece of change here," he says.

Almost 1984 American Express Co., which has been particularly aggressive in automating its back-office work, also uses monitoring systems. At the company's operating center, for instance, a computer keeps track of how long it takes workers to answer telephone calls. Employees answer questions about credit-card accounts using video display terminals, and the company expects them to pick up phones, on average, by the third ring. The computer hunts down the slowpokes for special attention from supervisors.

In many cases, automation can make back-office work more monotonous as well as more scrutinized. Workers who once performed a variety of tasks now do just one thing. Employers in some cases rearrange the work flow into an assembly-line operation. And computer systems render certain tasks superfluous.

In Syracuse, NY, health-insurance claims processors for Equitable Life Assurance Society of the United States needed a variety of skills when claims were processed manually. "I had to do all the figuring, making sure all the math was correct, and everything was in its proper place before the claim was typed up," says one worker. After the company began to automate three years ago, the computer assumed many of those tasks.

"All you have to do . . . is put a claim in front of you, punch some numbers, take another claim and punch some numbers," says Christine Gallagher, an Equitable dental-claims processor. "It's kind of an insult to anyone's intelligence."

Questions

1. Using the material from this chapter and this boxed feature, describe the impact computers are having on office work.
2. If management wants to introduce computer technology into office procedures, what key issues need to be addressed to maintain worker morale?
3. Using various definitions of work, describe how the claims processors at Equitable Life Assurance Society are experiencing their jobs. If you managed such a group, what advice would you follow?

In one Volvo plant in Sweden, a computer system was installed to monitor assembly operations. The computer was programmed to flash a red light signaling a quality-control problem. The workers protested the use of the red light, insisting that the supervisory function be returned to a foreman. They preferred to answer to a human being with whom they could interact, negotiate, discuss, argue, and explain, rather than to a computer whose only means of communication is unilateral.[34]

Computer-mediated Power Base   The authors of the book *Corporate Cultures* predict the coming of the "atomized organization."[35] They maintain that telecommunication networks and common cultures—not organization charts—will link the "atoms." There is a real argument for this scenario when we look at the redistribution of power because of computer technology.

One source of organizational power is the control of information.[36] Implementing computerized information systems redistributes data, and such implementation is sometimes intended to break up monopolies that exist in organizations. This is equivalent to redesigning parts of the organization, disrupting patterns of communication, and reallocating authority.

Consider the following example of the alteration of power relationships because of computer technology. "Bottom-up" power occurs where lower-level employees manage their superior's access to information. Secretaries can accrue power through various methods: use of lag time in communicating information and messages to their superiors or other personnel, selective reporting and even interpretation of information (filtering), and controlling the physical access to their superiors. What happens to the power source of the secretary when the memo is electronically sent to the executive's desk without any opportunity for personal mediation by the secretary? How will centralized data banks that are readily accessible at any time by the superior affect the superior's reliance on the secretary? What are the consequences of electronic time management and a master electronic scheduler (for meetings between individuals) on the secretary-supervisor relationship?

Prior to the introduction of computer technology, the secretary's power was positional (dependent on organizational location) and personal (dependent on individual skills, relationships, and experience). Now the power resides in the automated information system and the resulting electronic networks. The superior now has instantaneous and unmediated information. The secretary's role no longer includes being an information broker between the boss and the rest of the organization.

Similar shifts in power relationships can occur between geographically dispersed organizational units and their headquarters. What happens when the divisional vice president has the same information in the same time frame as the local plant manager? Will the superior reach the same interpretations as the plant manager even though the superior is 500 miles away with limited personal experience of local conditions confronting the subordinate?

Structural Implications of Computer Technology The following quote by Dr. Marvin Sirbu of MIT's Center for Policy Alternatives hints at the structural issues involved when computer technology is introduced:

> The company already had secretaries in a typing pool when they gave the secretaries word-processing equipment. A study found that 90 percent of the saving was from centralization; only 10 percent of the increase was from the new equipment. In other words, the results of the new equipment are often not attributable to automation but to the reorganization. In this way, technology's not totally neutral, it's the way in which it is used. Office automation is both an excuse and a cause of reorganizing work.[37]

While most managers and academicians agree that the bureaucratic, multi-layered organization is a dinosaur, there is little agreement about whether computer technology will result in very centralized or decentralized organizations. There is also disagreement about the impact on the structural configuration itself. Will it become flatter or more diamond shaped (see Figure 13–1)?

Some feel that the organizational structure will lose some of its layers as the functions of middle management become computerized. "We made the layers because we couldn't move information fast enough," notes one manager. "If information becomes available instantaneously, then you have to ask why you need all those layers. If the answer is, 'Maybe we don't,' then the impact will be on middle management."[38] A similar view is offered by a management consultant. "What has happened in the relatively small number of organizations . . . is that they've seen a flattening of the management pyramid."[39] Even robotics may

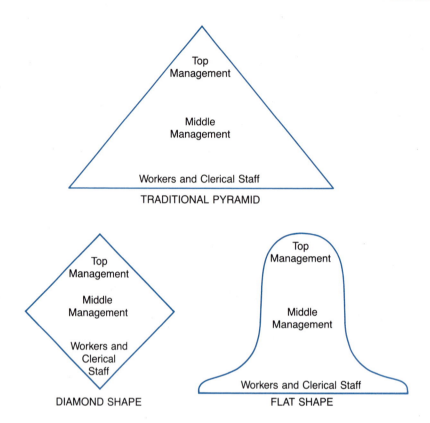

WHICH IS THE NEW STUCTURE FOR ORGANIZATION?

FIGURE 13–1
Structural implications of computer technology

influence the structure by allowing a greater span of control at the bottom of the organization.[40]

On the other hand, some feel that the impact for the organization's structure will be in the form of a basic change in configuration from a pyramid to a diamond shape. One researcher states: "We are likely to see a gradual shift in the overall shape of the organization from a pyramid to something closer to a diamond shape, with a diminishing clerical support staff, swelling numbers of professionals and middle managers, and a continually more remote, elite, policy-making group of senior managers."[41]

One final structural implication of computer technology is the effect on organizational boundaries. Part of the organization structure is the direct result of spatial and physical constraints. Tasks, activities, and the resulting information are utilized to form departments, work groups, and functions such as manufacturing, sales, and finance. These organizational units required physical, spatial, and even psychological boundaries to delineate one from the other.[42] With the advent of computers, individuals can communicate with one another electronically and are not limited by virtue of physical proximity. To the extent that boundaries are physical as well as emotional or political, electronic communication can reduce barriers between units.

Summary of Key Concepts

1. Computer-mediated work affects all types of jobs. The results can be seen as either positive or negative from the individual's perspective. The important point is that information technology has made the handling of symbols the definition of work and, as a result, has made certain aspects of work abstract.

2. Computer technology has restricted the amount of control exerted by the worker and as such may contribute to worker stress. Some workers are responding by creating problems so that control and variety are reinstated in their jobs.

3. Computers and communications have mixed results. Computers allow for more indepth communications between individuals, which can help generate novel ideas and suggestions. However, the lack of physical "presence" makes the communication of important information difficult; many managers would rather make a phone call or set up a meeting.

4. Computers can reduce the complexity of decision making by establishing logical rules in using data. But this can lead to an over reliance on computer decisions where safety and health conditions need multiple systems—human and machine.

5. Computers and computer-generated data may not necessarily be faster but the decisions seem to be better in terms of costs and speed of taking action based on the decisions.

6. Leadership and computers is an area that may pose special problems for the individual worker and the organization. Employees can feel additional stress if the computer system allows constant monitoring of their performance. Additionally, the management information system may create difficulties of who should manage what information. The term for this situation is remote supervision.

7. Computers can redistribute the organization's power in the form of information. These shifts in power and location of information may affect the structural configuration of the organization to become more diamond shaped or flattened.

Key Terms

Communication via computer technology

Computer-mediated power

Computer-mediated work

Computer-related stress

Decision making and computers

Individual versus computer control

Information society

Remote supervision

Structural consequences of computers

MANAGERIAL IMPLICATIONS

In the first part of this chapter, we talked about the impact of the computer upon the world as we now know it, specifically looking at the effect the increasing use of computers has had upon how we define and organize work, the impact of computers on individuals in the work force, how computers have affected communication, and the ways in which the advent and increasing use of computers have changed the styles of management used in organizations. And, of course, we stressed that computers will continue to be used at an increasing rate, and in ways that we cannot now even begin to imagine.

In this section, we look at the efforts to educate executives about computer usage. We also discuss what the effects are for subordinates whose bosses use computers as another method to manage those subordinates. Next, we review some polls that show the impact on us to be a two-edged sword. Another aspect to explore is the ability to work at home because of computer technology. Just as important to understand are the phases with which employees respond to the introduction of computer technology. Finally, we present some interesting and funny tidbits about computers.

Executives at Computer School

For those individuals who were born too soon to become part of the computer boom as a child, unique efforts are being made to permit them to rapidly acquire computer skills. Many of these individuals currently hold high positions in business and various kinds of organizations.

As reported in *Time* magazine, many organizations are providing opportunities for their executives to become grounded in computer skills.[43] And they often need that grounding! Complained one frustrated computer novice, "I run a $300 million division on a daily basis, and I can't even find the 'A' on the keyboard."[44]

At newly established learning centers, executives of such companies as United Technologies take three-day courses designed to provide them with basic computer skills. At United Technologies, executives are given IBM computer "packages" upon completion of the courses to use in any way that will help them effectively manage their businesses.

Many top-level executives who spend a major portion of their time determining organizational strategy do not find the computer to be an often used managerial tool. In fact, the computer is noted more by its absence than its presence in many executive suites. Top executives depend upon subordinates to do the data processing and manipulation that computers do so very effectively, devoting their attention to other matters. But with more realization of the kinds of things that microcomputers are now capable of doing, the trend is for much heavier computer usage at the very highest levels of organizations. Nevertheless, the trend may not be rapid. The experience of organizations involved in teaching upper-level executives computer skills has been that many top-level executives had difficulty learning to use the computer. They needed a lot of practice to use the computer effectively, and some individuals were reluctant to display a lack of computer skills in front of subordinates.

Many executives, having "mastered" the computer, felt that it had limited usefulness for them and that their time could be used more effectively interacting with subordinates rather than entering data on a keyboard (Remember some of Kotter's findings, presented in chapter 5, about what executives really do). Early estimates of computer use by graduates of the courses referred to in the *Time* article were optimistic. Less than 20 percent of executives who have completed the courses use their personal computers daily on their jobs; about the same number do so occasionally; and the balance say that they use the computer infrequently. Only one manager said that he did not want to use the computer at all.[45]

For executives in these high-level positions, frequent computer use may depend upon the development and availability of multifunctional computers activated by voice command. The day when this technology is widely available is not too far distant, but the issue of how useful computers will be at the policy-making level in organizations is still open to discussion. According to one CEO, one of the most difficult things to learn is when to ignore the stacks of computer printouts and rely on your intuition and creativity in making decisions. In large measure, most decisions of significance made at the top level are decisions in which organizational and individual values are a major component. Computers are of less help in this kind of decision.

Management by Computing Around

In chapter 5, on leadership, we talked about how executives and managers are using a more informal as well as more visible manner of managing—wandering around. With the advent of computers and executives learning how to use the computer, some top managers are managing their subordinates by computing around.

We mentioned that Ben Heineman of Northwest Industries was able to access his firm's data base and was therefore able to access low-level information, such as inventory control in a subsidiary. This phenomenon is becoming wide-spread. One article has termed this capability Executive Information System.[46] This system allows an executive to bypass the usual paperwork systems and channels of communication and quickly discover how the company or the industry is doing. Depending on the system's abilities and the executive's needs, a boss may call up information as detailed as the name of a bank officer who authorized a specific loan and as general as total sales per dollar expenditure from sales' entertainment costs.

"If you believe information is power, anytime you change the information flow you change the power structure," says John Rockart, director of Sloan School of Management's Center for Information Systems Research. "The CEO is potentially in a much more powerful situation. The question is how he uses it. The good guys use it with knowledge of human effects."[47]

With the new computers and simplified software, executives can now collect data at home or on trips with compatible portable units. Many subordinates now fear that the boss will know as much as they do and maybe before they do. Mr. Keen, a consultant on executive information systems, recalls one situation in which the chief operating officer of an oil-equipment supply firm discovered, through his home computer hookup, that the pricing policy for one of the company's products was far below competitors' prices. His analysis showed that the company could have made a couple of million dollars more by bringing its prices closer to the competition. "His reaction was 'If I can find out in an afternoon or two, where was the manager of this division? What was he doing all year?' " Mr. Keen adds that the manager wasn't fired but his career was severely damaged.[48]

It is obvious from this discussion that computer technology can have a profound impact on the function of managing. How will a manager handle this new tool? Will the manager use it to help subordinates learn and develop more as future managers? Or will a manager use computer technology to bypass "normal" methods of collecting data and making decisions because the manager can't trust his subordinates to do it "right"?

A Deep Wedge and a Two-edged Sword

We mentioned some of the impacts that increased use of computer technology would have on individuals in organizations. Another impact is indicated in a recent study by Louis Harris and Associates that finds that computers are driving a deep wedge into our society, separating us into classes of information-rich and information-poor.[49]

The study reported that while 68 percent of college graduates state they they know how to use the computer, only 16 percent of those who didn't finish high school are computer literate. Sixty-seven percent of those with incomes over $35,000 can operate computers compared with 23 percent of those making less than $7,500.

"Technology is becoming a structural barrier against poor people, one more thing that's holding them back. Those who don't know how to use computers are being left behind," states Robert Smith, publisher of the *Privacy Journal*.[50] "These people without knowledge of computers are often victims of credit abuse, improper arrest, and inaccurate employment records."

The study further states that while many of us are not certain what impact computers will have, those surveyed believe that computers can make our economy competitive with Japan's. But 74 percent fear that other high-tech products— nuclear, chemical, and biological weapons—could destroy the human race. Eighty-eight percent of those polled believe computer technology will improve our lives, yet many see technology-related threats that could threaten our jobs, our dignity, and our privacy.[51]

As with most new innovations, there are supporters of computer technology and there are critics concerned about its uses. The following is a summary of some of our beliefs according to the Harris study.

The Bad News

- *Computers.* Fifty-one percent consider them a threat to privacy. Two-thirds believe that there is a secret computer file on everyone somewhere and that closed-circuit TV will be used by government to record compromising activities by individuals.
- *Information Abuse.* Seventy percent believe we'll be threatened with disclosure of damaging facts about us by the federal government. That's one reason why 77 percent favor laws against information abuse, including impeachment of any public official who violates our privacy.
- *Robots.* Sixty-one percent are convinced that robots will make things much worse for us, and 71 percent believe that factory automation will eliminate thousands of jobs in the U.S.

The Good News

- *The Computer Revolution.* It's catching on! Ten percent of us have a home computer, and 45 percent of us know how to use one. Thirty-nine percent plan to buy one within five years.
- *Students.* Sixty-six percent favor computer instruction for elementary school students and 83 percent favor it in high schools.
- *Leisure.* Over half of us think computers will give us more leisure time, open up job opportunities, and help personal growth and development.
- *Electronic Mail.* Seventy-three percent look forward to the prospect of electronic mail—which may tell us something about how we feel about the current system.[52]

Thus we see some very interesting reactions and beliefs about the increasing impact of computers on our daily lives. It will be interesting to observe this kind of data five or six years from now. Is this trend another that will follow the pattern of great inventions of the past and provide neither all the benefits nor all the terrors that were predicted, or is the computer of a different nature with powers so pervasive that it will fundamentally change the way in which we live?

Working at Home

One of the impacts of computers on individuals that is most often discussed is the possibility of people doing productive work away from the organization, but linked into the communications network via some kind of remote terminal arrangement. There is no real need for physical proximity of those doing many jobs in the organization. Many workers function independently in large measure, and their physical presence in an office situation is primarily a matter of tradition. Writers, editors, in fact almost anyone whose job requires the extensive use of a VDT could conceivably work away from an office. Has this possibility really materialized? Let's take a look at some of the experiences that have been reported.

The *Wall Street Journal* recently published a report on several such experiences.[53] One Chicago bank recently dropped its experimental homebound secretarial pool because of problems of transferring correspondence typed on a home computer onto the stationery of its various departments. It took three people at the office to transfer the work of four people at home. The bank may try again in the future, using a newly developed printer.

Legal considerations are starting to appear. One Chicago publisher hesitates to provide computers for employees working at home. This organization uses employees working at home to summarize and extract business and science stories for data base subscribers. Currently they are working away at typewriters, with their product being entered into computers by other people at the office. Computers at each employee's home would be a perfect way to increase productivity, but the government has said that if the publisher provides computers for the people working at home, they are no longer considered to be independent contractors and the publisher must pay them Social Security benefits. The publisher doesn't want to get involved in this process.

Insurance issues must also be considered. If an employee working at home trips over a light cord or suffers a burn, is the company responsible? The answer to that question is not clear.

An increasing number of stories about dissatisfactions of working at home are starting to surface. Some people find the pressure of working around young family members to be particularly trying, other than doing simple work, such as company correspondence while the children are napping, for example. Some people find that they miss the social stimulation provided in an office setting. In fact, some organizations are experimenting with a system that has people working at home for three or four days and spending the remainder of the time in the office. There are some problems with this approach; one organization reports that the day on which everyone appeared at the office took on some of the aspects of a collegiate homecoming.

But for certain individuals with special circumstances, working at home via computers is an important if not essential condition of work. People with arthritis, for instance, report that they can start work in their pajamas and "warm up" to a full-time effort. Without this opportunity, they would be unable to hold a regular job. Some people have no other options available. George Chamberlain is a computer programming instructor for Control Data's home work course. He communicates with his students by computer from his prison cell at Stillwater

State Prison near Minneapolis, where he is serving a thirty-five-year sentence. He notes that he wouldn't mind a day at the office.[54]

Merrill Thompson has moved his work home and still functions as a partner in a big city law firm. In a remodeled building in a small town some two hundred miles away from the firm's Chicago offices, Mr. Thompson handles the same cases he did when he worked on the eighty-fifth floor of the Sears Tower. In fact, some clients don't even know the difference, as calls to the old office are transferred by direct telephone line from Chicago by Mr. Thompson's secretary of many years.

Mr. Thompson's practice is such that he works with a great deal of independence. He researches food and drug laws to see if they apply to a client's new product or new application of existing products. He visits clients as necessary, but usually handles client contact by phone. The direct line eliminates the cost of long-distance charges.

Clients say the move hasn't caused any foul-ups, and Mr. Thompson's partners seem pleased with the arrangement. He did agree to assume any additional expenses when he made the move and, in fact, bought his desk and office furniture from the firm. The only concern at the law firm is that Mr. Thompson's move will start a stampede. While he is the only one who has moved thus far, it's apparent that with computers and word processors, lawyers, accountants, and consultants can put themselves just about wherever they want to be.[55]

Computers and Management Systems

We've talked about the impact of computers on work and on individuals, but how about the impact of computers on management systems? What changes will be necessary to incorporate the computer smoothly into the management system?

In an article entitled "Computerization Without Fear," Michael Potts and Joel Beak of the Caspar Institute, a California consulting firm, outline some strategies for minimizing the trauma of office automation.[56] According to these consultants, there is a predictable pattern of behavior of an organization during the changeover to computerization. This pattern has six stages—initiation, resistance, acknowledgment, enchantment, disillusionment, and integration.

Initiation During the introduction of computers there is a very real threat to many of the existing systems and structures, and those employees who were not involved in the planning for the changeover may find themselves overwhelmed and embittered by the immediate effects. Often overlooked in this process is the fact that a decision to computerize often amounts to a decision to reorganize the business from top to bottom.

Resistance The second phase is one of resistance, for the pace of business doesn't slacken, yet employees are expected to tend to the business as well as master the intricacies of the new system. Office morale may plunge and emotional anxiety during this phase is usually high. If employees see the computer as a real threat, resistance may be very high. Sometimes this depends upon where the computer is located. A remote main-frame system is often more threatening because it tends to demand conformity to exterior procedures and implies invisible review of an employee's performance.

Acknowledgment   In this phase, employees recognize that the computer is here, and probably to stay. They do not support it, but feel that it is something that must be accepted. The anxiety level usually drops but is replaced with overtones of bitterness, guilt, and a tendency to self-depreciate. The energy level of the system in this phase is usually very low. The breakout from this stage for many people begins with a "hands on" experience with the computer, a time at which the task flows as promised and the results reward the worker's efforts. "It really works!"

Enchantment   Employees finally glimpse the profound vistas that computers may bring to their jobs. Anxiety vanishes but may be replaced with a desire to computerize *everything*. The world revolves around the computer.

Disillusionment   Enchantment is followed by disillusionment, a phase in which it is realized that the computer cannot do everything. Most likely, it will not make work easier, just different. The concerns growing out of constant use of VDTs attest to the reality of this phase. Many workers feel tied to their machines, with no opportunity for relaxation, and develop real physical problems because of improperly designed equipment and furniture systems.

Integration   Acceptance of the computer as a tool with no supernatural powers marks the beginning of the final stage in the changeover process. Of course, some organizations never get to this stage, but become mired in one of the preceding stages—usually acknowledgement or disillusionment. But if an organization does get to this final stage, it realizes the strengths and limitations of computer systems, and the transition to computerized systems is well on the way to being accomplished.

Potts and Beak feel that much can be done to help an organization progress through these stages. Many of their recommendations revolve around establishing a team of internal and external people who can become involved in both the planning and implementation of the various steps in the change process. As we discussed in chapter 11, Management of Change, a change agent can play an important role in successfully introducing change into an organization, and teams of the kind described could be a very effective way to perform the functions of a change agent.

Tidbits of Computer Lore

As a final note to this seemingly inexhaustible flow of information about computers, we thought you would enjoy learning some fascinating facts from computer lore. Published in the book *The Naked Computer*, some of the more interesting gems include the following:

- The first computer "bug" was a dead moth found in the 1940s inside a calculator at Harvard University. The bug was stuck in a relay which prevented the proper operation of the machine. Thus, the term bug was coined to mean a problem with the operation of the computer or its program. The carcass can still be viewed. It's taped to a page in a log book in a Navy museum in Virginia.
- Lockheed Missile and Space Company transfers computer data every day from its Sunnyvale, California, office to its research center in the Santa Cruz Mountains by carrier pigeon.
- One of the world's fastest computers, used by the Mead Corporation, a service bureau, can print 45,000 lines in a minute, or a 225-page book in thirty seconds. It's primarily used for printing junk mail.
- During the Iranian crisis, U.S. spy satellites distinguished among mullahs by the shape and fullness of their beards—from 23,000 miles away.
- One evening while playing Merlin, an electronic game for kids, a friend of the inventor found that the game's beeps could dial a number on a touch-tone phone. The result? The IXO Telecomputer, a bestselling communications terminal.
- Bill Gates was playing poker one night in January 1975 in a Harvard dorm when a friend showed him a copy of *Popular Mechanics* with a cover story about Altair, the world's first popular personal computer. On a whim, Gates came up with the application of BASIC, one of the world's most popular programming languages, for the personal computer. Their company, Microsoft, is now one of the leaders in the software industry.[57]

DISCUSSION QUESTIONS

1. Why did the opening short stories about individual reactions differ from negative to positive? What significance might your conclusions have for managers?
2. In what ways could computer technology enhance the communication processes in organizations? Give examples.
3. What is your reaction to the term "remote supervision"? What are positive aspects of this concept? What are negative aspects?
4. Most researchers agree that organizational structures will be affected as a result of computer technology, becoming diamond shaped or flatter shaped. Which do you feel is the most realistic possibility? Why?
5. If you were called in to consult with a firm implementing computer technology, what advice would you offer?

EXERCISE

From reading this chapter, you are aware that while the exact effects of computer technology aren't known, we do have some hints that organizational processes (communication, decision making, and leadership) will be affected. This exercise will help you understand some of these possible changes.

Using the following set of questions as a guide for constructing your own questionnaire, interview individuals who are currently using computer technology on the job or are planning on implementing computer technology. Other interviewees might include students at your school's computer center who are currently enrolled in a computer programming course. After gathering your own data, share your results and identify any general trends or issues you think should be addressed.

Possible Questions

1. What is your job like using the computer?
2. Do you consider yourself a novice, somewhat knowledgeable, or very experienced with computer technology?
3. How important is it for you to understand and be able to use the computer in your job (study)? Why?
4. What difficulties have you experienced? Please give some examples.
5. How are others around you responding to this same experience? If it is different, what do you think accounts for the differences?
6. If you did the same tasks before the advent of the computer, how does it compare? Harder? Easier? Better? Worse?
7. How much control do you have now with the computer? How does it feel to have (no control/control)?
8. Is your performance better or worse as a result of using the computer? Why?
9. What would you do differently if you had a say about how the computer was introduced to you?
10. Would you recommend that others use computers on their jobs? Why?

NOTES

1. This and preceding examples from Shoshana Zuboff, "Problems of Symbolic Toil," *Dissent* (Winter 1982): 51–61.
2. Personal interview, 14 December 1983.
3. Personal interview, 12 November 1983.
4. Personal interview, 15 June 1984.
5. Coined by Shoshana Zuboff.
6. *Scientific American* (September 1982).
7. John Naisbitt, *Megatrends* (New York: Warner Books, 1982).
8. Harley Shaiken, "A Robot Is After Your Job," *The New York Times*, (3 September 1981).
9. Gunn Johannson and Gunnar Aronsson, "Stress Reactions in Computerized Administrative Work," *Journal of Occupational Behavior* 5 (1984): 158–181.

10. Patrick C. Herdman, "High Tech Anxiety," *Management Focus* (May–June 1983): 29–31.

11. Linda Argote, Paul S. Goodman and David Schkade, "The Human Side of Robotics: How Workers React to a Robot," *Sloan Management Review*, 24, no. 3 (Spring 1983): 31–41.

12. Daniel Coleman, "The Electronic Rorschach," *Psychology Today* (February 1983): 37–43.

13. Ibid, p. 41.

14. Sara Kiesler, Jane Siegel, and Timothy W. McGuire, "Social Psychological Aspects of Computer-Mediated Communication," *American Psychologist* (in press).

15. L. A. Welsch, "Using Electronic Mail as a Teaching Tool," *Communications of the* ACM 23 (1982): 105–108.

16. Kiesler et al., "Social Psychological Aspects."

17. Valerie Geller, personal communication, September 1983.

18. Nickolas Negroponte, personal communication, January 1984.

19. John Dearden, "SMR Form: Will the Computer Change the Job of Top Management?" *Sloan Management Review*, vol. 25, no. 1 (Fall 1983): 57–60.

20. John P. Kotter, "What Effective General Managers Really Do," *Harvard Business Review* (November–December 1982): 156–167.

21. Geller, personal communication, September 1983.

22. Margrethe H. Olson and Henry C. Lucas, Jr., "The Impact of Office Automation on the Organization: Some Implications for Research and Practice," *Communication of the* ACM, vol. 25, no. 11 (November 1982): 838–847.

23. Viktor Belenko, "What Really Happened to KAL Flight 007," *Reader's Digest* (January 1984): 72–78.

24. I. Benbasat and R. G. Schroeder, "An Experimental Investigation of Some MIS Design Variables," *The Management Information System Quarterly* (March 1977).

25. H. L. Cherany and G. W. Dickson, "An Experimental Evaluation of Information Overload in a Production Environment," *Management Science* (June 1974): 1335–1344.

26. Ibid.

27. *Business Week* (25 April 1983): 68.

28. Shoshana Zuboff, "Problems of Symbolic Toil," p. 53.

29. Glen and Feldberg, "The Clerical Labor Process and Worker Response," unpublished draft for the Conference on the Labor Process, May 1980.

30. Personal interview, 14 December 1983.

31. *Business Week* (25 April 1983): 69.

32. Shoshana Zuboff, "New Worlds of Computer-mediated Work," *Harvard Business Review* (September–October 1983): 148.

33. Shoshana Zuboff, "Computer-mediated Work: The Emerging Managerial Challenge," *Office: Technology and People*, vol. 1 (1983) 237–243.

34. International Federation of Automation Control, Newsletter #6 (September 1978).

35. Terrence E. Deal and Allan A. Kennedy, *Corporate Cultures* (Reading, MA: Addison-Wesley, 1982): 137.

36. A. M. Pettigrew, "Implementation Control as a Power Source," *Sociology*, vol. 6, no. 2 (May 1972): 187–204.

37. Marvin Sirbu, personal communication, March 1984.

38. *Business Week* (25 April 1983): 68.

39. Ibid.

40. C. A. Meyers, ed. *The Impact of Computers on Management* (Cambridge, MA: The MIT Press, 1967).

41. D. Coleman, "The Electronic Rorschach," p. 43.

42. R. E. Callahan, "A Management Dilemma Revisited: Must Businesses Choose between Stability and Adaptability?" *Sloan Management Review* (Fall 1979): 25–33.

43. "Finding the A on the Keyboard," TIME (16 May 1983): 64.

44. Ibid.

45. Ibid.

46. *The Wall Street Journal, Educational Edition*, vol. 4, no. 1 (1984): 9.

47. Ibid.

48. Ibid.

49. U.S.A. TODAY (8 December 1983).

50. Ibid.

51. Ibid.

52. Ibid.

53. *The Wall Street Journal* (29 June 1983): 29.

54. Ibid.

55. *The Wall Street Journal* (15 July 1983): 21.

56. Michael Potts and Joel Beak, "Computerization Without Fear." A report published by the Caspar Institute, Caspar, CA, November 1982.

57. Jack B. Rochester and John Gantz, *The Naked Computer* (New York: Morrow, 1983).

RECOMMENDED READINGS

Harvey L. Poppel, "Who Needs the Office of the Future?" *Harvard Business Review* (November–December 1982): 146–155.

Poppel describes how white-collar productivity could be improved by using new office systems. He considers how conferencing, information transfer, information retrieval, personal processing (word-processing and interactive graphics), and activity management (electronic files and automated scheduling) might reduce the amount of unproductive activities managers face during a typical work day.

Linda Argote, Paul S. Goodman, and **David Schkade,** "The Human Side of Robotics: How Workers React to a Robot," *Sloan Management Review* (Spring 1983): 31–41.

This article examines workers' reactions to the introduction of a robot in one factory. It focuses on understanding workers' psychological reactions to this technology and to the manner in which it was introduced. The article concludes with a set of strategies for introducing robots into the factory.

New Technology and Job Design in a Phone Company

In the late 1970s a phone company began to automate a major part of the customer repair system. Previously, customer requests for repair service had been handled as follows:

1. Customer calls were connected with the local repair bureau which serviced the area;
2. The request was received in the repair bureau by a repair clerk who recorded all details on a form, initiated a manual test of the phone service to locate the trouble, and made a tentative time commitment for completing the repairs;
3. The clerk handed the form to a supervisor of the field repairman; and
4. If a customer called the bureau again, the clerk could readily check the status of the repair order.

Repair clerks engaged in a number of additional work activities, such as filing and assisting other personnel in the bureau.

The new system utilized on-line computer technology with the objectives of reducing the time taken to process requests and the number of clerks required. The new system operated in the following way:

1. The clerical task of receiving customer repair requests was removed from local bureaus and centralized in one answering center, connected by on-line computer to a large number of repair bureaus over a four-state area. One hundred answering personnel, designated as RSAs, manned the centralized answering cen-

ter over three shifts. The floor plan is shown in Figure A. Any phone call could be routed to any desk.

2. Customers with repair requests were connected to the answering center where the calls were directed to one of the available RSAs, and the RSA receiving the call elicited precisely the information required and recorded the details on a visual display console.
3. This information was dispatched automatically via computer to the appropriate repair bureau which received it in printout form. At the same time, the RSA initiated an automatic test of the customer's service.
4. Following prescribed guidelines, the RSA provided the customer with a schedule commitment for the repair.
5. The incoming repair requests and test results were received by operators in the repair bureau and passed on to supervisors, who dispatched field personnel to restore or repair subscriber service.

Organizationally, the answering centers and the repair bureaus reported to company headquarters by different chains of command. Employees in the answering center were represented by the same union which represented all nonsupervisory employees in the repair bureaus.

Technically, the new system promised to reduce both the time taken to process repair requests and the number of answering personnel required, but these objectives were not being achieved. Nor did the quality of service meet performance objectives. The system was plagued by three sets of problems:

1. Problems of task performance and work dissatisfaction among employees of the

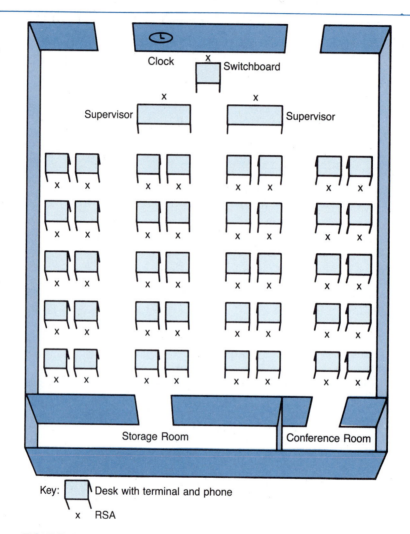

Key: ▢ Desk with terminal and phone

x   RSA

FIGURE A
Floor plan of answering center

answering center. Symptoms included conflict, turnover, tension, low morale, and the "worst labor relations in the company."
2. Coordination difficulties and conflicts, particularly at the interface between the answering

center and the repair bureaus.
3. Some new sources of customer dissatisfaction.

Some of these problems could be associated with the introduction of a new system, but others arose from the effects this particular system was having on the organization and performance of work. These problems were likely to persist.

Questions

1. What impact does computer technology have on the job definition and kinds of tasks performed by the repair clerks?
2. At which of the six stages outlined by Potts and Beak is the company in this case? What would need to happen to move the organization to the next stage?
3. If you were presented with this problem as a consultant, what would you recommend to improve the situation for the organization and the worker?

CHAPTER FOURTEEN
Productivity

OBJECTIVES

- Identify some of the issues that make productivity hard to define and measure

- List the major research conclusions from the Sentry Study, Chamber of Commerce Survey, New York Stock Exchange Survey, and Seattle University Survey

- Describe the six strategies organizations have used to improve their productivity

- Discuss the various aspects of incremental implementation of a productivity program

- Identify and explain the major managerial implications surrounding productivity in organizations

Wanted: Japan's Toyota Know-how

Toyota City, Japan—In every direction, as far as the eye can see, the unmistakable imprint of Japan's largest automaker is evident in this city that fittingly bears the company name. . . .

But recently, visitors have been most interested in another side of Toyota City: It is, by nearly all accounts, the most efficient car-making operation in the world.

Indeed, the General Motors Corp., the world's biggest car producer, is interested in buying access to Toyota's manufacturing know-how. Last month, the two companies announced they have been discussing the possibility of the joint production of small cars in the United States, presumably at one of GM's idled plants. . . .

Despite restraints on its exports to the United States and Western Europe, Toyota keeps making money while Detroit struggles with losses. Toyota earnings rose 16 percent in the six months ended Dec. 31 to $277 million, figured at current exchange rates.

The magnitude of the Japanese edge in manufacturing costs has become apparent with recent studies done by consultants, academics and the auto companies.

The findings indicate that major producers in Japan can manufacture and ship a small car to the United States for $1,300 to $1,700 less than American companies can make a similar car. Furthermore, the higher hourly wage and benefit rates paid to American auto workers—$19.65 at GM compared with $11 at Toyota—apparently are not the biggest part of the cost difference.

According to a study by James Harbour, a management consultant, the hourly labor costs difference is probably less than $500 a car, and that is nearly offset by the shipping and duty costs of bringing an auto from Japan to the United Sates.

Even after transport charges, Harbour's estimate is that the Japanese advantage is still about $1,500 because of more efficient manufacturing methods.

The Toyota advantage is a manufacturing system that in its constituent elements is neither visionary nor dependent upon sophisticated technology. But taken as a whole, the Toyota system represents a revolutionary change from certain tenets of mass production and assembly-line work originally applied to the auto industry by Henry Ford.

The Toyota approach has three main objectives: keeping inventory to an absolute minimum; making sure each step of the manufacturing process is done correctly the first time, even though the assembly line runs slower as a result; and continually reducing the amount of human labor that goes into each car.

The methods used to achieve these goals seem mundane, though implementing them is not simple. For example, American auto executives and consultants recently have been examining Toyota's production control system known as kanban—literally, "sign board."

. . . Containers tailored to hold a certain number of parts are delivered by a supplier and the parts are removed as needed. A kanban—an index card-sized label—is attached to the container, inscribed with instructions directing the supplier how many parts to put in the empty container, and when to return to the plant—to the minute, not before not after.

"Kanban is symptomatic of a fundamentally different philosophy of making cars," said James Abegglen, vice president of the Boston Consulting Group in Tokyo. "It's a constant search for waste and ways to eliminate it."

In another corner of the plant, one man fastens parts to a car chassis with specially designed tools. After the work is done, the chassis is lifted and placed at the next work station by a mechanical contraption that looks ungainly and homemade.

In fact, a handful of workers designed the automated transportation system and other improvements, with the assistance of company production engineers. Five persons used to be at the work station, and now there is one. Because of Toyota's practice of permanent employment, common among most large Japanese companies, the displaced workers are moved to other jobs, not laid off.

By now, eagerness of Toyota workers to make cost-cutting suggestions is legendary. But analysts say the current level of participation is the result of decades of nurturing with financial incentives and a long track record of proving to workers that their recommendations would be adopted.

Moreover, Toyota's manufacturing-cost advantage is not attributable to space-age technology. For instance, the Kamigo engine plant, where 70 percent of the company's engines are produced, is 15 years old. . . .

What the Toyota manufacturing advantage means in terms of saving time, space and money on the factory floor is illustrated by the results of an April 1980 study by Ford, meant for its internal use, that compared Ford plants in Western Europe and the United States with Toyota plants.

Over all, it found that Toyota's output per worker was three times the level at Ford. Because of the Japanese company's inventory-paring techniques, a Toyota engine plant took up 300,000 square feet, while a comparable Ford factory covered 900,000 square feet. The ability to do the same job with one third the factory space yields considerable savings in building and operating costs.

Between 80 and 85 percent of the Toyotas coming off the final assembly line had no defects, the study found. At Ford, cars averaged seven to eight defects in each. Because of Toyota's huge investment in back-up tooling, the time required to change a standard die was five to 10 minutes, while it took three to four hours at Ford.[1]

The Japanese advantage: All Japanese companies compared with American companies
(Source: Harbour & Associates)

		Japan	U.S.
Manufacturing (Machine stamping operations)	Parts stamped per hour	550	325
	Manpower per press line	1	7-13
	Time needed to change dies	5 minutes	4-6 hours
	Average production run	2 days	10 days
	Time needed to build a small car	30.8 hours	59.9 hours
Personnel (Average automobile plant)	Total workforce	2,360	4,250
	Average number absent (vacations, illness, etc.)	185	500
	Average absentee rate	8.3%	11.8%

UNDERSTANDING PRODUCTIVITY

We could say from the opening story that the issue of productivity looks easy when you have a productive organization; but, as we shall see, becoming more productive can be very complex and difficult. The lack of basic research makes the study of productivity difficult, compared to the subjects of earlier chapters of this book. Yet even though the systematic study of productivity is fraught with problems, we feel that the issue needs to be addressed because by its very nature it calls for integration. Examining productivity can provide us an opportunity to see how the various other aspects of organizations—communication, motivation, decision making, conflict management, leadership, group dynamics, job and organization design, and management of change—interact as they do in reality.

In this chapter we look at the issues of defining and measuring productivity. We review some of the literature that tells us how management and workers view productivity. Next we discuss some strategies organizations have used to increase productivity. Finally, we look at some of the managerial implications and examples of approaches to productivity.

Introduction

"How many people work in your organization?" one executive asked another. "About half." This old joke is still repeated in corporate boardrooms across the nation, but it probably produces fewer chuckles today than it did in the past. Growing concern about the United States' relatively sluggish productivity record of recent years has made worker performance a topic of intense scrutiny and debate.

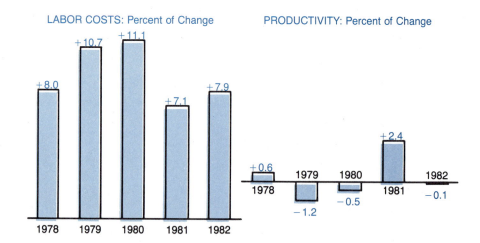

FIGURE 14–1
Labor costs versus productivity (Source: Based on data supplied by the U.S. Department of Labor, Bureau of Labor Statistics.)

It is easy to list figures to support the view that productivity is a problem. For instance, the U.S. Department of Labor has compiled various indices to help keep track of productivity and other relevant variables, such as labor costs, inflation rates, and output per hour worked. Figure 14–1 depicts some of their findings. One can go further and compare the U.S. with other nations to see how well or poorly we are doing. Table 14–1 shows some of those comparisons.

While these facts seem to indicate that U.S. productivity needs to be addressed from a national, regional, industrial, and organizational perspective, there seems to be a lack of clear agreement on the seriousness of the issue, much less on how to address it. One study polled various leadership groups here and abroad about how serious productivity problems are. Over 75 percent of the public said that declining productivity will continue to be a serious problem for the next several years. Business leaders voiced a greater concern for this view by agreeing 92 percent. Yet labor union leaders felt that, while it is a problem, it's one that's often exaggerated (41 percent).[2]

This difference in views (which has some basis in how the various leadership groups perceive the importance of productivity) and its popularity in the media has influenced us to include this chapter on productivity. It is our belief that some of the disagreements about the seriousness of and the methods to solve the productivity problems is inherently a human problem that can not be divorced from the study of organizational behavior. In addition, there are a multitude of questions usually raised when one talks about productivity. What is productivity? Is it doing better work, more work, or doing more work better? Do employees agree with the claim that productivity is down? Does productivity mean to them the same thing it means to top management? Do employees have an incentive to

TABLE 14–1

U.S. manufacturing productivity growth as compared to other nations

Country	Average Annual Percent Growth 1960–1966	1966–1976	Percent Change
Japan	8.8	8.9	+1
Denmark	5.4	8.0	+48
Belgium	5.0	8.1	+62
Netherlands	5.6	7.4	+32
Germany	6.0	5.8	−3
Italy	6.7	5.3	−21
Sweden	6.5	5.2	−20
France	5.5	5.8	+5
Switzerland	2.9	5.1	+56
Canada	4.3	3.5	−19
United Kingdom	3.7	3.1	−16
United States	4.0	2.2	−45

Source: Based on Timothy Hannan, "The Productivity Perplex," *Business Review of the Federal Reserve Bank of Philadelphia* (March–April 1980): 9–10.

increase their productivity? If so, what is that incentive? The creativity needed to address these issues will be the result of a joint effort by both the management and the employees of a firm.

What Is Productivity?

While there are numerous definitions of productivity, the fundamental problem is that, by and large, they all fall into one of two "camps"—the quantitative or the qualitative. The statistics released periodically by the federal government, similar to the previous table and figure, are purely quantitative. They measure the rate of output divided by the rate of consumption of labor, capital, and material. The human factor, together with the quality of the products and services produced, is simply not relevant to this measurement technique. One executive stated that "three major studies on the American economy have found that technology and capital are the two biggest drivers for productivity improvement. Depending on which study you believe, the quality of the workforce accounts for only 10 to 18 percent of the improvement. People associate productivity with people and that is not necessarily so. It's a fact that an unhappy man with a bulldozer will get more done than a happy man with a shovel." At the same time, however, this executive acknowledged that "the human being is the one element that can shut the whole thing down. All the state-of-the-art technology in the world, together with un-limited capital, will not succeed in increasing productivity unless it is endorsed and applied by people."[3]

Difficult to Define   This still leaves us with the question of what is productivity and how do we measure it? Productivity is the ratio of some output to some input. Productivity is not a measure of production or output produced. It is a measure of how well resources are combined and utilized to accomplish specific, desirable results.

$$\text{Productivity} = \frac{\text{output}}{\text{input}} = \frac{\text{results achieved}}{\text{resources consumed}}$$

The output, or results achieved, may be related to many different inputs, or resources, in the form of various productivity ratios—for example, output per labor hour, output per unit of material, or output per unit of capital. But the actual concept of productivity is the result of interplay between various factors in the work place. These influencing factors include the quality and the availability of materials, the scale of operations and the rates of capacity utilization, the availability and throughput capacity of capital equipment, the attitude and skill level of the work force, and the motivation and effectiveness of the management. The manner in which these factors interrelate has an important bearing on the resulting productivity.

This interplay of forces can be seen in a problem that faced Burger King—how to keep Whoppers really hot without warming the iced drinks stationed next to them. To combat this problem a Burger King manager in Des Moines came up with the answer by sculpting a $25 piece of sheet metal to concentrate heat in the Whopper bin. The manager's idea was a major contribution to the Whopper Hotness Program, which is part of Burger King's productivity drive. Food researchers have calculated that hotness is what sells Burger King's hamburgers, and they set about calibrating that hotness to a precise 130 degrees. Having a consistently hot Whopper and ice in the drinks means more sales per hour, and in the fast-food industry, that is higher productivity.[4]

Difficult to Measure　But measuring productivity is easier said than done. There is still no simple, steadfast rule to tell one how to measure productivity except in general terms of output divided by input. The judgement of what comprises output and input still appears to be more of an art than a science. The output measure needs to relate to the individual worker's or department's or the total organization's objectives. For instance, in an automobile plant, the individual's output could be the number of windshields installed; a department's output could be transmissions assembled; and the total organization's output could be cars completed.

　Some typical problems encountered in establishing any measurement process follow.

Activity-oriented rather than result-oriented measurement.　Sometimes managerial focus drifts to the hustle and bustle of activities with diminished regard for results—for example, when booking sales for the sake of booking sales takes precedent over booking sales to contribute to the organization's profit. Pricing and profit margins must be a part of results-oriented measurement. This problem is especially prevalent in the upper levels of management, where specific results are hard to establish because of the manager's job—managing people.

Complex work processes.　Most organizations are a complex web of people, equipment, and work processes. As a result, there is a large degree of interdependence between people, processes, and functions that can even be partially hidden from the organization's management. This interdependency is especially evident in an assembly line where each subsequent work station is dependent on the prior station for timeliness and quality.

Short-term gains versus long-term results.　There are many ways to achieve short-term productivity gains. For example, quality control and training can be neglected for a period to increase output and immediate sales or profits. Many employees and managers are of the opinion that good quality and high productivity are mutually exclusive; you can not have both at the same time.

Overemphasizing one measurement.　It is not uncommon for an organization to overemphasize a single facet of performance to the detriment of other facets. For instance, a city business manager might establish tons of garbage picked up per vehicle day as the productivity measurement related to its garbage pickup activities. To look good when judged by the movement of tons per vehicle day, the garbage crew might schedule less frequent pickups. Their increased productivity is at the expense of sanitation, the public's health, and the public's nose.

Measurements for service organizations.   The determination of what constitutes an organization's output is often difficult, particularly so with a service organization. For example, what is a police department's output? What is a hospital's output? Is it the number of bed-days or released patients or any of the many other tasks performed? How does one measure professionalism in an educational department? How do we measure your learning from this course: Your grade on the final? Getting a job? Holding a job? Promotion in the future?

Some Conclusions from Research

In recent years there has been an increased interest in the issue of productivity. Many of the resulting studies have tried to discover how workers, management, various leadership groups, and the general public feel about productivity and the attempts to increase it within organizations.

But as consumers of research and data, we must be wary of what the studies mean and understand any potential limitations. In particular, most of the following are called "polls" in the more popular press. These studies are basically self-reports by those participating. In contrast to more traditional research, which may utilize multiple methods to collect data, polls are one-time collections of personal perceptions as the data base. In addition, the polls usually ask the population sampled general questions about issues with which they may not be intimately knowledgeable, whereas a serious study might inquire about the specific organization in which they work.

While these conditions may limit our ability to generalize, the data is worth studying to gain a perspective about the complex issue of productivity. The following are four typical studies and some of their conclusions.

Sentry Study   The Sentry study surveyed over 4,700 individuals in five countries through interviews.[5] The sample included the general public, and selected leadership groups (business leaders, union leaders, members of Congress, and other leaders from environmental, consumer, state, and federal regulatory groups). The following are the major conclusions of the study:

1. There is widespread recognition of the need to improve the country's productivity performance. Seventy-nine percent of Americans feel that declining productivity is at least a serious problem for the next several years. A majority of employees think that both management (60 percent) and employees (58 percent) would be among the groups benefiting most from better productivity.

2. A majority (59 percent) of the respondents believe government encouragement of greater cooperation among business, labor, government, and special interest groups would make a major contribution to improved economic growth.

3. There is widespread support for two different approaches to improving productivity: steps to increase investment, and steps to increase employee motivation. Business leaders believe use of better equipment (65 percent), employees' receiving financial rewards for productivity gains (63 percent), and better management/labor relations (44 percent) would do more to increase productivity. While employees agree these are important methods, they focused on other areas that they felt would be important stimulants to greater productivity—having more say in decisions that affect them (22 percent versus 8 percent), more job security (21 percent versus 1 percent), and better fringe benefits (20 percent versus 1 percent).

4. The survey points out the need for more consensus to improve productivity in the U.S. International comparisons strongly suggest that cooperation among management, labor, and government is a major factor in increasing productivity in West Germany and Japan. For example, Japanese business leaders (50 percent) believe that in the last ten years labor unions in their country have become more helpful in assisting business to grow and become more efficient. This is in sharp contrast to the beliefs of U.S. executives (4 percent).

Chamber of Commerce Survey   Another study by the Gallup Organization was commissioned by the Chamber of Commerce of the United States.[6] The results are based on interviews of 1,500 individuals across the U.S. The study also arrived at some major conclusions about the issue of productivity:

1. Unlike the previous study, the results indicate that U.S. workers feel that they would benefit least (9 percent) and the consumer would benefit most (39 percent) from improved productivity. At the same time, these same workers were generally optimistic and enthusiastic about doing a good job (70 percent).

2. A majority of workers (53 percent) believed it would be possible to change worker attitudes and abilities to bring about the greatest improvement in productivity. The other major factor to influence productivity from their perspective was managements' attitudes and abilities (37 percent). As an indication of these attitudes, almost nine out of ten workers said it is personally important to work hard on their jobs and do their best.

3. Worker involvement seems to be of great concern to workers and may provide a basis for improving productivity. Sixty percent of the workers responded that they would like to be more involved in efforts to help

people do their best on the job. In addition, 84 percent of the workers believed that if they were involved in the decision-making process that affected their jobs they would work harder and do a better job.

4. One area that proved to have variation in opinions was identifying the most important aspect of the job—job security, promotion, money/salary, work quality, or job satisfaction. Forty percent of the unskilled workers said that money is the most important aspect of their job. In contrast, 39 percent of the skilled workers said that job satisfaction is the most important, while 31 percent of semiskilled workers believed job security to be most important. All of the various groups felt that promotion was the least important aspect.

New York Stock Exchange Survey   This study was conducted by using questionnaires directed at organizations rather than the general public.[7] Out of over 6,000 questionnaires, 26.7 percent of the organizations responded. In certain cases, a telephone follow-up was conducted to validate the representativeness of the returns. The following are the major results from this study:

1. Only a small percentage (14 percent) of corporations have human resource programs to stimulate productivity. A "program" refers to the full scope of a corporation's efforts to involve its employees. Each program may encompass several activities, such as quality circles, formal training courses, job rotation, and an incentive plan. Even in companies with programs, four out of every ten employees do not participate.

2. Corporations stated several reasons for initiating human resource programs. But the driving force is the desire to improve competitiveness. Sixty percent of the firms mentioned cost cutting, and 40 percent mentioned productivity improvement, as prompting their programs. The most significant response in 36 percent of the firms was a shift in management philosophy as a partial explanation for starting productivity programs. Part of this shift in thinking was attributed to the favorable press on quality-of-work-life programs.

3. There are a variety of human resource activities used by the responding firms who have programs. They include formal training (76 percent), employee appraisal (72 percent), goal setting (64 percent), job redesign (46 percent), attitude surveys (45 percent), quality circles (44 percent), workflow scheduling (43 percent), suggestion systems (38 percent), task forces (35 percent), profit sharing (25 percent), and labor/management committees (25 percent). Of these programs, quality circles, job redesign, task forces, and group incentive plans are the fastest growing.

Seattle University Survey   This survey utilized a questionnaire directed at a specific geographic area of the U.S., the Pacific Northwest. The questionnaire was administered to thirty-four randomly selected firms. Fifteen organizations responded, with 284 individuals completing the questionnaire. The respondents ranged from the workers to top management. The following conclusions resulted from the study:

1. A majority (69.6 percent) at all levels in the organizations agreed that productivity was a serious problem that U.S. firms are facing. Only 23 percent felt that it was a problem that was exaggerated or not a problem at all.

2. The perception of the seriousness of the productivity problem for one's own organization declined as the management level increased.

3. Over half (57.1 percent) of top management selected organized labor as responsible for productivity decline in the U.S. This was also the most popular response for middle management. First-level supervisors blamed the federal government and organized labor. Nonsupervisors blamed organized labor and economic conditions.

4. Top management agreed that management (57.1 percent) and the federal government (28.6 percent) has the most potential for improving U.S. productivity. Middle management selected management (25.9 percent) and government (22.4 percent). First-level supervisors selected the workers themselves (20.5 percent), management (18.2 percent), and the government (25 percent). Nonsupervisory personnel selected management (20.8 percent), workers (17 percent), and economic conditions (17 percent).

5. The most popular productivity definition for middle management and first-level supervisors was efficiency. Top management's definition was financial. The nonsupervisory definition was output.

6. When asked how much respondents could improve their own productivity, only 23.2 percent said that they could only increase it 5 percent or less; 26.9 percent said they could increase it 6 to 10 percent; 25.6 percent said they could increase it 11 to 20 percent; and 14.4 percent said they could increase it 21 to 30 percent.

7. Personal recognition and participation in decision making were the most popular means of improving organizational productivity for all levels of management.

All four surveys identified productivity as an important problem needing to be addressed by U.S. firms if they are to remain competitive in the world economy. The studies also point out that the various groups surveyed (top management, supervisors, and workers) view the problem from their own perspective. This showed up in the last survey around the definition of productivity (financial, efficiency, or output). Having different views of productivity obviously makes it more difficult to create solutions. However, there was some agreement that one way to increase employee morale and productivity centers around involving workers more in their jobs. The most often suggested means was to increase workers' say in decisions that affect them.

Finally, from these surveys we can derive some hope that we have begun a journey to improve our productivity performance as suggested by the New York Stock Exchange Survey. What is sobering is the fact that we still have a long way to go to improve productivity and humanize our work place.

Organizational Strategies

At this point, it seems obvious that the issue of productivity is complex and pervasive in U.S. industry. At the same time, certain organizations have begun to address the productivity issue at the operational level. One study asked managers, "What techniques do you use to improve productivity in your firm?" Their responses included:

- Bonuses related to output or quality of work (56 percent)
- Profit-sharing, stock option, or employee stock ownership plans (52 percent)
- Quality circles of specially trained workers who identify problems and suggest solutions (14 percent)
- Sharing of profits linked to productivity gains (13 percent)[9]

In this section, we consider a model to understand how the different programs affect the organization, and we explore some of the methods used by organizations to improve productivity. Besides the techniques mentioned in the previous study, we also look at teamwork, flexitime, and the Scanlon Plan.

Model for Understanding Programs' Effects   A key element in the search for increased productivity is the organization's management and their sensitivity to the complexity of implementing any program. While managers are seriously concerned about their organization's performance and even survival, in many instances, these same managers feel that they only have to say "Let's start a Quality Circles Program here." It is very akin to the old image of a manager standing over an employee with a club. Any technique being offered out of either academic or consulting meccas is of little value when superimposed on an outdated organizational system. A productivity program that does not change rules, rewards, management practices, and the job itself is doomed.

The authors feel strongly that organizations must consider incremental improvements much like the Japanese have over the last thirty years. One way to accomplish this is first to assess the organization—the structural, process, and leadership factors and their impact on the people who work in the organization. Assessment has been recommended throughout this book, but it may be appropriate to suggest one model to stimulate one's thinking in terms of where we are and where we want to go. Figure 14–2 provides such a model.

The model indicates that the external environment as well as the causal variables of structure, process, and leadership are the key determinants influenc-

EXTERNAL ENVIRONMENT INFLUENCES

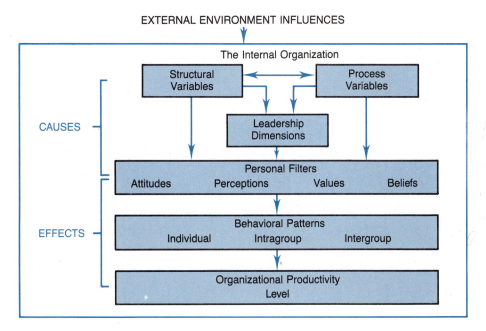

FIGURE 14–2

Organizational productivity model (Source: Jon English and Anthony R. Marchione, "Productivity: A New Perspective." Copyright © 1983 by the Regents of the University of California. Adapted from *California Management Review,* vol. 25, no. 2, p. 60, by permission of the Regents.)

ing emerging employee behavioral patterns.[10] In turn, these behaviors influence the organization's productivity level. Therefore, the ultimate aim of management to improve productivity must include an assessment and redirection of the causal factors to make the productivity program really work.

To understand the following organizational strategies and productivity programs, let us look at the model in more depth. The ultimate aim of the programs is to increase the organization's productivity level, presumably through other cause and effect relationships. For instance, according to the model, the program may be aimed at changing various causes such as structural, process, or leadership variables. These changes in turn affect the personal filters, which influence employee behavior patterns. Improved behavioral patterns should lead to increased productivity.

Consider the institution of the Scanlon Plan. This program is process-oriented (rewards are tied to decreased costs) and structural (various committees are created to evaluate ideas to cut costs) in nature. In addition, there has to be a leadership philosophy to involve employees in runnng the business. Through such a program, it is expected that employees will accept the belief that their efforts count and therefore will contribute ideas individually and within groups to increase productivity of the organization.

It is interesting to note that the strategies to improve productivity listed in this chapter are not new. They have been around for the past ten to fifteen years; some have been successfully adopted and implemented. But for these programs to be effective, management needs to be motivated to do a realistic appraisal and assessment with some model to judge critically what they are doing incorrectly as well as correctly. The model in Figure 14–2, which gives a realistic view of the complexity involved in changing or implementing a productivity program, can help.

Teamwork The Cadillac engine plant in Livonia, Michigan, is not typical of most auto factories. Hourly workers and supervisors dress much the same and cooperate closely on "business teams" that organize the work and make other decisions normally left to management. "It makes you feel like a part of what's going on," says Gary L. Andrews, an hourly worker and assistant team coordinator. A 14-year Cadillac veteran, Andrews says he would return to a traditional auto plant "only if it was a choice between that and hitting the streets."[11]

What are these "teams" that excite Mr. Andrews? Teams are the result of a group developing as an effective work unit. In organizational behavior terminology this group development is called team building—"Any planned event with a group of people who have or may have common organization relationships and/or goals which are designed to improve the way in which work gets done by them in some way or another."[12]

There are several ways to classify teams:

1. Groups reporting to the same hierarchical supervisor
2. Groups involving people with common organizational aims
3. Temporary groups formed to do a specific, but temporary, task
4. Groups consisting of people whose work roles are interdependent
5. Groups whose members have no formal links in the organization but whose collective purpose is to achieve tasks they cannot accomplish as individuals.[13]

The preceding list indicates the many ways teams can work in organizations. They could help design a new procedure for reducing rejects on a production line, develop a better method to process paperwork in a financial department, create a new use for the declining sales of a product, develop cost-cutting ideas in a financially troubled department, or tackle a number of other situations calling for creative problem solving.

But, teams are not magically organized by just putting people together. As a matter of fact, teams are effective only when those organizing them have paid careful attention to the attitudes and skills of team members, including the following:

- How leadership is exercised in the group
- How decision making is accomplished in the group
- How group resources are utilized
- How new members are integrated into the group

Teamwork and team building are important to organizations and managers as a method to improve productivity, for a number of reasons. An organization's very survival may depend upon its members being creative and having a mechanism for using that creativity. Flexibility, the ability to adapt to the changing environment surrounding all of our organizations, is also essential. Futhermore, we must fully use the human resources and talents available to us in the organization. It has been estimated that we use approximately 20 to 35 percent of available talent in an organization.[14] The remaining 65 to 80 percent lies dormant and unused. Another advantage of effective teams is their speed in solving problems. A difficulty facing many organizations today is their inability to come up with solutions to problems that should have been solved yesterday. It is, moreover, important to have *quality* solutions to the basic problems facing organizations. Not every solution is a good one. Finally, the inefficiency and ineffectiveness of poor teams manifests itself throughout the organization in the form of conflict and loss of interest among team members and general boredom among people working together.

Quality Circles   Gerald Swanson knows all about quality circles, though he's never set foot in Japan. Mr. Swanson runs the quality circles program at Lockheed Shipbuilding Company. One example Mr. Swanson proudly recites occurred in the sandblasting area. The workers in this unit noticed a couple of years ago that the sand was unusually light and dusty. It takes a lot of steel to build ships, and a lot of sandblasting to keep the steel from rusting. But the boss ignored complaints about the dusty sand. "The manager figured they were just bitching," Mr. Swanson said, and the manager told them, "Well, blasting's a dusty business." Enter quality circles. For the first time, the company listened. The sand mixture was analyzed and found to be below standards, and Lockheed was able to collect $68,000 from the supplier. "That paid for the first year of our program," Swanson said.[15]

Quality circles are one specific application of the teamwork approach. The quality circle concept involves a "comprehensive program for improving productivity through improved methods of human resource management that stress employee development and employee involvement in work-area decision making."[16]

At the heart of the quality circle approach is the assumption that motivation comes from within the individual and that management's task is to create the proper work environment for allowing the employee's inner motivation to respond. The quality circle utilizes work-area problem solving as its vehicle and provides the employee with training and development necessary for effective participation.

BOX 14–1

Honing the Competitive Edge

Looking at the old Weyerhaeuser lumber mill at Snoqualmie, one sees a huge, squat monster, hissing and howling, breathing steam. Inside, immense machines toss entire logs into the screeching blades of saws. People move about the ancient equipment, intent on their jobs. This is the mill everyone thought had closed forever when it was shut down in the early '80s. Among the reasons: a declining lumber market, its out-of-the-way location and an inefficient operation. But 11 months later, the 66-year-old mill was brought back to life. A new program was introduced, cutting manpower but increasing output through a team concept of production.

George VanVleet, Weyerhaeuser's Wood Products manager, was in charge of several mills in the Pacific Northwest. This burly, white-haired lumber veteran started working when he was 12 years old as a whistle punk. He knew the mill's problems. It was old. It had too many employees who didn't produce enough lumber to make the mill competitive. So he pondered the problem and came up with an idea. It was based partly on the attitudes and production methods he'd seen in the lumber business when he was a boy, partly on his confidence in the ability of America's working people and partly on his belief that

productivity makes profit. "It was a team concept," he said. "People say industry in the old days was autocratic. I don't remember it that way. It was a pretty open organization with everybody working together."

VanVleet began applying these thoughts to the situation with the Snoqualmie mill. "I knew if I could run this operation with 35 fewer people, I'd have some chance to make it," he said. He also knew it was unlikely that Weyerhaeuser would invest new money in the old mill. Making it competitive would be a workers' effort. "People need to know where and how they fit into the process," he continues. "The flip side of that was to ask myself what production can I make with that mill." A study showed that the mill's best production in the 10 years before it was closed was 24,000 board feet an hour. VanVleet figured the mill could squeak by at that rate. He decided that, at 25,000 board feet per hour, he could do pretty well. So if the mill were to reopen, it would be with fewer people who would have to equal, at the least, the best productivity the mill ever had achieved.

His plan called for increasing production by revamping the way people worked together. He organized them into small groups. Instead of each group having its own supervisor, one of the members would be a "lead man" who worked with the others and acted as a kind of chairman. Instead of the groups being told what to do and

Source: *The Herald,* Everett, WA. (Sunday, 13 February 1983): 1D. Reprinted by permission.

The quality circle concept centers on the total involvement of all employees in improving the way work is done. Employees voluntarily meet in "circle" groups to identify problems, analyze them, recommend solutions to management, and implement solutions when possible. It is an effective method for involving an organization's employees in assuming responsibility for "quality"—the quality of

how to do it by a foreman, they were given responsibility for getting the job done their own way. Instead of each individual having only one function, they all shared the entire task. If one member of a team got behind, the others would help him catch up. Management's function was to tell the workers what was needed. The workers' function was to do it in the best way possible and keep management informed. "The team is the basic part of the program," VanVleet said. "One guy gets the information and spreads it to the others. And he gets the information on their problems and ideas and gets it back to management. It is a beautiful, two-way communication."

VanVleet got approval from Weyerhaeuser and discussed it with the union. The mill reopened. "We said we'd give them a one-shot incentive. If they averaged 24,000 board feet of production over a 20-day period, we'd give them a bonus of $50. For 25,000, $75, and for 26,000, $100. That first day, they fell on their can. But from then on, they hit 29,000 feet per hour, and I'll be damned if they didn't get that $100 bonus in the first 18 days," recalled VanVleet.

After a year of operation, the workers are hitting 31,000 to 32,000 board feet consistently. One eight-hour shift set a record of 39,000 board feet per hour. "I have great respect for the average worker. They have good thoughts, good ideas, good understanding. They are better educated now than they used to be. And they are interested in what is going on and how they can help."

An example of the team concept can be observed during a tour of the mill: two men worked together to free a log that jammed a machine. The head sawyer left his machine to help. Under the old system, he might not have done that, a company official explained. He might have just waited.

Upstairs, in the saw filer's shop, Joe Brandenburg talked about his new situation. "In the old days, we had another guy, but now we are down to four," he said. "But now we chip in and help each other. One guy gets behind, and somebody else will take up the slack." He adds, "We used to have a foreman on the job here. I'm the lead man, but we don't have a foreman right on the job. There is only one for all three mills. He shows up and sees what's going on and away he goes. It is a lot better now. Nobody is looking down your neck all the time. You get more done. You don't need all those bosses."

VanVleet thinks the concept works so well that it can strengthen much of America's weakening industry. The union also believes in the concept. It voted by a 3-to-1 margin to put a similar program in operation at another Weyerhaeuser mill.

Questions

1. How did Mr. VanVleet's attitudes affect the program instituted in the Snoqualmie mill?
2. How does the team concept of production used by Weyerhaeuser compare with the concept of teamwork presented in the chapter? How would you classify Mr. VanVleet's teams, using material in the chapter?
3. What role did the bonuses play in worker motivation? Which motivational theory (chapter 3) best explains this result?

their work, their work environment, their professional growth, and their personal development. The name quality circles was so derived.

The program structure of quality circles will vary from firm to firm, but a typical structure is organized as shown in Figure 14–3. The organization is comprised of circles, leaders, facilitators, and a steering committee.

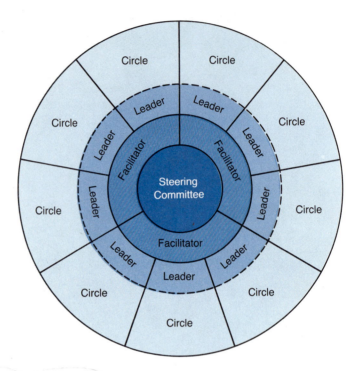

FIGURE 14–3

Quality circles structure (Source: Robert E. Callahan, "Quality Circles: A Program for Productivity Improvement through Human Resources Development," from Sang M. Lee and Gary Schwendiman, eds., *Management by Japanese Systems*, p. 86. Copyright © 1982 Praeger Publishers. Reprinted and adapted by permisision of Praeger Publishers.)

Circles.   Each circle can consist of three to fifteen members who share a common work-related experience and most often report to the same supervisor. Membership in the circle is strictly voluntary. Circles usually meet for an hour each week on company time. Members receive training in problem-solving techniques (brain storming, cause-effect relationship, statistical analysis, etc.) and presentation techniques. Members use this knowledge to identify problems and develop solutions.

Leaders.   The leader is most often the supervisor of the work group. The leader receives extensive training from the facilitator so that the leader can train his or her own circle members. The leader helps the group by preparing agendas and making sure members use good group practices (see chapter 6).

Facilitators.   Facilitators are a key element in this program. They work closely with the steering committee and the circle leaders to coordinate the program. They attend all of the circle meetings, provide leader training, obtain support and input from other functions, keep management informed of circle progress and accomplishments, and promote the program to other units who do not have a quality circle program.

Steering committee. The steering committee forms the hub of the quality circle's structure. The committee is generally composed of representatives of all major functional areas of the operation plus the facilitators. Under the committee's direction, the policies and procedures of the entire program are established and implemented. The committee determines what areas are off-limits to circle activities, coordinates the training program for the members, guides the program's expansion, and publicizes to employees the activities and progress of the individual circles.

The quality circle process refers not only to the way circles operate but, more importantly, to the management process that is involved in a circle's operation. The fundamental quality circle process is shown in Figure 14–4.

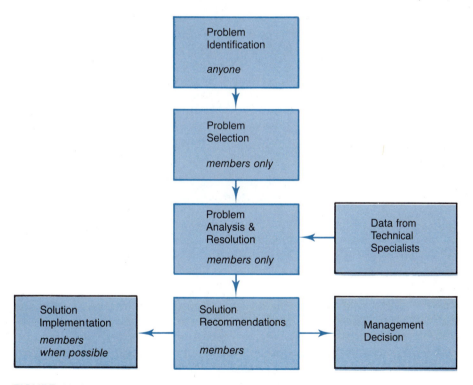

FIGURE 14–4

Quality circle process (Source: Robert E. Callahan, "Quality Circles: A Program for Productivity Improvement through Human Resources Development," in Sang M. Lee and Gary Schwendiman, eds., *Management by Japanese Systems,* p. 89. Copyright 1982 Praeger Publishers. Reprinted and adapted by permission of Praeger Publishers.)

BOX 14–2

Quality of Life at the Workplace Is Starting to Come Full Circle

He stood at the end of the table, his blue North American Tug of War Championship T-shirt spilling over his belt a bit, ready to record what the steelworkers wanted to do next. "How about tool holders in the mill," one worker said. "Then you don't have to waste time running around looking for a tool." Another wondered about suggestions from workers in the mill. "Don't you think we should respond to some of the suggestions from the guys down there," he wondered.

Wally Olecik, the man in the T-shirt, recorded the suggestions on a board. Other suggestions followed and Olecik dutifully wrote them down. "What you want to do," he joked at one point, "is redesign the whole mill." And so it went one afternoon recently at Bethlehem Steel Mill as a group of steelworkers sat around a table and tried to decide what it would recommend management tackle next to improve the working conditions un-

der which they labored.

The group was part of a growing movement in the country toward more quality circles or worker involvement in what traditionally have been management decisions. The use of quality circles as a management technique was developed in Japan. Basically, they encourage the cooperation of workers and management, meeting together to find ways to improve products or the workplace.

"We're changing an entire culture," said Jack McRae, supervisor of employee and community relations at Bethlehem. "We're changing that worker-boss relationship." But not all companies are that enthusiastic about the circles. Patricia Barber, vice president of a chapter of the International Association of Quality Circles, said her firm, Pay'n Save Corp., "runs hot and cold" on the idea. Management is not "totally committed" to the concept of quality circles, she said. Nonetheless, there are about nine circles in operation at the company.

Quality circles usually are associated with new high-technology companies, the newly emerging

Source: *The Seattle Times* (Wednesday, 12 January 1983): 1D. Reprinted by permission.

Problem identification. Identification of problems and themes for the circle to work on can come from members themselves, from management, or from any other source in the organization. The greater the number of problems that the circle has to choose from, the greater its opportunity to select a meaningful and challenging problem to work on.

Problem selection. Problem selection is a definite prerogative of the circle. The circle group itself, with each member including the circle leader having but one equal vote, arrives at such decisions on a democratic basis. This process of self-selection assures members that this is their program.

firms that can put in modern management techniques as they grow. And many high-technology firms use them. Boeing has an extensive quality circle program, according to Rod Motonaga, a circles coordinator at the Boeing Commercial Airplane Co. Eldec, an electronics firm, has just recently given the green light for extending quality circles throughout the entire operation. But the experience of Bethlehem Steel shows the circle concept can work with older traditional industries.

During the recent Bethlehem quality circle meeting, the steelworkers were trying to decide what problem they would attack next. They had just finished making a proposal to management to spend more than $10,000 to improve the air conditioning in part of the mill. Through a process of elimination and consensus, the group decided the next thing to tackle was a piece of machinery that was not working properly. It is a measure of the success of the quality circle concept that you have unionized steelworkers deciding to help the company save some money by fixing a machine. "We thought we did a good job on the air conditioning proposal," said John Massuco, coleader of the group. "But we haven't heard anything yet."

Gary Diebert, who is paid full-time by the steelworkers union to help coordinate the teams, said the program is not just a "gripe session" for the workers, but a problem-solving effort. That is in keeping with the concept of quality circles—to bring the knowledge and talents of all workers in a factory together to improve things, both products and working conditions. "Now they're learning how to solve their own problems," Diebert said. "There used to be a lot of head-butting around the plant between the union and management. They have another way of solving problems now and I enjoy seeing people realize they can work out their problems without butting heads." McRae put it another way, "If the only tool you give your foreman is a hammer, everyone is going to look like a nail."

Questions

1. Discuss the statement "Quality circles usually are associated with new high-technology companies."
2. How can the concept of conflict and conflict resolution (chapter 8) explain the results of Bethlehem's program and Mr. Diebert's comment, "I enjoy seeing people realize they can work out their problems without butting heads?"
3. Discuss the possible consequences of Ms. Barber's comment, "Management is not 'totally committed' to the concept of quality circles." What advice would you give this organization?

Problem analysis and resolution.   Having selected a problem to work on, the circle then proceeds to analyze it. The circle uses the various techniques received in its initial training. If other information is needed from technical specialists, the facilitator arranges to have them present at a session to help the circle complete its data collection and analysis. As with problem selection, all decisions concerning the problem resolution are made on a democratic basis.

Solution recommendation.   Having arrived at the solution, the circle members make their recommendation directly to management, using a powerful communication technique called the 'management presentation.' The facilitator and circle leader invite the appropriate management to attend. During the management presentation, the leader and members of the circle describe to management the project they have been working on and what recommendations they wish to make concerning it. The members even tell management how much the solution will save the company in terms of costs. The management presentations serve as one of the strongest means of providing recognition to circle members for their accomplishments. The members consider it an honor during which they can communicate directly, face-to-face, with management.

Flexitime   In West Germany, a department store, Ludwig Beck am Rathauseck, has taken the concept of flexible working hours to a new level—to flexiyears. The result is a radical new approach to schedules that allows employees to work pretty much when they want during the year as long as they put in an agreed-upon minimum number of hours. It is known in-house as "Individual Working Time." Store managers say the system works well. Sales by the staff increased an average of 9 percent when the system was implemented in 1978 and the following year sales increased another 6 percent.

Again, we must consider the figures suggesting such improvement in sales. Another possible explanation for the increase could be the institution of some other technology, such as computerized cash registers that monitor inventory and make sure that stock is on hand for all possible sales. Or we might be looking at a store that increased 9 percent, but the average industry increase was 12 percent. With these cautions in mind, let us examine the program in some depth.

A contract is drawn up between the store and the employee stipulating the minimum number of hours to be worked each year. Actual working time is arranged by department and each employee has an account in the computer, which allows the account to be overdrawn or stuffed with extra hours. Some accumulate enough hours to take a three-month vacation. The flexiyear concept has proved especially helpful to women trying to work and run households—"If it weren't for IWT (Individual Working Time), I couldn't work at all because I have to take care of my 6-year-old son," said Susanne Kuerzinger. The concept was recently introduced at the firm's New York branch.[17]

The concept of flexible work schedules, flexitime, is at least fifteen years old. The fundamental design of flexitime is a fairly simple concept that is adapted by each firm to meet its unique conditions. Whatever the local modifications, a flexitime program establishes a "core time" during which all workers are required to be present (for example, 9:00 to 3:30), and "window" or "quiet" times during which workers have flexibility to establish their own hours (7:00 to 9:00 and 3:30 to 5:00). Although workers may establish their own hours during "window" times, the traditional notion of flexitime includes both an eight-hour work day and a forty-hour week. The German department store originally found that the entire staff was in the store at 8:30 A.M., but there were no customers. This time became a "window" and the "core" was the peak customer period in the afternoon. In addition, all personnel were required to be on duty during the Christmas holiday sales.

Some of the advantages of flexitime include reduced rush-hour traffic; reduced absenteeism; improved productivity and employee attitudes; flexibility for employees to attend to personal matters; and expanded full-time work opportunities for homemakers. The disadvantages include problems in assembly line operations; adversely affected employee scheduling and supervision; increased energy costs by requiring facilities to remain operational over a longer period of the day; and making conformity to wage and hour laws difficult.[18]

But won't employees exploit the company by showing up and leaving at odd hours? It doesn't seem so from a few studies done recently. One such study involved 162 Israeli workers in several governmental agencies. Before implementing flexitime, the normal work hours were from 7:30 A.M. to 3:00 P.M. Time-clock records showed that the average worker shaved a few minutes off either end of the work schedule. After implementation of flexitime, workers got to work eight minutes later but stayed an average of twenty-two minutes longer, which resulted in a net gain for the employer of fourteen minutes of working time. This result and similar findings in the U.S. have concluded that most workers do not vary their starting and quitting times by more than an hour. The main reason seems to be the inflexibility of the "normal" world, such as demands of car pools, commuting, and families.[19]

Scanlon Plan   Rocky Mountain Data Systems' president, Mr. Schulhof, relates the story behind RMDS adopting the Scanlon Plan:

> Who are the hardest workers? . . . What was the difference between us and everyone else? . . . Was it that we were men with family responsibilities and they were women? . . . Or was it because we were part-owners of the company, knowing that we would benefit directly if the company was a success? Well, we set out to restructure our compensation so that each worker would have the same *zeal* we did.
>
> We considered stock ownership . . . *but* the payoff was 5 to 10 years in the future. . . . We considered a profit sharing and pension program . . . *but* we had no profits to share. . . . We had tried piece-work . . . *but* it resulted in everyone for himself. . . . We had tried job-enrichment and shared decision making . . . *but* it wasn't feasible for the workers to be involved in all decisions because of time constraints, and besides decisions can't be made by a committee but by the best qualified person. So!
>
> [RMDS started a Scanlon Plan.] We noticed immediately that the cases began going out faster. People were not only working harder, but smarter; since it was now their business, they wanted to make their customers happy. . . . In addition, discussions changed from, "Why haven't you repainted the bathrooms?" to "Is there money in the budget to repaint the bathrooms, or should we wait? We certainly don't want to cut into the profits."[20]

The company's Scanlon Plan developed from management's desire to create an improved work-place environment. Top management was committed to a program of employee participation that would improve communications and encourage better job performance. The company and the union created twenty-six production committees, as well as a twenty-four-member committee to screen suggestions. First-line supervision was encouraged, trained, and expected to take a leading role in the implementation and operation of the production committees. In the first three and a half years of the program 1,884 suggestions were submitted, of which 70 percent were accepted. In the first three years of the plan, bonuses averaged 5.6, 6.8, and 6.6 percent of earnings.[21]

A Scanlon Plan is a combination of a profit-sharing plan and an employee suggestion system. While a Scanlon Plan usually increases efficiency and productivity, it also is advocated as a means of reducing union-management conflict. Joseph Scanlon developed the Scanlon plan in the 1930s to save a failing company. Three general principles underlie the plan: employee involvement, bonus payment, and identity with the firm.

Employee involvement is accomplished through a formalized suggestion system and two overlapping committee systems. Elected employee representatives meet at least monthly with their departmental supervisor to review productivity, cost reductions, or quality improvement suggestions. These committees, often called production committees, have certain decision-making authority for less costly suggestions. More costly suggestions, or those affecting another department, are referred to a higher-level committee. This committee, called the screening committee, meets monthly to discuss suggested activity, bonus results, and other items such as backlogs and quality problems. Again, membership includes elected employee representatives and appointed management representatives.[22]

The payment of a bonus is based on increased productivity. The following ratio is typical of Scanlon Plans:

$$\text{Base Ratio} = \frac{\text{Payroll costs}}{\text{Value of Production or Sales}}$$

For example, assume that the normal monthly ratio of payroll costs to sales is 50 percent. (Thus if sales are $600,000, payroll costs are $300,000.) Assume a suggestion is implemented and results in payroll costs of $250,000 in a month where sales were $550,000 (payroll costs therefore should have been $275,000 — 50 percent of sales). The saving attributable to the suggestion is $25,000 ($275,000 − $250,000). The employee would typically share in 75 percent of this ($18,750) while the rest ($6,250) would go to the firm. In practice a portion of this is set aside for months in which labor costs exceed the ratio.

Identity with the firm is developed through education, communication, and discussion of the plan's goals, objectives, problems, and opportunities. Considerable management development is necessary at the supervisory level regarding how to manage groups. In addition, employee contributions are clearly evident in performance feedback about the ratio and this underscores the relationship between the firm's success and the employees' success.

The Scanlon Plan tends to be more effective where there is a relatively small number of participants (fewer than 1,000). It is more successful where there are stable product lines and costs. Finally, it is crucial that there be strong commitment to the plan on the part of management, especially during the confusing phase-in period.[23]

Profit Sharing The Facom Company, a French mechanical tool manufacturer, has achieved a growth rate that has made it internationally known for its quality products.[24] Its profit-sharing program involves employees at all levels. Its 1,300 employees enjoy salaries in the upper range of their industry and, in addition, earn shares of the profit ranging from 18 to 25 percent of their annual wages. The business is split into 100 sections, with a maximum of 20 members in each section. These sections operate as responsibility centers, making a wide variety of operational decisions, including the development of the budget and the establishment of section wages and all costs. The sections receive meaningful feedback on all operations.

When Facom initiated its plan in 1948, it had no profits. In 1972 it earned a profit of 18 percent on sales (the average rate for the 500 largest firms in France for 1972 was about 4 percent). Using a productivity index (1962 figures act as a base of 100) of the main European countries that produce hand tools, Facom had achieved a figure of 337 in 1972, as compared to 194 for Germany and 153 for England.

A profit-sharing plan is essentially any procedure whereby employees receive a share of the company's profits in addition to their regular pay. The major types of profit-sharing plans are cash plans, deferred plans, or some combination of cash and deferred plans. Under a cash plan, payments are made to employees at the end of each period (usually quarterly or annually). Profit-sharing plans are increasing in popularity, particularly among small companies.

One of the earliest movements toward profit sharing occurred in France. In 1842, a Paris house painter and decorator, E. J. Leclaire, paid his workers a share of his profits, just as he had promised them at the beginning of the year. Leclaire's employees obviously liked the plan but his competitors thought it was unfair and criticized Leclaire's generosity. The oldest profit-sharing plan still operating in the United States is Proctor and Gamble's plan, which was started in 1887.[25]

Over 100,000 companies have installed profit-sharing plans tailored to their own specific conditions. Consequently, many different kinds of plans exist. Some have a constant proportion of profits that are contributed by the company, usually 20 to 25 percent. Other plans have a discretionary arrangement whereby the company's contribution is decided each year by its board of directors. Other plans have ascending or descending scale formulas whereby the percentage of profits designated for a profit-sharing plan increases or decreases as a company's profits increase or decrease.

Many companies have claimed that their plans have succeeded in creating a sense of partnership between employees and management and in increasing

BOX 14–3

How to Improve Your Company's Productivity? Don't Go to Japan! Go to Cleveland!

Our image of Cleveland is probably one of a dying midwest industrial city. This is enhanced by the broken factory windows and abandoned plants. But continue just beyond the city limits and you will come upon a thriving eighty-seven-year old manufacturer that counters the stories of lazy American workers. It's Lincoln Electric, which produces arc-welding equipment and induction motors.

Last year it paid its 2,624 workers an average of about $44,000. Many of the production workers, who are paid on piecework, did even better. The company hasn't had a layoff in over thirty years. And this isn't Japan and its guaranteed employment.

While the total labor costs including benefits of the auto workers closely match the pay of Lincoln Electric, the Lincoln Electric workers haven't priced themselves out of a job. In arc-welding equipment, Lincoln is the world market leader, with much of its market overseas. The main reason for that is Lincoln's extraordinary productivity gains. In 1915 Lincoln was selling one of its earliest arc welders for $1,550. The price of a comparable model today is $996. In the intervening sixty-seven years, Lincoln's average factory pay has climbed 100-fold, to about $21 an hour, including a year-end bonus that effectively doubles base pay.

What accounts for Lincoln's productivity? "They don't give anything away. You work for it," says a sixteen-year veteran at Lincoln. Unlike the tonnage bonuses common in the steel industry, Lincoln piece rates are not a supplement to base pay, they are the base pay. If a worker calls in sick, the worker doesn't get paid. If a worker lets a defective machine through, he or she fixes it on personal time.

If one were to try to describe Lincoln's management system, "incentive management" might be the term, resulting in the expectation that the worker is self-motivated. If the worker can arrange work space or tasks to get a job done faster, that person is free to do so—and will pocket more money. The company doesn't object if someone figures out a way to beat the times figured into the piecework rates, since the higher volume will spread overhead costs over more pieces. The worker will get rich, but so will the company. Or the worker could turn in a suggestion for restructuring the job, losing the piecework windfall but gaining bonus points in return. Bonuses, awarded for teamwork and suggestions, average something close to 100 percent of base pay in most years, but vary widely from worker to worker.

While this type of work environment isn't for everyone, the turnover rate is only 6 percent a year, about one-sixth the rate for electric man-

Source: Adapted from *Forbes* (5 July 1982): 51–52. Used by permission.

employee interest in the company. In turn, many profit-sharing plans have contributed to the financial security of employees. Profit-sharing plans also have certain limitations. Because a worker's share of the profit is not directly tied to the individual's productivity, a profit-sharing plan does not effectively motivate some

ufacturing in general. The employees are constantly reminded that there is no free lunch. They once voted down a dental insurance plan, fearing it would cut too deeply into profits and thus their bonus checks. For the same reason they don't challenge the lack of air conditioning. When orders are slack or machines broken, workers accept arbitrary job reassignments. Sometimes the substitute assignment pays worse than the regular one, since there are no seniority rights.

The system would be a sure formula for factory revolt if management had not built up a certain amount of trust and esprit de corps. The company has an employee-elected advisory board and doesn't hire executives from the outside. Chairman William Irrang, age seventy-four, started out fifty-three years ago on piecework in the armature-winding department. He gets no fringe benefits his workers don't get and eats in the same spare cafeteria. Of course, he gets paid on a formula based on a percentage of sales that netted him $510,665 in 1981.

The contortions the company goes through to smooth output pays off in several ways. First, it prevents the peaks and valleys that cause so many firms to hire and layoff employees. Second, this smooth operation is reflected in a system of inventory called "kanban" in Japan—on-time delivery that allows a manufacturing firm to store only several hours of inventory. Lincoln has no central stockroom; supplies are delivered directly to a work area through one of the many loading docks in the oblong factory. Since Lincoln is a steady customer in good and bad times, it can demand reliable supplies.

James Lincoln was the inspirational dynamo who instituted the piecework system in 1914 and the bonuses in 1934. And his rugged Darwinism lives on. It's not uncommon to hear a factory worker spout Lincolnesque diatribes against featherbedding and paid holidays. Irrang, Lincoln's hand-picked successor, need not fear a takeover upsetting the delicate community of interest between worker and company. Better than 80 percent of Lincoln Electric stock is controlled by employees, retirees, or sympathetic Lincoln heirs, who sometimes offer shares to the company at below market value for resale to employees.

In its own unique way, Lincoln Electric remains one of the best-managed companies in the U.S. and is probably as good as anything across the Pacific. Indeed, Harvard's Professor Berg recently lectured a group of Japanese businessmen on the Lincoln success story. Says Berg, "Their reaction was, 'What's so unusual about this? It seems to us like a typical Japanese firm.' " Maybe he should lecture closer to home.

Questions

1. Using the organizational productivity model, Figure 14-2, identify the various factors that Lincoln Electric has that compare to the model's parts. Which are missing?
2. Which organizational strategy or strategies describe Lincoln's approach to productivity? Would Lincoln's program work for other firms? List conditions that might prevent a successful implementation.
3. If a company's management asked you to develop a program similar to Lincoln's, how would you go about it?

employees. Immediate rewards directly tied to specific individual behaviors are more motivating than profit-sharing plans, which may not provide immediate gratifications that some employees may want. Furthermore, profit-sharing programs must have profits to share. Occasionally, profits are eliminated by economic forces outside the control of either management or the workers. A profit-sharing plan may also not be very motivating because of the size of the firm. As an organization grows, workers may feel that their influence on the overall profit level is insignificant. Deferred plans are especially poor for providing employees with immediate incentives to work hard.

Employee Ownership Art Parrish, president of Parrish Power Products, Inc., of Toledo, Ohio, believes in Employee Stock Ownership Plans (ESOP). "If you buy a car, you treat it differently because it's yours," he says. "The work ethic is damn near dead. Giving a man a piece of the pie revives it." Seven years ago, Parrish and four others started their own company, and they installed an ESOP at the very start. Today the company manufactures and sells more than $4 million a year worth of industrial drive shafts, universal joints, and related products. The eighteen employees who later joined the five founders now own approximately a third of the company, about the same as the founders. Outsiders hold the rest.

Tom Jahns, a machine operator at Parrish Power, compares his job now with the several years he spent working for Chrysler. "At Chrysler," he says, "you would just come and put in your eight hours a day. To have people with that attitude here would tear the whole place apart. You've got to earn your way here—and be part of it—or you'll ruin it for everybody." Terry Bishop, a materials control manager, describes one of the ways that the ESOP affects productivity: "We've got guys in shipping and receiving who come back and say, 'I spent so-and-so many dollars on lumber. Did you realize it costs so much to pack stuff the way we're doing it?"[26]

An ESOP provides company-wide incentive because employees who have an ownership interest in a firm will probably be more concerned about the efficiency and profitability of the firm than employees who do not share in the ownership. But there are other reasons for ESOPs. They can be used to finance corporate growth, increase cash flow, raise capital, provide alternatives to mergers, and provide employee benefits. The designer and principal spokesman, Louis Kelso, insists that firms that adopt them will "enhance worker productivity, raise the capital needed to accelerate economic growth and reduce unemployment, and defuse the conflict between management and labor that underlies the wage-price spiral."[27]

Corporate giants like General Motors and American Telephone and Telegraph have instituted ESOPs, but the amount of their outstanding stock held by employees is miniscule. While both the company and the employees are expected to benefit from the ESOP arrangement, the overall effect on company operating capabilities and employee morale is quite small. Like profit-sharing plans, ESOPs have some disadvantages for employee morale and productivity. First, size may reduce their effectiveness, as in the case of GM and AT&T. Next, the gratification is not immediate but at best on a quarterly basis if dividends are issued. Finally, the real pay-off is at selling time when the employee leaves the firm or retires. The motivation is oriented more toward future security.[28]

Summary of Key Concepts

1. Productivity as an organizational issue needs to be considered from many perspectives—motivation, communication, decision making, job and organization design, leadership, group dynamics, and management of change.

2. The actual definition of productivity will vary according to the job holder's responsibilities and the context in which that job exists. Likewise, measurement will vary depending on the situation.

3. Some studies have been conducted to see how we view this issue of productivity. Most agree that productivity is an important problem to address.

4. The studies point out that various organizational levels view the productivity issue differently, therefore their proposed solutions also differ.

5. There seems to be some agreement that workers need to be more involved in their work-area decisions to increase motivation.

6. Designing and implementing a productivity program requires consideration of three areas—structural, process, and leadership—to develop a realistic approach.

7. Organizational strategies to improve productivity include teamwork, quality circles, flexitime, Scanlon Plan, profit sharing, and employee ownership.

Key Terms

Employee ownership

Flexitime

Organizational productivity model

Poll survey

Productivity program

Profit sharing

Quality circles

Scanlon plan

Teamwork

MANAGERIAL IMPLICATIONS

In this section we look in more depth at how managers and organizations are dealing with the issue of productivity. First, an article describes some of the reasons for our declining productivity. Then, we discuss how a large manufacturer sets up various programs to increase productivity. We also consider a group of American executives who visited Japan and what they learned. We see how various incentive programs stimulate self-interest for productivity. We then look at some attempts to increase white-collar productivity. Finally, we review how one approach—the work team—did not provide the increased productivity for which it was designed.

Some Reasons for Declining Productivity

"The percentage increase of productivity for the United States has been declining steadily for years, while the Japanese show a 7 to 9 percent increase from one year to the next. West Germany holds at a yearly increase of about 5 percent. Even Great Britain, with all its problems, shows a yearly increase of from 2 to 3 percent. But in the United States the trend goes steadily downward toward the vanishing point. Productivity is stagnant, not increasing. Our competitors improve while we do not."[29]

Thus starts an article by Benjamin Tregoe, chairman of one of the consulting firms most active in efforts to increase productivity in the United States today. In an intriguing analysis, he states that American managers have mostly created the productivity problem for themselves over the past three decades. But he also holds out great hope that with five years of concerted effort the nation could get itself headed toward high productivity again.

The article lists five important factors that have caused the decline in productivity in the United States.[30] The first of these factors is the extreme emphasis on individualism and specialization that has taken place in the U.S. during the past three decades. The expectation is that everyone will make it on his or her merits, independent of any one else. Be the expert in your chosen field, but don't share with anyone else, for knowledge is power. This is just the opposite of the Japanese philosophy, which stresses cooperate effort and deemphasis of the importance of the individual. People in Japan tend to subordinate themselves to the collectivity of which they are part.

The second factor has to do with the way in which work is organized in the United States. Building upon the notions of "scientific management" developed early in the century, much of work is concerned with procedures, job descriptions, process flows, charts, boxes, and standard operating procedures. Little or no attention has been paid to the people who actually do the work—they are treated simply as machines, another part of the total system. Consequently, work has been dehumanized and an adversarial relationship has developed between management and the nonmanagerial people in an organization.

The third factor relates to the ways in which we have tended to measure our performance. The rise of performance measurements such as Return on Investment (ROI) has created a concern for short-term results that has deemphasized the opportunities for growth and development of the human factors in organizations. Quality concerns are subordinated to concerns for short-term output, and the pursuit of immediate results has almost eliminated the element of judgement in evaluating performance.

Fourth, the advent of the business computer made it possible to obtain and process much more numerical data than ever before. This capability combined with the enthusiasm for short-run performance results created a preoccupation with numbers and printouts. Managers spent more time analyzing numerical data than they did with the people in their organizations. Production and quality control were downgraded and financial experts became very powerful in most organizations. The computer made it possible to obtain numerical data concerning almost any conceivable aspect of the operation and this data became the primary focus of management's attention.

Finally, the extremely favorable economic times following World War II made it appear that these management techniques were working effectively. Demand for new goods and services was so great that little attention was devoted to the longer-range implications of prevalent management practices. Because profits were so high, few people took the opportunity to critically assess the impact of these practices from a long-range point of view.

The article quotes C. Jackson Grayson, director of the American Institute for Productivity, "American management coasted off the great R&D gains made during World War II and the prosperity that followed."[31] Because everyone was enjoying such profitable times, little attention was given to the negative effects of current management styles.

But organizations have recently started to take steps to improve productivity. We look at several examples of efforts to increase productivity shortly, but there seem to be some conditions for success in such efforts. Tregoe suggests the following as fundamental to such success:

- The organization has an unshakeable, totally sincere commitment to improve quality
- The organization provides new problem-solving skills to everyone, from top to bottom
- The organization provides opportunity for problems to be solved
- The organization provides leadership in the use of problem-solving techniques
- The organization provides appropriate rewards for successful problem solving[32]

With the preceding list as background, suggesting why the United States has lagged in productivity and what the critical aspects of success are for any attempt to increase productivity, let's look at some of the experiences various organizations have had in dealing with the productivity issue.

Productivity at a Large Manufacturer

The Boeing Company is one of the world's major manufacturers of aircraft. The airplane industry is highly competitive, with manufacturers clawing at each other with lowball offers to airlines. "If you don't build as efficiently as you can, you can't compete in this world," stated Malcolm Stamper, Boeing's president. "You either have to work faster or use more mechanical advantages."[33]

According to industry observers, Boeing has been able to do just that. Boeing is renowned for its productivity, and one recent chronicler of the aircraft industry, John Newhouse, notes: "Boeing has astonishing productivity, which gives it the ability to assemble airliners faster than any competitor in the world."[34]

Boeing has been concerned with productivity for a long time, and its efforts are not simply an adaptation of some of the recent Japanese techniques we've talked about. Using the concept of the "learning curve," which states that the most recent unit produced should be produced more efficiently than earlier units, the company has always made productivity an integral part of its manufacturing operations, using an assumption of productivity improvements in its basic planning. But it has also adopted some of the newer approaches to productivity in addition to its fundamental belief in the learning curve.

Boeing attempts to promote productivity with a variety of programs. For instance, it pays an employee up to $10,000 for a cost-saving suggestion. In 1982, 22,000 employees submitted 51,000 suggestions and the company paid $4.3 million in awards. One employee has averaged $1,000 a month in extra take-home pay by making cost-saving suggestions.

According to John Black, productivity manager for the 757 Airplane Program, "Employee involvement is a key to the process of change." Black says that the first thing that he did when he took charge of productivity planning for the 757 Program was to examine what he calls the "Boeing culture." "We spent quite a while looking at what the Japanese are doing and what the West Europeans are doing. And their culture. And recognizing that we're not going to bring the Japanese culture here or the West European culture here. We have our own culture in the Boeing Company."[35]

An important element of that culture is the spirit of cooperation between management and the workforce on issues of productivity. Boeing officials note that the cooperative spirit must be nourished and maintained, and with changes in the nature of the work force—more formal education, a growing percentage of minority and female workers, and a rising age due to layoffs that have reduced the ranks of younger workers—this represents a current and future challenge.

Pride in both the company and its airplanes must be retained, according to Black; and to help in that retention, he wrote a country-western song, "757 Fly," which the company has had published. He calls the song a statement of the Boeing culture.[36]

In addition to borrowing the notion of a company song from the Japanese, Boeing has also been using other productivity techniques that originated in Japan. In the 757 Division the company sponsors a series of productivity workshops in which employees are asked to think about ways they can improve both productivity on their jobs and the quality of their lives within the company. In another effort, the company has established a unique program in which individual work areas in the division, using videotape, can tell their own job story.

In this project, volunteers from an area talk about their job to an interviewer, each coworker offering his or her perception of what is taking place and what processes are important in the production activities. These interviews are combined and edited and after approval by the participants the finished videotape is shown throughout the division, going through the entire chain of command. Boeing feels that this activity helps build a team spirit and provides the opportunity for people to develop a close association with both the product and with other people who are involved in producing it.[37]

Quality circles are also an important part of Boeing's productivity effort. In addition to the "standard" quality circle, Boeing has added some new dimensions. For example, Boeing has productivity teams from a cross section of disciplines, drawing people from several different areas of responsibility. One such team is looking at factory operations while another is analyzing the office environments at Boeing, evaluating how office systems might be more productive, whether some functions should be consolidated, or whether there are ways that existing systems might be made more compatible. These new approaches to the quality circle concept have the advantage of permitting teams to look beyond their immediate areas of responsibility and to draw from a wide variety of functional skills.

It is evident that Boeing has a strong commitment to productivity. Part of the commitment may be a matter of necessity, given the competitive situation in the airplane industry, but also present is a managerial attitude that encourages development of people and that provides an opportunity for growth on the job.

We have talked a great deal about Boeing because of the extensiveness and scope of its activities, but other organizations are also very active in efforts to improve productivity.

Lessons from Japan

An article entitled "Japan's Lessons," which appeared in *Industry Week*, related the experiences of a group of American executives who had visited Japan to observe productivity efforts. The focus of the trip was quality circles, and the interest of the Americans centered around the adaptability of that concept to their organizations in the United States. Some of their observations follow, obtained several months after the trip had concluded and after the executives had had an opportunity to analyze their activities in light of the Japanese tour.

At Precision Airmotive Corporation, a small organization that rebuilds piston aircraft engines, the quality circle concept was applied somewhat differently. Feeling that the work force was perhaps too small to install the concept as viewed in Japan, Precision reorganized the plant operations so that each employee relates to one of four work groups—a marked difference from previous structures in which there was a single loosely defined production group. In essence, the company installed a series of small work units with which individual employees could identify—but not a series of quality circles as defined by the Japanese. The results? ". . . a great sense of individual identification with the work units and an emergence of a 'healthy' kind of competition between groups. Improved productivity is coming from the smaller groups. The groups know that this unit is producing this sub-component and that another group is readying another part, and there's competition to get the sub-components for a particular work order finished together."[38] Overall, the company has experienced a 20 percent productivity improvement in the last year.

Another executive who made the trip to Japan, Norma C. Neal of Bechtel Group's San Francisco Power Division, inaugurated a productivity program shortly after returning. Currently, it involves more than 850 employees participating in 131 quality control circles. The unique aspect of this program, aside from the fact that it was established so rapidly, is that the quality circles are composed primarily of technical and professional people, considered by quality circle experts to be among the most difficult to involve in a program.

At Bechtel, quality circles are kept small, and membership is voluntary. The circles identify the problems they want to work on, and the activities of all circles are coordinated by a productivity council. Minutes of circle meetings are distributed to the group leader's supervisor, to the function manager, to the project engineer, to Ms. Neal, and to the productivity council. In the opinion of those involved, such wide reporting gives people up and down the line a good idea of what is going on and also takes the "mystery" out of the process. It also helps the circles to see the relationship of their efforts to a broader picture. For example, under this system a circle might bring in technical help earlier in the process rather than waiting until later when the plans had progressed to a somewhat final stage.

Omark Industries had had about six years of experience with quality circles before Don Cobb, plant manager for the company's Hydraulic Materials Handling Division, took the trip to Japan. Although a strong supporter of the system, Mr. Cobb feels that it would not be effective to attempt to make a carbon copy of the Japanese experience in the United States. In his judgement, it's vital that a company look at all the quality circle options and select those that make the most sense for its particular situation. It's also important not to expect bottom-line results in a few months. According to Mr. Cobb, the greatest benefit that might be observable at the end of twelve months would be improved communication, and perhaps less absenteeism or fewer rejects at a given work station.

This kind of thinking comes through very strongly from most knowledgeable people who have observed the Japanese experience first hand. Typical advice is not to copy exactly, but adapt what makes sense to your situation. Be aware of the culture of your organization and relate any productivity improvement effort to that culture. Don't expect too much too soon; early improvements may not show up on the bottom line. Any program that is seen simply as a tool of management will not be fully accepted by employees. Individual growth is also important. Thus it seems that U.S. organizations have learned from Japan, but those who have been successful have been aware of the differences between their situations and the situations in Japan and have made useful adaptations to the basic Japanese model.

Almost all of what we have been discussing so far concerning productivity has been related to efforts to increase productivity by providing opportunities for employees to become involved in improvements by offering specific suggestions how things might be done more efficiently. But there are other ways of attempting to increase productivity.

Paying for Productivity

Although much of the research suggests that financial rewards fall well below other factors in motivating people on the job, some organizations have taken a very direct approach to improving productivity by offering more pay for increased productivity. Sometimes the amount of pay is significant. Consider the situation of Radio Shack.

As reported in a recent story in *Business Week*, at the heart of Radio Shack's efforts to improve productivity is a profit-sharing program that awards "a piece of the action" to every store manager who obtains profits of 10 percent or more.[39] A manager whose store produced a 15 percent profit margin would receive a bonus of 15 percent of those profits. And not only managers are included in the plan. Salespeople are paid a salary of $5 to $6 an hour or a 6 percent commission on sales, whichever is higher.

John F. Pyktel, manager of one of the first of Radio Shack's computer centers, is an example of how lucrative the profit-sharing plan can be. Over his desk hang two plaques, one welcoming him to the "$350,000 Club," an honor he earned by selling $384,000 of microcomputers in 1982. The second plaque is a replica of Pyktel's 1982 earnings of $103,900.

The other side of the coin is that managers pay for their own mistakes under the system. They pay out of their earnings for shoplifting losses, bad checks, and carrying charges on excessive inventories. The company keeps a close watch on sales, and the manager of each of the 5,779 stores must file a daily sales report, on penalty of discharge. Operating statements for each store are distributed shortly after the first of each month.

Radio Shack also has an employee stock purchase plan that can be very rewarding to employees. Twenty-five percent of the company's stock is now owned by employees, some of whom have become millionaires because of the plan. For this organization, at least, the concept of increased pay for increased productivity has worked very well.

Many high-tech organizations have also adopted the use of various financial incentives to encourage productivity and build team spirit. A report in the *Christian Science Monitor* notes the findings of a recent study performed by the Hay Group, a Philadelphia based firm that specializes in salary, benefit, and pension consulting.[40] After looking at several of the country's largest high-tech companies, Hay found that stock purchase plans were used by 67 percent of the companies, often reaching down to all employee levels. This is about double the use of such programs in American industry generally.

The Hay study also found that high-tech companies were very likely to use front-end bonuses to attract management and technical professionals because of the stiff competition for such people. Again, this kind of inducement is sometimes made available to all levels of employees. At Apple Computers, for example, anyone who comes to work for the company gets an Apple II computer to take home after sixty days on the job. If the employee is still with the company a year later, he or she gets to keep the computer.

Half of the companies studied have a special reward program for key contributors, many involving substantial cash awards. Because of the young age of the industry, only 58 percent of the companies have pension plans, as compared with about 95 percent in other industries. Yet, about 40 percent of the high-tech firms have profit-sharing plans. Because of their positions in the growth cycle, many high-tech organizations have not had to deal with the issue of pension programs yet. It will be interesting to look at the industry ten or fifteen years from now and observe the status of bonus and pension plans.

According to William White, director of Strategic Compensation Services at Hay, "The emphasis in the high-tech industries is on building a team and a cooperative spirit in a high-risk situation . . . these firms have tried to tie everyone together in one common vehicle (stock plans) and will let them all become wealthy if the company is successful."[41] White notes that some perks are not as important to high-tech executives because of their intense involvement in their work and the excitement involved in seeing a product developed and sold. Indeed, many companies deemphasize perks for individuals except those related to financial reward. Typically, perks such as country club memberships, reserved parking, company cars, and special office facilities are not used. In one high-tech company, for example, the CEO shares his office with three other executives. Emphasis is put on the group rather than the individual because of the nature of high-tech development efforts and the need for synergistic activity in a highly competitive industry.

The necessity of keeping valuable employees has led to the phenomenon of "golden handcuffs." Through such devices as deferred bonuses, financing of homes for employees, and gifts of shares of stock, many organizations are trying to keep their valued employees from moving to competitors. The main ingredient of most of these plans is that they provide payment to the employees several years in the future, and only if they stay with the company. The objective is to make working for the organization so profitable that employees will not even consider leaving. Again, this kind of program is seen most often in industries like the high-tech industries where productive employees are especially valuable and where continued success may depend upon the constant development of new products.

White-collar Productivity

What about productivity in white-collar occupations? What kinds of efforts are underway to improve handling of the great amount of paperwork that seems to be integral to the operation of almost any organization?

Generally, productivity improvement programs have been focused on so-called blue-collar occupations. Currently blue-collar workers make up about 31 percent of the country's nonfarm labor force. By the year 2000, they'll be only about 20 percent. The trend is obviously away from blue-collar type activities, and in some organizations the trend is much more rapid than it is nationally. As reported in *The Wall Street Journal*, ". . . 40 percent of the workers of TRW are now involved in manufacturing activities. In 2000, the number will be about 5 percent."[42]

TRW is one of those organizations that is attempting to do something to increase white-collar productivity. The company decided to make productivity a high priority because it realized that the nature of its work force was changing substantially—and rapidly. One of the main focuses of TRW's programs was to improve the ways employees used their time. For example, the company wanted to eliminate time that software writers spent tracking down people on the telephone, filing, attending meetings, or just staring out the window.

Toward this end, TRW placed several of its best software writers into private, windowless offices equipped with state-of-the-art computer terminals that talk to the company computer network, use electronic mail, use teleconferencing facilities, and use sophisticated programs that help write other programs. While the company had expected some increases in productivity, it was surprised at the 39 percent increase in the program's first year.

Especially surprising were the reasons for the increases in productivity. The programmers liked the new electronic devices, but simple changes such as privacy, quiet, and comfortable chairs were even more important. While some programmers reported the loss of a feeling of team membership, the privacy resulted in greatly increased productivity. Reports were not uncommon of employees shutting their office doors, then becoming so engrossed in work that it was 6 P.M. before they knew it.

To find out how to improve productivity, TRW asked the programmers. As a result of these consultations, the company designed an office system that featured beige, soundproof, windowless spaces of Spartan efficiency. A chair built to fit the human body, a white board, a bookshelf, a work table, and a computer terminal were the only furnishings. To eliminate time-consuming filing and phone calls, files are stored and messages are exchanged by computer. The programmer doesn't have to move from the chair.

Before this productivity effort began in 1981, TRW's software division posted productivity increases of about 40 percent a decade. With the success of the software project, TRW now expects productivity increases of 400 to 500 percent in the next ten years. To achieve that level of improvement, TRW is installing similar setups in all of its new facilities, at an estimated cost of approximately $10,000 per programmer.

The United States government has also taken steps to improve white-collar productivity. A few years ago, the Treasury Department launched a pilot program that might be the forerunner of new performance appraisal programs throughout the civil service. Under the program, about 600 senior-level employees earned cash awards totaling $150,000 by improving productivity.[43]

The new program begins with a lengthy conference between the employee and the supervisor. Together, they discuss and write down the responsibilities of the position and formulate an individual work plan that describes the goals to be reached during the rating period and the standards that will be used to determine if the goals have in fact been reached. If the employee meets or exceeds the agreed upon goals by the end of the rating period, the supervisor recommends the award of a cash bonus. The final determination of the amount of the bonus is determined by a committee of higher-ranking managers.

While the program is still in its experimental stages, early indications are that the program has initiated a process of communication between supervisor and employee that had not been occurring before. Under the new system, employees have a clear indication of what is expected of them and what standards will be used to determine if their performance meets those expectations.

A Work Team Concept That Failed

Not all attempts to improve productivity through employee involvement are successful. At General Motor's Oklahoma City assembly plant, for instance, workers recently voted for representation by the United Auto Workers of America by a two to one margin. To management, this vote represented a defeat for a job enrichment program that was expected to enhance productivity and reduce labor strife.[44]

Actually, some aspects of the program did work, but a central concept—a system of work teams—not only failed to increase employee satisfaction but became a major issue in the union's successful organizing campaign. A few months after the workers voted the UAW in, the team approach was discarded at the union's insistence.

Prior to opening the plant in 1978, the work team concept was carefully structured by GM specialists. The work force was divided into teams, each of which elected leaders. Teams were given authority to make decisions related to work conduct and attendance. In essence, each team was responsible for the conduct of its members if it felt that that conduct was out of line. Teams were given authority to vote on members' requests for time off—whether for personal reasons or for illness. But this approach evidently played into the hands of the union organizers, who told the workers that they had no real authority and that the system was simply a ruse to cut down on absences.

When confrontations occurred, news of them spread rapidly. In one case, a worker called in sick, and his team leader insisted he come in so that the team could decide whether he was sick or not. The worker shouted over the phone that if he was well enough to come in, he would come in and work. Another worker was told that she could not take a day off to take her sick child to the doctor because the plant operation was more important.

After such denials for time off, workers would attempt to poll the team members to determine who had voted for or against their request. Obviously, such actions lead to disharmony and retribution. In some instances, team leaders felt they had special privileges and took actions that exceeded their authority.

While the team concept was in place, the company instituted a program of training in the hope of reducing the number of standby workers needed. Evidently there was no problem in employees getting time off for the training while the plant was in the early stages of production and not working at full capacity.

Furthermore, working at less than full capacity reduced the need for backup personnel. When full production was reached, however, no backup personnel were available, and the workers became angry. The union timed the election for two weeks after full production was instituted, and won handily.

GM is attempting to install other productivity programs at Oklahoma City, but there is reluctance to push new programs in the face of local resistance.

This example vividly illustrates that all productivity improvement programs are not successful. It appears that some of the conditions mentioned earlier in this chapter for successful initiation of work team projects may have been missing in the GM experience in Oklahoma City. Can you identify some of these and think of ways the program might have been redesigned to increase its chances of success?

DISCUSSION QUESTIONS

1. Given that organizations need to improve their productivity to remain competitive, discuss why productivity programs are difficult to start. What organizational issues may hamper the introduction of such programs?

2. Where should a manager start who is interested in improving his or her organization's productivity?

3. Why are there differences in the results reported by the surveys presented in this chapter?

4. Why is the Scanlon Plan more effective in a smaller firm? What about profit sharing? What about employee ownership?

5. The chapter states that the organizational strategies listed are not new; they have been around for the past ten to fifteen years. Discuss why these strategies are so important for organizations to consider now. What type of organizations will try some of these programs now? Why?

EXERCISE: PRODUCTIVITY

Form small groups of three or four members. Using the following questionnaire, interview individuals from several levels in a firm. Try to choose three supervisors and/or managers and three workers from the organization. Write a summary report to present to the class. Discuss your results and the results obtained by the other class groups to form some conclusions about the issue of productivity. Be sure to compare your results with those of studies cited in this chapter.

Note: The organization you studied may ask for a summary report. If you supply such a report, make sure that the report does *not* reveal who said what. Remove all names of individuals and any comments that could be traced to one person.

SAMPLE QUESTIONNAIRE

1. What does productivity mean to you? How would you define productivity? Give some examples of what you mean by productivity.

2. Is productivity improving, remaining the same, or decreasing in this organization? Can you give some examples? What are some reasons for this change?

3. Do you think that you, personally, could increase your productivity? By how much? What would it take to motivate you to increase productivity by that amount? What things would help you accomplish this improvement?

4. Do you think the rest of the organization could also increase its productivity? How much? What things would help accomplish this improvement?

5. If your organization has some programs to increase productivity, what are they? How are they working? If not, why?

6. Rank the following items that you think would be the most effective way to encourage people in your organization to come up with good ideas to improve the company's productivity.

( ) Personal recognition
( ) Monetary rewards (e.g., profit sharing, suggestion box, cost-savings plans)
( ) Promotion
( ) Paid time-off rewards other than vacation
( ) Threat of job-security/lay-off
( ) Participation in decisions directly affecting your work (e.g., quality circles)
( ) Flexible work schedules (e.g., flexitime, four-day work week, job sharing)
( ) Other: _____

NOTES

1. Article and table from *The Herald,* Everett, WA. (1 April 1982): 3D, reprinted from "The Company That Stopped Detroit," by Steve Lohr, *The New York Times* (21 March 1982). Copyright © 1982 by the New York Times Company. Reprinted by permission.

2. *A Sentry Study: Perspective on Productivity: A Global View,* conducted by Louis Harris & Associates, Inc., 1981.

3. From a personal interview with the author, 26 July 1983.

4. The editors of *Fortune* magazine, *Working Smarter* (New York: Viking Press, 1982): 33.

5. *A Sentry Study.*

6. *Worker's Attitudes Toward Productivity,* by Ronald Clarke and James Morris, U.S. Chamber Survey and Productivity Center, 1980.

7. *People and Productivity: A Challenge to Corporate America,* conducted by New York Stock Exchange, Inc., 1982.

8. Robert E. Callahan and Diane Lockwood, "Seattle University Survey," *Working Paper* (Fall 1983).

9. "Unlocking the Productivity Door," *Nation's Business* (December 1981): 55.

10. Jon English and Anthony R. Marchione, "Productivity: A New Perspective," *California Management Review,* vol. 25, no. 2 (January 1983): 57–66.

11. "A Plant Where Teamwork Is More Than Just Talk," *Business Week* (16 May 1983).

12. S. J. Liebowitz and K. P. DeMeuse, "Application of Team Building," *Human Relations,* vol. 35, no. 1 (1982): 2.

13. Ibid., p. 6.

14. The authors have continually over the years heard this figure from a multitude of academicians and practicing managers alike.

15. "Quality Circles: One Company Is Much Better Off Because of Them," *Seattle Post-Intelligence* (13 April 1983).

16. Robert E. Callahan, "Quality Circles: A Program for Productivity Improvement through Human Resources Development," in Sang M. Lee and Gary Schwendiman, eds., *Management by Japanese Systems* (New York: Praeger, 1982): 80.

17. "German Store Raises Flexible Work Hours to New Highs," *The Herald,* Everett, WA. (Monday, 23 May 1983): 24.

18. Cary B. Barad, "Flexitime under Scrutiny: Research on Work Adjustment and Organizational Performance," *The Personnel Administrator* (May 1980): 69–74.

19. "Inflexible Flexitimers," *Psychology Today* (August 1982): 13.

20. Robert J. Schulhof, "Five Years with a Scanlon Plan," *The Personnel Administrator* (June 1979): 55–62.

21. Michael Schuster, "The Impact of Union-Management Cooperation on Productivity and Employment," *Industrial and Labor Relations Review* (April 1983): 415–430.

22. James W. Driscoll, "Working Creatively with a Union: Lessons from the Scanlon Plan," *Organizational Dynamics* (Summer 1979): 61–79.

23. J. D. Dunn and F. Rachel, *Wage and Salary Administration* (New York: McGraw-Hill, 1972): 253.

24. Jean Bedel, "Twenty-five Years of Participation," *Management* (November 1972): 66–73.

25. Bert Metzger and Jerome Colletti, "Does Profit Sharing Pay?" in David Belcher, *Compensation Administration* (Englewood Cliffs, NJ: Prentice Hall, 1974): 353.

26. Doran Howitt, "Employee Ownership: A Capital Idea," *INC.* (April 1982): 35–42.

27. *Business Week* (1 March 1976): 58.

28. David J. Toscano, "Toward a Typology of Employee Ownership," *Human Relations,* vol. 36, no. 7 (1983): 581–602.

29. Benjamin B. Tregoe, "Productivity in America: Where It Went and How to Get It Back," *Management Review* (February 1983).

30. Ibid.

31. Ibid.

32. Ibid.

33. *Boeing News* (6 May 1982): 8.

34. Ibid.

35. Ibid.

36. Ibid.

37. Ibid.

38. "Japan's Lessons," *Industry Week* (23 February 1981): 71.

39. *Business Week* (12 September 1983): 64.

40. *Christian Science Monitor* (24 February 1983): 4.

41. Ibid.

42. *The Wall Street Journal* (22 September 1983): 26.

43. *Management Practice* (November 1979): 47.

44. *Engineering Times* (10 October 1983): 31.

RECOMMENDED READINGS

Thomas H. Melohn, "How to Build Trust and Productivity," *Harvard Business Review,* vol. 61, no. 1 (January–February 1983).

Melohn argues that the connection between financial results and employee morale is far from casual. He describes a strategy for building trust between employees and owners of North American Tool & Die Company.

Robert N. Lehner, ed., *White Collar Productivity* (New York: McGraw-Hill, 1983).

This book is written to help the reader understand some of the issues around measuring productivity for white-collar workers. It also describes some programs geared to improve white-collar productivity.

David Bain, *The Productivity Prescription: The Manager's Guide to Improving Productivity and Profits* (New York: McGraw-Hill, 1982).

This book is a "how-to" book for improving productivity. It is based on the premise that there can be compatibility between individual needs and organizational needs.

Savemore Food Store 5116

The Savemore Corporation is a chain of four hundred retail supermarkets located primarily in the northeastern section of the United States. Store 5116 employs over fifty persons, all of whom live within suburban Portage, New York, where the store is located.

Wally Shultz served as general manager of store 5116 for six years. Last April he was transferred to another store in the chain. At that time the employees were told by the district manager, Mr. Finnie, that Wally Shultz was being promoted to manage a larger store in another township.

Most of the employees seemed unhappy to lose their old manager. Nearly everyone agreed with the opinion that Shultz was a "good guy to work for." As examples of his desirability as a boss the employees told how Wally had frequently helped the arthritic black porter with his floor mopping, how he had shut the store five minutes early each night so that certain employees might catch their busses, of a Christmas party held each year for employees at his own expense, and his general willingness to pitch in. All employees had been on a first-name basis with the manager. About half of them had begun work with the Savemore Corporation when the Portage store was opened.

Wally Shultz was replaced by Clark Raymond. Raymond, about twenty-five years old, was a graduate of an Ivy League college and had been with Savemore a little over one year. After completion of his six-month training program, he

served as manager of one of the chain's smaller stores before being advanced to store 5116. In introducing Raymond to the employees, Mr. Finnie stressed his rapid advancement and the profit increase that occurred while Raymond had charge of his last store.

I began my employment in store 5116 early in June. Mr. Raymond was the first person I met in the store, and he impressed me as being more intelligent and efficient than the managers I had worked for in previous summers at other stores. After a brief conversation concerning our respective colleges, he assigned me to a cash register, and I began my duties as a checker and bagger.

In the course of the next month I began to sense that relationships between Raymond and his employees were somewhat strained. This attitude was particularly evident among the older employees of the store, who had worked in store 5116 since its opening. As we all ate our sandwiches together in the cage (an area about twenty feet square in the cellar fenced in by chicken wire, to be used during coffee breaks and lunch hours), I began to question some of the older employees as to why they disliked Mr. Raymond. Laura Morgan, a fellow checker about forty years of age and the mother of two grade-school boys, gave the most specific answers. Her complaints were:

1. Raymond had fired the arthritic black porter on the grounds that a porter who "can't mop is no good to the company."
2. Raymond had not employed new help to make up for normal attrition. Because of this, everybody's work load was much heavier than it ever had been before.

Source: This case was developed and prepared by Professor John W. Hennessey, Jr., Amos Tuck School of Business, Dartmouth College. Reprinted by permission. At the time of this case, the author, a college student, was employed for the summer as a checker and stockboy in store 5116.

3. The new manager made everyone call him "mister . . . he's unfriendly."
4. Raymond didn't pitch in. Wally Shultz had, according to Laura, helped people when they were behind in their work. She said that Shultz had helped her bag on rushed Friday nights when a long line waited at her checkout booth, but "Raymond wouldn't lift a finger if you were dying."
5. Employees were no longer let out early to catch busses. Because of the relative infrequency of this means of transportation, some employees now arrived home up to an hour later.
6. "Young Mr. Know-it-all with his fancy degree . . . takes all the fun out of this place."

Other employees had similar complaints. Gloria, another checker, claimed that, ". . . he sends the company nurse to your home every time you call in sick." Margo, a meat wrapper, remarked "everyone knows how he's having an affair with that new bookkeeper he hired to replace Carol when she quit." Pops Devery, head checker who had been with the chain for over ten years, was perhaps the most vehement of the group. He expressed his views in the following manner: "That new guy's a real louse . . . got a mean streak a mile long. Always trying to cut corners. First it's not enough help, then no overtime, and now, come Saturday mornings, we have to use boxes[1] for the orders 'til the truck arrives. If it wasn't just a year 'til retirement, I'd leave. Things just aren't what they used to be when Wally was around." The last statement was repeated in different forms by many of the other employees. Hearing all this praise of Wally, I was rather surprised when Mr. Finnie dropped the comment to me one morning that Wally had been demoted for inefficiency, and that no one at store 5116 had been told this. It was important that Mr. Shultz save face, Mr. Finnie told me.

---

[1] The truck from the company warehouse bringing merchandise for sale and store supplies normally arrived at ten o'clock Saturday mornings. Frequently, the stock of large paper bags would be temporarily depleted. It was then necessary to pack orders in cardboard cartons until the truck was unloaded.

A few days later, on Saturday of the busy weekend preceding the July 4 holiday, store 5116 again ran out of paper bags. However, the delivery truck did not arrive at ten o'clock, and by 10:30 the supply of cardboard cartons was also low. Mr. Raymond put in a hurried call to the warehouse. The men there did not know the whereabouts of the truck but promised to get an emergency supply of bags to us around noon. By eleven o'clock, there were no more containers of any type available, and Mr. Raymond reluctantly locked the doors to all further customers. The twenty checkers and packers remained in their respective booths, chatting among themselves. After a few minutes, Mr. Raymond requested that they all retire to the cellar cage because he had a few words for them. As soon as the group was seated on the wooden benches in the chicken wire enclosed area, Mr. Raymond began to speak, his back to the cellar stairs. In what appeared to be an angered tone, he began, "I'm out for myself first, Savemore second, the customers third, and you last. The inefficiency in this store has amazed me from the moment I arrived here. . . ."

At about this time I noticed Mr. Finnie, the district manager, standing at the head of the cellar stairs. It was not surprising to see him at this time because he usually made three or four unannounced visits to the store each week as part of his regular supervisory procedure. Mr. Raymond, his back turned, had not observed Finnie's entrance.

Mr. Raymond continued, "Contrary to what seems to be the opinion of many of you, the Savemore Corporation is not running a social club here. We're in business for just one thing . . . to make money. One way that we lose money is by closing the store on Saturday morning at eleven o'clock. Another way that we lose money is by using a 60-pound paper bag to do the job of a 20-pound bag. A 60-pound bag costs us over 2 cents apiece; a 20-pound bag costs less than a penny. So when you sell a couple of quarts of milk or a loaf of bread, don't use the big bags. Why do you think we have four different sizes anyway? There's no great intelligence or effort required to pick the right size. So do it. This store wouldn't be closed right now if you'd used your common sense. We started out this week with enough bags to last 'til Monday . . . and they would have lasted 'til Monday if you'd only used your brains. This kind of thing doesn't look good for the store, and it doesn't look good for me. Some of you have been bagging for over five years . . . and you ought'a be able to do it right by now. . ." Mr. Raymond paused and then said, "I trust I've made myself clear on this point."

The cage was silent for a moment, and then Pops Devery, the head checker spoke up: "Just one thing, Mistuh Raymond. Things were running pretty well before you came around. When Wally was here we never ran out'a bags. The customers never complained about overloaded bags or the bottoms falling out before you got here. What're you gonna tell somebody when they ask for a couple of extra bags to use in garbage cans? What're you gonna tell somebody when they want their groceries in a bag, and not a box? You gonna tell them the manager's too damn cheap to give 'em bags? Is that what you're gonna tell 'em? No sir, things were never like this when Wally Shultz was around. We never had to apologize for a cheap manager who didn't order enough then. What'ta you got to say to that, Mistuh Raymond?"

Mr. Raymond, his tone more emphatic, began again. "I've got just one thing to say to that, Mr. Devery, and that's this: store 5116 never did much better than break even when Shultz was in charge here. I've shown a profit better than the best he ever hit in six years every week since I've been here. You can check that fact in the book upstairs any time you want. If you don't like

the way I'm running things around here, there's nobody begging you to say . . ."

At this point, Pops Devery interrupted and, looking up the stairs at the district manager, asked "What about that, Mr. Finnie? You've been around here as long as I have. You told us how Wally got promoted 'cause he was such a good boss. Supposin' you tell this young fellar here what a good manager is really like? How about that, Mr. Finnie?"

A rather surprised Mr. Raymond turned around to look up the stairs at Mr. Finnie. The manager of store 5116 and his checkers and packers waited for Mr. Finnie's answer.

Questions

1. What measures of productivity might be appropriate for this organization? Would the employees use the same measures? How will the customers view these various measures of productivity (e.g., the use of bags)?

2. What methods has Mr. Raymond, the store manager, used to increase the store's productivity? What has been the reaction of the employees? Why? Explain your position.

3. How do you explain the employees' praise of the former store manager, Mr. Shultz, and his being demoted by Mr. Finnie, the area manager? Isn't morale a measure of an organization's productivity?

4. If you were Mr. Finnie, how would you handle the situation at the end of the case? How would you respond to Mr. Devery? Mr. Raymond?

CHAPTER FIFTEEN
International Aspects of Organizational Behavior

OUTLINE

OBJECTIVES

- Identify and discuss the major cultural dimensions used to describe various cultures

- Describe what culture is and how it affects behavior

- Explain how values, norms, and roles influence and interact with culture

- Contrast three cultures along several dimensions: communication, decision making, motivation, leadership, conflict resolution, negotiation, and organization

- Discuss the managerial implications of dealing with Colombia, Japan, and Sweden

The 100% American

Our solid American citizen awakens in a bed built on a pattern which originated in the Near East but which was modified in Northern Europe before it was transmitted to America. He throws back covers made from cotton, domesticated in India, or linen, domesticated in the Near East, or wool from sheep, also domesticated in the Near East, or silk, the use of which was discovered in China. All of these materials have been spun and woven by processes invented in the Near East. He slips into his moccasins, invented by the Indians of the Eastern woodlands, and goes to the bathroom, whose fixtures are a mixture of European and American inventions, both of recent date. He takes off his pajamas, a garment invented in India, and washes with soap invented by the ancient Gauls. He then shaves, a masochistic rite which seems to have been derived from either Sumer or ancient Egypt.

Returning to the bedroom, he removes his clothes from a chair of southern European type and proceeds to dress. He puts on garments whose form originally derived from the skin clothing of the nomads of the Asiatic steppes, puts on shoes made from skins tanned by a process invented in ancient Egypt and cut to a pattern derived from the classical civilizations of the Mediterranean, and ties around his neck a strip of bright-colored cloth which is a vestigial survival of the shoulder shawls worn by the seventeenth-century Croatians. Before going out for breakfast he glances through the window, made of glass invented in Egypt, and if it is raining puts on overshoes made of rubber discovered by the Central American Indians and takes an umbrella, invented in southeastern Asia. Upon his head he puts a hat made of felt, a material invented in the Asiatic steppes.

On his way to breakfast he stops to buy a paper, paying for it with coins, an ancient Lydian invention. At the restaurant a whole new series of borrowed elements confronts him. His plate is made of a form of pottery invented in China. His knife is of steel, an alloy first made in southern India, his fork a medieval Italian invention, and his spoon a derivative of a Roman original. He begins breakfast with an orange, from the eastern Mediterranean, a cantaloupe from Persia, or perhaps a piece of African watermelon. With this he has a cup of coffee, an Abyssinian plant, with cream and sugar. Both the domestication of cows and the idea of milking them originated in the Near East, while sugar was first made in India. After his fruit and first coffee he goes on to waffles, cakes made by a Scandinavian technique from wheat domesticated in Asia Minor. Over these he pours maple syrup, invented by the Indians of the Eastern woodlands. As a side dish he may have the egg of a species of bird domesticated in Indochina, or thin strips of the flesh of an animal domesticated in eastern Asia, which have been salted and smoked by a process developed in northern Europe.

When our friend has finished eating he settles back to smoke, an American Indian habit, consuming a plant domesticated in Brazil, in either a pipe, derived from the Indians of Virginia, or a cigarette, derived from Mexico. If he is hardy enough he may even attempt a cigar, transmitted to us from the Antilles by way of Spain. While smoking he reads the news of the day, printed in characters invented by the ancient Semites upon a material invented in China by a process invented in Germany. As he absorbs the accounts of foreign troubles he will thank a Hebrew deity in an Indo-European language that he is 100 percent American.[1]

This chapter was written by Gary D. Robinson, Ph.D., of the Boeing Company.

UNDERSTANDING CULTURAL DIFFERENCES

This admittedly contrived scenario underscores the theme of this chapter: the interdependence of culture, organizations, and people in the modern world. Even if one wished to be isolated from other cultures, it is becoming literally impossible to do so (barring moving to a mountain top, making clothing and shelter from animal hides, and eating nuts and berries).

But if we are so dependent on other cultures, why isn't it just common sense to treat them as we would like to be treated? Don't other peoples want to make money from their business opportunities like we do? Aren't they motivated in a similar fashion as we are? Don't they have to communicate and make decisions like we do? Don't they have to organize their people like we do?

In one sense we are all citizens of the world, but as we know from the initial chapters we all view our worlds differently. Our intention in this chapter is to expose the reader to some of the issues, opportunities, and responsibilities faced by managers and organizations in the arena of culture.

Cultural Differences in Values and Norms

It has been stated that no person can be truly educated until he or she has had an in-depth experience in another culture. In-depth by definition means other than a tourist experience. Americans who have experienced an in-depth cross-cultural experience have come away with generally one of two responses: they enjoyed it immensely, feel themselves to be better educated and better world citizens; or they are relieved to be back among their fellow countrymen, shaking their heads in disbelief that anyone could think so differently and so wrongly about the way things get done. In fact, most individuals who must operate in different cultures are afflicted to some degree by a malady called "culture shock."

Culture shock is a condition brought on by the anxiety that results from losing one's familiar signs and symbols of social relating. To describe it another way, we suffer from trying to deal with social interaction on the basis of our set of values and norms in a culture that has a different set of values and norms. Or to put it within a managerial perspective, consider the statement of a high-level manager who had spent over 180 days and six trips within the past year in an Asian culture. He returned shaking his head, saying, "I thought I knew how they think but it's apparent that I don't understand them at all. Please find me someone that can explain to me how they think and how they do business." Business negotiations across cultures can be compared with a card game where players have different card decks and play by their own sets of rules.

Americans are not the only victims of this phenomenon, of course. Reflect upon the experience of an exchange Peace Corps volunteer, related in Box 15–1.[2]

Both the opening story, which identifies the source of "American" as other than American, and the experience of Sr. Montana in the boxed feature illustrate the degree to which social behavior in different cultures is both overlapping and perplexing. It is important to understand this dilemma from two perspectives:

BOX 15-1

What America Really Looks Like!

After completion of training I was assigned immediately to a small town in the Appalachian section of Kentucky. My dialect training was really inappropriate, but I thought this was a small problem which I understand Peace Corps volunteers invariably confront. I was assigned as a community worker to the local antipoverty agency.

The countryside was the most beautiful of any I had ever seen. Every opportunity I had I spent out of doors. Following community development philosophy, I spent my time listening and talking, but never telling and trying to remain in the background.

For six months I listened and gathered facts, focusing in on the most serious problems felt by the Appalachian community. I read every article and publication I could find.

My elation soon gave way to depression. The people in this Kentucky coal country lived on some of the richest earth in the world, yet they were among the poorest and deprived of any people I have encountered. Even in my country, where the per capita income is under $400 per year, we do not have such a single and contained ghetto of deprivation. Here there were many suffering from malnutrition, particularly the young and the old. Coal miners who were 45 looked to be 65, and invariably they had lost a limb or were suffering from respiratory disease. There were few services in health or welfare available and these were highly restrictive and bureaucratic.

My study of the economy made all of this incongruous. The profits coming to the land-holding companies were some of the highest in the country. Yet, those same companies demonstrated almost no responsibility for the conditions of the people or the preservation of the natural surroundings. Like many of the wealthy in my country, the owners of the companies were absentee landlords who were interested only in profit.

I diligently studied the complex problems from both an economic and community development point of view. I committed myself to come up with a plan of action that would bring relief and perhaps prosperity to the people. As a foreigner, I realized the necessity of formulating a proposal that would be in the context of American culture.

Fortunately, I had brought with me many of the papers and speeches by outstanding Americans addressing themselves to similar kinds of issues of poverty in my country.

Following these particular American notions, I developed a comprehensive land reform measure for Appalachia. The thrust of my proposal would require the absentee landlords to divide the property they now owned in such enormous quantities among the Appalachia poor who now lived there. It was not a revolutionary document for in fact it repaid the absentee landlords very substantially for the property rights they had purchased. In many cases they had only paid a mule or a barrel of whiskey for hundreds of acres of mineral rights. Under my measure they would be

Source: Jose de Montana, "A Reverse Peace Corps Volunteer on Assignment to the United States of America," *Guidelines for Peace Corps Cross-cultural Training, Part III Supplementary Readings,* (Washington, DC: Peace Corps).

entitled to a 20 percent return on their initial investment.

After many days and nights of hard labor, I presented my proposal to the county board of supervisors. I was not at all prepared for the reaction I received. To a man, the local government officials accused me of being a socialistic, communistic, outside agitator. Their wrath was considerable and I left feeling both dejected and alone.

The word soon spread through the community that I was undesirable. Doors that had been opened were now closed. Still, I would not let my despair get the best of me. There were others who would surely listen to me.

The mine workers union had a courageous history of working in the interest of the miners. They had fought hard against the irresponsible landlords, surely they would support land redistribution for their people. After several days of trying to get an appointment, I finally was admitted to see the president of the "local." He listened impatiently to my proposal and then brusquely lectured me for interfering in the internal affairs of this country. He said that I could do much more if I went back home and worked on my own problems. If I did this, maybe then they wouldn't have to pay so "god-damned many taxes to us commie sympathizers." My interview ended in less than ten minutes.

Where had I made such serious errors in judgement? Had not Presidents Eisenhower, Kennedy, and Johnson urged land reform on my country and others in the underdeveloped free world? Had not the great names in the United States Senate—Fulbright, McGovern, Hatfield, McCarthy, and Morse—demanded land reform if we were to continue receiving a foreign aid allocation? Why was it that land reform was seen as the correct procedure in my country and dismissed as communism and agitation in this most underdeveloped section of America?

I took my meager savings and purchased a bus ticket for Washington so that I might present my modest proposal to at least one of America's outstanding liberal senators.

Upon arrival in Washington, I went at once to the Senate Office Building. After many attempts I was ushered in to see the administrative assistant of a famous senator. He listened to me very carefully and told me of the deep interest the senator had in my country, the reverse Peace Corps, and, of course, the poor of Appalachia. After a twenty-minute discussion he gave me the name of a hotel and told me to wait there for a call.

I stayed by the phone and within thirty minutes received a call, but not from the senator. It was from the State Department official responsible for the RPC program. He was quite excited and told me not to leave, he would be right over.

The next day I was on the way home to my country. My tour as a reverse Peace Corps volunteer had only lasted eight months. The State Department had been quite understanding and in fact has offered me a volunteer assignment in the flower arrangement program in Atlanta, Georgia. I felt that I had seriously failed in one program and I certainly did not want to stir up the flower arrangers in Atlanta, so I returned home.

Questions

1. What were the critical aspects of our culture that affected Sr. Montana?
2. What could have been done to properly prepare Sr. Montana for experiencing our culture?
3. Are there any lessons from this story for Americans going abroad? Explain.

first, trying to comprehend one's culture, values, and norms in the context of one's own culture, and secondly, trying to comprehend the same phenomena as they appear in another culture.

A popular topic debated by American managers today is the degree to which Japanese managerial strategies are appropriate to United States business. There are those who believe that there is much to be learned and those who reject these same strategies because of their perceived cultural incompatibility. What is culture? Why are cultures compatible or incompatible?

Culture   The definitions of culture are as varied as the perception of culture itself. In fact, it is not unusual to hear culture defined as things that are educated, refined, or sophisticated. For our purposes we will define culture as the "complex whole which includes knowledge, belief, art, morals, law, custom, and any other capabilities and habits acquired by man as a member of society."[3] It should be conceived of as a dynamic system in equilibrium and something more than an accidental collection of traits. It is a unified whole, with its constituent parts consistent with and adjusting to one another. A useful way of understanding this phenomenon is to conceive of culture as determining the identity of a human group in the same way as personality determines the identity of an individual.[4]

As the definition indicates, all of culture's elements emphasize behaviors. However, culture is not behavior but rather an environment in which behavior occurs. Several researchers itemize the following characteristics of culture:

1. Culture is learned behavior.
2. This learned behavior is oriented to the attainment of ends or satisfying needs.
3. Culture takes place in situations.
4. Culture is shared with others.
5. Culture is normatively regulated.[5]

Many of us have been led to believe that some cultures are "better" than others. A culture is not really deficient in anything. It is not "backward," "out-dated," or "out of step." The concept of culture really fits the systems concept applied by many management theorists today. For example, the weakest culture may be in reality a successful system—a delicately balanced organism that has been adapting successfully for thousands of years, surviving all kinds of changes and making those modifications necessary to preserve its equilibrium over time.

The five characteristics of culture and behavior are important for our understanding of the international aspects of organizational behavior. First, as we have noted in other chapters of the text, organizations are consciously coordinated activities for the attainment of certain objectives, and management involves the coordination of resources for the accomplishment of organizational objectives. Managerial activities and behavior, no matter in which culture they are found, are thus always directed toward the attainment of ends or goals.

Moreover, organizational behavior takes place within situations that are usually prescribed within the boundaries of the organization. This behavior is also normatively regulated (according to certain role expectations) and includes personal motivation as a key to managerial success and organizational efficiency. Conflict thus arises when trying to apply one set of cultural behavior to another culture because of the different role expectations based upon contradictory or contrasting cultural values.

This brings us to a framework for considering culture, values, norms, roles, and behavior. The concept of values within the milieu of culture and behavior is shown in Figure 15-1. Culture and its normative qualities are expressed in an individual through the values held about life and the surrounding world. These values in turn help shape attitudes concerning appropriate behavior in given situations. Continually changing patterns of individual and group behavior, however, eventually have an impact on a society's culture; and thus the cycle begins all over again.

Values We have referred in passing to values. What is a value and how does it affect our behavior in a work setting, both here and abroad? In your opinion, is the military draft right or wrong? How about prostitution, long hair, sexual preference, and ridicule of the handicapped? Your response to these questions gives an indication of your values and these values differ according to the culture in which you have been raised or are now living. In each of these examples, there is an opposite answer depending upon the culture in which the questions are asked. Values give us our perception of reality. When we speak of people not being able to cope with reality, we are indicating that their value system has been sufficiently threatened or overloaded, and that they are unable to deal with the situation. They become immobilized, incapable of taking action. If one is overseas, culture shock can result when values are threatened. The victim of culture shock displays defensive behaviors so as to keep the world in equilibrium.

Yankelovich, Skelly, and White found two sets of values in a national survey of United States workers: traditional and new.[6] In the traditional pattern, they identified the following profiles:

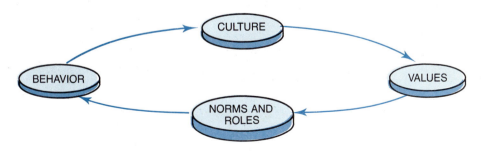

FIGURE 15-1
Culture and behavior

- *The uncommitted worker*. These persons seek maximum earnings in return for minimal commitment. They are least motivated to work and would be the first to stop working altogether if it were viable economically.
- *The job-oriented worker*. The working in a job (almost any job, it appears) is an end in itself. These workers are committed to working but not in any particular job. They are not ambitious in the traditional sense.
- *The work-oriented worker*. This worker holds what many in management believe to be the best of the traditional work values: those that are associated with the American dream. Psychic rewards are most important but must derive from the intrinsic character of the work. There is an overriding concern about excellence and, in general, doing the best job possible, not because of external rewards but because of strongly held internal values. As a by-product these workers may become managers.

In the new work values patterns, the researchers found the following:

- *The fulfillment seeker*. Essentially, these workers seek psychic rewards and the internal cues that indicate they are realizing their full potential. They must feel personal growth in the job.
- *The money seeker*. This worker does not seek money as an end but looks to money as a means of participating in what has been characterized as the "full, rich life."

While the preceding descriptions are useful in better understanding American work value patterns, they do not describe broader social values. Edward C. Steward describes these by contrasting our values with the generalized values of other cultures. He states that the particular American middle-class predispositions fall in the general categories of (1) Activity—forms of self-expression ("doing" in the American culture as opposed to "being" in the contrast culture); (2) Social Relationships (the American emphasis on equality, informality, and depersonalization in relationships); (3) Motivation (personal achievement as opposed to traditionally fixed status, material and visible signs of success); (4) Perception of the World ("The world is material," man is unique, man should strive for control and integration with nature, exploration of his environment rather than unity and integration with nature, optimism as opposed to fatalism); (5) Perception of Self and the Individual (the individualistic self, resistant to formal authoritative control, tendency "to fragment personalities" as opposed to others as total or whole persons, thus "an American does not have to accept the other person in totality to be able to work with him," since thoughts and intents are evaluated separately); and (6) Generalized Cultural Forms (linear concept of time, cause and effect, space; the world is matter rather than "a network of living forces"; rational rather than intuitive perception of the world).[7]

Stanley Davis, however, in considering this issue stated: "Because societies differ greatly in their value orientations, it is difficult to generalize in the face of

TABLE 15–1
Traditional versus modern societies

Traditional Societies	Modern Societies
High proportion of the labor force engaged in subsistence agriculture	Complex division of labor with less than 10 percent on the farm
Customary techniques handed down from generation to generation	A sophisticated use of technology and science
Local markets	An economy based on complex commercial markets and high per-capita production and consumption
A majority of the population living in rural areas	Population concentrated in urban areas
A system of social stratification that is sharply divided between a few rulers and a great many peasants, with little mobility between strata	A greater range of social strata, with a more equalitarian distribution of wealth, status, and power, and increased mobility
A high level of illiteracy	High literacy rates and emphasis on teaching pragmatic skills
Low level of participation in the mass media	Mass media aimed at the bulk of the population

Source: Joseph A. Kahl, *The Measurement of Modernism* (Austin, TX: University of Texas Press, 1968): 4-6. Copyright © 1968. Used by permission.

such diversity."[8] To make comparative statements, most social scientists differentiate between values in traditional and modern societies. These are described in Table 15–1.

Joseph Kahl contrasted these values as follows: "Traditional values are compulsory in their force, sacred in their tone, and stable in their timelessness. They call for fatalistic acceptance of the world as it is, respect for those in authority and submergence of the individual in the collectivity. Modern values are rational and secular, permit choice and experiment, glorify efficiency and change, and stress individual responsibility."[9]

Davis elaborated that a man with a modern value orientation, by contrast, is an activist: "He believes in making plans in advance for important parts of his life, and he has a sense of security that he can usually bring those plans to fruition. He values individualism and his own initiative, he is willing to move away from his relatives, he prefers to live in the city, he avails himself of the mass media, and he seeks to improve both his social and material status."[10]

These values are described by Rhinesmith in contrasting values of human nature relations across three different cultures in Figure 15–2. These values are expressed in the orientation of the populace toward dealing with nature. The society can attempt to control nature, live in harmony with it, or adopt a fatalistic stance. In all three cultures each orientation exists within a certain percentage of the population, but each culture has a dominant pattern or profile.

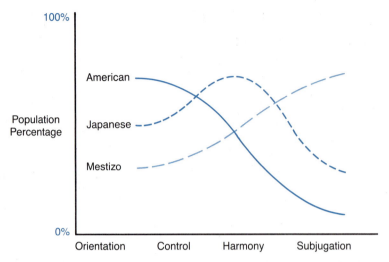

FIGURE 15–2

Human-nature relations in three cultures (Source: Stephen H. Rhinesmith, *Cultural Organizational Analysis* (Cambridge, MA: McBer and Company, 1970): 7. Reprinted by permission.)

Norms   There was a time in U.S. culture when no one thought twice about seeing two women dancing with each other on a dance floor. In some parts of the country they may still not. However, in most communities dancing is considered to be a heterosexual activity. In other cultures two men dancing with each other, as in Greece, is considered acceptable. Why this variation in the acceptability of behavior? Norms. Norms are the generally accepted standards of individual and group behavior. Even when we feel that we are independent of social pressures (norms), we are subtly and unconsciously influenced towards the perceived acceptable standard of conduct.

What then is the difference between a value and a norm? Values are the more generalized ideological justifications and aspirations while norms are general expectations of behavior. Norms are constructs through which a culture actualizes its values. They are the rules by which social interaction may occur. Transgression of these rules results in corrective action.

The applicability, then, of organizational behavior concepts across cultures becomes more complex. It is necessary to understand a culture not only through its value system but also in the ways that values are enforced through norms.

For example, an Indonesian value is that one must always be in concert with the world around one. Life has a constant spiritual value. One norm through which this value is enforced is through the concept of "Malu" or losing face. In Indonesia one never confronts or becomes angry with another. To do so would cause the person doing the confronting or losing temper to lose face. If a person loses face then that person has violated a norm and must be punished. In this case the punishment would be coolness, aloofness, and isolation by others.

Schein describes norms as pivotal or peripheral.[12] The former are mandatory for continual membership in the cultural subgroup while the latter are desirable but not essential. Knowledge and acceptance of pivotal norms is necessary to successful social interaction in any culture.

Consider the following more elaborate illustration of differences in cultural norms. An American at a cocktail party in Java tripped over the invisible cultural rope that marks the boundaries of acceptable behavior. He was seeking to develop a business relationship with a prominent Javanese and seemed to be doing very well. Yet as the cocktail party ended, so apparently did a promising beginning. For the North American spent nearly six months trying to arrange a second meeting. He finally learned, through pitying intermediaries, that at the cocktail party he had momentarily placed his arm on the shoulder of the Javanese—and in the presence of other people. Humiliating! Almost unpardonable in traditional Javanese etiquette.

In this particular case, the unwitting breach was mended by a graceful apology. It is worth noting, however, that a truly cordial business relationship never did develop.[13]

Norms may differ from situation to situation within a value system and be dependent upon the individual's role. Values derive from culture; norms derive, in turn, from values; and roles from norms. The preceding situation typifies the difference in United States and Javanese values and introduces the concept of roles.

Roles   Roles may be conceived of as a bottom part of the pendulum of a clock (see Figure 15-3). At the top the culture provides for little variation or deviation from what is acceptable. As we move down the pendulum more possible variation is introduced, though each level is influenced by the prior levels. Roles are influenced by the culture, values, and norms.

Roles come in as many variations as there are categories of people to fill them. We have biological roles (sex, kinship, and age); occupational roles; training roles (students); ceremonial roles (student body president); and others. In many cases one role may be complementary to another. For example, the functions prescribed for a teacher must be stated in terms of a student, and vice versa.

The importance of roles varies according to the culture, its values, and its norms. It is not an accident that we speak of roles when we discuss actors. Roles are "a set of expected behavior patterns attributed to someone occupying a given position in a social unit."[14]

In U.S. culture, most individuals know their work roles and the behavior that goes along with them. Jackall has described the behavior patterns that are associated with corporate bureaucrats in U.S. corporations, which among other requirements include loyalty to one's superior.[15] When an individual is confronted with divergent role expectations by others, that person suffers role con-

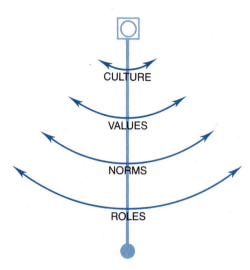

FIGURE 15-3
Aspects of culture

flict. To the extent an individual knows the attitudes and behavior consistent with expectations in a given situation, there should be no role conflict. To the extent that the individual's role perception, identity, or others' expectations differ, we can expect a problem.

The carrying of norms and roles into other cultures is fraught with difficulty. For example, most U.S. citizens hold a value of egalitarianism, which determines the norms and roles they expect others to play. In other cultures this may cause considerable difficulty. Consider the following case: An executive of a major manufacturing company was sent to Bolivia on assignment. While there, the family followed custom and hired a maid. They proceeded to have her sit and eat dinner with them at the dining room table. At one point the family invited executives from a Bolivian company to have dinner with them. The guests were greatly offended when the maid sat down and had dinner with them. One of them later confided to the couple that it was not within the maid's role to eat with the family. Upon questioning her, they found that not only was she uncomfortable in eating dinner with them but was greatly relieved and delighted to eat by herself in the kitchen. They had violated a Bolivian norm while respecting a North American norm, and the maid felt severe role conflict.[16]

In this section of the chapter we have tried to show that culture, values, norms, and roles all derive from one another and constitute a system in equilibrium. To the extent that we must deal with someone from another culture, the situation becomes more complex, requiring all involved to know as much about themselves and the other culture as possible to enhance the enrichment that the interaction may bring. It is only as we encounter other cultures, values, norms, and roles that we are fully able to perceive our own.

Pervasiveness of International Effect on Management and Organizations

Interest in the international effect on management and organizations received major impetus after World War II. As various countries tried to reconstruct their industries and economies, Western management practices were introduced. The academic community sought to determine whether this transfer of management practices and technology was value-free.

Perhaps a more succinct estimate of the problems facing this adaptation and transferability of American management methods was stated by Ross Weber, who said "on no subject are Americans more self-centered and ethnocentric than on management of economic enterprise."[17]

Two scholars, Fred Harbison and Charles Myers, after reviewing many cultural differences came to the conclusion in 1959 that "unless basic rather than trivial or technical changes in the broad philosophy of organization building are forthcoming, Japan is destined to fall behind in the ranks of modern industrial nations."[18] Such seemingly value-laden statements raise the question of whether management and behavioral science concepts can free themselves of their ethnocentric baggage.

The case of Japan provides us with one answer. Harbison and Myers did not know that another American, Edward Deming, had been in Japan for eight years laying the groundwork to prove that certain concepts of quality control and other management systems could be adapted and used to increase the efficiency and effectiveness of Japanese business organizations. He was so successful that to this day the annual prize for excellence in management awarded by the Japanese government is called the Deming Award.

A number of aspects highlight the pervasiveness of the international effect on management and organizations. First, there is no common understanding of what management is. In Germany, the concept of management is more akin to the concept of entrepreneurship; in Japan and other Asian countries, it emphasizes groups and consensus; and in Scandinavia and some other European countries, it is called "industrial democracy." In such locations as Hong Kong, Singapore, and the Philippines, management is based on the sociological concept of the extended family. In the more centrally controlled countries of the Eastern bloc, it is identified as economic planning and implementation. To a large degree the latter view is being followed by most developing nations, and the United States is contributing to this effort through its foreign aid program.

It is reasonable to conclude that there is much to be learned from other countries and cultures. The importance of the Japanese quality circle concept to the United States is an example. Unfortunately, political bias often restricts us from considering contributions from others of differing political ideologies.

United States management concepts are based on efficiency and other broad principles such as participative management. They are generally technology intensive and becoming more so. In the third world, however, many enterprises are based on a labor-intensive concept, and the concern is more for an employed

TABLE 15–2
Contrasting company profiles

Japanese Company Profile	Theory Z Company Profile	American Company Profile
Lifetime employment	Long-term employment	Short-term employment
Slow evaluation and promotion	Slow evaluation and promotion	Rapid evaluation and promotion
Nonspecialized career paths	Moderate career specialization	Specialized careers
Consensus decision making	Consensus decision making	Individual decisions
Collective responsibility	Individual responsibility	Individual responsibility
Informal implicit control	Informal implicit control	Explicit formal control
Holistic concern	Holistic concern	Segmented concerns

Source: William Ouchi, *Theory Z* © 1981, Addison-Wesley, Reading, MA. p. 58 (adapted material). Reprinted with permission.

worker who can feed his family than for the higher aims of the Maslow model of motivation. The stage of economic development has a direct bearing on the degree to which management and organizational concepts can be implemented elsewhere.

Let us take a case in point, the concept of the "Theory Z" organization. William Ouchi in his work studied a cross section of U.S. companies with operations in Japan and an equal number of Japanese companies with operations in the U.S. He found that companies such as IBM, Procter and Gamble, and Hewlett Packard were a blend of the American and Japanese organizations.[19] It is not lost on the reader that these companies are also some of the most "excellent" companies in the United States.[20] Table 15–2 presents the profiles of the American, Japanese, and Theory Z organizations. The lesson from the Theory Z organization is that we have had management concepts introduced and adapted abroad and then reintroduced to the United States as an operational concept.

Behavioral Implications

The purpose of studying organizational behavior is to learn to explain and predict human behavior. By examining key variables and relationships, a manager may apply these concepts and help the organization achieve its goals and objectives. Many managers have found this difficult and uncomfortable in their own culture let alone trying to apply these concepts to other cultures. What is the potential for transferring these concepts and how valid are they when examined in the light of another culture with its attendant values, norms, and roles?

It has been charged that, since American theories are based on a primarily American and western European experience, their export to other cultures amounts to cultural imperialism. Others have stressed the universality of these same theories and suggest that they are a means by which other nations, including the developing nations, may achieve modernity or "development."

Hofstede Study   A Dutch scholar, Geert Hofstede, undertook a study from 1967 to 1973 to examine this problem and provide us with both a framework and data from which to work. He sought to discover whether differences found among 116,000 employees of a large multinational corporation in 40 countries were a result of their different cultures.[21]

Through a review of other studies, theoretical reasoning, and the application of statistical techniques to the data from a single psychological questionnaire, Hofstede derived four criteria by which to compare differences among cultures: power distance, uncertainty avoidance, individualism/collectivism, and masculinity/femininity.

Power distance is the extent to which a society accepts the fact that power is unequally distributed and measures the degree to which there is psychological distance between people. Power distance may be considered as a continuum, with small power distance on the left and large power distance on the right. Examples of the differences that characterize these two ends of the continuum are given in Table 15–3. Most countries fall somewhere between the extremes.

Uncertainty avoidance is the extent to which a society is able to deal with threatening, ambiguous, or anxiety-provoking situations. The continuum for the various aspects that characterize weak uncertainty avoidance and strong uncertainty avoidance is shown in Table 15–4.

Individualism/collectivism is the third dimension. Individualism implies a loosely knit social framework in which people are supposed to take care of

TABLE 15–3

The power distance dimension

Small Power Distance	Large Power Distance
Inequality in society should be minimized	There should be an order of inequality in this world in which everyone has a rightful place; high and low are protected by this order
All people should be interdependent	A few people should be interdependent; most should be dependent
Superiors and subordinates consider each other to be just like themselves	Superiors and subordinates consider each other to be different kinds of people
Those in power should look less powerful than they are	Those in power should try to look as powerful as possible
Latent harmony exists between the powerful and the powerless	Latent conflict exists between the powerful and the powerless

Source: *Culture's Consequences* by Geert Hofstede, p. 122. Copyright © 1980. Reprinted by permission of Sage Publications, Inc.

TABLE 15–4
The uncertainty avoidance dimension

Weak Uncertainty Avoidance	Strong Uncertainty Avoidance
The uncertainty inherent in life is more easily accepted and each day is taken as it comes	The uncertainty inherent in life is felt as a continuous threat that must be fought
Conflict and competition can be contained on the level of fair play and used constructively	Conflict and competition can unleash aggression and should therefore be avoided
There should be as few rules as possible	There is a need for written rules and regulations
The authorities are there to serve the citizens	Ordinary citizens are incompetent compared with the authorities

Source: *Culture's Consequences* by Geert Hofstede, p. 184. Copyright © 1980. Reprinted by permission of Sage Publications, Inc.

themselves and their immediate families only, while collectivism is characterized by a tight social framework in which people distinguish between in-groups and out-groups. They expect their in-group to look after them, and in exchange for that they feel they owe absolute loyalty to the group. Table 15–5 provides a more complete picture of this dimension.

Masculinity is the degree to which values and traits in society are perceived as those associated with masculine qualities: independence, assertiveness, acquisition of material goods, and callousness towards others. On the other hand, qualities of *femininity* include nurturance and sympathy. This dimension is shown in Table 15–6.

Hofstede found that on the power distance dimension America ranked fifteenth out of forty countries, below the average but not as low as other wealthy

TABLE 15–5
The individualism dimension

Collectivist	Individualist
In society, people are born into extended families or clans who protect them in exchange for loyalty	In society, one is supposed to take care of oneself and one's immediate family
"We" consciousness holds sway	"I" consciousness holds sway
The emphasis is on belonging to organizations; membership is the ideal	The emphasis is on individual initiative and achievement; leadership is the ideal
Belief is placed in group decisions	Belief is placed in individual decisions
Value standards differ for in-groups and out-groups (particularism)	Value standards should apply to all (universalism)

Source: *Culture's Consequences*, by Geert Hofstede, p. 235. Copyright © 1980. Reprinted by permission of Sage Publications, Inc.

TABLE 15–6
The masculinity dimension

Feminine	Masculine
Men needn't be assertive, but can assume nurturing roles	Men should be assertive; women should be nurturing
There should be equality between the sexes	Men should dominate in society
People and environment are important	Money and things are important
Unisex and androgeny are ideal	Ostentatious manliness (machismo) is appreciated

Source: *Culture's Consequences,* by Geert Hofstede, p. 295. Copyright © 1980. Reprinted by permission of Sage Publications, Inc.

countries. On uncertainty avoidance, the U.S. ranked ninth, well below average. On individualism/collectivism, the U.S. ranked fortieth, which qualifies the country as the most individualistic in the sample. U.S. masculinity ranking was twenty-eighth out of forty—well above the average. In summary, United States managers cultivate a medium power distance, are very able to deal with ambiguity, are very individualistic, and score fairly high on the masculinity dimension.

Hofstede went on to examine the four dimensions from a number of viewpoints, attempting to determine if the dimensions showed cultural differences with respect to American theories of motivation, leadership, or organization.

Motivation Theory   Hofstede found that there is a strong relationship between McClelland's theory of achievement motivation and countries with a combination of weak uncertainty avoidance and strong masculinity. That is to say that the countries in which achievement motivation may be applicable are those that have individuals characterized by a willingness to accept risk and a concern with performance. Interestingly, the concept of achievement is difficult to translate into any language other than English, which in itself tells much about the transferability of the concept.

In contrasting Maslow's theory of a hierarchy of needs, Hofstede found that different countries would emphasize a level of the hierarchy according to where they fell on the continuum of the four dimensions. For example, he found that countries with strong uncertainty avoidance would place security high, that those high on femininity had social motivation; and that self-actualization is not consistent with a universal motivation process but is rather a description of the U.S. middle-class value system, of which Maslow was a part. In summary, countries *COLOMBIA* with strong uncertainty avoidance and strong masculine dimensions would be motivated by security, while countries with weak uncertainty avoidance and strong feminine dimensions would be motivated by social needs; for a country with strong uncertainty avoidance and strong femininity, both security and social needs would be important. Finally, countries exhibiting weak uncertainty avoidance and weak masculinity would enshrine the concept of self-actualization.

Leadership Theory Leadership is the second area of management theories contrasted via the four dimensions. Leadership depends on the cultural conditioning of the followers. While each of the dimensions contributes something to the understanding of leadership when considered in the perspective of other cultures, it is perhaps best summed up in Table 15–7. It describes the type of "subordinateship" that, other things being equal, a leader can expect to meet in societies at three different levels of power distance.

TABLE 15–7
Subordinateship for three levels of power distance

Small Power Distance (United States)	Medium Power Distance	Large Power Distance
Subordinates have weak dependence needs	Subordinates have medium dependence needs	Subordinates have strong dependence needs
Superiors have weak dependence needs toward their superiors	Superiors have medium dependence needs toward their superiors	Superiors have strong dependence needs toward their superiors
Subordinates expect superiors to consult them or may rebel or strike if superiors are seen as not staying within their legitimate roles	Subordinates expect superiors to consult them but will accept autocratic behavior as well	Subordinates expect superiors to act autocratically
Ideal superior to most is a loyal democrat	Ideal superior to most is a resourceful democrat	Ideal superior to most is a benevolent autocrat or paternalist
Laws and rules apply to all and privileges for superiors are not considered acceptable	Laws and rules apply to all, but a certain level of privileges for superiors is considered normal	Everybody expects superiors to enjoy privileges; laws and rules differ for superiors and subordinates
Status symbols are frowned upon and will easily come under attack from subordinates	Status symbols for superiors contribute moderately to their authority and will be accepted by subordinates	Status symbols are very important and contribute strongly to the superior's authority with subordinates

Source: *Culture's Consequences*, by Geert Hofstede, p. 379. Copyright © 1980. Reprinted by permission of Sage Publications, Inc.

Structural Considerations We have considered motivation and leadership and the extent to which the four cultural dimensions affect their applicability in cultures other than the one in which they were conceived. We now turn to the question of organizational structure and the degree to which these dimensions affect such variables as centralization and formalization. Hofstede found that power distance relates to centralization, and uncertainty avoidance relates to formalization, the degree to which rules and procedures are used. This means that people in large power distance cultures prefer centralization while those in small power distance cultures seek decentralization. Those with strong uncertainty avoidance favor formalization while those with weak uncertainty avoidance favor a more organic approach.

Communication The four dimensions affect other aspects of organizational behavior as well. Consider the effect on communication, conflict resolution, and negotiation. Power distance affects communication in the sense that, in a culture with large power distance, communication is formalized, channeled, and always appropriate with the proper protocol. In a small-power-distance country, it will be more informal, with fewer prescribed behaviors.

One example of these differences is illustrated by the following story. One U.S. company had totally different experiences with "Smith" and "Jones" in the handling of its labor relations. The local union leaders were bitterly hostile to Smith, whereas they could not praise Jones enough. These were puzzling reactions to higher management. Smith seemed a fair-minded and understanding man; it was difficult to fathom how anyone could be bitter against him. At the same time, Jones did not appear to be currying favor by his generosity in giving away the firm's assets. To management, he seemed to be just as firm a negotiator as Smith.

The explanation was found in the two men's communication characteristics. When the union leaders came in to negotiate with Smith, he would let them state their case fully and freely—without interruption, but also without comment. When they had finished, he would say, "I'm sorry. We can't do it." He would follow this blunt statement with a brief and entirely cogent explanation of his reasons for refusal. If the union leaders persisted in their arguments, Smith would paraphrase his first statement, calmly and succinctly. In either case, the discussion was over in a few minutes. The union leaders would storm out of Smith's office complaining bitterly about the cold and heartless man with whom they had to deal.

Jones handled the situation differently. His final conclusion was the same as Smith's—but he would state it only after two or three hours of discussion. Furthermore, Jones participated actively in these discussions, questioning the union leaders for more information, relating the case in question to previous cases, philosophizing about labor relations and human rights, and exchanging stories about work experiences. When the discussion came to an end, the union leaders would leave the office, commenting on how warmhearted and under- standing he was, and how confident they were that he would help them when it was possible for him to do so. They actually seemed more satisfied with a negative decision from Jones than they did with a hard-won concession from Smith.[22]

Conflict Resolution   Conflict resolution, however, would be handled somewhat differently. In a country with large power distance and strong uncertainty avoidance, one finds that conflict is to be avoided. This can be seen in the earlier example of "Malu" in the Indonesian culture. The idea that one from a culture such as the United States (small power distance and weak uncertainty avoidance), with an open, confrontational manner, would seek to utilize these behaviors is a prescription for disaster, particularly in the manner in which we carry out negotiations. Negotiations in the U.S. tend to be conflictful. The weak power distance and weak uncertainty avoidance culture stresses open, candid exchanges. By contrast, the culture with strong uncertainty avoidance and large power distance stresses indirect ways of handling the conflict in negotiations. For example, the Javanese would not come to a meeting if they knew that the answer they were to give was negative and would cause loss of face to the other side. Indirectly though, they would communicate this by not coming or by sending someone else.

Behavioral Aspects—Three Selected Countries

Three countries are presented to provide the reader with specific behavioral implications of the international aspects of organizational behavior: Colombia, Japan, and Sweden. Colombia represents a developing (third-world) country in the western hemisphere. Sweden is a developed European country, and Japan is a developed oriental (far eastern) country. We use these countries to compare and contrast behavioral science or western management methods in specific cultures. A brief socioeconomic description of each country is presented,[23] followed by a review of the cultural consequences for managers of Hofstede's four dimensions (see also Table 15–8).

General Descriptions

Colombia.   Colombia is a lush country of 440,000 square miles, one and two-thirds the size of Texas and three-fourths the size of Alaska. It has a population of 27.03 million (1981) with an annual growth rate of 2.1 percent. It was settled by the Spanish and is known as the country in the western hemisphere where the Spanish language is purest and closest to Spain's. The dominant religion is Roman Catholic. Schools offer five years of compulsory education, but 77 percent of the school-age population enter and 28 percent finish. It has a work force of nine million, an infant mortality rate of 65/1000 and a life expectancy of sixty-two years. It has a republican form of government with three major parties covering the spectrum from conservative to liberal. The central government budget was $4.8 billion in 1981, with a per capita income of $1,296 (in U.S. dollars). It is rich in natural resources, including petroleum, natural gas, iron ore, and gold, and is the foremost producer of fine emeralds in the world.

TABLE 15–8
Comparative study of Colombia, Japan, and Sweden

	Colombia	Japan	Sweden
General Description			
Size	440,000 sq. mi.	147,470 sq. mi.	179,986 sq. mi.
Population	27.03 million	118.45 million	8.3 million
Governmental form	Republican with 3 major parties	Parliamentary democracy with 8 political parties	Constitutional monarchy with multitude of political parties
Major products	Natural resources include oil; exports coffee, bananas, sugar, flowers, corn, and tobacco	No natural resources; imports energy; exports various industrial and electronic products	Has natural resources for hydroelectricity; exports agricultural products and nonelectronic machinery and steel
Religion	Roman Catholic	Shintoism with Buddhism	Lutheran
Hofstede Indicators			
Power distance	67	54	31
Uncertainty avoidance	80	92	29
→ Individualism/ collectivism	13	46	71
→ Masculinity/ femininity	64	95	5

handwritten notes in right margin:
U.S.
BELOW AVERAGE
WELL BELOW AVERAGE
HIGHEST
WELL ABOVE AVERAGE

Source: General description from *Background Notes* (Washington, DC: U.S. Department of State, Colombia: November 1982; Sweden: October 1982; Japan: May 1983). Hofstede indicators from Geert Hofstede, *Culture's Consequences* (Beverly Hills, CA: Sage Publications, 1980): 315.

Coffee is the most important agricultural crop and export. Also important are bananas, rice, corn, sugar cane, flowers, and tobacco. Industry is 22 percent of the GNP and accounts for 21 percent of the work force. Colombia's balance of trade was a $3.2 billion deficit in 1981. Colombia is also characterized by an underground drug trade that contributes to the GNP and the guerrilla activity in some of the rural areas.

Japan. Japan is an island country comprising 147,470 square miles, about the size of Montana and one-third the size of Colombia. Its population is 118,450,000 with an annual growth rate of 0.8 percent. The primary religion is Shintoism with Buddhism. It has a literacy rate of 99 percent and compulsory education between the ages of six and fifteen. The infant mortality rate is 7.5/1000; life expectancy is seventy-three years for males and seventy-eight for females. It is a parliamentary democracy with eight political parties ranging from conservative to communist. The workforce totals 59.3 million. The GNP for 1982 was $1.046 trillion. It has negligible natural resources; the most important agricultural crops are rice, vegetables, fruits, milk, meat, and silk. Its industry depends primarily on imports

BOX 15–2

Preparing For Overseas

"Many of Gulf's operations overseas are not located in or near large urban centers, so living in a small and isolated community may also present problems. . . . This should be considered very carefully before undertaking an overseas assignment—Have you and your family the inner resources and ability to meet the challenge of adjusting to a new way of life in a foreign country?"

That statement comes from the first paragraph of the Gulf Oil Corporation handbook *Your Overseas Assignment.* Supplementing that work is a series of booklets on individual countries and cities to which an employee could be assigned.

For example, one booklet, *Assignment Tokyo,* has the following headings:

Preparing for the Trip
- Physical examination and immunization
- Documents
- Travel
- Custom hints for Japan
- Mail and cables
- Tokyo international airport terminal
- Business cards

Living Conditions
- Housing
- Furnishings
- Clothing
- Food
- Domestic help
- Basic community services
- Religious activities

Source: Adapted from Norman B. Sigband, *Communication for Management and Business,* 3rd ed. (Glenview, IL: Scott, Foresman, 1982): 59–61. Used by permission. Gulf material from Gulf Oil Corporation, Overseas Personnel Office, *Your Assignment Overseas* (1974), and *Assignment Tokyo* (1975). BASF material from BASF-Germany, *Employee Handbook* (1977).

and consists of machinery and equipment, metal and metal products, textiles, autos, chemicals, and electrical and electronic equipment. Its exports are based on its industry, and it had a surplus balance of trade of $10 billion (U.S. dollars) in 1981.

Sweden. Sweden comprises an area of 179,986 square miles, about the size of Montana and Oregon combined and slightly larger than Japan. It has a population of 8.3 million and an annual growth rate of 0.2 percent. The country is 95 percent Lutheran. It has a literacy rate of 99 percent and nine compulsory years of education. The infant mortality rate is 7.5/1000; life expectancy is seventy-five years for men and eighty-one for women. The government is a constitutional monarchy, and the country has a spectrum of political parties ranging from the Moderate Coalition (conservative) to the Communist Party. The central government budget for 1982 was $14.82 billion with an annual inflation rate of 9 percent. Sweden's natural resources are forests, iron ore, and hydroelectric power. Agriculturally it stresses dairy products, grains, sugar beets, potatoes, and wood. Its

- Education
- Transportation
- Communication
- Health and medical care
- Recreation and social activities

In contrast, BASF USA produces a booklet for its German employees who come to work in the U.S. The booklet's headings let us know something of our culture as seen by foreigners:

- Purchasing an automobile
- Charge accounts
- Installment purchases
- Credit cards
- Saving and investing
- Taxes
- Schools
- Relationship between parent and school
- Adult education
- Homes
- Helpful hints to make the new surroundings feel more like home faster
- Helpful hints of what and what not to bring from home

- Household hints
- Clothing sizes
- Religion—in and out of church

Needless to say, BASF Germany also produces a booklet for Americans coming to Germany. One problem—related by an American—is that the booklet is in German.

Questions

1. Besides what was provided by Gulf's materials, what other preparation might be in order for prospective overseas employees? What specific advice would you offer the new manager who is going to Japan? What would you tell his or her spouse as preparation for the transfer?
2. What do the BASF USA booklet headings suggest about the American culture?
3. How would you respond to the American who complained about the "Helpful Hints to Living in Germany," being written in German? What message is being conveyed here?

industry is concentrated in machinery and it imports and exports nonelectric machinery, transport equipment, iron and steel, chemicals, and food stuffs.

It is apparent that there are some wide disparities among the three countries. Principal among these is the infant mortality rate, which is generally taken as a prime indicator of the health of a country's population. The dominant religions are clearly different, and of differential importance in the social power structure. Land size and natural resources also vary, with Colombia having more than either Japan or Sweden but also having a central government budget and GNP strikingly smaller. Annual growth rate would not be a problem for Colombia were it a developed country, but 2.4 percent is considered to be excessive considering the country's resources. Industry also shows marked contrasts. For example, Colombia has considerably more than either of the other two but continues to rely on the agriculture sector for its primary source of foreign exchange. Finally, the literacy rate and degree of compulsory education are indicators of the general fitness of the work force and affect the degree to which a developed country's management technology is appropriate.

What difference do the dimensions that we examined earlier in this chapter make when comparing these countries? To what degree do power distance, individualism/collectivism, uncertainty avoidance, and masculinity/femininity affect the manner in which a manager would approach problems of human behavior in these countries? Let's reexamine them from that perspective.

Hofstede's Dimensions: Colombia

Power distance. As a Latin, Catholic country, Colombia scores 67 on the power distance index. What this means for managers is that in Colombia there is a basic sense in the culture of a defined social order, and that generally people know their place within it. The authoritative nature of the Catholic Church reinforces this by emphasizing the traditional values of God and the role of the church in determining an individual's fate, both on earth and in the afterlife. In practical terms, this means that Colombians seek a high congruence between their actual and expected roles in society, including their work organizations. As employees, they give authorities their due publicly, though not necessarily privately nor in a political context.

Much of the perceived power distance is derived from the Spanish heritage, which emphasized an ordered environment and one in which all persons had a "patron" to look after them, provided that the person being looked after gave the proper deference and accepted the basic roles as defined by the values and norms of the society.

Uncertainty avoidance. Colombia fits the pattern of a traditional culture in the sense provided in Table 15–1 and shows a strong uncertainty avoidance score of 80. This operates in tandem with the large power distance score and indicates a Colombian tendency towards "personalism," translated as a high personalistic orientation.

At first glance this would appear to be a contradiction. That is, how could there be such a strong tendency towards uncertainty avoidance juxtaposed with a personalistic view towards life? The answer is that individuals depend upon the "cacique," an informal leader found in most communities and to some degree in organizations, to be the interface between themselves and the legal authorities. They depend upon these power figures to protect them and to obtain for them those things that they feel are needed to keep their lives in concert with perceived reality. Often when indicating a preference for a desired outcome the Colombian uses the phrase "si Dios quiere"—"if God wills it." This is somewhat moderated in the modern organization where the technocrats may take a more "modern" (a value term) view towards life.

Individualism/collectivism. Colombia has one of the lowest scores on the individualism index, indicating a collective orientation towards life. This is reflected through a strong emphasis on family and an orientation toward privacy. Most homes in Colombia are of the traditional Spanish layout, with the house placed close to the street and with a large patio on the inside. This desire for privacy, coupled with need to operate as a unit, carries over to the community at large. Reinforcing this was the undeclared civil war of 1948–1958 between the liberals and the conservatives, in which over 300,000 were killed in political violence. This left a residue in Colombia of "bandoleros" who roamed selected rural areas, killing and pillaging. This has evolved to the present guerrila activity that continues in Colombia. One of the effects of this activity has been the tendency to act collectively as a means of protection towards the threat of violence. In general one would perceive that their low score indicates a preference to be part of a group and not be out front as an individual taking charge, or taking risk.

Masculinity/femininity. Colombia scores far to the right on the masculinity index. Interesting to note is that masculinity is associated with Roman Catholicism. It indicates a preference for keeping women in their place to do "women's work." The man in Colombian society is one who always takes care of his family. He may participate in the double standard when it comes to sexual conduct but he must adhere to the value that stipulates that one always provides for his wife and children. Machismo, the Spanish word describing the extreme masculinity found in Colombia and other Latin countries, has joined the international vocabulary. Machismo is more than a word. It provides a code by which a man perceives when he has transgressed and the rules by which he will respond. Many times this may take a violent expression. In organizations this means that the traits of masculinity and male domination prevail.

Hofstede's Dimensions: Japan

Power distance. Japan scores 54 on the power distance index, almost midpoint between Colombia and Sweden. Hierarchy and a stratified society characterize the Japanese. Power inequality is the result of a long cultural heritage in which individuals were born into a certain social stratum and socialized through their cultures' values to adhere to certain norms. Each person in the Japanese culture knows his or her role and its accompanying responsibilities. If you are a high-level manager, you know that your role is to manage in the Japanese way. The Japanese way requires that you take an interest in your employees from both an organizational and a personal basis, including an understanding of and interest in the employees' families.

Uncertainty avoidance. Japan scores 92 on uncertainty avoidance, as compared with 80 by Colombia and 29 by Sweden. Proponents of Japanese management often neglect to point out that it is a very controlling style of management. Consensus is used as a means of obtaining control over the enterprise. This control is necessary to respond to the Japanese need for uncertainty avoidance. The subordinate employee knows that he or she will have a say in what happens, that the resultant action will be correct, and the decision will allow the employee and the enterprise to continue functioning successfully. The personal world of the

Japanese must be in harmony with the universe, and a primary way such harmony is achieved is through membership in an organization that controls the immediate work environment.

Individualism/collectivism.   Japan scores 46 on the individualism/collectivism index, about halfway between Colombia (13) and Sweden (71). Important to remember when considering this index is that the individual is not necessarily inner-directed in the need for collectivism but rather in the need to avoid losing face. Face is lost when one takes action inconsistent with one's expected role. In Japan's stratified society, each person has certain roles to play and actions to contribute to the betterment of the collective whole. To fail in these results in embarrassment and the losing of face. Japanese society has always stressed the importance of the group. With the advent of modern technology and the preeminence of the industrial organization in Japan, Japanese workers have shifted their loyalty from the collectivist organization that raised rice to the industrial organization that now provides much of the same nurturance that the agricultural collective did.

It is interesting to note that the Japanese individualism index is increasing. This is seen as a result of the shift to greater industrialization and socioeconomic progress. Individuals are beginning to question the degree to which they or the organization are more important.

Masculinity/femininity.   Japan is the most masculine country on Hofstede's index. It scores a 95 in comparison with a 64 for Colombia and a 5 for Sweden. Consider the following quote by Kunaiki Nagai, a Tokyo management consultant, in an interview on American society:

> In Japan the home has traditionally been the place where a man relaxed. When he returns home from the rough world of business, he is free to behave and dress any way he wants. [But in America] There is just as much tension at home as at work. It is as if the American husband punches off the time clock at 5 P.M. and punches on again for work at home. The American wife doesn't greet her returning husband with a cold beer and a steaming bath.[24]

In Japan a man's work and organization is of predominant importance to both him and his family. As he does well in his organization so does his family in society. In terms of the masculine characteristics such as "live to work," highly differentiated sex roles in society, high emphasis on tradition, and others, Japan is at the forefront. The role of the women in Japanese society is not only traditional but very controlled.

Hofstede's Dimensions: Sweden

Power distance.   Sweden scores a low 31 on the power distance index, equaled by Norway and exceeded only by Austria (11), Denmark (18), and Israel(13).[25] The pragmatic result of this low score is an emphasis on participation and informal consultation among workers and between workers and management. In fact, a deliberate effort is often made by managers in Sweden not to appear powerful. The low power distance score is reflected by the development of "industrial democracy" in which power over the corporate enterprise is shared by the unions, workers, and the state. Because of this orientation there has been a propensity by the government to assume responsibility for failing companies. There is reason to believe that this is changing now, and Sweden has made it clear that if a company is unprofitable it will be on the selling block. The impact of this on the concept of power distance is unclear, except that it signals a philosophic change in terms of the degree to which all assume responsibility for the various companies. In keeping with the low power distance index, the overall concern is with the ultimate success of the enterprise.

The low score is also a chief reason for the development of the autonomous work group technique developed by such Swedish companies as Volvo. In these situations, the power for the accomplishment of work is shared by the group and entails high interpersonal relations.

Uncertainty avoidance. Sweden scores a low 29 on the uncertainty avoidance index, equal to Hong Kong and exceeded only by Singapore (8).[26] In Sweden there is a tendency to be less concerned about the future because of a basic confidence in the individual and the society. This confidence creates a willingness to proceed with projects or issues without a clear vision of where they will end. Thus, for the Swede, uncertainty is a raw material with which to explore and expand reality. The high longevity rate for the population in general is indicative of the degree to which they can accommodate stress and anxiety in the process of exploring their collective reality. Case studies from Sweden show a proclivity for wishful (positive) thinking, which is useful in keeping the organization going during periods of uncertainty. New ideas are greeted with enthusiasm, and even if they are unsuccessful, the old thinking will be modified.

Individualism/collectivism. Sweden shows a moderately strong individualism index of 71, exceeded by the U.S. (91), Netherlands (80), Italy (76), Great Britain (89), Canada (80), and Australia (90).[27] This strong individualism score derives in large part from the values of the culture. It indicates a feeling that individuals are responsible for themselves, a personal preference for interesting work as opposed to earnings, and that work in a large organization is generally not more desirable than in a small company. How can a country that stresses autonomous work groups be high on the individualism index? Because individual responsibility within the group is also emphasized.

Masculinity/femininity. Sweden scores the lowest on this scale with a 5. In a Swedish school Dick and Jane do not exhibit the clear masculine and feminine activities that they do in the United States or Japan. An analysis of children's readers showed that Sweden emphasized girls in the leading role and showed boys in nontraditional roles. Interesting to note is that Sweden has an educational policy for training both girls and boys in nontraditional sex roles. It is this dimension that most sets Sweden apart from other countries, although less so from other Scandinavian countries and the Netherlands, which also scored low on the masculinity index.[28] It is because of this feminine orientation that we are able to explain some of the perceived anomalies such as a high individualism score while emphasizing collective types of work organization. The feminine orientation indicates a preference (remember the definition of a value: that which is preferred) for cooperation and concern in the working environment. In Sweden, the terms "mother" and "daughter" are used when referring to headquarters and foreign subsidiaries.

Summary of Key Concepts

1. To understand another culture, we must understand our own culture.
2. A culture is composed of values, norms, and roles. These elements are the collective consciousness of the participants and a guide for the interactions among a culture's members.
3. There is no universal concept of what management is. It can vary from "entrepreneurship" in Germany to "industrial democracy" in Scandinavia.
4. While we attempt to study the role of manager in other cultures, we must remember that the study itself is culturally bound and may not accurately portray what we want to study.
5. One of the most extensive studies of cultures and organizations within those cultures was done by Geert Hofstede. He utilized four dimensions to compare cultures: power distance, uncertainty avoidance, individualism/collectivism, and masculinity/femininity.
6. Further study allowed Hofstede to compare cultures using other behavioral concepts: motivation, leadership, communications, conflict resolution, and structural considerations.
7. Three countries were compared using Hofstede's dimensions: Colombia, Japan, and Sweden.

Key Terms

Culture	Norms
Culture shock	Power distance
Hofstede's study	Roles
Individualism/collectivism	Traditional society
Masculinity/femininity	Uncertainty avoidance
Modern society	Values

MANAGERIAL IMPLICATIONS

Having an understanding of the subtle differences between the three countries, we now can examine in more detail the effects of culture that managers need to consider when working with organizations and their employees in those countries. In this section we look at some of the managerial implications of dealing with Colombia, Japan, and Sweden in terms of communication, decision making, motivation, leadership, conflict resolution, negotiation, and organization.

Colombia

Communication   In Colombia, communication must be considered within the perspective of other cultural characteristics. The individual Colombian male has a tendency to be verbally expressive. The educated Colombian places an emphasis on philosophy and the arts and it is not unusual to hear a Colombian man recite his own poetry. A good deal of time is spent talking and discussing a topic from many different perspectives. This is also true of the less-educated "campesinos" (peasants), only the subject matter is different. Women, by the role definition given them in Colombia, are verbally expressive but only in a "woman's" setting and not in the work setting.

Another interesting note concerning communication in Spanish is the syntax of the language. For example, when a Colombian wishes to say "I dropped it," he says "se me cayo" which means literally, "it fell from me." This indicates the effect of uncertainty avoidance on communication. That is, there is something greater at play here that would assume the responsibility for what has happened. The style of communication in an interpersonal sense is determined by the values that the person holds. If the person has more traditional values, then communication styles would be more self-denying. If the values are more modern and the situation appropriate, then the person would be more self-bargaining. In addition, one's perceived or expected role in society will indicate the style of communication. For example, a campesino when talking to a political official, a priest, or other in authority, would demonstrate the appropriate deference.

Group communication in Colombia follows the same rules but may also be described in terms of the five communication networks described earlier, in chapter 4. Group communication by definition occurs more in an organizational setting and is important to the manager. In most cases the network used in Colombia is the "star" or the "Y" pattern. Both of these have a high degree of centralization and leadership predictability, consistent with the dimensions of power distance, uncertainty avoidance, and masculinity. Individualism influences it only to the extent to which a collective decision was sanctioned by the authorities.

Decision Making   The actual translation of decision making in Spanish also tells something about the culture. In Spanish you "tomar una decicion"—you take a decision, as opposed to "making" a decision in English. By definition, decisions in Colombia are aligned with authority—hence, power distance, and are more consistent with uncertainty avoidance. The dimension of individualism exists but only in the sense of "personalismo," not collectivity. Masculinity also influences decision making greatly since males are generally the decision makers in the work setting. In most cases, the manager makes the decision and announces it and most of the workers get in line with the decision. If they do not like it, then the only alternative is clandestine opposition.

Motivation In Colombia, motivation is a function of the type of values that the person holds—modern or traditional. In most organizations the values are somewhere between these two, depending on the organization and the leadership style of those in charge. For Colombia, with its strong uncertainty avoidance and masculinity dimensions, security ranks highest in the Maslow model of motivation. This is also consistent with the power distance dimension and individualism. In other words, given the socioeconomic level of the population, they tend to be more concerned with satisfying the basic needs. Employees tend to be more concerned with pay, job security, work conditions, and relationships with the boss than with recognition from others, achievement, or advancement.

Leadership Leadership in Colombia is probably most typified by the individual who is in control, and in whom subordinates can put their faith. Leadership is boss-centered, as opposed to subordinate-centered (see chapter 5, Tannenbaum and Schmidt's model). This means that the manager is the source of authority and determines what will be. It is expected both by subordinates and society that the manager will provide a modicum of "hygiene" factors and that the manager will demonstrate a paternalistic approach to management. All know their roles and fulfill them. To the extent that they do not, the leadership pattern will be disturbed and the resulting conflict will have to be resolved.

Something other than McGregor's Theory X (see chapter 5) may describe the leader's (manager's) attitudes towards workers, who are perceived as being responsible but only within the limits of the role that they are expected to fulfill. In this sense they fit most with the bureaucratic pattern of providing an allegiance to the leader, for as the manager prospers, so should the workers.

Conflict Resolution Conflict resolution in an organizational setting in Colombia ranges somewhere between avoidance and forcing, compromise and accommodation. As a subordinate, the employee avoids conflict. If that isn't possible, then the employee accommodates. The manager may favor forcing the conflict and only use compromise as a back-up style. As a leader in Colombia, you are expected to be assertive and compromise only to the extent that circumstances may force you. The previously discussed aspects of communication and leadership influence the manner in which conflict is resolved. In most cases you resolve conflict with authority or with verbiage. If this should fail, then compromise with honor would be the resulting alternative. Compromise would be seen as the least desirable. Recall the incident of Smith and Jones and the manner in which they resolved conflict with the union officials.

Negotiation   The concept of negotiation in United States culture has been described as the John Wayne style. In other words, you ride in on a white horse and you resolve conflict through pure personal power. Shoot first and ask questions later. In Colombia, as in most other (nonwestern) cultures, negotiation is an art and not a rational science. As the Smith and Jones example illustrated, it is like the old American song, "it ain't what you do, it's how you do it." Colombians have a concept of negotiation and it includes the proper "pomp and circumstance." You never just get to the point. You always take time for the cultural niceties, which might include having a "tinto" (cup of expresso coffee) before starting and usually involves talking about those things that are important in life, including the family or others that may be important to those present. What you say is not as important as how you say it. In particular, there are many ways to say "no," and unlike the American's tendency to be direct, the Colombian can be very circuitous about saying it.

Listening is important in communication and negotiation is done through communication. Most American managers are not adept at listening and observing the nonverbal cues given in a negotiation setting. Rather, we have been raised to believe that the world operates basically in a universally rational fashion. However, other cultures have other forms of "rationality." While Colombia's view is closer to the American than Japan's, to negotiate in Colombia, one must be articulate, poised, and willing to take the time to reach an agreement. To this extent, the dimension of individualism is important in the negotiation process. In Colombia the end must generally represent a collectivist end. Things must be said indirectly, one must recognize the status of the person with whom one is negotiating, and negotiation must conclude with less certainty for all.

Organization   In previous chapters, we have discussed the different types of organizational structures that may be appropriate or used in different enterprises. Chief among these is the bureaucracy, which combines other structural forms to various degrees. In Colombia the bureaucratic form is the most prevalent, consistent with the power distance, uncertainty avoidance, and masculinity dimensions. It offers impersonality combined with the "personalismo" of the manager. In short, what one finds is a paternalistic approach to bureaucracy in which individuals know when they are to behave in an impersonal way and when they are the subject of personal attention.

Japan

Communication   Communication in an interpersonal sense in Japan is open to the extent that it is task oriented. Relationships have already been defined by society and communication on this basis is not considered to be in the public domain. Thus interpersonal communication in Japan would fit the self-denying style. The giving and receiving of feedback is one of the most important facets of interpersonal communication. Hofstede states in citing Cox and Cooper: "In

Japan, the giving and receiving of personal feedback appeared virtually impossible, and, when tried, resulted in what the authors perceived as ritualized behavior. The receiver of feedback felt that he must have insulted the sender in some way."[29]

In group communication the Japanese stress the circle or all-channel network when dealing with issues concerning the job because these are task issues. In fact, the success of the quality circle technique of management is a task-oriented, problem-solving approach. Incorporated into the premise for using such networks may be a high concern for task. Thus in Japan it is safe to deal with peers on task issues but not on relationships. These are regulated by society and are generally taboo.

Decision Making   Quality circles are a form of decision making regarding problems in the workplace. These are at a peer level, however, and lower in the hierarchy. How are decisions made at higher levels of the hierarchy? By consensus, just as they are at the quality circle level. What then is the difference and how does this relate to the Japanese culture? In fact, all decisions in the Japanese organization are made by consensus. All individuals are socialized to this means and no one is satisfied until consensus is reached, no matter how long it takes. It is an effective means for managers to control their organizations.

Motivation   One of the motivation theories discussed earlier was McClelland's theory of achievement motivation. The word *achievement* is difficult in most languages other than English, thus making the concept itself questionable in other cultures. Japanese workers, because of their high score on uncertainty avoidance and masculinity, seem to place security needs as the strongest motivator. The scores on power distance and individualism/collectivism support them. However, we must remember that the individualism index is increasing in Japan and that managers must take this into consideration. For the near future, however, workers in Japan will continue to be concerned with their place in society as facilitated by their role in the organization and to focus more on the hygiene factors associated with them.

Leadership   Leadership is associated with the introduction of new technologies, particularly industrial technology transfer. One of the problems that has most perplexed western providers of development is the desire by developing nations for new technologies on the one hand, and on the other the inability to achieve the transfer of these technologies because of the values that they carry with them. In this case, Japan appears to serve as an example for the rest of the world of the successful introduction of what has been called "appropriate technology." Hofstede says: "Making these technologies work means that people in the receiving countries must learn new leadership and subordinateship skills, change old institutions. . . . Probably the country which has most successfully done this so far is Japan."[30] In practical terms this means that Japan has been able to "find a cultural synthesis which retains from the old local values those elements deemed essential but which allows the new technologies to function."[31] Quality circles in Japan are an example—they do not upset the old values of hierarchy and uncertainty avoidance and they reinforce the collectivist approach. Leadership in Japan takes the form of the manager presenting ideas and inviting questions. The manager may have a fairly well-formed notion of which idea he believes will prevail but will not present that idea fully until consensus concerning it has been achieved.

Conflict Resolution   Conflict in Japan is resolved in favor of the organization to which the parties belong. Even if the conflict is a union-management conflict, the result is one that benefits the organization as a whole. It is the holistic concern that individuals have for the organization and the implicit concept they have of the enterprise that allows this to happen. The results must allow both parties to win and will generally revolve around task issues. It is difficult to imagine conflict resolution concerning relationship issues because the culture defines relationships. It does not necessarily define tasks except as they may relate to roles or hierarchy. Conflict is generally avoided because this is inconsistent with the need for uncertainty avoidance.

Negotiation   On an evening television newscast that we observed, the feature was about the negotiations between the U.S. and Japan on a trade issue. The chief of the U.S. negotiating party described the negotiations something like this: "They come over here and sit across the table from us, they smile, and many times don't say anything. They don't know how to negotiate." He had just flunked the course on negotiations with the Japanese. Probably no other culture has done more to show Americans that there is another style of negotiation than that of Japan. The two negotiation styles could be described as follows:[32]

United States	Japan
An individualistic approach	A team approach
An informal-equalitarian approach	A formalized cultured approach
We will speak English	We will speak both languages
I can make the decision	We will check with the home office
Task orientation	Formality orientation
Here's my best deal	Let's see what's best
Talk, talk, talk	Silence, silence, silence
No means NO	No means let's talk some more
Step-by-step agreement	We will decide it all at the end

It is clear that when it comes to negotiations between two cultures the understanding necessary is drastically compounded by the different perceptions of reality by each. An American faced with a silence by a person from another culture during negotiations usually begins to talk and in the process possibly will "give away the company store."

Organization   The organization in Japan is best described as a benevolent bureaucracy. One might be tempted to think that this is the best of both worlds. However, we need to remember that any organizational structure is only as good as the cultural values underlying it. Japan's personalized bureaucracy is also a paternalistic bureaucracy. For Americans that is good if you are on the benefiting end. In general, however, such an organizational structure is not in keeping with our values. Our beliefs in individualism and independence are practically the opposite of Japan's. Both structures have attained some degree of success. In fact, many properties of the Japanese organizational structure and management are being adopted in the U.S., as described in Table 15–2.

Sweden

Communication   Interpersonal communication in Sweden would be characterized by others as indirect but by Swedes as very direct. There is an implicit sense in communications among Swedes that allows them to be "implicitly direct." This seeming contradiction is understood within the Swedish culture. One author described it thus: "The Swede is a straightforward person, but impossible to understand for a non-Swede."[33] Group communication is somewhat clearer. It is organic and consensus based and takes a long time, but results in a high commitment to that which has been decided. The circle or all-channel communication network would come closest to describing group communication in Sweden. Both are low in the degree of centralization, are high in the number of possible channels, and provide high group satisfaction. These communication networks complement the four dimensions of Hofstede's study.

Decision Making   According to many non-Swedes, decision making by Swedes is enough "to drive you up the wall." Swedes are viewed as prolonging decisions or making decisions difficult to interpret for non-Swedes. Decision making is characterized by lengthy consensus building that concentrates on detailed examination of the situation before committing to a course of action. But the process results in a decision that is understood by all and that elicits a commitment to implement it quickly (similar to the Japanese decision making results). Decision making is made in an informal personalized manner and is probably more intuitively than factually based. In the perspective of Tannenbaum and Schmidt, the manager builds consensus toward the decision and then makes the decision unilaterally. The manager can do this because there is inherent built-in commitment to the decision.

Motivation   Social needs and esteem are the elements of Maslow's hierarchy that best characterize motivation in Sweden. In Herzberg's terminology both hygiene factors and motivators are important, with emphasis on the motivators. Hygiene factors, such as a desired work environment, are important, perhaps more so than earnings. The elements of the work environment that emphasize both the individualism and femininity dimensions are important. McClelland's concept of achievement motivation is not consistent with the feminine dimension and, secondly, it is not translatable into Swedish as a concept. Taken within the perspective of Swedish values, the expectancy model may have some application, but to this point research hasn't been done in that area.

Leadership   The concept of leadership can only be considered in the feminine context of the Swedish culture. Leadership is defined as the ability to take action unilaterally after intuition and consensus have been utilized. Facts do not exist independently from the people who define them, and reality is in the eye of the perceiver. As a result, leadership in the Swedish culture is better understood by Swedes than by others. It means following a slow process to take action indirectly. It also means that one must be open to inputs from subordinates and be without a predisposition as to where the process is going to lead. It is an organic process where the ability to manage the means is more important than the end.

Conflict Resolution   The collaborative model best describes conflict resolution in Sweden, albeit slow collaboration. There appears to be a national trait to avoid open conflict. It expresses itself in deferring corrective action for a subordinate and avoiding embarrassing or difficult situations. The softer, more gentle manner usually prevails and may mean frustration for non-Swedes trying to understand the norms for conflict resolution.

Negotiation   As the reader can surmise, the negotiation style of the Swedish culture is one that seeks to resolve issues in such a way that the parties increase the resources available for allocation. For example, the very nature of the Swedish mind assumes that the result sought is not necessarily known at the onset but is developed through the consensual, consultative manner in which negotiations are carried out. The industrial democracy concept assumes that there is a greater good that can be achieved through reasoning together.

Organization   Organizational structure in Sweden follows the industrial democracy concept and contains an implicit acceptance of the value of the individual to the organization. The notion of autonomous work groups allows for freer interpretation of organizational goals and different paths to get there. It emphasizes the individualism, low uncertainty avoidance and femininity of the culture and concentrates more on the work atmosphere than on strict hierarchies or pyramidal structures. The organization may appear to outsiders as sluggish and one in which opportunities are missed because it cannot respond as rapidly as others believe it should. More than anything else, it is based upon cooperation among workers, unions, and the state.

Summary

From this discussion of Colombia, Japan, and Sweden, we can appreciate the subtle and intricate balance needed to relate to different cultures. As managers, we need to stop and consider what our values are and whether a host culture would share these same values. If the value system is different, then the behavior required will probably be different. As citizens of the world, to take a global view may mean to stop, look, and listen before we act.

DISCUSSION QUESTIONS

1. To what degree does the wealth (as measured by per capita income or GNP) influence the individualism index of a country?
2. Explain how the Theory Z organization is compatible with the egalitarian value of power distance and individualism in the United States.
3. What is the effect of power distance on the applicability of organizational behavior concepts in other countries?
4. What advice would you give a manager who is being transferred to Colombia? Japan? Sweden? What are some of the difficulties that the manager should think about before the transfer?
5. Explain the reasons for the successful transfer of U.S. management methods to the Japanese culture.

EXERCISE: CULTURAL DIFFERENCES

Assign yourself to either of two roles, American or contrast culture. Read each role description and try to become that individual with those beliefs and mannerisms. Take ten minutes to prepare your part.

After your preparation, meet with your counterpart and discuss the following issues:

1. Role of women in society and work
2. Use of authority to get the job done in a company

Try to convince the other person that your point of view is correct. Use five minutes for each issue.

Debrief the exercise by looking for areas of contrast and conflict that arose during the exercise. See if you can determine some of the reasons for the differences. How would you address the contrast culture in future interactions, based on your new insights?

ROLE DESCRIPTIONS FOR AMERICAN AND CONTRAST CULTURE

	American	Contrast Culture
1. *How do people approach activity?*	Concern with "doing," progress, change Optimistic, striving	Concern with "being" Fatalistic
2. *What is the desired pace of life?*	Fast, busy Driving	Steady, rhythmic Noncompulsive, evolving
3. *How important are goals in planning?*	Stress means, procedures, techniques	Stress final goals
4. *What are important goals in life?*	Material goals Comfort and absence of pain	Spiritual goals Fullness of pleasure and pain
5. *Where does responsibiity for decisions lie?*	Responsibility lies with each individual	Responsibility is the function of a group or resides in the role a person plays
6. *On what basis do people evaluate?*	Utility (does it work)	Essence (what is the ideal)
7. *Who should make decisions?*	The people affected	Those with proper authority
8. *What is the nature of learning?*	Learner is active (student-centered learning)	Learner is passive
9. *How are roles defined?*	Attained Loosely Generally	Ascribed by position in life Tightly Specifically
10. *How do people relate to others whose status is different?*	a. Stress equality Minimize differences b. Stress informality and spontaneity	Stress hierarchical ranks Stress differences, especially with supervisors Stress formality, behavior more easily anticipated
11. *How are sex roles defined?*	Similar, overlapping Sex equality Friends of both sexes	Distinct Male superiority Friends of same sex only
12. *What are member's rights and duties in a group?*	Assumes limited liability Joins group to seek own goals Active members influence group	Assumes unlimited liability Accepts constraints of group Leader runs group, members do not
13. *What is the meaning of friendship?*	Social friendship (short commitment, friends are shared)	Intense friendship (long commitment, friends are exclusive)
14. *What is the (natural) world like?*	Physical Mechanical Use of technology	Spiritual Organic Disuse of technology

15. *What are the relationships between people and nature?*	Resource is unlimited Modify nature for human ends Good health and material comforts expected and desired	Resource is limited Accept the natural order Some disease and material misery are natural, expected
16. *How is time defined? Valued?*	Future (anticipation) Precise units Limited resource Linear	Past (remembrance) or present (experience) Undifferentiated Not limited (not a resource) Circular
17. *On whom should a person place reliance?*	Self Impersonal organizations	Status, superiors, patrons, others Persons
18. *What kind of person is valued and respected? What qualities?*	Youthful (vigorous)	Aged (wise, experienced)
19. *What is the basis of social control?*	Persuasion, appeal to the individual Guilt	Formal, authoritative Shame

NOTES

1. Ralph Linton, *The Study of Man: An Introduction* © 1936, renewed 1964, pp. 326–327. Reprinted by permission of Prentice-Hall, Inc., Englewood Cliffs, NJ.

2. In late 1965 the United States Department of State sponsored an exchange Peace Corps Program. Modeled after its own successful Peace Corps program, volunteers from twenty-six countries came to the United States to serve as change agents in areas of critical need—health, welfare, education. This is an excerpt by Señor Montana, who served as one of those volunteers and relates some of the difficulties stemming from his experience in the United States culture.

3. Edward B. Tylor, *Primitive Culture*, 3rd English ed. (London: Murray, 1981): 6.

4. Bernard Berelson and Gary A. Steiner, *Human Behavior*, shorter ed. (New York: Harcourt, Brace, and World, 1967): 15.

5. Talcott Parsons and Edward Shils, eds., *Toward a General Theory of Action* (New York: Harper & Row, 1962): 53.

6. *Work Values Signal* (New York: Yankelovitch, Skelly and White, Inc., 1980).

7. Edward C. Steward, *Guidelines for Peace Corps Cross-Cultural Training, Part II, Specific Methods and Techniques* (Washington, DC: Peace Corps, 1970): C-764.

8. Stanley M. Davis, *Comparative Management* (Englewood Cliffs, NJ: Prentice-Hall, 1971): 13.

9. Joseph A. Kahl, *The Measurement of Modernism* (Austin, TX: University of Texas Press, 1968): 6.

10. Davis, *Comparative Management*, p. 14.

11. Stephen H. Rhinesmith, *Cultural Organizational Analysis* (Cambridge, MA: McBer and Company, 1970): 13.

12. Edgar H. Schein, *Organizational Behavior* (Englewood Cliffs, NJ: Prentice-Hall, 1970).

13. Related to the author in a personal interview.

14. Edward T. Hall and William Foote Whyte, "Intercultural Communication: A Guide to Men of Action," *Human Organization*, vol. 19 no. 1 (1960): 9.

15. Robert Jackall, "Moral Mazes: Bureaucracy and Managerial Work," *Harvard Business Review* (September–October 1983): 118–130.

16. Author's personal interview with Maria Antezana, Inlinqua, Inc.

17. Author's personal communication with Ross Weber, Case Western Reserve University, Cleveland, Ohio.

18. F. H. Harbison and C. A. Myers, *Management in the Industrial World* (New York: McGraw-Hill, 1959): 264.

19. William Ouchi, *Theory Z* (Reading, MA: Addison-Wesley, 1983).

20. Thomas J. Peterson and Robert H. Waterman, Jr., *In Search of Excellence* (New York: Harper & Row, 1982).

21. Geert Hofstede, *Culture's Consequences* (Beverly Hills, CA: Sage Publications, 1980).

22. Hall and Whyte, "Intercultural Communication."

23. *Background Notes* (Washington, DC: United States Department of State, 1983).

24. *The Wall Street Journal* (23 July 1983): 23.

25. Hofstede, *Culture's Consequences*, p. 315.

26. Ibid.

27. Ibid.

28. Ibid.

29. Hofstede, *Culture's Consequences*, p. 387.

30. Ibid., p. 380.

31. Ibid.

RECOMMENDED READINGS

W. G. **Ouchi**, *Theory Z* (Reading, MA: Addison-Wesley, 1981).

Ouchi describes various aspects of the Japanese and American cultures and organizational practices. He further describes U.S. firms that have adapted a modified culture and organizational practices that are termed "Theory Z," or the best of both cultures for a U.S. firm.

S. M. **Lee** and G. **Schwendiman,** eds., *Management by Japanese Systems* (New York: Praeger, 1982).

This book is a series of readings about trying to understand Japanese management systems and their transferability to U.S. firms. Titles include "Experiences of U.S. Corporations with the Japanese Systems," "Transfer and Diffusion of Technology," "Comparative Analysis of Japanese and American Management," and "Various Aspects of Quality Circles."

Paley of Japan

The Paley Corporation* had administered questionnaires to 7,500 of its employees in 19 countries outside of Europe. These questionnaires, within the restraints imposed by the difficulties of translation, included many of the same questions asked periodically of Paley's employees within the U.S.

The Paley management was shocked by the results from Japan in that they indicated a very high level of dissatisfaction among Paley employees there. Some suggested that the explanation was the introduction of U.S. management practices into a highly traditional and different pattern of social relations and values. A social scientist, one of Paley's researchers, was dispatched to Japan to look at the situation more closely. Normally such a level of dissatisfaction was associated with a high rate of attrition, but this was not so in Japan, which of all of Paley's affiliates had one of the lowest attrition rates.

Because of the similarity of Paley's operations worldwide, the people responding to the questionnaires in all countries were doing essentially the same things. The questionnaires were focused basically on two areas, (1) morale and (2) basic organizational behavior. The questionnaires were administered by organizational units, that is, departments, which normally consisted of about 20 people. In the domestic company, each plant was surveyed once every three years unless some special problem became evident, in which

case it might be done once a year for a given length of time. Questionnaire answers were tabulated on a departmental basis. The response in all cases was virtually 100 percent since the questionnaires were administered during working hours on an anonymous basis. Only those persons absent from their place of work on the day on which the questionnaire was administered were missed. The results were made known to the departmental management about one month after the questionnaire was administered. No one other than the tabulators saw the data for any subordinate unit until the responsible manager had had an opportunity to study them. In each case, he was also given comparable enterprise-wide and company-wide data. He was expected to make this data known to his department's members and to discuss it with them. He was also required to write a report to his immediate superior on what he saw in the data and what he planned to do about it. It was company policy to discourage management at any level from using the data for punitive purposes. (Admittedly, this policy was not completely successful.) Rather, managers were encouraged to evaluate a subordinate manager on the basis of how he responded to the data.

One set of questions had to do with what employees wanted from a job, for example, job security, security against transfer, opportunity for advancement, opportunity to develop personal skills, personal independence or autonomy, high earnings, challenging work, good working conditions, company security, working for a growth company, working for a technically advanced company. Each of these goals was rated on a five-point scale from ''utmost importance'' to ''no

*The name of the company is fictitious but the data are accurate.

Source: From *International Business Management: A Guide to Decision Making,* 2d ed., by Richard D. Robinson. Copyright © 1978 by Dryden Press. Reprinted by permission of CBS College Publishing.

importance." A European survey undertaken during the previous year of 6,500 salesmen and systems engineers (which constituted 85 percent of such employees in Europe) produced several interesting results when compared with comparable U.S. employees. For example:

1. Europeans were more interested in skill development than their U.S. counterparts.
2. Europeans were more interested in job security.
3. U.S. employees felt that personal time was more important (that is, regular working hours that did not impinge on family or personal life).
4. U.S. employees ranked residence in a desirable area more important (which implied that the Europeans were more mobile).

In regard to this fourth finding, the European survey revealed that 46 to 63 percent (depending upon the particular country) would accept foreign assignment and 25 to 35 percent "probably" would. Another relevant finding was that some 65 percent of the Europeans preferred to have the most competent individual assigned as his manager, even though of foreign nationality. Some 80 percent indicated that nationality made no difference if the choice were between equally qualified individuals speaking the local language. Unfortunately, comparable U.S. data on international mobility and management nationality were not available since these questions had not been included in the domestic survey.

It was found that in ranking job goals employees within certain countries tended to cluster with those of others. There was a Latin American cluster, a Chinese cluster (Taiwan, Hong Kong, Singapore), and an Anglo cluster (United Kingdom, Canada, U.S., Australia, New Zealand, Jamaica, Philippines—and Japan). The inclusion of Jamaica was rationalized on the basis of its association with the United Kingdom; the Philippines, because of its association with the U.S. In addition, there was a Scandinavian cluster, though this was somewhat rougher. Disparities were somewhat greater within the group. Other countries fell in between these clusters; for example, France came between the Latin American and Anglo clusters.

The hypothesis was advanced that differentials among these clusters were due to different levels of economic development, as measured by gross national product per capita. The highest correlations developed between job goals and GNP per capita involved (1) working for a financially secure company (which goal became of lesser importance as per capita GNP increased) and (2) the desire for challenging work (which goal increased in importance as per capita GNP went up). The major exceptions were South Africa and Germany. In the former case, it was probably true that the relevant GNP/capita was that of the white population only, which would cause a shift in the relationships. In the latter case, Germany, a hypothesis was that the wartime experience of the Germans had something to do with their greater concern for company security and lesser concern with challenging work. It was known that South Africa had the highest attrition rate in the world insofar as Paley companies were concerned. It was thought that the higher the desire for a challenging job and the lower the desire for security the higher the attrition rate was likely to be.

As already mentioned, the Japanese response clustered with the Anglo countries in that employees rated high on the challenge and income goals, relatively low in respect to the security goal. But the overall employee response showed a very low level of satisfaction. Interviews elicited the following Japanese complaints: (1) work pressure, (2) large scale and arbitrary movement of people, (3) inability to get complaints handled. It was true that, as a U.S. company in Japan, there was considerable pressure for efficiency and production from Paley's Asian area headquarters, which was located in Tokyo. It was also true that the all-Japanese management of Paley's Japanese manufacturing company had introduced certain U.S. practices, such as a performance promotion system and restricting the firm's involvement in providing employee housing. But certain traditional Japanese policies had been retained, for example, discouraging employees from taking a full vacation (the president of Paley-Japan had not taken a vacation in 40 years), paying salesmen a fixed salary rather than having a commission plan, paying employees the traditional low wages (about one-fourth that paid in the U.S.). Paley sold its technologically complex products at the same price around the world. About 15 percent of the Paley's Japanese employees had been trained in the U.S. Japanese salesmen participated in the 100 percent club for salesmen filling quotas 100 percent, which resulted periodically in big international affairs at which the 100 percenters from all over the world met.

Paley-Japan was relatively new, but had grown rapidly.

Questions

1. What is the most likely explanation for the relatively high level of dissatisfaction among Paley's Japanese employees?
2. As a member of Paley's international headquarters, what steps might you recommend to correct this situation?

CHAPTER SIXTEEN
Future Directions for People in Organizations

OUTLINE

WHAT LIES AHEAD?

Stimulants for the Future?

What, How, When, and Where Work Is Done Will Change

Wanted: Organizational Behavior Skills for the Future

The Continuous Challenge of Increasing Productivity, Quality, and Quality of Work Life

Summary of Key Concepts

OBJECTIVES

- Compare characteristics of today's organizations with those that might exist in the future

- Identify specific organizational behavior skills that will likely be emphasized in the future and explain why

- Describe and discuss what, how, when, and where work will change in the future

- Explain why productivity, quality, and quality of work life are interrelated

A Day in the Life of an Employee in the Year 2001

Mary Barker is a data entry supervisor for Business Information Systems Inc., a data base firm specializing in up-to-the-minute computerized business information for clients (stock reports, commercial real estate transactions, new patents filed). She woke up at seven o'clock one morning and looked over her "things to do today" time management work list. The top priority item was to provide her data entry operators with their weekly computer printouts listing errors and productivity rates. The operators themselves monitored their own performance with these printouts and were responsible as well for contacting clients directly to correct any routine mistakes. Mary's primary responsibility was to design and implement the actual feedback system.

Since Mary had a computer at home with a modem hook-up to her office downtown, she reasoned that she could just as easily work at home and send the feedback reports via computer directly to her operators, who all had their own portable computers. The operators, in turn, could decide whether to work at home or go down to the office if they needed to. "What a relief not to fight traffic jams today," Mary thought to herself. "Besides, I will save one hour round-trip commuting time, and I can sure use that time to review the cost savings suggestions that my operator quality circle team submitted earlier this week."

While sipping on her second cup of coffee, Mary recalled a conversation with her parents the previous evening about some of the differences in organizations of today (year 2001), compared with those in which her parents had worked in the 1980s.

WHAT LIES AHEAD?

What differences from today do you think will exist in the work world of 2001? What will the nature of supervision be? How will performance appraisals be conducted? What kinds of compensation or reward systems will exist? How will hiring decisions be made? What would a typical work schedule look like? What will the physical layout of space be like? Will there be any difference in technology, policy making, unions, and governmental regulation systems?

From the preceding futuristic story, we get a glimpse of what may happen. Granted, the story does not portray what a day would look like for top management or a production worker but the scenario helps set the tone for their changes as well. For example, operators' jobs, as suggested by the story, will entail more self-directed behavior and be more technologically based than are those of current office workers. Mary's manager probably has the responsibility for coordinating Mary's work with groups outside the organization and planning what additional opportunities exist for their services for other clients.

As we consider these future jobs, we may be asking ourselves some other questions besides the ones mentioned previously. What are some of the stimulants for these changes? Are we facing some of those issues today, but with

This chapter was written by Professor Diane Lockwood of Seattle University.

yesterday's perspective? In what ways will the experience of work change? What will be required of the employee of the future? What will be required of the manager to deal with the organization of the future? What organizational issues will be raised as a result of the changes that will occur? These are some of the questions that will guide us as we explore the possible future, today.

In this chapter we look at some of the current forces that, if they continue, will mean certain changes in the way work will be defined from the worker's and the organization's perspective. We examine how the concept of work may be changed and what will be required of the manager to accomplish the organization's objectives. In addition, we suggest what individual skills might be needed to be effective in the future. Finally, we discuss the continuing challenge of increasing productivity and the quality of work life.

Stimulants for the Future?

When we consider the future, we must ask ourselves "What changes are occurring today that may indicate what tomorrow will be like?" Given that we can't know the future in fact, and that change is progressive from one phase to another, what trends are happening today that can give us a glimpse into the future?

Trends Affecting Our Lives   One of the most talked about books concerning future possibilities is *Megatrends*.[1] In this book, several trends are discussed that have consequences for employees and organizations of the future.

Informational society.   The first trend is the shift from an industrial society to an informational society. We hinted at this trend in chapter 13, when we discussed how computer technology is being introduced on the factory floor as well as in the office and home. But, in addition to the actual technology involved, this change is concerned with the need for increasing amounts of information in all areas of our lives. It is estimated that scientific and technical information, which now increases 13.3 percent per year, will jump to 40 percent with the advent of more powerful management information systems.[2] This means that data may double every twenty months.

In the opening story, Mary's operators will have to continually learn about new technology to process such information. Mary also will have to learn new products and services for her customers, and she will have to stimulate her workers to continue to learn and develop to just stay competitive.

High tech/high touch.   Another trend associated with increased amounts of information is the resulting need for more technology and its seemingly corresponding need for "high touch." This concept simply means that whenever new technology is introduced into an organization, there must be a counterbalancing human response (high touch)—or the technology may be rejected. We saw this phenomenon in chapter 11 on change. When we introduce changes, individuals may resist for many reasons, one of which may be the threat to job security or self-esteem. Similarly, the introduction of sophisticated technology may be resisted by those having to use the technology.

The operators in the opening story, while familiar with the technology, may still feel somewhat threatened. Mary may thus want to remain sensitive to that possibility and carefully involve the operators to reduce the rejection.

Decentralization. "The decentralization of America has transformed politics, business, our very culture."[3] This quote hints at the increased diversity underlying our country. While Japan has a fairly homogeneous culture that allows more focused and accepted direction from authority, America prides itself on being a melting pot. A consequence in a society that supports individual rights is that groups and individuals want to be distinct and to have choices that reflect their situations.

The trend of decentralization is one response to this diversity. Diversity is evident in the press for women's rights, gay rights, states' rights, and so on. Each group has a set of needs they feel should be addressed. As we know from the chapters on groups and conflict, diversity needs to be managed to address not only the individual group's needs but those of the large system with which it is affiliated. In a similar vein, organizations are creating small work units or self-sufficient organizations to handle unique client needs or market segments. This decentralization calls for creative negotiations to allocate limited resources.

Self-help. As individuals, we have relied on various institutions to protect us and provide for our wants. We have relied on the government to help us in retirement (social security); the medical profession to provide cures or treatment even beyond our "normal" life expectancy; and organizations to continue to grow and provide prosperity, through increased benefits and wages. But we have begun to wean ourselves away from this form of institutional dependency and toward self-help.

We have made great strides to create self-awareness of our own ability to prevent or minimize disease. Smoking is down substantially, wine is replacing hard liquors, health food stores and products are the norm. We looked at one area of health in the chapter on stress; a number of organizations realize that health of the individual corresponds to the health of the organization in terms of productivity.

This growing self-reliance or self-help affects the organization in subtle ways. People aren't as willing as in the past to move for a promotion. Individuals are willing to blow the whistle on misconduct in organizations and not fear being fired. People are leaving large organizations and starting their own businesses as entrepreneurs. The trend is toward more self-reliant individuals who want to and will strive to meet their own needs.

Networks. A final trend to consider is that the pyramid structure of organizations is being threatened, if not directly through alternative structures then indirectly by more reliance on networking than on formal structures. Networking is the informal sharing of ideas, information, and resources.[4] It can be direct—talking to one another—or indirect—using computer technology.

In the formal organization, individuals are hierarchically related; someone reports to somebody else from the bottom to the top. The most important thing about a network is that each individual is at its center, structurally.[5]

While we are suggesting that this trend will affect individuals, like Mary Barker, and organizations in the future, some organizations today have attempted to avoid bureaucratic hierarchy. Intel Corporation, a leading semiconductor manufacturer, is characterized as "network management."[6] Some of the features are as follows:

- Workers have several bosses.
- Functions such as purchasing and quality control are the responsibility of a committee or council, not of a hierarchical staff reporting to an individual leader.
- There are no offices, only shoulder-high partitions separating office work space.
- The company is run by a tribune of top executives, an "outside man," a long-range planner, and an inside administrator.

While the five trends we mentioned are not all-inclusive, they are the more significant ones that are beginning *now*. They will have more impact by the year 2001, if we believe the Mary Barker story.

Shifting Values and Work Ethics   Another potential insight into the future is indicated by the shifts occurring in our values regarding life, work, and the work ethic. (Recall that this shifting is discussed in chapter 1).

Many studies have attempted to identify what shifts are occurring and how they will affect work and organizations. One study developed a typology to describe two groups—the "outer directeds" and the "inner directeds."[7] The outer directeds are concerned with external conditions, behave according to established norms, and respond to peer pressure. The inner directeds are more motivated by their own inner wants and desires, instead of responding to the norms of others. The study's opinion survey showed that the outer directeds, while previously comprising 71 percent of the population, have declined to 65 percent. The inner directeds were 17 percent but are approaching 27 percent.

Another study about how work is viewed in terms of motivation also gives us some clues as to the shift in values. A survey of managers and professionals yielded the following list of the top motivators:

Men	Women
Good chance for advancement	Good chance for advancement
Great deal of responsibility	Job that enables *me* to develop
Recognition for good work	*my* abilities

Men	Women
Job where I can think for *myself*	Recognition for good work
	Great deal of responsibility
Job that enables *me* to develop *my* abilities	Job where I can think for *myself*

Some managers would describe these shifts as resulting in a work ethic decline—"People just don't want to work hard anymore . . . the young people of today have had everything handed to them on a silver platter and they expect the moon!" While it is true that the previous material does suggest a work force more concerned with self-direction and self-satisfaction, this does not necessarily mean that people no longer feel a sense of work ethic. People may indeed want to work hard, but what has changed is the acceptability of conditions under which they will put forth the effort.

Jerome Rosow, president of the Work America Institute, suggests that the following six categories of attitude change have affected the quality of work life:[9]

Challenge to authority.   Permissive society created a group of people who learned to question traditional values and goals. What began as a minority attitude spread to a large proportion of the population and subsequently to the workplace, where workers questioned the authority of managers. In addition, most of the younger workers in today's organizations have never served in the military, where obedience to authority is emphasized.

Declining confidence in institutions.   Public scandals such as Watergate and the Ford Pinto scandal have reduced trust and confidence in both government and business.

Resistance to change.   Mistrust of organizations led to a resistance to technological innovations. Workers were tired of having no input into organizational decisions that directly affected their job security.

Changing attitudes toward work.   Traditional attitudes toward work upheld the Protestant work ethic of work as both a duty and a privilege. With the declining influence of the church, these attitudes have changed. Leisure activities have become more popular, partly because they avoid the stressful problems employees experience at work.

Work and family relationships.   The changing nature of marital and family relationships is also having an effect at work. There are more two-income families, more working single-parent families, and more people who choose to remain single. All of these place considerable stress on traditional work requirements.

Faster societal than workplace changes. Many significant changes in society occurred over a relatively short period. Attitudes toward minorities, civil rights, sexual norms, and other social issues preceded changes in organizations' attitudes and behaviors toward the same things. The "new" attitudes place considerable pressure upon traditional organizational values.

What, How, When, and Where Work Is Done Will Change

Having reviewed some of the trends and shifts in values, we can now define, from Mary Barker's point of view, some of the differences between yesterday's organizations (in the 1980s) and today's organizations (2001) that Mary might have shared with her parents. We compare several categories: nature of supervision, performance appraisal systems, pay systems, hiring decisions, work schedules, physical design, technology, policy making, unions, and government regulation compliance. Examining these differences from the viewpoint of the future will allow us to further develop what the concept of work will be in the future.

Nature of Supervision In the 1980s a supervisor's main job was to assign daily work schedules, monitor employee performance, correct errors, and solve daily crises.

Now, in 2001, supervisors are relieved of many of the mundane supervisory responsibilities (e.g., correcting routine errors and daily scheduling), which are now done by autonomous work groups. Today a supervisor's primary responsibilities are to develop feedback systems, set up work groups, oversee departmental planning, and interdepartmental coordination, and staff development.

Performance Appraisal Systems In the 1980s performance appraisal forms had a lot of one-to-five scales for such items as "shows initiative," and "is responsible." Employees typically received little immediate feedback on performance. Formal performance appraisals were conducted once a year by the employee's immediate supervisor.

Performance appraisals in 2001 have taken on an entirely different form. Instead of vague rating scales, we now have BARS (behaviorally-anchored rating scales), the performance-based MBO, and other productivity measurement schemes. Work group peers as well as the immediate supervisor provide input into performance appraisals. Formal performance appraisals are conducted at least twice a year, and informal feedback is provided on an ongoing basis.

Pay Systems In the 1980s the pay system for line operators was geared to their seniority and the type of job they performed (work was specialized). Pay itself was seldom directly tied to performance. All employees with the same job classification and seniority got the same pay every two weeks. Annual cost-of-living adjustments were routinely figured into pay raises. Fringe benefits were fixed, without any allowances for individual differences in needs. Executives were rewarded on short-term profits.

In 2001 pay systems are geared to the number of *different* jobs a person can perform (work is generalized), thus encouraging rotation and flexibility. Pay raises are directly related both to the quantity and quality of performance. Bonuses are proportionately allocated to both individuals and groups to encourage a sharing of ideas while maintaining individual incentives. Cost-of-living adjustments have been replaced by profit sharing (and loss sharing) or with employee stock ownership plans. "Cafeteria-style" benefit plans are commonplace. Executives are rewarded for long-term performance.

Hiring Decisions   In the 1980s screening of job applicants was done by the personnel department, and the final hiring decision was made by the appropriate supervisor.

Today, in 2001, the screening of job applicants is also done by the work group in cooperation with the human resources department and the appropriate supervisor. The theory is that the job applicant must also be acceptable to the group and the various group norms must be acceptable to the job applicant, since the organization desires to encourage a team effort. The human resources department is still responsible for ensuring compliance with affirmative action guidelines.

Work Schedules   In the 1980s the customary approach to work schedules was "eight to five" Mondays through Fridays, a forty-hour work week. The vast majority of people were full-time employees.

In 2001, many organizations have no set working hours. Work schedules are determined by individual needs and task requirements. Emphasis is put on getting the job done by a specified date, not on how many *hours* it takes or *when* people work. Part-time employment and job sharing are also commonplace.

Physical Design   In the 1980s the physical design of the organization typically reinforced status differences among employees. For example, there were different parking lots, restrooms, and cafeterias for managers and for line people. Machines and office furniture were typically designed without much consideration for the human element.

In 2001 physical design and office layout attempt to minimize status differences among people. All have the same cafeterias, and so forth. Ample room is set aside for group meetings. Machines, lighting, and office furniture are designed for maximum efficiency and comfort.

Technology   In the 1980s work was generally routine, standardized, and labor intensive before the "age of automation."

In 2001 automation (for example, computers and robots) has relieved people of much of the mundane work and has created exciting new careers. At the same time, automation has created a whole set of problems that we are finally beginning to tackle. (See chapter 13 for a review of this topic.)

Policy Making   In the 1980s organizational policy decisions were determined solely by a board of directors and top management, with little direct input from company employees. The board made all of its decisions by majority rule.

In 2001 there is a joint policy-making board that governs the total operation of the company. The workers elect representatives to sit on this board. Two members from the local community also serve on the board. While there are only three worker representatives on the twelve-person board, it is understood that any board member has a right to veto any proposal or decision. The board makes all of its decisions by consensus, not by majority vote.

Unions   In the 1980s union-management relationships were adversarial in nature and were primarily found in blue-collar manufacturing settings. The major collective bargaining issues centered around wages, hours, and grievance procedures.

In 2001 unions are still around, especially in the white-collar and public service sectors. The nature of their relationships with management, however, has taken on a more cooperative tone. Major bargaining items now include profit sharing, job training and retraining, employment security, and expanded benefits in lieu of wage increases (for example, dental plans, legal and financial services, and job placement help).

Government Regulation Compliance   In the 1980s a punishment-centered approach was used to force organizations to comply with government regulations, such as those issued by the EPA, OSHA, and EEOC. That is, if an organization was not in compliance with the laws, then the government would file suit against the company and a costly legal battle would ensue. The costs of compliance to the company (reporting, hiring costs, and so on) were often considered burdensome and were usually passed on to consumers in the form of higher prices.

In 2001 a positive reinforcement approach to compliance is used. For example, if an organization can demonstrate compliance, then they are allowed a tax write-off to cover compliance costs, plus some additional tax incentives. Similarly, for every worker that the company functionally retrains and places, the company receives a certain amount of tax incentives. This keeps people employed and prevents the loss in tax revenues that the government would accrue if those same workers were unemployed. Today's regulations are also more streamlined and all computerized reports go to one centralized government processing agency.

Let us now return to the present and ask what the future trends and shifting values and work ethic mean for our future concept and experience of work. Can we begin to define how work will be viewed by individuals in the future? We use these questions to guide us further into the future.

Concept of Work   As we saw in Mary Barker's case, the very nature of a manager's job will change toward managing information more and people less, as employees will be under self-management and control systems. "What" kind of work is done will also change dramatically. Exciting new careers are opening up almost daily. "How" work gets done will be altered significantly by new automated technologies, work methods, physical layouts, and job designs. "When" work is done will be altered by flexible work schedules and job sharing to better meet individual and family schedules. Consequently, the emphasis will be put on getting the job done by a specified date, but it will be primarily up to the individual to determine a daily work schedule. This may, for example, translate into working five eight-hour days per week or three ten-hour days, depending on individual needs and how the use of time is maximized. Concurrently, pay will depend on job performance rather than hours worked. "Where" work is done, depending on the nature of the task and individual needs, will also vary. Some people may prefer to work at home when their jobs lend themselves to this. Others who value social interaction and whose tasks require face-to-face group decision making may prefer to work in an office. Being physically located close to offices may no longer be a critical issue for some jobs, and this may cut down on relocation and other transportation expenses. It is difficult to generalize about future work conditions, but we do know that many of these changes will depend upon individual needs.

We can now begin to offer a definition of work in the future, which we can compare to today's and yesterday's concept of work. As we can see from Table 16-1, the concept of work will continue to change as we progress to the twenty-first century. Jobs involving data manipulation and information generation will become increasingly more common. This can easily be conceptualized about office work. But it will also be more common in factory settings where robots will

TABLE 16-1
Mechanized work versus year 2001 work

	Mechanized Work	Year 2001 work
Prime Examples	Production line	Data manipulation and information generation
Sources of Energy	Mechanical power	Electrical power from new sources, such as the sun
Types of Technology	Mechanized tools and complex machines	Information and decision systems, computer-generated work, and individual-controlled technology
Task Characteristics	Narrow, quasi-mechanical, indirect feedback, and human contribution	Multi-faceted job knowledge, continual learning for changing technology
Human Requirements	Physical parts of self	Mental concentration
Source of Control	External regulation by superior or machine	Self-generated feedback and regulation
Source of Motivation	Extrinsic rewards	Intrinsic rewards

do more of the physical work and humans will control and guide the robots depending on product specifications. In addition, more information will be used by operators to plan shipments, inventory control, and like procedures. The day of the "white coat" worker is approaching.

The task characteristics will also change. Individuals will be responsible for knowing several jobs which will lead to more organizational flexibility and individual stimulation. Workers as well as managers will have to continually learn new technologies and methods to generate information. As a result, control and motivation will be more self-directed, as the conditions are changing too rapidly for present-day performance appraisal systems built on consistency.

The Manager's Job We can now attempt to predict some of the changes required of managers as they supervise tomorrow's workers. Mary Barker gives us some indication of what a manager's job may be like. Considering the value shifts and the changing technology, workers are definitely the task experts and, as such, a manager will have to allow more employee participation in daily and weekly activities and decisions. As more employees become generalists in terms of the number of jobs they can perform, managers will need to spend more time planning and developing feedback systems to coordinate the continual shifting of employees as the tasks require it. The revolution in technology and communications systems necessitates more preparation and continual updating for the employee. This results in a more educational and developmental function for management.

Those managerial responsibilities just described are not entirely new to American companies. One article suggests several characteristics of high-tech firms it identifies as successful.[10] One is adaptability—willingness to undertake major and rapid change when necessary. Obviously, this requires certain skills in the management of change to be successful. Organizational flexibility entails frequent realignments of people and responsibilities. To manage such a firm requires skills to manage conflict and changing goals and roles of different work units. Fostering an "entrepreneurial culture" is another facet of successful high-tech firms. This refers to the firm's ability to innovate and create a supportive atmosphere for internally suggested changes. One aspect of this innovation process is the tolerance of failure. Managers must build a culture where employees are willing to suggest and develop alternatives to the way things are currently being done.

While these characteristics have been identified as present in a few organizations today, the future will require that these managerial responsibilities become commonplace.

Wanted: Organizational Behavior Skills for the Future

Up to this point we have looked at some of the stimulants for change in what, how, when, and where work will be done in the future. In addition, we have discussed how the concept of work will possibly change and what impact that may

Strategies for Successful Leadership in Changing Times

Tomorrow's leaders, and those who aspire to leadership, must become comfortable with the changing and uncertain times in which we live. They must be willing to develop behavioral skills that may not make an overt short-term impact on the bottom line, and must promote career development activities for themselves and others.

Michael Bisesi suggests that the following characteristics may be the keys to successful leadership in changing times.

Leaders must understand the environment outside the organization. Organizations are part of and interact with a larger environment composed of customers, suppliers and competitors, and economic, legal, political, and social forces. If "no man is an island," then no organization is ever autonomous.

Leaders must understand how to manage conflict. Individuals and groups within organizations often compete for attention and resources, especially when budgets get tight during recessionary times. A leader must be willing to negotiate to get individuals and groups to accomplish organizational goals.

Leaders must have a heightened sense of corporate social responsibility and business ethics. Businesses exist to make a profit, without which they could not survive. However, it is equally true that businesses are part of the larger society on whom they depend for support, and thus they have responsibilities to that society. A leader therefore must not be afraid to say "no" when "yes" (or no response) would be so much easier.

Leaders must be willing to give up some authority. Power is best assured when it is shared. Although quality circles may cause some short-term discomfort among middle managers, it will enable employees to be more productive. By delegating authority, managers give employees the freedom to develop and learn from their mistakes as well as their successes.

Leaders must take greater responsibility for the career development of people. Leaders must recognize that successful work is accomplished when there is a match between the requirements of the job and the talents of the individual. Thus, a leader must be willing to "let go" of valuable staff members who have outgrown their jobs and help them move on to more challenging positions.

Finally, leaders should not become obsolete—or worse yet, dull. Leaders must be lifelong learners. A college degree is just an introduction to a continuing professional education. They should spend some time studying behavioral sciences and other disciplines that probably do not readily appear in financial reports, but nevertheless make a significant difference in the assessment of profit or loss. Lastly, a broad education in a diversity of nonbusiness topics will make them more interesting people.

Questions

1. Are there any characteristics of successful leadership in the future that you would add to this list?
2. Given that leaders should be broadly educated, what (if any) courses would you add or delete from your current business school curriculum? Why?

Source: Adapted from Michael Bisesi, "Strategies for Successful Leadership in Changing Times," *Sloan Management Review*, vol. 25, no. 1 (Fall 1983): 61–64, by permission of the publisher. Copyright © 1983 by the Sloan Management Review Association. All rights reserved.

have on the managerial functions. Next, we consider what skills are needed to effectively participate in tomorrow's organizations.

The opening story in this chapter identified only a few of the organizational changes that we are likely to confront in the future. Besides the obvious need for computer literacy and other technical skills, what specific organizational-behavior-oriented skills will managers need for the work environment of the future and why? Five specific application areas of critical importance are (1) the management of change, (2) sensitivity to international differences, (3) conflict management, (4) group dynamics, and (5) the performance-reward connection. While these topics were discussed in detail elsewhere in this book, what is new is the probable emphasis on these skills in the future.

Management of Change   Someone once said that the only thing that does not change is change itself! While changes have been with us throughout history, what is different today perhaps is the unparalled rate of change confronting us in this post-industrial age or informational revolution age. Our lives are constantly being transformed by developments such as computer information technology, the evolution of a global economy, decentralization and deinstitutionalization of American life, increased educational levels, shifting values, changes in the work force composition to include more women and other minorities, demographic changes toward an aging society, and a multitude of consumer choices in the market place. The management of change, including methods of reducing resistance to change, will assume critical importance in this highly turbulent environment. Implementing change will require change agents who are knowledgeable about intervention strategies. Training and retraining methods will have to be designed around individual learning styles. Corporate managers will be forced to think about long-term results rather than just the next quarterly report. Government policy makers will also have to consider the long-range impact and cost-benefit tradeoffs of their decisions. Indeed, change must be consciously planned and managed if we are to avoid a management by crisis atmosphere in the future.

International Differences   We are rapidly becoming globally interdependent and can no longer afford the price of isolationism. For example, unemployment in Detroit is tied to an active Japanese export policy. American farm income is related to Soviet weather. Even driving one's car or heating one's home may depend on the political stability of the Middle East. The enormity of the impact of multinational corporations on the global economy becomes apparent when one considers an estimate made by the International Chamber of Commerce that U.S. multinationals, by themselves, account for one-third of the gross world product! A "global society," though hardly unified, is a reality. Thus, it becomes critical to understand cultural differences in the values and norms of other countries. Specific training programs in language, customs, decision making, and international business negotiations will receive increased attention. Participation in

BOX 16–2

Dying Factory Gets New Lease on Life

An electronic "heart transplant" has been given to an aging factory in an industry and in a region that many had given up for dead.

The General Electric Company is investing $316 million over the next three years to revitalize its locomotive plant in Erie, Pennsylvania. When all of the robots, computerized machine tools, and other automation systems are in place, the Erie "factory with a future" will have increased its production capacity by one-third.

One of the first automation projects to come on line is a $16 million flexible machining system for traction motor frames. With this system, two workers operating nine machine tools can do in sixteen hours what used to take seventy workers sixteen days to do using twenty-nine aging machine tools.

But increased productivity through automation means more rather than fewer jobs, says Carl J. Schlemmer, vice president and general manager of GE's Transportation Systems and Business Operations, who predicts the higher level of production will require a 10 percent increase in employment in the Erie plant.

"There may be some initial dislocations, but long-term automation is going to have a positive effect on the employment situation here," says Mr. Schlemmer. "We're confident that the growth we've projected, coupled with the competitive edge derived from productivity improvements, will serve to provide growth in jobs—not loss in jobs."

Work in the automated factory will be different. Sophisticated, highly automated factories need skilled labor to run them. To train its workers in the newly required skills, GE has built a $6 million Learning and Communications Center.

The learning center has four fully equipped classrooms; a high-technology laboratory for training in machine tool control and system applications; laboratories for computer study; diesel engine maintenance; rotating electrical machinery; and a high-bay lab that can accommodate an entire locomotive for hands-on maintenance training.

But there is more at stake than just this factory: GE is not only automating its own plants but is also helping other companies automate—with GE equipment.

Source: Adapted from Marvin J. Cetron, "Getting Ready for the Jobs of the Future." *The Futurist* (June 1983): 15–22. Used by permission.

Questions

1. If you were Mr. Schlemmer and felt as strongly about the long-term aspects of automation and new jobs, what would you tell some laid-off citizens who come to see you about possible employment? (You don't have any openings right now.)

2. The Learning and Communications Center is described in the article as mainly a technical facility. What other courses might be offered to enhance the workers' skills?

international student exchange programs will definitely be an asset on job resumes, as will fluency in foreign languages.

Conflict Management   We will live in an era of increasing scarcity of natural resources coupled with shrinking shares of an economic pie as more and more players (domestic and foreign competition) get into the act. Traditionally, American business values have reflected a growth bias—"bigger is better." Understandably, businesses favor growth because it increases the likelihood of survival and translates into real financial and political power. Newspaper headlines in the recent past, however, have been replete with instances of failing (or at least declining) businesses, including Braniff Airlines, Continental Airlines, Penn Square Bank, Seattle First National Bank, and Osborne Computers. Declines typically follow stages. First, the decline is ignored or denied. Second, when the decline is evident, managers react as if it were a temporary crisis. Finally, over time, management begins realistically to make decisions as if they were confronting a prolonged decay. There are several potential problems that managers face when organizations decline, and many of these have behavioral implications. For example, one would expect increased conflict among individuals and groups who are fighting for critical resources that become more scarce. Consistent with our approach in chapter 8, we are not suggesting that the increased conflict evident in decline is necessarily bad. If managed properly, it can lead to new ideas, clarify organizational goals, and in fact bring people closer together. Managed improperly, conflict can increase resistance to change, increase turnover, and result in declining employee motivation and morale. Realistically, since most organizations can be expected to face at least periods of decline, it becomes imperative that we develop conflict management skills. With careful management, decline can be turned from a nightmare into an opportunity.

Group Dynamics   Increasingly, important business decisions are being made by groups of people, rather than by individuals. Yet our classroom assignments and grades tend to emphasize the individual. This is precisely why it is so important to have group experiences in student organizations, team sports, and community volunteer associations. It is in these organizations that the critical skills of group decision making are practiced and developed. It is also true that anyone who has the experience of being graded on a classroom group project usually finds it difficult because they have to rely on others, and performance is evaluated, in part, on the total group's effort. Similarly, in organizations we have to work with others, yet our performance is often evaluated and rewarded on an individual basis. We need to develop evaluation and reward systems that combine incentives for both individual and group efforts. An increasing emphasis on group-oriented productivity improvement programs such as quality circles also means that we need to develop skills in group interaction and active listening.

BOX 16–3

Interviews with Practicing Managers

The following is a summary of comments made by two managers who shared with us their views about what the future holds. John Durbin is president and owner of Durbin Corporation, a financial holding company with a variety of investments in real estate and equipment distribution, which has fewer than twenty-five employees. John Bates is managing director at Marsh and McLennan, Inc., an insurance brokerage with offices throughout the U.S.

QUESTION: Design the ideal educational curriculum/experience for students to prepare them for general management jobs in the year 2001. What specific skills or knowledge will they need and why?

DURBIN: A student will need a specific skill such as accounting or finance. I would like to see a broader spectrum of background to handle different types of jobs. Students need to know how to work and get along in society, and a liberal arts background really helps here.

BATES: There will not be an office that isn't operating with computers, so computer literacy will be required. Everyone will need a strong financial background. They will also need a much broader "global perspective."

QUESTION: What will be the potential for middle management jobs in the year 2001, given that there currently appears to be a middle management glut in the labor market?

DURBIN: A lot of the middle management jobs are just not going to be in existence. There will be fewer middle managers and fewer blue-collar workers—even less than today.

BATES: Not as big a need for middle management in the future. The labor force is changing. A lot of skills at lower levels will be needed, and importantly, workers will be more self-sufficient and won't require as much direction; therefore, we won't have as great a need for middle managers to direct the workers.

QUESTION: What will be the likely impact of office automation and factory automation on the

Source: Interview statements used by permission of the participants.

The Performance-Reward Connection Employee motivation is fostered by having clear and challenging goals, continual feedback and valued rewards that are continually linked to performance. This has always been the case, but changing work values discussed earlier in this chapter and productivity growth concerns will mandate the critical necessity of translating these concepts into ongoing organizational practices. Management by objectives, behavior modification, behaviorally anchored rating scales for performance appraisals, Scanlon plans, and profit sharing are only a few of the applications that can go a long way toward clarifying this missing link between performance and rewards.

nature of the superior-subordinate relationships in the future?

DURBIN: This trend of automation has given us better tools for managing the company. There will be more robots and fewer blue-collar workers in the future. The *Megatrends* kinds of stuff will be a reality. We will have more service industries and more information industries. What we need to remember is that we will also need more "high touch" to help the worker accept this automation.

BATES: Subordinates will need to have a better handle on office automation. And as a result there will not be much of a gap between management levels. Maybe it will help us become more of a "we" organization than it is now (us versus them).

QUESTION: What will reward/incentive systems look like in the future?

DURBIN: The systems used in the past will continue, like hourly wage, profit sharing, and bonuses. And this will continue unless there are dramatic changes in the tax laws.

BATES: In the past, people have always looked for the big title in a big corporation, now we are moving toward the feeling that smallness is not so bad. Therefore, we will see more entrepreneurial types who find satisfaction in running their own businesses. I also see some "disincentives" and the need to get back to basics, that is, hard work and merit.

QUESTION: What other thoughts do you have about the future?

DURBIN: In the future we will see a better balance of women and minorities in the workplace, and the need for more equal opportunities for them.

BATES: I don't see the computer eliminating jobs but creating more jobs. What will be different is that the job created will require more skills than present jobs. I also see workers wanting more to say than in the past about how things are done. There needs to be more goal congruency between labor and management and definitely more of a bottoms-up approach to management.

Questions

1. What key points raised by the two managers should organizations and managers be considering today?
2. If you had a chance to interview these two managers, what questions might you ask them about the future?

The Continuous Challenge of Increasing Productivity, Quality, and Quality of Work Life

Improvements in U.S. productivity growth rates will help reduce unemployment, stem inflation, raise the standard of living, strengthen the dollar in international money markets, and improve the balance of trade. Exactly how to improve productivity rates is a complex issue without any single best solution. Most productivity scholars, however, would agree that this involves a balance between "humanware" and "hardware" (automation) approaches. No matter how much capital is invested in sophisticated equipment, if the workers cannot operate it and if they fear the loss of their jobs, then effective use of sophisticated equipment will never be realized. Similarly, it does not do much good to increase quantity without maintaining or improving quality. Poor quality, regardless of whether it is related to defective items purchased from suppliers of defective material or introduced in-house, is expensive! When quality deteriorates, it contributes to disrupted schedules, delayed deliveries, increased rework, wasted material and labor, higher customer dissatisfaction, and decreased productivity. The point here is that productivity, quality, and quality of work life must be inseparable in any future work environment.

Applications of organizational behavior concepts discussed throughout this book (goal-setting, behavior modification, active listening, conflict management, power strategies, NGT and Delphi techniques, strategies for managing change, job enrichment, profit sharing, flexitime, quality circles, and training for the international arena) will all help contribute to the attainment of both individual quality of work life and organizational productivity. None of these applications promise instant "miracle cures." They take time, money, education, and perhaps most importantly, everyone's commitment. It is now up to you, as future employees, managers, and citizens, to meet the exciting challenges that lie ahead.

Summary of Key Concepts

1. There are several trends occurring today that may help us predict the future: information society, high tech/high touch, decentralization, self-help, and networking.
2. Tomorrow's employees will be more inner-directed and less responsive to others around them. This will create some challenging opportunities for managers to structure work differently in the future.
3. The concept of work will continue to change as we move closer to the information age. Much of this change will create choices for employees in terms of what, how, when, and where work is done.
4. In the future, certain knowledge and skills will be critical: management of change, international perspective, conflict management, living in and managing groups, and designing more effective performance-reward systems.

Key Terms

Conflict resolution	Management of change
Decentralization	Networks
Group dynamics	Performance reward connection
High tech/high touch	Quality of Work Life (QWL)
Information society	Self-help
International differences	Work ethic

DISCUSSION QUESTIONS

1. If you were called in to consult with a firm that was concerned about whether or not its organizational practices were consistent with the changing values of its work force, what things would you consider?

2. If you were to design a course in organizational behavior in the year 2001, what topics would you include and why?

3. Many students today are understandably concerned about whether or not there will be jobs when they graduate. What could you say to reassure them?

4. What does the term *quality of work life* mean to you?

NOTES

1. John Naisbitt, *Megatrends* (New York: Warner Books, 1982).

2. Ibid, p. 24.

3. Ibid, p. 97.

4. Jessica Lipnack and Jeffrey Stamps, *Networking* (New York: Doubleday, 1982).

5. Marilyn Ferguson, *Aquarian Conspiracy* (New York: J. P. Tarcher, 1980).

6. Steve Lahr, "Overhauling America's Business Management," *New York Magazine* (4 January 1981).

7. Arnold Mitchell and Christine MacNulty, "Changing Values and Life Styles," *Long Range Planning*, vol. 14 (April 1981): 37–41.

8. Julia Kagin, "Surveys: Work in the 1980s and 1990s," *Working Woman*, July 1983, p. 17–18.

9. Jerome M. Rosow, "Changing Attitudes to Work and Lifestyles," *Journal of Contemporary Business*, vol. 8, no. 4 (1977).

10. Modesto A. Mandique and Robert H. Hayes, "The Art of High-Technology Management," *Sloan Management Review*, vol. 25, no. 2 (Winter 1984): 17–31.

RECOMMENDED READINGS

Craig Brod, *Technostress* (Reading, MA: Addison-Wesley, 1984).

Brod describes the impact of computer technology on the organization and the individual's sense of work. He also defines how computer technology has affected the way we raise our children and the way people interact. He does suggest methods of implementing computer technology that take into account the social effects.

John Naisbitt, *Megatrends* (New York: Warner Books, 1982).

The book clearly portrays how we as a society are changing. It describes ten major trends that will transform what we see today into our future. The uniqueness of the author's position is his heuristic approach of analyzing the political, societal, and economic trends that will shape our future.

GLOSSARY

Absenteeism   absence from work during appropriate work hours.

Achievement motivation   a disposition or behavioral tendency to strive for successful acts.

Action research   inquiry that involves those from whom data are collected in the data analysis and solution generation.

Aesthetic value orientation   orientation of one seeking to achieve a state of pleasure.

Alternative generation   a process of creating as many different solutions to a problem as possible.

Ambient stimuli   group characteristics influencing members to want to maintain group membership so they can be with people they like. Possible reasons include: extra compensation, status and prestige, exposure to influential people, possibility of getting away from the day-to-day routine of one's regular job, or finding the group task interesting or important. These stimuli are automatically possessed by members by virtue of their membership.

American management styles   Theory X or Theory Y (explained in chapter 5). Theory X emphasizes (1) the individual rather than the group; (2) functional relationships and specific role relationships (e.g. management versus workers); and (3) top management as decision makers and specialists. Theory Y, by contrast, stresses employee self-direction, responsibility, and creativity.

Analysis-for-the-top (AFT) type   a change agent who uses rational, analytical approaches to organizational change.

Attitudes   evaluative statements or feelings concerning objects, people, or events.

Autocratic   a leadership style in which the manager exercises almost unlimited power or authority over the individual workers.

Avoiding conflict   neglecting all concerns by ignoring the issue or delaying a response.

Behavior modification   the systematic application of reinforcement theory to worker behavior to attain organizational goals.

Behavioral channeling   individuals entering or leaving situations based upon their understanding that a specific situation either matches or does not match their needs (values).

Behavioral leadership theory   the set of theories developed in the early 1950s and 1960s that attempted to identify how effective leaders acted and behaved.

Bodily reactions to stress   the complex biochemical responses to a "fight or flight" situation.

Brainstorming   a process whereby a problem is presented to a group, which proposes as many solutions to the problem as possible without any evaluation of the suggestions.

Cafeteria fringe benefits   a benefit system that allows the individual some discretion to choose either the type of, or the level of participation in, selected benefits.

Centralization   a structural variable, characterized by the location and level in an organization where recurring decisions are made.

CEO (chief executive officer)   usually the head or president of the organization.

Change agent   an individual or team responsible for designing and implementing change.

Coercive power   a form of power based on the ability to punish noncompliance.

Cognitive consistency   stability of attitudes when emotions, cognitions, and behaviors associated with a situation seem consistent.

Cognitive dissonance theory   the theory that people dislike inconsistency (dissonance) and that they will reduce the dissonance by changing their attitudes or rationalizing that their behaviors are not truly inconsistent with their attitudes.

Cohesiveness   the amount of attractiveness of group members toward one another. High cohesiveness can result in group unity and members pulling in the same direction.

Collage   an individual or group technique of using drawing and combinations of images to illustrate a perceived aspect of the organization.

Communication   information flow between individuals that results in shared meaning and common understanding.

Communication network   the pattern of communication (written or verbal) between individuals. The network can be centralized or decentralized.

Competing conflict   conflict characterized by an individual's own concerns being paramount and at the expense of the opposition.

Complexity/specialization   the number of specific components or units within the organization that have a distinct and limited function or set of tasks to perform. Complexity can also refer to the comparison of the number of levels in an organization to those of another organization (four levels is less complex than six levels).

Compliance   acceptance of influence in the hope that there will be some favorable reaction from the influencer.

Computational decision-making techniques   algorithmic decision-making approaches available to the manager, such as payoff matrices, linear programming, and decision trees.

Computer-mediated power   a shift in organizational structure brought about by altered information flow.

Computer-mediated work   the reorganization of interaction between an individual and job activities because of computer technology (for example, from physical contact to manipulation of electronic symbols).

Computer networks   interaction between individuals using the computer and data lines as the medium, rather than face-to-face interaction or voice interaction over phone lines.

Computer-related stress   discomfort and concern created by computer-mediated work.

Computer technology   all aspects of electronic data processing and data handling (including computer terminals, data transmission lines, microcomputers, mainframe computers).

Computerized work   work previously done by workers either using machines or processing paper, redesigned to be handled by electronic technology. The individual worker now types symbols that instruct the electronic device to machine a part or process information.

Configuration   a series of measurements to describe an organization (number of levels, number of separate units, span of managerial control, ratio of direct to indirect workers). A tall organization has several hierarchical levels and narrow spans of control; a flat organization has few managerial levels and wide spans of control at those levels.

Conflict   any type of opposition or antagonistic interaction between individuals, groups, or organizations.

Conflict accommodation   satisfaction of the other party's concern at the expense of one's own.

Conflict assertiveness   attempts to satisfy one's own concerns.

Conflict collaboration   attempts to fully satisfy the needs of both parties.

Conflict compromising   a solution that leaves both parties with some concerns unsatisfied.

Conflict cooperativeness   attempts to satisfy the other party's concerns (but not necessarily at one's own expense).

Conflict management   a set of activities to help organizations and individuals creatively handle differences between parties.

Conflict resolution   the active management of conflict through defining and solving unresolved issues between individuals, groups, or organizations.

Conformity   the degree to which group members adhere to the rules and practices of the group.

Consideration   a term used in the 1940 Ohio State studies that applied to behaviors exhibited by leaders who tried to support their employees and to develop trust and respect between themselves and their employees.

Constructive or desirable conflict   conflict of individuals or organizations that results in creativity and productivity through dealing with the unresolved issues.

Content theories of motivation   theories that focus on the question of what arouses individual behavior.

Corporate culture   a consensus of beliefs, customs, value systems, behavioral norms, and ways of doing business that are unique to an organization.

Craft-oriented work   work organized according to specific skill categories. This type of organizational structure was widespread during the Middle Ages. Examples included the cobbler guild, furniture guild, and blacksmith guild.

Criteria and standards approach   a three-step process to develop a performance outline: (1) identify groups of similar jobs, (2) develop performance criteria, and (3) develop standards of performance for each criteria. Also referred to as BARS (behaviorally-anchored rating scales).

Criteria only approach   a performance appraisal process that measures employees on a rating scale for each predetermined criterion.

Culture   the complex whole of a society including knowledge, beliefs, art, morals, laws, customs, and any other capabilities and habits of that society.

Culture shock   a condition of anxiety that results from losing one's familiar signs and symbols of social relating.

Cyberphobia (computer phobia)   fear, distrust, or hatred of computer technology.

Data collection approaches   various methods to obtain data, such as interviewing, questionnaires, sensing, polling, collages, and drawing.

Decentralization   a trend to diversify and create smaller self-determining groups either at work or in society.

Decoding   the translation by the receiver of messages into interpreted or perceived messages.

Delphi technique   a survey method involving people in decision making who do not come together physically. Through questionnaires, problems and questions are presented to these individuals, who analyze and respond in absence.

Destructive conflict   conflict resulting in bitterness, hostility, and spite between parties involved.

Diet   the food, liquids, and food supplements an individual needs to live a healthy existence.

Differentiation   the degree to which an organization is segmented (both vertically and horizontally) into identifiable components.

Discretionary stimuli   group characteristics influencing members to want to maintain group membership because of a supportive environment, social acceptance, and information possessed by the group members. Unlike ambient stimuli, discretionary stimuli are awarded by group members for compliance to group rules and regulations.

Dissonance   the result of inconsistent or contradictory components in a person's attitude framework.

Divisional organization   an organization with a structure characterized by units that specialize by product or service.

Downward communication   information transmitted by a supervisor to a subordinate.

Earned time off   a program allowing employees to leave the work site once they have completed a certain amount of work.

Effective communication   the information flow that results in a shared meaning and a common understanding for both the information sender and the information receiver.

Emotional state   an individual's set of emotions, whether positive or negative, which can affect that person's view of what is happening.

Empathy awareness of another's needs and motives from the other's perspective.

Employee ownership a form of compensation that allows employees to purchase, or receive in lieu of money, shares of company stock.

Employee participation employees taking an active part in organizational processes, such as designing a performance appraisal system.

Encoding the transferring of a sender's thoughts, motives, and emotions into symbols for transmission as communication.

Environment factors, conditions, and other organizations that surround an organization and affect its structure and processes. Environmental factors include technology, culture, political processes, and competition.

Equity theory a social comparison of an existing condition against some standard.

Essay approach a method of performance appraisal requiring the rater to respond to one or more open-ended questions concerning the performance of the employee.

Exercise the physical exertion needed to live an active healthy life.

Expectancy the level of belief that a particular individual effort will result in a certain performance level.

Expert power influence based on special ability and/or knowledge possessed by one person and needed by another.

Extinction a type of conditioning used to reduce or eliminate certain behaviors.

Extrinsic reward a reward mediated or granted by external agents, such as the organization, supervisor, or friends.

Feedback a responding message or action initiated by the receiver of the previous communication.

Felt conflict conflict that reaches the level of consciousness and is experienced as anxiety, frustration, or feelings of hostility.

Fight-or-flight response the reaction, both biochemical and physical, associated with stressful situations.

Filtering the passing of only partial information by the sender of a communication. This can be either unintentional or intentional on the part of the sender.

Formal group a collection of individuals in a group assigned by the organization (for example, a research team, production committee, or board of directors).

Formalization the degree to which rules and regulations are spelled out for organizational members.

Force field analysis a technique for portraying various conditions pushing for a change (driving forces) and conditions hindering the change (restraining forces).

Flexitime (flex-time) a system of scheduling work allowing each employee to select a starting and quitting time that best meets personal needs and preferences while maintaining some core time during which all employees are present.

Frame of reference a base of experience by which an individual reads the situation in which communication takes place. If the sender and receiver have a common experience base, there is a better chance that effective communication will occur.

Functional organization an organization with a structure characterized by the grouping of activities by specialization (such as sales, engineering, finance, computer operations).

Gainsharing   an incentive system whereby employees share in the monetary gain from increased productivity due to worker suggestions and ideas.

Group   a collection of individuals who interact with each other on a regular basis and see themselves to be mutually dependent with respect to the attainment of one or more common goals.

Group dynamics   the processes and activities of functioning within a group, including how behavior is rewarded and how leadership and roles are assigned.

Group productivity incentive   rewards given to group members based on their collective output.

Groupthink   a possible stage in a group's life where the group is so cohesive that its norms become paramount to its functioning. The group members do not take outside reality into account and merely focus on themselves as the arbiters of reality.

Halo effect   the process whereby one's impression (either favorable or unfavorable) of a person in one area tends to influence one's judgement about that person in other areas.

High-tech/high-touch   the need for individuals to receive specific attention to their needs as new technologies are adopted, if those new technologies are to be accepted and, therefore, successful.

Hofstede's study   a series of research studies conducted by Geert Hofstede in 40 countries to discover cultural differences.

Human-potential movement   movement during the 1950s and 1960s when people attended training sessions geared to help them break down barriers between individuals. During these sessions, individuals tried to improve their self-esteem, become more assertive about meeting their needs, and effectively communicate their feelings to others.

Hygiene factors   conditions related to the job environment or context that can become dissatisfiers if not present to a certain degree.

Identification   the adoption of a specific behavior because that behavior is associated with a role relationship perceived to be part of a group's expected behavior. This adoption process goes as far as becoming part of one's self-image.

Incentive plan   system of matching performance outcomes with specific reward schemes on a continual basis.

Incrementalism   the process of building upon the past and making only marginal changes in the existing situation.

Individualism/collectivism   a cultural definition of people as either self-oriented or group-oriented.

Individual productivity incentive   a reward given to an individual based on his or her performance.

Influence   the process of affecting the thoughts, feelings, or behaviors of others.

Informal group   a group that emerges naturally from the interaction of individuals over time. The group's functioning may not relate to organizational purposes or goals.

Information society   the trend that as a society we are shifting from being industrially based (machines) to informationally based (computer technology).

In-group language   specialized words or vocabularies prevalent among occupational groups, such as medical, military, or other professions; jargon.

Initiating structure   a term used in the 1940 Ohio State studies that describes a leader who is very directive about what the employee should do on the job.

Instrumentality   the relationship between performance (individual work effort) and the performance's consequences (various rewards).

Integration   the degree of coordination and control in an organization.

Intergroup conflict   conflict that arises between groups, departments, or work units.

Internalization   acceptance of influence because it is congruent with one's value system.

Intervention   a method or means to initiate or manage change more successfully.

Intrinsic reward   a reward that occurs directly as a result of performing an activity; an outcome that an individual grants to himself or herself.

Japanese management style   characterized by (1) an emphasis on the group rather than the individual; (2) an emphasis on human rather than functional relationships; and (3) a view of top management as generalists and facilitators rather than as decision makers.

Job design   the relationship of activities and tasks in a job.

Job enlargement   expansion of a job horizontally by addition of related activities to mitigate the negative effects of job specialization.

Job enrichment   expansion of a job vertically by addition of activities with greater responsibility and decision authority (such as quality checking, scheduling time, setting up training).

Job rotation   changing work assignments periodically rather than changing the task itself.

Job satisfaction   the degree of positive feelings one has towards one's job situation.

Job sharing   the process of splitting jobs among part-time workers; usually involves two people dividing the job responsibilities of a single position.

Kinesics   ways in which facial expressions and body positions affect communication.

Laboratory training   an intensive workshop where individuals increase their self-awareness and become more sensitive to their impact on others.

Latent conflict   the conditions underlying a potential disagreement (such as scarcity of resources or different views of management styles).

Lateral communication   information exchange between individuals who are peer-related within the organization.

Leadership   a process involving two or more individuals in which one party attempts to influence the other's behavior with respect to accomplishing some goal(s).

Legitimate power   influence an individual has because of position, role, or status in the organization. Occupying such a position automatically gives the individual the right to direct others.

Life planning   a series of activities to help individuals assess their values, life experiences, goals, and actions, to prepare them to be more effective in achieving future goals.

Life stressors   events in one's life that cause one to experience tension (see Social Readjustment Rating Scale).

Line and staff conflict   conflict between production/sales-oriented individuals and the organization's support units (labor relations, finance, accounting).

Management by objectives (MBO)　a process that integrates goals of the individual and the organization by a systematic and mutual discussion and the setting of new plans or objectives.

Management of change　systematic planning and implementation of new techniques, procedures, or materials.

Manifest conflict　conflict that is expressed through behavior.

Masculinity/femininity　a cultural dimension that characterizes people along a continuum from assertive and independent at one extreme, to nurturant and sympathetic at the other extreme.

Matrix organization　a form of structure in which an employee has two bosses at the same time. One supervises the functional aspects (sales, engineering, quality control) while the other supervises the product or project aspects.

Maturity　the capacity to set high but attainable goals, the willingness and ability to take responsibility. Also the education and experience of an individual or group.

Mechanistic organization　a structure that is relatively rigid and inflexible to external and internal changes. Such organizations are best suited to stable, slowly changing environments.

Mechanized work　the replacement, during and after the Industrial Revolution, of man and beast as primary sources of physical work. Instead, steam power and various kinds of mechanical equipment were used, and individuals were assigned to assist a machine. As a result, individual workers performed routine repetitive tasks that were machine-determined.

Merit pay　a monetary increase for employees who have improved their performance.

Modern society　a society marked by values and characteristics associated with more recent cultures (for example, a population concentrated in urban areas).

Moralist value orientation　tendency of a person to act in a "right" or "just" manner.

Motivation　the process that causes behavior to be energized, directed, and sustained.

N-Achievement　a desire, motive, or need to do something better or more efficiently than it has been done before.

N-Affiliation　a desire, motive, or need to be with other people regardless of whether there is anything else to gain by the contact.

N-Power　a desire to have impact, to be influential, and to control others.

Need hierarchy　the relative importance of various needs from physiological to self-actualization.

Negative reinforcement　a desired response being followed by the termination or withdrawal of something unpleasant, thereby theoretically causing the desired response to be repeated.

Networks　informal structuring of relationships by sharing information, ideas, and resources either directly, or indirectly through computer technology.

Nominal group technique (NGT)　a process whereby a problem is presented to a group in which members individually contribute ideas and solutions in writing before interacting with others to evaluate the suggestions.

Nonverbal communication　information inferred from gestures, body language, and patterns of movement. This information may reinforce or conflict with the actual words spoken.

Norms   standards of behavior expected by members of a group or a society as a whole (could be termed a set of rules of conduct).

Operant conditioning   the creation of pleasing consequences to follow desired behavior so that the frequency of the behavior will increase, or using unpleasant consequences to decrease undesirable behavior.

Organic organization   a structure that is relatively adaptable and flexible to demands for change both internally and externally. Such organizations are best suited to changing and dynamic environments.

Organizational behavior   a subset of management activities concerned with understanding, predicting, and influencing individual behavior in organizational settings.

Organizational development (OD) type   an individual who focuses attention on the entire organization when attempting to bring about change (through intergroup relations, problem solving methods, communications, and decision making).

Organizational interface   the meeting ground where organizational units interact.

Organizational mirroring   an intervention technique that helps groups identify their biases and what they feel another group's biases might be. After collecting this data, the groups share their views and begin to resolve issues that may prevent them from working together.

Organizational politics   the mobilization, through influence, of resources, energy, and information on behalf of a preferred goal or objective by an individual or group.

Organizational productivity model   a conceptual framework to identify how variables, such as structure, process, and leadership, affect the organization's productivity.

Organizational structure   the patterning of relationships and activities in an organization.

Outside pressure (OP) type   an individual who tries to change the organization while remaining outside the organization.

Overload   a condition whereby an individual or unit becomes bogged down with too much information or data.

Paralanguage   sounds (grunts, whistles, shouts, bells, or other noises). Many of these are used in the organization as warning signals of a change in conditions to which the worker should attend.

Parallel channels of communication   use of more than one method to communicate the same message. The additional method acts as a reinforcement for the information.

Participative management   a management philosophy that allows increased participation by workers in the decision-making process.

People-change-technology (PCT) type   a change agent who focuses the change effort on the individual worker to increase worker morale and productivity.

Perceived conflict   the awareness of latent conditions that surround unresolved issues.

Perceptual process   the process by which individuals select, organize, and interpret sensory stimuli, such as from seeing, hearing, and touching, into meaningful information about their surroundings. The result of this process can be beliefs, ideas, or attitudes.

Perceptual screening   the influence of values on perceptions, on both what we select to see and hear and how we interpret what we see and hear.

Persuasive communication   a technique for inducing attitude change in a listener.

Performance appraisal system   a method of assessing work performance and output of individual workers.

Performance discrepancy   a perceived difference between the employee's actual performance and the supervisor's expectations of the desirable performance.

Performance planning   a system that incorporates future-oriented performance development goals.

Performance-reward connection   the development of a clear and concise linkage between the individual worker's output and a reward for increasing such output.

Planned change   a model for viewing the change process sequentially from pressures for change to evaluation of the change.

Poll survey   a type of research in which randomly selected individuals in a large population are asked their opinions about a particular subject.

Polling   a variation of voting, whereby a group quickly asks members to evaluate an issue by raising hands or writing their opinions on a piece of paper.

Positive reinforcement   a desired response being followed by something pleasant, thereby increasing the chance of the desired response occurring again.

Power   the capacity to influence others to get things done.

Power distance   a cultural dimension that measures the degree to which influence and psychological distance between individuals is narrow (equality) or great (specific classes).

Pragmatic value orientation   the orientation of a person who seeks success and deals primarily with facts and reality.

Primary value orientation   description of an individual's important values.

Process consultant   an individual who, on an ongoing basis, helps a group assess its own effectiveness.

Productivity   a term that symbolizes the measurement of individual, work group, or organization output (number of units produced or people serviced) per input (resources used to produce units or service people).

Productivity program   a set of activities geared to improve the organization's efficiency (such as teamwork, new incentive system, new equipment).

Profit sharing   the sharing of certain surplus organization revenues with employees.

Projection   the tendency to attribute one's own characteristics and feelings to others.

Proxemics   the study of the physical environment of communication, including distance between individuals as they talk to one another and the characteristics of the location in which communication takes place.

Psychological effects of stress   the mental discomfort associated with stressful situations, which can be manifested as depression, anxiety, nervous exhaustion, disorientation, apathy, or increased irritability.

Punishment   an unpleasant condition produced in an attempt to eliminate an undesirable behavior.

Quality circles   a systematic and ongoing problem-solving process involving small work groups trained to analyze problems, plan solutions, and make formal presentations to management about their progress.

Quality of work life programs (QWL)   a broad range of programs designed to improve employee satisfaction and motivation.

Transmission in communication, a physical action to accomplish the sending of information.

Turnover a term to describe employees leaving the employment of an organization at the discretion of the employee (voluntary) or at the discretion of the firm (involuntary).

Uncertainty avoidance a cultural dimension that characterizes the extent to which a society is able to deal with threatening, ambiguous, or anxiety-provoking situations.

Upward communication information transmitted from one individual to another who occupies a higher position in the organization.

Valence the strength of a person's preference for a particular outcome or reward.

Values an individual's ideas about what is right, good, or desirable.

Value system a set of interacting and interrelating values that a person possesses. The priority of these values depends upon their importance to the person's self-concept.

Work ethic the value of work to an individual or society.

NAME INDEX

SUBJECT INDEX